SQL Server Database Programming with Java

Ying Bai

SQL Server Database Programming with Java

Concepts, Designs and Implementations

Ying Bai
Charlotte, NC, USA

The additional materials will be available on: sn.pub/lecturer-material

ISBN 978-3-030-92687-8 ISBN 978-3-031-06553-8 (eBook)
https://doi.org/10.1007/978-3-031-06553-8

This Springer imprint is published by the registered company Springer Nature Switzerland AG
The registered company address is: Gewerbestrasse 11, 6330 Cham, Switzerland

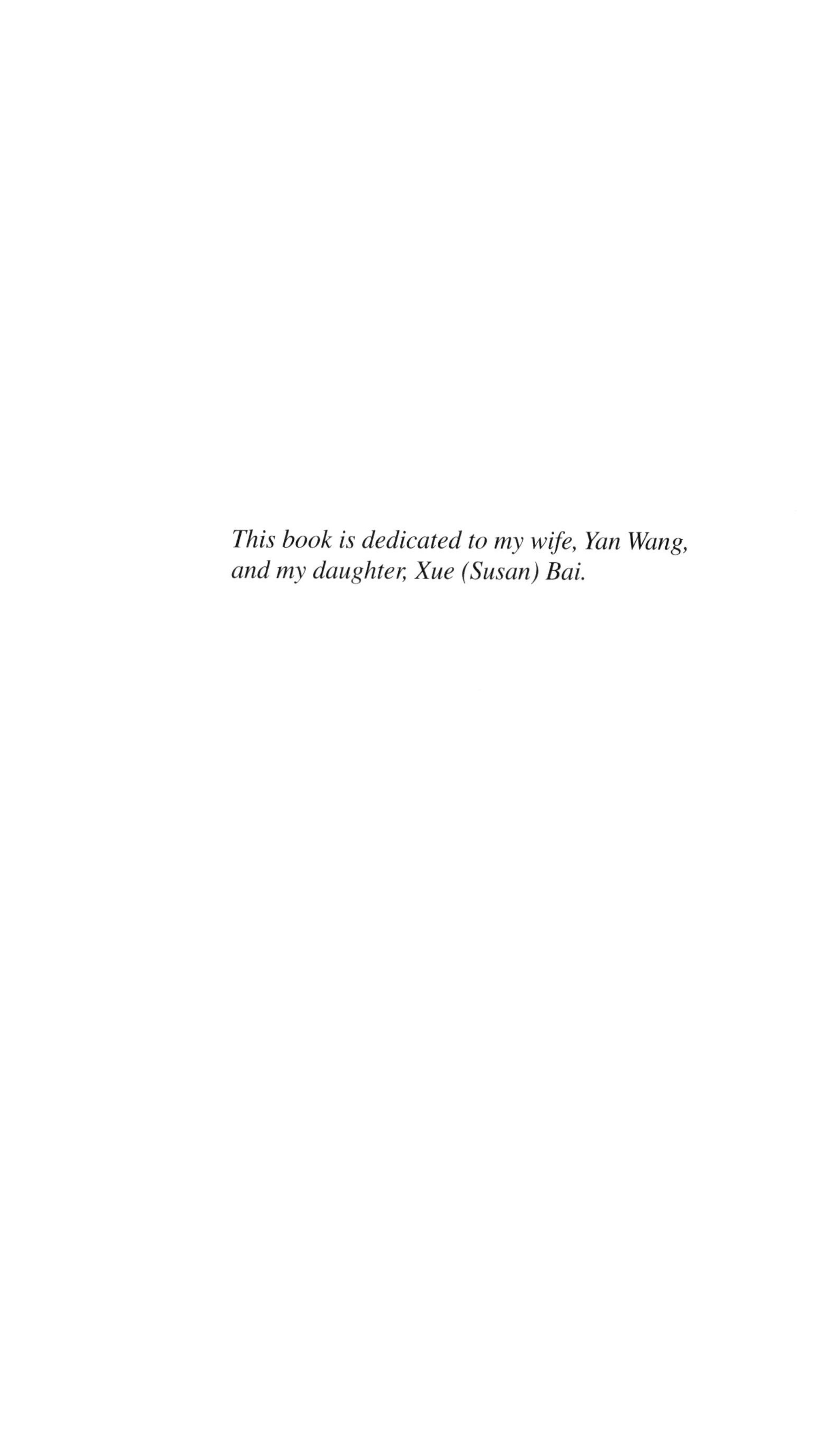

This book is dedicated to my wife, Yan Wang,
and my daughter, Xue (Susan) Bai.

Preface

Databases have become an integral part of our modern-day life. We are in an information-driven society today. Database technology has a direct impact on all aspects our daily lives. Decisions are routinely made by organizations based on the information collected and stored in databases. A record company may decide to market certain albums in selected regions based on the music preference of teenagers. Grocery stores display more popular items at the eye level and reorders are based on the inventories taken at regular intervals. Other examples include patients' medical records in hospitals, customers' account information in banks, book orders by the libraries or bookstores, club memberships, auto part orders, winter cloth stock by department stores, and many others.

In addition to database management systems, in order to effectively apply and implement databases in real industrial or commercial systems, a good graphic user interface (GUI) with an appropriate programming language is needed to enable users to access and manipulate their records or data in databases. NetBeans IDE with Java is an ideal candidate to be selected to provide this GUI with programming functionality. Unlike other programming languages, Java is a kind of language that has advantages such as being easy to learn and easy to understand with little learning curves. More importantly, Java is a truly Object Oriented Programming (OOP) language compared with other popular programming languages, such as C++ and C#.

Beginning from Java 1.0, Sun has integrated a few programming languages such as C++, JavaFX, and PHP with some frameworks into dynamic models that make Internet and Web programming easier and simpler, and any language integrated in this model can be used to develop professional and efficient Web applications that can be used to communicate with others via the Internet.

This book is mainly designed for college students and software programmers who want to develop practical and commercial database programming with Java and relational databases such as Microsoft SQL Server. The book provides a detailed description about the practical considerations and applications in database programming with Java and authentic examples as well as detailed explanations. More specially, some advanced Java Web related topics, such as Java Web Applications and Java Web Services, are discussed with quite a few of real project examples in this book, to provide readers with a clear picture as how to handle the database programming issues in NetBeans IDE environment.

The outstanding features of this book include, but no limited to, the following:

1. A real sample database, **CSE_DEPT**, which is built with Microsoft SQL Server 2019 Express, is provided and used for the entire book. Step by step, detailed illustration and description about how to design and build a practical relational database are provided.
2. Both fundamental and advanced Java database-programming techniques are covered to aide both beginning students and experienced programmers.
3. Updated Java database-programming techniques, such as Java Enterprise Edition 7, JavaServer Pages, JavaServer Faces, and Enterprise Java Beans, are discussed and analyzed with real projects to provide readers a clear picture and an easy-to-learn path for Java database applications.
4. Thirty (30) real database programming projects are covered in the book with detailed illustrations and explanations to help students understand key techniques and programming technologies.
5. Various actual JDBC APIs and JDBC drivers are discussed and presented with the coding explanations for real example projects. The working structure and principle of using JDBC driver to establish a valid database connection, and build an SQL statement and process the query results, are introduced in detail with example codes. One of the useful tools, JDBC RowSet, is also discussed and analyzed with some example codes.
6. Homework and selected solutions are provided for each chapter to strengthen and improve students' learning and understanding of topics they studied.
7. PowerPoint teaching slides are also provided to help instructors with their teaching and organizing of their classes.
8. A Good textbook for college students, and a good reference book for programmers, software engineers, and academic researchers.

I sincerely hope this book can provide useful and practical help and guidance to all readers or users who adopted this book, and I will be more than happy to know that you would be able to develop and build professional and practical database applications with the help of this book.

Copyrights and Trademarks

Acknowledgment

First and foremost, special thanks go to my wife, Yan Wang. I would not have finished this book without her sincere encouragement and support.

Special thanks go to Dr. Satish Bhalla who made great contributions to Chap. 2. Dr. Bhalla is a specialist in database programming and management, especially in SQL Server, Oracle, and DB2. Dr. Bhalla spent a lot of time to prepare materials for the first part of Chap. 2, and he deserves to be acknowledged.

Many thanks go to Ms. Susan Lagerstrom who made this book available to the public. This book would not have found its place in today's market without Susan's deep perspective and hard work. The same thanks are extended to the editorial team. Without their contributions, it would have been impossible to publish this book.

Thanks should also be extended to the following book reviewers for their precious opinions on this book:

- Dr. Jiang Xie, Professor, Department of Electrical and Computer Engineering at the University of North Carolina at Charlotte
- Dr. Daoxi Xiu, Application Analyst Programmer at North Carolina Administrative Office of the Courts
- Dr. Dali Wang, Professor, Department of Physics and Computer Science at Christopher Newport University
- Dr. Nailong Guo, Associate Professor, Department of Mathematics and Computer Science at Benedict College

Finally, I thank all those who support me to finish this book.

Contents

Part I Building Two-Tier Client-Server Applications

About the Author

Ying Bai is a professor in the Department of Computer Science and Engineering at Johnson C. Smith University. His special interests include artificial intelligences, soft-computing, mix-language programming, fuzzy logic and deep learning, robotic controls, robots calibrations, and database programming.

His industry experience includes positions as software engineer and senior software engineer at companies such as Motorola MMS, Schlumberger ATE Technology, Immix TeleCom, and Lam Research.

Since 2003, Dr. Bai has published 17 books with publishers such as Prentice Hall, CRC Press LLC, Springer, Cambridge University Press, and Wiley IEEE Press. The Russian translation of his first book titled *Applications Interface Programming Using Multiple Languages* was published by Prentice Hall in 2005. The Chinese translation of his eighth book titled *Practical Database Programming with Visual C#.NET* was published by Tsinghua University Press in China in 2011. Most books are about artificial intelligence and soft computing, software interfacing and serial port programming, database programming, fuzzy logic controls, microcontroller programming, as well as classical and modern controls.

During recent years, Dr. Bai has also published more than 65 academic research papers in *IEEE Trans.* journals and international conferences.

Chapter 1
Introduction

For some years when I taught database programming-related courses in my college, I found that it is so hard to find a good textbook for this kind of topic that I have to combine a few of different professional books as references to teach this course. Most of those books are specially designed for database programming software engineers or programmers, in which a lot of database programming strategies and huge blocks of codes are involved, and which is a terrible headache to the college students or beginning programmers who are new to the Java-related tools, such as NetBeans IDE, and database programming-related applications. In most times, I have to prepare the class-related presentations and figure out all homeworks as well as exercises or projects myself for my students. I once dreamed that one day I can find an appropriate textbook that is good and suitable for the college students or beginning programmers and help them to learn and master the database programming with Java easily and conveniently. After a long time waiting, eventually I decided that I need to do something for this dream myself.

Another reason to write this book is the job market. As we know, most operating companies or businesses in the United States, either industry or commerce, belong to database applications or implementations-related businesses, such as manufactures, banks, hospitals, hotels, airports, and retails. The majority of them need professional technicians or engineers to develop and build database-related applications, instead of building database management and design systems. To enable our college graduates to become good and qualified candidates, and to be able to handle those database-related programming jobs for those companies, we need to create a good book like this one.

There are so many different database programming books available on the market, but most of them are written for software engineers or programmers, starting

Supplementary Information The online version contains supplementary material available at [https://doi.org/10.1007/978-3-031-06553-8_1].

Y. Bai, *SQL Server Database Programming with Java*,
https://doi.org/10.1007/978-3-031-06553-8_1

from theoretical introduction to some coding developments with few actual examples. This kind of writing style made big headache and huge learning curve for college students who are new to database programming and applications. Without a complete and detailed introduction to database development environment and related tools, it is very hard to enable students to learn and understand related topics easily and quickly. Rarely can you find a book like this one, it starts from an introduction and discussion about database structures and principles, detailed analysis on database programming-related environment or integrated development environment (IDE – NetBeans IDE), discussions about various tools, such as Java Database Connection (JDBC) components, JDBC API, JDBC Data Sources, JDBC Drivers, two and three-tier client-server models, then more detailed implementations of using that IDE to build various database programming project examples with different components, such as Java Beans, Java Server Pages (JSP), and Java Enterprise Edition (Java EE), are provided. More importantly, the Java Web Applications and Java Web Service-related database programming techniques are also included in this book with some updated technologies, such as Enterprise Java Beans (EJB), REST-Based Web Services, and SOAP-Based Web Services. Two kinds of popular Web servers, Glssfish and TomCat, are also discussed and implemented in those related projects.

The most updated NetBeans IDE, Apache NetBeans IDE 12, is adopted and used in most database programming examples in this book. These implementations are discussed and introduced in Chaps. 5, 6, and 7. Starting from Chaps. 8 and 9, NetBeans IDE 8.2 is adopted to match the current versions of some tools, such as Glassfish and TomCat Web servers, to enable users to develop and build example projects successfully.

1.1 Outstanding Features About This Book

1. Covered both fundamental and advanced Java database programming techniques to convenience both beginning and experienced students as well as programmers.
2. A sample database, **CSE_DEPT**, which is equivalent to a Computer Science Department and built with Microsoft SQL Server 2019 Express, is used for all program examples developed in the entire book.
3. Different types of database projects, including the standard Java desktop applications, Java with Ant, Java class library, Java EE7 applications, Java Web Applications, and Java Web Services, are discussed, analyzed, and implemented in actual projects with line-by-line explanation.
4. Updated Java database programming techniques, such as Java Enterprise Edition 7, JavaServer Pages, Java Beans, Enterprise Java Beans, Glassfish, and TomCat Web servers, are discussed and analyzed with real projects to enable readers to have a clear picture and easy-to-learn path for Java database applications.
5. A detailed introduction and discussion to Apache NetBeans IDE 12 are provided in Chap. 5. Starting from a simple Java application, all different project types

built in NetBeans IDE are discussed and presented to give readers a detailed but global picture about the working structure and operational principles of NetBeans IDE.
6. Thirty (30) real sample database programming projects are covered in the book with detailed illustrations and explanations to help students to understand key techniques and programming technologies.
7. Homework and selected solutions are provided for each chapter to strengthen and improve students' learning and understanding abilities for topics they studied.
8. PowerPoint teaching slides are also provided to help instructors for their teaching and organizing their classes.
9. Good textbook for college students, good reference book for programmers, software engineers, and academic researchers.

1.2 Who This Book Is For

This book is designed for college students and software programmers who want to develop practical and commercial database programming with Java and relational database such as Microsoft SQL Server 2019 Express. Fundamental knowledge and understanding about Java language and Java programming techniques are required.

1.3 What This Book Covers

Nine chapters are included in this book. The contents of each chapter can be summarized as below.

- Chapter 1 provides an introduction and summarization to the entire book.
- Chapter 2 provides detailed discussions and analyses of the structures and components about relational databases. Some key technologies in developing and designing database are also given and discussed in this part. The procedure and components used to develop a practical relational database with Microsoft SQL Server 2019 Express is analyzed in detail with some real data tables in our sample database **CSE_DEPT**.
- Chapter 3 provides discussions on JDBC APIs and JDBC drivers. A detailed introduction to components and architecture of JDBC is given with step-by-step illustrations. Four popular types of JDBC drivers are discussed and analyzed with both their advantages and disadvantages emphasized in actual database applications. The working structure and operational principle of using JDBC drivers to establish a valid database connection, build a SQL statement, and process the query result are also discussed and presented in detail. One of the most useful tools, JDBC RowSet, is also discussed and analyzed with some example codes.

- Chapter 4 provides a detailed discussion and analysis about JDBC design and actual application considerations. Fundamentals of using JDBC to access and manipulate data against databases are discussed and introduced with example codes. Different JDBC interfaces, including the ResultSet, ResultSetMetaData, DatabaseMetaData, and ParameterMetaData, are introduced and discussed with example codes.
- Chapter 5 provides a detailed description about the Apache NetBeans IDE 12, including the components and architecture. This topic is necessary for college students who have no knowledge of NetBeans IDE. Starting from an introduction to installing the Apache NetBeans IDE 12, this chapter goes through each aspect of NetBeans IDE 12, including the NetBeans Platform, NetBeans Open Source, and all plug-in tools. Different projects built with NetBeans IDE are also discussed and presented in detail with three example projects.
- Starting from Chapter 6, the real database programming techniques with Java, query data from database, are provided and discussed. This chapter covers the so-called runtime object method to develop and build professional data-driven applications. Detailed discussions and descriptions about how to build professional and practical database applications using this runtime method are provided combined with a real project. In addition to basic query techniques, advanced query methods, such as PreparedStatement, CallableStatement, and stored procedure, are also discussed and implemented in this chapter with a real sample project.
- Chapter 7 provides detailed discussions and analyses on how to insert, update, and delete data from the popular databases – Microsoft SQL Server 2019. This chapter covers some techniques to manipulate data in our sample database using runtime object method. Nine real projects are used to illustrate how to perform the data manipulations against our sample database: Microsoft SQL Server 2019 Express. Professional and practical data validation methods are also discussed in this chapter to confirm the data manipulations. Some advanced data manipulation techniques and methods, such as Updatable ResultSet and Callable Statements, are introduced and discussed in this Chapter with some real projects.
- Chapter 8 provides introductions and discussions about the developments and implementations of three-tier Java Web applications in NetBeans IDE 8.2 environment. At the beginning of this chapter, a detailed and completed historical review about Java Web application development is provided, and this part is especially important and useful to college students or programmers who do not have any knowledge or background in the Java Web application developments and implementations. Following the introduction section, different techniques used in building Java Web applications are introduced and discussed in detail. The target database, Microsoft SQL Server 2019 Express, is utilized as the objective databases for those development and building processes. JavaServer Pages and Java Beans techniques are also discussed and involved in those real Web application projects.
- Chapter 9 provides introductions and discussions about the developments and implementations of Java Web Services in NetBeans IDE 8.2 environment. A

detailed discussion and analysis about the structure and components of the Java Web services is provided at the beginning of this chapter. Each Web service contains different operations that can be used to access different databases and perform the desired data actions such as Select, Insert, Update, and Delete via the Internet. To consume those Web services, different Web service client projects are also developed in this chapter. Both Windows-based and Web-based Web service client projects are discussed and built for each kind of Web service listed above. Totally twelve (12) projects, including the Web service projects and the associated Web service client projects, are developed in this chapter. All projects have been debugged and tested and can be run in any Windows compatible operating systems such as Windows 10.

1.4 How This Book Is Organized and How to Use This Book

This book is designed for both college students who are new to database programming with Java and professional database programmers who have some experience on this topic.

Chapters 2 and 3 provide the fundamentals on database structures and components, JDBC API, and related components. Chapter 4 covers an introduction to JDBC design and application considerations. Chapter 5 provides a detailed introduction to Apache NetBeans IDE 12 and its working environment with some actual project examples. Starting from Chaps. 6 and 7, the runtime object method is introduced with detailed coding developments for some real projects to perform different data actions against our sample SQL Server database, such as data query, data insertion, data updating, and deleting. All projects discussed in these two chapters belong to Java Ant Applications or Java Desktop database applications.

Chapters 8 and 9 give a full discussion and analysis about the developments and implementations of Java Web applications and Web services. These technologies are necessary to students and programmers who want to develop and build Web applications and Web services to access and manipulate data via Internet.

Based on the organization of this book as we described above, this book can be used as two categories, such as Level I and Level II, which are shown in Fig. 1.1, in the following ways.

- For undergraduate college students or beginning software programmers, it is highly recommended to learn and understand the contents of Chaps. 2, 3, 4, 5, 6 and 7 since those are fundamental knowledge and techniques used in database programming with Java. For Chaps. 8 and 9, they are optional to instructors and depend on the time and schedule.
- For experienced college students or software programmers who have already had some knowledge and techniques in database programming and Java language, it is highly recommended to learn and understand the contents of Chaps. 4, 5, 6, 7, 8 and 9 since the run-time data objects method and some sophisticated Web

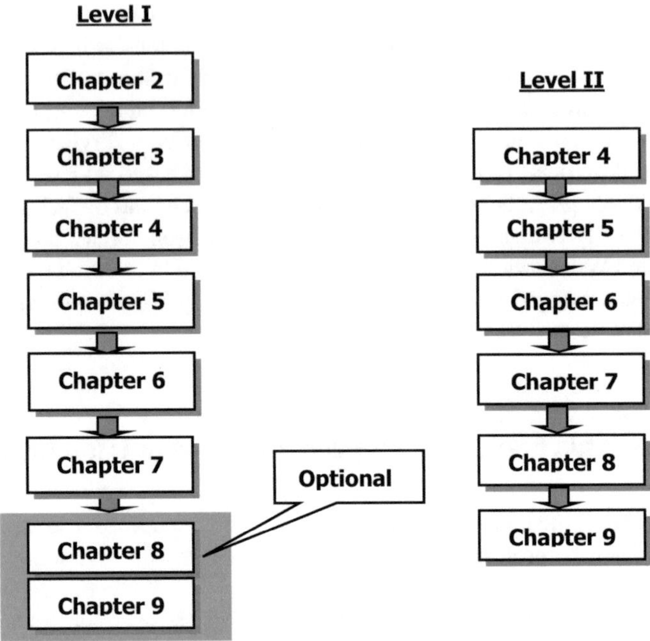

Fig. 1.1 Two possible teaching levels used for this book

database programming techniques such as Java RowSet object, Callable Statements, stored procedures, Java Beans, JSP and EJB are discussed and illustrated with real examples.

1.5 How to Use the Source Codes and the Sample Database

All source codes of each real class project developed in this book are available. All projects are categorized into the associated chapters that are located at the folder **Class DB Projects** that is located under the **Students** folder at the Springer ftp site https://doi.org/10.1007/978-3-031-06553-8_1. You can copy or download those codes into your computer and run each project as you like. To successfully run those projects on your computer, the following conditions must be met:

- Apache NetBeans IDE 12, JDBC 8, and JDK 14 must be installed in your computer for all projects categorized in Chaps. 2, 3, 4, 5, 6 and 7. NetBeans IDE 8.2, JDBC 4.2, and JDK 8 must be installed in your computer for all projects categorized in Chaps. 8 and 9.
- A SQL Server database management systems, Microsoft SQL Server Management Studio 18, must be installed in your computer.

- A sample SQL Server database, CSE_DEPT.mdf, must be installed in your computer in the appropriate folder. Refer to Appendix D to get more details about how to use this sample database.
- To run projects developed in Chaps. 8 and 9, in addition to conditions listed above, a Web server such as Glassfish v4 and a J2EE must be installed in your computer.

The following appendices are useful when one needs some references and practical knowledge to install database management systems and develop actual database application projects:

Appendix A: Install and Configure SQL Server 2019 Express Database and SQL Server Management Studio
Appendix B: Download and Install JDK 14 and Apache NetBeans IDE 12
Appendix C: Download and Install DevExpress .NET UI Controls
Appendix D: How to Use Sample Database
Appendix E: Data Type Mappings Between SQL Statements and Java Applications
Appendix F: Download and Install Java JDK 8
Appendix G: Download and Install JDBC 4.2
Appendix H: Download and Install NetBeans IDE 8.2 and Glassfish Server
Appendix I: Modify the HTTP Port Number for Tomcat Server

All of these appendices can be found from a folder **Appendix** that is located under the **Students** folder at the Springer ftp site https://doi.org/10.1007/978-3-031-06553-8_1.

A sample database file, **CSE_DEPT.mdf**, is located at a folder **Sample Database** that is located under the **Students** folder at the Springer ftp site https://doi.org/10.1007/978-3-031-06553-8_1. To use these databases for your applications or sample projects, refer to Appendix D.

The detailed distributions of above teaching and learning materials located at the Springer ftp site are shown in Fig. 1.2 on next page. Refer to that figure to get more details about them.

1.6 Instructors Materials and Customers Supports

All teaching materials for all chapters have been extracted and represented by a sequence of Microsoft PowerPoint files, each file for one chapter. The interested instructors can find those teaching materials from a folder **Teaching PPT**, which is located under the **Instructors** folder at the Springer ftp site sn.pub/lecturer-material. These teaching materials are password protected and only available to instructors who adopted this book as their textbook. All of these materials can be requested from the book's listing on the Springer ftp site sn.pub/lecturer-material.

The homework solutions are provided and they are divided into two parts: **Project Solutions** and **Question Solutions**. At the end of each chapter, a related

The Book Related Materials on the Web Sites

FOR INSTRUCTORS:

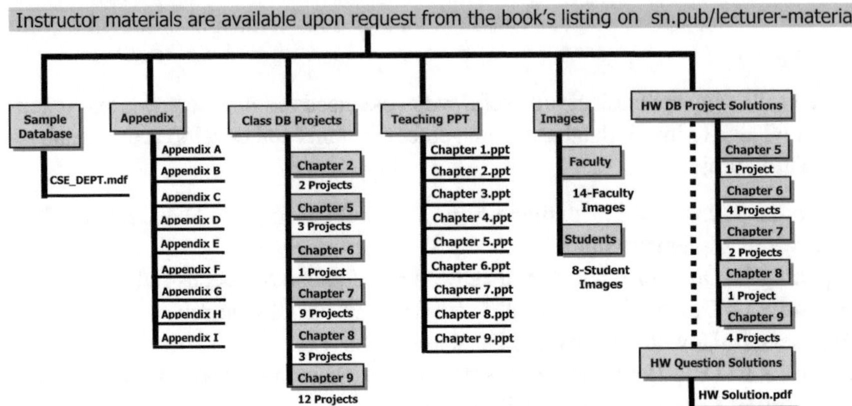

FOR STUDENTS:

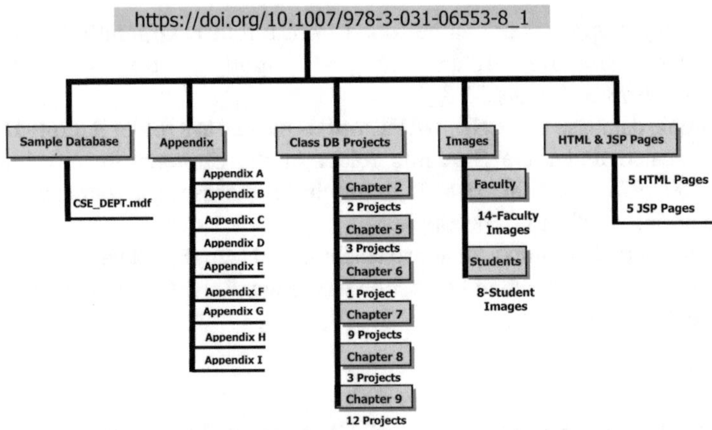

Fig. 1.2 Book-related materials on the web sites

homework is assigned with two parts: Question Answering part and Project Development part. Therefore the solutions are also divided into two parts. For solutions to Question part, they are located under a folder **HW Question Solutions**, and for solutions to Project part, they are located under a folder **HW DB Project Solutions**. Both folders are under a folder **Instructors** located at the Springer ftp site. The selected homework solutions are available upon request from the book's listing on Springer ftp site sn.pub/lecturer-material.

E-mail support is available to all readers of this book. When you send e-mail to us, please provide the following information:

- The detailed description about your problems, including the error message and debug message as well as the error or debug number if it is provided.
- Your name, job title, and company name.

Please send all questions to the e-mail address: ybai@jcsu.edu.

Chapter 2
Introduction to Databases

Databases have become an integral part of our modern-day life. Today we are an information-driven society. Large amounts of data are generated, analyzed, and converted into different information at each moment. A recent example of biological data generation is the Human Genome project that was jointly sponsored by the Department of Energy (DOE) and the National Institute of Health (NIH). Many countries participated in this venture for more than ten years. The project was a tremendous success. It was completed in 2003 and resulted in generation of huge amount of genome data, currently stored in databases around the world. The scientists will be analyzing this data in years to come.

Database technology has a direct impact on our daily lives. Decisions are routinely made by organizations based on the information collected and stored in the databases. A record company may decide to market certain albums in selected regions based on the music preference of teenagers. Grocery stores display more popular items at the eye level, and reorders are based on the inventories taken at regular intervals. Other examples include book orders by the libraries, club memberships, auto part orders, winter cloth stock by department stores, and many others.

Database management programs have been in existence since the sixties. However, it was not until the seventies when E. F. Codd proposed the then revolutionary Relational Data Model that database technology really took off. In the early eighties it received a further boost with the arrival of personal computers and microcomputer-based data management programs like dBase II (later followed by dBase III and IV). Today we have a plethora of vastly improved programs for PCs and mainframe computers, including Microsoft Access, SQL Server, IBM DB2, Oracle, Sequel Server, MySQL, and others.

Supplementary Information The online version contains supplementary material available at [https://doi.org/10.1007/978-3-031-06553-8_2].

Y. Bai, *SQL Server Database Programming with Java*,
https://doi.org/10.1007/978-3-031-06553-8_2

This chapter covers the basic concepts of database design followed by the implementation of a specific relational database to illustrate the concepts discussed here. The sample database, **CSE_DEPT**, is used as a running example. The database creation is shown in detail by using Microsoft Access and Microsoft SQL Server. The topics discussed in this chapter include:

- What are databases and database programs?
  - File Processing System
  - Integrated Databases
- Various approaches to developing a Database
- Relational Data Model and Entity-Relationship Model (ER)
- Identifying Keys
  - Primary Keys, Foreign Keys, and Referential Integrity
- Defining Relationships
- Normalizing the Data
- Implementing the Relational Sample Database
  - Create Microsoft SQL Server 2019 Express Sample Database

2.1 What Are Databases and Database Programs?

A modern-day database is a structured collection of data stored in a computer. The term structured implies that each record in the database is stored in a certain format. For example, all entries in a phone book are arranged in a similar fashion. Each entry contains a name, an address, and a telephone number of a subscriber. This information can be queried and manipulated by database programs. The data retrieved in answer to queries become information that can be used to make decisions. The databases may consist of a single table or related multiple tables. The computer programs used to create, manage, and query databases are known as a DataBase Management Systems (DBMS). Just like the databases the DBMSs vary in complexity. Depending on the need of a user one can use either a simple application or a robust program. Some examples of these programs were given earlier.

2.1.1 File Processing System

File Processing System (FPS) is a precursor of the integrated database approach. The records for a particular application are stored in a file. An application program is needed to retrieve or manipulate data in this file. Thus various departments in an organization will have their own file processing systems with their individual programs to store and retrieve data. The data in various files may be duplicated and not available to other applications. This causes redundancy and may lead to inconsistency meaning that various files that supposedly contain the same information may actually contain different data values. Thus duplication of data creates problems with data integrity. Moreover, it is difficult to provide access to multiple users with the file processing systems without granting them access to the respective application programs, which manipulate the data in those files.

The FPS may be advantageous under certain circumstances. For example, if data is static and a simple application will solve the problem, a more expensive DBMS is not needed. For example, in a small business environment you want to keep track of the inventory of the office equipment purchased only once or twice a year. The data can be kept in an Excel spreadsheet and manipulated with ease from time to time. This avoids the need to purchase an expensive database program, and hiring a knowledgeable database administrator. Before the DBMSs became popular, the data was kept in files and application programs were developed to delete, insert, or modify records in the files. Since specific application programs were developed for specific data, these programs lasted for months or years before modifications were necessitated by business needs.

2.1.2 Integrated Databases

A better alternative to a file processing system is an integrated database approach. In this environment all data belonging to an organization is stored in a single database. The database is not a mere collection of files, there is a relation between the files. Integration implies a logical relationship, usually provided through a common column in the tables. The relationships are also stored within the database. A set of sophisticated programs known as Database Management System (DBMS) is used to store, access, and manipulate the data in the database. Details of data storage and maintenance are hidden from the user. The user interacts with the database through the DBMS. A user may interact either directly with the DBMS or via a program written in a programming language such as Visual C++, Java, Visual Basic, or Visual C#. Only the DBMS can access the database. Large organizations employ Database Administrators (DBAs) to design and maintain large databases.

There are many advantages to using an integrated database approach over that of a file processing approach:

1. **Data sharing:** The data in the database is available to a large number of users who can access the data simultaneously and create reports, manipulate the data given proper authorization and rights.
2. **Minimizing data redundancy:** Since all the related data exists in a single database, there is a minimal need of data duplication. The duplication is needed to maintain relationship between various data items.
3. **Data consistency and data integrity:** Reducing data redundancy will lead to data consistency. Since data is stored in a single database, enforcing data integrity becomes much easier. Furthermore, the inherent functions of the DBMS can be used to enforce the integrity with minimum programming.

4. **Enforcing standards**: DBAs are charged with enforcing standards in an organization. DBA takes into account the needs of various departments and balances it against the overall need of the organization. DBA defines various rules such as documentation standards, naming conventions, update and recovery procedures, etc. It is relatively easy to enforce these rules in a Database System, since it is a single set of programs which is always interacting with the data files.
5. **Improving security:** Security is achieved through various means such as controlling access to the database through passwords, providing various levels of authorizations, data encryption, providing access to restricted views of the database, etc.
6. **Data independence:** Providing data independence is a major objective for any database system. Data independence implies that even if the physical structure of a database changes the applications are allowed to access the database as before the changes were implemented. In other words the applications are immune to the changes in the physical representation and access techniques.

The downside of using an integrated database approach has mainly to do with exorbitant costs associated with it. The hardware, the software, and the maintenance are expensive. Providing security, concurrency, integrity, and recovery may add further to this cost. Furthermore, since DBMS consists of a complex set of programs, trained personnel are needed to maintain it.

2.2 Develop a Database

Database development process may follow a classical Systems Development Life Cycle.

1. **Problem Identification** – Interview the user, identify user requirements. Perform preliminary analysis of user needs.
2. **Project Planning** – Identify alternative approaches to solving the problem. Does the project need a database? If so define the problem. Establish scope of the project.
3. **Problem Analysis** – Identify specifications for the problem. Confirm the feasibility of the project. Specify detailed requirements
4. **Logical Design** – Delineate detailed functional specifications. Determine screen designs, report layout designs, data models, etc.
5. **Physical Design** – Develop physical data structures.
6. **Implementation** – Select DBMS. Convert data to conform to DBMS requirements. Code programs; perform testing.
7. **Maintenance** – Continue program modification until desired results are achieved.

An alternative approach to developing a database is through a phased process which will include designing a conceptual model of the system that will imitate the real-world operation. It should be flexible and change when the information in the database changes. Furthermore, it should not be dependent upon the physical implementation. This process follows the steps shown below:

1. **Planning and Analysis** – This phase is roughly equivalent to the first three steps mentioned above in the Systems Development Life Cycle. This includes requirement specifications, evaluating alternatives, determining input, output, and reports to be generated.
2. **Conceptual Design** – Choose a data model and develop a conceptual schema based on the requirement specification that was laid out in the planning and analysis phase. This conceptual design focuses on how the data will be organized without having to worry about the specifics of the tables, keys, and attributes. Identify the entities that will represent tables in the database; identify attributes that will represent fields in a table; and identify each entity attribute relationship. Entity-relationship diagrams provide a good representation of the conceptual design.
3. **Logical Design** – Conceptual design is transformed into a logical design by creating a roadmap of how the database will look before actually creating the database. Data model is identified; usually it is the relational model. Define the tables (entities) and fields (attributes). Identify primary and foreign key for each table. Define relationships between the tables.
4. **Physical Design** – Develop physical data structures; specify file organization, and data storage, etc. Take into consideration the availability of various resources including hardware and software. This phase overlaps with the implementation phase. It involves the programming of the database taking into account the limitations of the DBMS used.
5. **Implementation** – Choose the DBMS that will fulfill the user needs. Implement the physical design. Perform testing. Modify if necessary or until the database functions satisfactorily.

2.3 Sample Database

We will use a sample database CSE_DEPT to illustrate some essential database concepts. Tables 2.1, 2.2, 2.3, 2.4 and 2.5 show sample data tables stored in this database.

The data in CSE_DEPT database is stored in five tables – LogIn, Faculty, Course, Student, and StudentCourse. A table consists of rows and columns (Fig. 2.1). A row represents a record and a column represents a field. A row is called a tuple and a column is called an attribute. For example, Student table has seven columns or fields – student_id, name, gpa, major, schoolYear, and email. It has five records or rows.

Table 2.1 LogIn table

user_name	pass_word	faculty_id	student_id
abrown	america	B66750	
ajade	tryagain		A97850
awoods	smart		A78835
banderson	birthday	A52990	
bvalley	see		B92996
dangles	tomorrow	A77587	
hsmith	try		H10210
terica	excellent		T77896
jhenry	test	H99118	
jking	goodman	K69880	
dbhalla	india	B86590	
sjohnson	jermany	J33486	
ybai	come	B78880	

Table 2.2 Faculty table

faculty_ id	faculty_ name	title	office	phone	college	email	fimage
A52990	Black Anderson	Professor	MTC-218	750-378-9987	Virginia Tech	banderson@college.edu	NULL
A77587	Debby Angles	Associate Professor	MTC-320	750-330-2276	University of Chicago	dangles@college.edu	NULL
B66750	Alice Brown	Assistant Professor	MTC-257	750-330-6650	University of Florida	abrown@college.edu	NULL
B78880	Ying Bai	Associate Professor	MTC-211	750-378-1148	Florida Atlantic University	ybai@college.edu	NULL
B86590	Davis Bhalla	Associate Professor	MTC-214	750-378-1061	University of Notre Dame	dbhalla@college.edu	NULL
H99118	Jeff Henry	Associate Professor	MTC-336	750-330-8650	Ohio State University	jhenry@college.edu	NULL
J33486	Steve Johnson	Distinguished Professor	MTC-118	750-330-1116	Harvard University	sjohnson@college.edu	NULL
K69880	Jenney King	Professor	MTC-324	750-378-1230	East Florida University	jking@college.edu	NULL

Table 2.3 Course table

course_ id	course	credit	classroom	schedule	enrollment	faculty_ id
CSC-131A	Computers in Society	3	MTC-109	M-W-F: 9:00-9:55 AM	28	A52990
CSC-131B	Computers in Society	3	MTC-114	M-W-F: 9:00-9:55 AM	20	B66750
CSC-131C	Computers in Society	3	MTC-109	T-H: 11:00-12:25 PM	25	A52990
CSC-131D	Computers in Society	3	MTC-109	M-W-F: 9:00-9:55 AM	30	B86590
CSC-131E	Computers in Society	3	MTC-301	M-W-F: 1:00-1:55 PM	25	B66750
CSC-131I	Computers in Society	3	MTC-109	T-H: 1:00-2:25 PM	32	A52990
CSC-132A	Introduction to Programming	3	MTC-303	M-W-F: 9:00-9:55 AM	21	J33486
CSC-132B	Introduction to Programming	3	MTC-302	T-H: 1:00-2:25 PM	21	B78880
CSC-230	Algorithms & Structures	3	MTC-301	M-W-F: 1:00-1:55 PM	20	A77587
CSC-232A	Programming I	3	MTC-305	T-H: 11:00-12:25 PM	28	B66750
CSC-232B	Programming I	3	MTC-303	T-H: 11:00-12:25 PM	17	A77587
CSC-233A	Introduction to Algorithms	3	MTC-302	M-W-F: 9:00-9:55 AM	18	H99118
CSC-233B	Introduction to Algorithms	3	MTC-302	M-W-F: 11:00-11:55 AM	19	K69880
CSC-234A	Data Structure & Algorithms	3	MTC-302	M-W-F: 9:00-9:55 AM	25	B78880
CSC-234B	Data Structure & Algorithms	3	MTC-114	T-H: 11:00-12:25 PM	15	J33486
CSC-242	Programming II	3	MTC-303	T-H: 1:00-2:25 PM	18	A52990
CSC-320	Object Oriented Programming	3	MTC-301	T-H: 1:00-2:25 PM	22	B66750
CSC-331	Applications Programming	3	MTC-109	T-H: 11:00-12:25 PM	28	H99118
CSC-333A	Computer Arch & Algorithms	3	MTC-301	M-W-F: 10:00-10:55 AM	22	A77587
CSC-333B	Comp Arch & Algorithms	3	MTC-302	T-H: 11:00-12:25 PM	15	A77587
CSC-335	Internet Programming	3	MTC-303	M-W-F: 1:00-1:55PM	25	B66750
CSC-432	Discrete Algorithms	3	MTC-206	T-H: 11:00-12:25 PM	20	B86590

(continued)

Table 2.3 (continued)

course_ id	course	credit	classroom	schedule	enrollment	faculty_ id
CSC-439	Database Systems	3	MTC-206	M-W-F: 1:00-1:55 PM	18	B86590
CSE-138A	Introduction to CSE	3	MTC-301	T-H: 1:00-2:25 PM	15	A52990
CSE-138B	Introduction to CSE	3	MTC-109	T-H: 1:00-2:25 PM	35	J33486
CSE-330	Digital Logic Circuits	3	MTC-305	M-W-F: 9:00-9:55 AM	26	K69880
CSE-332	Foundation of Semiconductor	3	MTC-305	T-H: 1:00-2:25 PM	24	K69880
CSE-334	Elec. Measurement & Design	3	MTC-212	T-H: 11:00-12:25 PM	25	H99118
CSE-430	Bioinformatics in Computer	3	MTC-206	Thu: 9:30-11:00 AM	16	B86590
CSE-432	Analog Circuits Design	3	MTC-309	M-W-F: 2:00-2:55 PM	18	K69880
CSE-433	Digital Signal Processing	3	MTC-206	T-H: 2:00-3:25 PM	18	H99118
CSE-434	Advanced Electronic Systems	3	MTC-213	M-W-F: 1:00-1:55 PM	26	B78880
CSE-436	Automatic Control & Design	3	MTC-305	M-W-F: 10:00-10:55 AM	29	J33486
CSE-437	Operating Systems	3	MTC-303	T-H: 1:00-2:25 PM	17	A77587
CSE-438	Adv Logic & Microprocessor	3	MTC-213	M-W-F: 11:00-11:55 AM	35	B78880
CSE-439	Special Topics in CSE	3	MTC-206	M-W-F: 10:00-10:55 AM	22	J33486

Table 2.4 Student table

student_ id	student_ name	gpa	credits	major	schoolYear	email	simage
A78835	Andrew Woods	3.26	108	Computer Science	Senior	awoods@college.edu	NULL
A97850	Ashly Jade	3.57	116	Info System Engineering	Junior	ajade@college.edu	NULL
B92996	Blue Valley	3.52	102	Computer Science	Senior	bvalley@college.edu	NULL
H10210	Holes Smith	3.87	78	Computer Engineering	Sophomore	hsmith@college.edu	NULL
T77896	Tom Erica	3.95	127	Computer Science	Senior	terica@college.edu	NULL

Table 2.5 StudentCourse table

s_course_id	student_id	course_id	credit	major
1000	H10210	CSC-131D	3	CE
1001	B92996	CSC-132A	3	CS/IS
1002	T77896	CSC-335	3	CS/IS
1003	A78835	CSC-331	3	CE
1004	H10210	CSC-234B	3	CE
1005	T77896	CSC-234A	3	CS/IS
1006	B92996	CSC-233A	3	CS/IS
1007	A78835	CSC-132A	3	CE
1008	A78835	CSE-432	3	CE
1009	A78835	CSE-434	3	CE
1010	T77896	CSC-439	3	CS/IS
1011	H10210	CSC-132A	3	CE
1012	H10210	CSC-331	2	CE
1013	A78835	CSC-335	3	CE
1014	A78835	CSE-438	3	CE
1015	T77896	CSC-432	3	CS/IS
1016	A97850	CSC-132B	3	ISE
1017	A97850	CSC-234A	3	ISE
1018	A97850	CSC-331	3	ISE
1019	A97850	CSC-335	3	ISE
1020	T77896	CSE-439	3	CS/IS
1021	B92996	CSC-230	3	CS/IS
1022	A78835	CSE-332	3	CE
1023	B92996	CSE-430	3	CE
1024	T77896	CSC-333A	3	CS/IS
1025	H10210	CSE-433	3	CE
1026	H10210	CSE-334	3	CE
1027	B92996	CSC-131C	3	CS/IS
1028	B92996	CSC-439	3	CS/IS

2.3.1 *Relational Data Model*

Data model is like a blueprint for developing a database. It describes the structure of the database and various data relationships and constraints on the data. This information is used in building tables, keys, and defining relationships. Relational model implies that a user perceives the database as made up of relations, a database jargon for tables. It is imperative that all data elements in the tables are represented correctly. In order to achieve these goals designers use various tools. The most commonly used tool is Entity-Relationship Model (ER). A well-planned model will give consistent results and will allow changes if needed later on. Following section further elaborates on the ER model.

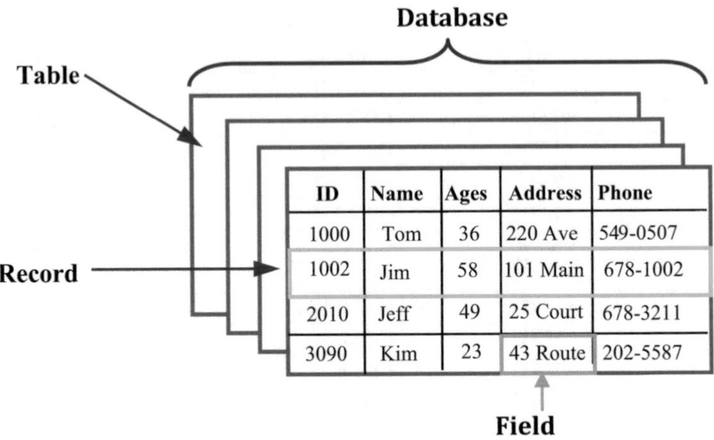

Fig. 2.1 Records and fields in a table

2.3.2 *Entity-Relationship Model (ER)*

ER model was first proposed and developed by Peter Chen in 1976. Since then Charles Bachman and James Martin have added some refinements the model was designed to communicate the database design in the form of a conceptual schema. The ER model is based on the perception that the real world is made up of entities, their attributes, and relationships. The ER model is graphically depicted as Entity-Relationship diagrams (ERD). ERDs are a major modeling tool; they graphically describe the logical structure of the database. ER diagrams can be used with ease to construct the relational tables and are a good vehicle for communicating the database design to the end user or a developer. The three major components of ERD are entities, relationships, and attributes.

Entities An entity is a data object, either real or abstract, about which we want to collect information. For example we may want to collect information about a person, a place, or a thing. An entity in an ER diagram translates into a table. It should preferably be referred to as an entity set. Some common examples are departments, courses, and students. A single occurrence of an entity is an instance. There are four entities in the CSE_Dept database, LogIn, Faculty, Course, and Student. Each entity is translated into a table with the same name. An instance of the Faculty entity will be Alice Brown and her attributes.

Relationships A database is made up of related entities. There is a natural association between the entities; it is referred to as relationship. For example,

- Students take courses
- Departments offer certain courses
- Employees are assigned to departments

The number of occurrences of one entity associated with single occurrence of a related entity is referred to as **cardinality**.

Attributes Each entity has properties or values called attributes associated with it. The attributes of an entity map into fields in a table. *Database Processing* is one attribute of an entity called *Courses*. The domain of an attribute is a set of all possible values from which an attribute can derive its value.

2.4 Identifying Keys

Primary Key and Entity Integrity
An attribute that uniquely identifies one and only one instance of an entity is called a primary key. Sometimes a primary key consists of a combination of attributes. It is referred to as a *composite key*. *Entity integrity rule* states that no attribute that is a member of the primary (composite) key may accept a null value.

A **faculty_id** may serve as a primary key for the Faculty entity, assuming that all faculty members have been assigned a unique FaultyID. However, caution must be exercised when picking an attribute as a primary key. Last Name may not make a good primary key because a department is likely to have more than one person with the same last name. Primary keys for the CSE_DEPT database are shown in Table 2.6.

Primary keys provide a tuple level addressing mechanism in the relational databases. Once you define an attribute as a primary key for an entity, the DBMS will enforce the uniqueness of the primary key. Inserting a duplicate value for primary key field will fail.

Candidate Key
There can be more than one attribute which uniquely identifies an instance of an entity. These are referred to as *candidate keys*. Any one of them can serve as a primary key. For example, ID Number as well as Social Security Number may make a suitable primary key. Candidate keys that are not used as primary key are called *alternate keys*.

Foreign Keys and Referential Integrity
Foreign keys are used to create relationships between tables. It is an attribute in one table whose values are required to match those of primary key in another table. Foreign keys are created to enforce ***referential integrity*** which states that you may not add a record to a table containing a foreign key unless there is a corresponding record in the related table to which it is logically linked. Furthermore, the referential integrity rule also implies that every value of foreign key in a table must match the primary key of a related table or be null. MS Access also makes provision for cascade update and cascade delete

which imply that changes made in one of the related tables will be reflected in the other of the two related tables.

Table 2.6 Faculty table

faculty_id	faculty_name	title	office	phone	college	email	fimage
A52990	Black Anderson	Professor	MTC-218	750-378-9987	Virginia Tech	banderson@college.edu	NULL
A77587	Debby Angles	Associate Professor	MTC-320	750-330-2276	University of Chicago	dangles@college.edu	NULL
B66750	Alice Brown	Assistant Professor	MTC-257	750-330-6650	University of Florida	abrown@college.edu	NULL
B78880	Ying Bai	Associate Professor	MTC-211	750-378-1148	Florida Atlantic University	ybai@college.edu	NULL
B86590	Davis Bhalla	Associate Professor	MTC-214	750-378-1061	University of Notre Dame	dbhalla@college.edu	NULL
H99118	Jeff Henry	Associate Professor	MTC-336	750-330-8650	Ohio State University	jhenry@college.edu	NULL
J33486	Steve Johnson	Distinguished Professor	MTC-118	750-330-1116	Harvard University	sjohnson@college.edu	NULL
K69880	Jenney King	Professor	MTC-324	750-378-1230	East Florida University	jking@college.edu	NULL

Consider two tables Course and Faculty in the sample database, CSE_DEPT. The Course table has a foreign key entitled faculty_id which is primary key in the Faculty table. The two tables are logically related through the **faculty_id** link. Referential integrity rules imply that we may not add a record to the Course table with a faculty_id which is not listed in the Faculty table. In other words there must be a logical link between the two related tables. Secondly, if we change or delete a faculty_id in the Faculty table it must reflect in the Course table meaning that all records in the Course table must be modified using a cascade update or cascade delete (Tables 2.7).

2.5 Define Relationships

Connectivity

Connectivity refers to the types of relationships that entities can have. Basically, it can be *one-to-one, one-to-many, and many-to-many*. In ER diagrams these are indicated by placing 1, M, or N at one of the two ends of the relationship diagram. Figures 2.2, 2.3, 2.4 and 2.5 illustrate the use of this notation.

Table 2.7 Course (Partial data shown), Faculty (Partial data shown)

Course (Partial data shown)		
course_id	course	faculty_id
CSC-132A	Introduction to Programming	J33486
CSC-132B	Introduction to Programming	B78880
CSC-230	Algorithms & Structures	A77587
CSC-232A	Programming I	B66750
CSC-232B	Programming I	A77587
CSC-233A	Introduction to Algorithms	H99118
CSC-233B	Introduction to Algorithms	K69880
CSC-234A	Data Structure & Algorithms	B78880

Faculty (Partial data shown)		
faculty_id	faculty_name	office
A52990	Black Anderson	MTC-218
A77587	Debby Angles	MTC-320
B66750	Alice Brown	MTC-257
B78880	Ying Bai	MTC-211
B86590	Davis Bhalla	MTC-214
H99118	Jeff Henry	MTC-336
J33486	Steve Johnson	MTC-118
K69880	Jenney King	MTC-324

LogIn

user_name	pass_word
ajade	tryagain
awoods	smart
bvalley	see
hsmith	try
terica	excellent

Student

user_name	gpa	credits	student_id
ajade	3.26	108	A97850
awoods	3.57	116	A78835
bvalley	3.52	102	B92996
hsmith	3.87	78	H10210
terica	3.95	127	J77896

Fig. 2.2 **One-to-**one relationship in the LogIn and the Student tables

- A ***one-to-one*** **(1:1)** relationship occurs when one instance of entity A is related to only one instance of entity B. For example, **user_name** in the LogIn table and **user_name** in the Student table (Fig. 2.2).
  A ***one-to-many (1:M)*** relationship occurs when one instance of entity A is associated with zero, one, or many instances of entity B. However, entity B is associated with only one instance of entity A. For example, one department can have many faculty members; each faculty member is assigned to only one department. In CSE_DEPT database, one-to-many relationship is represented by **faculty_id** in the Faculty table and **faculty_id** in the Course table, **student_id** in the Student table and **student_id** in the StudentCourse table, **course_id** in the Course table, and **course_id** in the StudentCourse table (Fig. 2.3).

Faculty

faculty_id	faculty_name	office
A52990	Black Anderson	MTC-218
A77587	Debby Angles	MTC-320
B66750	Alice Brown	MTC-257
B78880	Ying Bai	MTC-211
B86590	Davis Bhalla	MTC-214
H99118	Jeff Henry	MTC-336
J33486	Steve Johnson	MTC-118
K69880	Jenney King	MTC-324

Course

course_id	course	faculty_id
CSC-132A	Introduction to Programming	J33486
CSC-132B	Introduction to Programming	B78880
CSC-230	Algorithms & Structures	A77587
CSC-232A	Programming I	B66750
CSC-232B	Programming I	A77587
CSC-233A	Introduction to Algorithms	H99118
CSC-233B	Introduction to Algorithms	K69880
CSC-234A	Data Structure & Algorithms	B78880

Fig. 2.3 One-to-many relationship between Faculty and Course tables

Student

student_id	student_name	gpa	credits
A78835	Andrew Woods	3.26	108
A97850	Ashly Jade	3.57	116
B92996	Blue Valley	3.52	102
H10210	Holes Smith	3.87	78
T77896	Tom Erica	3.95	127

Course

course_id	course	faculty_id
CSC-132A	Introduction to Programming	J33486
CSC-132B	Introduction to Programming	B78880
CSC-230	Algorithms & Structures	A77587
CSC-232A	Programming I	B66750
CSC-232B	Programming I	A77587
CSC-233A	Introduction to Algorithms	H99118

StudentCourse

s_course_id	student_id	course_id	credit	major
1000	H10210	CSC-131D	3	CE
1001	B92996	CSC-132A	3	CS/IS
1002	T77896	CSC-335	3	CS/IS
1003	A78835	CSC-331	3	CE
1004	H10210	CSC-234B	3	CE
1005	T77896	CSC-234A	3	CS/IS
1006	B92996	CSC-233A	3	CS/IS

Fig. 2.4 Many-to-many relationship between Student and Course tables

- A ***many-to-many*** **(M:N)** relationship occurs when one instance of entity A is associated with zero, one, or many instances of entity B. And one instance of entity B is associated with zero, one, or many instances of entity A. For example, a student may take many courses and one course may be taken by more than one student, as shown in Fig. 2.4.

In CSE_DEPT database, a many-to-many relationship can be realized by using the third table. For example, in this case, the StudentCourse that works as the third table, set a many-to-many relationship between the Student and the Course tables.

This database design assumes that the course table only contains courses taught by all faculty members in this department for one semester. Therefore each course can only be taught by a unique faculty. If one wants to develop a Course table that contains courses taught by all faculty in more than one semester, the third table, say

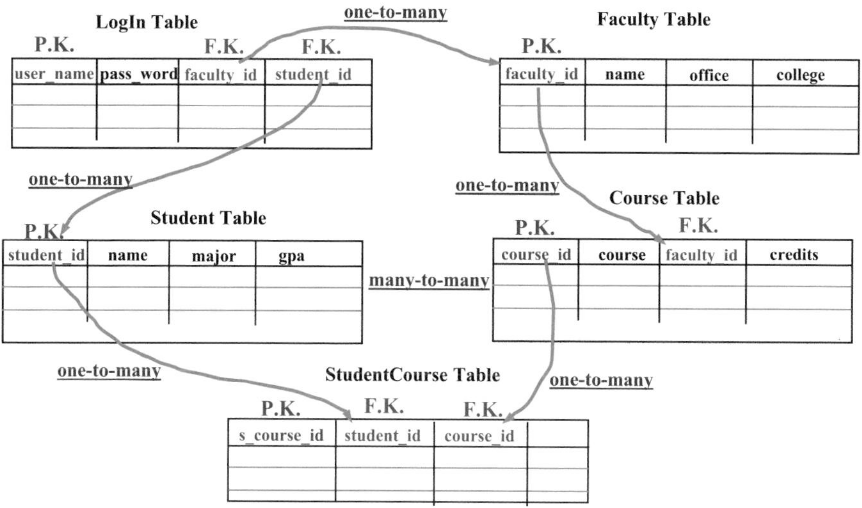

Fig. 2.5 Relationships in CSE_DEPT database

FacultyCourse table, should be created to set up a many-to-many relationship between the Faculty and the Course table since one course may be taught by the different faculty for the different semester.

The relationships in CSE_DEPT database are summarized in Fig. 2.5.

Database name: **CSE_DEPT**

Five entities are:

- LogIn
- Faculty
- Course
- Student
- StudentCourse

The relationships between these entities are shown below. **P.K.** and **F.K.** represent the primary key and the foreign key respectively.

Figure 2.6 displays the Microsoft Access relationships diagram among various tables in the CSE_Dept database. One-to-many relationships is indicated by placing 1 at one end of the link and ∞ at the other. The many-to-many relationship between the Student and the Course table was broken down to two one- to-many relationships by creating a new StudentCourse table.

2.6 ER Notation

There are a number of ER notations available including Chen's, Bachman, Crow's foot, and a few others. There is no consensus on the symbols and the styles used to draw ERD's. A number of drawing tools are available to draw ERDs. These include

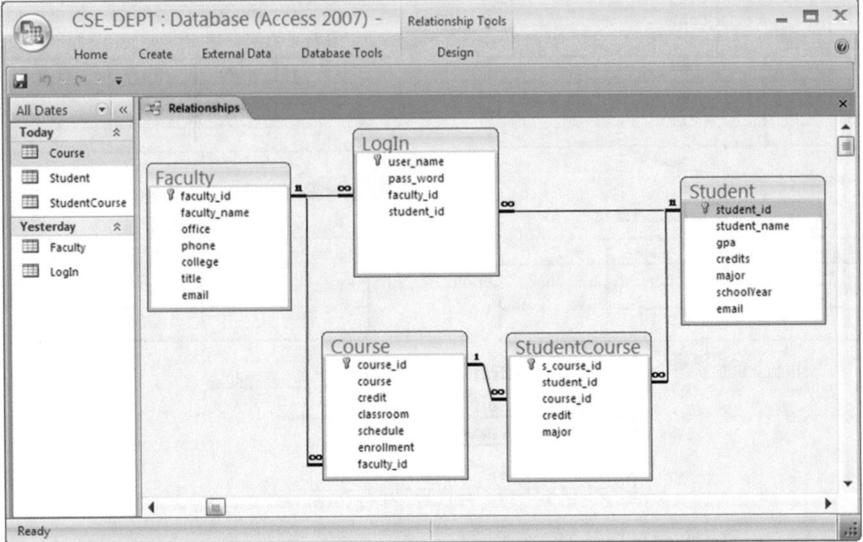

Fig. 2.6 Relationships are illustrated using MS Access in the CSE_DEPT database

ER Assistant, Microsoft Visio, and Smart Draw, among others. Commonly used notations are shown in Fig. 2.7.

2.7 Data Normalization

After identifying tables, attributes, and relationships the next logical step in database design is to make sure that the database structure is optimum. Optimum structure is achieved by eliminating redundancies, various inefficiencies, update and deletion anomalies that usually occur in the unnormalized or partially normalized databases. Data normalization is a progressive process. The steps in the normalization process are called normal forms. Each normal form progressively improves the database and makes it more efficient. In other words a database that is in second normal form is better than the one in the first normal form, and the one in third normal form is better than the one in second normal form. To be in the third normal form a database has to be in the first and second normal form. There are fourth and fifth normal forms but for most practical purposes a database meeting the criteria of third normal form is considered to be of good design.

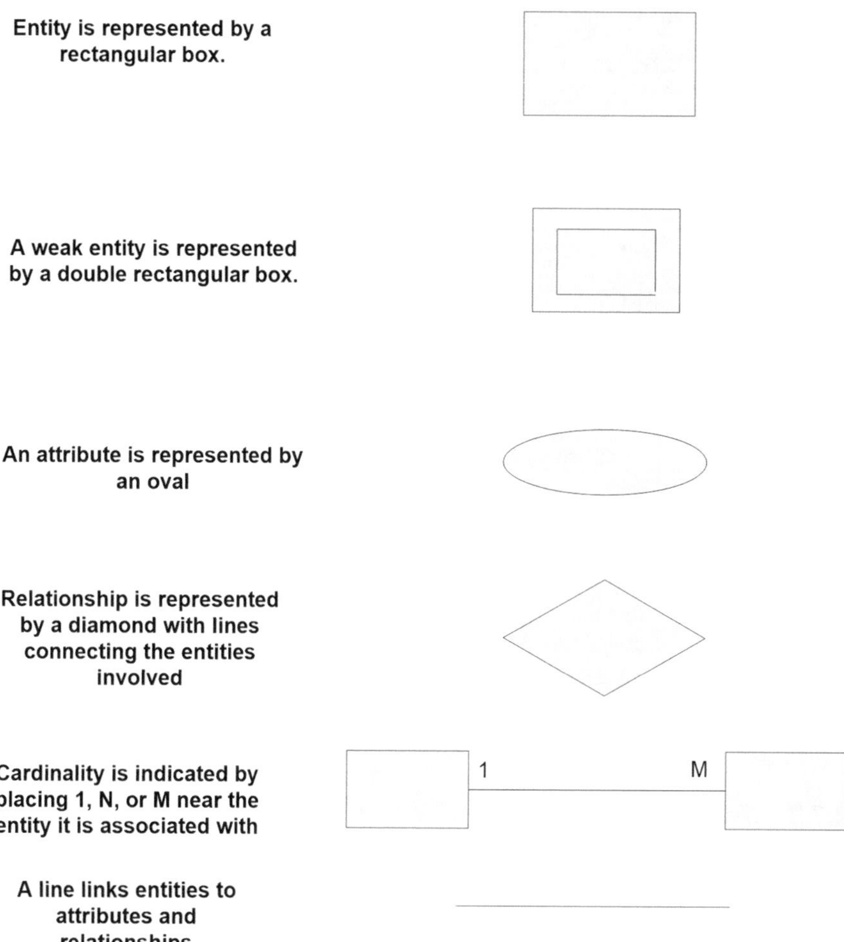
Entity is represented by a rectangular box.
A weak entity is represented by a double rectangular box.
An attribute is represented by an oval
Relationship is represented by a diamond with lines connecting the entities involved
Cardinality is indicated by placing 1, N, or M near the entity it is associated with
1
M
A line links entities to attributes and relationships

Fig. 2.7 Commonly used symbols for ER notation

2.7.1 First Normal Form (1NF)

A table is in first normal form if values in each column are atomic, that is there are no repeating groups of data.

The following Faculty table (Table 2.8) is not normalized. Some faculty members have more than one telephone number listed in the phone column. These are called repeating groups.

In order to convert this table to the First Normal Form (INF), the data must be atomic. In other words the repeating rows must be broken into two or more atomic rows. Table 2.9 illustrates the Faculty table in 1NF where repeating groups have been removed. Now it is in first normal form.

Table 2.8 Unnormalized Faculty table with repeating groups

faculty_id	faculty_name	office	phone
A52990	Black Anderson	MTC-218, SHB-205	750-378-9987, 555-255-8897
A77587	Debby Angles	MTC-320	750-330-2276
B66750	Alice Brown	MTC-257	750-330-6650
B78880	Ying Bai	MTC-211, SHB-105	750-378-1148, 555-246-4582
B86590	Davis Bhalla	MTC-214	750-378-1061
H99118	Jeff Henry	MTC-336	750-330-8650
J33486	Steve Johnson	MTC-118	750-330-1116
K69880	Jenney King	MTC-324	750-378-1230

Table 2.9 Normalized Faculty table

faculty_id	faculty_name	office	phone
A52990	Black Anderson	MTC-218	750-378-9987
A52990	Black Anderson	SHB-205	555-255-8897
A77587	Debby Angles	MTC-320	750-330-2276
B66750	Alice Brown	MTC-257	750-330-6650
B78880	Ying Bai	MTC-211	750-378-1148
B78880	Ying Bai	SHB-105	555-246-4582
B86590	Davis Bhalla	MTC-214	750-378-1061
H99118	Jeff Henry	MTC-336	750-330-8650
J33486	Steve Johnson	MTC-118	750-330-1116
K69880	Jenney King	MTC-324	750-378-1230

2.7.2 *Second Normal Form (2NF)*

A table is in second normal form if it is already in 1NF and every non-key column is fully dependent upon the primary key.

This implies that if the primary key consists of a single column then the table in 1NF is automatically in 2NF. The second part of the definition implies that if the key is composite then none of the non-key columns will depend upon just one of the columns that participate in the composite key.

The Faculty table in Table 2.9 is in first normal form. However, it has a composite primary key, made up of faculty_id and office. The phone number depends on a part of the primary key, the office, and not on the whole primary key. This can lead to update and deletion anomalies mentioned above.

By splitting the old Faculty table (Fig. 2.8) into two new tables, Faculty and Office, we can remove the dependencies mentioned earlier. Now the faculty table has a primary key, faculty_id, and the Office table has a primary key, office. The non-key columns in both tables now depend only on the primary keys only.

Old Faculty table in 1NF

faculty_id	faculty_name	office	phone
A52990	Black Anderson	MTC-218	750-378-9987
A52990	Black Anderson	SHB-205	555-255-8897
A77587	Debby Angles	MTC-320	750-330-2276
B66750	Alice Brown	MTC-257	750-330-6650
B78880	Ying Bai	MTC-211	750-378-1148
B78880	Ying Bai	SHB-105	555-246-4582
B86590	Davis Bhalla	MTC-214	750-378-1061
H99118	Jeff Henry	MTC-336	750-330-8650
J33486	Steve Johnson	MTC-118	750-330-1116
K69880	Jenney King	MTC-324	750-378-1230

New Faculty table

faculty_id	faculty_name
A52990	Black Anderson
A52990	Black Anderson
A77587	Debby Angles
B66750	Alice Brown
B78880	Ying Bai
B78880	Ying Bai
B86590	Davis Bhalla
H99118	Jeff Henry
J33486	Steve Johnson
K69880	Jenney King

New Office table

office	phone	faculty_id
MTC-218	750-378-9987	A52990
SHB-205	555-255-8897	A52990
MTC-320	750-330-2276	A77587
MTC-257	750-330-6650	B66750
MTC-211	750-378-1148	B78880
SHB-105	555-246-4582	B78880
MTC-214	750-378-1061	B86590
MTC-336	750-330-8650	H99118
MTC-118	750-330-1116	J33486
MTC-324	750-378-1230	K69880

Fig. 2.8 Converting Faulty table into 2NF by decomposing the old table in two, Faculty and Office

2.7.3 Third Normal Form (3NF)

A table is in third normal form if it is already in 2NF and every non-key column is non-transitively dependent upon the primary key. In other words all non-key columns are mutually independent, but at the same time they are fully dependent upon the primary key only.

Another way of stating this is that in order to achieve 3NF no column should depend upon any non-key column. If column B depends on column A, then A is said to functionally determine column B; hence the term determinant. Another definition of 3NF says that the table should be in 2NF and only determinants it contains are candidate keys.

Table 2.10 The old Course table

course_id	course	classroom	faculty_ id	faculty_name	phone
CSC-131A	Computers in Society	MTC-109	A52990	Black Anderson	750-378-9987
CSC-131B	Computers in Society	MTC-114	B66750	Alice Brown	750-330-6650
CSC-131C	Computers in Society	MTC-109	A52990	Black Anderson	750-378-9987
CSC-131D	Computers in Society	MTC-109	B86590	Davis Bhalla	750-378-1061
CSC-131E	Computers in Society	MTC-301	B66750	Alice Brown	750-330-6650
CSC-131I	Computers in Society	MTC-109	A52990	Black Anderson	750-378-9987
CSC-132A	Introduction to Programming	MTC-303	J33486	Steve Johnson	750-330-1116
CSC-132B	Introduction to Programming	MTC-302	B78880	Ying Bai	750-378-1148

For the Course table in Table 2.10, all non-key columns depend on the primary key – course_id. In addition name and phone columns also depend on faculty_id. This table is in second normal form but it suffers from update, addition, and deletion anomalies because of transitive dependencies. In order to conform to third normal form we can split this table into two tables, Course and Instructor (Tables 2.11 and 2.12). Now we have eliminated the transitive dependencies that are apparent in the Course table in Table 2.10.

2.8 Database Components in Some Popular Databases

All databases allow for storage, retrieval, and management of the data. Simple databases provide basic services to accomplish these tasks. Many database providers, like Microsoft SQL Server and Oracle, provide additional services which necessitate storing many components in the database other than data. These components such as views, stored procedures, etc., are collectively called database objects. In this section, we will discuss various objects that make up MS Access, SQL Server, and Oracle databases.

There are two major types of databases, *File Server* and *Client Server:*

In a File Server database, data is stored in a file and each user of the database retrieves the data, displays the data, or modifies the data directly from or to the file. In a Client Server database the data is also stored in a file; however, all these operations are mediated through a master program called a server. MS Access is a File Server database, whereas Microsoft SQL Server and Oracle are Client Server databases. The Client Server databases have several advantages over the File Server

Table 2.11 The new Course table

course_id	course	classroom
CSC-131A	Computers in Society	MTC-109
CSC-131B	Computers in Society	MTC-114
CSC-131C	Computers in Society	MTC-109
CSC-131D	Computers in Society	MTC-109
CSC-131E	Computers in Society	MTC-301
CSC-131I	Computers in Society	MTC-109
CSC-132A	Introduction to Programming	MTC-303
CSC-132B	Introduction to Programming	MTC-302

Table 2.12 The new Instructor table

faculty_id	faculty_name	phone
A52990	Black Anderson	750-378-9987
B66750	Alice Brown	750-330-6650
A52990	Black Anderson	750-378-9987
B86590	Davis Bhalla	750-378-1061
B66750	Alice Brown	750-330-6650
A52990	Black Anderson	750-378-9987
J33486	Steve Johnson	750-330-1116
B78880	Ying Bai	750-378-1148
A77587	Debby Angles	750-330-2276

databases. These include minimizing chances of crashes, provision of features for recovery, enforcement of security, better performance, and more efficient use of the network compared to the file server databases.

2.8.1 Microsoft Access Databases

Microsoft Access Database Engine is a collection of information stored in a systematic way that forms the underlying component of a database. Also called a Jet (Joint Engine Technology), it allows the manipulation of relational database. It offers a single interface that other software may use to access Microsoft databases. The supporting software is developed to provide security, integrity, indexing, record locking, etc. By executing MS Access program, MSACCESS.EXE, you can see the database engine at work and the user interface it provides. Figure 2.9 shows how a Java application accesses the MS Access database via ACE OLE database provider.

Database File

Access database is made up of a number of components called objects which are stored in a single file referred to as *database file*. As new objects are created or more

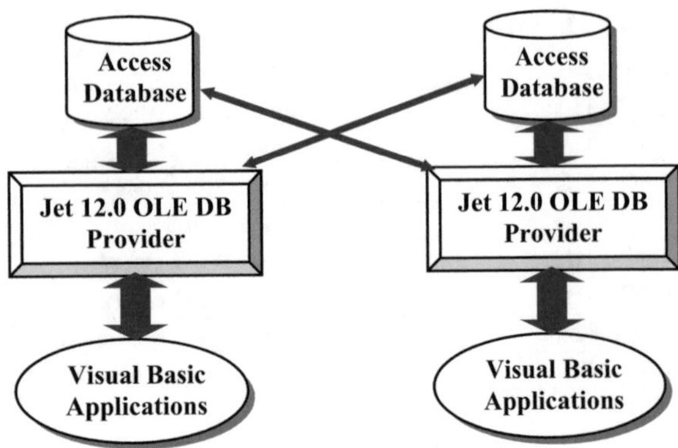

Fig. 2.9 Microsoft Access database illustration

data is added to the database, this file gets bigger. This is a complex file that stores objects like tables, queries, forms, reports, macros, and modules. The Access files have an .mdb (Microsoft DataBase) extension. Some of these objects help user to work with the database, others are useful for displaying database information in a comprehensible and easy-to-read format.

Tables

Before you can create a table in Access, you must create a database container and give it a name with the extension .mdb. Database creation is simple process and is explained in detail with an example, later in this chapter. Suffice it to say that a table is made up of columns and rows. Columns are referred to as fields, which are attributes of an entity. Rows are referred to as records also called tuples.

Queries

One of the main purposes of storing data in a database is that the data may be retrieved later as needed, without having to write complex programs. This purpose is accomplished in Access and other databases by writing SQL statements. A group of such statements is called a query. It enables you to retrieve, update, and display data in the tables. You may display data from more than one table by using a Join operation. In addition you may insert or delete data in the tables.

Access also provides a visual graphic user interface to create queries. This bypasses writing SQL statements and makes it appealing to beginning and not so savvy users, who can use wizards or GUI interface to create queries. Queries can extract information in a variety of ways. You can make them as simple or as complex as you like. You may specify various criteria to get desired information, perform comparisons, or you may want to perform some calculations and obtain the results. In essence, operators, functions, and expressions are the building blocks for Access operation.

2.8.2 *SQL Server Databases*

The Microsoft SQL Server Database Engine is a service for storing and processing data in either a relational (tabular) format or as XML documents. Various tasks performed by the Database Engine include:

- Designing and creating a database to hold the relational tables or XML documents
- Accessing and modifying the data stored in the database.
- Implementing Web sites and applications
- Building procedures
- Optimizing the performance of the database

The SQL Server database is a complex entity, made up of multiple components. It is more complex than MS Access database which can be simply copied and distributed. Certain procedures have to be followed for copying and distributing an SQL server database.

SQL Server is used by a diverse group of professionals with diverse needs and requirements. To satisfy different needs, SQL Server comes in five editions, Enterprise edition, Standard edition, Workgroup edition, Developer edition, and Express edition. The most common editions are Enterprise, Standard, and Workgroup. It is noteworthy that the database engine is virtually the same in all of these editions.

SQL Server database can be stored on the disk using three types of files – primary data files, secondary data files, and transaction log files. Primary data files are created first and contain user-defined objects like tables and views, and system objects. These files have an extension of .mdf. If the database grows too big for a disk, it can be stored as secondary files with an extension .ndf. The SQL Server still treats these files as if they are together. The data file is made up of many objects. The transaction log files carry .ldf extension. All transactions to the database are recorded in this file.

Figure 2.10 illustrates the structure of the SQL Server Database. Each Java application has to access the server, which in turn accesses the SQL database.

Data Files

A data file is a conglomeration of objects, which includes tables, keys, views, stored procedures, and others. All these objects are necessary for the efficient operation of the database.

Tables

The data in a relational database resides in tables. These are the building blocks of the database. Each table consists of columns and rows. Columns represent various attributes or fields in a table. Each row represents one record. For example, one record in the Faculty table consists of name, office, phone, college, title, and email. Each field has a distinct data type, meaning that it can contain only one type of data such as numeric or character. Tables are the first objects created in a database.

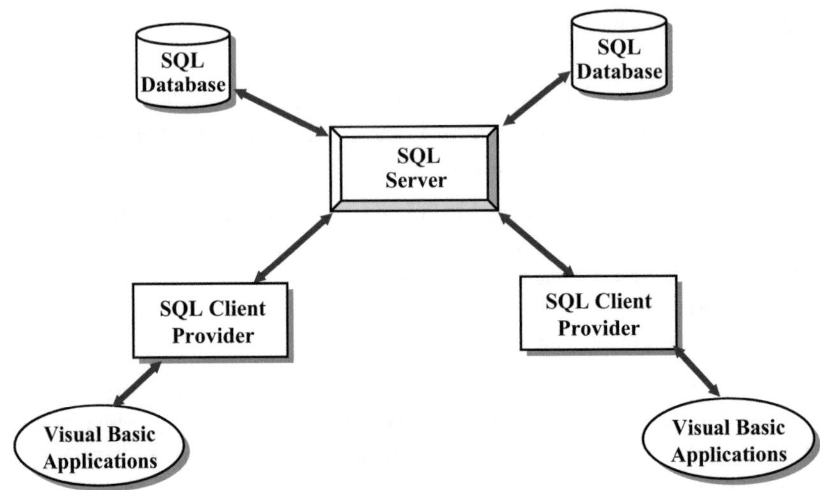

Fig. 2.10 SQL Server database structure

Views

Views are virtual tables, meaning that they do not contain any data. They are stored as queries in the database, which are executed when needed. A view can contain data from one or more tables. The views can provide database security. Sensitive information in a database can be excluded by including non-sensitive information in a view and providing user access to the views instead of all tables in a database. The views can also hide the complexities of a database. A user can be using a view that is made up of multiple tables, whereas it appears as a single table to the user. The user can execute queries against a view just like a table.

Stored Procedures

Users write queries to retrieve, display, or manipulate data in the database. These queries can be stored on the client machine or on the server. There are advantages associated with storing SQL queries on the server rather than on the client machine. It has to do with the network performance. Usually users use same queries over and over again, frequently different users are trying to access the same data. Instead of sending the same queries on the network repeatedly, it improves the network performance and executes queries faster if the queries are stored on the server where they are compiled and saved as stored procedures. The users can simply call the stored procedure with a simple command like *execute stored_procedure* A.

Keys and Relationships

A *primary key* is created for each table in the database to efficiently access records and to ensure *entity integrity*. This implies that each record in a table is unique in some way. Therefore, no two records can have the same primary key. It is defined as a globally unique identifier. Moreover, a primary key may not have null value, i.e., missing data. SQL server creates a unique index for each primary key. This ensures fast and efficient access to data. One or more columns can be combined to designate a primary key.

In a relational database relationships between tables can be logically defined with the help of *foreign keys*. A foreign key of one record in a table points specifically to a primary key of a record in another table. This allows a user to join multiple tables and retrieve information from more than one table at a time. Foreign keys also enforce *referential integrity*, a defined relationship between the tables which does not allow insertion or deletion of records in a table unless the foreign key of a record in one table matches a primary key of a record in another table. In other words, a record in one table cannot have a foreign key that does not point to a primary key in another table. Additionally, a primary key may not be deleted if there are foreign keys in another table pointing to it. The foreign key values associated with a primary key must be deleted first. Referential integrity protects related data, from corruption, stored in different tables.

Indexes

The indexes are used to find records, quickly and efficiently, in a table just like one would use an index in a book. SQL server uses two types of indexes to retrieve and update data – clustered and non-clustered.

Clustered index sorts the data in a table so that the data can be accessed efficiently. It is akin to a dictionary or a phone book where records are arranged alphabetically. So one can go directly to a specific alphabet and from there search sequentially for the specific record. The clustered indexes are like an inverted tree. The index's structure is called a B-tree for binary-tree. You start with the root page at the top and find the location of other pages further down at secondary level, following to tertiary level and so on until you find the desired record. The very bottom pages are the leaf pages and contain the actual data. There can be only one clustered index per table because clustered indexes physically rearrange the data.

Non-clustered indexes do not physically rearrange the data as do the clustered indexes. They also consist of a binary tree with various levels of pages. The major difference, however, is that the leaves do not contain the actual data as in the clustered indexes, instead they contain pointers that point to the corresponding records in the table. These pointers are called row locators.

The indexes can be unique where the duplicate keys are not allowed, or not unique which permits duplicate keys. Any column can be used to access data can be used to generate an index. Usually, the primary and the foreign key columns are used to create indexes.

Transaction Log Files

A transaction is a logical group of SQL statements which carry out a unit of work. Client server database use log file to keep track of transactions that are applied to the database. For example, before an update is applied to a database, the database server creates an entry in the transaction log to generate a before picture of the data in a table and then applies a transaction and creates another entry to generate an after picture of the data in that table. This keeps track of all the operations performed on a database. Transaction logs can be used to recover data in case of crashes or disasters. Transaction logs are automatically maintained by the SQL Server.

2.8.3 Oracle Databases

Oracle was designed to be platform-independent making it architecturally more complex than the SQL Server database. Oracle database contains more files than SQL Server database.

The Oracle DBMS comes in three levels: Enterprise, Standard, and Personal. Enterprise edition is the most powerful and is suitable for large installations using a large number of transactions in multi-user environment. Standard edition is also used by high-level multi-user installations. It lacks some of the utilities available in Enterprise edition. Personal edition is used in a single user environment for developing database applications. The database engine components are virtually the same for all three editions.

Oracle architecture is made up of several components including an Oracle server, Oracle instance, and an Oracle database. The Oracle server contains several files, processes, and memory structures. Some of these are used to improve the performance of the database and ensure database recovery in case of a crash. The Oracle server consists of an Oracle instance and an Oracle database. An Oracle instance consists of background processes and memory structures. Background processes perform input/output and monitor other Oracle processes for better performance and reliability. Oracle database consists of data files that provide the actual physical storage for the data.

Data files

The main purpose of a database is to store and retrieve data. It consists of a collection of data that is treated as a unit. An Oracle database has a logical and physical structure. The logical layer consists of tablespaces, necessary for the smooth operation of an Oracle installation. Data files make up the physical layer of the database. These consist of three types of files: *data files* which contain actual data in the database, *redo logfiles* which contain records of modifications made to the database for future recovery in case of failure, and *control files* which are used to maintain and verify database integrity. Oracle server uses other files that are not part of the database. These include *parameter file* that defines the characteristics of an Oracle instance, *password file* used for authentication, and *archived redo log* files which are copies of the redo log files necessary for recovery from failure. A partial list of some of the components follows.

Tables

Users can store data in a regular table, partitioned table, index-organized table, or clustered table. A *regular table* is the default table as in other databases. Rows can be stored in any order. A *partitioned table* has one or more partitions where rows are stored. Partitions are useful for large tables which can be queried by several processes concurrently. *Index organized tables* provide fast key-based access for queries involving exact matches. The table may have index on one or more of its columns. Instead of using two storage spaces for the table and a B-tree index, a single storage space is used to store both the B-tree and other columns. A *clustered table* or group of tables share the same block called a cluster. They are grouped together because they share common columns and are frequently used together. Clusters have a cluster key for identifying the rows that need to be stored together. Cluster keys are independent of the primary key and may be made up of one or more columns. Clusters are created to improve performance.

Views
Views are like virtual tables and are used in a similar fashion as in the SQL Server databases discussed above.

Stored Procedures
In Oracle functions and procedures may be saved as stored program units. Multiple input arguments (parameters) may be passed as input to functions and procedures; however, functions return only one value as output, whereas procedures may return multiple values as output. The advantages to creating and using stored procedures are the same as mentioned above for SQL server. By storing procedures on the server individual SQL statements do not have to be transmitted over the network, thus reducing the network traffic. In addition, commonly used SQL statements are saved as functions or procedures and may be used again and again by various users thus saving rewriting the same code over and over again. The stored procedures should be made flexible so that different users are able to pass input information to the procedure in the form of arguments or parameters and get the desired output.

Figure 2.11 shows the syntax to create a stored procedure in Oracle. It has three sections – a header, a body, and an exception section. The procedure is defined in

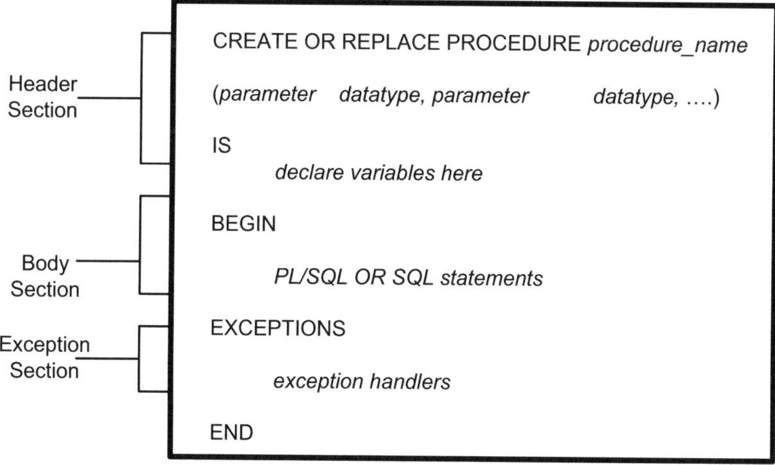

Fig. 2.11 Syntax for creating a stored procedure in Oracle

the header section. Input and output parameters, along with their data types, are declared here and transmit information to or from the procedure. The body section of the procedure starts with a keyword BEGIN and consists of SQL statements. The exceptions section of the procedure begins with the keyword EXCEPTION and contains exception handlers which are designed to handle the occurrence of some conditions that changes the normal flow of execution.

Indexes are created to provide direct access to rows. An index is a tree structure. Indexes can be classified on their logic design or their physical implementation. Logical classification is based on application perspective, whereas physical classification is based on how the indexes are stored. Indexes can be partitioned or nonpartitioned. Large tables use partitioned indexes, which spreads an index to multiple table spaces thus decreasing contention for index look up and increasing manageability. An index may consist of a single column or multiple columns; it may be unique or non-unique. Some of these indexes are outlined below.

Function-based indexes precompute the value of a function or expression of one or more columns and stores it in an index. It can be created as a B-tree or as a bit map. It can improve the performance of queries performed on tables that rarely change.

Domain Indexes are application-specific and are created and managed by the user or applications. Single column indexes can be built on text, spatial, scalar, object, or LOB data types.

B-tree indexes store a list of row IDs for each key. Structure of a *B-tree* index is similar to the ones in the SQL Server described above. The leaf nodes contain indexes that point to rows in a table. The leaf blocks allow scanning of the index in either ascending or descending order. Oracle server maintains all indexes when insert, update, or delete operations are performed on a table.

Bitmap indexes are useful when columns have low cardinality and a large number of rows. For example, a column may contain few distinct values like Y/N for marital status, or M/F for gender. A bitmap is organized like a B-tree where the leaf nodes store a bitmap instead of row IDs. When changes are made to the key columns, bit maps must be modified.

Initialization Parameter files

Oracle server must read the initialization parameter file before starting an oracle database instance. There are two types of initialization parameter files: static parameter file and a persistent parameter file. An initialization parameter file contains a list of instance parameters, and the name of the database the instance is associated with, name and location of control files, and information about the undo segments. Multiple initialization parameter files can exist to optimize performance.

Control Files

A control file is a small binary file that defines the current state of the database. Before a database can be opened control file is read to determine if the database is in a valid state or not. It maintains the integrity of the database. Oracle uses a single control file per database. It is maintained continuously by the server and can be maintained only by the Oracle server. It cannot be edited by a user or database administrator. A control file contains: database name and identifier, time stamp of database creation, tablespace name, names and location of data files and redo log-files, current log files sequence number, archive, and backup information.

Redo Log Files
Oracle's redo log files provide a way to recover data in the event of a database failure. All transactions are written to a redo log buffer and passed on to the redo log files.

Redo log files record all changes to the data, provide a recovery mechanism, and can be organized into groups. A set of identical copies of online redo log files is called a redo log file group. The Oracle server needs a minimum of two online redo logfile groups for normal operations. The initial set of redo log file groups and members are created during the database creation. Redo log files are used in a cyclic fashion. Each redo log file group is identified by a log sequence number and is overwritten each time the log is reused. In other words, when a redo log file is full then the log writer moves to the second redo log file. After the second one is full first one is reused.

Password Files
Depending upon whether the database is administered locally or remotely, one can choose either operating system or password file authentication to authenticate database administrators. Oracle provides a password utility to create password file. Administrators use the GRANT command to provide access to the database using the password file.

2.9 Create Microsoft SQL Server 2019 Express Sample Database

After you finished the installation of SQL Server 2019 Express database and SQL Server Management Studio (refer to Appendix A), you can begin to use it to connect to the server and build our database. Go to **Start|Microsoft SQL Server Tools 18|Microsoft SQL Server Management Studio 18**. A connection dialog is opened as shown in Fig. 2.12.

Your computer name followed by your server name should be displayed in the **Server name:** box. In this case, it is **YBSmart\SQL2019Express**. The Windows NT default security engine is used by selecting the **Windows Authentication** method from the **Authentication** box. The User name box contains the name you entered when you register for your computer. Click the **Connect** button to connect your client to the SQL database Server.

The server management studio is opened when this connection is completed, which is shown in Fig. 2.13.

To create a new database, right click on the **Databases** folder from the **Object Explorer** window, and select the **New Database** item from the popup menu. Enter

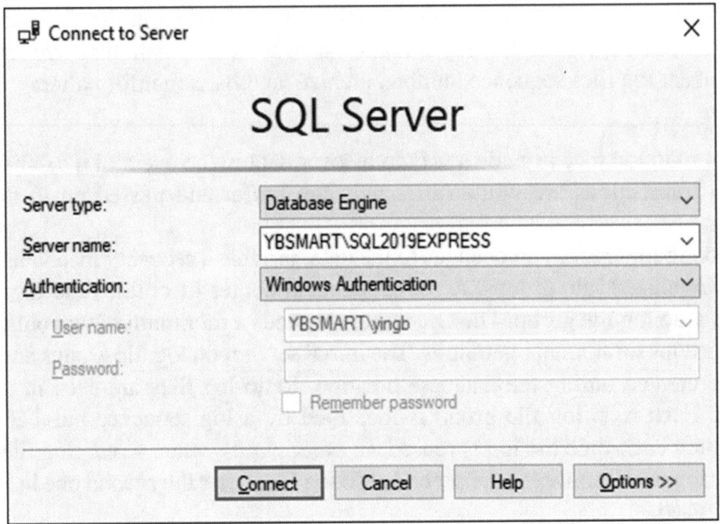

Fig. 2.12 Connect to the SQL Server 2019 Express database

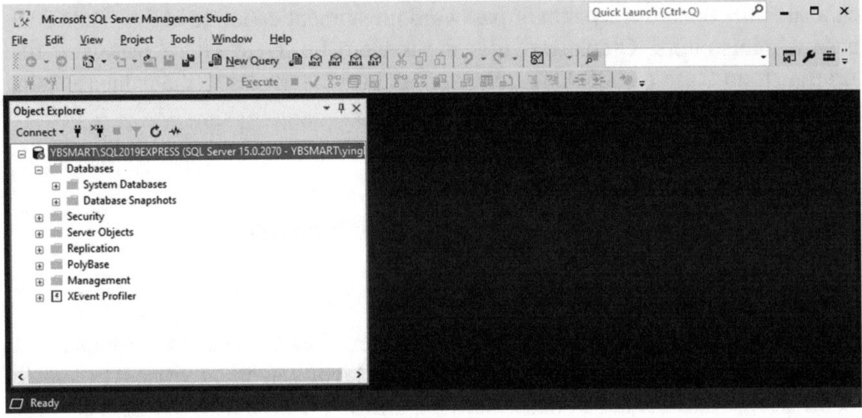

Fig. 2.13 The opened server management studio

CSE_DEPT into the **Database name** box in the New Database dialog as the name of our database, keep all other settings unchanged and then click the **OK** button. You can find that a new database named **CSE_DEPT** is created and located under the **Database** folder in the Object Explorer window.

Then you need to create data tables. For this sample database, you need to create five data tables: **LogIn, Faculty, Course, Student**, and **StudentCourse**. Expand the **CSE_DEPT** database folder by clicking the plus symbol next to it. Right click on the **Tables** folder and select the **New→Table** item, a new table window is displayed, as shown in Fig. 2.14.

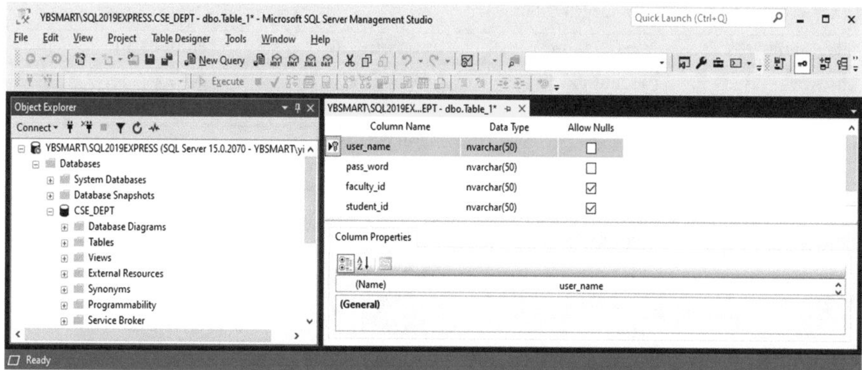

Fig. 2.14 The new table window

2.9.1 Create the LogIn Table

A default data table **dbo.Table_1** is created as shown in Fig. 2.14. Three columns are displayed in this new table: **Column Name**, **Data Type**, and **Allow Nulls**, which allows you to enter the name, the data type, and a null check mark for each column. You can check the checkbox if you allow that column to be empty, otherwise do not check it if you want that column to contain a valid data. Generally for the column that works as the primary key, you should not make check for the checkbox associated with that column.

The first table is **LogIn** table, which has four columns with the following column names: **user_name, pass_word, faculty_id**, and **student_id**. Enter those four names into four **Column Names** columns. The data types for these four columns are all **nvarchar(50)**, which means that this is a varied char type with a maximum letters of 50. Enter those data types into each **Data Type** column. The top two columns, **user_name** and **pass_word**, cannot be empty, so leave those checkboxes blank and check other two checkboxes.

To make the first column **user_name** as a primary key, click on the first row and then go to the Toolbar and select the **Primary Key** (displayed as a key) tool. In this way, a symbol of primary key is displayed on the left of this row, which is shown in Fig. 2.14.

Before we can continue to finish this **LogIn** table, we need first to save and name this table. Go to **File|Save Table_1** and enter the **LogIn** as the name for this new table. Click the **OK** button to finish this saving. A new table named **dbo.LogIn** is added into the new database under the **Tables** folder in the Object Explorer window.

To add data into this **LogIn** table, right click on this table (right-click on the **Tables** folder and select **Refresh** if you cannot find this **LogIn** table) and select **Edit Top 200 Rows** item from the popup menu. Enter all login data shown in Table 2.13 into this table. In fact, you can copy all data rows from Table 2.13 and paste them to the **LogIn** table directly. Your finished **LogIn** table should match one that is shown in Fig. 2.15.

Table 2.13 The data in the LogIn table

user_name	pass_word	faculty_id	student_id
abrown	america	B66750	NULL
ajade	tryagain	NULL	A97850
awoods	smart	NULL	A78835
banderson	birthday	A52990	NULL
bvalley	see	NULL	B92996
dangles	tomorrow	A77587	NULL
hsmith	try	NULL	H10210
terica	excellent	NULL	T77896
jhenry	test	H99118	NULL
jking	goodman	K69880	NULL
dbhalla	india	B86590	NULL
sjohnson	jermany	J33486	NULL
ybai	come	B78880	NULL

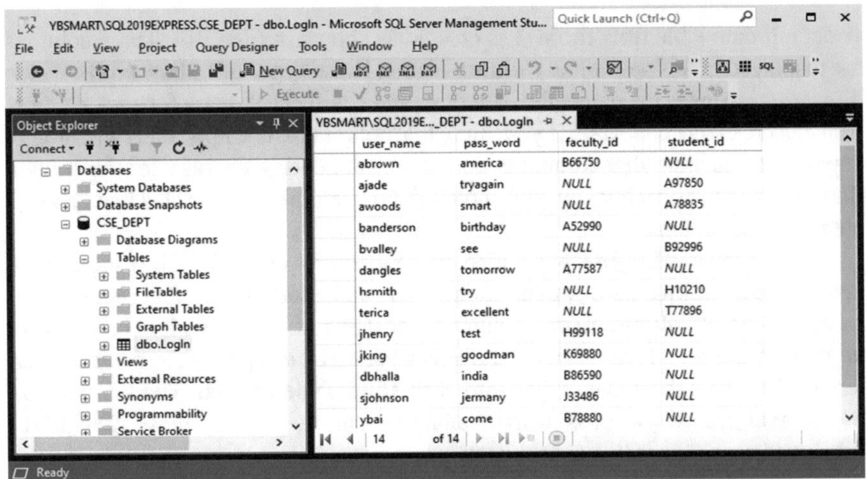

Fig. 2.15 The finished LogIn table

A point is that you must place an NULL for any field that has no value in this table since it is different with the blank field in the Microsoft Access file database. Go to the **File|Save All** item to save this table. Now let's continue to create the second table **Faculty**.

2.9.2 Create the Faculty Table

Right click on the **Tables** folder under the **CSE_DEPT** database folder and select the **Table** item to open the design view of a new table, which is shown in Fig. 2.16.

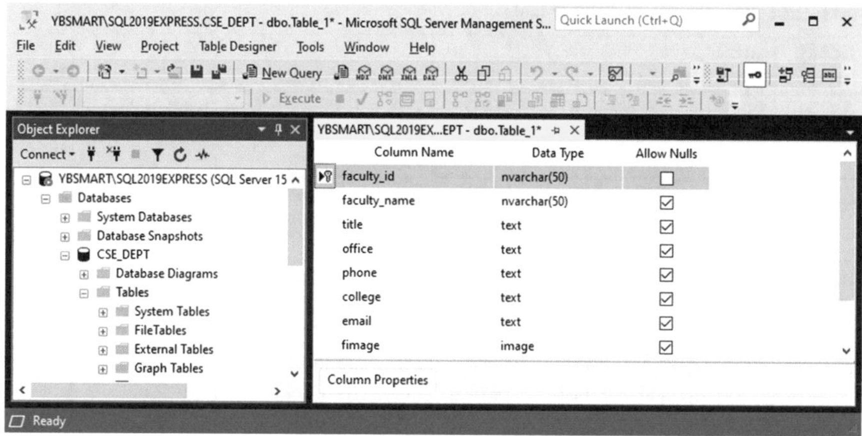

Fig. 2.16 The design view of the Faculty table

For this table, we have eight columns: **faculty_id, faculty_name, title, office, phone, college, email**, and **fimage**. The data types for the columns **faculty_id** and **faculty_name** are **nvarchar(50)**, and all other data types, except the **fimage** column, can be either **text** or **nvarchar(50)** since all of them are string variables. The data type for the **fimage** column is **image** since all faculty images are stored in this column. The reason we selected the **nvarchar(50)** as the data type for the **faculty_id** is that a primary key can work for this data type but it does not work for the **text**. The finished design-view of the **Faculty** table should match one that is shown in Fig. 2.16.

Since we selected the **faculty_id** column as the primary key, thus click on that row and then go to the Toolbar and select the **Primary Key** tool.

Now go to the **File** menu item and select the **Save Table_1**, and enter **Faculty** into the box for the **Choose Name** dialog as the name for this table, click **OK** to save this table.

Next you need to enter the data into this **Faculty** table. To do that, first open the table by right clicking on the **dbo.Faculty** folder under the **CSE_DEPT** database folder in the Object Explorer window, and then select **Edit Top 200 Rows** item to open this table. Enter the data that is shown in Table 2.14 into this **Faculty** table.

Your finished **Faculty** table should match one that is shown in Fig. 2.17.

Now go to the **File** menu item and select **Save All** to save this completed **Faculty** data table. Your finished **Faculty** data table will be displayed as a table named **dbo. Faculty** that has been added into the new database **CSE_DEPT** under the folder **Tables** in the Object Explorer window. At this moment just keep NULL for the **fimage** column and we will add actual faculty images later by using Visual Studio.NET and Devexpress controls.

Table 2.14 The data in the Faculty table

faculty_id	faculty_name	title	office	phone	college	email	fimage
A52990	Black Anderson	Professor	MTC-218	750-378-9987	Virginia Tech	banderson@college.edu	NULL
A77587	Debby Angles	Associate Professor	MTC-320	750-330-2276	University of Chicago	dangles@college.edu	NULL
B66750	Alice Brown	Assistant Professor	MTC-257	750-330-6650	University of Florida	abrown@college.edu	NULL
B78880	Ying Bai	Associate Professor	MTC-211	750-378-1148	Florida Atlantic University	ybai@college.edu	NULL
B86590	Davis Bhalla	Associate Professor	MTC-214	750-378-1061	University of Notre Dame	dbhalla@college.edu	NULL
H99118	Jeff Henry	Associate Professor	MTC-336	750-330-8650	Ohio State University	jhenry@college.edu	NULL
J33486	Steve Johnson	Distinguished Professor	MTC-118	750-330-1116	Harvard University	sjohnson@college.edu	NULL
K69880	Jenney King	Professor	MTC-324	750-378-1230	East Florida University	jking@college.edu	NULL

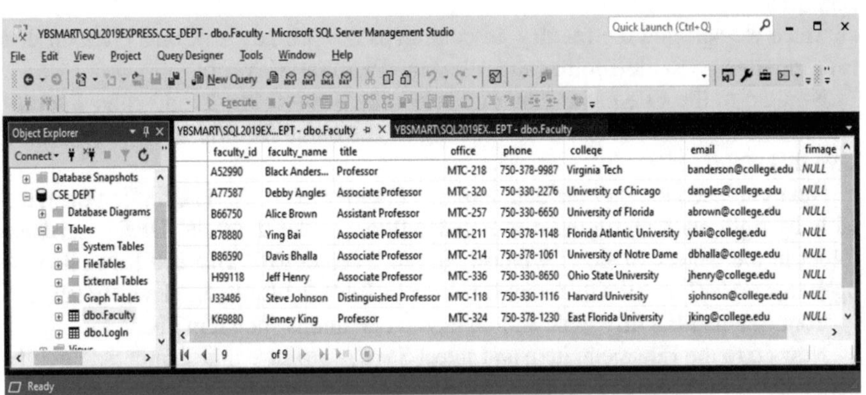

Fig. 2.17 The completed Faculty table

2.9.3 Create Other Tables

In a similar way, create the rest of three tables: **Course, Student**, and **StudentCourse**. Select **course_id, student_id**, and **s_course_id** as the primary keys for these tables (refer to Tables 2.15, 2.16, and 2.17). For the data type selections, follow the directions below:

Table 2.15 The data in the Course table

course_ id	course	credit	classroom	schedule	enrollment	faculty_ id
CSC-131A	Computers in Society	3	MTC-109	M-W-F: 9:00-9:55 AM	28	A52990
CSC-131B	Computers in Society	3	MTC-114	M-W-F: 9:00-9:55 AM	20	B66750
CSC-131C	Computers in Society	3	MTC-109	T-H: 11:00-12:25 PM	25	A52990
CSC-131D	Computers in Society	3	MTC-109	M-W-F: 9:00-9:55 AM	30	B86590
CSC-131E	Computers in Society	3	MTC-301	M-W-F: 1:00-1:55 PM	25	B66750
CSC-131I	Computers in Society	3	MTC-109	T-H: 1:00-2:25 PM	32	A52990
CSC-132A	Introduction to Programming	3	MTC-303	M-W-F: 9:00-9:55 AM	21	J33486
CSC-132B	Introduction to Programming	3	MTC-302	T-H: 1:00-2:25 PM	21	B78880
CSC-230	Algorithms & Structures	3	MTC-301	M-W-F: 1:00-1:55 PM	20	A77587
CSC-232A	Programming I	3	MTC-305	T-H: 11:00-12:25 PM	28	B66750
CSC-232B	Programming I	3	MTC-303	T-H: 11:00-12:25 PM	17	A77587
CSC-233A	Introduction to Algorithms	3	MTC-302	M-W-F: 9:00-9:55 AM	18	H99118
CSC-233B	Introduction to Algorithms	3	MTC-302	M-W-F: 11:00-11:55 AM	19	K69880
CSC-234A	Data Structure & Algorithms	3	MTC-302	M-W-F: 9:00-9:55 AM	25	B78880
CSC-234B	Data Structure & Algorithms	3	MTC-114	T-H: 11:00-12:25 PM	15	J33486
CSC-242	Programming II	3	MTC-303	T-H: 1:00-2:25 PM	18	A52990
CSC-320	Object Oriented Programming	3	MTC-301	T-H: 1:00-2:25 PM	22	B66750
CSC-331	Applications Programming	3	MTC-109	T-H: 11:00-12:25 PM	28	H99118
CSC-333A	Computer Arch & Algorithms	3	MTC-301	M-W-F: 10:00-10:55 AM	22	A77587
CSC-333B	Computer Arch & Algorithms	3	MTC-302	T-H: 11:00-12:25 PM	15	A77587
CSC-335	Internet Programming	3	MTC-303	M-W-F: 1:00-1:55 PM	25	B66750
CSC-432	Discrete Algorithms	3	MTC-206	T-H: 11:00-12:25 PM	20	B86590

(continued)

Table 2.15 (continued)

course_id	course	credit	classroom	schedule	enrollment	faculty_id
CSC-439	Database Systems	3	MTC-206	M-W-F: 1:00-1:55 PM	18	B86590
CSE-138A	Introduction to CSE	3	MTC-301	T-H: 1:00-2:25 PM	15	A52990
CSE-138B	Introduction to CSE	3	MTC-109	T-H: 1:00-2:25 PM	35	J33486
CSE-330	Digital Logic Circuits	3	MTC-305	M-W-F: 9:00-9:55 AM	26	K69880
CSE-332	Foundations of Semiconductor	3	MTC-305	T-H: 1:00-2:25 PM	24	K69880
CSE-334	Elec. Measurement & Design	3	MTC-212	T-H: 11:00-12:25 PM	25	H99118
CSE-430	Bioinformatics in Computer	3	MTC-206	Thu: 9:30-11:00 AM	16	B86590
CSE-432	Analog Circuits Design	3	MTC-309	M-W-F: 2:00-2:55 PM	18	K69880
CSE-433	Digital Signal Processing	3	MTC-206	T-H: 2:00-3:25 PM	18	H99118
CSE-434	Advanced Electronics Systems	3	MTC-213	M-W-F: 1:00-1:55 PM	26	B78880
CSE-436	Automatic Control and Design	3	MTC-305	M-W-F: 10:00-10:55 AM	29	J33486
CSE-437	Operating Systems	3	MTC-303	T-H: 1:00-2:25 PM	17	A77587
CSE-438	Advd Logic & Microprocessor	3	MTC-213	M-W-F: 11:00-11:55 AM	35	B78880
CSE-439	Special Topics in CSE	3	MTC-206	M-W-F: 10:00-10:55 AM	22	J33486

Table 2.16 The data in the Student table

student_id	student_name	gpa	credits	major	schoolYear	email	simage
A78835	Andrew Woods	3.26	108	Computer Science	Senior	awoods@college.edu	NULL
A97850	Ashly Jade	3.57	116	Info System Engineering	Junior	ajade@college.edu	NULL
B92996	Blue Valley	3.52	102	Computer Science	Senior	bvalley@college.edu	NULL
H10210	Holes Smith	3.87	78	Computer Engineering	Sophomore	hsmith@college.edu	NULL
T77896	Tom Erica	3.95	127	Computer Science	Senior	terica@college.edu	NULL

Table 2.17 The data in the StudentCourse table

s_course_id	student_id	course_id	credit	major
1000	H10210	CSC-131D	3	CE
1001	B92996	CSC-132A	3	CS/IS
1002	T77896	CSC-335	3	CS/IS
1003	A78835	CSC-331	3	CE
1004	H10210	CSC-234B	3	CE
1005	T77896	CSC-234A	3	CS/IS
1006	B92996	CSC-233A	3	CS/IS
1007	A78835	CSC-132A	3	CE
1008	A78835	CSE-432	3	CE
1009	A78835	CSE-434	3	CE
1010	T77896	CSC-439	3	CS/IS
1011	H10210	CSC-132A	3	CE
1012	H10210	CSC-331	2	CE
1013	A78835	CSC-335	3	CE
1014	A78835	CSE-438	3	CE
1015	T77896	CSC-432	3	CS/IS
1016	A97850	CSC-132B	3	ISE
1017	A97850	CSC-234A	3	ISE
1018	A97850	CSC-331	3	ISE
1019	A97850	CSC-335	3	ISE
1020	T77896	CSE-439	3	CS/IS
1021	B92996	CSC-230	3	CS/IS
1022	A78835	CSE-332	3	CE
1023	B92996	CSE-430	3	CE
1024	T77896	CSC-333A	3	CS/IS
1025	H10210	CSE-433	3	CE
1026	H10210	CSE-334	3	CE
1027	B92996	CSC-131C	3	CS/IS
1028	B92996	CSC-439	3	CS/IS

The data type selections for the **Course** table:

- **course_id** – nvarchar(50) (Primary key)
- **credit** – smallint
- **enrollment** – int
- **faculty_id** – nvarchar(50)
- All other columns – either nvarchar(50) or text

The data type selections for the **Student** table:

- **student_id** – nvarchar(50) (Primary key)
- **student_name** - nvarchar(50)
- **gpa** – float

- **credits** – int
- **simage** - image
- All other columns – either nvarchar(50) or text

The data type selections for the **StudentCourse** table:

- **s_course_id** – int (Primary key)
- **student_id** – nvarchar(50)
- **course_id** – nvarchar(50)
- **credit** – int
- **major** – either nvarchar(50) or text

Enter the data that are shown in Tables 2.15, 2.16, and 2.17 into each associated table, and save each table as **Course, Student**, and **StudentCourse**, respectively.

Similar to **Faculty** table, at this moment just keep NULL for the **simage** column in the **Student** table and we will add actual student images later by using Visual Studio.NET and Devexpress controls. The finished **Course**, **Student**, and **StudentCourse** tables are shown in Fig. 2.18, 2.19, and 2.20, respectively.

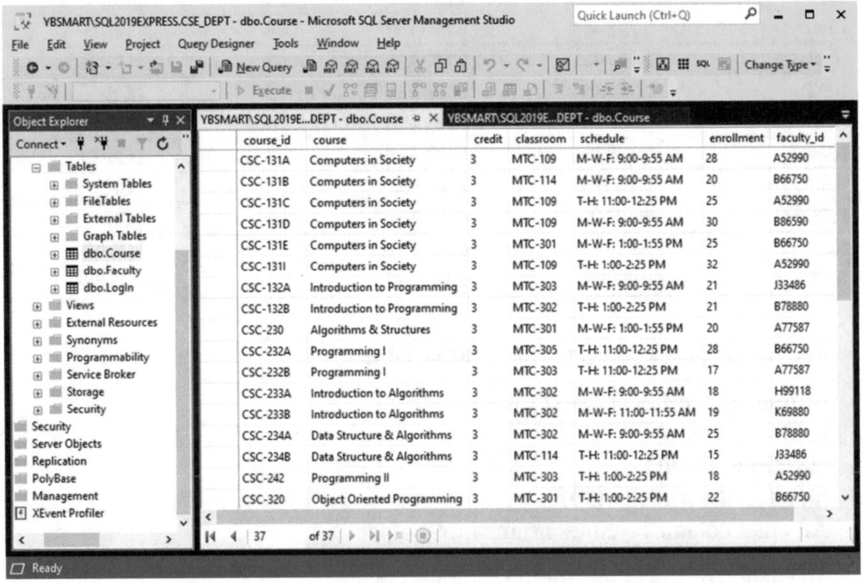
YBSMART\SQL2019EXPRESS.CSE_DEPT - dbo.Course - Microsoft SQL Server Management Studio
Quick Launch (Ctrl+Q)
File Edit View Project Query Designer Tools Window Help
New Query
Execute
Change Type
Object Explorer
Connect
Tables
System Tables
FileTables
External Tables
Graph Tables
dbo.Course
dbo.Faculty
dbo.LogIn
Views
External Resources
Synonyms
Programmability
Service Broker
Storage
Security
Security
Server Objects
Replication
PolyBase
Management
XEvent Profiler
YBSMART\SQL2019E...DEPT - dbo.Course
YBSMART\SQL2019E...DEPT - dbo.Course
course_id course credit classroom schedule enrollment faculty_id
CSC-131A Computers in Society 3 MTC-109 M-W-F: 9:00-9:55 AM 28 A52990
CSC-131B Computers in Society 3 MTC-114 M-W-F: 9:00-9:55 AM 20 B66750
CSC-131C Computers in Society 3 MTC-109 T-H: 11:00-12:25 PM 25 A52990
CSC-131D Computers in Society 3 MTC-109 M-W-F: 9:00-9:55 AM 30 B86590
CSC-131E Computers in Society 3 MTC-301 M-W-F: 1:00-1:55 PM 25 B66750
CSC-131I Computers in Society 3 MTC-109 T-H: 1:00-2:25 PM 32 A52990
CSC-132A Introduction to Programming 3 MTC-303 M-W-F: 9:00-9:55 AM 21 J33486
CSC-132B Introduction to Programming 3 MTC-302 T-H: 1:00-2:25 PM 21 B78880
CSC-230 Algorithms & Structures 3 MTC-301 M-W-F: 1:00-1:55 PM 20 A77587
CSC-232A Programming I 3 MTC-305 T-H: 11:00-12:25 PM 28 B66750
CSC-232B Programming I 3 MTC-303 T-H: 11:00-12:25 PM 17 A77587
CSC-233A Introduction to Algorithms 3 MTC-302 M-W-F: 9:00-9:55 AM 18 H99118
CSC-233B Introduction to Algorithms 3 MTC-302 M-W-F: 11:00-11:55 AM 19 K69880
CSC-234A Data Structure & Algorithms 3 MTC-302 M-W-F: 9:00-9:55 AM 25 B78880
CSC-234B Data Structure & Algorithms 3 MTC-114 T-H: 11:00-12:25 PM 15 J33486
CSC-242 Programming II 3 MTC-303 T-H: 1:00-2:25 PM 18 A52990
CSC-320 Object Oriented Programming 3 MTC-301 T-H: 1:00-2:25 PM 22 B66750
37 of 37
Ready

Fig. 2.18 The completed Course table

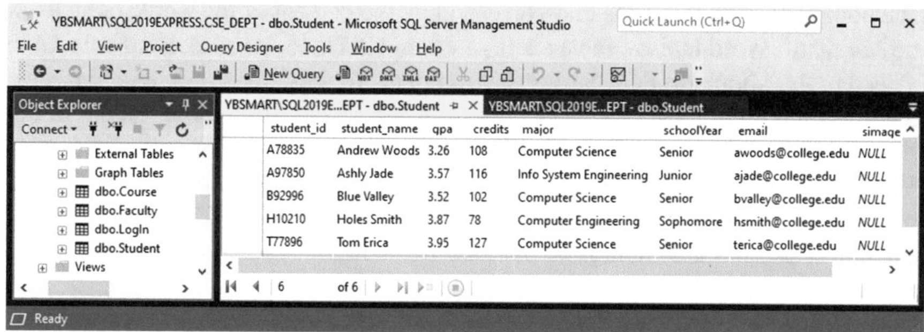

student_id	student_name	gpa	credits	major	schoolYear	email	simage
A78835	Andrew Woods	3.26	108	Computer Science	Senior	awoods@college.edu	NULL
A97850	Ashly Jade	3.57	116	Info System Engineering	Junior	ajade@college.edu	NULL
B92996	Blue Valley	3.52	102	Computer Science	Senior	bvalley@college.edu	NULL
H10210	Holes Smith	3.87	78	Computer Engineering	Sophomore	hsmith@college.edu	NULL
T77896	Tom Erica	3.95	127	Computer Science	Senior	terica@college.edu	NULL

Fig. 2.19 The completed Student table

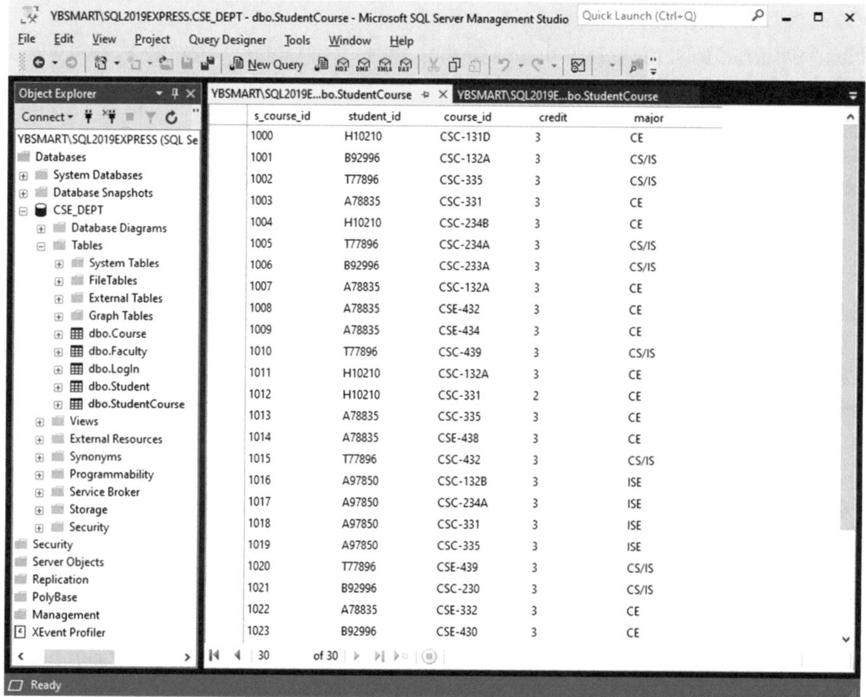

s_course_id	student_id	course_id	credit	major
1000	H10210	CSC-131D	3	CE
1001	B92996	CSC-132A	3	CS/IS
1002	T77896	CSC-335	3	CS/IS
1003	A78835	CSC-331	3	CE
1004	H10210	CSC-234B	3	CE
1005	T77896	CSC-234A	3	CS/IS
1006	B92996	CSC-233A	3	CS/IS
1007	A78835	CSC-132A	3	CE
1008	A78835	CSE-432	3	CE
1009	A78835	CSE-434	3	CE
1010	T77896	CSC-439	3	CS/IS
1011	H10210	CSC-132A	3	CE
1012	H10210	CSC-331	2	CE
1013	A78835	CSC-335	3	CE
1014	A78835	CSE-438	3	CE
1015	T77896	CSC-432	3	CS/IS
1016	A97850	CSC-132B	3	ISE
1017	A97850	CSC-234A	3	ISE
1018	A97850	CSC-331	3	ISE
1019	A97850	CSC-335	3	ISE
1020	T77896	CSE-439	3	CS/IS
1021	B92996	CSC-230	3	CS/IS
1022	A78835	CSE-332	3	CE
1023	B92996	CSE-430	3	CE

Fig. 2.20 The completed StudentCourse table

A possible problem you may encounter is that you cannot find the new created Table under the Tables folder in SSMS 2018 even you complete a table creation. A simple solution is that you need to refresh that Tables folder by right-clicking on that folder and select Refresh item from the pop-up menu.

One point you need to note is that you can copy the content of the whole table from the Microsoft Word tables (Tables 2.15, 2.16 and 2.17) to the associated data table opened in the Microsoft SQL Server environment. To make these copies and pastes, first you must select a whole blank row from your destination table – table in the Microsoft SQL Server database, and then select all data rows from your Microsoft Word tables by highlighting them and choose the **Copy** menu item. Next, you need to paste those rows by clicking that blank row in the Microsoft SQL Server database and then click the **Paste** item from the **Edit** menu item.

2.9.4 Create Relationships Among Tables

Next, we need to setup relationships among these five tables using the Primary and Foreign Keys. In Microsoft SQL Server 2019 Express database environment, the relationship between tables can be set by using the **Keys** folder under each data table from the Object Explorer window. Now let's begin to setup the relationship between the **LogIn** and the **Faculty** tables by using Microsoft SQL Server Management Studio 18.

2.9.4.1 Create Relationship Between the LogIn and the Faculty Tables

The relationship between the Faculty and the LogIn table is one-to-many, which means that the **faculty_id** is a primary key in the **Faculty** table, and it can be mapped to many **faculty_id** that are foreign keys in the **LogIn** table.

To setup this relationship, expand the **LogIn** table and the **Keys** folder that is under the **LogIn** table in an opened Microsoft SQL Server Management Studio 18. Currently, only one primary key, **PK_LogIn**, is existed under the **Keys** folder.

To add a new foreign key, right click on the **Keys** folder and select **New Foreign Key** item from the popup menu to open the **Foreign Key Relationships** dialog, which is shown in Fig. 2.21.

The default foreign relationship is **FK_LogIn_LogIn***, which is displayed in the **Selected Relationship** box. Right now we want to create the foreign relationship between the **LogIn** and the **Faculty** tables, so change the name of this foreign relationship to **FK_LogIn_Faculty** by modifying its name in the (Name) box that is under the **Identity** pane, and then press the **Enter** key from your keyboard.

Then select two tables by clicking on the **Tables And Columns Specification** item that is under the **General** pane. Click the expansion button ... that is located on the right of the **Tables And Columns Specification** item to open the **Tables and Columns** dialog, which is shown in Fig. 2.22.

Click the drop-down arrow from the **Primary key table** combobox and select the **Faculty** table since we need the primary key **faculty_id** from this table, then

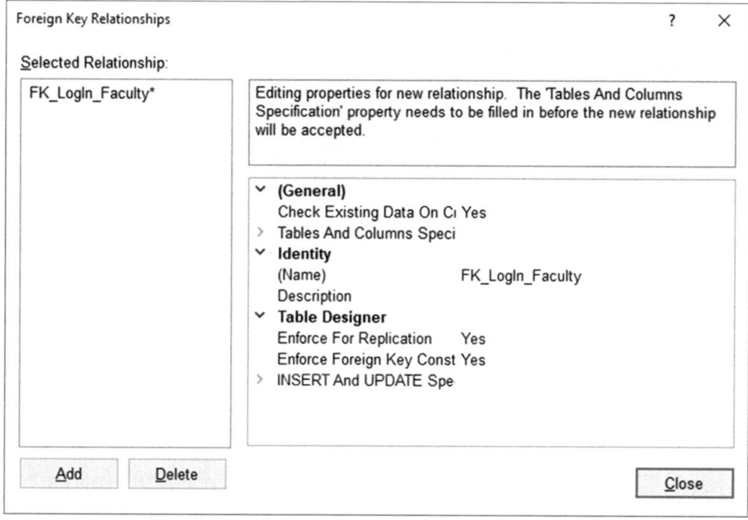

Fig. 2.21 The opened Foreign Key Relationships dialog box

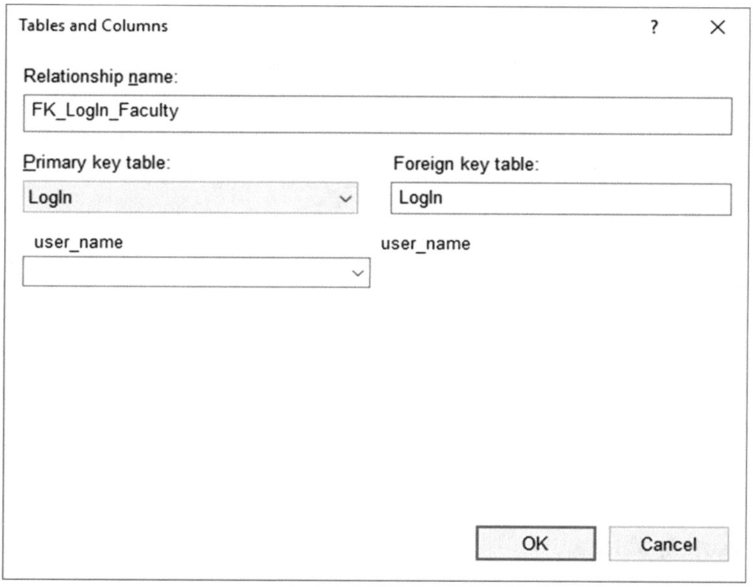

Tables and Columns

Relationship name:

FK_LogIn_Faculty

Primary key table: LogIn

Foreign key table: LogIn

user_name

user_name

OK Cancel

Fig. 2.22 The opened Tables and Columns dialog box

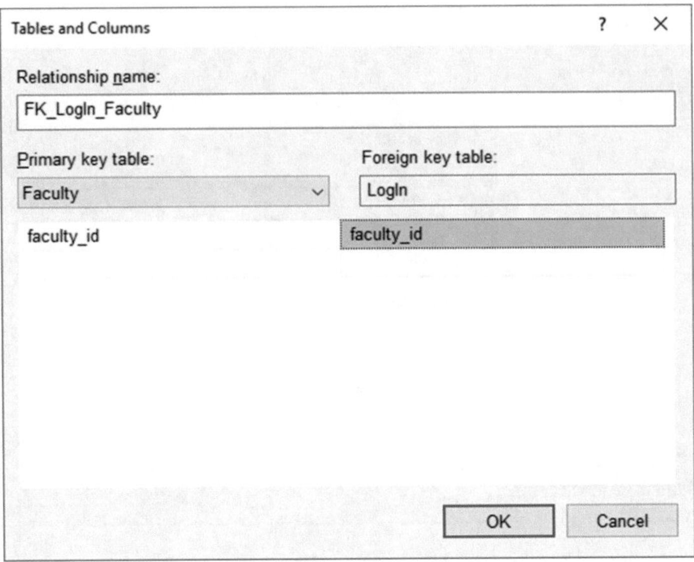

Fig. 2.23 The finished Tables and Columns dialog box

click on the blank row that is just below the **Primary key table** combobox and select the **faculty_id** column. You can see that the **LogIn** table has been automatically selected and displayed in the **Foreign key table** combobox. Click the drop-down arrow from the box that is just under the **Foreign key table** combobox and select the **faculty_id** as the foreign key for the **LogIn** table. Your finished **Tables and Columns** dialog should match one that is shown in Fig. 2.23.

Click on the **OK** button to close this dialog.

Before we can close this dialog, we need to do one more thing, which is to setup a cascaded relationship between the Primary key (**faculty_id**) in the parent table **Faculty** and the Foreign keys (**faculty_id**) in the child table **LogIn**. The reason we need to do this is because we want to simplify the data updating and deleting operations between these tables in a relational database such as **CSE_DEPT**. You will have a better understanding about this cascading later when you learn how to update and delete data against a relational database in Chap. 7.

To do this cascading, scroll down along this Foreign Key Relationships dialog and expand the item **Table Designer**, then you can find the **INSERT And UPDATE Specifications** item. Expand this item by clicking the small plus icon, two sub items are displayed, which are:

- **Delete Rule**
- **Update Rule**

The default value for both sub items is **No Action**. Click on the **No Action** box for the **Delete Rule** item and then click on the drop-down arrow, and select the **Cascade** item from the list. Perform the same operation for the **Update Rule** item.

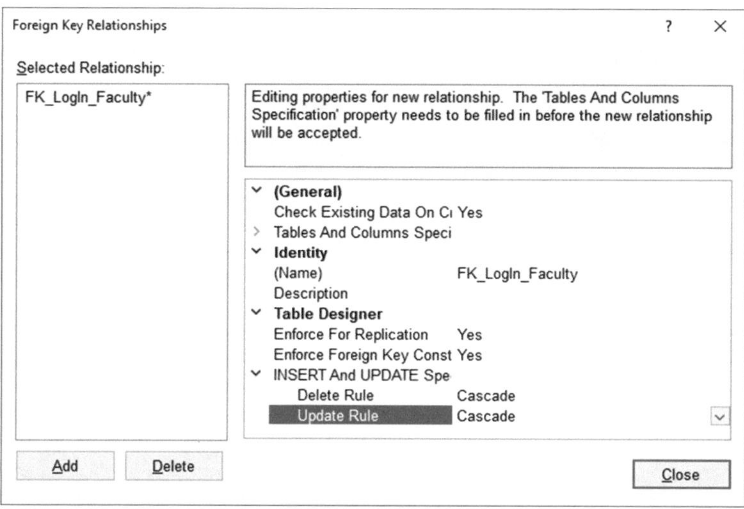

Fig. 2.24 The finished Foreign Key Relationships dialog

Your finished Foreign Key Relationships dialog should match one that is shown in Fig. 2.24.

In this way, we established the cascaded relationship between the Primary key in the parent table and the Foreign keys in the child table. Later on when you update or delete any Primary key from a parent table, the related foreign keys in the child tables will also be updated or deleted without other additional operations. It is convenient! Click the **Close** button to close this dialog.

Go to the **File|Save LogIn** menu item to open the **Save** dialog and click the **Yes** button to save this relationship. You can select **Yes** or **No** to the **Save Change Script** dialog box if it appears.

Now right click on the **Keys** folder under the **LogIn** table from the Object Explorer window, and select the **Refresh** item from the popup menu to refresh this **Keys** folder. Immediately you can find a new foreign key named **FK_LogIn_Faculty** appears under this **Keys** folder. This is our new created foreign key that sets the relationship between our **LogIn** and **Faculty** tables. You can also confirm and find this new created foreign key by right clicking on the **Keys** folder that is under the **Faculty** table.

2.9.4.2 Create Relationship Between the LogIn and the Student Tables

In a similar way, you can create a foreign key for the **LogIn** table and setup a one-to-many relationship between the **Student** and the **LogIn** tables.

Right click on the **Keys** folder that is under the **dbo.LogIn** table and select **New Foreign Key** item from the popup menu to open the **Foreign Key Relationships** dialog. Change the name to **FK_LogIn_Student** and press the **Enter** key from your

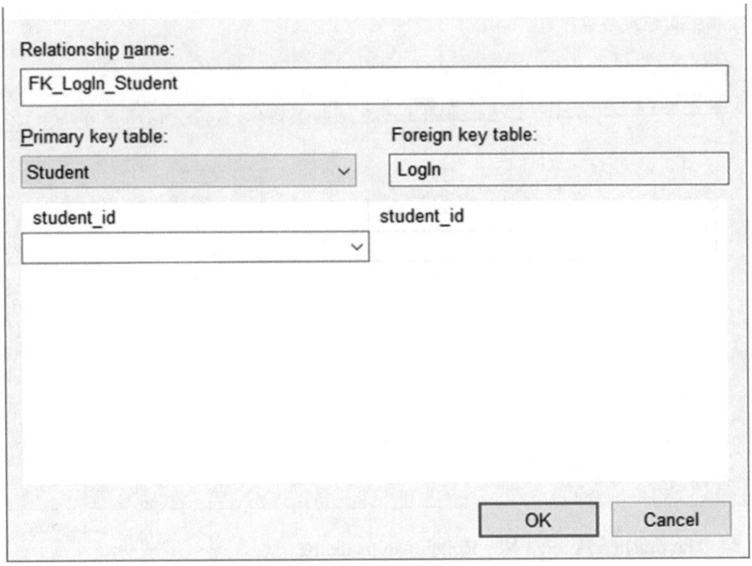

Fig. 2.25 The completed Tables and Columns dialog

keyboard. Go to the **Tables And Columns Specification** item to open the **Tables and Columns** dialog, then select the **Student** table from the **Primary key table** combobox and **student_id** from the box that is under the **Primary key table** combobox. Select the **student_id** from the box that is under the **Foreign key table** combobox. Your finished **Tables and Columns** dialog should match one that is shown in Fig. 2.25.

Click the **OK** to close this dialog box.

Do not forget to establish the cascaded relationship for **Delete Rule** and **Update Rule** items by expanding the **Table Designer** and the **INSERT And UPDATE Specifications** items, respectively. Click the **Close** button to close the **Foreign Key Relationships** dialog box.

Go to the **File|Save LogIn** menu item to save this relationship. Click **Yes** for the following dialog box to finish this saving. Now right click on the **Keys** folder that is under the **dbo.LogIn** table, and select **Refresh** item to show our new created foreign key **FK_LogIn_Student**.

2.9.4.3 Create Relationship Between the Faculty and the Course Tables

The relationship between the **Faculty** and the **Course** tables is one-to-many, and the **faculty_id** in the **Faculty** table is a Primary key and the **faculty_id** in the **Course** table is a Foreign key.

Right click on the **Keys** folder under the **dbo.Course** table from the Object Explorer window and select the **New Foreign Key** item from the popup menu.

On the opened **Foreign Key Relationships** dialog, change the name of this new relationship to **FK_Course_Faculty** in the (Name) box and press the **Enter** key from the keyboard.

In the opened **Tables and Columns** dialog box, select the **Faculty** table from the **Primary key table** combobox and select the **faculty_id** from the box that is just under the **Primary key table** combobox. Then select the **faculty_id** from the box that is just under the **Foreign key table** combobox. Your finished **Tables and Columns** dialog should match one that is shown in Fig. 2.26.

Click the **OK** to close this dialog and setup the cascaded relationship for the **Delete Rule** and the **Update Rule** items, and then click the **Close** button to close the **Foreign Key Relationships** dialog box. Go to the **File|Save Course** menu item and click **Yes** for the following dialog box to save this setting.

Now right click on the **Keys** folder under the **dbo.Course** table, and select the **Refresh** item. Immediately you can find our new created relationship key **FK_Course_Faculty**.

2.9.4.4 Create Relationship Between the Student and the StudentCourse Tables

The relationship between the **Student** and the **StudentCourse** tables is one-to-many, and the **student_id** in the **Student** table is a Primary key and the **student_id** in the **StudentCourse** table is a Foreign key.

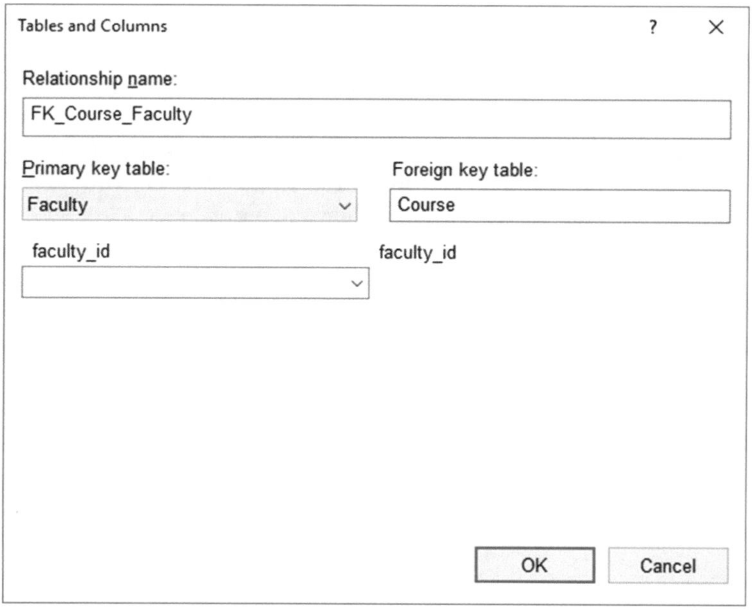

Fig. 2.26 The finished Tables and Columns dialog

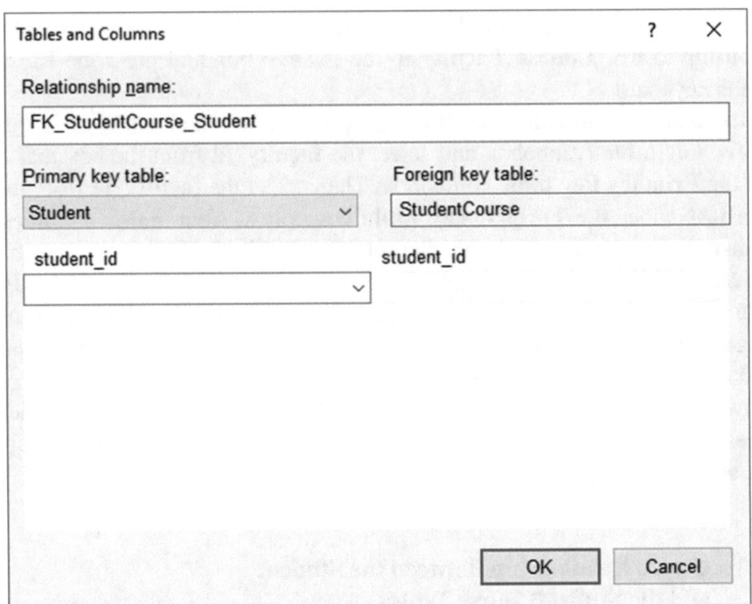

Fig. 2.27 The finished Tables and Columns dialog

Right click on the **Keys** folder under the **dbo.StudentCourse** table from the Object Explorer window and select the **New Foreign Key** item from the popup menu.

On the opened **Foreign Key Relationships** dialog, change the name of this new relationship to **FK_StudentCourse_Student** in the (Name) box and press the **Enter** key from the keyboard.

In the opened **Tables and Columns** dialog box, select the **Student** table from the **Primary key table** combobox and select the **student_id** from the box that is just under the **Primary key table** combobox. Then select the **student_id** from the box that is just under the **Foreign key table** combobox. The finished **Tables and Columns** dialog should match one that is shown in Fig. 2.27.

Click the **OK** to close this dialog and setup the cascaded relationship for **Delete Rule** and the **Update Rule** items, and then click the **Close** button to close the **Foreign Key Relationships** dialog box. Go to the **File|Save StudentCourse** menu item and click **Yes** for the following dialog box to save this relationship.

Now right click on the **Keys** folder under the **dbo.StudentCourse** table, and select the **Refresh** item. Then you can find our created relationship key **FK_StudentCourse_Student**.

2.9.4.5 Create Relationship Between the Course and the StudentCourse Tables

The relationship between the **Course** and the **StudentCourse** tables is one-to-many, and the **course_id** in the **Course** table is a Primary key and the **course_id** in the **StudentCourse** table is a Foreign key.

Right click on the **Keys** folder under the **dbo.StudentCourse** table from the Object Explorer window and select the **New Foreign Key** item from the popup menu.

On the opened **Foreign Key Relationships** dialog, change the name of this new relationship to **FK_StudentCourse_Course** in the (Name) box and press the **Enter** key from the keyboard.

In the opened **Tables and Columns** dialog box, select the **Course** table from the **Primary key table** combobox and select the **course_id** from the box that is just under the **Primary key table** combobox. Then select the **course_id** from the box that is just under the **Foreign key table** combobox. Your finished **Tables and Columns** dialog should match one that is shown in Fig. 2.28.

Click the **OK** to close this dialog and do not forget to establish a cascaded relationship for the **Delete Rule** and the **Update Rule** items, and then click the **Close** button to close the **Foreign Key Relationships** dialog box. Then go to the **File|Save StudentCourse** menu item and click **Yes** for the following dialog box to save this relationship.

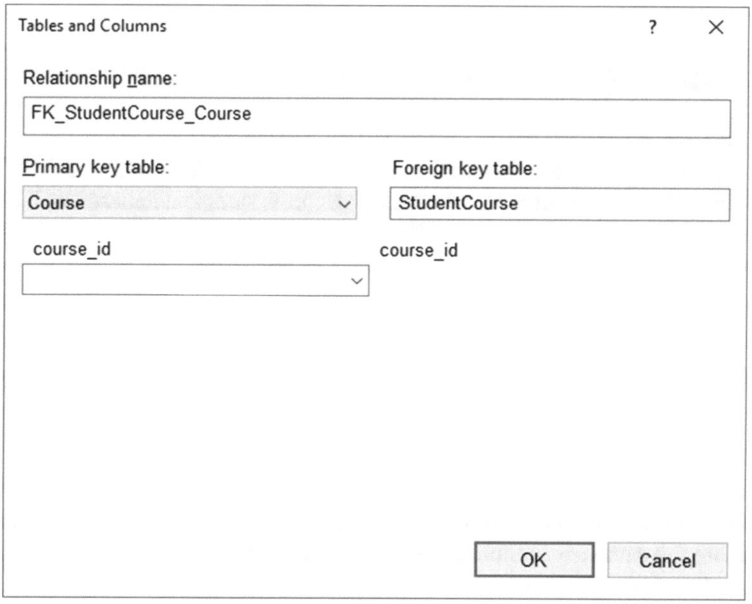

Fig. 2.28 The finished Tables and Columns dialog

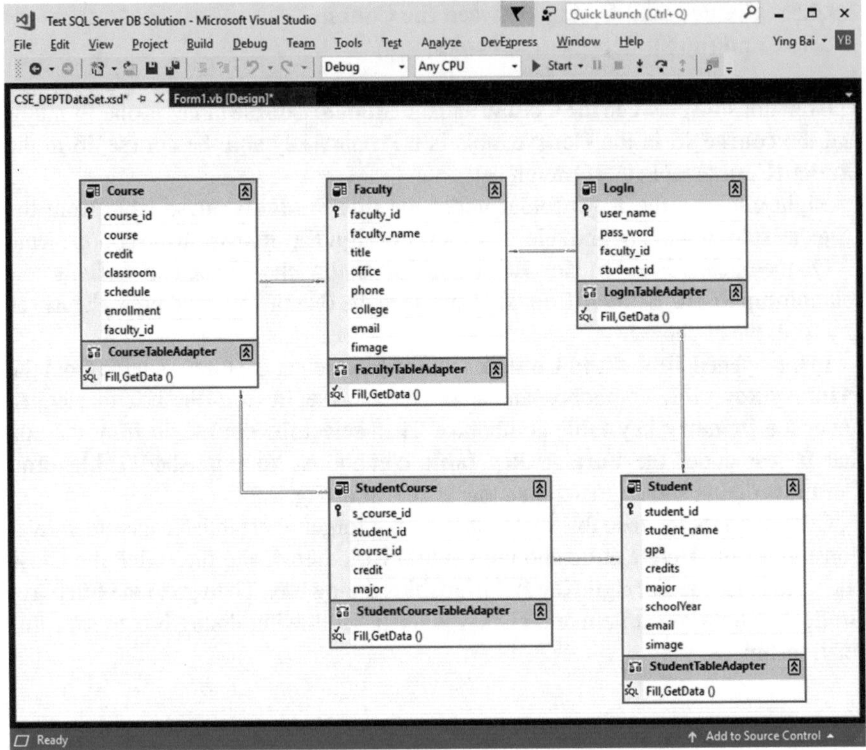

Fig. 2.29 Relationships among tables

Now right click on the **Keys** folder under the **dbo.StudentCourse** table, and select the **Refresh** item. Then you can find our created relationship key **FK_StudentCourse_Course**.

At this point, we complete setting the relationships among our five data tables.

A completed Microsoft SQL Server 2019 Express sample database **CSE_DEPT.mdf** can be found from the Springer ftp site (refer to Fig. 1.2 in Chap. 1). The completed relationships for these tables are shown in Fig. 2.29.

2.9.5 Store Images to the SQL Server 2019 Express Database

When building **Faculty** and **Student** tables in Sects. 2.9.2 and 2.9.3, we need to store faculty and student images into the SQL Server 2019 Express database directly. Due to the new property of SQL Server 2019 database, an image can be directly stored into the database column as an image object (in fact, it is a binary data type).

With the help of a product developed by Developer Express Incorporated, exactly a user interface component, WindowsUI, we can directly insert an image into a SQL

Server database's column via Microsoft Visual Studio.NET platform without any coding process. Follow Appendix C to finish the downloading and installation of the WindowsUI component in your computer.

Now open Visual Studio.NET 2019 and click the link: **Continue without code** at the bottom to open the Visual Studio.NET. Go to **File|New Project** to open the platform selection page. Then select the **Blank Solution** and click on the **Next** button. Enter **SQL Image Solution** into the **Solution name** box and click on the **Create** button to generate and save this blank solution in any folder in your computer.

1) To add a new project, just right click on the new created blank solution in the Solution Explorer window and select **Add|New Project** item from the popup menu to open the **Add New Project** wizard, as shown in Fig. 2.30.
2) Make sure to select the **Windows Forms App (.NET Framework) Visual Basic** on the left pane as the Template, and click on the **Next** button to continue.
3) Enter **SQL Image Project** into the **Project name:** box as the name for this project, and click on the **Create** button to add this project into our solution.
4) The added project wizard is shown in Fig. 2.31. Click on the **Add New Data Source** link in the **Data Sources** window located at the lower-left corner (if this window is not shown up, go to **View|Other Windows|Data Sources** to select it), to open the **Data Source Configuration Wizard** to connect to our designed SQL Server 2019 Express database CSE_DEPT.
5) Keep the default **Database** and **DataSet** selection on the next two wizards and click on the **Next** buttons to come to our database connection page. Check the **Show the connection string…** checkbox and click on the **New Connection…** button to open the Add Connection wizard, which is shown in Fig. 2.32.

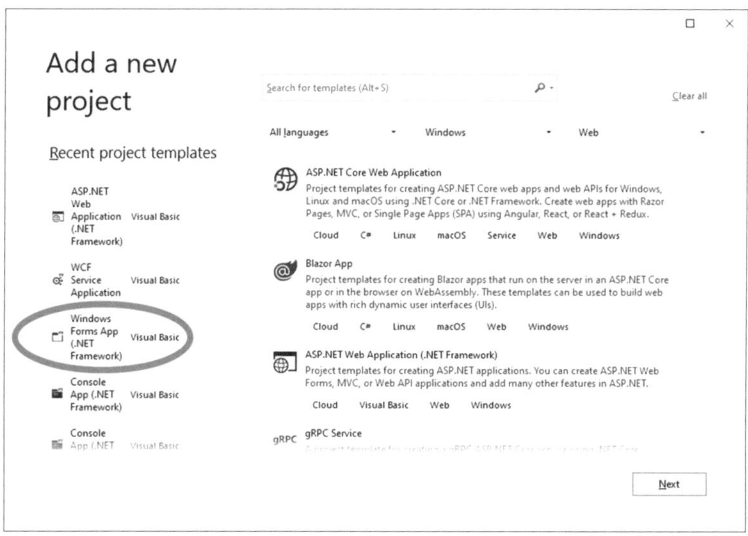

Fig. 2.30 The Add new project wizard

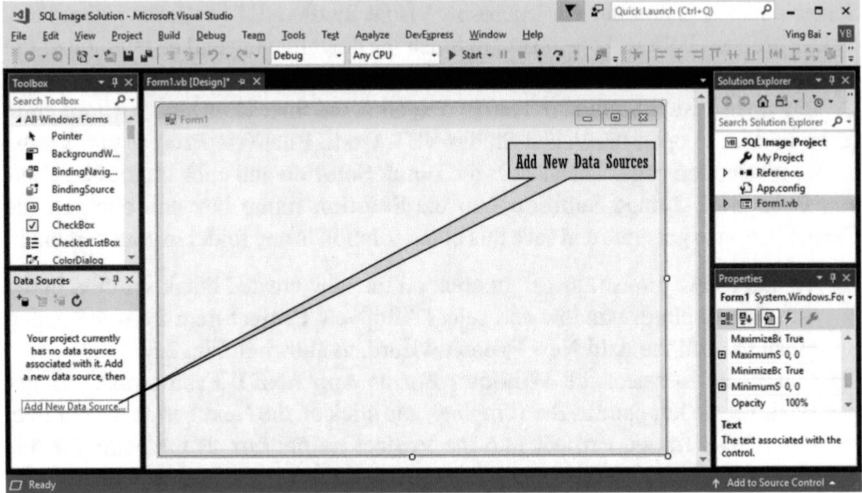

Fig. 2.31 The new added project SQL Image Project

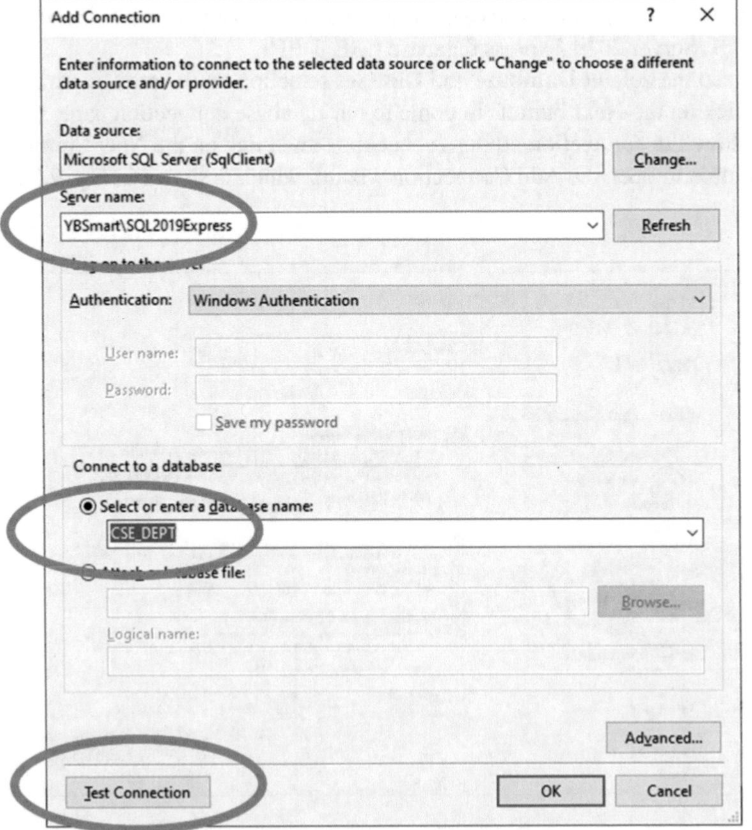

Fig. 2.32 The opened Add Connection wizard

6) Click on the drop down arrow on the **Server names** combo box and select our server name, **YBSMART\SQL2019EXPRESS**. You may need to enter this server name if it is not displayed in this combo box.
7) Click on the drop down arrow on the **Select or enter a database name** combo box and select our database **CSE_DEPT** from the combo box (Fig. 2.32).
8) Click the **Test Connection** button at the lower-left corner to test this connection. A successful connection message should be displayed if this connection is fine.
9) Click on the **OK** button for both MessageBox and the Add Connection wizard. Then click on the **Next** button to continue.
10) Click on the **Next** button again on the next page to save our connection string and open our connected database and dataset, which is shown in Fig. 2.33.
11) Expand our database and check our **Faculty** table, and select three columns, **faculty_id, faculty_name**, and **fimage**, by checking them one by one, as shown in Fig. 2.33. Then click on the **Finish** button to complete this database connection and dataset setup process.
12) Now return to our Visual Basic.NET project page, expand our DataSet and related Faculty table, **CSE_DEPTDataSet** and **Faculty**, in the Data Sources window. Click on the drop down arrow on the **Faculty** table combo box and select the **Details** item, and then drag this **Details** item and place it into the Form window, as shown in Fig. 2.34.
13) Now go to the **Image** object added on the Form window, **fimage**, and click on an arrow box ▶ located at the upper-right corner to open the **PictureEdit Tasks**

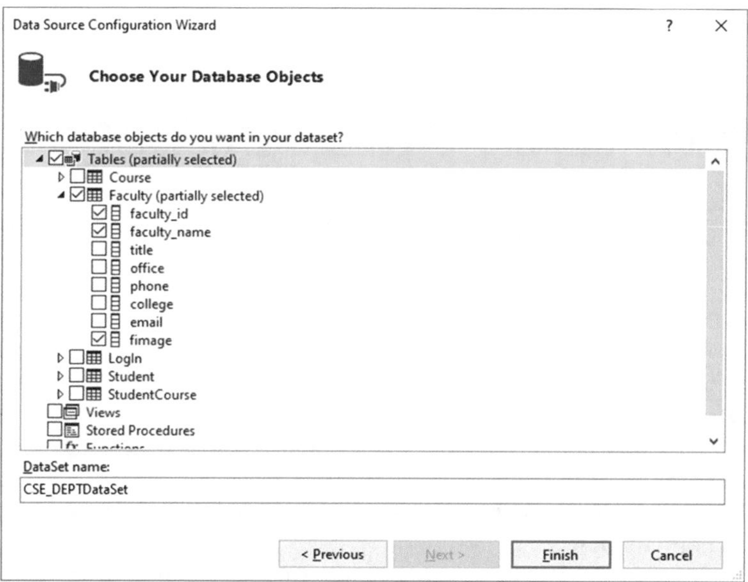

Fig. 2.33 The connected database and dataset CSE_DEPTDataSet

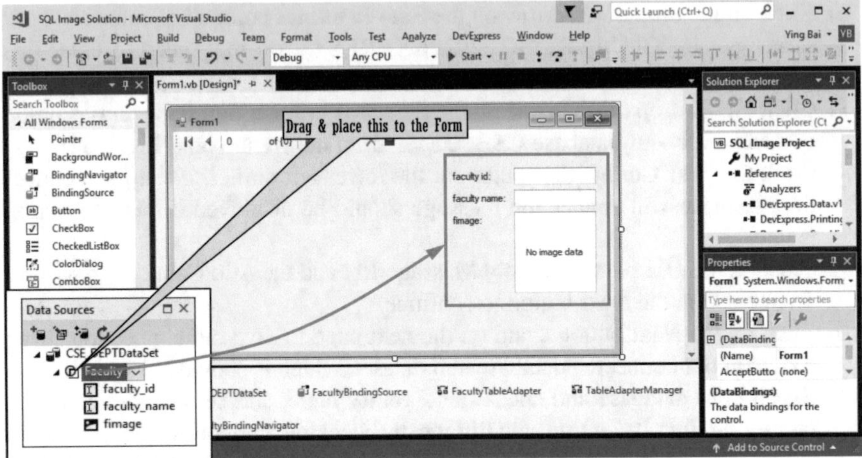

Fig. 2.34 Drag and place three columns in Details format on Faculty table

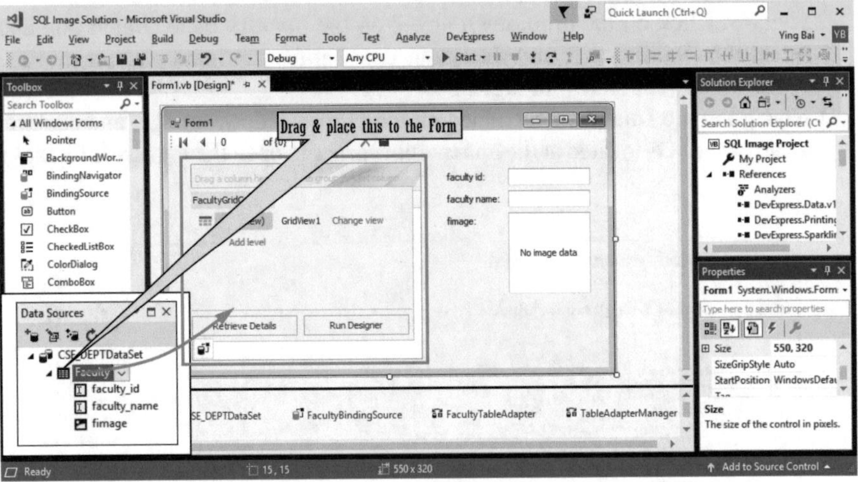

Fig. 2.35 Drag and place three columns in GridView format on Faculty table

dialog box, and select **Stretch** from the **Size Mode** combo box. Then click on any place on the Form window to close that PictureEdit Tasks dialog box.

14) Perform a similar operation as we did in step 13, click on the drop down arrow on the **Faculty** table combo box and select the **GridView** item, and then drag this GridView item and place it into the Form window, as shown in Fig. 2.35.
15) Now go to **File|Save All** item to save all of these additions and modifications to this Form window.
16) Then click on the **Start** button (green arrow on the tool bar) to run this Visual Basic project. As the project runs, the contents of three columns for all faculty

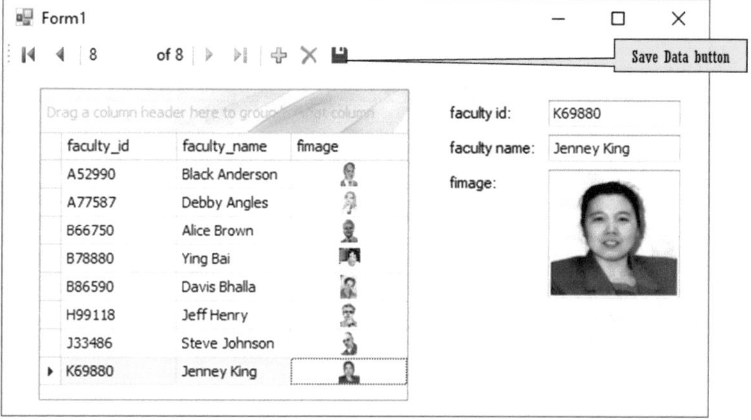

Fig. 2.36 The completed Form for adding faculty images

members in this **Faculty** table are displayed in both the Details and GridView except the faculty image **fimage**, as shown in Fig. 2.36.

17) To add an image to the **fimage** box for the selected faculty, click on an arrow for that faculty and first click (left-click) on the **fimage** column in the GridView, and then right-click on the **fimage** column again. On the popup menu, select the **Load** item to try to load and add an image for the selected faculty member.
18) Browse to the related faculty image, in our case, all faculty images are in the folder: **C:/SQL Java DB Programming\Instructors\Images\Faculty**, and select the associated faculty image, such as **Anderson.jpg** for the faculty member **Black Anderson**, by clicking on it, and click on the **Open** button to add it to the **CSE_DEPTDataSet**. All faculty images can be found under a folder **Students\Images\ Faculty** at the Springer ftp site (refer to Fig. 1.2 in Chap. 1). One can copy all of these images and save them to one desired folder on your machine.
19) Then click on the **Save Data** button located at the upper-right corner on the tool bar to save this image into the database. Perform similar operations to add all faculty images into our sample database **CSE_DEPT.mdf**.

Your finished Form window is shown in Fig. 2.36. Now you can stop running of the Visual Basic.NET project **SQL Image Project** by clicking on the **Close** button **X**.

The relationships between each faculty member and related name of image file are shown in Table 2.18.

Now if you open the Microsoft SQL Server Management Studio and the database **CSE_DEPT**, select and open the **Faculty** table with **Edit Top 200 Rows** item, you can find that all **NULL** in the **fimage** column become to **Binary data**, as shown in Fig. 2.37.

In a similar way, you can add all students' images into the **Student** table in our database **CSE_DEPT.mdf**. All students' images can be found under a folder

Table 2.18 The image files in the Faculty table

faculty_id	faculty_name	fimage
A52990	Black Anderson	Anderson.jpg
A77587	Debby Angles	Angles.jpg
B66750	Alice Brown	Brown.jpg
B78880	Ying Bai	Bai.jpg
B86590	Davis Bhalla	Davis.jpg
H99118	Jeff Henry	Henry.jpg
J33486	Steve Johnson	Johnson.jpg
K69880	Jenney King	King.jpg

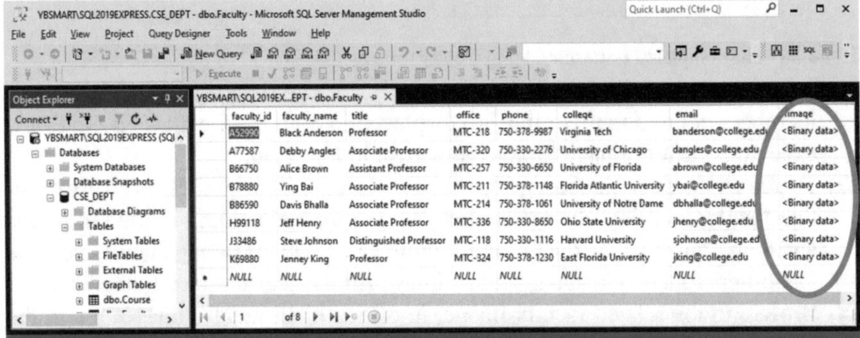

Fig. 2.37 The modified fimage column

Table 2.19 The image files in the Student table

student_id	student_name	simage
A78835	Andrew Woods	Woods.jpg
A97850	Ashly Jade	Jade.jpg
B92996	Blue Valley	Valley.jpg
H10210	Holes Smith	Smith.jpg
T77896	Tom Erica	Erica.jpg

Students\ Images\Students at the Springer ftp site (Fig. 1.2 in Chap. 1). One can copy and store them in a folder: **C:/SQL Java DB Programming\Students\Images** in your computer. The relationships between each student and related name of image file are shown in Table 2.19.

You need to create another new project and redo everything as we did above. Also you need to reconfigure the **CSE_DEPTDataSet** to select the **Student** table only with three columns, **student_id, student_name**, and **simage**. Follow steps below to complete this configuration.

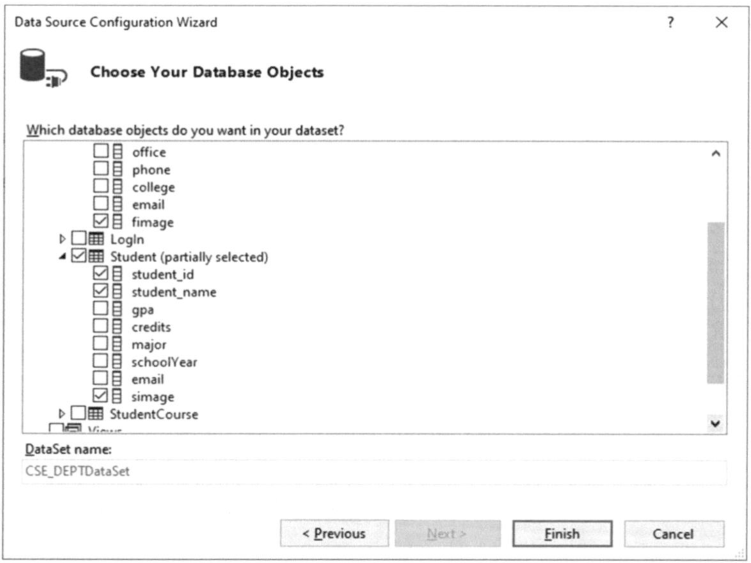

Fig. 2.38 The finished Student table in the Data Source Configuration Wizard

1) In the Visual Basic Form window, right click on the **CSE_DEPTDataSet** in the Data Sources window, and select **Configure Data Source with Wizard…** item from the popup menu to open that configuration wizard.
2) Expand the **Tables** folder and check the **Student** table with the **Faculty** table also checked (no change), and expand the **Student** table.
3) Uncheck five columns; **gpa, credits, major, schoolYear**, and **email**, and leave three columns, **student_id, student_name**, and **simage**, to be checked.

Your finished **Student** table in the Configuration Wizard is shown in Fig. 2.38. Click on the **Finish** button to complete this configuration.

In the Visual Basic.NET project window, exactly in the **SQL Image Project** Form window, replace the **Details** and **GridView** of the **Faculty** table with the **Details** and **GridView** of the **Student** table by deleting **Details** and **GridView** of the **Faculty** table first.

Now you can run the project to add all images for all students. Your finished Form window should match one that is shown in Fig. 2.39.

Two complete projects, **SQL Image Project** and **Student Image Project**, can be found from the folder **Class DB Projects\Chapter 2** under the **Students** folder in the Springer ftp site (refer to Fig. 1.2 in Chap. 1).

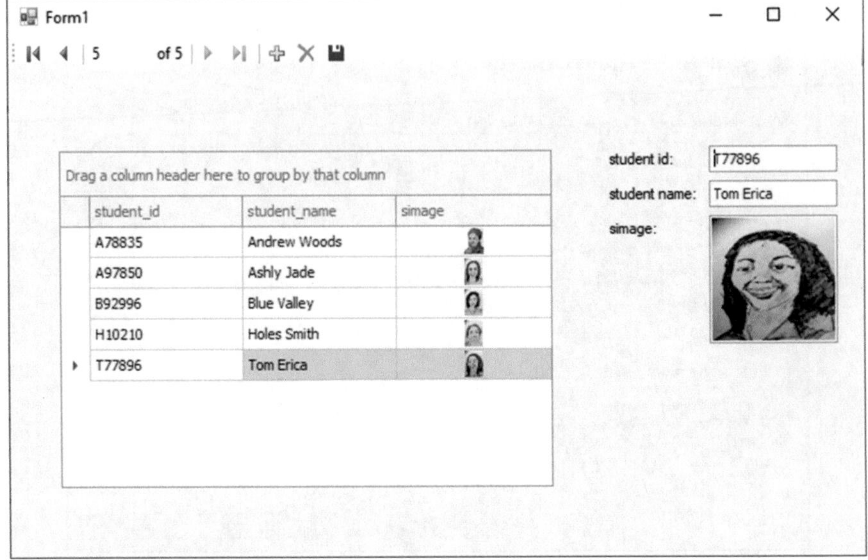

Fig. 2.39 The completed form for adding student images

2.10 A Short-Cut: How to Use the Sample Database without Building It

If some users, for some reasons, do not have time or do not like to create and build this sample database, **CSE_DEPT**, with these steps, they can take a short-cut way to directly use this sample database without spending any time or efforts. The pre-condition is that the following components must be installed:

- Microsoft SQL Server 2019 Express Database
- Microsoft SQL Server Management Studio

Refer to Appendix A to get more details in how to install Microsoft SQL Server 2019 Express Database and SQL Server Management Studio. Refer to Appendix D to get more details in how to copy, paste this sample database file and attach it into the SQL Server 2019 Express Database via the SQL Server Management Studio.

2.11 Chapter Summary

A detailed discussion and analysis of the structure and components about popular database systems are provided in this chapter. Some key technologies in developing and designing database are also given and discussed in this part. The procedure and components used to develop a relational database are analyzed in detail with some real data tables in our sample database **CSE_DEPT**. The process in developing and building a sample database is discussed in detail with the following points:

- Defining Relationships
- Normalizing the Data
- Implementing the Relational Database

In the second part of this chapter, a sample SQL Server 2019 Express database, **CSE_DEPT**, which is developed with an updated and popular database management system, Microsoft SQL Server Management Studio, is provided in detail. This sample database will be used in the following chapters throughout the whole book.

Homework

I. True/False Selections

____1. Database development process involves project planning, problem analysis, logical design, physical design, implementation, and maintenance
____2. Duplication of data creates problems with data integrity.
____3. If the primary key consists of a single column then the table in 1NF is automatically in 2NF.
____4. A table is in first normal form if there are no repeating groups of data in any column.
____5. When a user perceives the database as made up of tables, it is called a Network Model.
____6. Entity integrity rule states that no attribute that is a member of the primary (composite) key may accept a null value.
____7. When creating data tables for the Microsoft Access database, a blank field can be kept as a blank without any letter in it.
____8. To create data tables in SQL Server database, a blank field can be kept as a blank without any letter in it.
____9. The name of each data table in SQL Server database must be prefixed by the keyword dbo.
___10. In each relational database table, it can contain multiple primary keys, but only one unique foreign key.

II. Multiple Choices

1. There are many advantages to using an integrated database approach over that of a file processing approach. These include

   (a) Minimizing data redundancy
   (b) Improving security
   (c) Data independence
   (d) All of the above

2. Entity integrity rule implies that no attribute that is a member of the primary key may accept _______

   (a) Null value
   (b) Integer data type
   (c) Character data type
   (d) Real data type

3. Reducing data redundancy will lead to _____

   (a) Deletion anomalies
   (b) Data consistency
   (c) Loss of efficiency
   (d) None of the above

4. ______ keys are used to create relationships among various tables in a database

   (a) Primary keys
   (b) Candidate keys
   (c) Foreign keys
   (d) Composite keys

5. In a small university the department of Computer Science has six faculty members. However, each faculty member belongs to only the computer science department. This type of relationship is called _________

   (a) One-to-one
   (b) One-to-many
   (c) Many-to-many
   (d) None of the above

6. The Client Server databases have several advantages over the File Server databases. These include ________

   (a) Minimizing chances of crashes
   (b) Provision of features for recovery
   (c) Enforcement of security
   (d) Efficient use of the network
   (e) All of the above

7. One can create the foreign keys between tables ______

   (a) Before any table can be created
   (b) When some tables are created
   (c) After all tables are created
   (d) With no limitations

8. To create foreign keys between tables, first one must select the table that contains a _______ key and then select another table that has a _______ key.

   (a) Primary, foreign
   (b) Primary, primary
   (c) Foreign, primary
   (d) Foreign, foreign

9. The data type nvarchar(50) in SQL Server database is a string with _______

   (a) Limited length up to 50 letters
   (b) Fixed length of 50 letters
   (c) Certain number of letters
   (d) Varying length

10. For data tables in SQL Server Database, a blank field must be ________

   (a) Indicated by NULL Avoided
   (b) Kept as a blank
   (c) Either by NULL or a blank
   (d) Indicated by NULL

III. Exercises

1. What are the advantages of using an integrated database approach over that of a file processing approach
2. Define entity integrity and referential integrity. Describe the reasons for enforcing these rules.
3. Entities can have three types of relationships. It can be one-to-one, one-to-many, and many-to-many. Define each type of relationship. Draw ER diagrams to illustrate each type of relationship.
4. List all steps to create Foreign keys between data tables for SQL Server 2019 Express database in the SQL Server Management Studio. Illustrate those steps by using a real example. For instance, how to create foreign keys between the LogIn and the Faculty table.
5. List all steps to create Foreign keys between data tables for a SQL Server 2019 Express database in the SQL Server Management Studio. Illustrate those steps by using a real example. For instance, how to create foreign keys between the StudentCourse and the Course table.

Chapter 3
JDBC API and JDBC Drivers

This chapter discusses the fundamentals of JDBC and JDBC API, which include an overview of the JDBC and JDBC API, JDBC drivers, and related components used in JDBC API.

3.1 What Are JDBC and JDBC API?

JDBC is a standard *Java Database Connectivity* and JDBC API can be considered as a *Java Database Connectivity Application Programming Interface* (JDBC API). All components and techniques of JDBC are embedded and implemented in JDBC API. Basically, the JDBC API is composed of a set of classes and interfaces used to interact with databases from Java applications.

Generally, the JDBC API performs the following three functions:

1) Establishes a connection between your Java application and related databases
2) Builds and executes SQL statements
3) Processes the results

Different database vendors provide various JDBC drivers to support their applications to different databases. The most popular JDBC components are located at the following packages:

- **java.sql**: contains the standard JDBC components
- **javax.sql**: contains the Standard Extension of JDBC, which provides additional features such as **Java Naming and Directory Interface** (JNDI) and **Java Transaction Service** (JTS)

Supplementary Information The online version contains supplementary material available at [https://doi.org/10.1007/978-3-031-06553-8_3].

Y. Bai, *SQL Server Database Programming with Java*,
https://doi.org/10.1007/978-3-031-06553-8_3

- **oracle.jdbc**: contains the extended functions provided by the java.sql and javax.sql interfaces
- **oracle.sql**: contains classes and interfaces that provide Java mappings to SQL data types

All of these parts are combined together to provide necessary components and classes to build database applications using Java.

Generally, JDBC API enables users to access virtually any kind of tabular data sources such as spreadsheets or flat files from a Java application. It also provides connectivity to a wide scope of SQL or Oracle databases. One of the most important advantages of using JDBC is that it allows users to access any kind of relational database in a same coding way, which means that the user can develop one program with the same coding to access either a SQL Server database or an Oracle database, or MySQL database without coding modification.

The JDBC 4.0 and JDBC 4.3 specifications contain additional features, such as extensions to the support to various data types, MetaData components, and improvements on some interfaces.

3.2 JDBC Components and Architecture

The JDBC API is the only part of the entire JDBC product line.

The core of JDBC API is called a JDBC driver, which implements all JDBC components, including the classes and interfaces, to build a connection and manipulate data between your Java application and selected database. Exactly a JDBC driver, which is a class that is composed of a set of methods, builds a connection and accesses databases through those methods.

The JDBC API contains two major sets of interfaces: the first is the JDBC API for application writers (interface to your Java applications) and the second is the lower-level JDBC driver API for driver writers (interface to your database). JDBC technology drivers fit into one of four categories. Applications and applets can access databases via the JDBC API using pure Java JDBC technology-based drivers, as shown in Fig. 3.1.

As we mentioned, the JDBC API is composed of a set of classes and interfaces used to interact with databases from Java applications. Table 3.1 lists all classes defined in the JDBC API and their functions, and Table 3.2 shows all interfaces defined in the JDBC API.

It can be found from Table 3.1 that the most popular classes in JDBC API are top three classes: DriverManager, DriverPropertyInfo, and Type, and they are widely implemented in the Java database programming applications.

All interfaces listed in Table 3.2 are popular and widely implemented in the Java database applications. More detailed discussion and example applications of these interfaces will be provided in Chap. 5 with real project examples.

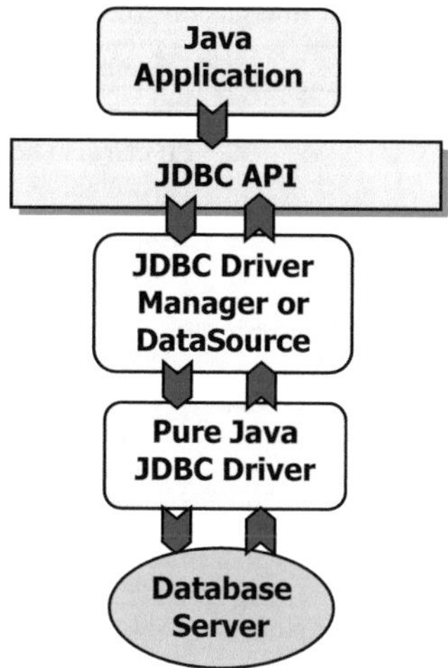

Fig. 3.1 The components and architecture of a JDBC API

Table 3.1 Classes defined in the JDBC API

Classes	Function
DriverManager	Handle loading and unloading of drivers and establish a connection to a database
DriverPropertyInfo	All methods defined in this class are used to setup or retrieve properties of a driver. The properties can then be used by the connection object to connect to the database
Type	The type class is only used to define the constants used for identifying the SQL types
Date	This class contains methods to perform conversion of SQL date formats and Java date objects
Time	This class is similar to the date class, and it contains methods to convert between SQL time and Java time object
TimeStamp	This class provides additional precision to the Java date object by adding a nanosecond field

The core of the JDBC API is the JDBC Driver that can be accessed and called from the DriverManager class method. Depending on the different applications, a JDBC driver can be categorized into four types: Type I, Type II, Type III, and Type IV. A more detailed discussion about the JDBC Driver and its types will be given in Sect. 3.4. An optional way to access the database is to use the DataSource object, which is a better way to identify and connect to a data source and makes code even more portable and easier to maintain.

Table 3.2 Interfaces defined in the JDBC API

Interface	Function
Driver	The primary use of the driver interface is to create the connection objects. It can also be used for the collection of JDBC driver metadata and JDBC driver status checking
Connection	This interface is used for the maintenance and status monitoring of a database session. It also provides data access control through the use of transaction locking
Statement	The statement methods are used to execute SQL statements and retrieve data from the ResultSet object
PreparedStatement	This interface is used to execute pre-compile SQL statements. Pre-compile statements allow for faster and more efficient statement execution, and more importantly, it allows to run dynamic query with querying parameters' variation. This interface can be considered as a subclass of the statement
CallableStatement	This interface is mainly used to execute SQL stored procedures. Both IN and OUT parameters are supported. This interface can be considered as a subclass of the statement
ResultSet	The ResultSet object contains the queried result in rows and columns format. This interface also provides methods to retrieve data returned by a SQL statement execution. It also contains methods for SQL data type and JDBC data type conversion
ResultSetMetaData	This interface contains a collection of metadata information or physical descriptions associated with the last ResultSet object
DatabaseMetaData	This interface contains a collection of metadata regarding the database used, including the database version, table names, columns, and supported functions

3.3 How Does JDBC Work?

As we mentioned in the last section, the JDBC API has three functions: (1) setup a connection between your Java application and your database; (2) build and execute SQL statements; and (3) process results. We will discuss these functions in more detail in this section based on the JDBC architecture shown in Fig. 3.1.

3.3.1 Establish a Connection

JDBC Driver class contains six methods and one of the most important methods is the **connect()** method, which is used to connect to the database. When using this Driver class, a point to be noted is that most methods defined in the Driver class never be called directly, instead, they should be called via the DriverManager class methods.

3.3.1.1 Using DriverManager to Establish a Connection

The DriverManager class is a set of utility functions that work with the Driver methods together and manage multiple JDBC drivers by keeping them as a list of drivers loaded. Although loading a driver and registering a driver are two steps, only one method call is necessary to perform these two operations. The operational sequence of loading and registering a JDBC driver is:

1) Call class methods in the DriverManager class to load the driver into the Java interpreter
2) Register the driver using the **registerDriver()** method

When loaded, the driver will execute the **DriverManager.registerDriver()** method to register itself. The above two operations will never be performed until a method in the DriverManager is executed, which means that even both operations have been coded in an application; however, the driver cannot be loaded and registered until a method such as **connect()** is first executed.

To load and register a JDBC driver, two popular methods can be used:

1) Use Class.forName() method:

Class.forName("com.microsoft.sqlserver.jdbc.SQLServerDriver");

2) Create a new instance of the Driver class:

Driver sqlDriver = new com.microsoft.sqlserver.jdbc.SQLServerDriver;

Relatively speaking, the first method is more professional since the driver is both loaded and registered when a valid method in the DriverManager class is executed. The second method cannot guarantee that the driver has been registered by using the DriverManager.

3.3.1.2 Using DataSource Object to Establish a Connection

Another and better way to establish a connection is to use the DataSouce object.

The DataSource interface, introduced in the JDBC 2.0 Standard Extension API, is a better way to connect to a data source to perform data actions. In JDBC, a data source is a class that implements the interface **javax.sql.DataSource** to connect to more than one desired databases. The `getConnection()` method is always used to setup this connection.

A DataSource object is normally registered with a Java Naming and Directory Interface (JNDI) naming service. This means that an application can retrieve a DataSource object by name from the naming service independently of the system configuration.

Perform the following three operations to deploy a DataSource object:

1. Create an instance of the DataSource class
2. Set its properties using setter methods
3. Register it with a JNDI naming service

After a valid connection has been setup using the DataSource object, one can use any data query methods listed in Tables 3.3 and 3.4 to perform data actions against the desired database.

3.3.2 Build and Execute SQL Statements

Once a valid connection is established and a Connection object is created, the JDBC driver is responsible for ensuring that an application has consistent and uniform access to any database. It is also responsible for ensuring that any requests made to the application are presented to the database in a way that can be recognized by the database.

To build a SQL statement, one needs to call the method createStatement() that belongs to the Connection class to create a new Statement object. Regularly, there are three types of Statement objects widely implemented in the JDBC API; Statement, PreparedStatement and CallableStatement. The relationship among these three classes is: the PreparedStatement and CallableStatement classes are the subclasses of the Statement class.

To execute a SQL statement, one of the following three methods can be called:

1) **execmuteQuery()**
2) **executeUpdate()**
3) **execute()**

All of these methods belong to the Statement and the PreparedStatement classes and used to access database to perform different data actions.

The differences between these three methods are dependents on the different data operations and actions. Table 3.3 lists the function for each method and the

Table 3.3 The function of three SQL statements execution methods

Method	Function
executeQuery()	This method performs data query and returns a ResultSet object that contains the queried results
executeUpdate()	This method does not perform data query, instead it only performs either a data updating, insertion, or deleting action against the database and returns an integer that equals the number of rows that have been successfully updated, inserted, or deleted
execute()	This method is a special method, and it can be used either way. All different data actions can be performed by using this method, such as data query, data insertion, data updating, and data deleting. The most important difference between the execute() method and two above methods is that this method can be used to execute some SQL statements that are unknown at the compile time or return multiple results from stored procedures. Another difference is that the execute() method does not return any result itself, and one needs to use getResultSet() or getUpdateCount() method to pick up the results. Both methods belong to the statement class

Table 3.4 The desired method used to pick up the SQL execution results

Execution method	Picking up method
executeQuery()	getResultSet(), getXXX(), where XXX equals to the desired data type of returned result
executeUpdate()	getUpdateCount() This method will return an integer that equals the number of rows that have been successfully updated, inserted, or deleted
execute()	getResultSet(), getUpdateCount() This method does not return any result itself, and one needs to use getResultSet() or getUpdateCount() method to pick up the results. Both methods belong to the statement class

situation under which the appropriate method should be utilized. Mode detailed discussion about these three methods and their implementations can be found in Chap. 5.

3.3.3 Process Results

After the desired SQL statement is executed, you need to retrieve the execution results. Depending on the different execution methods you called, you need to use the different methods to pick up the results.

Table 3.4 lists some necessary methods used to pick up the appropriate results based on the different execution methods utilized.

3.3.3.1 Using ResultSet Object

A ResultSet object will be created after the `executeQuery()` method is executed or a `getResultSet()` method is executed. A ResultSet object is a data structure that presents rows and columns returned by a valid query. It maintains a cursor pointing to its current row of data. Initially, the cursor is positioned before the first row. One can use the `next()` method to move the cursor to the next row, and continue this moving one can scan the entire ResultSet. With a loop, one can use the appropriate `getXXX()` method of the ResultSet class to pick up each row in the ResultSet object. The XXX indicates the corresponding Java data type of the selected row. A more detailed discussion about these methods will be provided in Chap. 4.

3.3.3.2 Using RowSet Object

A RowSet object contains a set of rows from a result set or some other source of tabular data, like a file or spreadsheet. Because a RowSet object follows the JavaBeans model for properties and event notification, it is a JavaBeans component that can be combined with other components in an application. As is compatible with other Beans, application developers can probably use a development tool to create a RowSet object and set its properties.

RowSets may have many different implementations to fill different needs. These implementations fall into two broad categories, connected and disconnected:

1) A connected RowSet is equivalent to a ResultSet, and it maintains a connection to a data source as long as the RowSet is in use.
2) A disconnected RowSet works as a DataSet in Visual Studio.NET, and it can connect to a data source to perform the data updating periodically. Most time, it is disconnected with the data source and uses a mapping memory space as a mapped database.

While a RowSet is disconnected, it does not need a JDBC driver or the full JDBC API, so its footprint is very small. Thus a RowSet is an ideal format for sending data over a network to a thin client.

Because it is not continually connected to its data source, a disconnected RowSet stores its data in memory. It needs to maintain metadata about the columns it contains and information about its internal state. It also needs a facility for making connections, for executing commands, and for reading and writing data to and from the data source. A connected RowSet, by contrast, opens a connection and keeps it open for as long as the RowSet is being used. A more detailed discussion about the RowSet object and its implementation will be given in Chap. 5.

Since the JDBC driver is a core for entire JDBC API, we will have a more detailed discussion about this component in the next section.

3.4 JDBC Driver and Driver Types

The JDBC driver builds a bridge between your Java applications and your desired database, and works as an intermediate-level translator to perform a double-direction conversion: convert your high-level Java codes to the low-level native codes to interface to the database, and convert the low-level native commands from the database to your high-level Java codes.

As we discussed in the last section, a JDBC driver class contains six methods and one of the most important methods is the **connect()** method, which is used to connect to the database. When using this Driver class, a point to be noted is that most methods defined in the Driver class never be called directly, instead, they should be called via the DriverManager class methods.

Generally, the JDBC API will not contain any JDBC driver and you need to download a desired JDBC driver from the corresponding vendor if you want to use a specified driver. Based on the different configurations, JDBC drivers can be categorized into the following four types:

3.4.1 Type I: JDBC-ODBC Bridge Driver

Open Database Connectivity (ODBC) is a Microsoft-based database Application Programming Interface (API) and it aimed to make it independent of programming languages, database systems, and operating systems. In other words, the ODBC is a database and operating system independent API and it can access any database in any platform without problem at all.

Figure 3.2 shows a typical architecture of JDBC-ODBC Bridge Driver application. Figure 3.2a is for a Java standard-alone application and 3.2b is a Java 2-tire application.

Basically, ODBC is built and based on various Call Level Interface (CLI) specifications from the SQL Access Group and X/Open techniques. To access an ODBC to interface to a desired database, a JDBC-ODBC Bridge is needed and this bridge works just like a translator or a converter, which interpreters the JDBC requests to the CLI in ODBC when a request is sent from the JDBC to the ODBC, and perform an inverse translation (from CLI in ODBC to JDBC) when a result is returned from the database. The advantage of using Type I driver is simplicity since we do not need to know the details inside ODBC and transactions between the ODBC and DBMS. Refer to Fig. 3.2a, it is a typical Java standard-alone application that uses JDBC-ODBC Bridge Driver to access a local database, and it will work fine. However, a problem will be exposed if applying this JDBC-ODBC Bridge Driver in

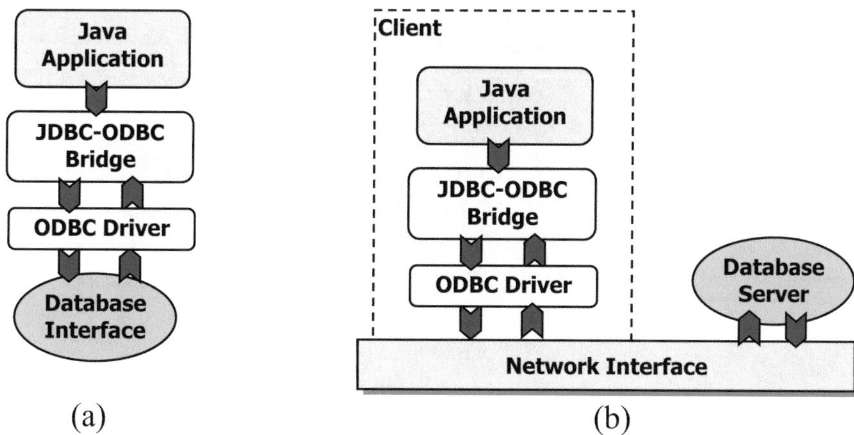

Fig. 3.2 JDBC-ODBC Bridge Driver

a 2-tier application that is shown in Fig. 3.2b. The problem is that the network standard security manager will not allow the ODBC that is downloaded as an applet to access any local files when you build a Java Applet application to access a database located in a database server. Therefore, it is impossible to build a Java Applet application with this JDBC-ODBC Bridge Driver configuration.

3.4.2 Type II: Native-API-Partly-Java Driver

The Native-API-Partly-Java driver makes use of local native libraries to communicate with the database. The driver does this by making calls to the locally installed native call level interface (CLI) using a native language, either C or C++, to access the database. The CLI libraries are responsible for the actual communications with the database server. When a client application makes a database accessing request, the driver translates the JDBC request to the native method call and passes the request to the native CLI. After the database processed the request, results will be translated from their native language back to the JDBC and presented to the client application. Figure 3.3 shows a Type II driver configuration.

Compared with Type I driver, the communications between the driver and the database are performed by using the native CLI without needing any translation between JDBC and ODBC driver, therefore the speed and efficiency of Type II driver is higher than that of Type I driver. When available, Type II drivers are recommended over Type I drivers.

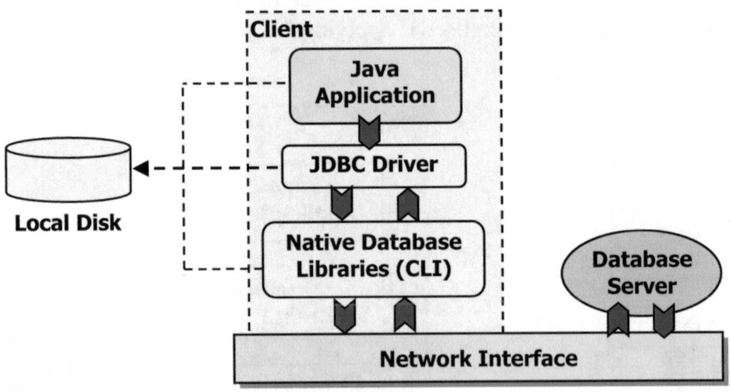

Fig. 3.3 Type II Driver

3.4.3 Type III: JDBC-Net-All-Java Driver

Basically, the Type III drivers are similar with Type II drivers and the only difference between them is the replacement of the native database access libraries.

For both Type I and Type II drivers, either the ODBC driver or the native CLI libraries must be installed and located on the client machine. All communications between the server processes and the JDBC driver have been through native program interface. However, in Type III driver configuration, the native CLI libraries are placed on a server and the driver uses a network protocol to facilitate communications between the application and the driver. The result of this modification is to separate the driver into two parts: (1) a part of JDBC driver that is an all-Java portion can be downloaded to the client and (2) a server portion containing both another part of JDBC driver and native CLI methods. All communications between the application and the database server are 100% Java to Java. However, the communication between the database and the server is still done via a native database CLI. Figure 3.4 shows this configuration.

It can be found from Fig. 3.4 that the client does not need to perform either database-specified protocol translation or a Java-to-CLI translation by using Type III drivers, and this will greatly reduce the working loads for the client machine and the client piece of a Type III driver only needs to translate requests into the network protocol to communicate with the database server. Another advantage of using a Type III driver is that the second part of the Type III driver, which is used to communicate with the database native libraries, does not need to be downloaded to the client, and as a result of this fact, Type III drivers are not subject to the same security restrictions found as Types I and II did. Since all database-related codes reside on the server side, a large driver that is capable of connecting to many different databases can be built.

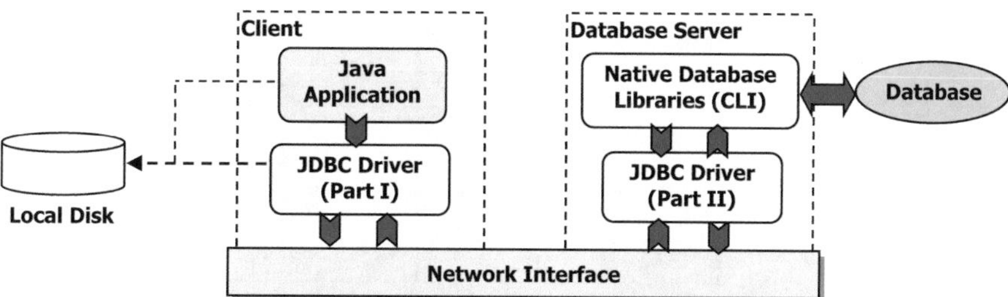

Fig. 3.4 Type III Driver configuration

3.4.4 *Type IV: Native-Protocol-All-Java Driver*

Type IV drivers are totally different with any drivers we have discussed so far. These types of drivers are capable of communicating directly with the database without the need for any type of translation since they are 100% Java without using any CLI native libraries. Figure 3.5 shows a typical Type IV driver configuration.

The key issue in the use of a Type IV driver is that the native database protocol will be rewritten to convert the JDBC calls into vendor-specific protocol calls, and the result of this rewritten is that the driver can directly interact with the database without needing any other translations. Therefore, Type IV drivers are the fastest drivers compared with all other three-type drivers, Types I ~ III. By using a Type IV driver, it will greatly simplify database access for applets by eliminating the need for native CLI libraries.

3.5 JDBC Standard Extension API

Besides the standard JDBC API (or core API), Sun added an extension package called JDBC 2.0 Standard Extension API to support extended database operations. This package contains the following components:

1) JDBC DataSource
2) JDBC driver-based connection pooling
3) JDBC RowSet
4) Distributed transactions

We will take a close look at these components and provide a more detailed discussion about these elements in the following sections.

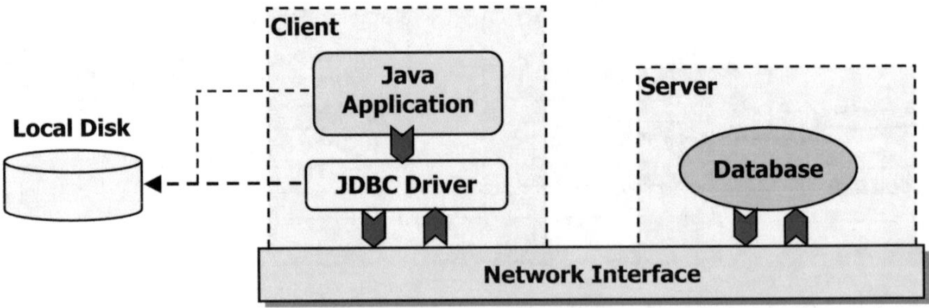

Fig. 3.5 Type IV driver configuration

3.5.1 JDBC DataSource

In Sect. 3.3.3.2, we have had a brief discussion about the DataSource object. Because of its specialty and advantage over JDBC drivers and DriverManagers, we will provide a more detailed discussion about this interface in this part.

As we know, the DataSource interface is introduced in the JDBC 2.0 Standard Extension API and it is a better way to connect to a data source to perform data actions. In JDBC, a data source is a class that implements the interface **javax.sql.DataSource** to connect to more than one desired databases. The **getConnection()** method is always used to setup this connection.

As we discussed in Sect. 3.3.1, to establish a connection by using a JDBC driver, you need to use the DriverManager to load a desired driver and register that driver to the driver list. You also need to know exactly the driver name and the driver URLs to complete this connection. In fact, the DataSource can provide an alternative and better way to do that connection in a fast and more efficient way.

The advantage of using a DataSource to perform this database connection is: a DataSource object is normally registered with a Java Naming and Directory Interface (JNDI) naming service. This means that an application can retrieve a DataSource object by the name of that DataSource only, without needing to know the driver name, database name, and driver URLs, even without needing to register any drivers. In other words, this naming service is independent of the system configurations and databases.

3.5.1.1 Java Naming and Directory Interface

Java Naming and Directory Interface (JNDI) provide naming and directory functionality and service to Java applications. It is defined to be independent of any specific directory service implementation so that different directories can be accessed in a common way.

Exactly, the JNDI can be analogous to a file directory that allows users to find and work with files by name. In this way, the JNDI is used to find the DataSource using the logical name assigned to it when it is registered with the JNDI.

The association of a name with an object is called a binding process. A DataSource object stores the attributes that tell it how to connect to a database, and those attributes are assigned when you bind the DataSource instance to its JNDI directory. The core JNDI interface that performs looking up, binding, unbinding, renaming objects, creating and destroying subcontexts is the Context interface.

The Context interface represents a naming context, which consists of a set of name-to-object bindings. It contains methods for examining and updating these bindings. Table 3.5 shows some most popular methods used by this interface.

In fact, using JNDI can significantly improve the portability of a Java application by removing the need to hard code a driver name and database name, and it is very similar to a file directory to improve file accessing by overcoming the need to

Table 3.5 The most popular methods used in the context interface

Method	Function
bind(String name, Object obj)	Binds a name to an object
createSubcontext(String name)	Creates and binds a new context
destroySubcontext(String name)	Destroys the named context and removes it from the namespace
listBindings(String name)	Enumerates the names bound in the named context, along with the objects bound to them
lookup(String name)	Retrieves the named object
unbind(String name)	Unbinds the named object
close()	Closes this context

```
Vendor_DataSource ds = new Vendor_DataSource();
ds.setServerName("localhost");
ds.setDatabaseName("CSE_DEPT");
ds.setDescription("CSE_DEPT Database");
Context ctx = new InitialContext();
ctx.bind("jdbc/CSE_DEPT", ds);
```

Fig. 3.6 An example coding for the creation of a new DataSource object

reference disk cylinders and sectors. To establish a valid database connection using the JNDI, the only information you need is the name of the DataSource, yes, that is all you need and it is so simple and easy, is it not?

3.5.1.2 Deploy and Use a Basic Implementation of DataSource

In this section, we will use a piece of codes to illustrate the implementation of a DataSource object. Perform the following three operations to deploy a DataSource object:

1) Create an instance of the DataSource class
2) Set its properties using setter methods
3) Register it with a JNDI naming service

The first step is to create a DataSource object, set its properties, and register it with a JNDI naming service. A DataSource object is usually created, deployed, and managed separately from the Java applications that use it. A point to be noted is that a DataSource object for a particular data source is created and deployed by a developer or system administrator, not the user. Figure 3.6 shows a piece of example codes to create a new DataSource object with some properties setting by using some setters. The class `Vendor_DataSource` would most likely be supplied by a driver vendor.

In Fig. 3.6, the first coding line is to create a new DataSource object based on the data source provided by the vendor. The following three lines are used to setup different properties using a setter. The last two lines are used to create an InitialContext object and to bind and register the new DataSource object `ds` to the logical name `jdbc/CSE_DEPT` with a JNDI naming service.

The JNDI namespace consists of an initial naming context and any number of subcontexts under it. It is hierarchical, similar to the directory/file structure in many file systems, with the initial context being analogous to the root of a file system and subcontexts being analogous to subdirectories. The root of the JNDI hierarchy is the initial context, here represented by the variable `ctx`. There may be many subcontexts under the initial context, one of which is `jdbc`, the JNDI subcontext reserved for JDBC data sources. The logical data source name may be in the subcontext `jdbc` or in a subcontext under `jdbc`. The last element in the hierarchy is the object being registered, analogous to a file, which in this case is a logical name for a data source.

The codes shown in Fig. 3.7 show how an application uses this to connect to a data source.

To get a connection using a DataSource object, create a JNDI Context instance and use the name of the DataSource object to its `lookup()` method to try to find it from a JNDI subcontext `jdbc`. The returned DataSource object will call its `getConnection()` method to establish a connection to the database.

As soon as a database connection has been established, you can execute any SQL statements as you want to perform any desired data action against the connected database.

3.5.2 JDBC Driver-Based Connection Pooling

By using a DataSource object, you can easily setup a connection with your database and perform any data operation you want. Sound good! Yes, this kind of operation is good for two-tier database applications without problem. However, a problem would come if you apply this operation is a three-tier database application. The main issue is the overhead in transactions between the application server and client. If you are running in a three-tier database application, each time when you communicate between your application server and your database via a database server

```
Context ctx = new InitialContext();
DataSource ds = (DataSource)ctx.lookup("jdbc/CSE_DEPT");
Connection con = ds.getConnection("myUserName", "myPassWord");

// Execute the SQL statements to perform data actions via database......
```

Fig. 3.7 An example coding for execution of the database connection via DataSource

to perform a connection or a disconnection, there would be quite a few communication traffics running between your server and your database, and this will introduce multiple opening and closing operations to your database and greatly reduce the efficiency of the database.

To solve this overhead problem, a Connection Pooling API has been provided by JDBC Standard Extension API. The pooling implementations do not actually close connections when the client calls the `close()` method, but instead return the connections to a pool of available connections for other clients to use. This avoids any overhead of repeatedly opening and closing connections, and allows a large number of clients to share a small number of database connections.

The connection pooling API is an extension of the regular connection API. The working principle of using a connection pooling is: when a resource or connection is no longer needed after a task has been completed, it is not destroyed but is added into a resource pool instead, making it available when required for a subsequent operation. In other words, we can temporarily store all unused connections to a connection pool, and reuse them as soon as a new data action is required for the target database. In this way, we can greatly improve the database performance by cutting down on the number of new connections that need to be created.

The JDBC API provides a client and a server interface for connection pooling. The client interface is `javax.sql.DataSource`, which is what application code will typically use to acquire a pooled database connection. The server interface is `javax.sql.ConnectionPoolDataSource`, which is how most application servers will interface with the PostgreSQL JDBC driver. Both interfaces are defined in the JDBC 2.0 Standard Extension (also known as the JDBC 2.0 Optional Package).

The server interface for connection pooling, `ConnectionPoolDataSource` object, is a factory for `PooledConnection` objects. All Connection objects that implement this interface are registered with a JNDI naming service.

To implement a DataSource object to create pooled connections, you need to perform the following operations:

- Create a `ConnectionPoolDataSource` object
- Set its properties to the data source that produced connections
- Register `ConnectionPoolDataSource` object with the JNDI naming service
- Create a DataSource object
- Set properties to the DataSource object by using setter

Figure 3.8 shows a piece of example codes to illustrate how to use the connection pooling API to create and deploy a DataSource object that an application can use to get pooled connections to the database.

The first coding line is used to create a new `ConnectionPoolDataSource` object, and this object is equivalent to a pool body to hold unused data sources later.

The following four lines are used to set appropriate properties to this created object. Then, in the sixth and seventh lines, the created `ConnectionPoolDataSource` object is registered with the JNDI naming

```
ConnectionPoolDataSource  cpds = new  ConnectionPoolDataSource();
cpds.setServerName("localhost");
cpds.setDatabaseName("CSE_DEPT");
cpds.setPortNumber(5000);
cpds.setDescription("CSE_DEPT Database");
Context ctx = new InitialContext();
ctx.bind("jdbc/pool/CSE_DEPT", cpds);
PooledDataSource  ds  = new  PooledDataSource();
ds.setDescription("CSE_DEPT database pooled connection source");
ds.setDataSourceName("jdbc/pool/CSE_DEPT");
Context  ctx = new InitialContext();
ctx.bind("jdbc/CSE_DEPT", ds);
```

Fig. 3.8 An example coding for the connection pooling DataSource

```
Connection con = null;
 try {
      con = ds.getConnection();
      // use connection
     }
catch(SQLException e)
    {
      // log error
     }
finally
    {
         if(con != null)
           try {con.close();}catch(SQLException e) {}
   }
```

Fig. 3.9 An example coding for retrieving and reusing a connection

service. The logical name associated with `cpds` has a subcontext pool added under the subcontext `jdbc`, which is similar to adding a subdirectory to another subdirectory in a file system.

Now we need to create our DataSource object implemented to work with it, or in other words, we can add this DataSource object into our pool, the `ConnectionPoolDataSource` object, when it is temporarily unused in an application. The coding lines between the eighth and the tenth are used to create our DataSource object `ds` with the `PooledDataSource` class. Note in the tenth coding line, the name of the DataSource is `jdbc/pool/CSE_DEPT`, which is identical with the logical name of our `ConnectionPoolDataSource` object we created before.

The last two coding lines are used to register our DataSource object with the JNDI naming service.

Now you can use this connection pooling for your data source object. The point is that when you finished a task to your current database, you must call the `close()` method from your client to inform the server that this database connection will be temporarily unused, and this will allow the Connection Pooling API to add this unused connection to the `ConnectionPoolDataSource` object. Later on if you want to reuse this database, you need to use the codes shown in Fig. 3.9 to get that connection from the pool.

Another situation to use a DataSource object is when you need to implement distributed transactions, which means that you need to use multiple databases synchronously in your applications. In that case, use of a DataSource object with built-in distributed transaction capabilities is the best solution.

3.5.3 Distributed Transactions

A *distributed transaction*, sometimes referred to as a *global transaction*, is a set of two or more related transactions that must be managed in a coordinated way. The transactions that constitute a distributed transaction might be in the same database, but more typically are in different databases and often in different locations. Each individual transaction of a distributed transaction is referred to as a *transaction branch*.

In the JDBC 2.0 extension API, distributed transaction functionality is built on top of connection pooling functionality, which we have discussed in the last section. This distributed transaction functionality is also built upon the open XA standard for distributed transactions. (XA is part of the X/Open standard and is not specific to Java).

3.5.3.1 Distributed Transaction Components and Scenarios

A typical distributed transaction can be composed of the following components and scenarios:

- A distributed transaction system typically relies on an external transaction manager, such as a software component that implements standard Java Transaction API (JTA) functionality, to coordinate the individual transactions. Many vendors will offer XA-compliant JTA modules. This includes Oracle, which is developing a JTA module based on the Oracle implementation of XA.
- XA functionality is usually isolated from a client application, being implemented instead in a middle-tier environment such as an application server. In many scenarios, the application server and transaction manager will be together on the middle tier, possibly together with some of the application code as well.
- The term `resource manager` is often used in discussing distributed transactions. A resource manager is simply an entity that manages data or some other kind of resource. Wherever the term is used in this chapter, it refers to a database.

By definition XA is a standard protocol that allows coordination, commitment, and recovery between transaction managers (e.g., CICS, Tuxedo, and even BEA

Web Logic Server) and resource managers (e.g., databases, message queuing products such as JMS or Web Sphere MQ, mainframe applications, ERP packages).

As with connection pooling API, two classes must be used for a distributed transaction:

- A XADataSource that produces XAConnections supporting distributed transactions.
- A DataSource object that is implemented to work with it.

The transaction manager is responsible for making the final decision either to `commit` or `rollback` any distributed transaction. A commit decision should lead to a successful transaction; rollback leaves the data in the database unaltered. JTA specifies standard Java interfaces between the transaction manager and the other components in a distributed transaction: the application, the application server, and the resource managers.

3.5.3.2 The Distributed Transaction Process

The transaction manager is the primary component of the distributed transaction infrastructure; however, the JDBC driver and application server components should have the following characteristics:

- The driver should implement the JDBC 2.0 API (including the Optional Package interfaces XADataSource and XAConnection) or higher and the JTA interface XAResource.
- The application server should provide a DataSource class that is implemented to interact with the distributed transaction infrastructure and a connection pooling module.

The first step of the distributed transaction process is to send a request to the transaction manager by the application. Although the final commit/rollback decision treats the transaction as a single logical unit, there can be many transaction branches involved. A transaction branch is associated with a request to each resource manager involved in the distributed transaction. Requests to three different RDBMSs, therefore, require three transaction branches. Each transaction branch must be committed or rolled back by the local resource manager. The transaction manager controls the boundaries of the transaction and is responsible for the final decision as to whether or not the total transaction should commit or rollback. This decision is made in two phases, called the Two-Phase Commit Protocol.

In the first phase, the transaction manager polls all of the resource managers (RDBMSs) involved in the distributed transaction to see if any of them is ready to commit. If a resource manager cannot commit, it responds negatively and rolls back its particular part of the transaction so that data is not altered.

In the second phase, the transaction manager determines if any of the resource managers have responded negatively, and, if so, rolls back the whole transaction. If there are no negative responses, the translation manager commits the whole transaction, and returns the results to the application.

The DataSource implemented to produce connections for distributed transactions is almost always implemented to produce connections that are pooled as well. The XAConnection interface extends the PooledConnection interface.

To begin a distributed transaction, a XADataSource object should be created first, and this can be done by creating a new instance of the XATransactionlDS and setting its properties.

Figure 3.10 shows an example coding for a distributed transaction.

The first coding line is used to create a new `XADataSource` object, and it produces XAConnections supporting distributed transactions.

The following four lines are used to set appropriate properties to this created object.

Then, in the sixth and seventh lines, the created `XADataSource` object is registered with the JNDI naming service. The logical name associated with `xads` has a subcontext `xa` added under the subcontext `jdbc`, which is similar to adding a subdirectory to another subdirectory in a file system.

Finally, the DataSource object is created to interact with `xads`, and other `XADataSource` objects are deployed.

Now that instances of the `TransactionlDS` and `XATransactionlDS` classes have been created, an application can use the DataSource to get a connection to the CSE_DEPT database, and this connection can then be used in any distributed transactions.

3.5.4 JDBC RowSet

A JDBC RowSet object is one of the JavaBeans components with multiple supports from JavaBeans and it is a new feature in the `java.sql` package. By using the RowSet object, a database query can be performed automatically with the data

```
XATransactionIDS  xads = new  XATransactionIDS ();

xads.setServerName("localhost");
xads.setDatabaseName("CSE_DEPT");
xads.setPortNumber(5000);
xads.setDescription("CSE_DEPT Database");

Context ctx = new InitialContext();
ctx.bind("jdbc/xa/CSE_DEPT", xads);

TransactionIDS  ds  = new  TransactionIDS();
ds.setDescription("CSE_DEPT distributed transaction connection source");
ds.setDataSourceName("jdbc/xa/CSE_DEPT");

Context  ctx = new InitialContext();
ctx.bind("jdbc/CSE_DEPT", ds);
```

Fig. 3.10 An example coding for the distributed transaction implementation

source connection and a query statement creation. In this section, we will provide a brief introduction about this new feature to reduce the coding load and improve the efficiency of the data query with the help of this RowSet object. A more detailed discussion with real project examples will be given in Sect. 6.4.6 in Chap. 6.

3.5.4.1 Introduction to Java RowSet Object

A RowSet object contains a set of rows from a result set or some other source of tabular data, like a file or spreadsheet. Because a RowSet object follows the JavaBeans model for properties and event notification, it is a JavaBeans component that can be combined with other components in an application. As it is compatible with other Beans, application developers can probably use a development tool to create a RowSet object and set its properties.

RowSets may have many different implementations to fill different needs. These implementations fall into two broad categories, connected and disconnected:

1) A connected RowSet is equivalent to a ResultSet, and it maintains a connection to a data source as long as the RowSet is in use.
2) A disconnected RowSet works as a DataSet in Visual Studio.NET, and it can connect to a data source to perform the data updating periodically. Most time, it is disconnected with the data source and uses a mapping memory space as a mapped database.

While a RowSet is disconnected, it does not need a JDBC driver or the full JDBC API, so its footprint is very small. Thus a RowSet is an ideal format for sending data over a network to a thin client.

To make writing an implementation easier, the Java Software division of Sun Microsystems, Inc., plans to provide reference implementations for five different styles of RowSets in the future. Among them, two components are very popular and widely implemented in Java database applications:

1) A CachedRowSet class—a disconnected RowSet that caches its data in memory; not suitable for very large data sets, but an ideal way to provide thin Java clients, such as a Personal Digital Assistant (PDA) or Network Computer (NC), with tabular data.
2) A JDBCRowSet class—a connected RowSet that serves mainly as a thin wrapper around a ResultSet object to make a JDBC driver look like a JavaBeans component.

To effectively apply RowSet objects to perform data actions against desired databases, the following operational sequence should be adopted.

3.5.4.2 Implementation Process of a RowSet Object

Generally, the operational procedure of using a RowSet object to query data can be divided into the following four steps:

1) Setup and configure a RowSet object
2) Register the RowSet Listeners
3) Set input and output parameters for the query command
4) Traverse through the result rows from the ResultSet

The first step is used to setup and configure the static or dynamic properties of a RowSet object, such as the connection `url`, username, password, and running command, to allow the RowSet object to connect to the data source, pass user parameters into the data source and perform the data query.

The second step allows users to register different Listeners for the RowSet object with different event sources. The RowSet feature supports multiple listeners to be registered with the RowSet object. Listeners can be registered using the **addRowSetListener()** method and unregistered through the **removeRowSetListener()** method. A listener should implement the `javax.sql.RowSetListener` interface to register itself as the RowSet listener. Three types of events are supported by the RowSet interface:

1) cursorMoved event: Generated whenever there is a cursor movement, which occurs when the next() or previous() methods are called.
2) rowChanged event: Generated when a new row is inserted, updated, or deleted from the row set.
3) rowsetChanged event: Generated when the whole row set is created or changed.

In this book, the Apache NetBeans IDE 12 is used and the event-listener model has been setup by NetBeans IDE. So we can skip this step and do not need to take care of this issue during our coding process in the following chapters.

Step 3 allows users to setup all static or dynamic parameters for the query statement of the RowSet object. Depending on the data type of the parameters used in the query statement, suitable **setXXX()** method should be used to perform this parameter setup process.

The fourth step is used to retrieve each row from the ResultSet object.

3.6 Chapter Summary

This chapter discusses the fundamentals of JDBC and JDBC API, which include an overview of the JDBC and JDBC API, JDBC drivers, and related components used in JDBC API.

The JDBC components and architecture are discussed and analyzed in detail in the first part of this chapter. All classes and interfaces defined in a JDBC API are discussed and presented with sequence tables. With some basic idea on JDBC and its components, the function and operational procedure of using JDBC API to perform data actions are described by three key steps:

1) Establish a connection between your Java application and related databases
2) Build and execute SQL statements
3) Process the results

To setup a valid database connection, two popular connection methods are introduced; using the DriverManager class method and using the DataSource object. Relatively speaking, the second method is simple and easy to be used in real applications since no detailed data source information is needed for this database connection.

To build and execute a typical SQL statement, the Statement, PreparedStatement, and CallableStatement components are discussed and introduced. Both PreparedStatement and CallableStatement classes are subclasses of the Statement class; however, both of them have more flexibility compared with the Statement component.

To process returned query result, different objects, such as ResultSet and RowSet, are introduced and discussed to provide users a clear picture about those objects and their functionalities.

Following the JDBC API and JDBC driver discussion, a detailed discussion about the types of JDBC Drivers is provided. Four popular types of drivers are analyzed and compared with architectures and their implementations.

Finally, four important components defined in the JDBC Standard Extension API, DataSource, Connection Pooling, Distributed Transactions, and RowSet are introduced and discussed with example coding.

The topics discussed in this chapter are prerequisites for the next chapter, and some components will be discussed and analyzed in more detail to give users a deeper understanding and a better picture about their roles in real Java database applications.

Homework

I. True/False Selections

____1. JDBC is a standard *Java Database Connectivity* and JDBC API can be considered as a *Java Database Connectivity Application Programming Interface*.

____2. JDBC API is not the only component included in a JDBC.

____3. JDBC API is composed of a set of classes and interfaces used to interact with databases from Java applications.

____4. JDBC Drivers are implementation dependent, which means that different applications need different drivers.

____5. The core of JDBC 4.0 API provides standard JDBC components that are located at the `java.sql` package, and some additional components such as JNDI and JTS are defined in JDBC 4.0 Standard Extension that is located at the `javax.sql` package.

____ 6. One can establish a database connection by directly calling the Driver class method `connect()`.

____ 7. To load and register a JDBC driver, two popular methods can be used; using either Class.forName() method or to create a new instance of the Driver class.

____ 8. Three components can be used to build a SQL statement: Statement, Prepared-Statement, and CallableStatement.

____ 9. To pick up the execution results, one can use the executeQuery() and executeUpdate() methods. The former returns an integer and the latter returns a ResultSet.

____10. There are four types of JDBC drivers, and Type IV driver is a pure Java driver with fast running speed and high efficiency in data actions.

II. Multiple Choices

1. Generally, the JDBC API performs the following three functions _____
   (a) Connect to database, load JDBC driver, perform the query
   (b) Perform the query, connect to database, load JDBC driver
   (c) Get result from ResultSet, connect to database, load JDBC driver
   (d) Establish a connection to database, execute SQL statements and get running results
2. To establish a connection with a DataSource object, you need to ________
   (a) Create a DataSource object, set properties, and use this object
   (b) Set properties, setup a connection, and perform queries
   (c) Create a DataSource object, set properties, and register it with JNDI naming service
   (d) Register a DataSource object, set properties, and create a DataSource object
3. To build and run a SQL statement, following components can be utilized ______
   (a) Statement
   (b) Statement, PreparedStatement
   (c) Statement, PreparedStatement, CallableStatement
   (d) None of them
4. To execute a SQL statement to get a query result, ________ method(s) should be used.
   (a) executeQuery()
   (b) executeUpdate()
   (c) execute() and executeUpdate()
   (d) executeQuery() and execute()

5. To perform an insert, update or delete operation, the ________ method(s) should be used.

   (a) executeUpdate()
   (b) executeQuery()
   (c) executeQuery() and execute()
   (d) executeQuery() and executeUpdate()

6. The ________ method can be used to either pick up a query result or update a datum.

   (a) executeUpdate()
   (b) execute()
   (c) executeQuery()
   (d) None of them

7. A *distributed transaction* is defined as to access _________ data source(s) at _______ location(s).

   (a) Single, single
   (b) Multiple, same
   (c) Multiple, different
   (d) Single, multiple

8. The execute() method can _____________.

   (a) Not return any result
   (b) Return some results
   (c) Be used either to return a result or not return any result.
   (d) None of above

9. A CachedRowSet class is a __________ that caches its data in __________.

   (a) Connected RowSet, database
   (b) Disconnected RowSet, database
   (c) Connected RowSet, memory
   (d) Disconnected RowSet, memory

10. The ResultSet object can be created by either executing the ___________ or __________ method, which means that the ResultSet instance cannot be created or used without executing a query operation first.

   (a) executeQuery(), getResultSet()
   (b) getResultSet(), execute()
   (c) createResultSet(), getResultSet()
   (d) buildResultSet(), executeQuery()

III. Exercises

1. Provide a detailed description about the JDBC API, which includes:
   (a) The definition of the JDBC and JDBC API
   (b) The components defined in a JDBC API, including all classes and interfaces
   (c) The architecture of the JDBC API
   (d) The regular functions of a JDBC API performed
   (e) The packages of the JDBC API is involved
2. Provide a brief discussion about database connection using JDBC API, which includes:
   (a) Two popular methods used to establish a connection
   (b) Operational procedure to establish a connection
   (c) How to use a DataSource object to establish a connection
   (d) Compare two popular method with the DataSource method in establishing a database connection
3. Explain the function of three different statement execution methods: executeQuery(), executeUpdate() and execute(). For each method, provides a way to retrieve the execution result.
4. Provides a brief introduction about four types of JDBC drivers and their architecture.
5. Provides a brief introduction about the connection pooling API.

Chapter 4
JDBC Application and Design Considerations

This chapter discusses the application fundamentals of JDBC and JDBC API, which include the application models and operational procedures of the JDBC API implemented in Java database applications.

4.1 JDBC Application Models

JDBC API supports both two-tier and three-tier models for database accesses. In a two-tier model, a Java application or an applet can communicate directly with the database.

In a three-tier model, commands are sent to a middle-tier, which sends the messages to the database. In return, the result of the database query is sent to the middle-tier that finally directs it to the application or applet. The presence of a middle-tier has a number of advantages, such as a tight control over changes done to the database.

4.1.1 Two-Tier Client-Server Model

In a two-tier client-server model, a Java application can directly communicate with the database. In fact, the so-called two-tier model means that the Java application and the target database can be installed in two components with two layers:

- Application layer, which includes the JDBC driver, user interface, and the whole Java application, installed in a client machine.

Supplementary Information The online version contains supplementary material available at [https://doi.org/10.1007/978-3-031-06553-8_4].

Y. Bai, *SQL Server Database Programming with Java*,
https://doi.org/10.1007/978-3-031-06553-8_4

- Database layer, which includes the RDBMS and the database, installed in a database server.

Figure 4.1 shows a typical configuration of a two-tier model.

It can be found from Fig. 4.1 that both Java application and JDBC API are located at the first layer, or the client machine and the DBMS and database are located at the second layer or the database server. A DBMS-related protocol is used as a tool to communicate between these two layers. The interface to the database is handled by a JDBC driver that is matched to the particular database management system being used. The JDBC driver has double-side functionality; it passes SQL statement to the database when a data action request is sent from the client, and returns the results of executing those statements to the client when the data action is done.

A client-server configuration is a special case of the two-tier model, where the database is located on another machine called the database server. The Java application program runs on the client machine that is connected to the database server through a network.

Most topics discussed in Chaps. 5, 6, and 7 in this book are about two-tier model applications. The Java application projects are built in the client machine and communicate with the database server through the network to perform all kinds of data actions. The inherent flexibility of Java JDBC approach to develop database applications enables you to access a variety of RDBMS systems, including Microsoft Access, SQL Server, and Oracle.

4.1.2 Three-Tier Client-Server Model

In a three-tier client-server model, a data action request is coming from an application GUI and sent to the application server that can be considered as a middle tier, and the application server that contains the JDBC API then sends SQL statements to the database located on a database server. When the data action is processed, the database sends the results back to the application server, which then sends them to the client. In fact, the so-called three-tier model is common in Web applications, in

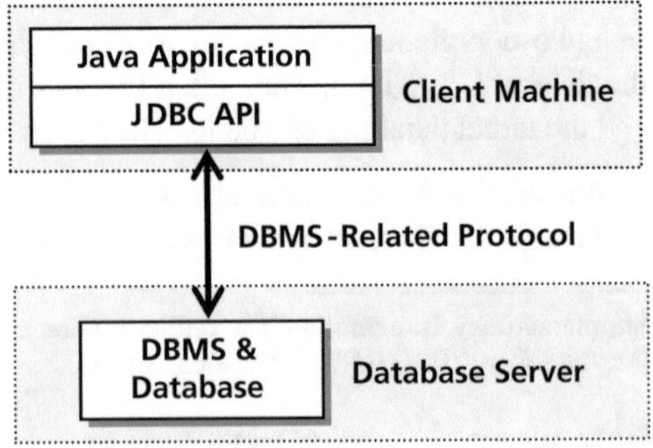

Fig. 4.1 A typical configuration of a two-tier model

which the client tier is implemented in a Web browser, the middle-tier is a Web server, and the database management system runs on a database server. This model can be represented by the following three layers:

- Client layer, which includes a Web browser with some language-specified virtual machines, installed in a client machine.
- Application server layer, which includes Java Web applications or Java Web services, installed in a Web server. This layer is used to handle the business logic or application logic. This may be implemented using Java Servlet engines, Java Server Pages, or Java Server Faces. The JDBC driver is also located in this layer.
- Database layer, which includes the RDBMS and the database, installed in a database server.

Figure 4.2 shows a typical configuration of a three-tier model.

Advantages of using a three-tier configuration over a two-tier counterpart include:

- Application performance can be greatly improved by separating the application server and database server.
- Business logic is clearly separated from the database.
- Client application can then use a simple protocol to access the server.

Topics discussed in Chaps. 8 and 9 in this book are about three-tier applications that use a Web browser as the client, a Java Server Face (JSF) or Java Server Page (JSP) as the middle-tier, and a relational database management system as the database server.

Now that we have a clear picture about the Java application running models, next we need to dig a little deeper about the Java database applications.

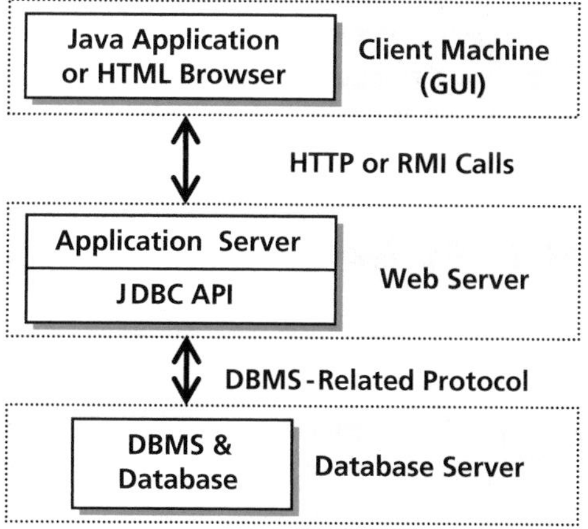

Fig. 4.2 A typical configuration of a three-tier model

4.2 JDBC Applications Fundamentals

As we discussed in Sect. 3.1 in Chap. 3, to run a Java database application to perform data actions against the selected database, a JDBC API needs to perform the following operations:

1) Establish a connection between your Java application and related databases
2) Build and execute SQL statements
3) Process the results

In fact, to successfully develop and run a Java database application, the above three operational steps need to be further divided into the following seven steps:

1) Import necessary Java packages, such as **java.awt, java.util, javax.swing, java.sql**, and **javax.sql**
2) Load and register the JDBC driver
3) Establish a connection to the database server
4) Create a SQL statement
5) Execute the built statement
6) Retrieve the executing results
7) Close the statement and connection objects

In all steps listed above, step 1 is a prerequisite step since all JDBC-related components and interfaces are defined in the **java.sql** and **javax.sql** packages. All GUI-related components are defined in the **java.awt** and **javax.swing** packages, and all other application-related components are defined in the **java.util** package. In order to use any component defined in those packages, you must first import those packages into your program to provide namespaces and locations for those components. Otherwise, a compiling error may be encountered since the compiler cannot find and identify those components when you used them but without providing the related packages.

In this and the following sections, we will provide a deeper and more detailed discussion about the data actions on Java database applications based on these seven fundamental steps.

4.2.1 Loading and Registering Drivers

As we studied in Chap. 3, to establish a valid database connection, first you need to load and register a JDBC driver. Then you can call the **connect()** method to establish a database connection to your desired database.

We provided a brief discussion about the JDBC Driver and DriverManager components in Chap. 3. In fact, the core of the JDBC API is the JDBC Driver that can be accessed and called from the DriverManager class method. However, the Driver class is under the control of the DriverManager class and the DriverManager is exactly a manager for the Driver class. When using this Driver class, you cannot call and run any method defined in the Driver class, instead, you need to call them via the DriverManager class methods.

The DriverManager class is a set of utility functions that work with the Driver methods together and manage multiple JDBC drivers by keeping them as a list of drivers loaded. Although loading a driver and registering a driver are two steps, only one method call is necessary to perform these two operations. The operational sequence of loading and registering a JDBC driver is:

1) Call class methods in the DriverManager class to load the driver into the Java interpreter
2) Register the driver using the **registerDriver()** method

When loaded, the driver will execute the **DriverManager.registerDriver()** method to register itself. The above two operations will never be performed until a method in the **DriverManager** is executed, which means that even both operations have been coded in an application; however, the driver cannot be loaded and registered until a method such as **connect()** is first executed.

To load and register a JDBC driver, two popular methods can be used:

1) Use **Class.forName()** method:

```
Class.forName("com.microsoft.sqlserver.jdbc.SQLServerDriver");
```

2) Create a new instance of the Driver class:

```
Driver sqlDriver = new com.microsoft.sqlserver.jdbc.SQLServerDriver;
```

Relatively speaking, the first method is more professional since the driver is both loaded and registered when a valid method in the **DriverManager** class is executed. The second method cannot guarantee that the driver has been registered by using the DriverManager.

A piece of sample codes that are used to load and register a Microsoft SQL Server JDBC driver using the first method is shown in Fig. 4.3.

```
import java.sql.*;
try
{
    //Load and register SQL Server driver
    Class.forName("com.microsoft.sqlserver.jdbc.SQLServerDriver");
}
catch(Exception e) {
    System.out.println("Class not found exception!" + e.getMessage());
}
```

Fig. 4.3 A sample coding for the driver loading and registering

In Fig. 4.3, the first coding line is used to import the JDBC API package **java.sql.***.

Then a **try.....catch** block is used to load and register a Microsoft SQL Server JDBC Driver. The **Class.forName()** method is utilized to make sure that our JDBC Driver is not only loaded but also registered when it is connected by running the **getConnection()** method later. The argument of this method, **com.microsoft.sqlserver.jdbc.SQLServerDriver**, is the name of this Microsoft SQL Server JDBC Driver class and it is created by the NetBeans when it is added to a Java database application project.

The `catch` block is used to track any possible error for this loading and registering. The related exception information will be displayed if any error occurred.

You can use the second method to replace this method to perform the same driver loading and registering operation if you like.

4.2.2 Getting Connected

To establish a connection to the desired database, two methods can be used:

1) Using **DriverManager.getConnection()** method
2) Using **Driver.connect()** method

Before we can take a closer look at these two methods, first let's have a quick review for all methods defined in these two classes, **DriverManager** and **Driver**.

4.2.2.1 The DriverManager and Driver Classes

All 12 methods defined in the DriverManager class are shown in Table 4.1.

Four methods in the **DriverManager** class are widely applied in most database applications; **getConnection(), getDriver(), registerDriver()**, and **deregisterDriver()**. Note that the **getConnection()** method has two more overloading methods with different arguments.

All six methods defined in the Driver class are shown in Table 4.2.

Most popular methods in the Driver class are **acceptsURL()** and **connect()**.

Most methods defined in the Driver class will not be called directly in most Java database applications, instead, they will be called indirectly by using the DriverManager class.

Now let's have a closer look at these two methods.

Table 4.1 Methods defined in the DriverManager class

Method	Function
deregisterDriver(Driver dr)	Remove a driver from the driver list
getConnection(String url, Properties login)	Attempt to establish a connection to the referenced database
getConnection(String url, String user, String pswd)	Attempt to establish a connection to the referenced database
getConnection(String url)	Attempt to establish a connection to the referenced database
getDriver(String url)	Locate an appropriate driver for the referenced URL from the driver list
getDrivers()	Get a list of all drivers currently loaded and registered
getLoginTimeout()	Get the maximum time (in seconds) a driver will wait for a connection
getLogStream()	Get the current PrintStream being used by the DriverManager
Println(String msg)	Print a message to the current LogStream
registerDriver(Driver dr)	Add the driver to the driver list. This is normally done automatically when the driver is instantiated
setLoginTimeout(int seconds)	Set the maximum time (in seconds) that a driver can wait when attempting to connect to a database before giving up
setLogStream(PrintStream out)	Set the PrintStream to direct logging message to

Table 4.2 Methods defined in the Driver class

Method	Function
acceptsURL(String url)	Return a true if the driver is able to open a connection to the database given by the URL
connect(String url, Properties login)	Check the syntax of the URL and the matched drivers in the driver list. Attempt to make a database connection to the given URL
getMajorVersion()	Determine the minor revision number of the driver
getMinorVersion()	Determine the major revision number of the driver
getPropertyInfo(String url, Properties login)	Return an array of DriverPropertyInfo objects describing login properties accepted by the database
jdbcCompliant()	Determine if the driver is JDBC COMPLIANT

4.2.2.2 Using the DriverManager.getConnection() Method

When using the first method **DriverManager.getConnection()** to establish a database connection, it does not immediately try to do this connection, instead, in order to make this connection more robust, it performs a two-step process. The **getConnection()** method first checks the driver and Uniform Resource Locator (URL) by running a method called **acceptsURL()** via DriverManager class to test the first driver in the driver list, if no matched driver returns, the **acceptURL()** method will go to test the next driver in the list. This process continues until each driver is tested or until a matched driver is found. If a matched driver is found, the **Driver.connect()** method will be executed to establish this connection. Otherwise, a SQLException is raised.

It looks like that this two-step connection is not efficient enough; however, a more robust connection can be set if more than one driver is available in the driver list.

The purpose of the **acceptsURL()** method is to check whether the current driver is able to open a valid connection to the given URL or not. This method does not create a real connection or test the actual database connections; instead, it merely examines the sub-protocol of the URL and determines if it understands its syntax. In this way, it can effectively reduce the chance of the misconnection and make sure the correctness of an established connection.

4.2.2.3 Using the Driver.connect() Method

The **Driver.connect()** method enables you to create an actual connection to the desired database and returns an associated Connection object. This method accepts the database URL string and a Properties object as its argument. A URL indicates the protocol and location of a data source while the properties object normally contains the user login information. One point to be noted is that the only time you can use this **Driver.connect()** method directly is that you have created a new instance of the Driver class.

A null will be returned if an exception is occurred when this **Driver.connect()** method is executed, which means that something wrong during this connection operation.

Comparing the **DriverManager.getConnection()** method with this **Driver.connect()** method, the following conclusions can be obtained:

- The **DriverManager.getConnection()** method can perform checking and testing each driver in the driver list automatically for all loaded drivers. As soon as a matched driver is found, it can be connected to the database directly by using the **Driver.connect()** method. This automatic process will greatly reduce the processing time.
- The **DriverManager.getConnection()** method has looser requirements for the arguments passed with this method. When applying the **Driver.connect()** method, you have to pass two arguments, the URL as a string and the login properties as a Properties object with strict syntax and grammar requirements. However, when using the **DriverManager.getConnection()** method, you can define login properties as either String, a Properties object, or even a null string, since the DriverManager can handle the converting these arguments to the appropriate Properties object when it is applied.

From this comparison, it can be found that the **DriverManager.getConnection()** method is over the **Driver.connect()** method; therefore, we will use this method to do our database connection in all example projects in this book.

After a driver has been loaded and registered, the next step is to establish a database connection using a URL. Before we can continue on the database connection, we need to have a clear picture and understanding about the JDBC connection Uniform Resource Locator (URL).

4.2.2.4 The JDBC Connection URL

The JDBC URL provides all information for applications to access to a special resource, such as a database. Generally, a URL contains three parts or three segments: protocol name, sub-protocol, and subname for the database to be connected. Each of these three segments has different function when they worked together to provide unique information for the target database.

The syntax for a JDBC URL can be presented as: **protocol:sub-protocol:subname**

The protocol name works as an identifier or indicator to show what kind of protocol should be adopted when connect to the desired database. For a JDBC driver, the name of the protocol should be **jdbc**. The protocol name is used to indicate what kind of items to be delivered or connected.

The sub-protocol is generally used to indicate the type of the database or data source to be connected, such as **sqlserver** or **oracle**.

The subname is used to indicate the address to which the item supposed to be delivered or the location of the database is resided. Generally, a subname contains the following information for an address of a resource:

- Network host name/IP address
- The database server name
- The port number
- The name of the database

An example of a subname for our SQL Server database is:

```
localhost\\SQL2019EXPRESS:5000
```

The network host name is **localhost**, and the server name is **SQL2019EXPRESS** and the port number the server used is **5000**. You need to use a double slash, either forward or back, to represent a normal slash in this URL string since this is a DOS style string.

By combining all three segments together, we can get a full JDBC URL. An example URL that is using a SQL Server JDBC driver is:

```
jdbc:sqlserver//localhost\\SQL2019EXPRESS:5000
```

The database's name works as an attribute of the connected database.

Now that we have a clear picture about the JDBC URL, next let's connect our application to our desired database.

4.2.2.5 Establish a Database Connection

Now we have a clear picture and understanding about the fundamentals in `DriverManager` and Driver classes as well as related database connection methods. As we discussed in the previous sections, to connect to a database, two methods, **DriverManager.getConnection()** and **Driver.connect()**, can be used. However, as we know, the first method is better than the second one, therefore in this section we will concentrate on the use of the first method to establish a database connection.

Figure 4.4 shows a piece of example codes to establish a connection using the **DriverManager.getConnection()** method. This piece of codes should be a follow up of the codes shown in Fig. 4.3; in other words, a valid driver has been loaded and registered before the following connection can be established.

Since the **DriverManager.getConnection()** method is an overloading method with three different signatures, here we used two of them and the first one is highlighted in bold and the second one is commented out.

To establish a database connection, a valid JDBC URL is defined in the first coding line with the following components:

- The protocol name **jdbc**
- The sub-protocol **sqlserver**
- The subname **localhost\\SQL2019EXPRESS:5000**
- The database name **CSE_DEPT**

Then a **try…catch** block is used to try to establish a connection using the **getConnection()** method with three arguments: URL, username, and password. After a valid connection is established, a Connection object is returned and this returned object has the following functions and properties:

1) The Connection object represents an SQL session with the database.

```
……. .
//A driver has been successfully loaded and registered

String url = "jdbc:sqlserver://localhost \\SQLEXPRESS:5000;databaseName=CSE_DEPT;";
//String url = "jdbc:sqlserver://localhost\\SQLEXPRESS:5000;
//              databaseName=CSE_DEPT;user=cse;password=mack8000";

//Establish a connection
try{
    con = DriverManager.getConnection(url,"cse","mack8000");
    //con = DriverManager.getConnection(url);
    con.close();
   }
   catch(SQLException e) {
   System.out.println("Could not connect!" + e.getMessage());
   e.printStackTrace();
   }
```

Fig. 4.4 An example coding for the database connection

2) The Connection object provides methods for the creation of Statement objects that will be used to execute SQL statements in the next step.
3) The Connection object also contains methods for the management of the session, such as transaction locking, catalog selection, and error handling.

By definition, the responsibility of a Connection object is to establish a valid database connection with your Java application, and that is all. The Connection object has nothing to do with the SQL statement execution. The SQL statement execution is the responsibility of the Statement, PreparedStatement, and CallableStatement objects. As we mentioned, both PreparedStatement and CallableStatement are subclasses of the Statement class and they play different roles for the statement execution.

In the next coding line in Fig. 4.4, a **close()** method that belongs to the Connection class is called to try to close a connection. In fact, it is unnecessary to close a connected database in actual applications. However, we used this method here to show users a complete picture of using the Connection object, which means that you must close a connection when it is no longer to be used in your application (even in the connection pooling situation, but it will not be really closed instead it is placed into a pool), otherwise a running error may be encountered when you reuse this connection in the future. Therefore, this coding line is only for the testing purpose and should be removed in a real application.

The **catch** block is used to detect any possible exception and display them if any of them occurred.

A Connection class contains 19 methods, and Table 4.3 lists 7 most popular methods.

Now a valid database connection has been established, and the next step is to execute the SQL statements to perform data actions against our connected database.

Table 4.3 Methods defined in the Connection interface

Method	Function
close()	Close the connection to the database
createStatement()	Create a Statement object for the execution of static SQL statements
getMetaData()	Retrieve all database related information stored in the DatabaseMetaData object for the current connection
isClosed()	Determine if the referenced Connection has been closed – True = closed
prepareCall(String sqlString)	Create a CallableStatement object for use with SQL stored procedures
prepareStatement(String sqlString)	Create a PreparedStatement object for use with SQL dynamic queries
commit()	Immediately commits all transactions to the database. All updates and changes are made permanent

4.2.3 *Executing Statements*

To successfully execute an appropriate Statement object to perform SQL statements, the following operational sequence should be followed:

1) Creating a **Statement** object based on the requirement of the data actions
2) Calling the appropriate execution method to run the SQL statements

In a simple word, the **Statement** object is used for executing a static SQL statement and returning the results stored in a ResultSet object.

4.2.3.1 Overview of Statement Objects and Their Execution Methods

By using the **Connection** object, three separate statement objects can be created, and they are:

- **Statement** object
- **PreparedStatement** object
- **CallableStatement** object

Table 4.4 Methods defined in the Statement interface

Method	Function
close()	Close the Statement and release all resources including the ResultSet associated with it
execute(String sqlString)	Execute an SQL statement that may have an unknown number of results. Returned a True means that the first set of results from the sqlString execution is a ResultSet. If the execution resulted in either no results or an update count, a False is returned
executeQuery(String sqlString)	Execute an SQL Select statement. A ResultSet object that contained the query results from the database will be returned
executeUpdate(String sqlString)	Execute an SQL Update, Insert or Delete statement. An integer will be returned to indicate the number of rows that have been affected
getMaxRows()	Determine the maximum number of rows that can be returned in a ResultSet object
getMoreResults()	Move to the Statements next result. Only in conjunction with the execute statement and where multiple results are returned by the SQL statement. A False is returned if the next result is null or the results are an update count
getResultSet()	Return the current result set for the Statement. Only used in conjunction with execute() method. The current ResultSet object will be returned
getUpdateCount()	Return the number of rows affected by the last SQL statement. Is only meaningful for INSERT, UPDATE or DELETE statements
setCursorName(String name)	Set the cursor name to be used by the Statement. Only useful for databases that support positional updates and deletes
setMaxRows(int rows)	Set the maximum number of rows that can be returned in a ResultSet. If more results are returned by the query, they are truncated

The **Statement** object is used to execute static SQL queries. The so-called static statements do not include any IN or OUT parameters in the query string and do not contain any parameters passing to or from the database.

The **Statement** interface contains more than 18 methods, and Table 4.4 lists 10 most popular methods.

Among those 10 methods in the `Statement` interface, three execution methods including the **executeQuery(), executeUpdate()** and **execute(),** and **getResultSet()** method are often used in Java database applications.

The **PreparedStatement** is a subclass of the **Statement** and it is mainly used to execute dynamic SQL queries with IN parameter involved. These kinds of

Table 4.5 Methods defined in the PreparedStatement interface

Method	Function
clearParameters()	Clear all parameters associated with a PreparedStatement. After execution of this method, all parameters have the value null
execute()	Execute the associated SQL Statement when the number of results returned is unknown. A False is returned if the returned result is null
executeQuery()	Execute an SQL Select statement. A ResultSet object that contained the query results from the database will be returned
executeUpdate()	Execute an SQL Update, Insert or Delete statement. An integer will be returned to indicate the number of rows that have been affected
getMetaData()	Return a set of meta data for the returned ResultSet object
getParameterMetaData()	Return the number, types, and properties of this PreparedStatement object's parameters
setBoolean(int index, Boolean value)	Bind a Boolean value to an input parameter
setByte(int index, Byte value)	Bind a byte value to an input parameter
setDouble(int index, double value)	Bind a double value to an input parameter
setFloat(int index, float value)	Bind a floating point value to an input parameter
setInt(int index, int value)	Bind an integer value to an input parameter
setLong(int index, long value)	Bind a long value to an input parameter
setNull(int index, int sqlType)	Bind a null value to an input parameter
setObject(int index, Object obj)	Bind an Object to an input parameter. The Object will be converted to an SQL data type before being sent to the database
setShort(int index, short value)	Bind a short value to an input parameter
setString(int index, String value)	Bind a String value to an input parameter
setTime(int index, Time value)	Bind a Time value to an input parameter

statements can be pre-parsed and pre-compiled by the database, and therefore have faster processing speed and lower running loads for the database server.

The **PreparedStatement** interface contains more than 20 methods, and Table 4.5 lists 17 most popular methods.

It can be found from Table 4.5 that three execution methods, **execute(), executeQuery(),** and **executeUpdate()**, look like a duplication with those methods defined in the Statement interface. However, a significant difference is: all of these three methods defined in the Statement interface have their query strings as an argument when these methods are executed, which means that the SQL statements have to be defined in those query strings and should be passed into the database as the arguments of those methods. In contract, all three methods defined in the PreparedStatement interface have no argument to be passed into the database when they are executed. This means that the SQL statements have been built and passed into the database by using the **PreparedStatement** object before these three methods are executed.

Two methods belong to the getters that are used to retrieve the metadata for the **ResultSet** and the **ParameterMetaData** objects. Both methods are very useful when the developer wants to get more detailed structure and properties information about a returned **ResultSet** object or **ParameterMetaData** object.

More than 10 methods defined in the **PreparedStatement** interface are setter methods, which means that these methods are used to set up an appropriate value to an input parameter with different data types. These methods are specially useful when a dynamic query is built with one or more dynamic input parameters that need to be determined in the SQL statements.

The **CallableStatement** is also a subclass of the **Statement** and the **PreparedStatement** classes and it is mainly used to execute the stored procedures with both IN and OUT parameters involved. As we know, stored procedures are built and developed inside databases, and therefore have higher running and responding efficiency in data queries and processing.

This interface is used to execute SQL stored procedures. The JDBC API provides a stored procedure SQL escape syntax that allows stored procedures to be called in a standard way for all RDBMSs. This escape syntax has one form that includes a result parameter and one that does not. If used, the result parameter must be registered as an OUT parameter. The other parameters can be used for input, output, or both. Parameters are referred to sequentially, by number or position, with the first parameter being 1.

```
{?= call <procedure-name>[(<arg1>,<arg2>, ...)]}
{call <procedure-name>[(<arg1>,<arg2>, ...)]}
```

The IN parameter values are set using the **setXXX()** methods inherited from the interface **PreparedStatement**. The type of all OUT parameters must be registered prior to executing the stored procedure; their values are retrieved after execution via the **getXXX()** methods defined in this **CallableStatement** interface.

Table 4.6 Methods defined in the CallableStatement interface

Method	Function
getBigDecimal(int index, int scale)	Return the value of parameter specified by the parameter index number as a BigDecimal
getBoolean(int index)	Return the value of parameter specified by the parameter index number as a Boolean
getByte(int index)	Return the value of parameter specified by the parameter index number as a byte
getBytes(int index)	Return the value of parameter specified by the parameter index number as an array of bytes
getDouble(int index)	Return the value of parameter specified by the parameter index number as a double
getFloat(int index)	Return the value of parameter specified by the parameter index number as a floating point number
getInt(int index)	Return the value of parameter specified by the parameter index number as an integer
getLong(int index)	Return the value of parameter specified by the parameter index number as a long integer
getObject(int index)	Return the value of parameter specified by the parameter index number as an Object. The object type is determined by the default mapping of the SQL data type to Java data type
getShort(int index)	Return the value of parameter specified by the parameter index number as a short integer
getString(int index)	Return the value of parameter specified by the parameter index number as a String object
getTime(int index)	Return the value of parameter specified by the parameter index number as a Time object
registerOutParameter(int index, int slqType)	Register the specified output parameter to receive the SQL data type indicated by the argument passed.
registerOutParameter(int index, int slqType, int scale)	Register the specified output parameter to receive the SQL data type indicated by the argument passed. If the output is registered as either DECIMAL or NUMERIC, the scale of the value may also be specified
wasNull()	Determine if the last value read by a **getXXX()** method was a SQL null value. A True is returned if the last read value contained a null value

A **CallableStatement** can return one ResultSet object or multiple ResultSet objects. Multiple ResultSet objects are handled using operations inherited from the **Statement** interface. The **CallableStatement** interface contains over 30 methods, Table 4.6 lists 15 most popular methods.

The **registerOutParameter()** method is an overloading method with two signatures and these methods are used to declare what SQL type the OUT parameter will return when a CallableStatement method is executed.

By default, only one ResultSet object per Statement object can be open at the same time. Therefore, if the reading of one ResultSet object is interleaved with the reading of another, each must have been generated by different Statement objects.

All execution methods in the Statement interface implicitly close a Statment's current ResultSet object if an open one exists.

The Statement interface contains three important query methods with different functions; **executeQuery(), executeUpdate(),** and **execute()**. For each method, different operations can be performed and different results will be returned.

Generally, the query methods can be divided into two categories; (1) the query method that needs to perform data query, such as **executeQuery()**, which returns an instance of **ResultSet** that contained the queried results, and (2) the query method that does not perform data query and only return an integer, such as **executeUpdate()**. An interesting method is the **execute()**, which can be used in either way.

Let's first concentrate on the creation of the Statement objects based on the different requirements of data actions.

4.2.3.2 Using the Statement Object

As we discussed in the last section, three separate statement objects can be created based on three different data actions; **Statement, PreparedStatement**, and **CallableStatement**. Let's discuss how to create a `Statement` object first.

4.2.3.2.1 Creating the Statement Object

The **Statement** object is the most common type of object and easy to be used in a static data query. The shortcoming of using this object is that all SQL statements must be pre-defined with definite parameters when a Statement object is created. In other words, by using a Statement object to execute a SQL statement, no parameter can be passed into or from the database.

The **Statement** object is created by using the **createStatement()** method defined in the **Connection** interface (refer to Table 4.3). Figure 4.5 shows an example of creation of a **Statement** object. The coding line that is used to create a **Statement**

```
String url = "jdbc:sqlserver://localhost\\SQL2019EXPRESS:5000;databaseName=CSE_DEPT;";
//Establish a connection
try{
    con = DriverManager.getConnection(url,"cse","mack8000");
}
catch(SQLException e) {
    System.out.println("Could not connect!" + e.getMessage());}
String query = "SELECT user_name, pass_word FROM LogIn";
try{
    Statement stmt = con.createStatement();
}
catch(SQLException e) {
    System.out.println("Error in Statement!" + e.getMessage());}
```

Fig. 4.5 An example coding for the creation of a Statement object

```
import java.sql.*;
static Connection con;
try{
     //Load and register SQL Server driver
     Class.forName("com.microsoft.sqlserver.jdbc.SQLServerDriver");
}
catch(Exception e) {
     System.out.println("Class not found exception!" + e.getMessage());}
String url = "jdbc:sqlserver://localhost\\SQL2019EXPRESS:5000;databaseName=CSE_DEPT;";
//Establish a connection
try{
     con = DriverManager.getConnection(url,"cse","mack8000");
}
catch(SQLException e) {
     System.out.println("Could not connect!" + e.getMessage());}
String query = "SELECT user_name, pass_word FROM LogIn";
try{
     Statement  stmt = con.createStatement();
     ResultSet rs = stmt.executeQuery(query);
}
catch(SQLException e) {
     System.out.println("Error in Statement!" + e.getMessage());}
```

Fig. 4.6 An example coding for the execution of a Statement object

object has been highlighted in bold. All other lines are prerequisite codes that are used to load and register a driver, establish a connection using the URL and build a SQL query string.

4.2.3.2.2 Executing the Statement Object

To execute the created **Statement** object to perform a data action, you need to call one of the execution methods defined in the `Statement` interface shown in Table 4.4. Figure 4.6 shows an example coding for the execution of a SQL query with this **Statement** object.

The coding line that is used to execute a **Statement** object has been highlighted in bold. All other lines are prerequisite codes that are used to load and register a driver, establish a connection using the URL, build a SQL query string, and create a **Statement** object. It can be found from this piece of codes that no parameter can be passed to or from the database when this query is executed. Therefore, the **Statement** object can only be used to perform static queries.

To overcome this shortcoming, we need to use **PreparedStatement** objects to perform dynamic queries with varied input parameters.

4.2.3.3 Using the PreparedStatement Object

To perform dynamic SQL statements, we need to use a **PreparedStatement** object. Generally, to use a **PreparedStatement** object to perform a dynamic SQL statement includes the following steps:

1) Create a **PreparedStatement** object
2) Set data types and values to the associated input parameters in the query string
3) Call appropriate execution method to perform this dynamic query

Let's first concentrate on the creation of a **PreparedStatement** object.

4.2.3.3.1 Creating the PreparedStatement Object

Referring to Table 4.3, the **prepareStatement()** method defined in the Connection interface is used to create a **PreparedStatement** object. An example code to create a PreparedStatement object looks like:

```
PreparedStatement pstmt = con.prepareStatement(query);
```

Unlike Statement objects, the **PreparedStatement** object takes the SQL statement to be executed as an argument. For dynamic SQL statements that contain input parameters to be passed into the database, you need to define a position for each input parameter in the query string. Regularly, a placeholder is used to inform the database that it can expect a variable in that position. Each placeholder that holds a position for a variable in the query string is represented by a question mark '**?**', which holds a place for the associated variable during compiling time. When compiled, the placeholder is part of the statement and therefore appears static to the compiler. In this way, no matter what value is later assigned to the variable, the database does not need to recompile the statement. At the run time, you can assign values to the variables by using any **setXXX()** method defined in the **PreparedStatement** interface shown in Table 4.5.

Before we can call an execution method to run the **PreparedStatement** to perform a dynamic query, let's first take a look at how to use **setXXX()** method to reserve a place for the input parameter with the correct data type settings.

4.2.3.3.2 Setting the Input Parameters

All input parameters used for a PreparedStatement interface must be clearly bound to the associated IN parameters in a dynamic query string by using a **setXXX()** method. This **setXXX()** method can be divided into three categories based on the different data types,

1) The primitive data type method
2) The object method
3) The stream method

For the primitive and the object method, the syntax is identical, and the difference between them is the type of value that is assigned. For the stream method, both the syntax and the data types are different.

Set Primitive Data Type and Object IN Values

The primitive data type means all built-in data types used in Java programming language. The syntax of setting a primitive data type or an object value method is,

```
setXXX(int position, data_type value);
```

where **XXX** means the associated value type to be assigned, the **position** that is an integer is used to indicate the relative position of the IN parameter in the SQL statement or the SQL stored procedure, and the **value** is the actual data value to be assigned to the IN parameter.

Some popular **setXXX()** methods defined in the `PreparedStatement` interface can be found from Table 4.5.

An example of using the **setXXX()** method is:

```
String query = "SELECT product, order_date FROM Order " +
                        "WHERE order_id = ? AND customer = ?";
PreparedStatement pstmt = con.prepareStatement(query);
setInt(1, 101);
setString(2, "Tom Johnson");
```

Two dynamic parameters are used in the query string and both of them are IN parameters. The data type of first IN parameter is an integer and the second one is a String, and both are represented by a placeholder '?'. The first setting method, **setInt(1, 101),** is to assign an integer value of 101 to the first IN parameter, which is indicated with a position number of 1, and the second setting method, **setString(2, "Tom Johnson")** is to assign a String value "**Tom Johnson**" to the second IN parameter, which is indicated with a position number of 2.

From this example, you can find that there is no difference between setting a primitive parameter and an object value to the IN parameters in a SQL statement.

Set Object Methods

The **setObject()** method has three protocols, which are:

```
setObject(int position, object_type object_value);
setObject(int position, object_type object_value, data_type
desired_data_type);
setobject(int position, object_type object_value, data_type
desired_data_type, int scale);
```

The first one is straightforward and it contains two parameters; the first one is the relative position of the IN parameter in the SQL statement, and the second one is the value of a desired object to be assigned to the IN object.

The second one adds one more input parameter, **desired_data_type**, and it is used to indicate a data type to which convert the object to.

The third one adds the fourth input parameter, **scale**, and it is used to make sure that the object conversion result contains a certain number of digits.

An example of the **setObject()** method is shown here,

```
pstmt.setObject(2, 101);
pstmt.setObject(2, 101, Type.FLOAT);
pstmt.setObject(2, 101, Type.FLOAT, 2);
```

The first method is to set an input parameter, which is the second one in a SQL statement, to an object (here is an integer) with a value of 101. The next method is to set the same input to the same object, however, it needs to convert the object (integer) to a float data type. The final method performs the same operation as the previous one, but it indicates that the conversion result should contain at least 2 digits.

Since set stream IN methods are not very popular in Java database applications, we skip this part in this section. If you want to get more detailed information for these methods, refer to some sections in Chap. 6.

Now let's begin to call some appropriate execution methods to run this PreparedStatement object to perform dynamic queries.

4.2.3.3.3 Executing the PreparedStatement Object

As we discussed in Sect. 3.3.2 in Chap. 3, three execution methods can be called to perform the data action against the database. Refer to Tables 4.4 and 4.5, it can be found that both **Statement** and **PreparedStatement** interfaces contain these three methods:

- **executeQuery()**
- **executeUpdate()**
- **execute()**

```
String url = "jdbc:sqlserver://localhost\\SQL2019EXPRESS:5000;databaseName=CSE_DEPT;";
//Establish a connection
try{
    con = DriverManager.getConnection(url,"cse","mack8000");
}
catch(SQLException e) {
    System.out.println("Could not connect!" + e.getMessage());}
String query = "SELECT user_name, pass_word FROM LogIn" +
               "WHERE user_name = ? AND pass_word = ?";
try{
    PreparedStatement pstmt = con.prepareStatement(query);
    pstmt.setString(1,"cse");
    pstmt.setString(2,"mack8000");
    ResultSet rs = pstmt.executeQuery();
}
catch (SQLException e) {
    System.out.println("Error in PreparedStatement!" + e.getMessage()); }
```

Fig. 4.7 A coding example for the execution of a PreparedStatement

The difference between these three methods in both interfaces is that all three execution methods defined in the Statement interface need an argument, which works as a query statement passed into the database. However, all three methods defined in the **PreparedStatement** interface have no argument, which means that the query statement has been built and passed to the database by using the **PreparedStatement** object when it is created.

Figure 4.7 shows a piece of example codes for calling of the **executeQuery()** method to perform a login process.

First the query statement **query** is created in which two placeholders (**?**) are used since we have two dynamic parameters, username and password, to be passed into our sample database **CSE_DEPT**.

Then with a **try…catch** block, a **PreparedStatement** object is created with the `query` statement as an argument. Two **setString()** methods defined in the **PreparedStatement** interface are used to initialize these two dynamic parameters (username = "**cse**", password = "**mack8000**"). Finally, the **executeQuery()** method defined in the **PreparedStatement** interface is called to run this query statement and the results are returned and stored in a **ResultSet** object.

In addition to using the **executeQuery()** method, the **PreparedStatement** object can also use another two methods, **executeUpdate()** and **execute()** to perform a data action. However, those methods have different functionalities and should be applied in different situations. For more detailed information about these methods, refer to Sect. 4.2.3.5.

Compared with the **Statement** interface, the advantage of using a **PreparedStatement** interface is that it can perform a dynamic query with some known or unknown dynamic parameters as inputs. Most time, those dynamic parameters are input parameters and can be defined as IN variables. However, you do not need to specify those parameters with an IN keyword when using a **PreparedStatement** interface.

4.2.3.4 Using the CallableStatement Object

As we discussed in the early part of this chapter, the **CallableStatement** is a subclass of both **Statement** and **PreparedStatement**, and this interface is mainly used to call stored procedures to perform a group data actions. The JDBC **CallableStatement** method provides a way to allow us to perform a complicated query. The speed and efficiency of a data query can be significantly improved by using the stored procedure since it is built in the database side.

The difference between a **PreparedStatement** and a **CallableStatement** interface is: unlike the **PreparedStatement** interface, the **CallableStatement** interface has both input and output parameters, which are indicated with IN and OUT keywords, respectively. In order to setup values for input parameters or get values from the output parameters, you have to use either a **setXXX()** method inherited from the **PreparedStatement** or a **getXXX()** method to do that. However, the point is that before you can use any **getXXX()** method to pick up the values of output parameters, you must first register the output parameters to allow the **CallableStatement** interface to know them.

Generally, the sequence to run a **CallableStatement** to perform a stored procedure is:

1) Build a **CallableStatement** query string
2) Create a **CallableStatement** object
3) Set the input parameters
4) Register the output parameters
5) Execute **CallableStatement**
6) Retrieve the running result by using different **getXXX()** method

Let's discuss this issue one by one in more detail in the following sections.

4.2.3.4.1 Building a CallableStatement Query String

The **CallableStatement** interface is used to execute SQL stored procedures. The JDBC API provides a stored procedure SQL escape syntax that allows stored procedures to be called in a standard way for all RDBMSs. This escape syntax has one form that includes an output parameter and one that does not. If used, the output parameter must be registered as an **OUT** parameter. The other parameters can be used for input, output, or both. Parameters are referred to sequentially, by number, with the first parameter being 1.

```
{?= call <procedure-name>[<arg1>,<arg2>, ...]}
{call <procedure-name>[<arg1>,<arg2>, ...]}
```

Two syntaxes are widely used to formulate a **CallableStatement** string: the SQL92 syntax and the Oracle syntax. The SQL92 syntax is more popular in most applications. We will concentrate on the SQL92 syntax in this section, and take care of the Oracle syntax later when we build data queries for the Oracle database.

For a standard alone stored procedure or packaged procedure, the SQL92 syntax can be represented as:

```
{call [schema.][package.]procedure_name[(?, ?, …)]}
```

For standard alone functions or packaged functions, the SQL92 syntax looks like:

```
{? = call [schema.][package.]function_name[(?, ?, …)]}
```

The definition and meaning of elements used in these syntaxes are:

- All elements enclosed inside the square brackets [] means that they are optional.
- The curly braces {} are necessary in building a **CallableStatement** string and they must be used to cover the whole string.

- The schema indicates the schema in which the stored procedure is created.
- The package indicates the name of the package if the stored procedure is involved in a package.
- The ***procedure_name*** or the ***function_name*** indicate the name of the stored procedure or the function.
- The question mark **?** is the placeholder for either an IN, IN/OUT, or OUT parameters used in the stored procedure, or the returned value of a function. The order of these placeholders, which starts from 1, is very important, and it must be followed exactly when using either a **setXXX()** method to setup input parameters or register the output parameters for the built **CallableStatement** string later.

A **CallableStatement** can either return a **ResultSet** object and multiple **ResultSet** objects by using **executeQuery()** method or return nothing by using **execute()** method. Multiple **ResultSet** objects are handled using operations inherited from the **Statement** interface. A suitable **getXXX()** method is needed to pick up the running result of a **CallableStatement**.

Now that we have built a **CallableStatement** query string, next we need to create a **CallableStatement** object to execute the associated method to run stored procedures.

4.2.3.4.2 Creating the CallableStatement Object

To create a **CallableStatement** object, you need to use one of methods defined in the **Connection** class (refer to Table 4.3), **prepareCall()**, to do that. When the SQL92 syntax is used to create this **CallableStatement** object, it will looks like:

```
CallableStatement cstmt = null;
try{
    String query = "{call dbo.FacultyCourse(?, ?)}";
    cstmt = con.prepareCall(query);
    .........
```

The operation sequence of this piece of codes to create a new **CallableStatement** object is:

1) A new null **CallableStatement** object **cstmt** is first declared.
2) A **try** block is used to create the query string with the SQL92 syntax. The name of the stored procedure to be called is **dbo.FacultyCourse()** with two argu-

```
String query ="{call dbo.FacultyCourse(?,?)}";
cstmt = con.prepareCall(query);
cstmt.setString(1,"Jones");
cstmt.setString(2,"CSC-132B");
```

Fig. 4.8 A coding example for the setting input parameters

ments; the first one is an input parameter, **faculty_name** and the second one is an output parameter used to store all **course_id** taught by the selected faculty. Both parameters are represented by placeholders and they are positional parameters.

3) The **CallableStatement** object is created by calling the **prepareCall()** method, which belongs to the **Connection** class, with the query string as the argument.

Next, let's take a look at how to setup the input parameter for this object.

4.2.3.4.3 Setting the Input Parameters

We have provided a very detailed introduction in setting the input parameters for the PreparedStatement object in Sect. 4.2.3.3.2. Refer to that section to get more detailed description about setting the input parameters for a query string in the CallableStatement object. Figure 4.8 shows a piece of example codes to set input parameters for two dynamic parameters, *faculty_name* and *class_name*, the data type for both input parameters is String. Therefore, a **setString()** method is used.

Now let's take a look at how to register output parameters for a query string when using the **CallableStatement** object to perform a stored procedure call.

4.2.3.4.4 Registering the Output Parameters

After a **CallableStatement** interface is executed, you need to use the associated **getXXX()** method to pick up the running result from the **CallableStatement** object since it cannot return any result itself. However, before you can do that, you must first register any output parameter in the SQL statement to allow the **CallableStatement** to know that the output result is involved and stored in the related output parameters in the SQL statement.

Once an output parameter is registered, the parameter is considered an OUT parameter and it can contain running results that can be picked up by using the associated **getXXX()** method.

To register an output parameter, the **registerOutParameter()** method that belongs to the **CallableStatement** interface should be used to declare what SQL type the OUT parameter will return. A point to be noted is that a parameter in a SQL statement can be defined as both an IN and an OUT at the same time, which means

```
String query ="{call dbo.FacultyCourse(?,?)}";
cstmt = con.prepareCall(query);
cstmt.setString(1,"Jones");
cstmt.setString(2,"CSC-132B");
cstmt.registerOutParameter(2, java.sql.Types.VARCHAR);
```

Fig. 4.9 A coding example for the registering of the output parameters

that you can setup this parameter as an IN by using the **setXXX()** method, and also you can register this parameter as an OUT using the **registerOutParameter()** method at the same time. In this way, this parameter can be considered as an IN/OUT parameter with both the input and the output functions.

The syntax to register an output parameter is:

```
registerOutParameter(int position, data_type SQL_data_type);
```

where the **position** is still the relative position of the OUT parameter in the SQL statement, and the **SQL_data_type** is the SQL data type of the OUT parameter, which can be found from the JDBC API class, **java.sql.TYPE**. An example of using this method is shown in Fig. 4.9.

There are two parameters in this **CallableStatement** interface in this example. The first one is an IN parameter, which is set by using the **setString()** method. The second one is an IN/OUT parameter, which is first setup by using the **setString()** method and then registered by using the **registerOutParameter()** method with the data type of **VARCHAR**. The SQL data type **VARCHAR** can be mapped to a data type of String in Java. Refer to Appendix E to get more detailed information about the data type mapping between the SQL and Java.

An interesting point to this **registerOutParameter()** method is that all OUT parameters can be registered by using this syntax except those OUT parameters with the **NUMERIC** and **DECIMAL** data types. The syntax to register those OUT parameters looks like:

```
registerOutParameter(int position, data_type SQL_data_type, int scale);
```

The only difference is that a third parameter **scale** is added and it is used to indicate the number of digits to the right of the decimal point for the OUT parameter.

4.2.3.4.5 Executing the CallableStatement Object

To run a **CallableStatement** object, three execution methods can be used: **executeQuery()**, **executeUpdate()**, and **execute()**. As we discussed in Sect. 4.2.3.1, the **executeQuery()** method can return a **ResultSet** object that contains the running or query results, and the **executeUpdate()** method can return an integer to indicate the

```
String query = "{call dbo.FacultyCourse(?,?)}";
cstmt = con.prepareCall(query);
cstmt.setString(1,"Jones");
cstmt.setString(2,"CSC-132B");
cstmt.registerOutParameter(2,java.sql.Types.VARCHAR);
cstmt.execute();
```

Fig. 4.10 A coding example for running of the CallableStatement object

number of rows that have been inserted, updated, or deleted against the target database. However, the **execute()** method cannot return any running result with itself, and you need to use associated **getXXX()** methods to pick up the query or running result. Another important point of using the **execute()** method is that it can handle an unknown result with undefined data type. Refer to Sect. 4.2.3.5 to get more detailed information about the **execute()** method.

An example of using the **execute()** method to run the **CallableStatement** object is shown in Fig. 4.10.

After finishing building the query string, creating the **CallableStatement** object, and setting and registering input and output parameters, the **execute()** method is called to execute this **CallableStatement** object to perform a stored procedure processing.

Before we can continue in how to retrieve the running result from the execution of a **Statement, PreparedStatement,** or **CallableStatement** object, we need to have a closer look at three execution methods.

4.2.3.5 More About the Execution Methods

The three statement objects are used to perform different data actions against the target database, and the type of statement object to be used is determined by the parameters of the SQL statement. To make it simple, the following strategy should be adopted for the given situation:

- For static statements without needing to pass any parameter into the database, a **Statement** object can be used to perform this kind of data action.
- For dynamic statements with some input parameters that are needed to be passed into the target database, a **PreparedStatement** object should be used to perform this kind of data action.
- For stored procedures with both input and output parameters needed to be passed into the target database, a **CallableStatement** object can be used to perform this kind of data action.

Similarly to statement objects, the execute method to be used is determined by the expected output of the SQL statement. There are three types of output that can be expected from a SQL statement:

- A **ResultSet** containing data in tabular format with certain rows and columns.
- An integer indicating the number of rows affected by the SQL statement.
- A combination of a **ResultSet** and an integer.

Each of these output types requires its own special output handling. Accordingly, three execute methods, **executeQuery(), executeUpdate(),** and **execute()**, can be used for each type of statement object.

Generally, the execute methods can be divided into two categories; (1) the execute method that needs to perform a data query, such as the **executeQuery()**, which returns an instance of **ResultSet** that contained the queried results, and (2) the execute method that does not perform a data query and only return an integer, such as the **executeUpdate()**. An interesting method is the **execute()**, which can be used in either way. In conclusion, the following points should be noted when using any of these execute methods:

- The **executeQuery()** method performs data query and returns a **ResultSet** object that contains the queried results.
- The **executeUpdate()** method does not perform data query, instead it only performs either a data updating, insertion, or deleting action against the database and returns an integer that equals the number of rows that have been successfully updated, inserted, or deleted.
- The **execute()** method is a special method, and it can be used either way. All different data actions can be performed by using this method, such as data query, data insertion, data updating, and data deleting. The most important difference between the **execute()** method and two above methods is that the former can be used to execute some SQL statements that are unknown at the compile time or return multiple results from stored procedures. Another difference is that the **execute()** method does not return any result itself, and one needs to use **getResultSet()** or **getUpdateCount()** method to pick up the results. Both methods belong to the **Statement** interface.

A confusion issue may come with the use of the **execute()** method. As we mentioned, since any SQL statement, either known or unknown at the compile time, can be used with this **execute()** method, how do we know the execution results? Yes, that indeed is a problem. However, fortunately, we can solve this problem by using some testing methods indirectly.

In fact, we can call either **getResultSet()** or **getUpdateCount()** method to try to pick up the running results from execution of the **execute()** method. The key point is:

- The **getResultSet()** method will return a **null** if the running result is an integer, which is a number of rows that have been affected, either inserted, updated, or deleted.
- The **getUpdateCount()** method will return a −1 if the running result is a **ResultSet**.

```
PreparedStatement pstmt = con.prepareStatement(query);
pstmt.setString(1, "faculty_name");
pstmt.execute();

int updateCount = pstmt.getUpdateCount();

if (updateCount == -1)
   System.out.println("execute() method returned a ResultSet object!");
else
   System.out.println("execute() method returned an integer!");
```

Fig. 4.11 A coding example to distinguish the returned result

Based on these two key points, we can easily determine whether a result is a **ResultSet** or an integer. Figure 4.11 shows a piece of example codes to illustrate how to distinguish what kind of result is returned by using these two methods.

A **PreparedStatement** object is created and the input parameter is initialized using the **setString()** method, and then the **execute()** method is called to run the SQL statement. In order to distinguish the running result, first we use the **getUpdateCount()** method to pick up the returned result. A **ResultSet** object is returned if a −1 is returned for the execution of the **getUpdateCount()** method. Otherwise, an integer is returned to indicate that a data update, insert, or delete action has been executed and the integer value is equal to the number of rows that have been affected.

Now that we have known how to create and execute different execute methods, let's have a closer look at the creation and execution of SQL statements by using those methods.

4.2.3.6 Creating and Executing SQL Statements

To execute any execution method we discussed in the last sections, exactly is to execute a string representing an SQL statement. In fact, the SQL statement and the JDBC representation are exactly the same thing from the point of view of the terminal execution results. However, in some cases, you have to modify the JDBC string to make sure that the database can receive the correct SQL statement.

All SQL statements can be divided into two categories:

- Data definition language (DDL) statements
- Data manipulation language (DML) statements

The DDL statements are used to create and modify the structure of your database tables and other objects related to the database. The DML statements are used to work and manipulate with data in the database tables.

Let's discuss the creation and execution of SQL statements based on these two categories in the following sections.

```
String  sqlString = (" CREATE TABLE  LogIn "
                    + " (user_name   VARCHAR2(10),"
                    + " pass_word   VARCHAR2(10), "
                    + " login_ID   int )";

Statement  stmt = con.createStatement();
stmt.execute(sqlString);
```

Fig. 4.12 A coding example to create a LogIn table using JDBC statement

4.2.3.6.1 Creating and Executing the DDL Statements

Since DDL statements are mainly used for the creation and modification of the structure of the database tables and related objects, therefore they do not perform any query and do not affect any rows in the database-related tables. Of course, they will never return any **ResultSet** object, neither. However, in order to keep DDL statements consistent with other types of SQL statements, the DDL statements always return a 0 in an actual application.

A standard DDL protocol used to create the structure of a table is:

```
CREATE TABLE <table name>
(<attribute name 1> <data type 1>,
…… .
<attribute name n> <data type n>);
```

Figure 4.12 shows a piece of example codes to illustrate how to create a **LogIn** table using the JDBC statement.

First, the protocol used to create the **Login** table is assigned to a JDBC statement string **sqlString**. The data type for both **user_name** and **pass_word** columns are **VARCHAR2**, which is a varied-length char. The argument 10 is used to define the length of those chars. The **login_ID** is an integer. Then a **Statement** object is created and the **execute()** method is called to perform the creation of this table with the **sqlString** as the argument that is passed to the database.

To add data into a created table, you need to use the DML statements to do that job.

4.2.3.6.2 Creating and Executing the DML Statements

The DML statements are used to build and complete the body of the database tables. These statements include the data query statements, insert, update, and delete statements. All of these statements need to return some execution results, either a **ResultSet** object or an integer.

A standard DML statement used to insert data into the created data table looks like:

```
String  sqlString = ("INSERT INTO LogIn "
                   + "VALUES('Tom Baker', 'come123', 100078, 'David Tim', 'test55', 100080)";
Statement  stmt = con.createStatement();
stmt.execute(sqlString);
```

Fig. 4.13 A coding example to insert data into the LogIn table using JDBC statement

```
String query = "SELECT user_name, pass_word FROM LogIn" +
               "WHERE user_name = ? AND pass_word = ? ";
try {
     PreparedStatement  pstmt = con.prepareStatement(query);
     pstmt.setString(1, "cse ");
     pstmt.setString(2, " mack8000");
     ResultSet rs = pstmt.executeQuery();
}
catch (SQLException e) {
      System.out.println("Error in PreparedStatement!" + e.getMessage());}
```

Fig. 4.14 A coding example to perform a SQL query using JDBC statement

Table 4.7 Keywords and their syntax supported by JDBC escape syntax

Keyword	Function	Syntax
Call	Execute stored procedures	{ call procedure_name [arg1, …]}
? = call	Execute stored functions	{ ? = call function_name [arg1, …] }
d	Define a date	{ d ‘yyy-mm-dd’ }
escape	Define the databases escape character	{ escape ‘escape character’ }
fn	Execute a scalar function	{ ‘fn function [arg1, …] }
oj	Define an outer join	{ oj outer-join }
t	Define a time	{ ‘hh:mm:ss’ }
ts	Define a time stamp	{ ‘yyyy-mm-dd hh:mm:ss.f….’ }

```
INSERT INTO <table name>
VALUES (<value 1>, <value 2>, … <value n>);
```

A standard DML statement used to update data from a created data table looks like:

```
UPDATE <table name>
SET <attribute> = <expression>
WHERE <condition>;
```

Figure 4.13 shows a piece of example codes to illustrate how to add some data items to the created `LogIn` table using the JDBC statement.

Figure 4.14 shows a piece of example codes to illustrate how to perform a select query to retrieve the desired username and password from the **LogIn** table.

4.2.3.6.3 JDBC Escape Syntax

When JDBC performs a SQL statement, it does not check the SQL grammar and you can send any SQL statement to your database. This gives you flexibility to allow you to use some extended functions that are not included in the entry-level SQL92 standard and provided by particular vendors. To support these extensions in a database-independent manner, JDBC implements an ODBC-style escape syntax for many of these extensions. By using escape syntax, applications can achieve total database independence and still take advantages of the additional functionalities provided by those extensions.

Escape syntax works much like the escape character, which contains a keyword and parameters all enclosed in curly braces.

```
{ keyword  [parameter], .... }
```

As JDBC finds a set of curly braces in an executable string, the driver maps the enclosed keyword and parameters to the database-specified syntax, and the mapped syntax is then sent to the database for execution.

JDBC escape syntax supports seven keywords, each of them indicates the type of extension that is enclosed within the braces. Table 4.7 shows a collection of the keywords and their syntax.

So far we have discussed most Statement components and interfaces in JDBC data actions and applications, now let's take care of retrieving the execution results.

4.2.4 Retrieving Results

Based on the different SQL statements, three execution methods can be used to run an associated SQL statement. As we discussed in Sect. 4.2.3.1, each execution method performs different data actions:

- The **executeQuery()** method is used to run a data query, and the expected returning result is a result set stored in a **ResultSet** object.
- The **executeUpdate()** method is used to perform an insert, update, or delete data action, and the returning result should be an integer that equals the number of rows that have been affected by running this data manipulation.
- The **execute()** method can be used in either way, but this method never returns any result and you need to use special methods to pick up the running results.

Table 4.8 Methods used to determine the types of returned result

Method	Return value	Testing result
getUpdateCount()	> 0	The result is an update count
getUpdateCount()	= −1	The result is not an update count
getUpdateCount()	= 0	Either the update count is zero or a data definition language (DDL) statement is executed, such as CREATE TABLE.
getResultSet()	= null	The result is not a ResultSet
getResultSet() getUpdateCount()	= −1 != null	The result is a ResultSet

To pick up the running results for different methods, the following rules should be followed:

1) For the **executeQuery()** method, the **getResultSet()** method defined in the **Statement** interface should be used since the running result is a result set stored in a **ResultSet** object.

Table 4.9 Methods defined in the ResultSet interface

Method	Function
close()	Close the ResultSet and release all resources associated with it
findColumn(String colName)	Return the column index number corresponding to the column name argument
getAsciiStream(int index)	Retrieve the value of the specified column from the current row as an ASCII stream. The column can be represented by either the column index or the column name
getBigDecimal(int index)	Return the value of the referenced column from the current row as a BigDecimal object
getBoolean(int index)	Return the value of the referenced column from the current row as a Boolean
getByte(int index)	Return the value of the referenced column from the current row as a byte
getBytes(int index)	Return the value of the referenced column from the current row as an array of bytes
getBlob(int column_Index)	Retrieves the value of the designated column in the current row of this ResultSet object as a Blob object in the Java programming language
getBlob(String column_Name)	Retrieves the value of the designated column in the current row of this ResultSet object as a Blob object in the Java programming language
getDouble(int index)	Return the value of the referenced column from the current row as a double
getFloat(int index)	Return the value of the referenced column from the current row as a floating point number
getInt(int index)	Return the value of the referenced column from the current row as an integer
getLong(int index)	Return the value of the referenced column from the current row as a long integer
getObject(int index)	Return the value of the referenced column from the current row as an Object. The object type is determined by the default mapping of the SQL data type
getShort(int index)	Return the value of the referenced column from the current row as a short integer
getString(int index)	Return the value of the referenced column from the current row as a String object
getTime(int index)	Return the value of the referenced column from the current row as a java.sql.Time object
getMetaData()	Return a metadata object from the ResultSet object
next()	Move the ResultSet row cursor to the next row
wasNull()	Determine if the last value read by a getXXX() method was a SQL null value. A True is returned if the last read value contained a null value

2) For the **executeUpdate()** method, the **getUpdateCount()** method defined in the **Statement** interface should be used since the running result is an integer that equals the number of rows that have been affected.
3) For the **execute()** method, since this method can handle both **ResultSet** and integer, also it never returns any result, you need to use special methods to retrieve the running result for the execution of this method.

Relatively speaking, for the first two methods, it is relatively easy to pick the running result since the result is known and definite. The challenge is the third method, **execute()**, since the result of execution of this method can be either a **ResultSet** or an integer. Another challenge is that this method can be used where the SQL statement to be executed is not known at the compile time or there is a possibility of multiple results being returned by a stored procedure. Unlike the first two methods, the **execute()** method never returns any result, and you must use either the **getResultSet()** or **getUpdateCount()** method to retrieve the running results.

To distinguish what kind of result is returned, we can use the method we discussed in the last section to do that. To handle multiple results, we need to use the **getMoreResults()** method defined in the **Statement** interface (refer to Table 4.4). When executing this method, a **True** will be returned if a **ResultSet** object is returned. If the result retrieved is an integer, then the **getMoreResults()** method returns a **False**. The confusing issue is that this method will also return a **False** if no result is received. In order to solve this confusion, you must use the **getUpdateCount()** method to test the possible results. Table 4.8 shows a full picture with associated testing condition and possible testing results.

It is easy to get the result of the execution of the `executeUpdate()` method since only an integer is returned as the result for this method. However, it needs more works to do for the result of the execution of the **executeQuery()** and **execute()** methods since a **ResultSet** object that contains a tabular set is returned. We will concentrate on the methods used to retrieve and process the actual data contained in the **ResultSet** object. First let's have a closer look at the **ResultSet** interface.

4.2.4.1 The ResultSet Interface

Data is stored in a **ResultSet** just as it is returned by the database, exactly, it is stored in tabular format. Each field of the database can be described by a unique combination of a row ID and a column ID. A column can be mapped to an array since all data in a single column have the same data type. Similarly, a row can be mapped to a Vector since all elements in a single row may have the different data types.

The **ResultSet** interface has more than 25 methods and Table 4.9 lists some most often used methods.

All **getXXX()** methods defined in this **ResultSet** interface, except the **getMetaData()**, are overloading methods with two signatures, which means that all of those methods can pass two types of arguments, either a column index that is an integer or a column name that is a String. To save space, here we only list the first signature for each of those methods.

Now we have a clear picture about the **ResultSet** interface, next we need to get the running results from the execution of an execute method. First, let's take care of how to get a `ResultSet` object after an execute method has been done.

4.2.4.2 Getting and Processing the ResultSet Object

When a SQL data query is executed, the returned result is stored in a **ResultSet** object, and this **ResultSet** object can be created by one of the following two methods:

- The **executeQuery()** method
- The **getResultSet()** method

When an **executeQuery()** method is executed, the result of the queried data is stored in a **ResultSet** object and returned. However, when an **execute()** method is used to retrieve a data query result, it will not return any result directly, instead you need to use the **getResultSet()** method to create a **ResultSet** to pick up the returned result.

Once the **ResultSet** object is created by using either method, an appropriate **getXXX()** method defined in the **ResultSet** interface can be used to access and retrieve data. Since the data is in a tabular format, any data can be retrieved by using the column and row ordinals. Two different ways can be used to select and access each column and row in a **ResultSet** object:

1) Using either column index or column name to select the desired column
2) Using the cursor that points to the current row to select a desired row

In order to scan the entire table in a **ResultSet** object, you can use the **next()** method defined in the **ResultSet** interface to move the cursor row by row until the

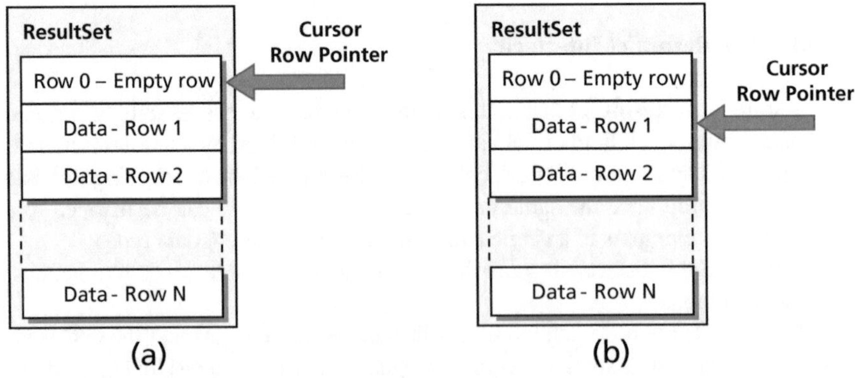

Fig. 4.15 The structure of a ResultSet with a row pointer positioning diagram

```
String query = "SELECT user_name, pass_word FROM LogIn" +
               "WHERE user_name = ? AND pass_word = ?";
PreparedStatement pstmt = con.prepareStatement(query);
pstmt.setString(1," cse ");
pstmt.setString(2," mack8000 ");
ResultSet rs = pstmt.executeQuery();
while (rs.next()){
   username = rs.getString(1);          // username = rs.getString(" user_name ");
   password = rs.getString(2);          // password = rs.getString(" pass_word ");
}
```

Fig. 4.16 An example coding of using the looped next() method

last record. To pick up a specified column from a given row, you can use an appropriate **getXXX()** method defined in the **ResultSet** interface with a column index or column name as the argument.

Let's have a closer look at accessing and processing each row and column from a **ResultSet** object with a little more discussion in the following sections.

4.2.4.2.1 Fetching by Row

In a **ResultSet** object, a cursor is used as a pointer to point to each row, and each row of data must be processed in the order in which they can be returned. At the beginning time, after an execution method is executed and a **ResultSet** object is returned, the cursor points the initial row, which is an empty row (refer to Fig. 4.15). To move the cursor to point to the first row of data, as we mentioned, the **next()** method can be used. Then an appropriate **getXXX()** method can be used to pick up desired column from the current row based on the column index or the column name as the argument of that method. Figure 4.15 shows a structure of a **ResultSet** object with a row pointer positioning diagram.

Figure 4.15a shows an initial cursor position of a **ResultSet** object, in which an execution method is just completed and a **ResultSet** object is created. The cursor now points to the initial row, row 0, and it is an empty row with no data included.

To access and retrieve a row of data, the **next()** method is executed to move the cursor to point to the next row, row 1 (shown in Fig. 4.15b), in which the first row of data is stored. An appropriate **getXXX()** method can be used to retrieve the desired column with the column index or column name as the argument. To navigate through the entire **ResultSet** and process each row, you can use the **next()** method again until the last row. A **true** will be returned from this **next()** method if it points to a row containing data, and a **false** will be returned if the cursor points to a null row, which means that the bottom of the **ResultSet** has been arrived and no more data available in this object.

In an actual program development and coding process, a **while()** loop can be used to execute the **next()** method to advance the cursor from the current row to point to the next row, until a **false** is returned, which means that the bottom of the **ResultSet** object has been arrived.

Figure 4.16 shows a piece of example codes to illustrate how to use a **while()** loop with the **next()** method to retrieve the related username and password from the LogIn table in our sample database **CSE_DEPT**.

Those non-highlighted codes are prerequisite codes used to create an SQL statement query string, create a **PreparedStatement** object, and set input parameters for the query string. The codes in bold are key codes used to create a **ResultSet** object, perform a **while()** loop with the **next()** method to retrieve all related usernames and passwords from the LogIn table in our sample database. Since most **getXXX()** methods defined in the **ResultSet** interface are overloading methods, alternatively, you can use the column name as an argument to pick up the desired column. Those alternative codes are shown on the right side with the comment out symbol in front of them.

4.2.4.2.2 Fetching by Column

When a valid data row has been retrieved, we need to get each column from that row. To do that, different **getXXX()** methods should be used based on the different data types of the returned data. One can use either the name of a column or the index of that column to get the data value. Inside the **while** loop in Fig. 4.16, we used a column index as the argument for the **getString()** method to retrieve the username and password columns from our LogIn table. As you know, the data type for both the **user_name** and the **pass_word** are String in our LogIn table, therefore a **getString()** method is used with the index of each column. A point to be noted is that the first column has an index of 1, not 0. If the name of each column, not an index, is used for the **getString()** method in this **while** loop, the codes can be re-written as

```
while (rs.next()){
        username = rs.getString("user_name");
        password = rs.getString("pass_word");
        }
```

One of the most important methods in **ResultSet** class is the **getObject()**. The advantage of using this method is that a returned datum, which is stored in a **ResultSet** object and its data type is unknown (a datum is dynamically created), can be automatically converted from its SQL data type to the ideal Java data type. This method out-perform any other **getXXX()** method since the data type of returned data must be known before a suitable **getXXX()** method can be used to fetch the returned data.

The **findColumn()** method is used to find the index of a column if the name of that column is given, and the **close()** method is used to close a **ResultSet** instance.

One of the very useful methods, or a pair of method, **getBlob()**, is crystal important when retrieving an image object from a table in a database. An image object is stored in a table with a Blob (Binary Large Object) format, thus one needs to use this method to access the table to retrieve any image object stored in a database.

The **getMetaData()** method is a very good and convenient method and it allows users to have a detailed and clear picture about the structure and properties of data returned to a **ResultSet**. A **ResultSetMetaData** object, which contains all pieces of necessary information about the returned data stored in a **ResultSet** instance, is returned when this method is executed. By using different methods of the R**esultSetMetaData** interface, we can obtain a clear picture about the returned data. For example, by using the **getColumnCount()** method, we can know totally how many columns have been retrieved and stored in the **ResultSet**. By using **getTableName(), getColumnName(),** and **getColumnType()**, we can know the name of the data table we queried, the name of column we just fetched and data type of that column. A more detailed discussion about the **ResultSetMetaData** component will be given in the following sections.

4.2.5 Using JDBC MetaData Interfaces

In addition to general and popular data information provided by three statement interfaces and execution methods, JDBC also provides useful and critical information and descriptions about the database, running result set, and parameters related

Table 4.10 Methods defined in the ResultSetMetaData interface

Method	Function
getCatalogName(int index)	Determine the name of the catalog that contains the referenced column
getColumnCount()	Return the total number of columns contained in the ResultSet object
getColumnDisplaySize(int index)	Return the maximum display width for the selected column
getColumnLabel(int index)	Return the preferred display name for the selected column
getColumnName(int index)	Return the name of the column for the selected column
getColumnType(int index)	Return the SQL data type for the selected column
getPrecision(int index)	Return the precision used for the selected column
getScale(int index)	Return the scale used for the selected column
getSchemaName(int index)	Return the name of the schema that contains the selected column
getTableName(int index)	Return the name of the table that contains the selected column
isAutoIncrement(int index)	Determine if the column is automatically numbered by the database (auto-number)
isCurrency(int index)	Determine if the column represents currency
isNullable(int index)	Determine if the column is able to accept null values
isSigned(int index)	Determine if the column contains signed numbers
isWritable(int index)	Determine if the column is writable by the user
isReadOnly(int index)	Determine if the column is read-only

to the JDBC drivers and database applications. All of these properties, structures, and descriptions can be categorized into three interfaces of so-called metadata interfaces, or

1) **ResultSetMetaData** interface
2) **DatabaseMetaData** interface
3) **ParameterMetaData** interface

In the following sections, we will concentrate on these three interfaces to illustrate how to use these interfaces to retrieve detailed descriptions and structures as well as properties related to the data action components, such as **ResultSet**, database, and parameters to facilitate database applications.

Let's start from the **ResultSetMetaData** interface.

4.2.5.1 Using the ResultSetMetaData Interface

In Sect. 4.2.4, we discussed how to retrieve running result stored in a **ResultSet** object and important methods of this interface. By using different fetching methods, either fetching by rows or columns, we can easily retrieve a whole set of returned results stored in a **ResultSet** object. However, in some applications, we may need more detailed information and properties about the returned result set, such as the total number of columns returned, each column name and data type, as well as some other structure information related to the returned result set. By using these structure information and properties, we can get a clear and full picture about the returned

ResultSet, and enable us to retrieve our desired data information more directly and conveniently. With the help of the metadata provided by the **ResultSetMetaData**, you can develop entire database applications without even knowing what RDBMS, table, or type of data to be accessed.

The **ResultSetMetaData** interface provides a collection of information about the structure and properties related to the returned **ResultSet** object, and this gives us a possibility to perform the functions we described above. The **ResultSetMetaData** interface contains more than 20 methods, and Table 4.10 shows 16 most popular methods.

It can be found from Table 4.10 that the top 10 methods in a **ResultSetMetaData** object are mainly used to retrieve the structure and properties for the specified

```
ResultSet  rs = pstmt.executeQuery();
ResultSetMetaData   rsmd = rs.getMetaData();
While (rs.next()){
   for (int m = 1; m< rsmd.getColumnCount(); m ++)
   {
       System.out.println( rs.getString(m));
   }
}
```

Fig. 4.17 A coding example of using the getColumnCount() method

column with the column index as an argument. The rest of the methods that return a Boolean value are used to determine some important properties that describe special functions provided by the database engine for the selected column. One of the advantages of using this metadata is that you can build dynamic applications that are independent of the data source. One possible way to achieve this is to remove the need for all direct column name references.

Because of the space limitation, we can only provide a brief discussion for some important methods that are widely implemented in most database applications.

After a data query is executed and a **ResultSet** object is returned, before we can retrieve our desired data from the **ResultSet**, we may need to get some structure information and properties related to columns we preferred. One of the most important properties is the total number of columns returned in the **ResultSet** object. By using the **getColumnCount()** method, we can get not only the total number of columns, but also the content of each column easily. Figure 4.17 shows a piece of example codes to illustrate how to use this method to scan the entire **ResultSet** to retrieve each column from it.

Table 4.11 Popular methods defined in the DatabaseMetaData interface

Method	Function
getCatalogs()	Return a ResultSet containing a list of all catalogs available in the database
getCatalogTerm()	Determine what the database-specific name for Catalog is
getDatabaseProductName()	Return the name of the database product
getDatabaseProductVersion()	Return the database revision number
getDriverName()	Return the name of the driver
getDriverVersion()	Return the revision number of the driver
getPrimaryKeys(String catalog, String schema, String table)	Return a ResultSet describing all of the primary keys within a table
getProcedures(string catalog, String schPatt, String proPatt)	Return a ResultSet describing all stored procedures available in the catalog
getProcedureTerm()	Determine the database-specific term for procedure
getSchemas()	Return a ResultSet containing a list of all schemas available in the database
getSchemaTerm()	Determine the database-specific term for schema
getTables(String catalog, String schePatt, String tablePatt, String[] types)	Return a ResultSet containing a list of all tables available matching the catalog, schema, and table type selection criteria
getTableTypes()	Return a ResultSet listing the table types available
getTypeInfo()	Return a ResultSet describing all of the standard SQL types supported by the database
getURL()	Return the current URL for the database
getUserName()	Return the current user name used by the database

The first coding line is used to create a ResultSet object by executing the **executeQuery()** method. Then a **ResultSetMetaData** object **rsmd** is created by calling the **getMetaData()** method defined the **ResultSet** interface. To pick up each returned column, a `while` loop is used combined with the **next()** method. By using this piece of codes, you even do not need to know how many columns returned in that **ResultSet** and what are the name for each column, in other words, you do not have to had prior knowledge about the table and database, you can retrieve all columns with their exact names! Yes, that is easy and fancy.

In some applications, you may need to know some other useful information about the columns, such as the data type of each column, the width of each column, the precision and scale of the selected column if a floating point or double data is stored in that column. To get those properties, you can call the appropriate methods, such as **getColumnType()**, **getColumnDisplaySize()**, **getPrecision()** and **getScale()**.

Besides to get some important information and properties about the returned ResultSet, sometimes we may need to get similar information for the connected database. In that case, you may need to use the **DatabaseMetaData** interface.

4.2.5.2 Using the DatabaseMetaData Interface

Compared with other metadata interfaces, the **DatabaseMetaData** is the largest metadata interface with over 150 methods. This interface is mainly used for by those developers who are building database applications that need to be fully RDBMS-independent, which means that the developers do not need to know anything about the database or do not have prior knowledge about the database they are using. In this way, the users can discover and retrieve structures and properties of the RDBMS dynamically as the application runs.

To create a **DatabaseMetaData** object, one needs to call the **getMetaData()** method defined in the **Connection** interface.

Relatively speaking, the **ResultSetMetaData** interface allows you to discover the structure of tables and properties of columns, but the **DatabaseMetaData** interface enables you to dynamically determine properties of the RDBMS. Table 4.11 shows some 16 most popular and important methods widely implemented by the **DatabaseMetaData** interface.

These 16 methods can be divided into 7 groups based on their functionalities:

1) Catalog Identification Methods
2) Database Identification Methods
3) Driver Identification Methods
4) Stored Procedure-Related Methods
5) Schema Identification Methods
6) Table Identification Methods
7) Database-Related Parameter Methods

Table 4.12 Popular methods defined in the ParameterMetaData interface

Method	Function
getParameterCount()	Return the number of parameters in the PreparedStatement object for which this ParameterMetaData object contains information
getPrecision(int param)	Return the designated parameter's number of decimal digits
getScale(int param)	Return the designated parameter's number of digits to the right of the decimal point
getParameterType(int param)	Return the designated parameter's SQL type
getParameterTypeName(int param)	Return the designated parameter's database-specific type name
getParameterMode(int param)	Return the designated parameter's mode
isNullable(int param)	Determine whether null values are allowed in the designated parameter
isSigned(int param)	Determine whether values for the designated parameter can be signed numbers

```
String query = "SELECT user_name, pass_word FROM LogIn " +
               "WHERE user_name = ? AND pass_word = ?";
PreparedStatement pstmt = con.prepareStatement(query);
pstmt.setString(1, "cse");
pstmt.setString(2, "mack8000");
ResultSet  rs = pstmt.executeQuery();
ParameterMetaData  pmmd = pstmt.getParameterMetaData();
System.out.println("The total number of parameter is" + pmmd.getParameterCount());
```

Fig. 4.18 A coding example of using the getParameterCount() method

To get the name and version of the current database being used, the **getDatabaseProduct-Name()** and **getDatabaseProductVersion()** methods can be used. Similarly, to get the name and revision number of the JDBC driver being used, the **getDriverName()** and **getDriverVersion()** methods can be executed.

In fact, the **DatabaseMetaData** interface provides methods that allow you to dynamically discover properties of a database as the project runs. Many methods in the **DatabaseMetaData** return information in the **ResultSet** component, and one can get those pieces of information from **ResultSet** object by calling related methods such as **getString()**, **getInt()** and **getXXX()**. A kind of **SQLException** would be thrown out if the queried item is not available in the **MetaData** interface.

Overall, the **DatabaseMetaData** interface provides an easy and convenient way to allow users to identify and retrieve important structure and properties information about the database dynamically.

```
try{
      stmt.close();
      if (!con.isClosed())
          con.close();
    }
catch(SQLException e){
    System.out.println("Could not close!" + e.getMessage());
    }
```

Fig. 4.19 A coding example of closing the Connection and Statement objects

4.2.5.3 Using the ParameterMetaData Interface

The detailed information about the parameters passed into or from the database can be obtained by calling the **getParameterMetaData()** method that is defined in the **PreparedStatement** interface. Although this interface is not as popular as **ResultSetMetaData** and **DatabaseMetaData**, it is useful in some special applications.

Basically the **ParameterMetaData** interface can be defined as: an object that can be used to get information about the types and properties of the parameters in a **PreparedStatement** object. For some queries and driver implementations, the data that would be returned by a **ParameterMetaData** object may not be available until the **PreparedStatement** has been executed. Some driver implementations may not be able to provide information about the types and properties for each parameter marker in a **CallableStatement** object.

The **ParameterMetaData** interface contains 7 fields and 9 methods. Table 4.12 shows 10 most popular methods that are widely implemented in most database applications.

Figure 4.18 shows a piece of example codes to illustrate how to retrieve the total number of parameters related to a **PreparedStatement** object.

After a **PreparedStatement** instance is created, the **getParameterMetaData()** method is executed to retrieve the total number of parameters returned in the `ParameterMetaData` object.

Finally, let's handle closing the connection object and releasing used resources including the statement objects.

4.2.6 Closing the Connection and Statements

After a set of data actions has been performed and the desired data have been acquired, the Connection object that is used to connect to our target database should be closed and the related data operational resources including all opened statement objects used for these data actions should also be released. Otherwise, you may encounter some possible exceptions when you try to open a database that has been opened but without being closed in the previous applications. To these cleanup jobs, it is very easy with a piece of codes shown in Fig. 4.19.

To do a closing operation, a **try…catch** block had better be used to track and monitor this closing process with possible exceptions warning.

4.3 Chapter Summary

The application fundamentals of JDBC and JDBC API, which include the application models and operational procedures of the JDBC API implemented in Java database applications, are discussed in detail in this chapter.

Starting with an introduction to two JDBC application models, two-tier and three-tier models, a detailed illustration and description about these two models are given in the first part of this chapter. A typical two-tier model contains an application server and a database server, in which a Java database application project resides in an application server and the target database is located at the database server. The so-called three-tier model places the application onto an application server that can be considered as a mid-tier, and installs database in a database server. To run this three-tier model application, the user needs to communicate the application server by using a Web browser that can be considered as a top tier with a GUI being installed in this browser. Then the application server can process requests sent from the browser via the target database via the database server. Finally, when requests have been done, results will be returned to the browser by the application server.

Following the application models, a complete operational procedure to perform a standard Java database application is discussed with some example codes, which includes:

- Load and register a JDBC Driver.
- Connect to the target database using either **DriverManager.getConnection()** method or **Driver.connect()** method.
- Execute an SQL statement by creating and calling an appropriate **Statement** object, which include:
  - **Statement object**
  - **PreparedStatement object**
  - **CallableStatement object**
- Distinguish different queries by running associated execute method.
- Execute DDL and DML SQL statements.
- Retrieve the running result by creating and getting a **ResultSet** object.
- Develop sophisticated Java database applications using different JDBC metadata interfaces, including the **ResultSetMetaData, DatabaseMetaData**, and **ParameterMetaData** interfaces.

- Close the connected database and opened statement objects to release data resource used for the application.

Combining the contents in this chapter and the last chapter, you should have had a complete and clear picture about the JDBC fundamentals and application procedure. Beginning from the next chapter, we will introduce and discuss some development tools and actual techniques used in Java database applications.

Homework

I. True/False Selections

____1. JDBC applications are made of two models: two-tier and three-tier models.

____2. In a three-tier model, the application is located at a Web server and the database is installed in a database server. The user can access the application server through a Web browser with a GUI being installed in the browser.

____3. To load and register a driver, the **creating a new instance of the Driver class** method is a better method compared with the **Class.forName()** method.

____4. When establish a database connection, the **DriverManager.getConnection()** method is a better method compared with the **Driver.connect()** method.

____5. A JDBC URL is composed of three parts: network host name, the database server name, and the port number.

____6. By using three methods defined in the Connection interface, **createStatement(), prepareStatement(),** and **prepareCall()**, one can create three statement objects: **Statement, PreparedStatement**, and **CallableStatement**.

____7. The **Statement** object can be used to perform both static and dynamic data queries.

____8. To create a **ResultSet** object, you can use either **getResultSet()** method or call the **executeQuery()** method.

____9. The **executeQuery()** method returns an integer that equals the number of rows that have been returned, and the **executeUpdate()** method returns a **ResultSet** object containing the running result.

____10. The **next()** method defined in the **ResultSet** interface can be used to move the cursor that points from the current row to the next row in a **ResultSet**.

II. Multiple Choices

1. The __________ object provides methods for the creation of Statement objects that will be used to execute SQL statements in the next step.

   (a) Statement
   (b) Connection
   (c) DriverManager
   (d) Driver

2. The relationship between three statement objects are: the ____________ is a subclass of the __________ that is a subclass of the __________.

   (a) CallableStatement, PreparedStatement, Statement
   (b) Statement, CallableStatement, PreparedStatement
   (c) PreparedStatement, Statement, CallableStatement
   (d) Statement, PreparedStatement, CallableStatement

3. The __________ method returns a(n) __________, and the _________ method returns a(n) __________.

   (a) execute(), ResultSet, executeQuery(), integer
   (b) executeQuery(), integer, execute(), nothing
   (c) executeUpdate(), integer, executeQuery(), ResultSet
   (d) execute(), integer, executeUpdate(), ResultSet

4. The __________ object is used to execute a static SQL query, but the _________ object is used to execute a dynamic SQL query with IN and OUT parameters.

   (a) PreparedStatement, Statement
   (b) Statement, PreparedStatement
   (c) CallableStatement, Statement
   (d) Statement, CallableStatement

5. Both interfaces, PreparedStatement and CallableStatement, are used to perform dynamic SQL statements, however, the ________ performs queries with only _____ parameters but the _______ calls stored procedures with both ______ and _______ parameters.

   (a) CallableStatement, OUT, PreparedStatement, IN, OUT
   (b) PreparedStatement, IN, CallableStatement, IN, OUT
   (c) CallableStatement, IN, PreparedStatement, IN, OUT
   (d) PreparedStatement, OUT, CallableStatement, IN, OUT

6. By using __________ method, we can get a collection of information about the structure and properties of the returned ResultSet object.

   (a) getResultSetMetaData()
   (b) getResultSet()
   (c) getMetaData()
   (d) ResultSetMetaData()

7. To create a ______________ object, one needs to call the _____________ method defined in the **Connection** interface.

   (a) ResultSet, getMetaData()
   (b) Statement, getStatement()
   (c) PreparedStatement, getPreparedStatement()
   (d) DatabaseMetaData, getMetaData()

8. The ______________ interface allows you to discover the structure of tables and properties of columns, but the _________________ interface enables you to dynamically determine properties of the RDBMS.
   (a) ResultSet, DatabaseMetaData
   (b) ParameterMetaData, ResultMetaData
   (c) DatabaseMetaData, ParameterMetaData
   (d) DatabaseMetaData, ResultSet
9. When using a CallableStatement object to run a stored procedure, you need to register the __________ parameters by using the _____________ method.
   (a) IN/OUT, getParameters()
   (b) IN, registerINParameter()
   (c) OUT, registerOUTParameter()
   (d) IN/OUT, registerINOUTParameter()
10. The placeholder used in the **setXXX()** and the **registerOUTParameter()** methods is used to ___________________.
    (a) Indicate the location of the input or output parameters
    (b) Reserve spaces for input or output parameters
    (c) Inform the compiler to hold memory spaces for those parameters
    (d) All of them

III. Exercises

1. Provide a brief description about seven basic steps to use JDBC.
2. Translate the above seven steps to Java codes.
3. Provide a detailed description about JDBC three-tier model and its function.
4. Provides a brief description about the JDBC URL.
5. Explain the operational sequence of retrieving results from a returned **ResultSet** object.
6. Explain the relationship between three Statement objects, and illustrate why and how the **CallableStatement** object can use **setXXX()** methods defined in the **PreparedStatement** interface.
7. Explain the advantages of using JDBC metadata for Java database applications.

Chapter 5
Introduction to Apache NetBeans IDE

Java was originally created by Sun Microsystems to try to overcome some complexities in C++ and to simplify the structure and architecture of applications developed by using object-oriented programming (OOP) languages such as C++. In the early days, Java developers need to use separate tools to build, develop, and run a Java application. The following tools are most popularly used when building a Java application:

- NotePad or WordPad—used to develop the Java source codes
- Java Compiler—used to compile the Java source codes to the Java bytecodes
- Java Interpreter—used to convert the bytecodes to the machine codes

There is no GUI tool available in the early days, and developers have to use the Java layout manager to design and build the GUI by using different layouts with various components, such as buttons, labels, textfields, checkboxes, and radio buttons. Even for Web-related Java, applications, such as Applets, must be built by using different tools, too. This brought a significant inconvenience and complicated development environment for Java developers in that age.

As more sophisticated and advanced techniques developed, the Java development environment and tools have been greatly improved. By combining Java Software Development Kits (SDK) and GUI components, such as Abstract Windowing Toolkit (AWT) and Swing API, Sun integrated those components and tools together to establish and build an Integrated Development Environment (IDE). This IDE is very similar to Visual Studio.NET, in which all program development tools and components have been integrated together and categorized into different packages. Developers can design, develop, build, and run a Java standard-alone or a Web application easily and conveniently inside this IDE without needing to use different tools.

Supplementary Information The online version contains supplementary material available at [https://doi.org/10.1007/978-3-031-06553-8_5].

Y. Bai, *SQL Server Database Programming with Java*,
https://doi.org/10.1007/978-3-031-06553-8_5

The Apache NetBeans IDE is one of the most current and updated IDEs and is widely implemented in a wide spectrum of Java applications. The Apache NetBeans IDE is actually written in Java and runs everywhere where a Java Virtual Machine (JVM) is installed, including Windows, Mac OS, Linux, and Solaris. A Java Development Kits (JDK) is required for Java development functionality, but is not required for development in other programming languages.

The Apache NetBeans project consists of an open-source IDE and an application platform that enable developers to rapidly create web, enterprise, desktop, and mobile applications using the Java platform, as well as JavaFX, PHP, JavaScript and Ajax, Ruby and Ruby on Rails, Groovy and Grails, as well as C/C++.

The Apache NetBeans IDE, which was originally called NetBeans IDE released by Sun Microsystems and later on taken over by Oracle, is a modular, standards-based integrated development environment (IDE), written in the Java programming language. The NetBeans project consists of a full-featured open-source IDE written in the Java programming language and a rich client application platform, which can be used as a generic framework to build any kind of application.

5.1 Overview of the Apache NetBeans 12

The Apache NetBeans, which exactly contains two parts: the Apache NetBeans IDE and the Apache NetBeans Platform, is a top-level Apache Project dedicated to providing rock-solid software development products that address the needs of developers, users, and the businesses who rely on NetBeans as a basis for their products, particularly, to enable them to develop these products quickly, efficiently, and easily by leveraging the strengths of the Java platform and other relevant industry standards.

Like NetBeans IDE, the Apache NetBeans IDE works as a free Java IDE and provides support for several other languages, such as Java, Maven, Ruby, PHP, JavaFX, JavaScript, and C/C++, but the latter provides more supports for Web and Internet applications.

Table 5.1 shows some most popular features provided by Apache NetBeans IDE 12.

The current version of the Apache NetBeans IDE is 12 and it is an IDE to offer complete support for the entire Java Enterprise Edition (EE) 8 and higher specifics with improved support for JSF 2.3/Facelets, Java Persistence 2.2, Enterprise JavaBean (EJB) 3.1 including using EJBs in web applications, RESTful web services, and GlassFish v3. It is also recommended for developing with the latest JavaFX SDK 14, and for creating PHP web applications with the new PHP 7.4 release or with the Symfony Framework.

As we know, the Apache NetBeans projects are composed of an open-source IDE and an application platform that enables developers to rapidly create web, enterprise, desktop, and mobile applications. Let's have a closer look at these two components to have a deeper understanding about this IDE.

Table 5.2 shows the most popular techniques supported by the Apache NetBeans IDE 12 and application servers adopted by the Apache NetBeans.

Table 5.1 Most popular features supported by Apache NetBeans IDE 12

Project category	Features
Java Enterprise Edition 8	Web Projects with Java EE 8 and Java EE 8 Web profiles, EJBs in web applications EJB 3.1 support, EJB project file wizard also supports Singleton session type RESTful web services (JAX-RS 2.1), GlassFish Metro 2.0 web services (JAX-WS 2.3), JAXB 2.2.8 Java Persistence JPA 2.2, deployment, debugging, and profiling with GlassFish v5 application server.
Web Projects with JavaServer Faces 2.3 (Facelets)	Code completion, error hints, namespace completion, documentation popups, and tag auto-import for Facelets Editor support for Facelets libraries, composite components, expression language, including generators for JSF and HTML forms Customizable JSF components palette generates JSF forms and JSF data tables from entities New File wizard generates customizable CRUD (create/read/update/delete) JSF pages from entities Broader usage of annotations instead of deployment descriptors
JavaFX	Added support for the latest JavaFX SDK 14 Improved code completion Editor Hints: Fix Imports, Surround With, Implements Abstract Methods, and more Improved navigation: Hyperlinks, Go to Type, Find Usages
Kenai.com: Connected Developer	Full JIRA support (plugin from update center) Project dashboard with more member and project details, improved search and navigation, easier project sharing Improved instant messenger integration: Online presence, private and group chat with Kenai members, easy to add links to code/files/issues/stack traces to messages Improved issue tracker integration
PHP	Full PHP 7.4 support: namespaces, lambda functions and closures, syntax additions: NOWDOC, ternary conditions, jump labels, __callStatic() Symfony Framework support: Symfony projects, Symfony commands, shortcuts, PHP syntax coloring in YAML files Create a PHP project from a remote PHP application PHPUnit, Code Coverage, FTP/SFTP integration improvements, exclude PHP project folders from scanning/indexing
Maven	New Project from Maven archetype catalog and improved support for Java EE 6, Groovy, Scala projects Customizable dependency exclusion in dependency graph Maven CheckStyle plugin "Update from Kenai" action for Kenai.com-hosted Maven projects

(continued)

Table 5.1 (continued)

Project category	Features
Ruby	Support for creating Rails 6.0 apps with dispatchers, JRuby 9.2.9, Ruby 2.7 debugging, and RSpec 3.7 Improved rename refactoring, type inference, and navigation Specifying arguments for Rails servers Run/Debug File with arguments, also for files not part of a project
C and C++	Profiling: New Microstate Accounting indicator, Thread Map view, Hot Spots view, Memory Leaks view, Sync Problems view Faster synchronization during remote development Support for gdbserver attach and easier attaching to already running processes
Miscellaneous improvements	Java Debugger: Mark an object in the variables tree with a name to refer to it in expressions Database integration: Code completion in SQL Editor now also for DELETE, DROP, UPDATE statements, and for reserved keywords Groovy 2.0 & Grails: Improved code completion, including methods introduced via AST Transformations

Table 5.2 Most popular techniques and application servers supported by Apache NetBeans

Category	Supported techniques and application servers
Supported technologies	Java EE 8 and higher JavaFX SDK 14 Java ME SDK 8.0 Struts 1.3.8 Spring 2.5 Hibernate 5.4 Java API for RESTful Web Services (JAX-RS) 2.1 PHP 7.4, 7.3, 7.1 Ruby 2.7 JRuby 9.2.9 Rails 2.3.4 Groovy 2.0 Grails 1.1 VCS CVS: 1.11.23 Subversion: 1.14 Mercurial: 5.x ClearCase V9.x
Tested application servers	GlassFish v5 Sun Java System Application Server PE 9.x WebLogic 14c (14.1.1) Tomcat 8 & 7 Tomcat 9 JBoss 7.2 & 7.3

5.1.1 The Apache NetBeans Platform

The Apache NetBeans Platform is a broad Swing-based framework on which you can base large desktop applications. The IDE itself is based on the NetBeans Platform. The Platform contains APIs that simplify the handling of windows, actions, files, and many other things typical in applications.

Each distinct feature in a NetBeans Platform application can be provided by a distinct NetBeans module, which is comparable to a plugin. An Apache NetBeans module is a group of Java classes that provides an application with a specific feature.

You can also create new modules for Apache NetBeans IDE itself. For example, you can write modules that make your favorite cutting-edge technologies available to users of Apache NetBeans IDE. Alternatively, you might create a module to provide an additional editor feature.

The Apache NetBeans platform offers reusable services common to desktop applications, allowing developers to focus on the logic specific to their application. Among the features of the platform are:

- User interface management (e.g., menus and toolbars)
- User settings management
- Storage management (saving and loading any kind of data)
- Window management
- Wizard framework (supports step-by-step dialogs)
- NetBeans Visual Library

The second part of an Apache NetBeans is the NetBeans open-source IDE.

5.1.2 The Apache NetBeans Open-Source IDE

The Apache NetBeans IDE is an open-source integrated development environment and it supports the development of all Java application types, such as Java Standard Edition (Java SE) including JavaFX, Java Mobile Edition (Java ME), Web, Enterprise JavaBean (EJB), and mobile applications, out of the box. This IDE also allows users to quickly and easily develop Java desktop, mobile, and web applications, as well as HTML5 applications with HTML, JavaScript, and CSS. The IDE provides a great set of tools for PHP and C/C++ developers. It is free and open source and has a large community of users and developers around the world. Among other features are an Ant-based project system, Maven support, refactorings, and version control.

All the functions of the IDE are provided by modules. Each module provides a well-defined function, such as support for the Java language, editing, or support for the Concurrent Versions System (CVS) versioning system, and Java Subversion (SVN). NetBeans contains all the modules needed for Java development in a single download, allowing the user to start working immediately. Modules also allow NetBeans to be extended. New features, such as support for other programming languages, can be added by installing additional modules. For instance, Sun Studio, Sun Java Studio Enterprise, and Sun Java Studio Creator from Sun Microsystems are all based on the NetBeans IDE.

Three main modules included in the NetBeans IDE and most often used are in Table 5.3.

Users can choose to download NetBeans IDE bundles tailored to specific development needs.

Users can also download and install all other features at a later date directly through the NetBeans IDE. A complete set of bundles that can be used by users when they download and install NetBeans IDE onto their computers is shown below:

- Apache NetBeans Base IDE
- Java SE, JavaFX
- Web & Java EE
- Java ME
- Ruby
- C/C++
- PHP (Version 6.5 and later)
- GlassFish
- Apache Tomcat

Figure 5.1 shows a typical structure and architecture of the Apache NetBeans IDE.

Table 5.3 Three main modules included in the Apache NetBeans IDE

Module name	Functions
NetBeans Profiler	This is a tool for the monitoring of Java applications: It helps you find memory leaks and optimize speed. Formerly downloaded separately, it is integrated into the core IDE since version 12.1 The Profiler is based on a Sun Laboratories research project that was named JFluid. That research uncovered specific techniques that can be used to lower the overhead of profiling a Java application. One of those techniques is dynamic bytecode instrumentation, which is particularly useful for profiling large Java applications. Using dynamic bytecode instrumentation and additional algorithms, the NetBeans Profiler is able to obtain runtime information on applications that are too large or complex for other profilers. NetBeans also supports Profiling Points that let you profile precise points of execution and measure execution time
GUI design tool	The GUI design-tool enables developers to prototype and design Swing GUIs by dragging and positioning GUI components The GUI builder also has built-in support for JSR 296 (Swing Application Framework), and JSR 295 (Beans Binding technology)
NetBeans JavaScript Editor	This module provides extended support for Javascript, Ajax, and Cascading Style Sheets (CSS) JavaScript editor features comprise syntax highlighting, refactoring, code completion for native objects and functions, generation of JavaScript class skeletons, generation of Ajax callbacks from a template; and automatic browser compatibility checks CSS editor features comprise code completion for styles names, quick navigation through the navigator panel, displaying the CSS rule declaration in a List View and file structure in a Tree View, sorting the outline view by name, type or declaration order (List & Tree), creating rule declarations (Tree only), refactoring a part of a rule name (Tree only)

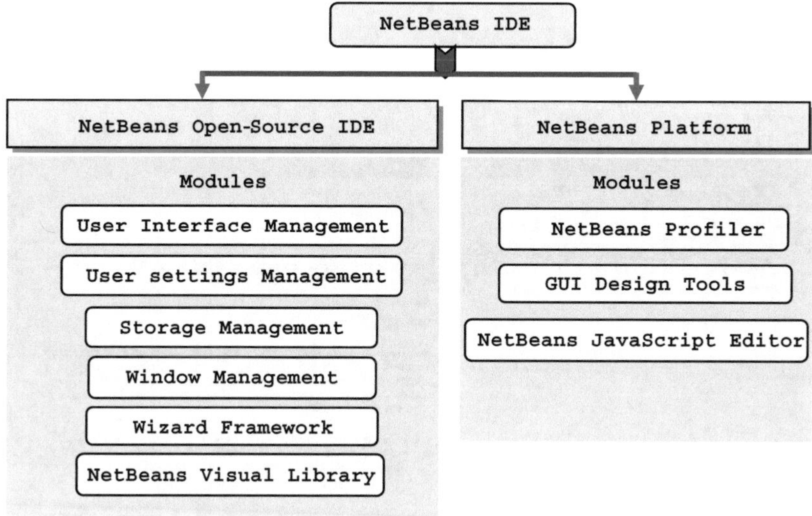

Fig. 5.1 A typical structure of the Apache NetBeans IDE

Now that we have had a clear picture and understanding about the NetBeans IDE, next we need to configure the Apache NetBeans IDE and build actual projects in our computers.

5.2 Installing and Confirming the Apache NetBeans IDE

Refer to Appendix B to download and install Apache NetBeans 12 and Java Development Kit (JDK) 14. Next, we need to check and confirm the installed NetBeans IDE to make it our desired development environment.

To launch the installed Apache NetBeans IDE 12, double click on the Apache NetBeans IDE 12 icon on the desktop. To configure this IDE, go to **Tools|Plugins** item to check and confirm all installed components used in the Java Applications, as shown in Fig. 5.2.

As the **Plugins** wizard appears, click on the **Installed** tab and check all desired components installed by this IDE, as shown in Fig. 5.2. The following components are needed for our projects:

- HTML5
- Java SE
- Tools
- PHP
- JavaFX 2
- Java Web and EE
- Developing NetBeans

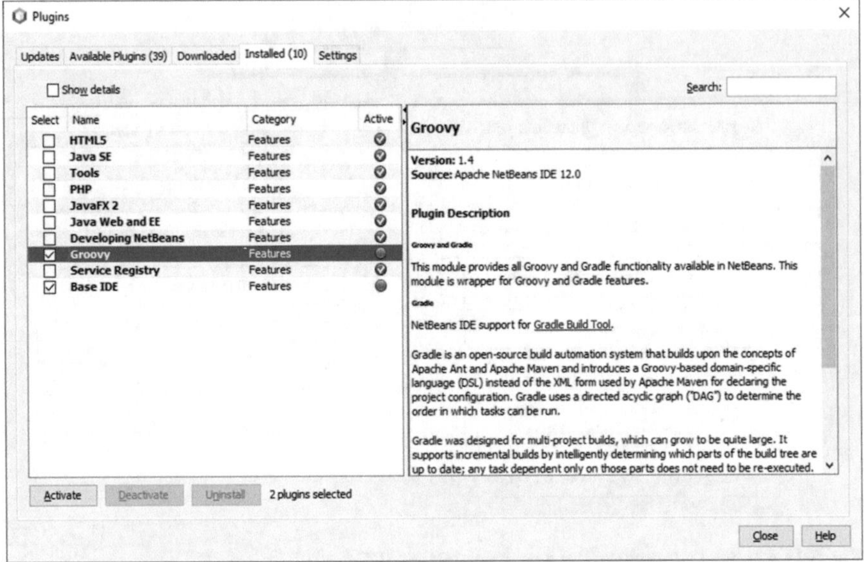

Fig. 5.2 The launched NetBeans IDE 12

- Groovy
- Service Registry
- Base IDE

From this installed list, it can be found that most components or tools have been activated. Now check both the **Base IDE** and the **Groovy** checkboxes to activate them. In fact, the **Base IDE** has been activated by default, and this activation action is just for the **Groovy**. Click on the **Activate** button for the next two wizards, and then the **Close** button to close this **Plugins** wizard.

Now that we have installed and confirmed the Apache NetBeans IDE 12, next we need to explorer it to find all useful features we will use to build our professional database applications in this integrated development environment.

5.3 Exploring Apache NetBeans IDE 12

By using Apache NetBeans IDE, the developers can design and build Java-related applications with different categories that are shown below:

- Java applications
- JavaFX applications
- Java Web applications
- Java Enterprise applications
- PHP applications

- Maven applications
- Grails applications
- NetBeans modules

To get a clear picture and detailed description about this IDE, first let's have a work-through overview for this product and its functionalities.

5.3.1 An Overview of Apache NetBeans IDE 12 GUI

When you first time launch the Apache NetBeans IDE 12, a main menu and some default windows are displayed, as shown in Fig. 5.3.

The first window or pane located at the upper-left corner is called **Projects|Files|Services** window that contains three different kinds of items:

1) All opened projects
2) All created files
3) All database services

These three different items can be displayed and switched by clicking on the corresponded tab on the top of this window.

The second window located at the lower-left corner, which is currently hidden, is called **Navigator** window that contains all components to enable users to scan and go through all different objects or parts of a file. In fact, the Navigator window

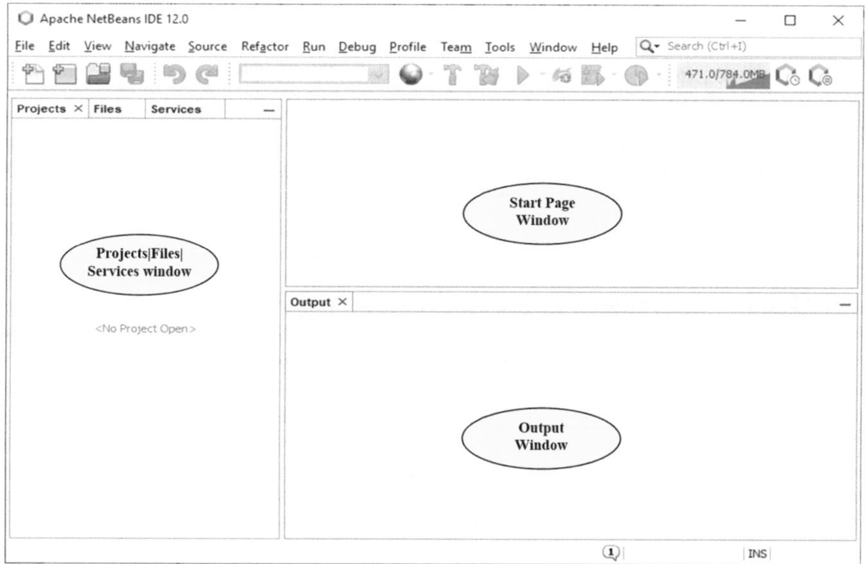

Fig. 5.3 The opened Apache NetBeans IDE 12

provides structured views of the file you are working with and lets you quickly navigate between different parts of the file.

The **Tasks** window, which is also hidden, is located at the bottom and it is mainly used to list all methods in your projects and allow you to enter the codes into those methods at any time when you building your project.

The **Start Page** is a main window when the IDE is opened and this window displays all recent projects you developed. All updated news and tutorials related to the NetBeans will also be displayed in this window.

Refer to Fig. 5.3, among all menu items, the following items are special items with the specific functionalities in the NetBeans IDE:

- **Navigate**: the NetBeans Navigator is used to navigate to any object, file, type of objects and symbol you created and built in your projects. With the name of each object or file, you can navigate to any of them as the development stage. Another important property of using the Navigate menu item is to enable you to inspect any member and hierarchy of those members defined in your project. In fact, the Inspect submenu item is used to inspect the members and hierarchy of any Java class in a convenient popup window that displays base classes, derived classes, and interfaces. Use filters to control the level of detail that is displayed.
- **Source:** the NetBeans Source is used to facilitate your source coding development by allowing you to insert codes, fix codes, fix imports, show method parameters, shift and move codes in your projects.
- **Refactor:** the NetBeans Refactor allows you to restructure code in your project without breaking it. For example, when you rename an identifier or move a class to another package, you do not need to use Search and Replace, instead, the IDE can identify and update all occurrences instantly.
- **Profile:** the NetBeans Profiler is a tool for the monitoring of Java applications: It helps you find memory leaks and optimize speed. The Profiler is based on a Sun Laboratories research project that was named JFluid. That research uncovered specific techniques that can be used to lower the overhead of profiling a Java application. One of those techniques is dynamic bytecode instrumentation, which is particularly useful for profiling large Java applications. Using dynamic bytecode instrumentation and additional algorithms, the NetBeans Profiler is able to obtain runtime information on applications that are too large or complex for other profilers. NetBeans also supports Profiling Points that let you profile precise points of execution and measure execution time.
- **Team:** the NetBeans Team provides the source code management and connected developer services to enable developers to perform the following functions:
    - Source Code Management (Subversion, Mercurial, CVS)
    - Local file history
    - Integrated Connected Developer features for projects hosted on Kenai.com:
        - Source code management (Subversion, Mercurial, and Git)
        - Issue tracking (Jira and Bugzilla)
        - Team wiki, forums, mailing lists
        - Document and downloads hosting

In the NetBeans IDE, you always work inside of a project. In addition to source files, an IDE project contains metadata about what belongs on the **Classpath**, how to build and run the project, and so on. The IDE stores project information in a project folder which includes an Ant build script and properties file that control the building and running settings, and a `project.xml` file that maps Ant targets to IDE commands.

The Apache Ant is a Java-based building tool used to standardize and automate building and running environments for development. The IDE's project system is based directly on Ant. All of the project commands, like **Clean and Build Project** and **Debug**, call targets in the project's Ant script. You can therefore build and run your project outside the IDE exactly as it is built and run inside the IDE.

It is not necessary to know Ant to work with the IDE. You can set all the basic compilation and runtime options in the project's **Project Properties** wizard, and the IDE automatically updates your project's Ant script. If you are familiar with Ant, you can customize a standard project's Ant script or write your own Ant script for a project.

The Apache NetBeans 12 IDE categories all Java-related applications into different groups based on related Template, such as Java with Ant, Java with Maven, HTML5/JavaScript, and PHP. Under Java with Ant, another four subgroups are involved:

1) JavaFX
2) Java Web
3) Java Enterprise
4) NetBeans Modules

Let's start with a new **Java with Ant** project since this is a popular type of Java applications.

5.3.2 Build a New Java with Ant Project

The NetBeans IDE allows you to create and build different projects based on different categories by selecting the right template for your project and completing the remaining wizard steps. First let's take care of creating a new Java with Ant project.

To create a new **Java with Ant** project under the Apache NetBeans IDE, go to **File|New Project** menu item. A **New Project** wizard is displayed and shown in Fig. 5.4.

Under the **Java with Ant** category, the IDE contains the following standard project templates for Java desktop and Web applications:

- **Java Application**: Creates a new skeleton Java Standard Edition (SE) project with a main class
- **Java Class Library:** Creates a skeleton Java class library without a main class

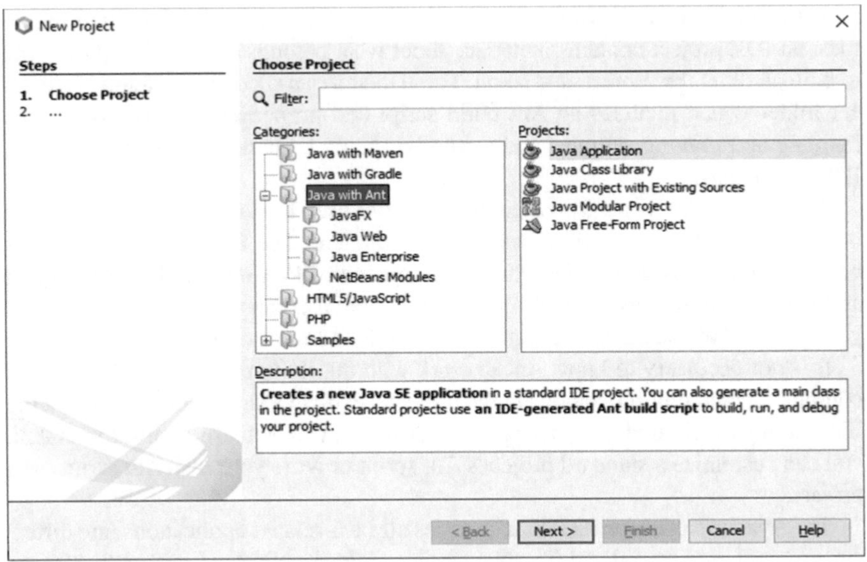

Fig. 5.4 The opened create New Project wizard

- **Java Project with Existing Sources:** Creates a Java SE project based on your own Java sources
- **Java Modular Project:** Create a new Java SE Modular Application in a standard IDE project. Multiple modules can be added into the project as Standard projects using an IDE-Generated Ant building script to build, run and debug the whole project. Java module is a new feature in Java 9 via the *Java Platform Module System* (JPMS)
- **Java Free-Form Project:** The free-form templates enable you to use an existing Ant script for a project but require manual configuration

Let's give a more detailed discussion for each of these projects one by one.

5.3.2.1 Build a Java Application Project

On the opened **New Project** wizard, select the **Java with Ant** from the **Categories** list and click on the **Java Application** node from the **Projects** list to create a new Java Application Project. Click on the **Next** to open the **New Java Application** wizard, which is shown in Fig. 5.5.

Perform the following operation to set up properties for this new project:

- Enter a desired project name, such as **JavaAppProject** in this example, into the **Project Name** box as the name for this project.

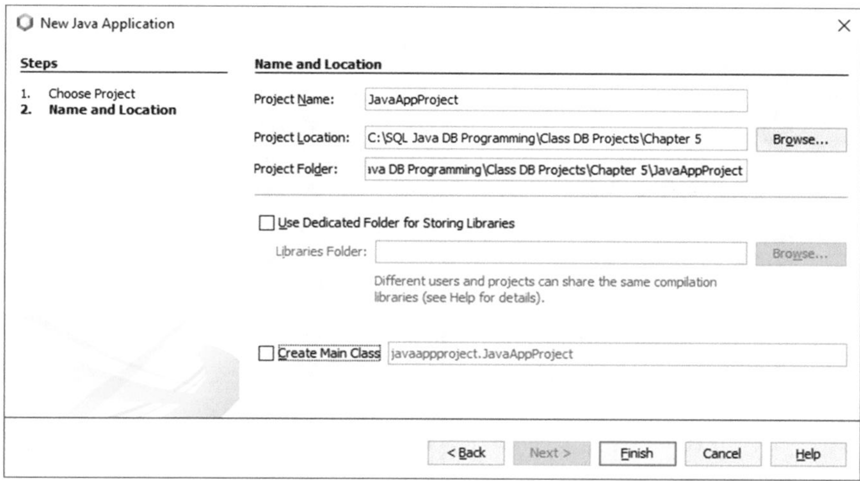

Fig. 5.5 The New Java Application wizard.

- Select a desired location to save this project. In this example, our desired location is **C:\SQL Java DB Programming\Class DB Projects\Chapter 5**. You can select any other valid folder to save your project if you like.
- Uncheck the **Create Main Class** checkbox since we do not want to use this class in this application.
- Keep all other default settings and click on the **Finish** button.

When you finish creating a project, it opens in the IDE with its logical structure displayed in the **Projects** window and its file structure displayed in the **Files** window, as shown in Fig. 5.6.

1) The **Projects** window is the main entry point to your project sources. It shows a logical view of important project contents such as Java packages and Web pages. You can right-click on any project node to access a popup menu of commands for building, running, and debugging the project, as well as opening the **Project Properties** dialog box. The **Projects** window can be opened by choosing **Window > Projects (Ctrl-1)**.
2) The **Files** window shows a directory-based view of your projects, including files and folders that are not displayed in the **Projects** window. From the **Files** window, you can open and edit your project configuration files, such as the project's build script and properties file. You can also view build output like compiled classes, JAR files, WAR files, and generated Javadoc documentation. The **Files** window can be opened by choosing the menu item **Window > Files (Ctrl-2)**.

If you need to access files and directories that are outside of your project directories, you can use the **Favorites** window. You open the **Favorites** window by choosing the menu item **Window > Favorites (Ctrl-3)**. You add a folder or file to

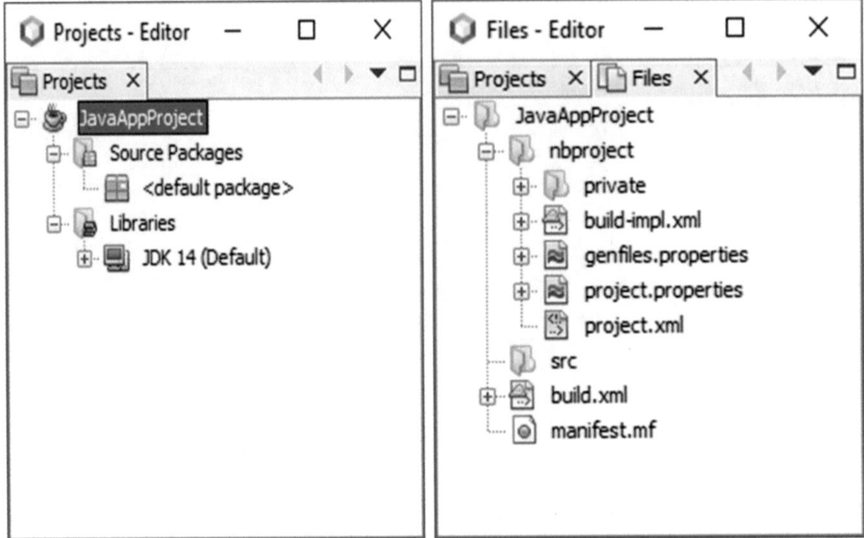

Fig. 5.6 The logical and file structures displayed in the Projects and the Files windows

the **Favorites** window by right-clicking on the **Favorites** window and choosing the **Add to Favorites** menu item.

It can be found from Fig. 5.6 that the **Java JDK 14** has been installed with the NetBeans IDE 12 and located in the **Libraries** folder in this project. If you want to use other Software Development Kits (SDK), JDK, project, or library with your projects, you can load them first, and then add them into your library by right-clicking on the **Libraries** node and select the associated operational menu item from the popup menu.

Next we need to add a graphical user interface (GUI) with other necessary GUI components to our project and use it as a user interface to communicate with our project during the project runs.

5.3.2.1.1 Add a Graphical User Interface

To proceed with building our interface, we need to create a Java container within which we will place the other required GUI components. Generally, the most popular Java GUI containers include:

- JFrame Form (Java Frame Form window)
- JDialog Form (Java Dialog Box Form window)
- JPanel Form (Java Panel Form window)

In this project, we will create a container using the **JFrame** component. We will place the container in a new package, which will appear within the **Source Packages** node.

Perform the following operations to complete this GUI adding process:

1. In the **Projects** window, right-click on our new created project **JavaAppProject** and choose the **New > JFrame Form** menu item from the popup menu.
2. Enter **JavaAppFrame** into the **Class Name** box as the class name, as shown in Fig. 5.7.
3. Enter **JavaAppPackage** into the **Package** box as the package name (Fig. 5.7).
4. Click on the **Finish** button.

Your finished **New JFrame Form** wizard should match one that is shown in Fig. 5.7.

The IDE creates the **JavaAppFrame** form and the `JavaAppFrame` class within the **JavaAppProject** application, and opens the **JavaAppFrame** form in the GUI Builder. The **JavaAppPackage** package replaces the default package.

When we added the **JFrame** container, the IDE opened the newly created **ContactEditorUI** form in an `Editor` tab with a toolbar containing several buttons, as shown in Fig. 5.8. The `ContactEditor` form opened in the GUI Builder's Design view and three additional windows appeared automatically along the IDE's edges, enabling you to navigate, organize, and edit GUI forms as you build them.

The GUI Builder's various windows include:

- **Design Area.** The GUI Builder's primary window for creating and editing Java GUI forms. The toolbar's `Source` and `Design` toggle buttons enable you to view a class's source code or a graphical view of its GUI components. The additional toolbar buttons provide convenient access to common commands, such as choosing between Selection and Connection modes, aligning components, setting component auto-resizing behavior, and previewing forms.
- **Navigator Window.** Provides a representation of all the components, both visual and non-visual, in your application as a tree hierarchy. Navigator API is good for

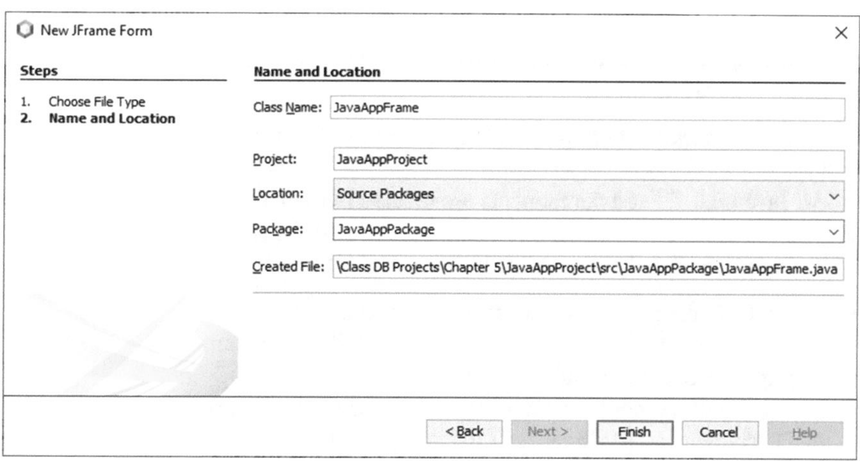

Fig. 5.7 The finished New JFrame Form wizard

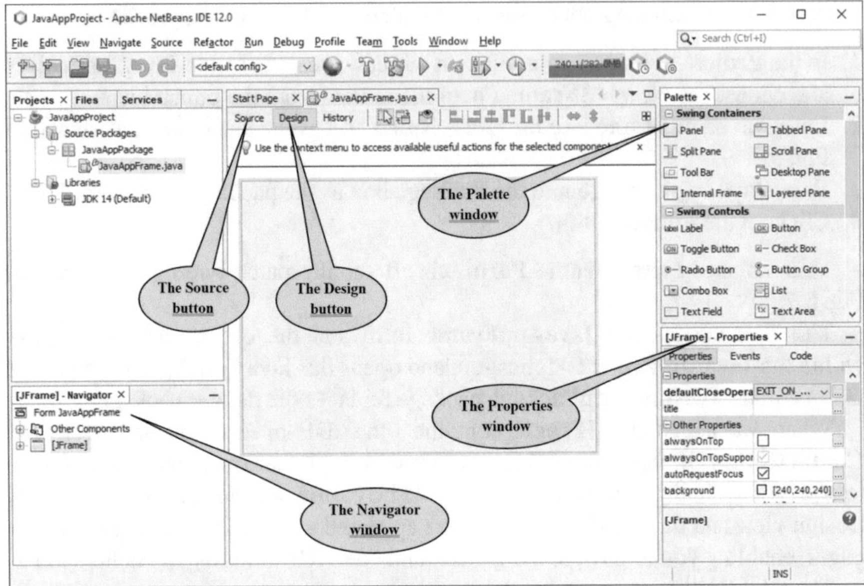

Fig. 5.8 The opened ContactEditor form

clients that want to show some structure or outline of their document in dedicated window, allowing end user fast navigation and control over the document. Navigator API also allows its clients to plug in their Swing-based views easily, which then will be automatically shown in specialized Navigator UI.

- **Palette Window.** A customizable list of available components containing tabs for JFC/Swing, AWT, and JavaBeans components, as well as layout managers. In addition, you can create, remove, and rearrange the categories displayed in the `Palette` using the customizer.
- **Properties Window.** Displays the properties of the component currently selected in the `GUI Builder`, `Inspector` window, `Projects` window, or `Files` window.

Two more points to be emphasized are about the `Palette` and the `Properties` windows.

All Java GUI-related components are located in the Palette window and distributed in the different packages or namespaces. This Palette window contains the following GUI-related components based on the different packages:

- Swing Containers: contains all Java container classes
- Swing Controls: contains all Swing-related GUI components
- Swing Menus: contains all Swing-related menu items
- Swing Windows: contains all Swing-related window classes
- AWT: contains all AWT-related GUI components
- Beans: contains all JavaBeans-related GUI components

- Java Persistence: contains all Java Persistence-related components

Relatively speaking, AWT-related GUI components are older compared with those components defined in the Swing package, in which all components are defined in a model view controller (MVC) style. The `java.awt` package contains all basic and fundamental graphic user interface components (AWT). However, the `javax.swing` package contains extensions of `java.awt`, which means that all components in the `javax.swing` package have been built into a Model-View-Controller (MVC) mode with more object-oriented properties (Swing).

The `Properties` window is used to setup and display all properties about GUI components you added into the container, such as appearances and physical descriptions. Let's illustrate how to use this window to setup and show each property for added GUI-related components on this container in the next section.

5.3.2.1.2 Add Other GUI-Related Components

Next let's finish this GUI by adding some GUI-related components into this GUI container. For this application, we want to add:

1) One JPanel object that can be considered as a kind of container.
2) Two JTextField objects to retrieve and hold the user's first and the last name.
3) Four JLabel objects to display the caption for each JTextFields and the user's full name as the **Display** button is clicked.
4) Three JButton objects, **Display**, **Clear**, and **Exit**. The **Clear** button is used to clean up all contents on two JTextField objects (user's first and last name), and the **Exit** button is used to exit the application.

Now let's begin to add those components one by one by dragging them from the `Palette` window. If you did not see the `Palette` window in the upper right corner of the IDE, choose the `Windows > IDE Tools` > `Palette` menu item to open it.

Let's add the JPanel object first in the following operational sequence:

1) Start by selecting a **JPanel** from the `Palette` window and drop it onto the **JFrame**.
2) While the **JPanel** is highlighted, go to the `Properties` window and click on the ellipsis (...) button next to the `Border` property to choose a border style.
3) In the `Border` dialog, select `TitledBorder` from the list, and type in `Display Full Name` in the `Title` field, and click on the `OK` to save the changes and exit the dialog.
4) You should now see an empty titled JFrame that says `Display Full Name` JPanel object. Now add the rest of GUI-related components, including four JLabels, two JTextFields and three JButtons, into this JPanel object as you see in Fig. 5.9.

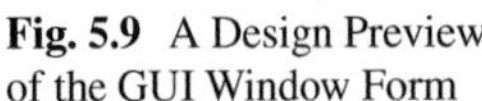

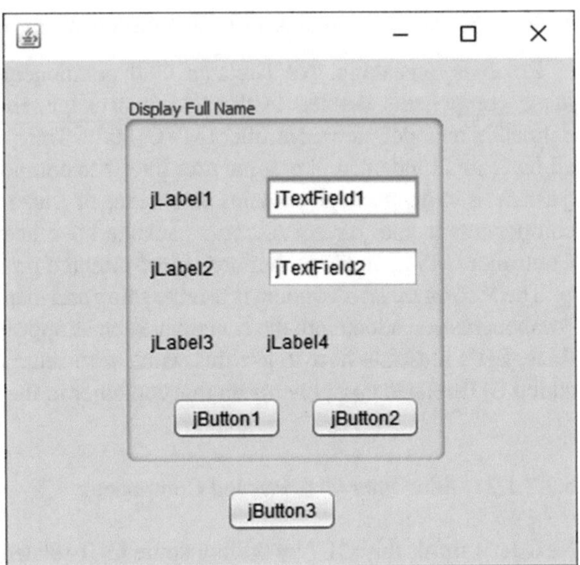

Fig. 5.9 A Design Preview of the GUI Window Form

Next let's rename all added components and modify **JLabel4** by setting the appropriate property for that label in the `Properties` window. Perform the following operational sequence:

1) Double-click on **jLabel1** and change the text property to **First Name**.
2) Double-click on **jLabel2** and change the text to **Last Name**.
3) Double-click on **jLabel3** and change the text to **Full Name**.
4) Click on **jLabel4** and click on the ellipsis (...) button next to the `Border` property to choose a border style. In the `Border` dialog, select `Line Border`, and change the border color to dark blue by clicking on the ellipsis (...) button next to the `Color` property, and click on the **OK** to save the changes and exit the dialog. Then go to the `Text` property to delete the default text `JLabel4` to make this an empty label. Set the **preferredSize** property to [100, 20] if you like.
5) Delete the sample text from **jTextField1**. You can make the display text editable by clicking on the `Text` field, pausing, and then clicking the `Text` field again. You may have to resize the **jTextField1** to its original size. Repeat this step for **jTextField2**.
6) Change the **name** of **jTextField1** to `FirstTextField`. To do that change, right click on the **jTextField1** object and select `Change Variable Name` menu item from the popup menu, then enter `FirstTextField` into the `New Name` box. Click on the **OK** to complete this rename operation.
7) Perform a similar operation to change the `Name` property of the **jTextField2** to `LastTextField`, and the `Name` property of the **jLabel4** to `FullNameLabel`.
8) Rename the display text of **jButton1** to `Display`. You can edit a button's `Text` property by right-clicking on the button and choosing the `Edit Text`

menu item from the popup menu. Or you can click on the button, pause, and then click again.

9) Rename the display text of **jButton2** to `Clear`.
10) Rename the display text of **jButton3** to `Exit`.
11) Change the `Name` property of the **jButton1** to `DisplayButton`, **jButton2** to `ClearButton` and **jButton3** to `ExitButton`, respectively.

Your Finished GUI should now look like one that is shown in Fig. 5.10.

Next let's develop the coding for each component to connect our GUI-related components with our coding to process and respond user's input and display the running result.

5.3.2.1.3 Develop the Codes for Three Buttons

In fact, only three JButton objects need to be coding process since both TextField objects are used to retrieve and hold the user's input without any other actions in this application. Similar situation happened to the JLabel4, which is used to display the running result of this application.

In order to give function to any button, we need to assign an event handler to each to respond to events. In our case we want to know what happened when a button is pressed, either by mouse clicking or via keyboard pressing. So we will use `ActionListener` responding to `ActionEvent`.

In the early days, the developers must do the connection between the `ActionListener` and `ActionEvent` manually in an application. Thanks to NetBeans IDE, in which this Listener and Event model has been setup and

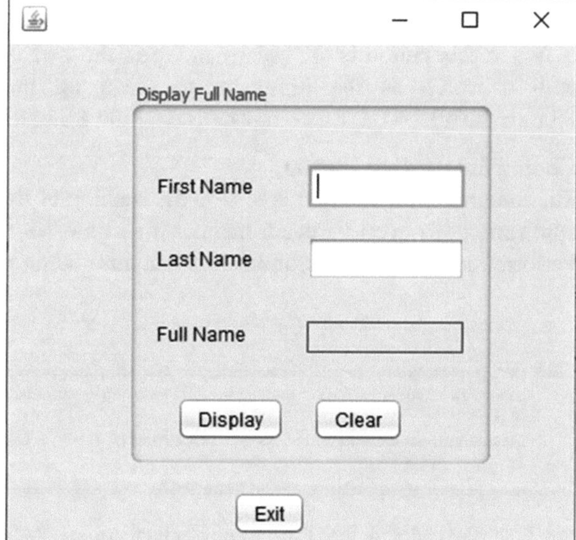

Fig. 5.10 The finished GUI design window

configured. To setup that connection, what the developer needs to do is just to perform a double click on the selected button. Is that easy? Yes, it is. Now let's do this Event-Listener action connection with our first button—`DisplayButton`.

Coding for the Display Button

The function of the `Display` button is to concatenate the first and the last names entered by the user and stored in the `FirstTextField` and the `LastTextField` TextFields, and display it in the `FullNameLable` when this `Display` button is clicked by the user as the project runs.

Double click on the `Display` button, you can open its callback method or event handler, `DisplayButtonActionPerformed()`. Enter the codes shown in Fig. 5.11 into this event handler to concatenate the first and the last names entered by the user and display it in the `FullNameLabel`.

Regularly, for most events and the associated event handler methods, you can do that connection by right clicking on the source object (`DisplayButton` in this application), and select the `Events` menu item from the popup menu. All events can be triggered by this source object will be displayed in a popup menu. By moving your cursor to the desired event, all event handlers responding to this event will be displayed in a popup submenu and you can select the desired event handler to open it, and a connection between that event and event handler has been setup simultaneously.

The coding for this **Display** button `ActionPerformed()` event handler is simple, and the `setText()` method is used to display the concatenated first and last name with a plus symbol.

Coding for the Clear Button

The function of this `Clear` button is to cleanup all contents in two TextFields,

`FirstTextField` and `LastTextField`, respectively to allow the user to enter a new name. Double click on the `Clear` button to open its event handler, and enter the codes shown in Fig. 5.12 into this event handler.

When this button is clicked by the user, the `setText()` method is executed with a `null` as the argument to clean up three objects' contents, the `FirstTextField`, `LastTextField`, and `FullNameLabel`.

Coding for the Exit Button

The function of this button is to stop the running of this project and exit from this application. To open its event handler, this time we use another way to do that. Perform the following operations to finish this coding process.

```
private void DisplayButtonActionPerformed(java.awt.event.ActionEvent evt) {
    // TODO add your handling code here:
    FullNameLabel.setText(FirstTextField.getText() + " " + LastTextField.getText());
}
```

Fig. 5.11 The codes for the DisplayButtonActionPerformed() event handler

```
private void ClearButtonActionPerformed(java.awt.event.ActionEvent evt) {
   // TODO add your handling code here:
   FirstTextField.setText(null);
   LastTextField.setText(null);
   FullNameLabel.setText(null);
}
```

Fig. 5.12 The coding for the ClearButtonActionPerformed() event handler

```
private void ExitButtonActionPerformed(java.awt.event.ActionEvent evt) {
   // TODO add your handling code here:
   System.exit(0);
}
```

Fig. 5.13 The coding for the ExitButtonActionPerformed() event handler

1) Right click on the `Exit` button. From the pop-up menu choose `Events > Action > ActionPerformed`. Note that the menu contains many more events you can respond to! When you select the `actionPerformed` event, the IDE will automatically add an `ActionListener` to the `Exit` button and generate a handler method for handling the listener's `actionPerformed` method.
2) The IDE will open up the Source Code window and scroll to where you implement the action you want the button to do when the button is pressed.
3) Enter the codes that are shown in Fig. 5.13 into this event handler.

A system method, `exit()`, is executed as this button is clicked by the user, and a 0 is used as an argument to be returned to the operating system to indicate that the application has been completed successfully. A returned non-zero value indicates that some exceptions may have been encountered when the application runs.

Before we can run the project to test functions we have built, we need to do one more coding, which is to locate the GUI window in the center when the project runs.

The NetBeans IDE has a default location for each GUI window, the upper-left corner, and will display those windows in that location as the project runs. To make our GUI window located in the center of the screen as the project runs, we need to put one line coding into the constructor of this class since the first thing we need to do is to display our GUI window after the project runs. Open the code window by clicking on the `Source` button and enter one coding line into the constructor of this class, which is shown in Fig. 5.14.

A system method `setLocationRelativeTo()` is used to set this form at the center of the screen as the project runs. A `null` argument means that no object can be referenced or relative to and the JFrame Form is set to the center.

Now we have finished the building process for this project and we are ready to run it to test functions we have built.

```
public class JavaAppProjectFrame extends javax.swing.JFrame {

  /** Creates new form JavaAppProjectFrame */
  public JavaAppProjectFrame() {
    initComponents();
    this.setLocationRelativeTo(null); // set the GUI form at the center
  }
  ........
}
```

Fig. 5.14 The coding for the constructor of the class JavaAppProjectFrame

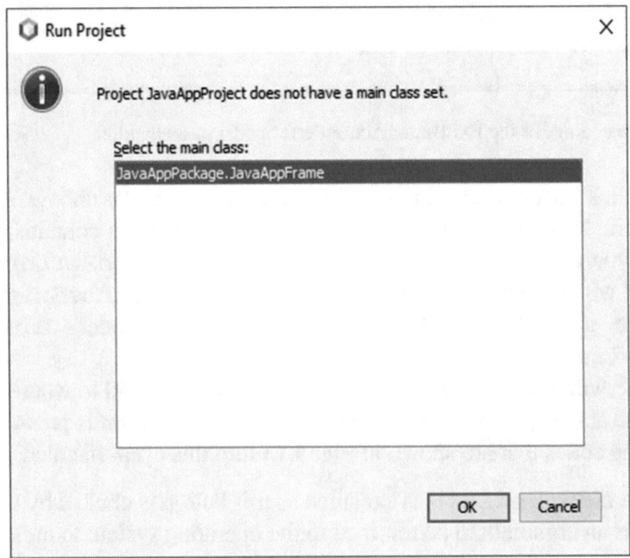

Fig. 5.15 Add the JFrame as the main class

5.3.2.1.4 Run the Project

Perform the following operations to run our project:

- Click on the `Clean and Build Main Project` button to compile and build our project.
- Choose the `Run > Run Main Project` menu item.
- If you get a window informing you that Project `JavaAppProject` does not have a main class set, then you should select `JavaAppPackage.JavaAppFrame` as the main class in the same window and click the **OK** button, as shown in Fig. 5.15.

A sample of our running project is shown in Fig. 5.16.

Enter your first and last name into the `First Name` and `Last Name` TextFields, respectively, and click on the `Display` button. Your full name will be displayed in the `Full Name` label, as shown in Fig. 5.16. Try to click on the `Clear` button to

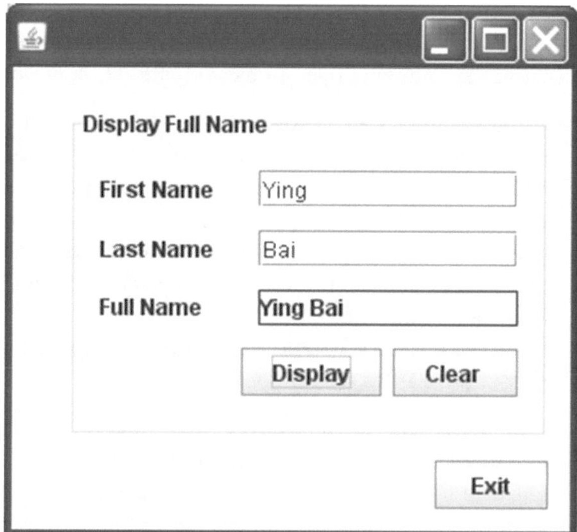

Fig. 5.16 The running result of our project

see what happened? Then you can click on the `Exit` button to stop our project. Yes, that is all for a typical Java Application project.

A complete Java Application project **JavaAppProject** can be found from the folder **Students\Class DB Projects\Chapter 5**, which is located at the Springer site (refer to Fig. 1.2 in Chap. 1).

5.3.2.2 Build a Java Class Library

As we mentioned, a Java Class Library is only a skeleton Java class library without a main class and it cannot be executed itself, instead it must be called or used by other Java applications. Similar to other general libraries, a Java Class Library can be statically or dynamically bound or connected with an application and to be used as a utility class.

Since a Java class library cannot be executed itself, we need to create a Java Application project to call or use that Java class library. Therefore, we need to create two projects to illustrate how to use a Java class library from a Java application:

- A Java Class Library project in which you will create a utility class.
- A Java Application project with a main class that implements a method from the library project's utility class.

The function of this Java class library is simple, which is just to add two integers together and return the sum result to the Java application project and the result will be displayed in the application project by calling some methods defined in the Java application project.

First let's create a Java Class Library project named **SumLib()**.

5.3.2.2.1 Create a Java Class Library Project

Perform the following operations to create this new Java Class Library project:

- Choose the `File > New Project` menu item. Under the `Categories`, select the `Java with Ant`. Under the `Projects`, select `Java Class Library`, and then click on the **Next** button.
- Enter **SumLib** into the `Project Name` field as the name of this class library. Change the `Project Location` to any directory as you want on your computer. From now on, this directory is **C:\SQL Java DB Programming\Class DB Projects\Chapter 5**.
- Click the `Finish` button. The **SumLib** project opens in both the **Projects** window and the **Files** window.

Next we need to create a new Java package and our class file. The Java package is used as a container or a namespace to hold the class file.

Perform the following operations to finish this Java package and class file:

1) Right-click on the **SumLib** project node from the **Projects** window and choose the `New > Java Class` item. Type **SumLibClass** as the name for the new class, type **org.me.sumlib** in the **Package** field as the package name for this class file, and click on the **Finish** button. The `SumLibClass.java` opens in the `Source Editor`.
2) In the opened `SumLibClass.java` file, place the cursor on the line after the class declaration, `public class SumLibClass {`.
3) Type or paste the codes shown in Fig. 5.17 as a new method **sumapp()**.
4) If the code that you pasted in is not formatted correctly, press **Alt-Shift-F** to reformat the entire file.
5) Go to `File > Save All` menu item to save this file.

This piece of codes is simple and straightforward. The input argument to this method should be a sequence of integers separated with commas (,), which can be considered as a String entered by the user as the project runs.

Let's have a closer look at this piece of codes to see how it works.

```
public class SumLibClass {
  public static  int  sumapp(String args) {
    int sum = 0;

    String[]temp;
    temp = args.split(",");
    int num[] = new int[temp.length];
    for(int  i = 0;  i < temp.length ;  i++){
      System.out.println(temp[i]);
      num[i] = java.lang.Integer.parseInt(temp[i]);
      sum = sum + num[i];
    }
    return  sum;
  }
}
```

Fig. 5.17 The codes for the class method sumapp()

First a temporary String array `temp` is created and it is used to hold the split input integers. Then the `split()` method is executed to separate the input argument into each separate number string. A `for` loop is used to display each separated number string and convert each of them to the associated integer number using the `parseInt()` method. Since this method is defined in the `java.lang.Integer` package, so a full name of the method must be used. A sum operation is performed to add all integers together and returned to the `main()` method in the Java application project `SumApp`.

Now that a Java class library project has been created and a Java class file has been coded, next we need to create our `Java Application` project to call or use that class library to perform a two-integer addition operation.

5.3.2.2.2 Create a Java Application Project

Perform the following operations to create a new Java Application project:

- Choose the `File > New Project` menu item. Under `Categories`, select `Java with Ant`. Under `Projects`, select `Java Application`. Then click on the **Next** button.
- Enter **SumApp** into the `Project Name` field. Make sure the `Project Location` is set to **C:\SQL Java DB Programming\Class DB Projects\Chapter 5**.
- Enter **sumapp.Main** as the main class.
- Ensure that the `Create Main Class` checkbox is checked.
- Click the **Finish** button. The **SumApp** project is displayed in the `Projects` window and `Main.java` opens in the `Source Editor`.

Now we have finished creating two Java projects.

After these two projects have been created, you need to add the Java class library project to the *classpath* of the Java application project. Then you can code the application. The library project will contain a utility class with a **sumapp()** method. This method takes two integers as arguments and then generates a sum based on those integers. The **SumApp** project will contain a main class that calls the **sumapp()**method and passes the integers that are entered as arguments when the application is run.

Now let's configure the compilation classpath in the Java application project to enable the application to know the location of the class library and execute it to perform the integer addition operation during the project runs.

5.3.2.2.3 Configure the Compilation Classpath

Since the **SumApp** Java application is going to depend on a class in **SumLib**, you have to add **SumLib** to the classpath of **SumApp**. Doing so also ensures that classes in the **SumApp** project can refer to classes in the **SumLib** project without causing compilation errors. In addition, this enables you to use code completion in the **SumApp** project to fill in code based on the **SumLib** project. In the Apache NetBeans IDE 12, the classpath is visually represented by the `Libraries` node.

Perform the following operations to add the **SumLib** library's utility classes to the application **SumApp** project classpath:

1) In the `Projects` window, right-click the `Libraries` node under the **SumApp** project and choose `Add Project` as shown in Fig. 5.18.
2) Browse to the folder **C:\SQL Java DB Programming\Class DB Projects\Chapter 5** and select the **SumLib** project folder, as shown in Fig. 5.19. The `Project JAR Files` pane shows the JAR files that can be added to the project. Notice that a JAR file for **SumLib** is listed even though you have not actually built the JAR file yet. This JAR file will get built when you build and run the `SumApp` project.
3) Click on the **Add Project JAR Files** button.
4) Now expand the `Libraries` node. The **SumLib** project's JAR file has been added to the **SumApp** project's classpath.

Before we can run our Java application project to call the Java class library, we need to add some codes to the **Main.java** tab in our Java application project.

5.3.2.2.4 Add Codes to the Main.java Tab in the Java Application Project

Now we need to add some code to **Main.java**. In doing so, you will see the Source Editor's code completion and code template (abbreviation) features.

1) Select the **Main.java** tab in the Source Editor. If it isn't already open, expand **SumApp > Source Packages > sumapp** in the `Projects` window and double-click on the item **Main.java**.

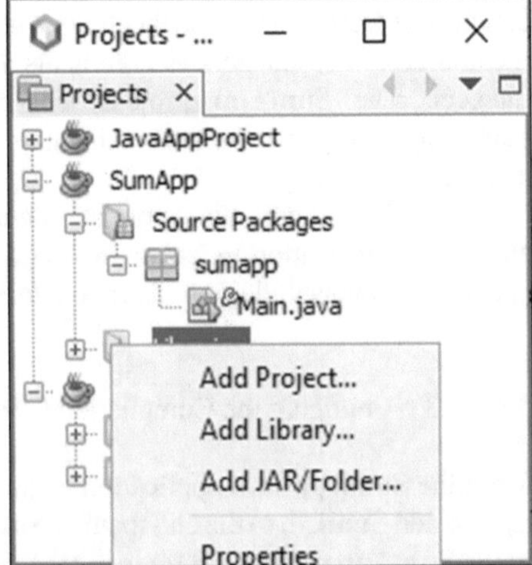

Fig. 5.18 To add the SumLib class to the classpath of the SumApp project

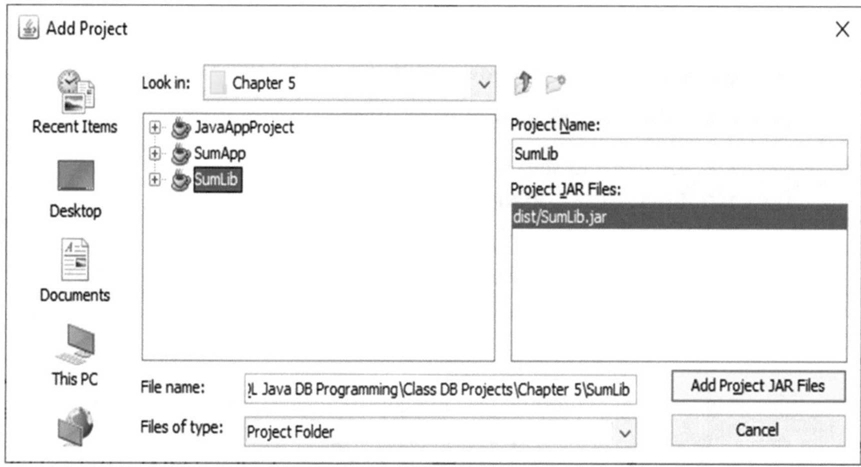

Fig. 5.19 The Add Project dialog box

2) Inside the **main()** method, replace the comment `//TODO code application logic here` with the following:

   int result = Sum

3) Leave the cursor immediately after **Sum**. In the next step you will use code completion to turn **Sum** into **SumLibClass**.
4) Press Ctrl-Space to open the code completion box. A short list of possible ways to complete the word appears. However, the class that you want, **SumLibClass** might not be there.
5) Press Ctrl-Space again to display a longer list of possible matches. The **SumLibClass** should be in this list.
6) Select the **SumLibClass** and press the **Enter** key. The Apache NetBeans IDE fills in the rest of the class name and also automatically creates an import statement for the class.

Note: The IDE also opens a box above the code completion box that displays Javadoc information for the selected class or package. Since there is no Javadoc information for this package, the box displays a "`Cannot find Javadoc`"

7) In the main method, type a period (.) after `SumLibClass`. The code completion box opens again.
8) Select the **sumapp(String args) int** method and press the `Enter` key. The IDE fills in the **sumapp()** method and highlights the input parameters.

9) Press the **Enter** key to accept the `args` as the parameter, and change this `null` to `args[0]`. Type a semicolon (;) at the end of this coding line. The final line should look like the following line.

   int result = SumLibClass.sumapp(args[0]);

10) Press the `Enter` key to start a new line. Then type the following coding line.
   System.out.println("The sum = " + result);
11) Go to the `File > Save All` menu item to save the file.

At this point, we are ready to run our Java application project **SumApp** to test its calling function to our Java library file **SumLibClass**.

5.3.2.2.5 Run the Application Project to Call the Java Library

The output of this application program **SumApp.java** is based on arguments that you provide when you run the application. As arguments, you can provide two or more integers, from which the adding result of those input integers will be generated. The adding process will be executed by the Java library file **sumapp()** located in the **SumLibClass** library, and the execution result will be returned to and displayed in the **main()** method in the Java application project **SumApp.java**.

Now let's run the application. Since this application needs arguments as inputs to the **main()** method, therefore we have to use an alternative way to run it. First let's perform the following operations to add the arguments for the IDE to use when running the application:

- Right-click on the **SumApp** project node, choose the `Properties` item, and select the **Run** node in the dialog's left pane. The main class should already be set to **sumapp.Main**.

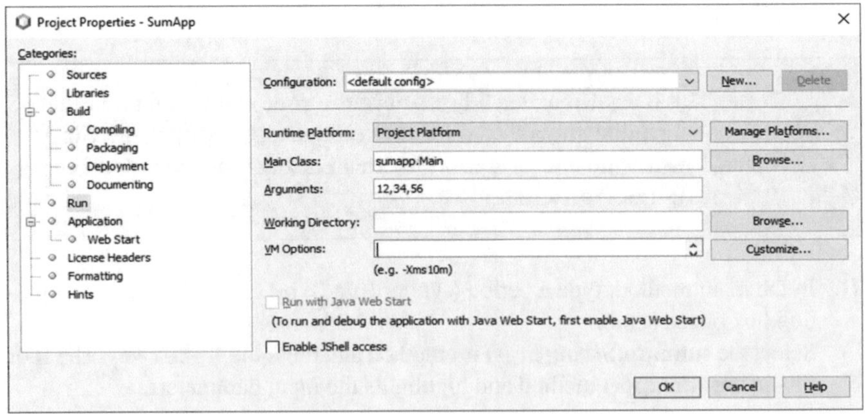

Fig. 5.20 The completed Project Properties window

- Enter some integers as input arguments to the `Arguments` field and each integer should be separated with a comma, such as `12,34,56` and click on the **OK** button.

Your finished `Project Properties` window should match one that is shown in Fig. 5.20.

Now that we have created the application and provided runtime arguments for the application, we can test and run the application in two ways: run the application inside the Apache NetBeans IDE 12, or run the application outside the NetBeans IDE 12.

To run the application inside the Apache NetBeans IDE 12, Click on the **Run** button in the menu item (or **F6** key). In the **Output** window shown in Fig. 5.21, you should see both the input arguments (`12`, `34,` and `56`) and the output result from the program (`The sum = 102`).

To run this application outside of the NetBeans IDE, you need first to build and deploy the application into a JAR file and then run the JAR file from the command line.

5.3.2.2.6 Build and Deploy the Application

The main build command in the NetBeans IDE is the **Clean and Build Main Project** command. This command deletes previously compiled classes and other build artifacts and then rebuilds the entire project from scratch.

Notes: There is also a `Build Main Project` command, which does not delete old building artifacts, but this command is disabled by default.

Perform the following operations to build the application:

1) Click on the **Run > Clean and Build Main Project (SumApp)** menu item (Shift-F11).

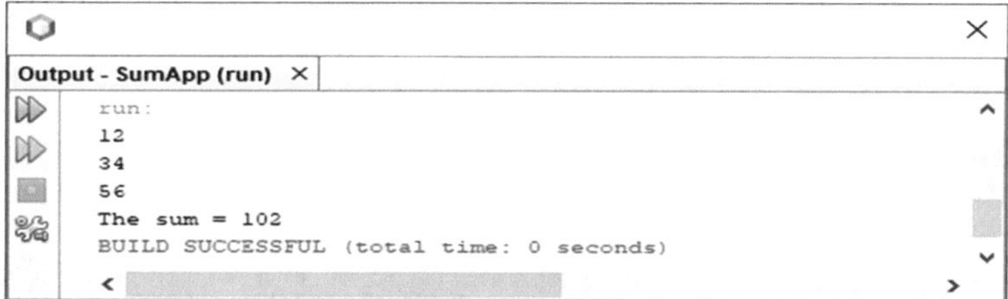

Fig. 5.21 The running result shown in the Output window

2) Output from the Ant build script appears in the **Output** window. If the **Output** window does not appear, you can open it manually by choosing **Window > Output**.
3) When you clean and build your project, the following things occur:
   (a) Output folders that have been generated by previous build actions are deleted ("cleaned"). In most cases, these are the `build` and `dist` folders.
   (b) The `build` and `dist` folders are added to your project folder, or hereafter referred to as the `PROJECT_HOME` folder.
   (c) All of the sources are compiled into `.class` files, which are placed into the `PROJECT_HOME/build` folder.
   (d) A JAR file `SumApp.jar` containing your project is created inside the `PROJECT_HOME/dist` folder.
   (e) If you have specified any libraries for the project (`SumLib.jar` in this case), a `lib` folder is created in the `dist` folder. The libraries are copied into `dist/lib` folder.
   (f) The manifest file in the JAR is updated to include entries that designate the main class and any libraries that are on the project's classpath.

Note: You can view the contents of the manifest in the IDE's Files window. After you have built your project, switch to the Files window and navigate to SumApp/ dist/SumApp.jar. Expand the node for the JAR file, expand the META-INF folder, and double-click MANIFEST. MF to display the manifest in the Source Editor.

```
Manifest-Version: 1.0
Ant-Version: Apache Ant 1.10.4
Created-By: 14.0.1+7 (Oracle Corporation)
Class-Path: lib/SumLib.jar
X-COMMENT: Main-Class will be added automatically by build
Main-Class: sumapp.Main
```

After building and deploying the application, now we can run this application outside the NetBeans IDE. To do that, perform the following operations:

1) On your system, open a command prompt or terminal window.
2) In the command prompt, change directories to the **SumApp/dist** directory.

```
Command Prompt

C:\SQL Java DB Programming\Class DB Projects\Chapter 5\SumApp\dist>java -jar SumApp.jar 12,34,56
12
34
56
The sum = 102

C:\SQL Java DB Programming\Class DB Projects\Chapter 5\SumApp\dist>
```

Fig. 5.22 The running result shown in the Command window

3) At the command line, type the following statement:

```
java -jar SumApp.jar 12,34,56
```

The application then executes and returns the outputs as shown in Fig. 5.22.

5.3.2.2.7 Distribute the Application to Other Users

Now that you have verified that the application works outside of the IDE, you are ready to distribute the application and allow other users to use it.

To distribute the application, perform the following operations:

1) On your system, create a zip file that contains the application JAR file (**SumApp.jar**) and the accompanying lib folder that contains **SumLib.jar**.
2) Send the file to the people who will use the application. Instruct them to unpack the zip file, making sure that the **SumApp.jar** file and the **lib** folder are in the same folder.
3) Instruct the users to follow the steps listed in the last section above to run this application outside the Apache NetBeans IDE.

Two complete Java projects, Java Class Library project **SumLib** and Java Application project **SumApp**, can be found from the folder **Students\Class DB Projects\Chapter 5**, which is located at the Springer site (refer to Fig. 1.2 in Chap. 1).

You can download these two projects and test them by calling the Java class library **SumLib** from the Java application project **SumApp**.

Next let's develop and build a Java Project with Existing Sources.

5.3.2.3 Build a Java Project with Existing Sources

To build a Java project with existing sources is mainly used for development of a new Java project but some existing sources, either GUIs or source codes that had been built in early Java or current Java JDK, must be involved in this new Java project to save developing efforts or the time. For Java projects developed outside of NetBeans, you can use an "Existing Sources" template in the New Project wizard to make a NetBeans project. In the wizard, you identify the location of the sources and specify a location for the NetBeans project metadata. You then use the `Project Properties` dialog box to configure the project.

Perform the following operations to set up a NetBeans project for an existing Java application:

1) Choose **File > New Project** (Ctrl-Shift-N).

2) Choose **Java with Ant > Java Project with Existing Sources**, then click on the **Next**.
3) In the **Name and Location** page of the wizard, perform these steps:
   (a) Type a project name as you like.
   (b) (Optional) Change the location of the project folder.
   (c) (Optional) Change the name of the build script used by the IDE. This might be desirable if there is already a build script called build.xml that is used to build the sources.
   (d) (Optional) Select the **Use Dedicated Folder for Storing Libraries** checkbox and specify the location for the libraries folder.
4) Click on the **Next** to advance to the **Existing Sources** page of the wizard.
5) In the **Source Packages Folder** pane and click **Add Folder**. Then navigate to your sources and select the source roots.
6) When you add a folder containing source code, you must add the folder that contains the highest folder in your package tree. For example, in the **com.mycompany.myapp.ui** package, you add the folder that contains the **com** folder.
7) (Optional) In the **Test Package Folders** pane, click **Add Folder** to select the folder containing the **JUnit** package folders. Click on the **Next** button to continue.
8) (Optional) In the **Includes & Excludes** page of the wizard, enter file name patterns for any files that should be included or excluded from the project. By default, all files in your source roots are included.
9) Click on the **Finish** button to complete this process.

The new built project is displayed in both the **Projects** window and the **Files** window.

Because of the simplicity of this kind of Java projects, no example project is involved in this chapter.

5.3.2.4 Build a Java Free-Form Project

There are also project templates available for Java free-form projects. In so-called free-form projects, the NetBeans IDE uses targets in an existing Ant script to build, run, clean, test, and debug your application. If the Ant script does not contain targets for some of these functions, the functions are unavailable for the project. To implement these functions you write targets either in your Ant script or in a secondary Ant script.

In general, it is better to use standard "**With Existing Sources**" project templates for importing projects. For Eclipse projects, it is best to use the Import Project feature, which creates and configures a standard project for you. Standard projects are easier to maintain in the long term. However, the free-form project templates can be useful if you have an existing Ant-based project with a complex or idiosyncratic configuration that cannot be replicated within a standard project. For example, if you are importing a project with multiple source roots, each of which has a different classpath, and you cannot split the source roots into different projects, it might be necessary to use a free-form project template.

Because the scope of this book is about database programming with Java, for more detailed information to set up free-form projects, refer to Advanced Free-Form Project Configuration.

5.3.3 *Build a Java Web Application Project*

Java Platform, either Standard Edition (SE) or Enterprise Edition (EE), provides rich and flexible tools and components to support Web applications and Web Services developments. With Java EE, developers can build professional, multitier and portable applications that can be run at cross-platform environments with improved efficiency.

We will provide a detailed discussion about the Java Web Applications development in Chap. 8 with real project examples. Refer to that chapter to get more detailed information for building this kind of application in NetBeans IDE.

5.4 Chapter Summary

The basic and fundamental knowledge and implementations of Apache NetBeans IDE 12 are discussed and presented with some real examples projects in this chapter. The components and architecture of Apache NetBeans IDE 12 are introduced and analyzed in detail at the beginning of this chapter. Following an overview of Apache NetBeans IDE 12, a detailed discussion and introduction of the Apache NetBeans IDE 12 platform is given. A detailed introduction and illustration in how to download and install Apache NetBeans IDE 12 are provided in this chapter.

Most popular technologies and applications supported by Apache NetBeans IDE 12 are discussed, which include:

- Java Ant Applications
- Java Class Library
- Build a Java Project with Existing Sources
- Build a Java Free-Form Project
- Build a Java Web Application Project

Each of these technologies and implementations is discussed and analyzed in detail with real project examples, and line-by-line coding illustrations and explanations. Each real sample project has been compiled and built in NetBeans IDE and can be downloaded and run at user's computer easily and conveniently.

All of these technologies and their implementations are discussed and illustrated by using real project examples in this chapter step by step, and line by line. By following these example projects, users can learn and master those key techniques easily and conveniently with lower learning curves.

All actual example projects discussed and developed in this chapter have been compiled and built successfully, and stored in the folder **Class DB Projects\Chapter 5** that is located under the **Students** folder at the Springer ftp site (refer to Fig. 1.2 in Chap. 1).

Homework

I. True/False Selections

____1. The Apache NetBeans Platform is a broad Swing-based framework on which you can base large desktop applications.

____2. Each distinct feature in a NetBeans Platform application can be provided by a distinct NetBeans module, which is comparable to a plugin.

____3. An Apache NetBeans module is a group of Java classes that provides an application with a specific feature.

____4. The NetBeans IDE is an open-source integrated development environment and it only supports the development of all Java application types.

____5. Three main modules included in the NetBeans IDE are: NetBeans Profiler, GUI Design Tool, and NetBeans JavaScript Editor.

____6. The Apache NetBeans IDE is mainly composed of NetBeans Open-Source IDE and NetBeans Platform.

____7. A Java Class Library is only a skeleton Java class library without a main class, but it can be executed itself.

____8. JavaFX, which is a kind of script language, is a Java platform for creating and delivering rich Internet applications. But starting from JDK 9, this platform has been removed from the JDK and no longer belongs to any Java JDK.

____9. Like VisualStudio.NET, one can build a Java Ant Application by adding a JFrame Form and use the Palette to add any GUI component to that Form.

___10. The Java EE differs from the Java SE in that it adds libraries which provide functionality to deploy fault-tolerant, distributed, multi-tier Java software, based largely on modular components running on an application server.

II. Multiple Choices

1. Each distinct feature in a NetBeans Platform application can be provided by a distinct NetBeans module, and an Apache NetBeans module is a: ____________________.

    (a) Java SE application
    (b) Group of classes with specific features
    (c) Java EE Application model and specifications
    (d) Enterprise JavaBeans (EJB) and Java Persistence API (JPA)

2. The Apache NetBeans IDE is an open-source integrated development environment and it supports development of all Java application types, which include________________.
   (a) Java desktop applications
   (b) Mobile and Web applications
   (c) HTML5 and Java Script applications
   (d) All of them
3. Three main modules included in the Apache NetBeans IDE are ___________________.
   (a) JEUS 7 application server, JBoss Application Server 6, Caucho Resin 4.0
   (b) Java EE, Java SE, Maven
   (c) NetBeans Profiler, GUI design tool, NetBeans JavaScript Editor
   (d) PHP, JavaScript, GlassFish
4. The major Java Bean used to handle or process message is called ______________.
   (a) Session Bean
   (b) Notification Bean
   (c) Message-Driven Bean
   (d) Manager Bean
5. The ______________ just work as a View for the Glassfish application server and setup a connection between the application server and the Session Bean in the Web tier.
   (a) Java EE 8
   (b) Enterprise Java Beans (EJB)
   (c) Java Server Faces (JSF)
   (d) Java Persistence API
6. To add new components or tools into the NetBeans IDE, one can use _______________.
   (a) JFrame tool
   (b) Plugins
   (c) PHP tool
   (d) JavaFX
7. The Apache NetBeans IDE is composed of two components, they are: _______________.
   (a) NetBeans Platform and NetBeans modules
   (b) NetBeans modules and Java EE
   (c) NetBeans Profiler and GUI design tools
   (d) NetBeans open-source IDE and NetBeans platform

8. The most popular Java GUI containers include: ___________________.

   (a) JFrame Form, JDialog Form, JPanel Form
   (b) JPanel Form, JPlugins Form, JCanvas Form
   (c) JPanel Form, JMaven Form, PHP Form
   (d) JFrame Form, JField Form, JDialog Form

9. To display an image in JFrame Form, one needs to use a ____________ object.

   (a) JImage
   (b) JPanel
   (c) Canvas
   (d) JPicture

10. A module can be considered as a(n) __________ object or unit that can be combined or bound together to form a __________________ application.

   (a) Dependent, big and complex
   (b) Dependent, small and easier
   (c) Independent, big and complex
   (d) Independent, small and easier

III. Exercises

1. Explain the advantages of using NetBeans Module for Java project development.
2. Provide a brief discussion about Apache NetBeans Platform.
3. Provide a brief description about Apache NetBeans Open Source IDE.
4. Refer to Sect. 5.3.2, build a similar Java Ant Application named **SumTwoNumbers** with the following functions:

   1) Build a GUI by adding a JFrame Form with two TextFields, **Num1Field** and **Num2Field**, one Label **ResultLabel** and two buttons, **CalculateButton** and **ExitButton**.
   2) Coding to the **CalculateButton** and **ExitButtons**' ActionPerformed() event handlers to perform summing of two input integers and display result on the **ResultyLabel**, as well as exit the project.

Part I
Building Two-Tier Client-Server Applications

Chapter 6
Query Data from Databases

Similar to querying data in Visual Studio.NET, when query data in the Java NetBeans IDE environment, two query modes or methods can be utilized: Java Persistence API (JPA) Wizards and runtime object codes. Traditional Java codes (SDK 1.x) only allow users to access databases with a sequence of codes, starting from creating a DriverManager to load the database driver, setting up a connection using the Driver, creating a query statement object, running the executeQuery object and processing the received data using a ResultSet object. This coding is not a big deal to the experienced programmers; however, it may be an issue for the college students or beginners who are new to the Java database programming. However, there is no significant difference between these two modes; in this chapter, we concentrate on the introductions and discussions on the second method, the regular Java runtime object method since it is more popular and widely implemented in our real world.

6.1 Setup Connection Between Microsoft SQL Server Database and Java Classes

In order to set a map between our Microsoft SQL Server database and Java classes, we need first to connect our database to NetBeans IDE. By using the NetBeans IDE connection functions, we can connect to different databases, such as Microsoft Access, SQL Server, or Oracle Database. This kind of connection belongs to project-independent connection, which means that no matter whether a project has been created or not or whether any NetBeans project will use this connection or not, the connection can be made for the entire IDE.

Supplementary Information The online version contains supplementary material available at [https://doi.org/10.1007/978-3-031-06553-8_6].

Y. Bai, *SQL Server Database Programming with Java*,
https://doi.org/10.1007/978-3-031-06553-8_6

As we discussed in Chap. 3, to access SQL Server Database from Apache NetBeans 12, a JDBC Driver is needed to provide a bridge or a connection between the SQL Server database engine and the Java programming language.

This connection can be divided into the following four sections:

1) Download and install Microsoft SQL Server JDBC Driver
2) Configure TCP/IP protocol and setup for SQL Server Express
3) Configure Authentication Mode for SQL Server 2019 Express
4) Use Apache NetBeans IDE 12 New Database Connection to setup a connection

Now let's start from the first part.

6.1.1 Download and Install Microsoft SQL Server JDBC Driver

Go to the site http://msdn.microsoft.com/data/jdbc/ and click on the link **Download JDBC Driver** to open the downloading page, as shown in Fig. 6.1. The current version of this JDBC Driver is 8.4, which supports Java SE 14. Click on the link: **Download Microsoft JDBC Driver 8.4 for SQL Server (zip)** to begin this process. The JDBC Driver file named **sqljdbc_8.4.1.0_enu.zip** is downloaded to the **Download** folder in your computer when this downloading process is done.

Now double click on this downloaded zip file to unzip this driver file. Make your selection for WinZip Update Checking or not to the popup Messagebox, and click on the Next button and continue this unzip process.

On the next WinZip wizard shown as in Fig. 6.2, make sure that the correct JDBC Driver is selected and click on the Next and then Unzip button to complete this unzip process. Click on the Finish button when this unzipping process is done.

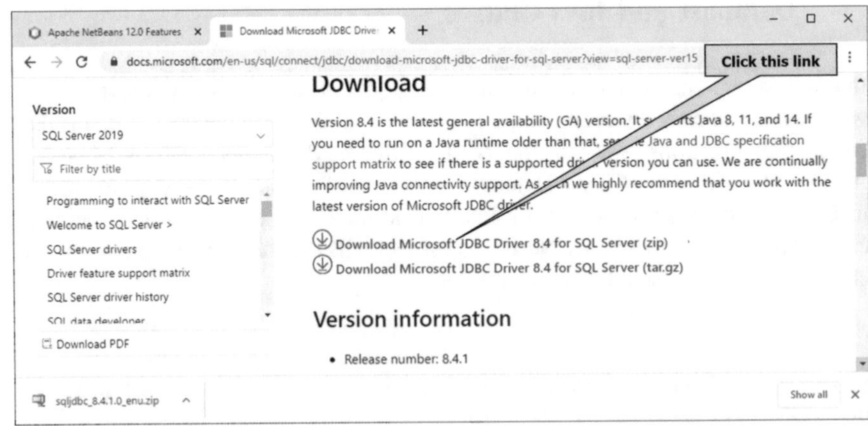

Fig. 6.1 The opened download site

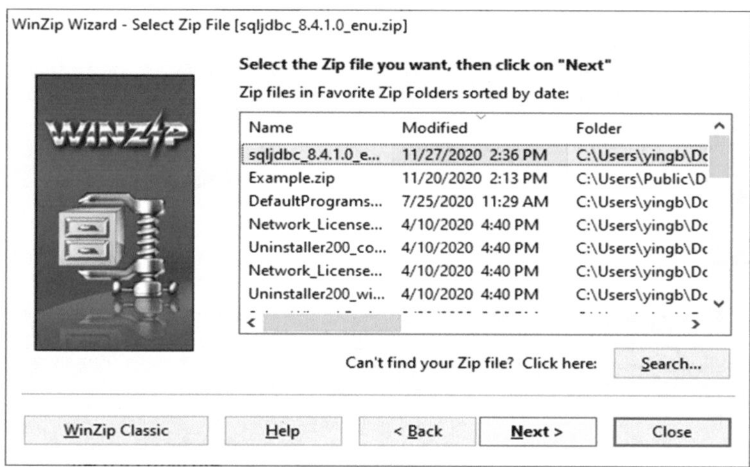

Fig. 6.2 The unzipping process

The SQL Server JDBC Driver is unzipped and stored in a folder **sqljdbc_8.4** under your default **Unzipped** folder in your computer if you did not specify the location for this unzipping process. One drive file, **mssql-jdbc-8.4.1.jre14.jar**, can be found from the subfolder **enu** and we will use this driver since it is an updated one and compatible with Java 14. It is recommended to move this **sqljdbc_8.4** folder to the system default folder **C:\Program Files**.

6.1.2 *Configure TCP/IP Protocol and Setup for SQL Server Express*

By default, the TCP/IP for *SQL Server* 2019 *Express* is disabled when a SQL Server Express

server is installed in your machine, therefore the JDBC cannot directly connect to it when a connection command is issued. Also the port used for TCP/IP to listen to the network has not been established when SQL Server 2019 Express server is installed in your machine. In order to fix these problems and make the TCP/IP work properly, we need to perform the following operations to meet our connection requirements:

1) Open the SQL Server Configuration Manager by going to **Start|Microsoft SQL Server 2019|SQL Server 2019 Configuration Manager**.
2) Expand the **SQL Native Client 11.0 Configuration** item and click on the sub-item **Client Protocols**, as shown in Fig. 6.3. Check and confirm the **Order** of the **TCP/IP** used for this SQL client, in this case it is **TCP/IP 2**. Remember this TCP/IP Order and also make sure that it is **Enabled**, as shown in Fig. 6.3.

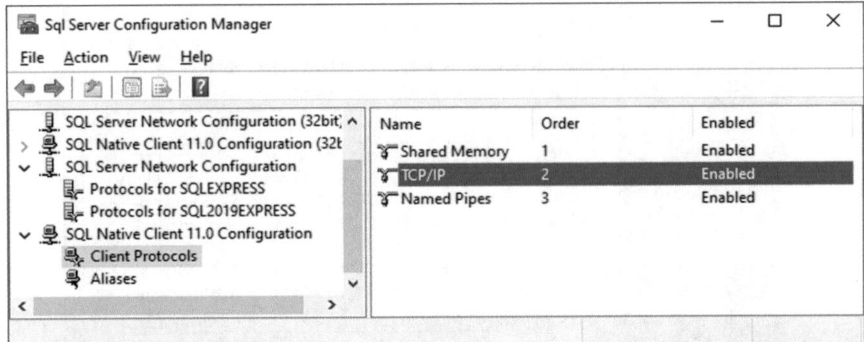

Fig. 6.3 Check the TCP/IP Order used for SQL Server 2019 Express

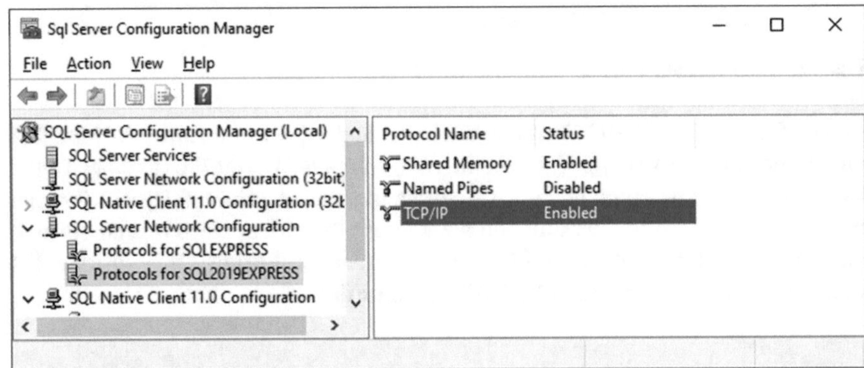

Fig. 6.4 Enable TCP/IP protocol for SQL Server 2019 Express

3) Then expand the **SQL Server Network Configuration** folder and click on the **Protocols for SQL2019EXPRESS** sub-item, as shown in Fig. 6.4, to open all protocols used for this SQL2019EXPRESS server on the right pane. Right click on the **TCP/IP** protocol and select **Enable** to enable it.
4) Double click on the **TCP/IP** protocol we just enabled on the right pane to open the **TCP/IP Properties** wizard, which is shown in Fig. 6.5a.

5) Click on the **IP Address** tab to display all valid IP addresses used for this machine. By default, all TCP Ports are blanks. Therefore, we need to setup one port number to the TCP/IP Order that is used for the SQL Server 2019 Express server manually. Recalled in step 2, the **TCP/IP 2** is used for our server. Thus just setup a desired port number to the TCP Port box under the **IP 2**, as shown in Fig. 6.5a. Here we used 5000 as our desired port number. Also enable this **IP 2** by selecting **Yes** for the **Enabled** property, as shown in Fig. 6.5a.

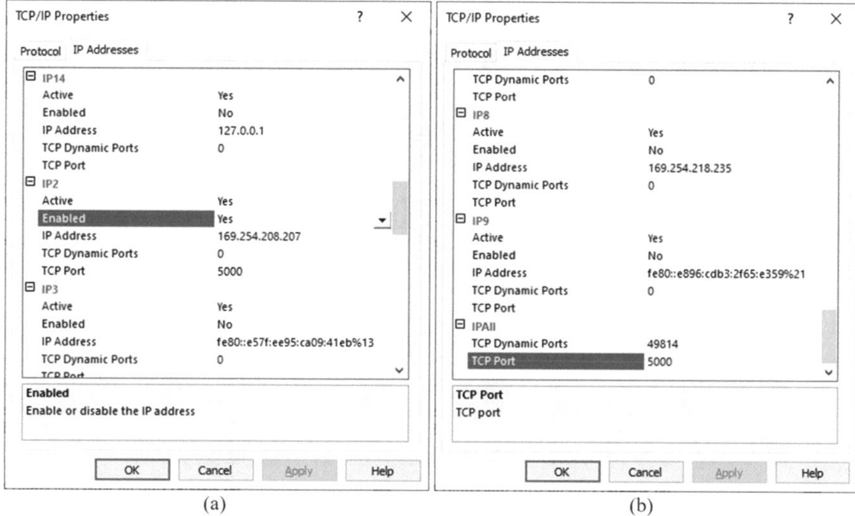

Fig. 6.5 The opened TCP/IP Properties wizard

6) Also still in this **TCP/IP Properties** wizard, scroll down to the bottom to find **IPAll** item, as shown in Fig. 6.5b. Enter **5000** into the **TCP Port** box to setup a port number for all dynamic opened ports.
7) To make this TCP/IP port effective, you should stop the SQL 2019 Server and then restart it. To do that, click on the **SQL Server Services** icon and right click on the **SQL Server (SQL2019EXPRESS)** item from the right list and select the **Stop** item to stop the server. Then right click on this server again and select the **Start** item to restart the server. Sometimes you may need to try to restart the Server one more time to start it.
8) To test this TCP Port number, open a command window and type: `netstat -an`. A running TCP/IP result window is displayed, as shown in Fig. 6.6. You can find that one of TCP/IP Ports, port **5000**, is working and it is displayed as a test result as:

TCP 0.0.0.0:5000 0.0.0.0:0 LISTENING

Now you can close the SQL Server Configuration Manager to complete this TCP/IP configuration.

6.1.3 *Configure Authentication Mode for SQL Server 2019 Express*

By default, *SQL Server 2019 Express* uses ***Windows Authentication*** *Mode* to authenticate connections when it is installed in your machine. However, if this SQL Authentication Mode is used by SQL Server JDBC Driver as it is connected to the Apache NetBeans IDE 12. Connection errors, such as

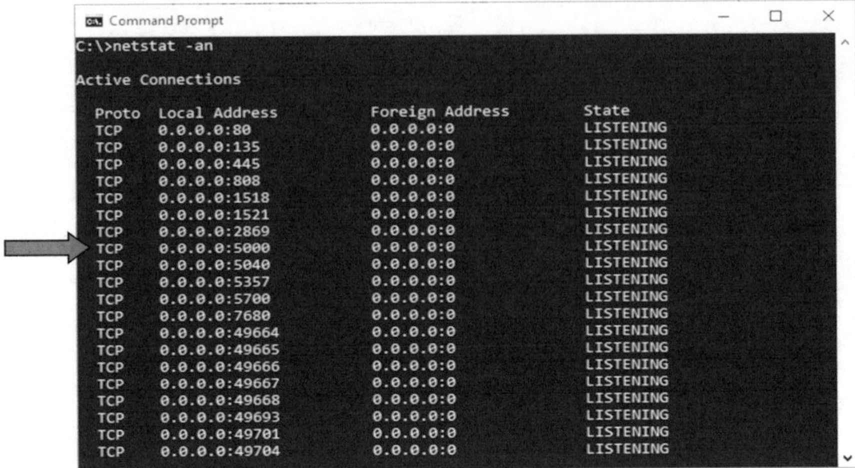

Fig. 6.6 Testing the TCP/IP Port number

```
Login failed for user '<User name>'. The user is not associated
with a trusted SQL Server connection
```

may be encountered if this default authentication mode is used for the connection. Perform the following operations to change the authentication to a mixed mode:

1) Launch Microsoft SQL Server Management Studio by going to **Start|Microsoft SQL Server Tools 18|Microsoft SQL Server Management Studio 18** item. Login and connect to your SQL Server using the Window Authentication mode.
2) Right click on our server icon **YBSMART\SQL2019EXPRESS** at the top of the Object Explorer window and click on the **Properties** from the pop up menu to open the **Server Proerties** wizard, which is shown in Fig. 6.7.
3) Click on the **Security** item to open the Security page, and check the **SQL Server and Windows Authentication mode** radio button to select this mixed mode, as shown in Fig. 6.7. Then click on the **OK** button to close this configuration.
4) In the *Object Explorer* pane, expand ***Security/Logins*** node. Now we want to add a new user to access this database via the SQL Server Express server.
5) Right click on the **Logins** folder and select `New Login` item to open the **Login – New** wizard, which is shown in Fig. 6.8.
6) Enter a desired username, such as **SMART**, into the **Login name** box and check the **SQL Server authentication** radio button since we need to use this mode to connect to the NetBeans using SQL Server JDBC driver. Enter a desired password, such as **Happy2020**, into the **Password** and **Confirm password** boxes. Uncheck all four checkboxes under the **Confirm password** box and select our sample database **CSE_DEPT** we developed in Chap. 2 from the **Default database** combo box.
7) Still in this **Login – New** wizard, click on the **Server Roles** icon from the left pane to open the `Server Roles` page, as shown in Fig. 6.9. Check the **sysad-**

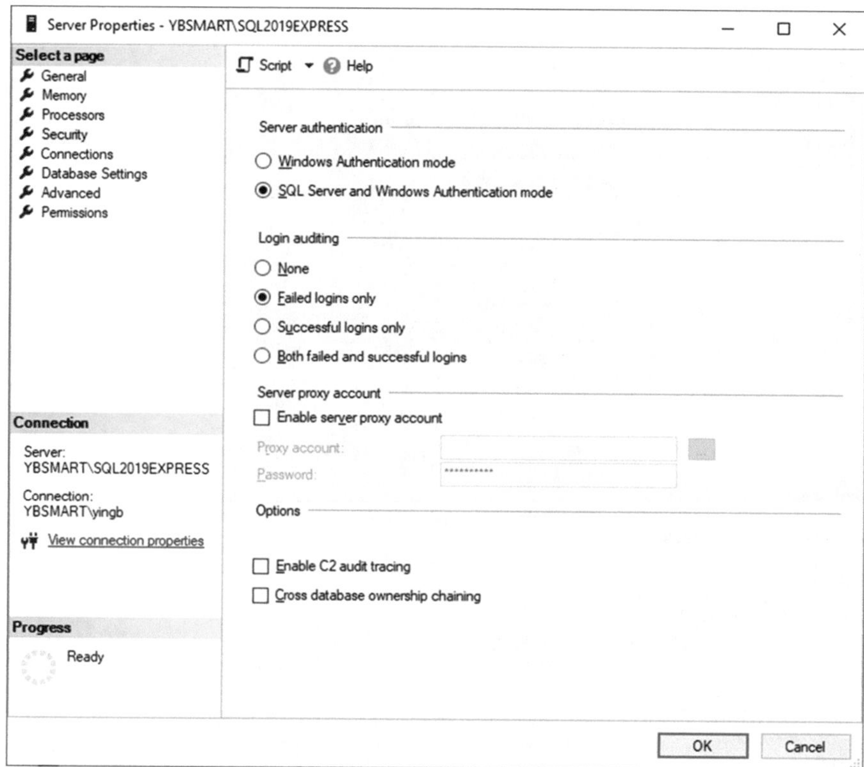

Fig. 6.7 The opened Server Properties wizard

min checkbox to make this new user as a system administrator to access this database (refer to Fig. 6.9).

8) Still in this **Login – New** wizard, click on the **Status** icon from the left pane to open the `Status` page, and then check the **Enabled** radio button under the **Login** item to enable this new user if it is disabled.
9) Click on the **OK** button to complete this authentication configuration.

Now go to **File|Save All** menu item to save these setups and close the Microsoft SQL Server Management Studio. Next, let us connect our sample database from Apache NetBeans IDE 12 using Microsoft SQL Server JDBC Driver.

6.1.4 Use the New Database Connection in Apache NetBeans to Setup a Connection

Before we can start the Apache NetBeans IDE 12, make sure that the following jobs have been performed and the following required components have been configured:

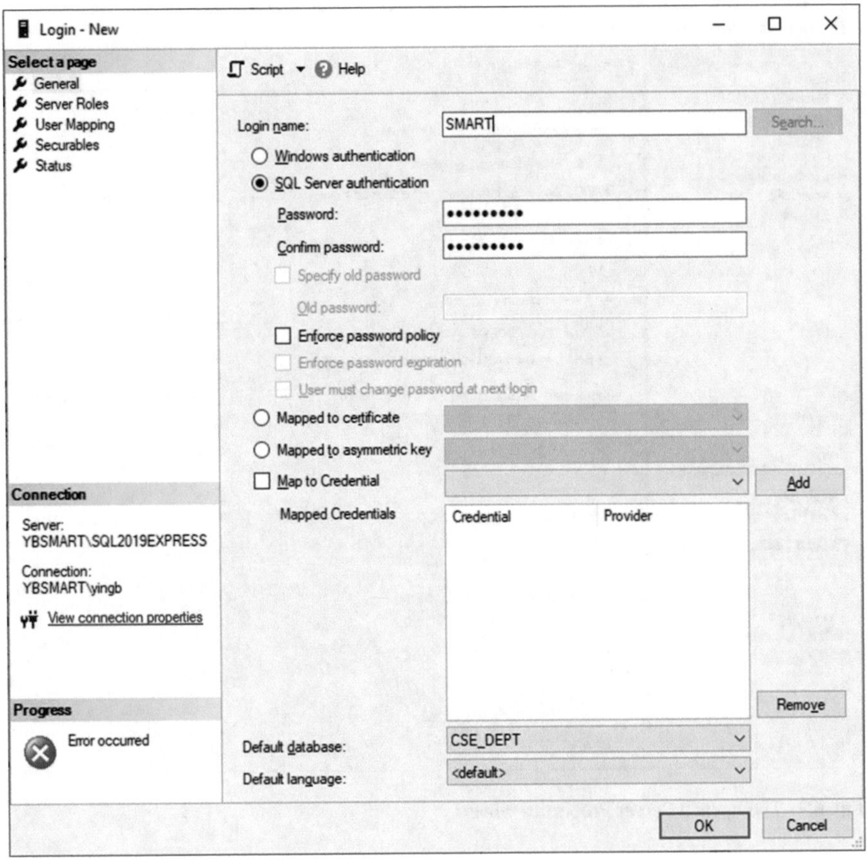

Fig. 6.8 The opened Login New wizard

- Make sure that the SQL Server 2019 Express has been running in your host computer.

To do that checking, open the Microsoft SQL Server 2019 Configuration Manager, and then click on the **SQL Server Services** item from the left pane. Make sure that both **SQL Server (SQL2019EXPRESS)** in the right pane are in the running status under the **State** tab. Close this Configuration Manager when this checking is finished.

Now let's launch Apache NetBeans IDE 12 to begin this database connection.

1) Click on the **Services** tab on the opened NetBeans and expand the **Databases** icon from the Object Explorer window. Now we need to add the Microsoft SQL Server JDBC Driver we downloaded above into the NetBeans IDE system.
2) Right click on the **Drivers** folder and select **New Driver** item to open the New JDBC Driver wizard, as shown in Fig. 6.10. Click on the **Add** button to browse to our driver's location, **C:\Program Files\sqljdbc_8.4|enu**, and click on our

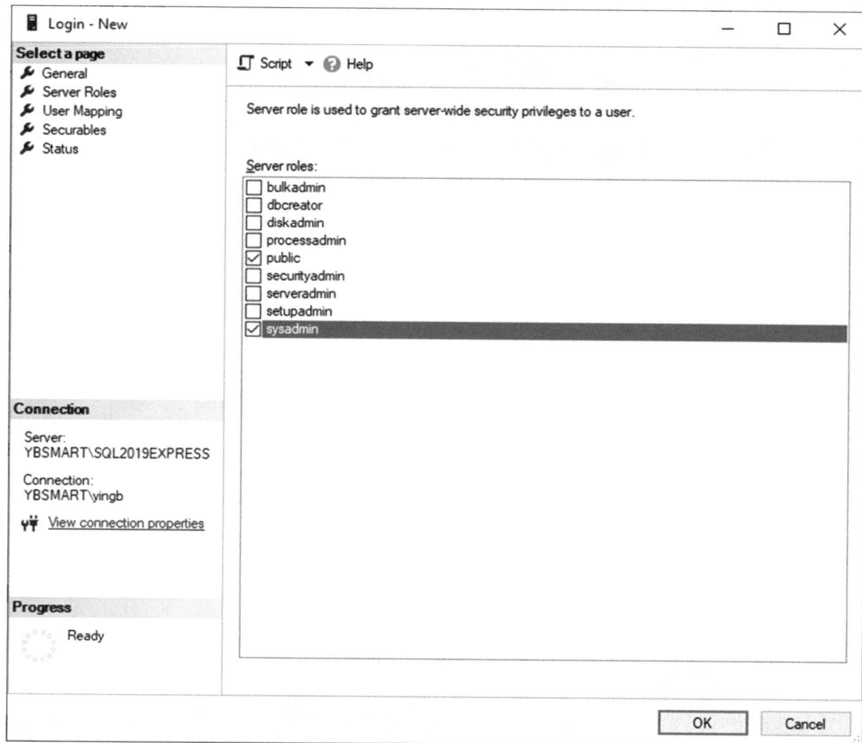

Fig. 6.9 The opened Server Roles page

installed driver **mssql-jdbc-8.4.1.jre14.jar**, and click on the **Open** button to add it into our NetBeans system. Your finished New JDBC Driver dialog box should match one that is shown in Fig. 6.10.

3) Click on the **OK** button to complete this process. Immediately you can find that a new driver named **Microsoft SQL Server 2019** has been added into the **Drivers** folder.
4) Now right click on the new added driver **Microsoft SQL Server 2019** and select the **Connect Using** item to open the **New Database Connection** wizard, as shown in Fig. 6.11.
5) Enter the following connection parameters into the associated boxes:

   a. **localhost** to the **Host** box since we are using a server that is installed in our local computer as our database server.
   b. **5000** into the **Port** box since we setup this number as our TCP/IP communication port number.
   c. **CSE_DEPT** into the **Database** box as we built this SQL Server database in Chap. 2.
   d. **CSE_DEPT** into the **Database** box since we developed this SQL Server database in Chap. 2.

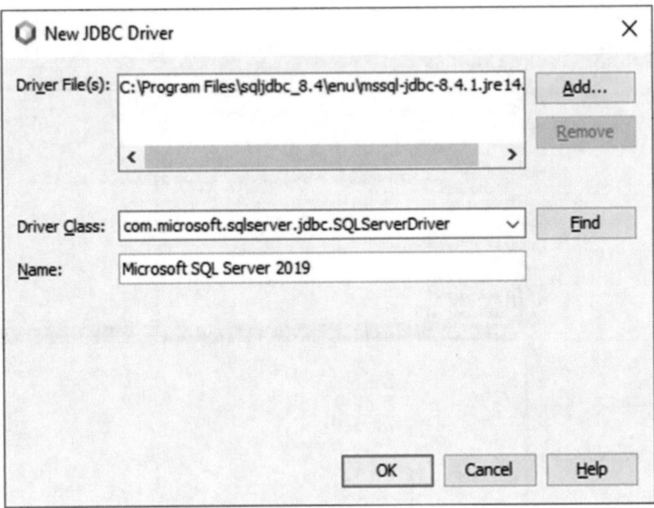

Fig. 6.10 The finished New JDBC Driver dialog box

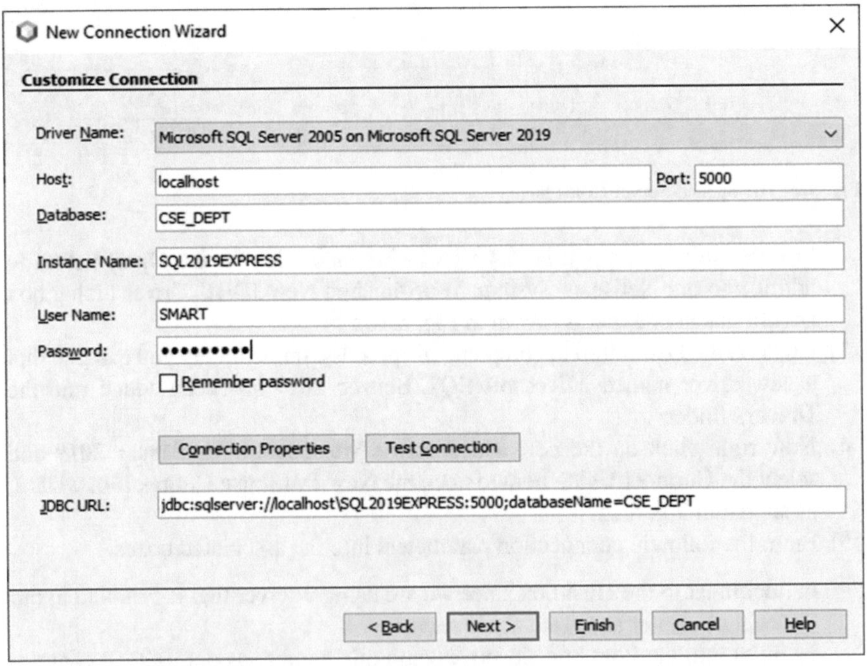

Fig. 6.11 The Finished New Database Connection wizard

e. **SQL2019EXPRESS** into the **Instance Name** box since the SQL2019EXPRESS is a default instance name when we install SQL Server 2019 Express server in our machine.

f. **SMART** and **Happy2020** into the **User Name** and **Password** boxes, respectively since we added a new user with this username and password when we configure our SQL Server 2019 server in the previous steps.
g. Check and confirm the contents on the **JDBC URL:** box, which is a full URL that will be used to setup this connection.

6) Your finished New Database Connection wizard is shown in Fig. 6.11.
7) You can click on the **Test Connection** button to test this connection. A **Connection Succeeded** message should be displayed if everything is fine. Click on the **Next** button to open the Database Schema Selection page to setup the schema for this connection.
8) Select the **dbo** from the **Select schema** combo box on this page, as shown in Fig. 6.12.
9) Click on the **Next** button to confirm this connection with a valid connection name.
10) In next page, **Choose name for connection**, you can find a new database connection URL

jdbc:sqlserver://localhost\SQL2019EXPRESS:5000;databaseName=CSE_DEPT [SMART on Default schema]

is displayed in the **Input connection name** box, as shown in Fig. 6.13.

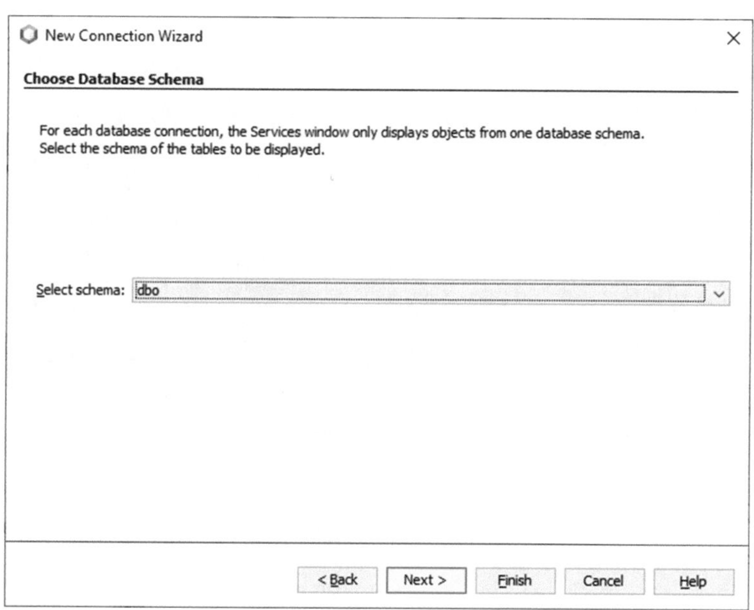

Fig. 6.12 The opened New Connection Wizard

11) Your finished **Choose name for connection** page should match one that is shown in Fig. 6.13. Click on the **Finish** button to complete this connection and close this wizard.

The contents inside the square bracket indicate that the user who setups and uses this connection is **SMART**, and the **dbo** is the database schema when we built our sample database **CSE_DEPT** in Chap. 2.

Immediately you can find this new connection icon that is located under the **Drivers** folder in the Object Explorer window in the NetBeans IDE 12.

Note: If you cannot make this connection or an error is returned, try to reboot your computer to disconnect to the SQL Server 2019 Express since the NetBeans IDE cannot connect to that database if it is still being used by the SQL Server 2019.

Now we have finished connecting to our sample database using Apache NetBeans IDE 12 Services. Next, let's discuss how to use Java runtime object method to build our database application projects.

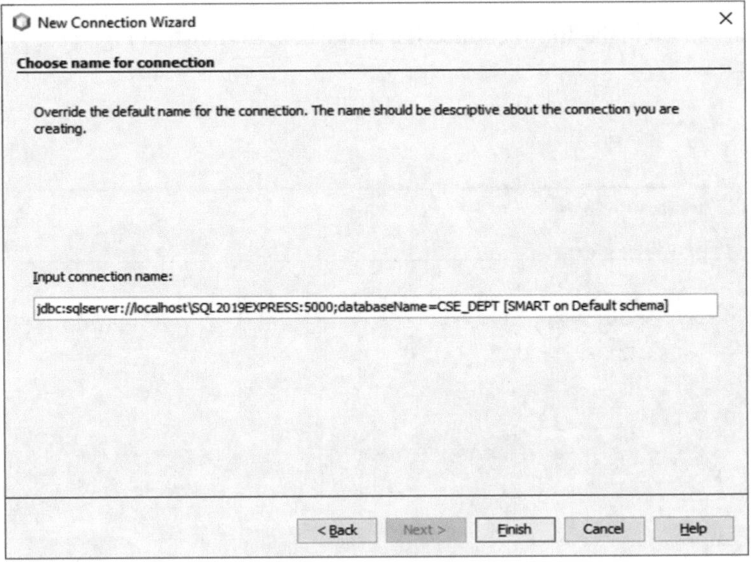

Fig. 6.13 The finished Choose name for connection page

6.2 Introduction to Runtime Object Method

The so-called Java runtime object method is to develop and build database accessing operations using runtime Java codes without touching JPA Wizards and Entity classes. In other words, no object-to-relational database mapping is needed and the project can directly access the database using Java codes.

As we discussed in Chap. 4, to access a database to perform data query, the following operational sequence should be followed:

1) Load and register the database driver using **DriverManager** class and **Driver** methods
2) Establish a database connection using the **Connection** object
3) Create a data query statement using the **createStatement()** method
4) Execute the data query statement using the **executeQuery()** method
5) Retrieve the queried result using the **ResultSet** object
6) Close the statement and connection using the **close()** method

In JPA Wizards method, the first and the second operations are combined together using JPA Entity classes. The Query Manager and Query components are also used in steps 3 through 5 to simplify the query operations. However, in Java runtime object method, all those operations are performed by developing the Java codes without touching any JPA Wizards. In the following sections, we will use an example project, **SQLSelectObject**, to illustrate how to use Java runtime object method to develop and build database query projects to access SQL Server database. To make these developments easy, we still use Apache NetBeans 12 as our development IDE.

6.3 Create a Java Application Project to Access the SQL Server Database

Perform the following operational steps to create this new Java with Ant Application project:

- Go to **File|New Project** to open the New Project wizard. Keep the default selection **Java with Ant** in the **Categories** box, and select **Java Application** from the **Projects** box. Click on the **Next** button to open the New Java Application wizard.
- Enter **SQLSelectObject** into the **Project Name** box and select an appropriate folder as the location to save this project. In this case, we used **C:\SQL Java DB Programming\Class DB Projects\Chapter** 6 as our project location.
- Make sure to uncheck the **Create Main Class** checkbox. Your finished Java New Application wizard should match one that is shown in Fig. 6.14.
- Click on the **Finish** button to create this new Java Application project.

Next we need to create four JFrame Form windows as our graphical user interfaces, **LogInFrame, SelectionFrame, FacultyFrame**, and **CourseFrame**, to perform the data queries to three data tables in our sample database. We also need to create a JDialog as our message box to display some running-time information.

6.3.1 Create Graphic User Interfaces

First let's create the LogInFrame Form window. Right click on our new project **SQLSelectObject** and select **New|JFrame Form** item from the popup menu to open **New JFrame Form** wizard. Enter the following values to this wizard to create this new JFrame Form:

1) **LogInFrame** to the Class Name box.
2) **SQLSelectObjectPackage** into the Package box.
3) Click on the **Finish** button.

Add the following GUI components with the appropriate properties shown in Table 6.1 into this Form. You need to drag each component from the **Palette** Windows and place it to the **LogInFrame** Form, and setup each property in the **Properties** Windows.

When setup property for each component, you need first to click on that component to select it and then go the **Properties** Windows to setup an appropriate property for that component. To setup a **Variable Name** for each component, you need to right click on that component and select **Change Variable Name** item from the

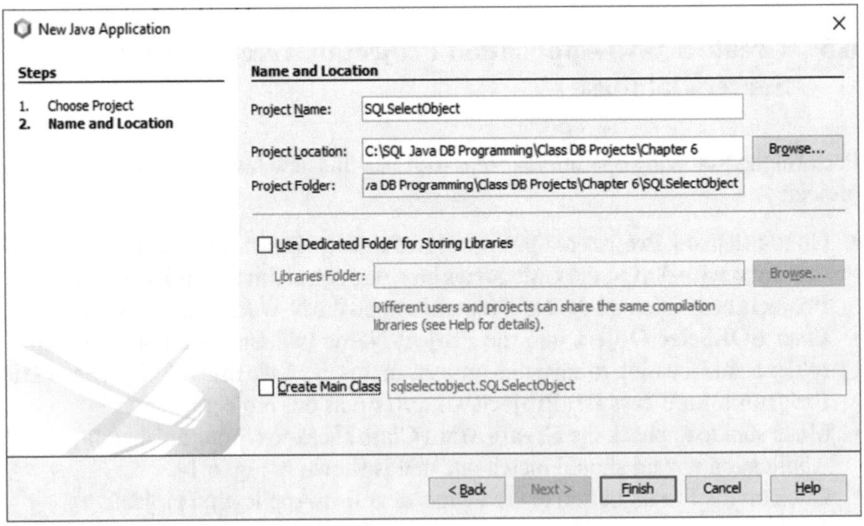

Fig. 6.14 The finished Java New Application wizard

Table 6.1 Objects and controls in the LogIn form

Type	Variable Name	Text
Label	Label1	Welcome to CSE Department
Label	Label2	User Name
Text Field	UserNameField	
Label	Label3	Pass Word
Text Field	PassWordField	
Button	LogInButton	LogIn
Button	CancelButton	Cancel
Title		CSE DEPT LogIn

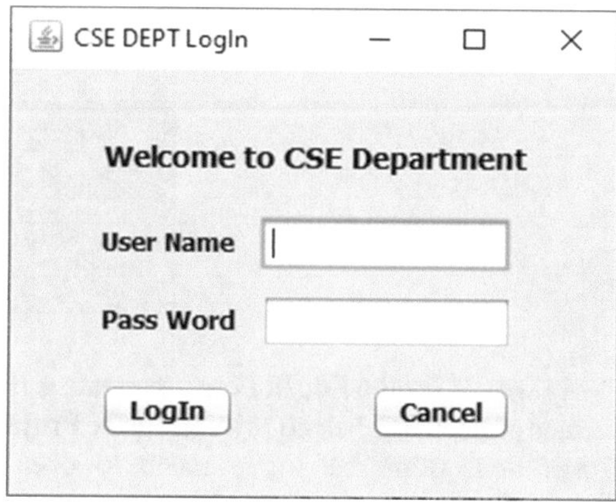

Fig. 6.15 The finished LogInFrame Form

pop-up menu, and then enter a desired name into the **New Name** box for that object. Your finished LogInFrame Form is shown in Fig. 6.15.

Now let's create the **SelectionFrame** Form window.

As we did for the **LogIn** Form, right click on our project **SQLSelectObject** from the **Projects** window and select **New|JFrame Form** item from the popup menu to open New JFrame Form wizard. Enter **SelectionFrame** into the **Class Name** box as the name of our new Frame Form class, and select **SQLSelectObjectPackage** from the **Package** box. Click on the **Finish** button to complete this creation.

Add the following objects and controls, which are shown in Table 6.2, into this **SelectionFrame** Form. One point to be noted is that you need to remove all default items located inside the **model** property of the Combo Box **ComboSelection**. To do that, click on the **ComboSelection** combo box from the Design View, and then go to the **model** property, click on the three-dot button to open the model pane. Select all four default items by highlighting them, and press the **Delete** button from the keyboard to remove all of those items. A preview of t**he completed SelectionFrame Form should match one that is shown in Fig. 6.16.**

Next let's create our **FacultyFrame** Form window.

Table 6.2 Objects and Controls in the SelectionFrame Form

Type	Variable Name	Text	Model	Title
Label	Label1	Make Your Selection		
ComboBox	ComboSelection			
Button	OKButton	OK		
Button	ExitButton	Exit		
SelectionFrame				CSE DEPT Selection

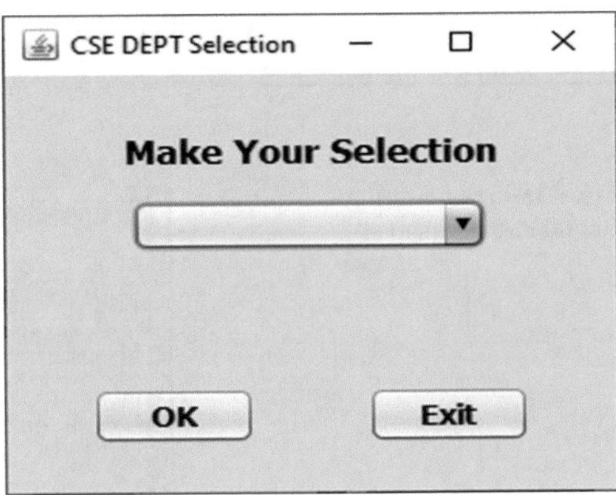

Fig. 6.16 A preview of the created SelectionFrame Form

As we did for the **LogIn** Form, to create a JFrame Form, right click on our new created project **SQLSelectObject** from the **Projects** window and select **New|JFrame Form** item from the popup menu to open New JFrame Form pane. Enter **FacultyFrame** into the Class Name box as the name of our

new Frame Form class, and then select the item **SQLSelectObjectPackage** from the Package box. Click on the **Finish** button to complete this creation.

Add the objects and controls shown in Table 6.3 into this FacultyFrame Form. One point to be noted is that you need to remove all default items located inside the **model** property of the Combo Box **ComboName** and **ComboMethod** as we did for the **ComboSelection** ComboBox above. Perform the similar operations for the **ComboMethod**. A preview of t**he completed FacultyFrame Form should match one that is shown in Fig. 6.17.**

A point to be noted is that when dragging a Canvas control from the Palette and place it into the FacultyFrame Form window, first you need to right click on the location where you want to place the Canvas on the **FacultyFrame** Form and select **Add From Palette > AWT > Canvas** item. Then a Canvas icon is displayed in that location. You can drag this Canvas icon to enlarge it to get the desired size. The purpose of adding this Canvas is that we need to use it to display a selected faculty image with it.

Next let's build our CourseFrame Form window.

Right click on our project **SQLSelectObject** from the **Projects** window, select **New|JFrame Form** item to open **New JFrame Form** pane. Enter **CourseFrame**

Table 6.3 Objects and controls in the FacultyFrame form

Type	Variable Name	Text	Border	Title
Canvas	ImageCanvas			
Panel	jPanel1		Titled Border	Faculty Name and Query Method
Label	Label1	Faculty Name		
ComboBox	ComboName			
Label	Label2	Query Method		
ComboBox	ComboMethod			
Panel	jPanel2		Titled Border	Faculty Image
Label	Label3	Faculty Image		
Text Field	FacultyImageField			
Panel	jPanel3		Titled Border	Faculty Information
Label	Label4	Faculty ID		
Label	Label5	Faculty Name		
Label	Label6	Title		
Label	Label7	Office		
Label	Label8	Phone		
Label	Label9	College		
Label	Label10	Email		
Text Field	FacultyIDField			
Text Field	FacultyNameField			
Text Field	TitleField			
Text Field	OfficeField			
Text Field	PhoneField			
Text Field	CollegeField			
Text Field	EmailField			
Button	SelectButton	Select	Button	SelectButton
Button	InsertButton	Insert	Button	InsertButton
Button	UpdateButton	Update	Button	UpdateButton
Button	DeleteButton	Delete	Button	DeleteButton
Button	BackButton	Back	Button	BackButton
FacultyFrame Form	FacultyFrame			CSE DEPT Faculty

into the **Class Name** box, and select the **SQLSelectObjectPackage** from the **Package** box. Click on the **Finish** button to create this new **CourseFrame** class.

Add the objects and controls shown in Table 6.4 into this CourseFrame Form window to finish the GUI design for this form.

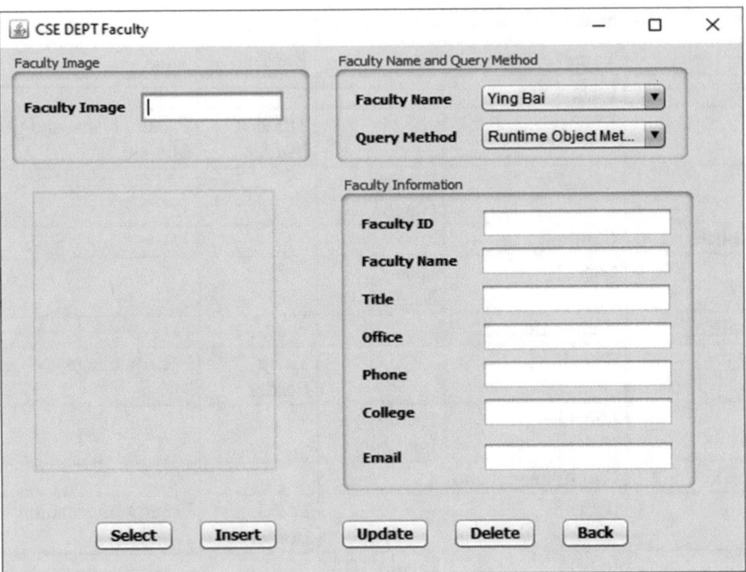

Fig. 6.17 A preview of the finished FacultyFrame Form window

Your finished **CourseFrame** Form window should match one that is shown in Fig. 6.18.

Finally, we need to create a JDialog box to work as our message box to display any exception or error information.

6.3.2 Use a JDialog as a MessageBox

In order to use this JDialog object as our MessageBox, first we need to create a new JDialog object based on the JDialog class. Then we need to add some codes to this class, exactly add codes into the constructor of this class, to make this dialog to be displayed at the center of the screen as the project runs.

First let's create a new JDialog object based on its class. Perform the following operational steps to create this JDialog object:

1) On the opened Projects window, right click on our project SQLSelectObject and select the New|Other item to open the New File wizard, as shown in Fig. 6.19.
2) Select the Swing GUI Forms from the Categories list and **OK/Cancel Dialog Sample Form** item from the File Types list, as shown in Fig. 6.19. Click on the **Next** button.
3) Enter **MsgDialog** to the **Class Name** box as our dialog box's name and select **SQLSelectObjectPackage** from the **Package** box to select it as our package in which our **MsgDialog** will be developed.

Table 6.4 Objects and controls in the CourseFrame form

Type	Variable Name	Text	Border	Title
Panel	jPanel1		Titled Border	Faculty Name and Query Method
Label	Label1	Faculty Name		
ComboBox	ComboName			
Label	Label2	Query Method		
ComboBox	ComboMethod			
Panel	jPanel2		Titled Border	Course ID List
ListBox	CourseList			
Panel	jPanel3		Titled Border	Course Information
Label	Label3	Course ID		
TextField	CourseIDField			
Label	Label4	Course		
TextField	CourseField			
Label	Label5	Schedule		
TextField	ScheduleField			
Label	Label6	Classroom		
TextField	ClassRoomField			
Label	Label7	Credits		
TextField	CreditsField			
Label	Label8	Enrollment		
TextField	EnrollField			
Button	SelectButton	Select		
Button	InsertButton	Insert		
Button	UpdateButton	Update		
Button	DeleteButton	Delete		
Button	BackButton	Back		
JFrame	CourseFrame			CSE DEPT Course

4) Click on the **Finish** button to create this **MsgDialog** Form.
5) Click on the **Design** tab from the top to open the Design View of our new created **MsgDialog** box. Reduce the size to an appropriate one, and add one label control to this dialog by dragging a Label from the **Palette** window and place it onto our dialog box.
6) Right click on this label and select **Change Variable Name** item from the popup menu to change it to **MsgLabel**. Go to the **text** property to remove the default text.
7) Set the **Font** to Bold and size to 12. Enter **MsgDialog** into the **Title** box.
8) A preview of this dialog box is shown in Fig. 6.20.

Next let's add some codes to this class to enable it to be displayed in the center of the screen as the project runs. To do that, keep the **MsgDialog.java** selected in the **Project** window and open the Code Window by clicking on the **Source** tab from the top and enter **this.setLocationRelativeTo(null);** just under the **initComponents();** method inside the constructor.

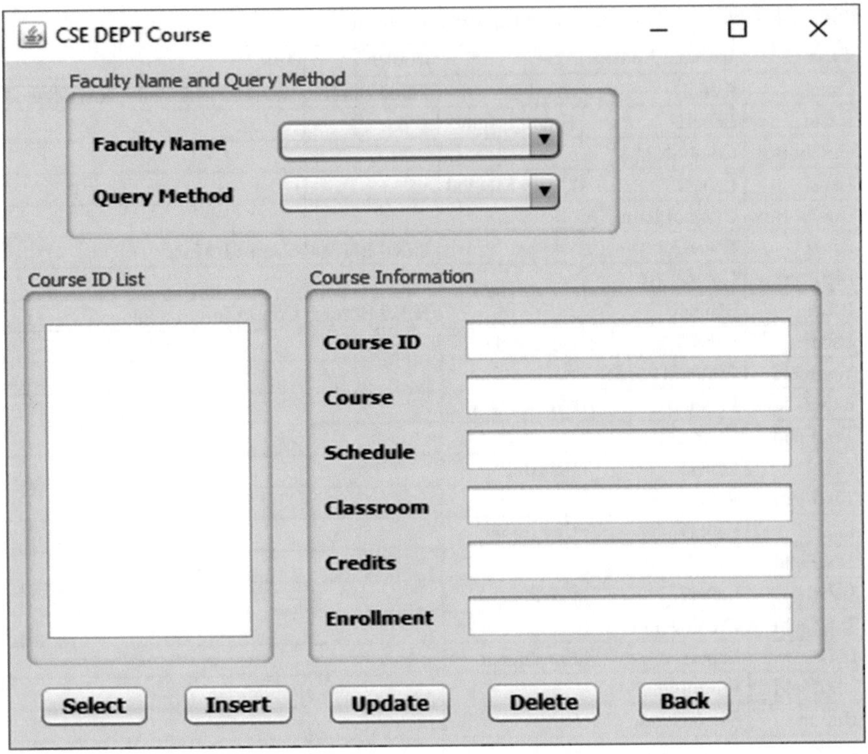

Fig. 6.18 The Finished CourseFrame Form window

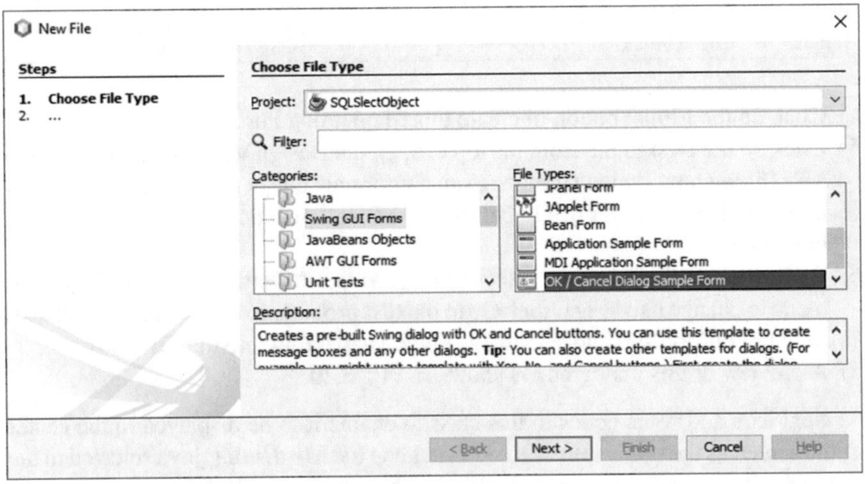

Fig. 6.19 The opened and finished New File wizard

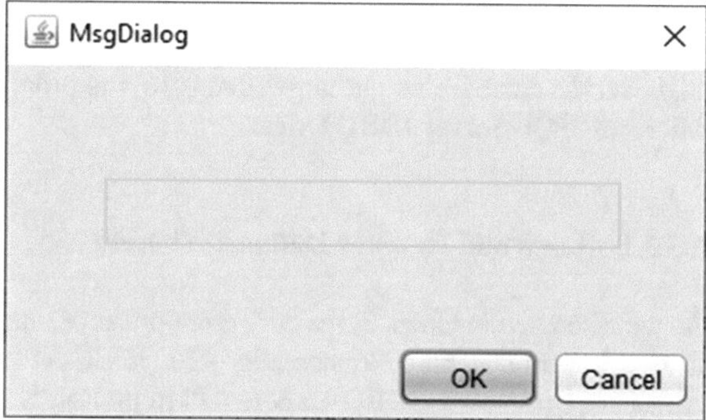

Fig. 6.20 A preview of the designed MessageBox

```
public class MsgDialog extends javax.swing.JDialog {

   public static final int RET_CANCEL = 0;

   public static final int RET_OK = 1;
   public void setMessage(java.lang.String msg){
          MsgLabel.setText(msg);
      }

   public MsgDialog(java.awt.Frame parent, boolean modal) {
      super(parent, modal);
      initComponents();
      this.setLocationRelativeTo(null);

      // Close the dialog when Esc is pressed
      String cancelName = "cancel";
      InputMap inputMap = getRootPane().getInputMap(JComponent.WHEN_ANCESTOR_OF_FOCUSED_COMPONENT);
      inputMap.put(KeyStroke.getKeyStroke(KeyEvent.VK_ESCAPE, 0), cancelName);
```

Fig. 6.21 Codes for the constructor and the setMessage() method

Then move your cursor just under the line: **@SuppressWarnings("unchecked")** and enter the codes shown in Fig. 6.21 to create a new method, **setMessage()**. Your finished codes for these two code adding, which have been highlighted, are shown in Fig. 6.21.

At this point, we have completed building in all graphical user interfaces we need in this project. Next let's concentrate on the coding development to perform the data query for each different data table in our sample SQL Server sample database **CSE_DEPT**.

6.3.3 Perform the Data Query for the LogIn Table

The function of this **LogInFrame** Form is to check and confirm the username and password entered by the user to make sure that both are correct. The user needs to enter both username and password, and then click on the **LogIn** button to begin this login process. An error message will be displayed if either an invalid username/password pair has been entered or both boxes are kept empty.

First let's start from loading and registering the database driver using DriverManager class and Driver methods. In this section, we want to use Microsoft SQL Server database as the target database, therefore we will concentrate on the Microsoft SQL Server JDBC Driver.

6.3.3.1 Load and Register Database Drivers

As we discussed in Chap. 3, the core component or interface of accessing databases in Java is Java Database Connectivity API (JDBC API), which is composed of two parts in two packages: JDBC 4.3 core API in **java.sql** and JDBC Standard Extension in **javax.sql**. Both parts are combined together to provide necessary components and classes to build database applications using Java.

Generally, JDBC API enables users to access virtually any kind of tabular data source such as spreadsheets or flat files from a Java application. It also provides connectivity to a wide scope of SQL or Oracle databases. One of the most important advantages of using JDBC is that it allows users to access any kind of relational database in a same coding way, which means that the user can develop one program with the same coding to access either a SQL Server database or an Oracle database, or even MySQL database without coding modification.

The JDBC 3.0 and JDBC 4.0 specifications contain additional features, such as extensions to the support to various data types, MetaData components, and improvements on some interfaces.

Exactly, the JDBC API is composed of a set of classes and interfaces used to interact with databases from Java applications. As we discussed in Chap. 3, the basic components of JDBC are located at the package **java.sql**, and the Standard Extension of JDBC, which provides additional features such as **Java Naming and Directory Interface** (JNDI) and **Java Transaction Service** (JTS), is in the **javax.sql** package.

6.3.3.2 Add Microsoft SQL Server JDBC Driver to the Project

Before we can load and register a JDBC driver, first we need to add the **Microsoft SQL Server JDBC Driver** we downloaded and installed in Sect. 6.1.1 as a library file into our current project **Libraries** node to enable our project to locate and find it when it is loaded and registered. To do that, follow steps below to finish this adding process:

1) Expand our project **SQLSelectObject** from the **Projects** window and right click on the **Libraries** folder.
2) Click on the **Add JAR/Folder** item from the popup menu to open the **Add JAR/Folder** wizard, which is shown in Fig. 6.22.
3) Browse to the location where we installed the **Microsoft SQL Server JDBC Driver**, which is **C:\Program Files\sqljdbc_8.4|enu**. Click on the driver **mssql-**

jdbc-8.4.1.jre14.jar, and click on the **Open** button to add this driver to our project **Libraries** node.

6.3.3.3 Load and Register Microsoft SQL Server JDBC Driver

The first step to build a Java database application is to load and register a JDBC driver. Two important components, DriverManager and Driver, are used for this process. As we discussed in

Chap. 3, Driver class contains six methods and one of the most important methods is the **connect()** method, which is used to connect to the database. When using this Driver class, a point to be noted is that most methods defined in the Driver class are never called directly, instead, they should be called via the DriverManager class methods.

The DriverManager class is a set of utility functions that work with the Driver methods together and manage multiple JDBC drivers by keeping them as a list of drivers loaded. Although loading a driver and registering a driver are two steps, only one method call is necessary to perform these two operations. The operational sequence of loading and registering a JDBC driver is:

1) Call class methods in the DriverManager class to load the driver into the Java interpreter.
2) Register the driver using the **registerDriver**() method.

When loaded, the driver will execute the **DriverManager.registerDriver()** method to register itself. The above two operations will never be performed until a method in the DriverManager is executed, which means that even both operations have been coded in an application, however, the driver cannot be loaded and registered until a method such as **connect()** is first executed.

To load and register a JDBC driver, two popular methods can be used:

1) Use Class.forName() method:

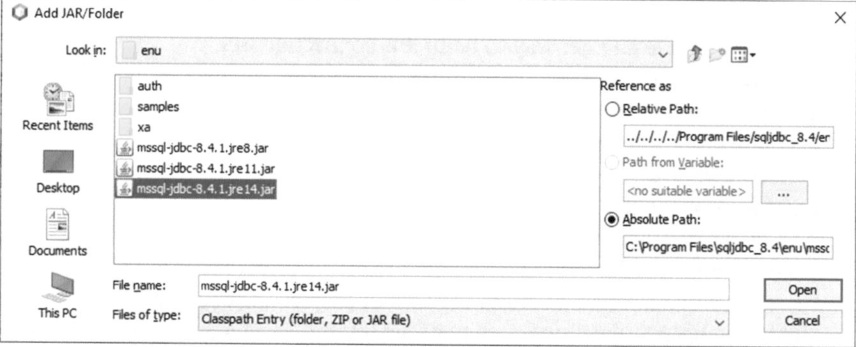

Fig. 6.22 The opened and finished Add JAR/Folder wizard

Class.forName("com.microsoft.sqlserver.jdbc.SQLServerDriver");

2) Create a new instance of the Driver class:

Driver sqlDriver = new com.microsoft.sqlserver.jdbc.SQLServerDriver;

Relatively speaking, the first method is more professional since the driver is both loaded and registered when a valid method in the DriverManager class is executed. The second method cannot guarantee that the driver has been registered by using the DriverManager.

Now let's develop the codes to load and register the Microsoft SQL Server JDBC Driver in our **LogInFrame** class. Open the Code Window of the **LogInFrame** by clicking on the **Source** tab from the top of the window, and enter the codes that are shown in Fig. 6.23 into this window.

Let's have a closer look at this piece of codes to see how it works.

A. Since all JDBC-related classes and interfaces are located in the **java.sql** package, thus we need first to import this package into our project.
B. A class instance **con** is declared here since we need to use this connection object in our whole project. A **MsgDialog** object is also created and we need to use it in this form.
C. The **setLocationRelativeTo()** method is called to setup this **LogInFrame** Form at the center of the screen as the project runs. A **null** argument means that no object can be referenced or relative to and the JFrame Form is set to the center.
D. A **try…catch** block is used to load and register our Microsoft SQL Server JDBC Driver. The **Class.forName()** method is utilized to make sure that our JDBC Driver is not only loaded but also registered when it is connected by running the **getConnection()** method in step **G** later. The argument of this method is the name of our Microsoft SQL Server JDBC Driver class and it is created by the NetBeans when we add this driver into our project in Sect. 6.1.1.
E. The **catch** block is used to track any possible error for this loading and registering. The related exception information will be displayed if any error occurred.
F. The connection **url**, which includes the protocol, subprotocol, and subname of the data source, is created to define a full set of the information for the database to be connected. An alternative **url**, which has been commented out, is also working and it is another way to build this connection **url**.
G. A **try…catch** block is used to perform the database connection by calling the **getConnection()** method. Three arguments are passed into this method; **url**, username, and password. Another way to call this method, which has been commented out, has only one argument that has combined three arguments together to make it simple.
H. The connected database is disconnected by calling the **close()** method. This instruction is only for the testing purpose for this **LogInFrame** Form, and it will be removed later when we build the formal project since we need to keep this single database connection for all our four JFrame Form windows until the project is terminated.

```
  package SQLSelectObjectPackage;
A import java.sql.*;

  public class LogInFrame extends javax.swing.JFrame {
B    static Connection con;
     MsgDialog msgDlg = new MsgDialog(new javax.swing.JFrame(), true);
     /** Creates new form LogInFrame */
     public LogInFrame() {
       initComponents();
C      this.setLocationRelativeTo(null);
       try
       {
          //Load and register SQL Server driver
D         Class.forName("com.microsoft.sqlserver.jdbc.SQLServerDriver");
       }
E      catch (Exception e) {
          msgDlg.setMessage("Class not found exception!" + e.getMessage());
          msgDlg.setVisible(true);
       }
F      String url = "jdbc:sqlserver://localhost\\SQL2019EXPRESS:5000;databaseName=CSE_DEPT;";
       //String url = "jdbc:sqlserver://localhost\\SQL2019EXPRESS:5000;
       //              databaseName=CSE_DEPT;user=SMART;password=Happy2020";
       //Establish a connection
G      try {
       con = DriverManager.getConnection(url,"SMART","Happy2020");
       //con = DriverManager.getConnection(url);
H      con.close();
       }
I      catch (SQLException e) {
          msgDlg.setMessage("Could not connect! " + e.getMessage());
          msgDlg.setVisible(true);
J         e.printStackTrace();
       }
  }
```

Fig. 6.23 Codes for loading and registering a JDBC Driver

I. Any possible exception that occurred during this connection will be displayed by using the **catch** block.
J. Prints this `Throwable` and its backtrace to the standard error stream. This method prints a stack trace for this `Throwable` object on the error output stream that is the value of the field `System.err`. The first line of output contains the result of the `toString()` method for this object. Remaining lines represent data previously recorded by the method `fillInStackTrace()`.

The reason we put this piece of codes that include the loading, registering, and connecting to our JDBC Driver inside the constructor of this **LogInFrame** class is that we need to setup and complete these operations first, or before other data actions can be performed since a valid database connection is a prerequisite for any database query operation.

Before we can continue to discuss database connection, first let's have a clear picture about the JDBC URLs.

6.3.3.3.1 The JDBC Uniform Resource Locators (URLs)

The JDBC **url** provides all information for applications to access a special resource, such as a database. Generally, a **url** contains three parts or three segments: protocol name, sub-protocol, and subname for the database to be connected. Each of these three segments has different function when they worked together to provide unique information for the target database.

The syntax for a JDBC **url** can be presented as:

```
protocol:sub-protocol:subname
```

The protocol name works as an identifier or indicator to show what kind of protocol should be adopted when connect to the desired database. For a JDBC driver, the name of the protocol should be **jdbc**. The protocol name is used to indicate what kind of items to be delivered or connected.

The sub-protocol is generally used to indicate the type of the database or data source to be connected, such as **sqlserver** or **oracle**.

The subname is used to indicate the address to which the item supposed to be delivered or the location of the database is resided. Generally, a subname contains the following information for an address of a resource:

- Network host name/IP address
- The database server name
- The port number
- The name of the database

An example of a subname for our SQL Server database is:

localhost\\SQL2019EXPRESS:5000

The network host name is **localhost**, and the server name is **SQL2019EXPRESS** and the port number the server used is **5000**. You need to use a double slash, either forward or back, to represent a normal slash in this **url** string since this is a DOS style string.

By combining all three segments together, we can get a full JDBC **url**. An example **url** that is using a SQL Server JDBC driver is:

jdbc:sqlserver//localhost\\SQL2019EXPRESS:5000

The database's name works as an attribute of the connected database.

Now that we have a clear picture about the JDBC **url**, next let's connect our application to our desired database.

6.3.3.4 Connect to Databases and Drivers

In step **G** of Fig. 6.23, we showed how to call the **getConnection()** method that belongs to the **DriverManager** class to connect to our sample database from our Java application. In fact, the retuned Connection object is not only used as a connection between our application and database, but also used for providing different ways to create SQL statements and methods for the different session managements, such as transaction locking, catalog selection, and except handling. The statement execution is performed by the associated components such as Statement, **PreparedStatement**, and **CallableStatement**.

The Statement object is used to execute static SQL queries. The so-called static statements do not include any IN or OUT parameters in the query string and do not contain any parameters passing to or from the database.

The **PreparedStatement** is used to execute dynamic SQL queries with IN parameter involved. These kinds of statements can be pre-parsed and pre-compiled by the database, and therefore have faster processing speed and lower running loads for the database server.

The **CallableStatement** is used to execute the stored procedures with both IN and OUT parameters involved. As we know, stored procedures are built and developed inside databases, and therefore have higher running and responding efficiency in data queries and processing.

6.3.3.5 Create and Manage Statement Object

The Statement class contains three important query methods with different functions: **executeQuery()**, **executeUpdate()**, and **execute()**. For each method, both different operations will be performed and different results can be returned. Generally, the execute methods can be divided into two categories: 1) the execute method that needs to perform a data query, such as **executeQuery()**, which returns an instance of **ResultSet** that contained the queried results, and 2) the execute method that does not perform a data query and only return an integer, such as the **executeUpdate()**. An interesting method is the **execute()**, which can be used in either way.

- The **executeQuery()** method performs data query and returns a **ResultSet** object that contains the queried results.
- The **executeUpdate()** method does not perform data query, instead it only performs either a data updating, insertion, or deleting action against the database and returns an integer that equals the number of rows that have been successfully updated, inserted, or deleted.
- The **execute()** method is a special method, and it can be used either way. All different data actions can be performed by using this method, such as data query, data insertion, data updating, and data deleting. The most important difference between the **execute()** method and two above methods is that the former can be

used to execute some SQL statements that are unknown at the compile time or return multiple results from stored procedures. Another difference is that the **execute()** method does not return any result itself, and one needs to use **getResultSet()** or **getUpdateCount()** method to pick up the results. Both methods belong to the **Statement** interface.

A confusion issue may come with the using of the **execute()** method. As we mentioned, since any SQL statement, either known or unknown at the compile time, can be used with this **execute()** method, how do we know the execution results? Yes, that indeed is a problem. However, fortunately, we can solve this problem by using some testing methods indirectly.

In fact, we can call either **getResultSet()** or **getUpdateCount()** method to try to pick up the running results from execution of the **execute()** method. The key point is that:

- The **getResultSet()** method will return a null if the running result is an integer, which is a number of rows that have been affected, either inserted, updated, or deleted.
- The **getUpdateCount()** method will return a -1 if the running result is a ResultSet.

Based on these two points, we can determine whether a result is a ResultSet or an integer.

Now let's first use the **executeQuery()** method to perform our data query from the **LogIn** table in our sample database. We will illustrate how to use the **execute()** method to perform the data query for the **FacultyFrame** Form in Sect. 6.3.5.

As we mentioned, a static statement does not contain any parameter passing into or from the database, therefore this kind of statement does not meet our requirement since we need to pass two parameters, username and password, into our sample database to perform the login process. To make a data query to our **LogIn** table to perform the login process, we need to use the second type of statement, **PreparedStatement**.

The advantages of using a **PreparedStatement** object to build and perform a dynamic query are that both the query flexibility can be increased and the query execution speed and efficiency can be significantly improved since the prepared statement can be pre-compiled and re-run again for a multiple query situation.

6.3.3.6 Use PreparedStatement Object to Perform Dynamic Query

In the Design View of the **LogInFrame** Form window, double click on the **LogIn** button to open its event handler, and enter the codes that are shown in Fig. 6.24 into this event handler.

Let's have a closer look at this piece of codes to see how it works.

A. Two local string variables, **username** and **password**, are declared first since we need to use them to hold the returned queries result later.

```
  private void LogInButtonActionPerformed(java.awt.event.ActionEvent evt) {
      // TODO add your handling code here:
A     String username = new String();
      String password = new String();
B     String query = "SELECT user_name, pass_word FROM LogIn " + "WHERE user_name = ? AND pass_word = ?";
C     try{
          PreparedStatement pstmt = con.prepareStatement(query);
D         pstmt.setString(1, UserNameField.getText());
          pstmt.setString(2, PassWordField.getText());
E         ResultSet rs = pstmt.executeQuery();
F         while (rs.next()){
            username = rs.getString(1);
            password = rs.getString(2);
          }
      }
G     catch (SQLException e) {
        msgDlg.setMessage("Error in Statement! " + e.getMessage());
        msgDlg.setVisible(true);
      }
H     if (UserNameField.getText().isEmpty() || PassWordField.getText().isEmpty()) {
        msgDlg.setMessage("Enter valid LogIn Information...");
        msgDlg.setVisible(true);
      }
I     else if ((username.equals(UserNameField.getText())) && (password.equals(PassWordField.getText()))) {
        msgDlg.setMessage("LogIn is Successful! ");
        msgDlg.setVisible(true);
        this.setVisible(false);
        this.dispose();
      }
J     else {
        msgDlg.setMessage("LogIn is failed!");
        msgDlg.setVisible(true);
      }
  }
```

Fig. 6.24 The codes for the LogIn button Click event handler

B. The query string is created with two dynamic parameters that are represented by using the positional parameter mode.
C. A **try…catch** block is used to perform the data query. First, a **PreparedStatement** object is created based on the Connection object we obtained from the database connection in the constructor of this **LogInFrame** class.
D. The **setString()** method of the **PreparedStatement** class is used to setup two dynamic parameters. The position of each parameter is indicated with the associated index of each parameter. The **getText()** method is used to get the username and password entered by the user from two text fields, **UserNameField** and **PassWordField**, respectively. A point to be noted is that different **setXXX()** methods should be used to perform this setup operation for the different types of the dynamic parameter. For example, here both **username** and **password** are String, so the **setString()** method is used. If the type of the parameter is integer, the **setInt()** method should be used to finish this parameter setting. Where **XXX** means the data type used for the dynamic parameter.

E. The **executeQuery()** method that belongs to the **Statement** class is called to perform this data query, and the query result is returned to the **ResultSet** object **rs**.

F. The **next()** method of the **ResultSet** class is utilized with a **while** loop to point to the next available queried row. This method returned a Boolean value, and a true indicates that more queried rows are in the **ResultSet**. A false means that no more queried row in the **ResultySet**. The **getString()** method is used to pick up each column from the **ResultSet** until a false is returned from the **next()** method. Similarly to the **setString()** method discussed in step **D**, different **getXXX()** methods should be used to pick up queried column with different data types. The argument **index** in the **getString()** method is used to indicate the position of the queried column in the **ResultSet**, which starts from 1, not 0.
G. The **catch** block is used to catch and display any possible error for this data query process.
H. If both **UserName** and **PassWord** text fields are empty, a warning message should be displayed to allow user to enter valid login information.
I. If both queried username and password match to those entered by the user, which means that the login process is successful. A successful message is displayed to indicate this. This message only works as a testing purpose and it will be removed later for the formal development of this project.

J. A login failed message will be displayed if any error occurred.

Before we can run this piece of codes to test it, make sure to remove or comment out the code in step **H** in Fig. 6.23, which is to close the connection to our sample database. Because when we make connection coding in Fig. 6.23, we need to close any connection to our sample database if a connection is successful to avoid possible multiple connections to our database. However, now we want to perform data queries, therefore we need to connect to our database to do a query since no data query can be performed if no database connection has been made.

After remove or comment out that **con.close()** coding line in Fig. 6.23, now we can build and run this **LogInFrame** Form to test our coding. Click on the **Clean and Build Main Project** button from the toolbar to build our project. Then right click on our **LogInFrame.java** file from the **Projects** window, and select the **Run File** item to run this object. A sample of running result is shown in Fig. 6.25.

Enter valid username and password, such as **ybai** and **come**, and click on the **LogIn** button to begin this login process. A login successful message should be displayed if this process is fine.

Before we can move to the next section, we need to finish developing the codes for the **Cancel** button Click event handler. The function of this handler is to close the **LogInFrame** Form window and the database connection if this button is clicked by the user. Open the Design View of the **LogInFrame** Form and double click on the **Cancel** button to open its event handler, and enter the codes that are shown in Fig. 6.26 into this event handler.

Let's have a closer look at this piece of codes to see how it works.

A. The **setVisible()** and **dispose()** methods are called to remove the **LogInFrame** Form window from the screen when this button is clicked by the user.

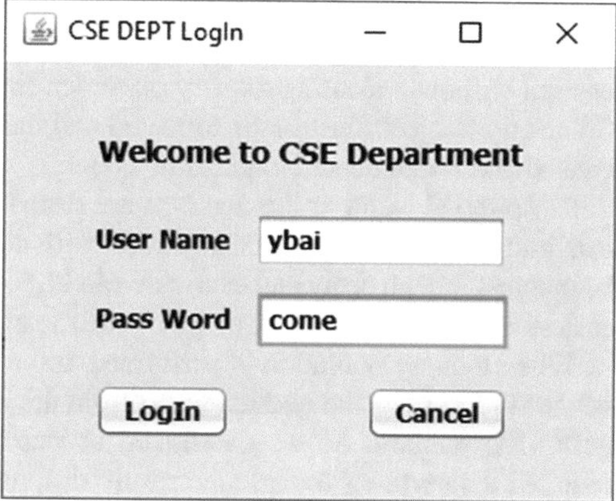

Fig. 6.25 A running sample of the LogInFrame Form

```
  private void CancelButtonActionPerformed(java.awt.event.ActionEvent evt) {
A         this.setVisible(false);
          this.dispose();
B         try {
              con.close();
          }
C         catch (SQLException e) {
              msgDlg.setMessage("Could not close!" + e.getMessage());
              msgDlg.setVisible(true);
          }
  }
```

Fig. 6.26 The codes for the Cancel button Click event handler

B. Also a **try…catch** block is used to try to close the database connection. A point to be noted is that a **try…catch** block must be used if one wants to perform a close action to a connected database.
C. The **catch** block will track and display any possible exception that occurred for this close action.

Next let's discuss how to retrieve the query result by calling **ResultSet** object.

6.3.3.7 Use ResultSet Object

The **ResultSet** class contains 25 methods and the most popular methods to be used are:

- **getXXX()**
- **getMetaData()**
- **next()**
- **findColumn()**
- **close()**

The **ResultSet** object can be created by either executing the **executeQuery()** or **getResultSet()** method, which means that the ResultSet instance cannot be created or used without executing a query operation first. Similar to a Statement object, a Connection object must be first created and then the Statement component can be created and implemented to perform a query.

The queried result or queried data are stored in the ResultSet with a certain format, and generally in a 2D tabular form with columns and rows. Each column can be mapped into an array and each row can be considered as a Vector. Therefore, the easiest way to map a ResultSet is to create an array of Vectors.

When a query operation is performed and a ResultSet instance is created, next we need to retrieve the queried result from the ResultSet object by using a suitable **getXXX()** method. As we mentioned in step **D** in Fig. 6.24, depending on the returned data type of the queried result, different method should be used, such as **getInt()**, **getString()**, **getByte()**, **getDouble()**, **getShort()**, and **getObject()**.

Two different ways can be used to get returned data from a ResultSet instance: fetching by row and fetching by column.

Fetching by Row:

Since the returned data can be stored in a ResultSet in a tabular form, the data can be picked up in row by row. The **next()** method in the ResultSet class is specially used for this purpose. Each row can be selected by using a cursor that can be considered as a pointer to point to each row. The **next()** method can move the row pointer from the current position to the next row. As we discussed in steps **E** and **F** in Fig. 6.24, when a login query is executed, a ResultSet instance **rs** is created and returned. Initially the cursor pointed to a row that is just above the first row, and you have to run the **next()** method once to allow it to point to the first data row, and then you can repeat to run this method by using a **while** loop to scan the whole table until the last row. A true will be returned by the **next()** method if a valid row has been found and pointed to, and a false is returned if the cursor points to null row, which means that no more valid row can be found and the bottom of the ResultSet has been touched.

Fetching by Column:

When a valid data row has been retrieved, we need to get each column from that row. To do that, different **getXXX()** methods should be used based on the different data types of the returned data. One can use either the name of a column or the index of that column to get the data value. In step **F** on Fig. 6.24, for our **LogIn** table, both the **user_name** and the **pass_word** are String, therefore a **getString()** method is used with the index of each column. A point to be noted is that the first column has an index of 1, not 0. If the name of each column, not an index, is used for the **getString()** method in step **F** in Fig. 6.24, the codes can be re-written as

```
while (rs.next()){
username = rs.getString("user_name");
password = rs.getString("pass_word");
}
```

One of the most important methods in ResultSet class is the **getObject()** method. The advantage of using this method is that a returned datum, which is stored in a ResultSet object and its data type is unknown (a datum is dynamically created), can be automatically converted from its SQL data type to the ideal Java data type. This method out-perform any other **getXXX()** method since the data type of returned data must be known before a suitable **getXXX()** method can be used to fetch the returned data.

The **findColumn()** method is used to find the index of a column if the name of that column is given, and the **close()** method is used to close a ResultSet instance.

The **getMetaData()** method is a very good and convenient method and it allows users to have a detailed and clear picture about the structure and properties of data returned to a ResultSet. A ResultSetMetaData object, which contains all pieces of necessary information about the returned data stored in a ResultSet instance, is returned when this method is executed. By using different methods of the ResultSetMetaData class, we can obtain a clear picture about the returned data. For example, by using the **getColumnCount()** method, we can know totally how many columns have been retrieved and stored in the ResultSet. By using **getTableName()**, **getColumnName()**, and **getColumnType()**, we can know the name of the data table we queried, the name of column we just fetched and data type of that column. A more detailed discussion about the **ResultSetMetaData** component will be given in Sects. 6.3.5.2.2 and 6.3.5.2.5.

Now that we have finished the coding development for the **LogIn** table, we are ready to perform the data query for the **Faculty** table using the **FacultyFrame** Form window. We need first to develop the codes for the **SelectionFrame** Form to allow users to select desired data query.

6.3.4 Develop the Codes for the SelectionFrame Form

Select the **SelectionFrame** class by clicking on it from the **Projects** window and open its Code Window by clicking on the **Source** tab from the top of the window. Enter the codes that are shown in Fig. 6.27 into the constructor of this class.

Let's have a closer look at this piece of codes to see how it works.

A. The Java JDBC Driver package is imported first since we need to use some classes located in that package to perform the data query.
B. A class-level object of the JDialog class **dlg** is created here since we need to use this **dlg** to display some debug and warning messages during the project runs.

```
  package SQLSelectObjectPackage;
A import java.sql.*;
  public class SelectionFrame extends javax.swing.JFrame {
B   MsgDialog dlg = new MsgDialog(new javax.swing.JFrame(), true);
    public SelectionFrame() {
      initComponents();
C     this.setLocationRelativeTo(null);
D     this.ComboSelection.addItem("Faculty Information");
      this.ComboSelection.addItem("Course Information");
      this.ComboSelection.addItem("Student Information");
    }
```

Fig. 6.27 The codes for the constructor of the SelectionFrame class

```
    private void OKButtonActionPerformed(java.awt.event.ActionEvent evt) {
      // TODO add your handling code here:
A     FacultyFrame facultyFrame = new FacultyFrame();
      CourseFrame courseFrame = new CourseFrame();

B     if (ComboSelection.getSelectedItem()== "Faculty Information"){
        facultyFrame.setVisible(true);
      } else if (ComboSelection.getSelectedItem()== "Course Information"){
        courseFrame.setVisible(true);
      } else {
        dlg.setMessage("Student Information is selected\n");
        dlg.setVisible(true);
      }
    }
```

Fig. 6.28 Codes for the OK button Click event handler

C. The **setLocationRelativeTo()** method is called to locate this SelectionFrame Form at the center of the screen as the project runs. A **null** argument means that no object can be referenced or relative to and the JFrame Form is set to the center.
D. The **addItem()** method is executed to add three pieces of information into the Combo Box ComboSelection to allow users to choose one of them as the project runs. Another method to add these three pieces of information is to directly add those pieces of information into the model box under the Combo Box Model Editor, which can be considered as a static adding (before the project runs). In that way, you do not need to enter these three lines of codes in this constructor. However, we prefer to use the **addItem()** method to add those pieces of information since it belongs to a dynamic adding.

Next let's do the coding for the **OK** and **Exit** command buttons, exactly for the event handlers of those buttons. The function for the **SelectionFrame** Form is: as the user selected a desired choice from the Combo Box and click the **OK** button to query the related information, the related information frame, such as **FacultyFrame** Form, CourseFrame Form, or StudentFrame Form, will be displayed to enable users to make related queries.

Now let's open the Design View of the **SelectionFrame** Form by clicking on the **Design** tab from the top and double click on the **OK** button to open its event handler. Enter the codes that are shown in Fig. 6.28 into this handler.

Let's have a closer look at this piece of codes to see how it works.

A. Two objects are created at the beginning of this handler, which include the **FacultyFrame** and **CourseFrame**, since we need to direct the program to the different frame when an associated frame is selected by the user.
B. An **if** selection structure is used to identify each selected item from the **ComboSelection** combo box. The MsgDialog is used if the **Student Information** item is selected since that Frame has not been built and we will build it later.

The rest coding includes two parts: coding for the **Exit** button Click event handler and coding for the creating a **getter** method. As you know, in the Object-Oriented Programming, in order to use the unique object created in a project, a popular way is to create a **setter** and a **getter** method in the target class. In this way, when other objects such as JFrames, JDialogs, or JWindows in the same project want to use the target object, they can call this **getter** to get the desired target object.

Let's create codes for both the **getter** method and the **Exit** button Click event handler by entering the codes that are shown in Fig. 6.29 into this **SelectionFrame** class.

Let's have a closer look at this piece of codes to see how it works.

A. The function of the **getter** method is simple; as this method is called, the current **SelectionFrame** object is obtained by returning **this** component that is a pointer point to the current Frame object to the calling object. A point to be noted is that the accessing mode of this method must be a **public** since we want this method to be called by any other objects to get this **SelectionFrame** object as the project runs.
B. In the **Exit** button Click event handler, a **try…catch** block is used to check whether the database connection we created in the **LogInFrame** Form window is still connected to our database by using the **isClosed()** method. A true will be returned if that connection has been closed, otherwise a false is returned to indicate that the connection is still active. The **close()** method of the Connection

```
A  public SelectionFrame getSelectionFrame(){
     return this;
   }
   private void ExitButtonActionPerformed(java.awt.event.ActionEvent evt) {
       // TODO add your handling code here:
B      try{
           if (!LogInFrame.con.isClosed()){ LogInFrame.con.close(); }
       }
C      catch(SQLException e){
          dlg.setMessage("Could not close!" + e.getMessage());
          dlg.setVisible(true);
          }
D      this.setVisible(false);
       this.dispose();
       System.exit(0);
   }
```

Fig. 6.29 Codes for the getter method and the Exit button Click event handler

class is called to close this connection if a false is returned. As you may remember, the Connection object **con** we created in the **LogInFrame** class is a class instance, therefore we can directly use the class name to access that instance without needing to create a new instance.

C. The **catch** block is used to track and display any error for this close process.
D. Then the **SelectionFrame** Form object is removed from the screen by calling the **setVisible()** and **dispose()** methods. The object **this** indicates the current Frame Form object, which is the **SelectionFrame**. A system **exit()** method is called to allow the project to be officially exited from the current process. An argument 0 means that no error for this exit operation.

At this point, we have completed all coding for the **SelectionFrame** Form window. Before we can continue to the next section, we need to modify some codes in both **SelectionFrame** and the **LogInFrame** classes to allow a smooth switching from either of them.

```
  private void LogInButtonActionPerformed(java.awt.event.ActionEvent evt) {
      String username = new String();
      String password = new String();
A     SelectionFrame selFrame = new SelectionFrame().getSelectionFrame();
      String query = "SELECT user_name, pass_word FROM LogIn " + "WHERE user_name = ? AND pass_word = ?";
      try{
        PreparedStatement pstmt = con.prepareStatement(query);
        pstmt.setString(1, UserNameField.getText());
        pstmt.setString(2, PassWordField.getText());
        ResultSet rs = pstmt.executeQuery();
        while (rs.next()){
          username = rs.getString(1);
          password = rs.getString(2);
        }
      }
      catch (SQLException e) {
        msgDlg.setMessage("Error in Statement!" + e.getMessage());
        msgDlg.setVisible(true);
      }
      if (UserNameField.getText().isEmpty() || PassWordField.getText().isEmpty()) {
        msgDlg.setMessage("Enter the LogIn Information...");
        msgDlg.setVisible(true);
      } else if ((username.equals(UserNameField.getText())) && (password.equals(PassWordField.getText()))) {
B       selFrame.setVisible(true);
C       //msgDlg.setMessage("LogIn is Successful! ");
        //msgDlg.setVisible(true);
        this.setVisible(false);
        this.dispose();
      } else {
        msgDlg.setMessage("LogIn is failed!");
        msgDlg.setVisible(true);
      }
  }
```

Fig. 6.30 Modified codes for the LogIn button Click event handler

6.3.4.1 Modify Codes to Transfer Between SelectionFrame and LogInFrame

First we need to add some codes into the **LogIn** button Click event handler in the **LogInFrame** class to direct the project to open the **SelectionFrame** Form window if the login process is successful. Open the **LogIn** button event handler and add the following codes into this handler, which is shown in Fig. 6.30.

Let's have a closer look at these modified codes to see how they work.

A. A new instance of the **SelectionFrame** class **selFrame** is created. However, the **getter** method **getSelectionFrame()** we built for the **SelectionFrame** class is called to retrieve the original **SelectionFrame** instance and assign it to the new created instance. In this way, we did not create any new instance of the SelectionFrame, instead we are still using the original SelectionFrame instance and it is a unique instance in this project.
B. Replace the old codes by using the code line **selFrame.setVisible(true)** to display our **SelectionFrame** Form window if the login process is successful. Also close and dispose this **LogInFrame** Form window since we have finished the login process.
C. Comment out all messages displayed by using the **msgDlg** object since those are only used for the testing purpose.

At this point, we have finished all coding jobs for the **LogInFrame** and the **SelectionFrame**. In the following sections, we will discuss how to perform data query to our **Faculty** table using the **FacultyFrame** class.

6.3.5 Perform the Data Query for the Faculty Table

The function of this form is: as the user selected a faculty member from the **ComboName** combo box and click the **Select** button, the detailed information with an image for the selected faculty should be displayed in seven text fields and a canvas. The development of this query can be divided into the following five parts:

1) Adding some necessary java packages and coding for the constructor of the **FacultyFrame** class to perform some initialization processes.
2) Coding for the **Select** button Click event handler to run the **executeQuery()** method to query data from the **Faculty** table in our sample database using the DatabaseMetaData interface and ResultSetMetaData interface.
3) Coding for the **Select** button Click event handler to run the **execute()** method to query data from our **Faculty** table in our sample database.
4) Adding a user-defined method **ShowFaculty()** to display an image for the selected faculty in the **FacultyFrame** Form window.
5) Coding for the **Back** button Click event handler to close the **FacultyFrame** Form window and return the control to the **SelectionFrame** Form.

Now let's start with the first part.

6.3.5.1 Add Java Package and Coding for the Constructor

Since we need to display an image of the selected faculty when a data query is executed, the **java.awt.*** package should be imported since some image-related classes, such as Image, Graphics, and MediaTracker, are located at that Abstract Windowing Tools (AWT) package.

Open the Code Window of the **FacultyFrame** class by clicking on the **Source** tab from the top of the window and add the codes that are shown in Fig. 6.31 into this source file.

Let's have a closer look at this piece of codes to see how it works.

A. Four java packages, **java.awt.***, **java.sql.***, **java.io.File**, and **javax.swing.JFileChooser**, are imported at the beginning of this file since we need to use some classes defined in the first two packages to display the selected faculty image, and use another two packages for the **File Chooser** object to allow users to select desired faculty image.
B. A JDialog object **msgDlg** is created here as a class level object because we need to use it in the whole class of the **FacultyFrame** to display some debug or warning messages.
C. The **addItem()** method is used to add all three query methods into the Query Method combo box. In this section, we only use the Runtime Object Method and the **execute()** method.

```
  package SQLSelectObjectPackage;
A import java.awt.*;
  import java.sql.*;
  import java.io.File;
  import javax.swing.JFileChooser;

  public class FacultyFrame extends javax.swing.JFrame {
B   MsgDialog msgDlg = new MsgDialog(new javax.swing.JFrame(), true);
    /** Creates new form FacultyFrame */
    public FacultyFrame() {
      initComponents();
      this.setLocationRelativeTo(null);   // set the faculty Form at the center
C     ComboMethod.addItem("Runtime Object Method");
      ComboMethod.addItem("Java execute() Method");
      ComboMethod.addItem("Java Callable Method");
D     ComboName.addItem("Ying Bai");
      ComboName.addItem("Davis Bhalla");
      ComboName.addItem("Black Anderson");
      ComboName.addItem("Steve Johnson");
      ComboName.addItem("Jenney King");
      ComboName.addItem("Alice Brown");
      ComboName.addItem("Debby Angles");
      ComboName.addItem("Jeff Henry");
    }
```

Fig. 6.31 Initialization codes for the FacultyFrame class

D. Also the **addItem()** method is utilized to add all eight faculty members into the Faculty Name combo box.

Now let's develop codes for the **Select** button Click event handler to perform the data query.

6.3.5.2 Query Data using JDBC MetaData Interface

In Sect. 6.3.3.7, we discussed how to use **ResultSet** component to retrieve the queried result. Relatively speaking, there are some limitations on using the ResultSet object to get the returned query result. In other words, it is hard to get a clear and detailed picture about the queried result, such as the structure and properties of the data stored in the ResultSet. For example, no information about the returned result, such as the name of the data table, the total number of columns, each column's name, and the data type, would be available when using ResultSet object to pick up the queried result. In order to solve that problem to get detailed knowledge of the data table structure, we need to use the **ResultSetMetaData** component.

The JDBC MetaData Interface provides detailed information about the database and its contents made available by the JDBC API, and it can be divided into the following three categories:

1) The DatabaseMetaData interface
2) The ResultSetMetaData interface
3) The ParameterMetaData interface

Each class has its special functions and operation sequences, and some of them are related when they are utilized in some specific ways.

6.3.5.2.1 The DatabaseMetaData Interface

The DatabaseMetaData interface contains more than 150 methods and provides detailed information about the database as a whole body, such as:

- General information about the database
- Data source limitations
- Levels of transaction support
- Feature support
- Information about the SQL objects that source includes

In fact, the DatabaseMetaData interface provides methods that allow you to dynamically discover properties of a database as the project runs. Many methods in the DatabaseMetaData return information in the ResultSet component, and one can get those pieces of information from ResultSet object by calling related methods such as **getString()**, **getInt()**, and **getXXX()**. A SQLException would be thrown out if the queried item is not available in the MetaData interface.

6.3.5.2.2 The ResultSetMetaData Interface

The detailed information about the structure of a queried data table can be obtained by calling the **getMetaData()** method that belongs to the **ResultSetMetaData** class, and a **ResultSetMetaData** object will be created when the **getMetaData()** method is executed. Some popular methods included in the **ResultSetMetaData** class are:

- **getColumnCount()** – returns the total number of columns in the ResultSet
- **getColumnName()** – returns the column name
- **getColumnType()** – returns the column data type
- **getTableName()** – returns the data table name

Similar to **DatabaseMetaData** interface, the **ResultSetMetaData** interface allows users to discover the structure of data tables and properties of columns in tables.

6.3.5.2.3 The ParameterMetaData Interface

The detailed information about the parameters passed into or from the database can be obtained by calling the **getParameterMetaData()** method that belongs to the **PreparedStatement** class. Although this interface is not as popular as **ResultSetMetaData** and **DatabaseMetaData**, it is useful in some special applications.

In this section, we will use the **DatabaseMetaData** and the **ResultSetMetaData** interfaces to illustrate how to improve the data query for our **Faculty** table.

6.3.5.2.4 Use DatabaseMetaData Interface to Query Database Related Information

Open the **Select** button Click event handler of the **FacultyFrame** class and enter the codes that are shown in Fig. 6.32 into this event handler.

Let's have a closer look at this piece of codes to see how it works.

A. The query string is declared first to query all columns from the **Faculty** table based on the selected faculty name.
B. An **if** selection structure is used to identify the desired data query method, **Runtime Object Method**, which will be used in this section. A prepared query statement is then created to query the detailed information for the selected faculty member.
C. First a **try…catch** block is utilized to perform the database-related information query using the DatabaseMetaData interface. A DatabaseMetaData object **dbmd** is created by calling the **getMetaData()** method that belongs to the

```
  private void SelectButtonActionPerformed(java.awt.event.ActionEvent evt) {
      // TODO add your handling code here:
A     String query = "SELECT faculty_id, faculty_name, title, office, phone, college, email, fimage " +
                     "FROM Faculty WHERE faculty_name = ?";
B     if (ComboMethod.getSelectedItem()=="Runtime Object Method"){
C        try{
            DatabaseMetaData dbmd = LogInFrame.con.getMetaData();
D           String drName = dbmd.getDriverName();
            String drVersion = dbmd.getDriverVersion();
E           msgDlg.setMessage("DriverName is: " + drName + ", Version is: " + drVersion);
            msgDlg.setVisible(true);
         }
F        catch (SQLException e) {
            msgDlg.setMessage("Error in Statement!" + e.getMessage());
            msgDlg.setVisible(true);
         }
      }
  }
```

Fig. 6.32 The codes for the Select button Click event handler

Connection class, and detailed information about the connected database is also returned and assigned to the **dbmd** object.

D. Two methods, **getDriverName()** and **getDriverVersion()**, are executed to pick up the retrieved driver name and version and assign them to the associated String variables.
E. The **msgDlg** is used to display retrieved driver name and version.
F. The **catch** block is used to collect and display all possible errors during this query process.

Here the **msgDlg** is only used for the testing purpose and it can be commented out as the project is finally built and deployed later. From this example, it is shown that some useful database-related information can be easily obtained by using the **DatabaseMetaData** interface.

6.3.5.2.5 Use ResultSetMetaData Interface to Query Table-Related Information

Still in the **Select** button Click event handler of the **FacultyFrame** class, add the codes that are in bold and shown in Fig. 6.33 into this handler to apply **ResultSetMetaData** interface to obtain the Faculty table-related information.

Let's take a closer look at this added piece of codes to see how it works.

A. A PreparedStatement object **pstmt** is created by calling the **prepareStatement()** method with the prepared query string as the argument.
B. The **setString()** method is used to setup the dynamic positional parameter in the prepared query statement. The actual value of this parameter, which is the selected faculty member by the user from the ComboName combo box, can be obtained by calling the **getSelectedItem()** method.

```
private void SelectButtonActionPerformed(java.awt.event.ActionEvent evt) {
      // TODO add your handling code here:
      String query = "SELECT faculty_id, faculty_name, title, office, phone, college, email, fimage " +
                    "FROM Faculty WHERE faculty_name = ?";
      if (ComboMethod.getSelectedItem()=="Runtime Object Method"){
         try{
            DatabaseMetaData dbmd = LogInFrame.con.getMetaData();
            String drName = dbmd.getDriverName();
            String drVersion = dbmd.getDriverVersion();
            msgDlg.setMessage("DriverName is: " + drName + ", Version is: " + drVersion);
            msgDlg.setVisible(true);
A           PreparedStatement pstmt = LogInFrame.con.prepareStatement(query);
B           pstmt.setString(1, ComboName.getSelectedItem().toString());
C           ResultSet rs = pstmt.executeQuery();
D           ResultSetMetaData rsmd = rs.getMetaData();
E           msgDlg.setMessage("Faculty Table has " + rsmd.getColumnCount() + " Columns");
            msgDlg.setVisible(true);
            }
         }
         catch (SQLException e) {
            msgDlg.setMessage("Error in Statement!" + e.getMessage());
            msgDlg.setVisible(true);
         }
      }
}
```

Fig. 6.33 The codes of using the ResultSetMetaData interface

C. The **executeQuery**() method is called to perform the prepared statement to get the queried result. The returned result is assigned to the ResultSet object **rs**.
D. The **getMetaData**() method is executed to query the detailed information about the structure of the Faculty table and properties of the columns in that table. The returned result is assigned to the ResultSetMetaData object **rsmd**.
E. The **msgDlg** is used to test and display the number of columns in the Faculty table.

Although we only use the **getColumnCount()** method to get the total number of columns in the **Faculty** table, in fact, you can use any other method to get more detailed description about the **Faculty** table as you like. Also as we mentioned before, here the **msgDlg** is only for the testing purpose and it can be commented out when the final project is debugged and implemented.

Next let's use this number of columns in our **Faculty** table to retrieve the detailed information for the selected faculty member.

Open the **Select** button Click event handler if it has not been opened, and enter the codes that are in bold and shown in Fig. 6.34 into this event handler.

Let's take a closer look at this added piece of codes to see how it works.

A. First a TextField array is created since we need to combine all seven TextField objects, **FacultyIDField, FacultyNameField, TitleField, OfficeField, PhoneField, CollegeField**, and **EmailField**, into this array and assign the queried results to these TextField objects one by one later to improve the assignment efficiency. Because the definition of the TextField class is different in the basic **java.awt** package and the **javax.swing** package, thus we need to indicate that this TextField belongs to the latter by using the whole package path.

```
    private void SelectButtonActionPerformed(java.awt.event.ActionEvent evt) {
        // TODO add your handling code here:
A       javax.swing.JTextField[] f_field = {FacultyIDField, FacultyNameField, TitleField, OfficeField,
                                            PhoneField, CollegeField, EmailField};
        String query = "SELECT faculty_id, faculty_name, title, office, phone, college, email, fimage " +
                       "FROM Faculty WHERE faculty_name = ?";
        if (ComboMethod.getSelectedItem()=="Runtime Object Method"){
          try{
              DatabaseMetaData dbmd = LogInFrame.con.getMetaData();
              String drName = dbmd.getDriverName();
              String drVersion = dbmd.getDriverVersion();
              msgDlg.setMessage("DriverName is: " + drName + ", Version is: " + drVersion);
              //msgDlg.setVisible(true);
              PreparedStatement pstmt = LogInFrame.con.prepareStatement(query);
              pstmt.setString(1, ComboName.getSelectedItem().toString());
              ResultSet rs = pstmt.executeQuery();
              ResultSetMetaData rsmd = rs.getMetaData();
              msgDlg.setMessage("Faculty Table has " + rsmd.getColumnCount() + " Columns");
              //msgDlg.setVisible(true);
B             while (rs.next()){
C               for (int i=1; i <=rsmd.getColumnCount() - 1; i++) {
                  f_field[i-1].setText(rs.getString(i));
                }
              }
          }
          catch (SQLException e) {
              msgDlg.setMessage("Error in Statement!" + e.getMessage());
              msgDlg.setVisible(true);
          }
        }
    }
```

Fig. 6.34 The codes for the ResultSetMetaData query method

B. As we did before, a **while** loop is used with the **next()** method as the argument to move the data table cursor from the initial position to the first row position in the ResultSet object, to allow us to pick up each column. The terminal column count is minus by one sine the last column is the faculty image and we do not need to display it on these fields.
C. A **for** loop is then used to pick up each column from the returned row and assign each of them to the associated TextField object in the TextField array **f_field**. The upper bound of the columns we used for this **for** loop is obtained from the calling of the **getColumnCount()** method that belongs to the ResultSetMetaData interface. A point to be noted is that the index used to indicate each column in the ResultSet object is different from that used in the TextField array. The former starts from 1, however the latter starts from 0. Therefore, an **i=1** is used for the index in the TextField array.

Now let's develop codes to display an image for the selected faculty.

6.3.5.3 Display an Image for the Selected Faculty in Canvas

There are different ways to store and display images in a database-related project. One professional way is to store all images as binary files in a database with all queried data together. As we did in Chap. 2 when we built our sample database

CSE_DEPT, all faculty members' images have been stored in the **fimage** column as a sequence of binary data in our sample database, exactly in the **Faculty** table.

In this part, we want to use a **File Chooser** object to allow users to select a desired faculty image and display it in a Canvas object, **ImageCanvas**, we added into the **FacultyFrame** Form when we built our **FacultyFrame** Form instance.

Unlike Visual Studio.NET, such as Visual Basic.NET and Visual C#.NET, there is no PictureBox class available in the Java to display an image or a picture. One needs to use a Canvas object as an image holder, a Graphics object as a tool to display an image, and a MediaTracker class as a monitor to coordinate the image processing. In Java, the main package containing the key image processing classes, such as **Image**, **Toolkit**, **Graphics**, and **MediaTracker**, is **java.awt**. Currently, the Java graphics programming library (AWT) supports GIF and JPEG images. Format considerations include local color palettes, feature restrictions (compression, color depth, and interlacing, for example), and dithering.

We divide this section into the following three parts to make the image displaying in Java more illustrative and straightforward:

1) Show the operational sequence to display an image in Java
2) Create a user-defined method **ShowFaculty()** to select and display a desired faculty image
3) Develop the additional codes to coordinate this image displaying

Now let's start with the first part.

6.3.5.3.1 Operational Sequence to Display an Image in Java

Regularly, to display an image in Java, two steps are necessary to be performed:

1) Loading an image from an image file
2) Displaying that image by drawing it in a Graphics context

For example, to load an image named "**faculty.jpg**", use the **getImage()** method that belongs to the Toolkit class and it looks as:

```
Image img = myWindow.getToolkit().getImage("faculty.jpg");
```

where **MyWindow** is a Java GUI container, such as a JFrame, Jdialog, or a JWindow, in which the image will be displayed. The **getToolkit()** method that belongs to the Java GUI container is used to get the Toolkit object. One point to be noted when this instruction is executed is that both Image and Toolkit classes are abstract classes, which means that you cannot directly create new instances by invoking those classes' constructors. Instead, you have to use some methods related to those abstract classes to do that.

After an image is loaded, display the image by drawing it in a Graphics context by using

```
g.drawImage(img, x, y, width, height, imageObserver);
```

where object **g** is an instance of the Graphics class.

As you know, every AWT component object has a Graphics context, and the real drawing is done in the **paint()** method of a component because **paint()** is called by AWT automatically when the image is finished in loading. However, an important issue is that the image loading is an asynchronous process, which means that the loading does not necessarily occur until you attempt to display the image via **drawImage()**. The last parameter to **drawImage()** specifies which component to repaint when the image is finally ready. This is normally the component that calls **drawImage()** in the Java GUI container.

In fact, when the first step – loading an image starts, the **getImage()** method kicks off a new thread to load and fetch the image, and this thread does not start immediately or synchronously as you run this loading method. Instead, this thread will not begin its process until the **drawImage()** method is called. Therefore, it is not guaranteed that the required image will be loaded and ready to be displayed as the **drawImage()** is executed.

In order to solve this asynchronous problem in the image loading and displaying, another image-related class, **MediaTracker**, should be used to monitor and track the running status of the image loading process. The MediaTracker is a utility class designed to track the status of media objects. In theory, media objects could include audio clips and other media as well as images. You can use a media tracker object by instantiating an instance of MediaTracker for the component that you want to be monitored, and invoking its **addImage()** method for each image that you want to track. Each image can be assigned a unique identifier starting from 1, or groups of images can be assigned with the same identifier. You can determine the status of an image or group of images by invoking one of several methods on the MediaTracker object and passing the identifier as a parameter to the method.

Another way you can use the MediaTracker object is that you can cause MediaTracker to block and wait until a specified image or group of images completes loading. We will use this approach in this project to make certain that a desired faculty image has completed loading before we attempt to draw it.

Before we can start this image displaying process with codes, we need first to create a user-defined method to identify, select, and display the desired faculty image via the File Chooser object defined in the Swing windows group.

6.3.5.3.2 Create a User-Defined Method to Select and Display Desired Faculty Image

Open the Code Window of the **FacultyFrame** class by clicking on the **Source** tab from the top of the window, and enter the codes that are shown in Fig. 6.35 to create this new method **ShowFaculty()**.

Let's have a closer look at this piece of codes to see how it works.

```
  private boolean ShowFaculty(Blob bimg) throws SQLException, IOException{
A     Image img;
      int imgId = 1, timeout = 1000;
      FileOutputStream imgOutputStream = null;
      MediaTracker tracker = new MediaTracker(this);
B     String imgPath = System.getProperty("user.dir");
C     String fimgName = ComboName.getSelectedItem().toString() + ".jpg";
D     try {
          imgOutputStream = new FileOutputStream(imgPath + "/" + fimgName);
E       }catch (FileNotFoundException ex) {
            Logger.getLogger(FacultyFrame.class.getName()).log(Level.SEVERE, null, ex);
      }
F     imgOutputStream.write(bimg.getBytes(1, (int)bimg.length()));
G     imgOutputStream.close();
H     img = this.getToolkit().getImage(fimgName);
      Graphics g = ImageCanvas.getGraphics();
I     tracker.addImage(img, imgId);
J     try{
        if(!tracker.waitForID(imgId, timeout)){
          msgDlg.setMessage("Failed to load image");
          msgDlg.setVisible(true);
          return false;
        }
K       }catch(InterruptedException e){
          msgDlg.setMessage(e.toString());
          msgDlg.setVisible(true);
          return false;
        }
L       g.drawImage(img, 0, 0, ImageCanvas.getWidth(), ImageCanvas.getHeight(), this);
        return true;
  }
```

Fig. 6.35 Detailed codes for the user-defined method ShowFaculty()

A. Some local variables and objects used in this method are declared and defined first. The **imgId** and **timeout** are used as the ID of the tracked image and the maximum waiting time for that tracking process. A local Image object **img**, which is used to temporarily hold the selected faculty image, is created and initialized here. Since we need to retrieve our faculty image and store it as an output stream format, thus a **FileOutputStream** object, **imgOutputStream**, is declared and initialized here to null. A new instance of MediaTracker class, **tracker**, is created since we need to use it in this ShowFaculty() method.
B. In order to store our retrieved faculty image into our current project folder, the system method, **getProperty()** with our current directory (**user.dir**), is used and this current folder is assigned to a local string variable **imgPath**.
C. To get the selected faculty image, we need to get the current selected or queried faculty name from the Faculty Name combo box, convert this item to a string and attach a "**.jpg**" as the image file name. We need to use this faculty image name later to store and display this selected faculty image in the Canvas.
D. A **try-catch** block is used to activate and initialize a new instance for the **FileOutputStream** class, **imgOutputStream**, by attaching our current project folder with the name of the selected faculty image since we need to store this image file to that folder, and later on to retrieve it back to display it on our Canvas in this **FacultyFrame** Form. The forward slash **"/"** is necessary to separate the current folder with the image name.

E. Any possible error, including the **file not found** exception, is collected by this catch block.
F. If this **imgOutputStream** instance is initialized successfully, our retrieved faculty image, **bimg**, which is a Blob and passed argument to this **ShowFaculty()** method, is written or stored into our current folder with the selected faculty image name, **fimgName**. This writing operation is performed by executing a method **getBytes()** with the length of this Blob, which means that the entire Blob is retrieved and written byte by byte into our current folder with the image name.
G. This **imgOutputStream** should be closed when this writing operation is completed.
H. To display the selected faculty image, the **getImage()** method that belongs to the abstract class Toolkit is executed to load the selected image. Since the Toolkit class is an abstract class, we used a method **getToolkit()** to create it instead of generating it by invoking its constructor. The **getGraphics()** method is called to get a Graphics context and our **ImageCanvas** works as an image holder for this faculty image.
I. The **addImage()** method that belongs to the MediaTracker class is called to add our image with its ID into the tracking system.
J. A **try catch** block is used to begin this tracking process and the **waitForID()** method is called to execute this tracking. If a timeout occurred for this tracking process, which means that the selected faculty image has not been loaded into the project, a warning message is displayed using our MsgDialog object.
K. Any possible exception or error will be caught by the **catch** block and to be displayed in our **msgDlg** dialog.
L. If no timeout error happened, which means that the selected faculty image has been loaded into our project and ready to be displayed, the **drawImage()** method is executed to display it in the FacultyFrame Form window. We want to display this image starting from the origin of the Canvas object, which is the upper-left corner of the canvas (0, 0), with a width and height that are identical with those of the canvas. Therefore, the **getWidth()** and **getHeight()** methods are called to get both of them from the canvas object. A **true** is returned to the main program to indicate that the execution of this method is successful.

Now we have finished coding process for this method. Next let's finish the coding process to call this user-defined method to select and display the selected faculty image by adding the additional codes into the **Select** button event handler.

6.3.5.3.3 Develop Additional Codes to Coordinate This Image Displaying

Open the Design View of our **FacultyFrame** Form by clicking on the **Design** tab from the top of the window, and double click on the **Select** button to open its event handler. Add the codes that are in bold and shown in Fig. 6.36 into this handler.

```
  private void SelectButtonActionPerformed(java.awt.event.ActionEvent evt) {
A     Blob fimgBlob = null;
      javax.swing.JTextField[] f_field = {FacultyIDField,FacultyNameField,TitleField,OfficeField, PhoneField,
                                          CollegeField,EmailField};
      String query = "SELECT faculty_id, faculty_name, title, office, phone, college, email, fimage " +
                     "FROM Faculty WHERE faculty_name = ?";
      if (ComboMethod.getSelectedItem()=="Runtime Object Method"){
         try{
             PreparedStatement pstmt = LogInFrame.con.prepareStatement(query);
             pstmt.setString(1, ComboName.getSelectedItem().toString());
             ResultSet rs = pstmt.executeQuery();
             ResultSetMetaData rsmd = rs.getMetaData();
             while (rs.next()){
B               for (int i = 1; i <=rsmd.getColumnCount(); i++) {
C                  if (i == rsmd.getColumnCount()){
                      fimgBlob = rs.getBlob("fimage");
                      break;
                   }
                   f_field[i-1].setText(rs.getString(i));
                }
             }
D        } catch (SQLException e) {
             msgDlg.setMessage("Error in Statement!" + e.getMessage());
             msgDlg.setVisible(true);
         }
      }
E     try {
          if (!ShowFaculty(fimgBlob)){
             msgDlg.setMessage("No matched faculty image found!");
             msgDlg.setVisible(true);
          }
F     } catch (SQLException | IOException ex) {
          Logger.getLogger(FacultyFrame.class.getName()).log(Level.SEVERE, null, ex);
      }
  }
```

Fig. 6.36 The new added codes to the Select button Click event handler

Let's have a closer look at these new added codes to see how they perform their works.

A. Some new local variable and object are added and declared here, which include a Blob object, **fimgBlob**, and it is used to hold the retrieved faculty image that exactly is a Binary Large Object (Blob) used in Java database programming techniques.

B. A modification is made for this **for** loop, which is that the terminating count number is changed to our max column number, 8, by removing the original minus-1 since we need to get the last column, which is the faculty image column, **fimage**.
C. As the **for** loop works, it picks up all first seven columns and assign them to the related TextFields to display queried faculty information, until it gets the last column, which is the faculty image column. Then we need to use **getBlob()** method to retrieve this image as a binary large object and assign it to our local object **fimgBlob**.
D. The **catch** block is used to collect any SQL program-related errors.
E. The **ShowFaculty()** method is called with the selected faculty image **fimgBlob** as the argument to pick up and display the selected faculty image in the Canvas.

This method should return a Boolean value to indicate whether it is executed successfully or not. A true means that this method is executed successfully, otherwise a false is returned and is displayed in our **MsgDialog**.

F. Since this **ShowFaculty()** method contains a Blob object as its argument, thus a **try-catch** block is used to throw any possible SQLException error if it did occur.

Another piece of coordinating codes to be added into this FacultyFrame Form is the related Import commands for all new classes we used, such as **FileOutputStream**, **IOException**, and **FileNotFoundException**. Add these Imports commands on the top of this FacultyFrame Form code window, as shown in Fig. 6.37. An easy way to add these Imports clauses is to right click on the code window, and select the **Fix Imports** item from the popup menu.

The final coding job for this FacultyFrame class is the **Back** button Click event handler. This coding is very easy and the FacultyFrame object should be closed and disposed as the user clicks on this button, and the control should be directed to the SelectionFrame Form to allow users to continue selecting other functions.

6.3.5.4 Develop the Codes for the Back Button Click Event Handler

The coding for this event handler is simple. The FacultyFrame Form window should be closed and removed from the screen as this button is clicked by the user. Open the **Back** button Click event handler and enter the codes that are shown in Fig. 6.38 into this event handler.

Both the **setVisible()** and the **dispose()** methods are called to close and remove this FacultyFrame Form window as this button is clicked.

Now we can build and run our project to test the functionalities of the **LogInFrame** Form, **SelectionFrame** Form, and **FacultyFrame** Form. Click on the **Clean and Build Main Project** button on the toolbar to build our project, and click on the **Run Main Project** button from the toolbar to run our project. Select **SQLSelectObjectPackage.LogInFrame** as the main class set for our project, and click on the **OK** button to run our project.

```
package SQLSelectObjectPackage;
import java.awt.*;
import java.io.FileNotFoundException;
import java.io.FileOutputStream;
import java.io.IOException;
import java.sql.*;
import java.util.logging.Level;
import java.util.logging.Logger;
/**
 *
 * @author yingb
 */
```

Fig. 6.37 The added Imports clauses

```
private void BackButtonActionPerformed(java.awt.event.ActionEvent evt) {
        // TODO add your handling code here:
        this.setVisible(false);
        this.dispose();
}
```

Fig. 6.38 The codes for the Back button Click event handler

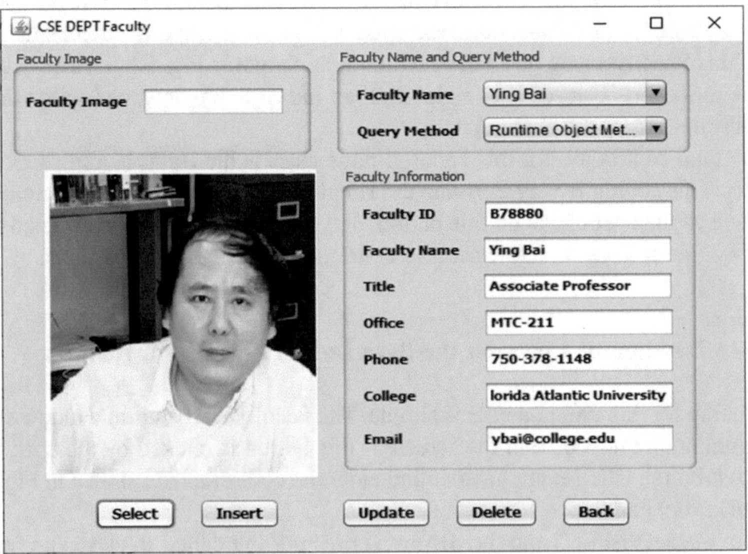

Fig. 6.39 A running result of the project

Enter the correct username and password, such as **jhenry** and **test** to the **LogInFrame** to complete the login process. Select the **Faculty Information** from the **SelectionFrame** Form window to open the **FacultyFrame** Form window. Select the default faculty member **Ying Bai** from the Faculty Name combo box and the **Runtime Object Method** from the Query Method combo box, and click on the **Select** button to get detailed information for this selected faculty.

Immediately the detailed information of the selected faculty is displayed in seven text fields with the faculty image, which is shown in Fig. 6.39. You can try to select other faculty members to perform different queries to test the function of this form.

Click on the **Back** and the **Exit** buttons to terminate our project.

But wait for moment, the story is not finished. As we discussed in Sect. 6.3.3.5, both **executeQuery()** and **execute()** methods can be used to perform a data query operation; however, the **execute()** method is more popular since it can perform not only a query-related action, but also a non-query-related action. In the next section, we will discuss how to use the **execute()** method to perform a query-related action against our sample database.

6.3.5.5 Query Data Using the execute() Method to Perform a Query-Related Action

As we mentioned in Sect. 6.3.3.5, the **execute()** method will not return any result itself, and one needs to use either **getResultSet()** or **getUpdateCount()** method to pick up the results. Both methods belong to the Statement class. The key point is:

- The **getResultSet()** method will return a null if the running result is an integer, which is a number of rows that have been affected, either inserted, updated, or deleted.
- The **getUpdateCount()** method will return a -1 if the running result is a ResultSet.

Based on these two key points, we can easily determine whether a result is a ResultSet or an integer.

Now let's modify the codes in the **Select** button Click event handler to use the **execute()** method to perform this data query. Open the **Select** button Click event handler and add the codes that are in bold and shown in Fig. 6.40 into this event handler.

Let's have a closer look at this piece of new added codes to see how it works.

A. If the user selected the **Java execute() Method** from the Query Method combo box, a **try…catch** block is used to create a prepared statement using the **prepareStatement()** method with the query string as the argument. Then the **setString()** method is used to setup the positional dynamic parameter, which is obtained from the ComboName combo box and selected by the user.
B. The **execute()** method is called to perform this data query. The advantage of using this method is that both a query-related action and a non-query-related action can be performed by using this method. The disadvantage of using this method is that the running result cannot be determined when this method is done since this method can execute either a data query and return a ResultSet object or an updating, insertion, and deleting action and return an integer.
C. Suppose we do not know what kind of data will be returned by running this **execute()** method, we assume that a non-query-related action has been performed by calling this method. So we try to use the **getUpdateCount()** method to pick up the running result, which is supposed to be an integer.
D. If the returned result of calling of the **getUpdateCount()** method is -1, which means that the running result of the **execute()** method is not an integer, instead it is a ResultSet object, The **getResultSet()** method will be called to pick up that result.
E. A **while** loop combined with the **next()** method is used to move the cursor to point to the first row of the data stored in the returned ResultSet object. Also a **for** loop is used to pick up each column obtained from the Faculty table and assign each of them to the associated text field to display them. The eighth's column **fimage** is a faculty image, and it is assigned to the local object **fimgBlob** to be temporarily stored in there.

```
private void SelectButtonActionPerformed(java.awt.event.ActionEvent evt) {
    Blob fimgBlob = null;
    javax.swing.JTextField[] f_field = {FacultyIDField,FacultyNameField,TitleField,OfficeField, PhoneField,
                                        CollegeField,EmailField};
    String query = "SELECT faculty_id, faculty_name, title, office, phone, college, email, fimage " +
                   "FROM Faculty WHERE faculty_name = ?";
    if (ComboMethod.getSelectedItem()=="Runtime Object Method"){
      try{
          PreparedStatement pstmt = LogInFrame.con.prepareStatement(query);
          pstmt.setString(1, ComboName.getSelectedItem().toString());
          ResultSet rs = pstmt.executeQuery();
          ResultSetMetaData rsmd = rs.getMetaData();
          while (rs.next()){
            for (int i = 1; i <=rsmd.getColumnCount(); i++) {
              if (i == rsmd.getColumnCount()){
                 fimgBlob = rs.getBlob("fimage"); break;
              }
              f_field[i-1].setText(rs.getString(i));
            }
          }
      } catch (SQLException e) {
          msgDlg.setMessage("Error in Statement!" + e.getMessage());
          msgDlg.setVisible(true);
      }
    }
A   if (ComboMethod.getSelectedItem()=="Java execute() Method"){
      try{
            PreparedStatement pstmt = LogInFrame.con.prepareStatement(query);
            pstmt.setString(1, ComboName.getSelectedItem().toString());
B           pstmt.execute();
C           int updateCount = pstmt.getUpdateCount();
D           if (updateCount == -1){
              ResultSet rs = pstmt.getResultSet();
              ResultSetMetaData rsmd = rs.getMetaData();
E             while (rs.next()){
                for (int i=1; i <=rsmd.getColumnCount(); i++){
                   if (i == rsmd.getColumnCount()){
                      fimgBlob = rs.getBlob("fimage"); break;
                }
                 f_field[i-1].setText(rs.getString(i));
                }
              }
            }
F           else{
              msgDlg.setMessage("execute() method returned an integer!");
              msgDlg.setVisible(true);
            }
          }
G         catch (SQLException e) {
             msgDlg.setMessage("Error in Statement!" + e.getMessage());
             msgDlg.setVisible(true);   }
      }
      try {
          if (!ShowFaculty(fimgBlob)){
             msgDlg.setMessage("No matched faculty image found!");
             msgDlg.setVisible(true);
          }
      } catch (SQLException | IOException ex) {
         Logger.getLogger(FacultyFrame.class.getName()).log(Level.SEVERE, null, ex);
      }
}
```

Fig. 6.40 The codes for the execute() method

F. If the returned result from running of the **execute()** method is not -1, which means that a non-query-related action has been performed, the **msgDlg** is used to display this situation.

G. The **catch** block is used to track and monitor any possible error that occurred during this query operation and display it if any error has occurred.

Now you can re-build our project and run it to test this piece of new added codes. Select the **Java execute() Method** from the Query Method combo box as the FacultyFrame Form is opened, and click on the **Select** button to test the function of this new coding.

Next let's move to the **CourseFrame** class to build some data actions using the Callable Statement method to query detailed information for the courses taught by the selected faculty and related course information.

6.3.5.6 Query Data Using the CallableStatement Method

The JDBC CallableStatement method provides a way to allow us to call a stored procedure to perform a complicated query. The speed and efficiency of a data query can be significantly improved by using the stored procedure since it is built in the database side. A more detailed discussion of developing and implementing the CallableStatement method will be given in the next section for the CourseFrame class.

6.3.6 Perform the Data Query for the Course Table

As we discussed, the function of this CourseFrame Form is to allow users to get all courses taught by the selected faculty member and detailed information for each course. First, all courses, exactly all **course_id**, taught by the selected faculty member from the Faculty Name combo box will be displayed in the **Course ID** List listbox as the user clicks on the **Select** button. Second, the detailed information for each course (**course_id**) selected from the Course ID List listbox will be displayed in six text fields as each **course_id** is clicked by the user.

In this section, only two buttons, **Select** and **Back**, are used for this **CourseFrame** Form and the **Insert** button will be used later for the data insertion query.

The codes development in this section can be divided into the following four parts:

1) Importing some necessary Java packages and coding for the constructor of the **CourseFrame** class to perform some initialization processes.
2) Coding for the **Select** button Click event handler to perform a **CallableStatement** to run a stored procedure to query data from the **Course** table in our sample database.
3) Coding for the **CourseList** box to handle an event when a **course_id** in the CourseList box is selected to display the detailed information for that **course_id** in six text fields.
4) Coding for the **Back** button Click event handler to close the **CourseFrame** Form window

and return the control to the **SelectionFrame** Form.

Now let's start with the first part.

6.3.6.1 Import Java Packages and Coding for the CourseFrame Constructor

Open the Code Window of the **CourseFrame** class by clicking on the **Source** tab from the top of the window and add the codes that are shown in Fig. 6.41 into this source file.

Let's have a closer look at this piece of codes to see how it works.

A. The **java.sql.*** package is added into this file since we need to use some JDBC API classes and interfaces that are located in that package.
B. A class-level object **msgDlg**, which is an instance of the JDialog class, is created since we need to use it to display some debug and exception information to track and monitor the running status of our project during its running.
C. Three query methods are added into the Query Method combo box to enable users to perform different queries with desired methods. In this project, we only take care of the third method, **JPA Callable Method**.
D. Eight faculty members are also added into the Faculty Name combo box to allow users to select all courses taught by the different faculty members.

Next let's have a detailed discussion about the CallableStatement method.

```
   package SQLSelectObjectPackage;
A  import java.sql.*;
   public class CourseFrame extends javax.swing.JFrame {
B    MsgDialog msgDlg = new MsgDialog(new javax.swing.JFrame(), true);
     /** Creates new form CourseFrame */
     public CourseFrame() {
       initComponents();
       this.setLocationRelativeTo(null);
C      ComboMethod.addItem("Runtime Object Method");
       ComboMethod.addItem("Java execute Method");
       ComboMethod.addItem("Java Callable Method");
D      ComboName.addItem("Ying Bai");
       ComboName.addItem("Davis Bhalla");
       ComboName.addItem("Black Anderson");
       ComboName.addItem("Steve Johnson");
       ComboName.addItem("Jenney King");
       ComboName.addItem("Alice Brown");
       ComboName.addItem("Debby Angles");
       ComboName.addItem("Jeff Henry");
     }
```

Fig. 6.41 The coding for the constructor of the CourseFrame class

6.3.6.2 Query Data From Course Table Using CallableStatements

When a faculty member has been selected from the Faculty Name combo box and the **Select** button is clicked by the user, all courses (**course_id**) taught by the selected faculty member should be displayed in the Course ID List listbox. As we know, there is no **faculty_name** column available in the **Course** table, instead, the only connection between each course and the faculty who teaches that course is the **faculty_id**, which is a foreign key in the **Course** table. Therefore, in order to get the **course_id** that is taught by the selected faculty, two queries are needed to be performed; first, we need to perform a query to the **Faculty** table to get the **faculty_id** based on the selected faculty name, and second, we can perform another query to the **Course** table to get all **course_id** based on the **faculty_id** obtained from the first query.

To save time and space, a good solution for these two queries is to combine both of them into a stored procedure. As you know, stored procedures are developed and built inside a database. The execution speed and efficiency of stored procedures can be significantly improved compared with a normal query. In JDBC API, a CallableStatement interface is used for this purpose.

As we discussed in the last section, compared with the Statement interface, the advantage of using a PreparedStatement interface is that it can perform a dynamic query with some known or unknown dynamic parameters as inputs. Most time, those dynamic parameters are input parameters and can be defined as **IN** variables. However, you do not need to specify those parameters with an **IN** keyword when using a PreparedStatement interface.

The difference between the **PreparedStatement** and the **CallableStatement** interfaces is: unlike the PreparedStatement interface, the CallableStatement interface has both input and output parameters, which are indicated with **IN** and **OUT** keywords, respectively. In order to setup values for input parameters or get values for the output parameters, you have to use either a **setXXX()** method or a **getXXX()** method to do that. However, the point is that before you can use any **getXXX()** method to pick up the values of output parameters, you must first register the output parameters to allow the **CallableStatement** interface to know them.

Generally, the sequence to run a CallableStatement to call a stored procedure is:

1) Build and formulate the CallableStatement query string
2) Create a CallableStatement object
3) Set the input parameters
4) Register the output parameters
5) Execute CallableStatement
6) Retrieve the running result by using different **getXXX()** methods

Let's discuss this issue in more detail in the following sections.

6.3.6.2.1 Build and Formulate the CallableStatement Query String

The CallableStatement interface is used to execute SQL stored procedures. The JDBC API provides a stored procedure SQL escape syntax that allows stored procedures to be called in a standard way for all RDBMSs. This escape syntax has one form that includes an output parameter and one that does not. If used, the output parameter must be registered as an **OUT** parameter. The other parameters can be used for input, output, or both. Parameters are referred to sequentially, by number, with the first parameter being 1.

```
{?= call <procedure-name>[<arg1>,<arg2>, ...]}
{call <procedure-name>[<arg1>,<arg2>, ...]}
```

Two syntaxes are widely used to formulate a CallableStatement string: the SQL92 syntax and the Oracle syntax. The SQL92 syntax is more popular in most applications. We will concentrate on the SQL92 syntax in this section, and take care of the Oracle syntax in some other sources when we build data queries for the Oracle database.

For a standard alone stored procedure or packaged procedure, the SQL92 syntax can be represented as:

```
{call [schema.][package.]procedure_name[(?, ?, …)]}
```

For standard alone functions or packaged functions, the SQL92 syntax looks like:

```
{? = call [schema.][package.]function_name[(?, ?, …)]}
```

The definition and meaning of elements used in these syntaxes are:

- All elements enclosed inside the square brackets [] means that they are optional.
- The curly braces { } are necessary in building a CallableStatement string and they must be used to cover the whole string.
- The schema indicates the schema in which the stored procedure is created.
- The package indicates the name of the package if the stored procedure is involved in a package.
- The **procedure_name** or the **function_name** indicate the name of the stored procedure or the function.
- The question make ? is the place holder for either an **IN, IN/OUT** or **OUT** parameters used in the stored procedure, or the returned value of a function. The order of these placeholders, which starts from 1, is very important, and it must be followed exactly when using either a **setXXX()** method to setup input parameters or register the output parameters for the built CallableStatement string later.

A CallableStatement can either return a ResultSet object and multiple ResultSet objects by using **executeQuery()** method or return nothing by using **execute()** method. Multiple ResultSet objects are handled using operations inherited from

Statement. A suitable **getXXX()** method is needed to pick up the running result from the execution of a CallableStatement.

6.3.6.2.2 Create a CallableStatement Object

To create a CallableStatement object, you need to use one of the methods defined in the Connection class, **prepareCall()**, to do that. When the SQL92 syntax is used to create this CallableStatement object, it will look like:

```
CallableStatement cstmt = null;
try{
        String query = "{call dbo.FacultyCourse(?, ?)}";
        cstmt = LogInFrame.con.prepareCall(query);
        .........
```

The operation sequence of this piece of codes to create a new CallableStatement object is:

1) A new null CallableStatement object **cstmt** is first declared.
2) A **try** block is used to create the query string with the SQL92 syntax. The name of the stored procedure to be called is **dbo.FacultyCourse()** with two arguments: the first one is an input parameter, **faculty_name** and the second one is an output parameter used to store all **course_id** taught by the selected faculty. Both parameters are represented by placeholders and they are positional parameters.
3) The CallableStatement object is created by calling the **prepareCall()** method, which belongs to the Connection class, with the query string as the argument.

Next let's take a look at how to setup the input parameter for this object.

6.3.6.2.3 Set the Input Parameters

All input parameters used for a CallableStatement interface must be clearly bound to the associated **IN** parameters in a stored procedure by using a **setXXX()** method. This **setXXX()** method can be divided into three categories based on the different data types:

1) The primitive data type method
2) The object method
3) The stream method

For the primitive and the object method, the syntax is identical, and the difference between them is the type of value that is assigned. For the stream method, both the syntax and the data types are different.

Set Primitive Data Type and Object IN Values

The primitive data type means all built-in data types used in Java programming language. The syntax of setting a primitive data type or an object value method is,

```
setXXX(int position, data_type value);
```

where **XXX** means the associated value type to be assigned, the **position** that is an integer is used to indicate the relative position of the **IN** parameter in the SQL statement or the SQL stored procedure, and the **value** is the actual data value to be assigned to the **IN** parameter.

Some popular **setXXX()** methods are:

```
setBoolean(), setByte(), setInt(), setDouble(), setFloat(),
setLong(), setShort(), setString(),
setObject(), setDate(), setTime() and setTimeStamp()
```

An example of using the **setXXX()** method is:

```
String query = "SELECT product, order_date FROM Order " +
               "WHERE order_id = ? AND customer = ?";
PreparedStatement pstmt = con.prepareStatement(query);
setInt(1, 101);
setString(2, "Tom Johnson");
```

Two dynamic parameters are used in the query string and both of them are **IN** parameters. The data type of the first **IN** parameter is an integer and the second one is a String, and both are represented by a placeholder '?'. The first setting method, **setInt(1, 101)**, is to assign an integer value of 101 to the first **IN** parameter, which is indicated with a position number of 1, and the second setting method, **setString(2, "Tom Johnson")** is to assign a String value "**Tom Johnson**" to the second **IN** parameter, which is indicated with a position number of 2.

From this example, you can find that there is no difference between setting a primitive parameter and an object value to the **IN** parameters in a SQL statement.

Set Object Methods

The **setObject()** method has three protocols, which are:

```
setObject(int position, object_type object_value);
setObject(int position, object_type object_value, data_type desired_data_type);
setobject(int position, object_type object_value, data_type desired_data_
type, int scale);
```

The first one is straightforward and it contains two parameters: the first one is the relative position of the **IN** parameter in the SQL statement, and the second one is the value of a desired object to be assigned to the **IN** object.

The second one adds one more input parameter, **desired_data_type**, and it is used to indicate a data type to which convert the object to.

The third one adds the fourth input parameter, **scale**, and it is used to make sure that the object conversion result contains a certain number of digits.

An example of the **setObject()** method is shown here,

```
pstmt.setObject(2, 101);
pstmt.setObject(2, 101, Type.FLOAT);
pstmt.setObject(2, 101, Type.FLOAT, 2);
```

The first method is to set an input parameter, which is the second one in a SQL statement, to an object (here is an integer) with a value of 101. The next method is to set the same input to the same object; however, it needs to convert the object (integer) to a float data type. The final method performs the same operation as the previous one, but it indicates that the conversion result should contain at least 2 digits.

Set Stream IN Methods

When transferring images between an application and a database, it needs a large size for the **IN** parameters. In that situation, an **InputStream()** method should be used to perform that kind of operation. The syntax of using this method is:

```
setXXXStream(int position, data_type input_stream, int number_of_bytes);
```

where **XXX** means the InputStream type: ASCII, Binary, or Unicode. The first parameter is the relative position of the **IN** parameter in the SQL statement, and the second parameter is the data stream to be read from. The third parameter indicates the number of bytes to be read from the data stream at a time.

A simple example of using the **InputStream()** method is:

```
FileInputStream picFile = new FileInputStraem("new_file");
String query = "INSERT INTO picture (image) VALUES (?) WHERE pic_id = 101 ";
PreparedStatement pstmt = prepareStatement(query);
pstmt.setUnicodeStream(1, picFile, 2048);
```

This piece of code is used to set the first **IN** parameter to read 2KB bytes from a picture file, which is a Unicode file, named **picFile** at a time.

6.3.6.2.4 Register the Output Parameters

As we discussed in Sect. 6.3.6.2, after a CallableStatement interface is executed, you need to use the associated **getXXX()** method to pick up the running result from the CallableStatement object since it cannot return any result itself. However, before you can do that, you must first register any output parameter in the SQL statement to allow the CallableStatement to know that the output result is involved and stored in the related output parameters in the SQL statement.

Once an output parameter is registered, the parameter is considered an **OUT** parameter and it can contain running results that can be picked up by using the associated **getXXX()** method.

To register an output parameter, the **registerOutParameter()** method that belongs to the **CallableStatement** interface should be used to declare what SQL type the **OUT** parameter will return. A point to be noted is that a parameter in a SQL statement can be defined as both an **IN** and an **OUT** at the same time, which means that you can setup this parameter as an **IN** by using the **setXXX()** method, and also you can register this parameter as an **OUT** using the **registerOutParameter()** method at the same time. In this way, this parameter can be considered as an **IN/OUT** parameter with both the input and the output functions.

The syntax to register an output parameter is:

```
registerOutParameter(int position, data_type SQL_data_type);
```

where the **position** is still the relative position of the **OUT** parameter in the SQL statement, and the **SQL_data_type** is the SQL data type of the **OUT** parameter, which can be found from the JDBC API class, **java.sql.TYPE**.

An example of using this method is shown here:

```
String query = "{call dbo.FacultyCourse(?, ?)}";
cstmt = LogInFrame.con.prepareCall(query);
cstmt.setString(1, ComboName.getSelectedItem().toString());
cstmt.setString(2, "CSC-230A");
cstmt.registerOutParameter(2, java.sql.Types.VARCHAR);
```

There are two parameters in this CallableStatement interface in this example. The first one is an **IN** parameter, which is set by using the **setString()** method. The second one is an **IN/OUT** parameter, which is the first setup by using the **setString()** method and then registered by using the **registerOutParameter()** method with the data type of **VARCHAR**. The SQL data type **VARCHAR** can be mapped to a data type of String in Java. Refer to Appendix E to get more detailed information about the data type mapping between the SQL and Java.

An interesting point to this **registerOutParameter()** method is that all **OUT** parameters can be registered by using this syntax except those **OUT** parameters with the **NUMERIC** and **DECIMAL** data types. The syntax to register those **OUT** parameters look like:

```
registerOutParameter(int position, data_type SQL_data_type, int scale);
```

The only difference is that a third parameter **scale** is added and it is used to indicate the number of digits to the right of the decimal point for the **OUT** parameter.

6.3.6.2.5 Execute CallableStatement

To run a CallableStatement object, three methods can be used; **executeQuery()**, **executeUpdate()**, and **execute()**. As we discussed in Sect. 6.3.3.5, the **executeQuery()** method can return a ResultSet object that contains the running or query results; however, the **execute()** method cannot return any running result with itself, and you need to use associated **getXXX()** methods to pick up the query or running result. Another important point of using the **execute()** method is that it can handle an unknown result with undefined data type. Refer to Sects. 6.3.3.5 and 6.3.5.5 to get more detailed information about the **execute()** method.

An example of using the **execute()** method to run the CallableStatement object is:

```
String query = "{call dbo.FacultyCourse(?, ?)}";
cstmt = LogInFrame.con.prepareCall(query);
cstmt.setString(1, ComboName.getSelectedItem().toString());
cstmt.registerOutParameter(2, java.sql.Types.VARCHAR);
cstmt.execute();
```

Now let's handle how to retrieve the running result from the execution of a CallableStatement object.

6.3.6.2.6 Retrieve the Running Result

To pick up the running results from the execution of a CallableStatement object, one needs to use an associated **getXXX()** method to do that. Two popular ways to get back a running result from a CallableStatement are: **getXXX()** method and **getObject()** method. The former is based on the returned data type of the result, and the latter is more general to get any kind of result.

All of the **getXXX()** methods and **getObject()** use the same syntax, which looks like:

```
getXXX(int position);
getObject(int position);
```

where **XXX** indicates the **OUT** value Java data type and the position is the relative position of the **OUT** parameter in the SQL statement. Same syntax is used for the **getObject()** method.

An example of using **getXXX()** method to pick up the running result from the execution of a CallableStatement object is shown below:

```
  private void SelectButtonActionPerformed(java.awt.event.ActionEvent evt) {
      // TODO add your handling code here:
A     if (ComboMethod.getSelectedItem()=="Java Callable Method"){
         CallableStatement cstmt;
         try{
B            String query = "{call dbo.FacultyCourse(?, ?)}";
C            cstmt = LogInFrame.con.prepareCall(query);
D            cstmt.setString(1, ComboName.getSelectedItem().toString());
E            cstmt.registerOutParameter(2, java.sql.Types.VARCHAR);
F            cstmt.execute();
G            String cResult = cstmt.getString(2);
H            //String cResult = (String)cstmt.getObject(2);
I           String[] result = cResult.split(",");
J           CourseList.setListData(result);
         }
K        catch (SQLException e){
            msgDlg.setMessage("Error in CallableStatement! " + e.getMessage());
            msgDlg.setVisible(true);
         }
      }
  }
```

Fig. 6.42 The codes for the Select button Click event handler

```
String query = "{call dbo.FacultyCourse(?, ?)}";
cstmt = LogInFrame.con.prepareCall(query);
cstmt.setString(1, ComboName.getSelectedItem().toString());
cstmt.registerOutParameter(2, java.sql.Types.VARCHAR);
cstmt.execute();
String cResult = cstmt.getString(2);
```

Since the **OUT** parameter is a String and is located at position of 2, therefore an argument of 2 is used in the **getString()** method to pick up the running result. An alternative way to get the same running result is to use the **getObject()** method, which looks like:

```
String cResult = (String)cstmt.getObject(2);
```

The returned result must be casted by using the String data type since an object can be any data type.

Ok, that is enough for the theoretical discussion, now let's go to our real staff, developing the codes for the Select button Click event handler to perform this CallableStatement object to call a SQL stored procedure to make the course query from our Course table in our sample database.

6.3.6.3 Coding for the Select Button Click Event Handler to Perform CallableStatement Query

Open the **CourseFrame** Form window by clicking on the **Design** tab from the top of the window, then open the **Select** button Click event handler by double clicking on the **Select** button. Enter the codes that are shown in Fig. 6.42 into this event handler.

Let's have a closer look at this piece of codes to see how it works.

A. First we need to check whether a Java Callable Method has been selected or not. If it is, a new null object of the CallableStatement class, **cstmt**, is created.
B. A **try…catch** block is used to perform this CallableStatement query. A SQL92 syntax is used to build a query string to try to call a SQL stored procedure **dbo. FacultyCourse**, which will be developed in the next section, to query all courses, exactly all **course_id**, taught by the selected faculty member. Two parameters are used in this SQL statement; the first one is an **IN** parameter, **faculty_name** obtained from the Faculty Name combo box **ComboName**, and the second one is an **OUT** parameter that contains all **course_id** taught by the selected faculty member.
C. The real CallableStatement object is created by calling the **prepareCall()** method and assigned to the null object **cstmt** we created in step **A**. One point to be noted is that the **prepareCall()** method belongs to the Connection class; therefore, we need to call our Connection object **con**, which is a class instance defined in the **LogInFrame** class, to perform this creation.
D. The first parameter in this SQL statement is a String **faculty_name**, which is an **IN** parameter and bound using the **setString()** method. The value of this input parameter is obtained by calling the **getSelectedItem()** method from the Faculty Name combo box **ComboName**.
E. The second parameter in this query string, which is an **OUT** parameter and contains all queried **course_id** taught by the selected faculty member, is registered using the **registerOutParameter()** method. The SQL data type of this **OUT** parameter is **VARCHAR**.
F. The **CallableStatement** object is executed by calling the **execute()** method.
G. The **getString()** method is used to pick up the running result with a position of 2. The SQL data type **VARCHAR** can be mapped to a String in Java (refer to Appendix E).
H. An alternative way to pick up this running result is to use the **getObject()** method. However, it must be casted to a String object before it can be picked up.
I. The running result stored in the **cResult** contains all **course_id** that are separated by a comma, so the **split()** method is executed to separate each of **course_id** and assign them to a String array **result**.
J. The **setListData()** method is used to add all **course_id** that are stored in the String array **result** into the Course ID List listbox, **CourseList**, to display them.
K. The **catch** block is used to catch any possible errors and display them if they indeed occurred.

Now that we have a clear picture about the coding for the CallableStatement in the Java side, let's begin to deal with the stored procedure in the SQL side.

6.3.6.4 Build the SQL Stored Procedure dbo.FacultyCourse

Stored Procedures are nothing more than functions or procedures applied in any project developed in any programming language. This means that stored procedures can be considered as functions or subroutines, and they can be called easily with any arguments and they can also return any data with certain type. One can integrate multiple SQL statements into a single stored procedure to perform multiple queries at a time, and those statements will be pre-compiled by the SQL Server to form an integrated target body. In this way, the pre-compiled body is insulated with your coding developed in Java environment. You can easily call the stored procedure from your Java application project as the project runs. The result of using the stored procedure is that the performance of your data-driven application can be greatly increased and the data query's speed can be significantly improved. Also when you develop a stored procedure, the database server automatically creates an execution plan for that procedure, and the developed plan can be updated automatically whenever a modification is made to that procedure by the database server.

Regularly there are three types of stored procedures: System stored procedures, extended stored procedures, and custom stored procedures. The system stored procedures are developed and implemented for administrating, managing, configuring, and monitoring the SQL server. The extended stored procedures are developed and applied in the dynamic linked library (dll) format. This kind of stored procedures can improve the running speed and save the running space since they can be dynamically linked to your project. The custom stored procedures are developed and implemented by users for their applications.

Some possible ways can be used to create a stored procedure.

1) Using SQL Server Enterprise Manager
2) Using Visual Studio.NET – Real-Time Coding Method
3) Using Visual Studio.NET – Server Explorer

For our current application, I prefer to use the Server Explorer in Visual Studio. NET. A more complicated but flexible way to create the stored procedure is to use the real-time coding method from Visual Studio.NET. In this section, we will concentrate on the fifth method listed above.

```
CREATE PROCEDURE [dbo].[Stored Procedure's name]

        @Param1's name    Param1's data type  Input/Output,
        @Param2's name    Param2's data type  Input/Output
        .......
AS
    (DECLARE Your local variables.... If you have)
    (Your SQL Statements)
    RETURN
```

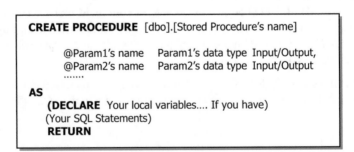

Fig. 6.43 The structure and syntax of a SQL stored procedure

```
CREATE PROCEDURE [dbo].[StudentInfo]

    @StudentName  VARCHAR(50)

AS
    SELECT student_id FROM Student
    WHERE name LIKE @StudentName
    RETURN
```

Fig. 6.44 An example of a SQL stored procedure

6.3.6.4.1 Structure and Syntax of a SQL Stored Procedure

The prototype or syntax of creating a SQL stored procedure is shown in Fig. 6.43.

For SQL Server database, the name of the stored procedure is always prefixed by the schema **dbo**. A sample stored procedure StudentInfo is shown in Fig. 6.44.

The parameters declared inside the braces are either input or output parameters used for this stored procedure, and an @ symbol must be prefixed before the parameter in the SQL Server database. Any argument sent from the calling procedure to this stored procedure should be declared in here. The other variables, which are created by using the keyword DECLARE located after the keyword AS, are local variables and they can only be used in this stored procedure. The keyword RETURN is used to return the queried data columns.

6.3.6.4.2 Return Multiple Rows from a SQL Stored Procedure to the Java CallableStatement

As we know, in a SQL stored procedure, regularly only one piece of data or one row can be returned to the calling procedure. In order to return multiple rows, a cursor must be used to hold those multiple data rows. A cursor works as a data table and it can hold data in a certain format. A problem is that there is no mapped data type for the cursor in the Java environment! Therefore, we cannot use the cursor to return the queried result from a SQL stored procedure to our Java applications. When we perform a query to our **Course** table to get multiple courses taught by the selected faculty, we need to return multiple rows or multiple **course_id** to our Java CourseFrame class.

In JDBC API 4.0, it indeed added more components to facilitate the interface between the SQL Server database and Java applications; however, unfortunately, it still has not covered this topic. To solve this problem and allow multiple rows to be returned from a SQL stored procedure to the Java applications, we need to perform the following operations:

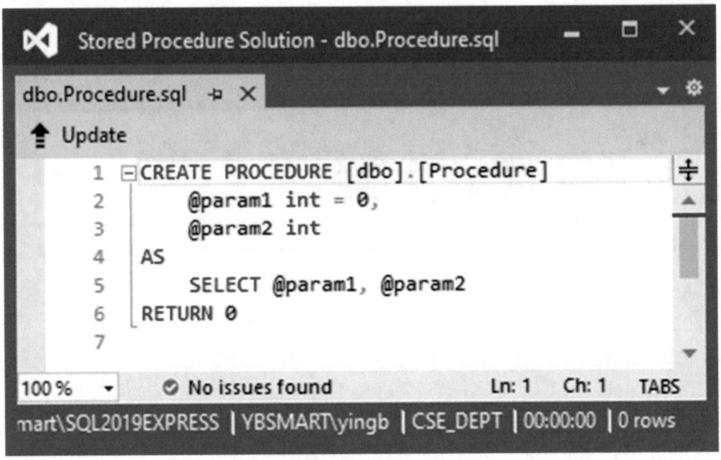

Stored Procedure Solution - dbo.Procedure.sql

dbo.Procedure.sql

Update

```
CREATE PROCEDURE [dbo].[Procedure]
    @param1 int = 0,
    @param2 int
AS
    SELECT @param1, @param2
RETURN 0
```

100 % No issues found Ln: 1 Ch: 1 TABS

mart\SQL2019EXPRESS | YBSMART\yingb | CSE_DEPT | 00:00:00 | 0 rows

Fig. 6.45 The opened New Stored Procedure window

```
  CREATE PROCEDURE [dbo].[FacultyCourse]
A         @facultyName VARCHAR(50),
          @result VARCHAR(800) OUTPUT
  AS
B         DECLARE @courseID CURSOR
          DECLARE @facultyID VARCHAR(50)
C         DECLARE @courseid1 VARCHAR(100)
          DECLARE @courseid2 VARCHAR(100)
          DECLARE @courseid3 VARCHAR(100)
          DECLARE @courseid4 VARCHAR(100)
          DECLARE @courseid5 VARCHAR(100)
D         DECLARE @message VARCHAR(800)
E         SET @facultyID = (SELECT faculty_id FROM Faculty
          WHERE faculty_name LIKE @facultyName)
F         SET @courseID = CURSOR FOR (SELECT course_id FROM Course WHERE faculty_id LIKE @facultyID)
G         OPEN @courseID
H         FETCH NEXT FROM @courseID INTO @courseid1
          FETCH NEXT FROM @courseID INTO @courseid2
          FETCH NEXT FROM @courseID INTO @courseid3
          FETCH NEXT FROM @courseID INTO @courseid4
I         IF @@FETCH_STATUS = 0
          FETCH NEXT FROM @courseID INTO @courseid5
J         IF @@FETCH_STATUS = -1
            SET @result = @courseid1 + ',' + @courseid2 + ',' + @courseid3 + ',' + @courseid4
K         ELSE IF @@FETCH_STATUS = 0
            SET @result = @courseid1 + ',' + @courseid2 + ',' + @courseid3 + ',' + @courseid4 + ',' + @courseid5
L         CLOSE @courseID
    PRINT ' '
M   SELECT @message = '----- ResultSet =: ' + @result
N   PRINT @message
    RETURN
```

Fig. 6.46 The codes for the stored procedure dbo.FacultyCourse

1) The data type of the **OUT** parameter in the SQL statement or in the SQL stored procedure should be defined as a **VARCHAR**, which can be mapped to a String in the Java code.

2) Inside the SQL stored procedure, we need to declare a local cursor variable and use that local cursor to collect the queried multiple rows or multiple **course_id**.
3) Fetch each queried row from the cursor into each associated local variable.
4) Combine all fetched rows into the **OUT** parameter that has a data type of **VARCHAR**.

A key point to build this SQL stored procedure is that our sample database **CSE_DEPT.mdf** should have been built and located at the default location, which is **C:\Program Files\Microsoft SQL Server\MSSQL15.SQL2019EXPRESS\MSSQL\DATA**. Refer to Chap. 2 to build this sample database if it has not been built.

Perform the following operational steps to create this stored procedure:

1) Open the Microsoft Visual Studio.NET 2019 and open the Server Explorer by going to the **View|Server Explorer** menu item.
2) Make sure that our sample database **CSE_DEPT** has been connected to the Visual Studio.NET 2019. If not, you need to use the **Data Source** window to first connect it by adding a new data source.
3) The point to be noted is that you need to check the Data Source you are connecting is **SQL2019EXPRESS**. To do this checking, click on the **Advanced** button in the **Add Connection** wizard and then the **Data Source** property.
4) Expand our sample database **CSE_DEPT.mdf** from the Server Explorer window, and right click on the **Stored Procedures** folder, select **Add New Stored Procedure** item from the popup menu to open the **New Stored Procedure** wizard, which is shown in Fig. 6.45.
5) Remove all comment-out marks and replace the name of this stored procedure with the **[dbo].[FacultyCourse]**. Add the codes that are shown in Fig. 6.46 into this stored procedure to make it as our target stored procedure.

Let's have a closer look at this new added piece of codes to see how it works.

A. Both **IN** and **OUT** parameters are first declared in the parameter section. The @**facultyName** is an input parameter with a data type of **VARCHAR(50)** and the @**result** is an output parameter with a data type of **VARCHAR(800)**. The keyword **OUTPUT** must be attached after the **OUT** parameter to indicate that this is an output parameter in this stored procedure.
B. Two local variables, @**courseID** and @**facultyID**, are declared here since we need to use them inside this stored procedure only. The data type for the first one is the **CURSOR** since we need to query multiple rows and store them into this cursor later. The second one is a **VARCHAR** variable.
C. Another five local variables are created and declared after these two local variables, and each of them is related to one **course_id** queried from this stored procedure. As we know, all faculty members in this CSE dept teach either four or five courses, so the maximum number of **course_id** should be five. If more courses were taught by some selected faculty members, the number of these local variable should also be increased based on the actual courses taught by the related faculty members.

D. The local variable **@message** is used for the testing purpose of this stored procedure.
E. As we remember, there is no **faculty_name** column available in our **Course** table and the only relationship between each faculty and each course is made by the **faculty_id** column, which is a primary key in the **Faculty** table, but a foreign key in the **Course** table. In order to get the **faculty_id**, we need to perform a query to the **Faculty** table based on the **faculty_name**, which is an input to this stored procedure. Then we can perform another query to the **Course** table to get all courses taught by the selected **faculty_id** obtained from the first query. So you can see that we need to perform two queries to get our desired **course_id**. To save the time and space, here we used a stored procedure to combine these two queries together to speed up this query process.
F. Here we used a cursor **@courseID** to collect multiple rows (**course_id**) returned from this query. To perform an assignment operation in SQL, a **SET** instruction must be used.
G. After a query is performed and the result has been stored into the cursor. To fetch each row from the cursor, the cursor must be first opened.
H. A **FETCH** command is used to fetch the first four courses into four local variables, **@courseid1** through **@courseid4**.
I. By checking the global variable **@@FETCH_STATUS**, we can know whether the last fetch operation is successful or not. If this status returned a 0, which means that the last fetch is fine, and then we can try to fetch the fifth course into the local variable **@courseid5**. Because all faculty members in this CSE dept teach either four or five courses, therefore the maximum number of queried courses should be five.
J. If the fetch status **@@FETCH_STATUS** returned a -1, which means that the last fetch is unsuccessful or there is no fifth course to be fetched, we need to combine only the first four fetched courses into the **OUT** parameter **@result**. In order to make it convenient to separate this combined string in the Java application, we combine these fetched rows with a comma mark as a separator.
K. If the fetch status **@@FETCH_STATUS** returned a 0, which means that the last fetch is successful or the fifth course is indeed existed, we can combine all

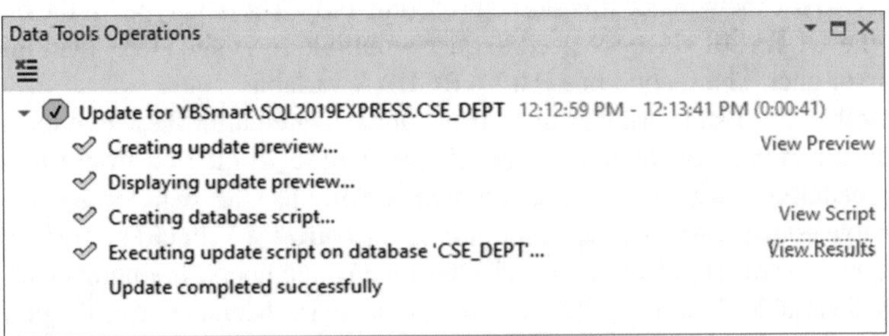

Fig. 6.47 The updating result of our new created stored procedure

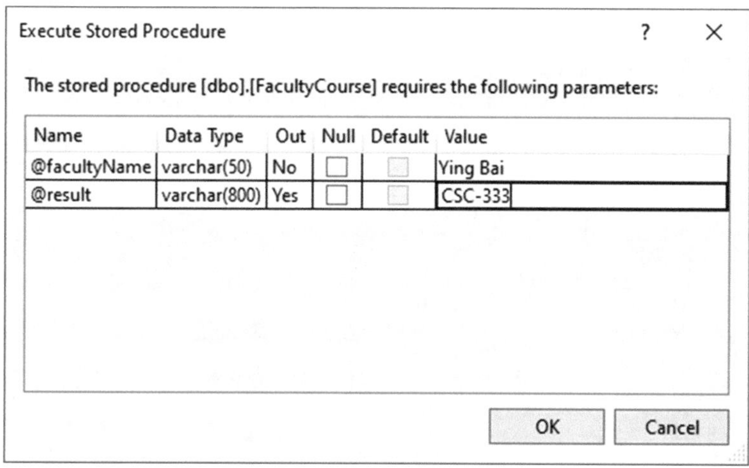

Fig. 6.48 The running status of the stored procedure

T-SQL | Results | Message

```
----- ResultSet =: CSC-132B,CSC-234A,CSE-434,CSE-438
   (1 row(s) affected)
   (1 row(s) affected)
```

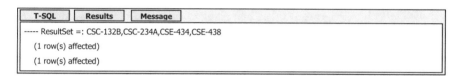

Fig. 6.49 The running result of the stored procedure

five fetched courses together into the **OUT** parameter **@result**, and separate them with a comma mark.

L. After all fetches have been completed, the cursor is closed.
M. To test this stored procedure, we use a **SELECT** statement to collect the values of the **OUT** parameter and
N. Use the **PRINT** command to display it.

Now let's save this procedure and add it into our database by clicking on the **Update** icon located at the upper-left corner on this wizard. On the opened **Preview Database Updates** wizard, click on the **Update Database** button to begin this process. Immediately you can find that this updating operation is successful, as shown in Fig. 6.47.

Now let's run this store procedure to test it in the Server Explorer environment. Perform the following operations to run this procedure:

1) Go to the Server Explorer window, and expand the **Stored Procedures** folder under our sample database to try to find our new stored procedure, **FacultyCourse**.
2) You may need to refresh this **Stored Procedures** folder by right-clicking on this folder, and select the **Refresh** item to find our procedure.

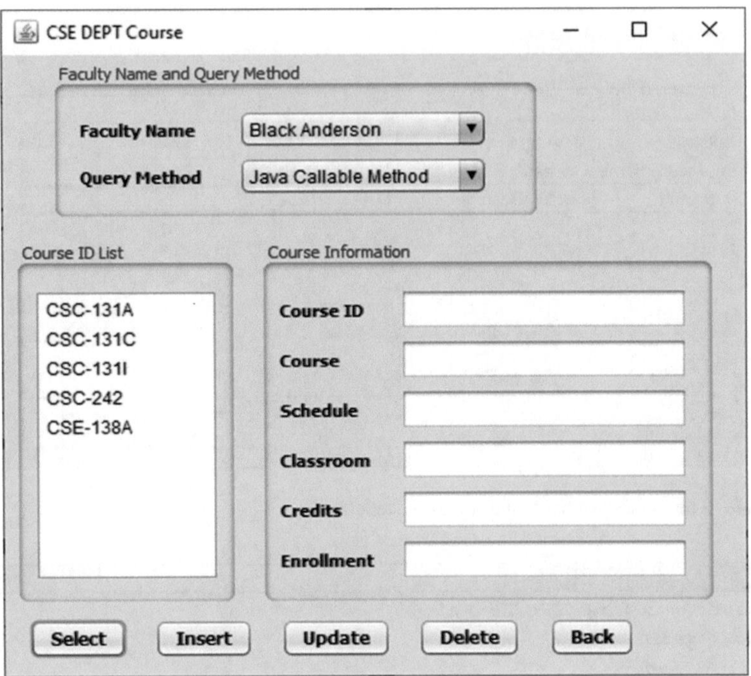

Fig. 6.50 The running result of the CourseFrame Form

3) Right click on our new stored procedure **FacultyCourse** and select the **Execute** item to run our procedure. The Execute Stored Procedure wizard is shown up, as shown in Fig. 6.48.
4) Enter faculty name, **Ying Bai**, into the **Value** column for **@facultyName** box, and **CSC-333** to the **Value** column for the **@result** box, as shown in Fig. 6.48, and click on the **OK** button to run this procedure.

The running result is shown in the mi-pane, which is shown in Fig. 6.49.

Before we can call this stored procedure from our **CourseFrame** Form to test the **CallableStatement** interface, make sure that you have closed the connection between our sample database **CSE_DEPT.mdf** and the Visual Studio.NET 2019. To do that, right click on our sample database **YBSmart\SQL2019EXPRESS.CSE_DEPT.dbo** from the Server Explorer window, and select the **Close Connection** item from the popup menu. Otherwise, you may encounter a connection exception when you run our Java application project.

Now we can test the CallableStatement object we built in our CourseFrame class. Open our project and the CourseFrame Form window, click on the **Clean and Build Main Project** button from the toolbar to build our project. Then click on the **Run Main Project** button to run our project.

Enter the suitable username and password, such as **jhenry** and **test**, to complete the login process. Then select the **Course Information** from the SelectionFrame

```
  private void CourseListValueChanged(javax.swing.event.ListSelectionEvent evt) {
      // TODO add your handling code here:
A     javax.swing.JTextField[] c_field = {CourseIDField, CourseField, ScheduleField, ClassRoomField,
                                          CreditsField, EnrollField};
B     if(!CourseList.getValueIsAdjusting() ){
        String courseid = (String)CourseList.getSelectedValue();
C       if (courseid != null){
           String cQuery = "SELECT course_id, course, schedule, classroom, credit, " +
                           "enrollment FROM Course WHERE course_id = ?";
D       try{
           PreparedStatement pstmt = LogInFrame.con.prepareStatement(cQuery);
E          pstmt.setString(1, courseid);
F          ResultSet rs = pstmt.executeQuery();
G          ResultSetMetaData rsmd = rs.getMetaData();
H          while (rs.next()){
              for (int i=1; i <=rsmd.getColumnCount(); i++) {
                 c_field[i-1].setText(rs.getString(i));
              }
           }
        }
I       catch (SQLException e) {
           msgDlg.setMessage("Error in Statement!" + e.getMessage());
           msgDlg.setVisible(true);
        }
      }
    }
  }
```

Fig. 6.51 The coding for the CourseListValueChanged() event handler

Form window to open the CourseFrame Form window. Select the **Java Callable Method** from the Query Method combo box, and click on the **Select** button to run our CallableStatement object to query all **course_id** taught by the default faculty member **Ying Bai**. A sample running result is shown in Fig. 6.50.

Click on the **Close** button that is located at the upper-right corner of this CourseFrame Form window to terminate our project.

Next let's develop the codes to display the detailed information for each course shown in the Course ID List listbox.

6.3.6.5 Coding for the CourseList Box to Display Detailed Information for the Selected Course

The function of this event handler is simple, which is listed below:

1) After the user selected a faculty member from the Faculty Name combo box, a **Java Callable Method** from the Query Method combo box, and clicked on the **Select** button, all courses, exactly all **course_id**, taught by the selected faculty should be displayed in the Course ID List listbox.
2) As the user clicks on a **course_id** from the Course ID List listbox, the detailed information for the selected **course_id** should be displayed in six text fields on the right side.

Based on the function description listed above, the coding for this event handler is easy and straightforward. Open the Design View of the **CourseFrame** Form window by clicking on the **Design** tab on the top of the window, and right click on the **CourseList** listbox and select the **Events > ListSelection > valueChanged** item to open its **CourseListValueChanged()** event handler. Enter the codes that are shown in Fig. 6.51 into this event handler.

Let's have a closer look at this piece of codes to see how it works.

A. A text field array **c_field** is created here since we need to assign the queried detailed course information to six text fields to display them, therefore it is easy to use an array to do that assignment.
B. Since JList component belongs to the javax.swing package, not java.awt package, therefore any clicking on an entry in the CourseList box causes the itemStateChanged() method to fire twice: Once when the mouse button is depressed, and once again when it is released. Therefore, the selected course_id will appear twice when it is selected. To prevent this from occurring, the getValueIsAdjusting() method is used to make sure that no any item has been adjusted to be displayed twice. Then the selected course_id is assigned to a local String variable courseid by calling the getSelectedValue() method of the CourseList Box class.
C. Before we can proceed to the query operation, first we need to confirm that the selected **courseid** is not a null value. A null value would be returned if the user did not select any **course_id** from the **CourseList** box, instead, the user just clicked on the **Select** button to try to find all **course_id** taught by other faculty members. Even the user only clicked on the **Select** button without touching any **course_id** in the **CourseList** box; however, the system still considers that a null **course_id** has been selected and thus a null value will be returned. To avoid that situation from occurring, an **if** selection structure is used to make sure that no null value has been returned from the **CourseList** box. A SQL query string is created if no null value has been returned.
D. A **try…catch** block is used to perform this PreparedStatement query operation. First, a PreparedStatement object is created with the query string as the argument.
E. The **setString()** method is executed to use the real query criterion **courseid** to replace the nominal position parameter.
F. The dynamic query is actually executed by calling the **executeQuery()** method and the query result is returned and stored in a ResultSet object.
G. The **getMetaData()** method is called to return the detailed information about the returned ResultSet object, including the column number, column name, and data type.

```
private void cmdBackActionPerformed(java.awt.event.ActionEvent evt) {
        // TODO add your handling code here:
        this.setVisible(false);
        this.dispose();
}
```

Fig. 6.52 Coding for the Back button Click event handler

H. A **while** and **for** loops are used to retrieve the queried columns from the ResultSet object and assign them one by one to the associated Text Field to display them.
I. The **catch** block is used to track and monitor the running status of this piece of codes. An error message will be displayed if any exception has occurred.

Next, we need to take care of the coding for the **Back** button Click event handler to switch from the **CourseFrame** Form back to the **SelectionFrame** Form to allow users to perform other query operations.

6.3.6.6 Coding for the Back Button Click Event Handler

When this **Back** button is clicked, the **CourseFrame** Form should be closed and the control will be returned to the **SelectionFrame** Form. Open the Design View of the CourseFrame Form window by clicking on the **Design** tab from the top of the window and double click on the **Back** button to open its event handler. Enter the codes that are shown in Fig. 6.52 into this event handler.

The function of this piece of codes is straightforward, the CourseFrame Form will be closed by calling the **setVisible()** method with a **false** argument, and the **dispose()** method is used to remove the CourseFrame Form from the screen.

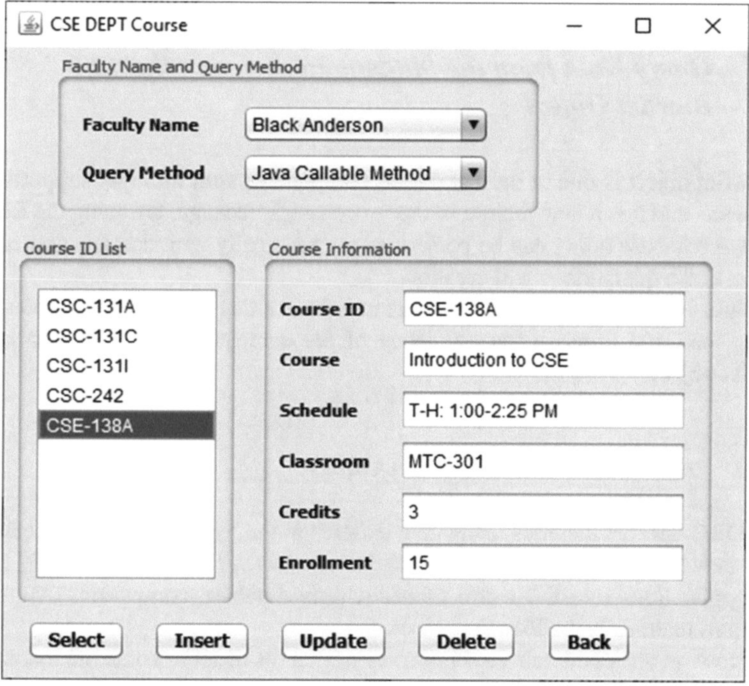

Fig. 6.53 The running result of the CourseFrame Form window

At this point, we have finished all coding jobs for the CourseFrame Form object. Now we can build and run our project to test its function. Click on the **Clean and Build Main Project** button on the top of the window to build our project. Then click on the **Run Main Project** button to run the project.

Enter suitable username and password, such as **jhenry** and **test**, to the LogInFrame Form to complete the login process. Select the **Course Information** item from the SelectionFrame Form window to open the CourseFrame Form window. Then select the **Java Callable Method** from the Query Method combo box, keep the default faculty member **Ying Bai** from the Faculty Name combo box, and click on the **Select** button. All courses, exactly all **course_id**, taught by the selected faculty member are shown in the Course ID List listbox, which is shown in Fig. 6.53.

Click on any **course_id** from the **Course ID** List listbox, the detailed course information about the selected **course_id** is displayed in six text fields, which is also shown in Fig. 6.53. Our course query using the CallableStatement with the stored procedure is successful!

Click on the **Back** and then **Exit** buttons to terminate our project.

A complete project **SQLSelectObject** can be found from the folder **Class DB Projects\Chapter** 6 that is located under the **Students** folder at the Springer ftp site (see Chap. 1).

Next, let's discuss how to perform data queries from the Student table in our sample database using the RowSet object.

6.3.7 Query Data from the Student Table Using the Java RowSet Object

A RowSet object is one of the JavaBeans components with multiple supports from JavaBeans and it is a new feature in the `java.sql` package. By using the RowSet object, a database query can be performed automatically with the data source connection and a query statement creation.

In this section, we will show readers how to use this new feature to reduce the coding load and improve the efficiency of the data query with the help of this RowSet object.

6.3.7.1 Introduction to Java RowSet Object

The JDBC 4.0 API includes many new features in the `java.sql` package as well as the new Standard Extension package, `javax.sql`. This new JDBC API moves Java applications into the world of heavy-duty database computing. One of the important features is the RowSet object.

A RowSet object contains a set of rows from a result set or some other source of tabular data, like a file or spreadsheet. Because a RowSet object follows the

JavaBeans model for properties and event notification, it is a JavaBeans component that can be combined with other components in an application. As it is compatible with other Beans, application developers can probably use a development tool to create a RowSet object and set its properties.

RowSets may have many different implementations to fill different needs. These implementations fall into two broad categories, connected and disconnected:

1) A connected RowSet is equivalent to a ResultSet, and it maintains a connection to a data source as long as the RowSet is in use.
2) A disconnected RowSet works as a DataSet in Visual Studio.NET, and it can connect to a data source to perform the data updating periodically. Most time, it is disconnected from the data source and uses a mapping memory space as a mapped database.

While a RowSet is disconnected, it does not need a JDBC driver or the full JDBC API, so its footprint is very small. Thus a RowSet is an ideal format for sending data over a network to a thin client.

Because it is not continually connected to its data source, a disconnected RowSet stores its data in memory. It needs to maintain metadata about the columns it contains and information about its internal state. It also needs a facility for making connections, for executing commands, and for reading and writing data to and from the data source. A connected RowSet, by contrast, opens a connection and keeps it open for as long as the RowSet is being used.

To make writing an implementation easier, the Java Software division of Oracle, Inc., plans to provide reference implementations for five different styles of RowSets. The following list of planned implementations gives you an idea of some of the possibilities.

1) A CachedRowSet class—a disconnected RowSet that caches its data in memory; not suitable for very large data sets, but an ideal way to provide thin Java clients, such as a Personal Digital Assistant (PDA) or Network Computer (NC), with tabular data
2) A JDBCRowSet class—a connected RowSet that serves mainly as a thin wrapper around a ResultSet object to make a JDBC driver look like a JavaBeans component
3) A WebRowSet class—a connected RowSet that uses the HTTP protocol internally to talk to a Java Servlet that provides data access; used to make it possible for thin web clients to retrieve and possibly update a set of rows.
4) A FilteredRowSet is an extension to WebRowSet that provides programmatic support for filtering its content. This enables you to avoid the overhead of supplying a query and the processing involved. The SQL implementation of FilteredRowSet is **javax.sql.rowset.FilteredRowSet**. The Oracle implementation of FilteredRowSet is **oracle.jdbc.rowset.OracleFilteredRowSet**. The OracleFilteredRowSet class in the **ojdbc14.jar** file implements the standard JSR-114 interface javax.sql.rowset.FilteredRowSet.

5) A JoinRowSet is another extension to WebRowSet that consists of related data from different RowSets. There is no standard way to establish a SQL **JOIN** between disconnected RowSets without connecting to the data source. A JoinRowSet addresses this issue. The SQL implementation of JoinRowSet is the javax.sql.rowset.JoinRowSet class. The Oracle implementation of JoinRowSet is the **oracle.jdbc.rowset**. OracleJoinRowSet class. This class, which is in the **ojdbc14.jar** file, implements the standard JSR-114 interface javax.sql. rowset.JoinRowSet. Any number of RowSet objects, which implement the Joinable interface, can be added to a JoinRowSet object, provided they can be related in a SQL **JOIN**. All five types of RowSet support the Joinable interface. The Joinable interface provides methods for specifying the columns based on which the **JOIN** will be performed, that is, the match columns.

Next, let's have a closer look at the operational sequence for the RowSet object.

6.3.7.2 The Operational Procedure of Using the JDBC RowSet Object

A compliant JDBC RowSet implementation must implement one or more standard interfaces specified in this package and may extend the BaseRowSet abstract class. For example, a CachedRowSet implementation must implement the CachedRowSet interface and extend the BaseRowSet abstract class. The BaseRowSet class provides the standard architecture on which all RowSet implementations should be built, regardless of whether the RowSet objects exist in a connected or disconnected environment. The BaseRowSet abstract class provides any RowSet implementation with its base functionality, including property manipulation and event notification that is fully compliant with JavaBeans component requirements. As an example, all implementations provided in the reference implementations (contained in the **com. sun.rowset** package) use the BaseRowSet class as a basis for their implementations.

Table 6.5 Features of the BaseRowSet abstract class

Feature	Details
Properties	Provides standard JavaBeans property manipulation mechanisms to allow applications to get and set `RowSet` command and property values. Refer to the documentation of the `javax.sql.RowSet` interface (available in the JDBC 3.0 specification) for more details on the standard `RowSet` properties.
Event notification	Provides standard JavaBeans event notifications to registered event listeners. Refer to the documentation of `javax.sql.RowSetEvent` interface (available in the JDBC 3.0 specification) for more details on how to register and handle standard RowSet events generated by compliant implementations.
Setters for a RowSet object's command	Provides a complete set of setter methods for setting RowSet command parameters.
Streams	Provides fields for storing of stream instances in addition to providing a set of constants for stream type designation

Table 6.5 illustrates the features that the BaseRowSet abstract class provides.

In this application, we will concentrate on the implementation of the CachedRowSet component since we preferred to use a disconnected RowSet.

Generally, the operational procedure of using a RowSet object to query data can be divided into the following four steps:

1) Setup and configure a RowSet object
2) Register the RowSet Listeners
3) Set input and output parameters for the query command
4) Traverse through the result rows from the ResultSet

The first step is used to setup and configure the static or dynamic properties of a RowSet object, such as the connection **url**, username, password, and running command, to allow the RowSet object to connect to the data source, pass user parameters into the data source, and perform the data query.

The second step allows users to register different Listeners for the RowSet object with different event sources. The RowSet feature supports multiple listeners to be registered with the RowSet object. Listeners can be registered using the **addRowSetListener()** method and unregistered through the **removeRowSetListener()** method. A listener can implement the **javax.sql.RowSetListener** interface to register itself as the RowSet listener. Three types of events are supported by the RowSet interface:

1) **cursorMoved event**: Generated whenever there is a cursor movement, which occurs when the **next()** or **previous()** methods are called.
2) **rowChanged event**: Generated when a new row is inserted, updated, or deleted from the row set.
3) **rowsetChanged event**: Generated when the whole row set is created or changed.

In our applications, the Apache NetBeans IDE 12 is used and the event-listener model has been setup by NetBeans IDE. So we can skip this step and do not need to take care of this issue during our coding process.

Step 3 allows users to setup all static or dynamic parameters for the query statement of the RowSet object. Depending on the data type of the parameters used in the query statement, a suitable **setXXX()** method should be used to perform this parameter setup process.

The fourth step is used to retrieve each row from the ResultSet object.

A point to be noted when using any RowSet object to perform data query is that most RowSet classes are abstract classes and cannot be instantiated directly. One needs to use a suitable RowSet Implementation class to create a RowSet implementation object to perform a data query. Also a RowSet can be implemented in two ways, the direct implementation and distributed implementation via a ResultSet. We will use the first way in our project.

Now let's follow the four steps listed above to develop a data query operation using the CachedRowSet object to query data from the Student table in our sample database **CSE_DEPT**. First, let's build a GUI named **StudentFrame** Form using Apache NetBeans 12.

Table 6.6 Objects and controls in the StudentFrame form

Type	Variable Name	Text	Border	Title
Canvas	ImageCanvas			
Panel	jPanel1		Titled Border	Student Name and Query Method
Label	Label1	Student Name		
ComboBox	ComboName			
Label	Label2	Query Method		
ComboBox	ComboMethod			
Panel	jPanel2		Titled Border	Course Selected
ListBox	CourseList			
Panel	jPanel3		Titled Border	Student Information
Label	Label3	Student ID		
Text Field	StudentIDField			
Label	Label4	Student Name		
Text Field	StudentNameField			
Label	Label5	School Year		
Text Field	SchoolYearField			
Label	Label6	GPA		
Text Field	GPAField			
Label	Label7	Major		
Text Field	MajorField			
Label	Label8	Credits		
Text Field	CreditsField			
Label	Label9	Email		
Text Field	EmailField			
Button	SelectButton	Select		
Button	InsertButton	Insert		
Button	UpdateButton	Update		
Button	DeleteButton	Delete		
Button	ExitButton	Exit		
StudentFrame Form	StudentFrame			CSE DEPT Student

6.3.7.3 Build a Graphical User Interface StudentFrame Form

As we did for the other JFrame Forms, right click on our project **SQLSelectObject** from the **Projects** window, and then select **New|JFrame Form** item from the popup menu to open **New JFrame Form** dialog box. Enter **StudentFrame** into the **Class Name** box as the name for our new class, and select the **SQLSelectObjectPackage**

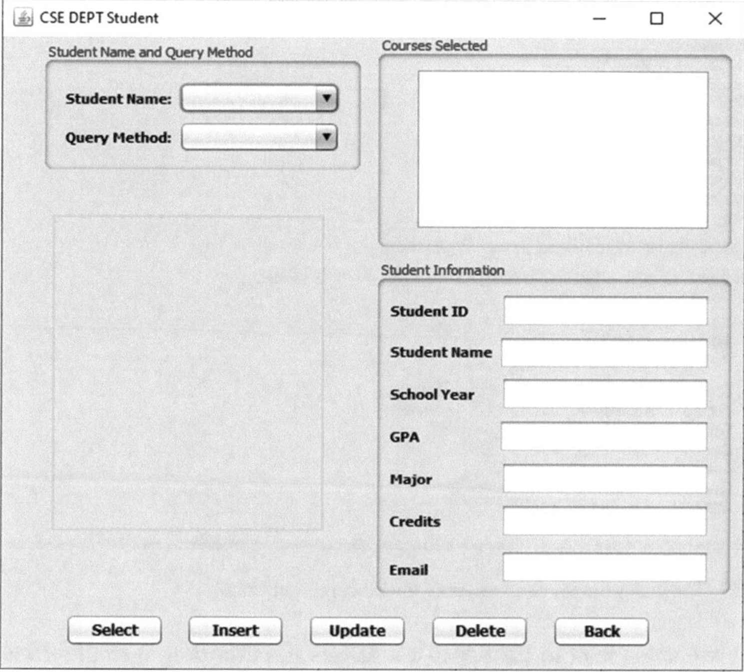

Fig. 6.54 A sample window of the StudentFrame Form

from the **Package** box, and click on the **Finish** button to create this new **StudentFrame** class.

Add the following objects and controls shown in Table 6.6 into this StudentFrame Form window to finish the GUI design for this form. Your finished StudentFrame Form window should match one that is shown in Fig. 6.54.

The function of this StudentFrame Form class is:

1) As this StudentFrame Form runs, the user can select the desired student and query method from the Student Name and Query Method combo boxes, respectively. As the **Select** button is clicked by the user, all courses, exactly all **course_id**, taken by the selected student will be displayed in the Course Selected ListBox. Also the detailed information about the selected student will be displayed in six text fields.
2) When the user clicks on the **Exit** button, the StudentFrame Form project will be terminated and the database-related connection will be closed, too.
3) In this section, we only use the Java JDBC RowSet Method as our data query method, and the **Select** and the **Exit** buttons as our coding objectives.

A point to be noted is that when drag a Canvas control from the Palette and place it into the StudentFrame Form window, first you need to click on the Canvas from the Palette. Then you need to click a location where you want to place it in the **StudentFrame**. A Canvas icon is displayed in that location you clicked. You must

```
  package SQLSelectObjectPackage;
A import java.sql.*;
  import javax.sql.rowset.*;
  import java.io.IOException;
  import java.util.logging.Level;
  import java.util.logging.Logger;
  import java.awt.Graphics;
  import java.awt.Image;
  import java.awt.MediaTracker;
  import java.io.FileNotFoundException;
  import java.io.FileOutputStream;
  public class StudentFrame extends javax.swing.JFrame {
B   MsgDialog msgDlg = new MsgDialog(new javax.swing.JFrame(), true);
    /** Creates new form StudentFrame */
    public StudentFrame() {
      initComponents();
      this.setLocationRelativeTo(null);
C     ComboMethod.addItem("Runtime Object Method");
      ComboMethod.addItem("CachedRowSet Method");
D     ComboName.addItem("Tom Erica");
      ComboName.addItem("Ashly Jade");
      ComboName.addItem("Holes Smith");
      ComboName.addItem("Andrew Woods");
      ComboName.addItem("Blue Valley");
   }
```

Fig. 6.55 The codes for the constructor of the StudentFrame class

drag this Canvas icon to the upper-left direction, never drag it to the lower-right direction, to enlarge it.

Another point to be noted is that you need to remove all default items located inside the **model** property of the combo boxes **ComboName** and **ComboMethod**. To do that, click on each combo box from the Design View, and then go the **model** property, click on the three-dot button to open the model pane. Select all four default items, and press the **Delete** button from the keyboard to remove all of those items.

6.3.7.4 Coding for the Constructor of the StudentFrame Class

Open the Code Window of the **StudentFrame** class by clicking on the **Source** tab from the top of the window and enter the codes that are shown in Fig. 6.55 into the top of this window and the constructor of this class. Let's have a closer look at this piece of codes to see how it works.

A. Ten useful java packages are added first since we need to utilize some classes defined in those packages. The first package, **java.sql.***, provides all classes and interfaces used in JDBC API for SQL Server database. The next two packages contain all related classes and interfaces used for the CachedRowSet component and CachedRowSet Implementation classes. As we mentioned, the CachedRowSet is an abstract class and we have to use its implementation class to perform any data query.

```
  private void SelectButtonActionPerformed(java.awt.event.ActionEvent evt) {
A     Blob simgBlob = null;
      CachedRowSet rowSet = null;
B     try{
        rowSet = RowSetProvider.newFactory().createCachedRowSet();
      }catch (SQLException ex) {
        Logger.getLogger(StudentFrame.class.getName()).log(java.util.logging.Level.SEVERE, null, ex); }
C     String strStudent = "SELECT student_id, student_name, gpa, credits, major, schoolYear, email, simage " +
                          "FROM Student  WHERE student_name = ?";
D     String strStudentCourse = "SELECT course_id FROM StudentCourse WHERE student_id = ?";
E     if (ComboMethod.getSelectedItem()== "CachedRowSet Method"){
        try{
          String url = "jdbc:sqlserver://localhost\\SQL2019EXPRESS:5000;databaseName=CSE_DEPT;";
          rowSet.setUrl(url);
          rowSet.setUsername("SMART"); rowSet.setPassword("Happy2020");
          rowSet.setCommand(strStudent);
F         rowSet.setString(1, ComboName.getSelectedItem().toString());
G         rowSet.execute();
H         while (rowSet.next()){
            StudentIDField.setText(rowSet.getString(1));
            StudentNameField.setText(rowSet.getString(2));
            GPAField.setText(Float.toString(rowSet.getFloat(3)));
            CreditsField.setText(Integer.toString(rowSet.getInt(4)));
            MajorField.setText(rowSet.getString(5));
            SchoolYearField.setText(rowSet.getString(6));
            EmailField.setText(rowSet.getString(7));
          } // end while
I         rowSet.setCommand(strStudentCourse); rowSet.setString(1, StudentIDField.getText());
J         rowSet.execute();
K         int i = 0; String Result[] = {null, null, null, null, null, null, null, null};
L         while (rowSet.next()){
            String sResult = rowSet.getString(1);
            Result[i] = sResult;
            i++;
          }
M         CourseList.setListData(Result);
N         rowSet.close();
O         PreparedStatement pstmt = LogInFrame.con.prepareStatement(strStudent);
          pstmt.setString(1, ComboName.getSelectedItem().toString());
          ResultSet rs = pstmt.executeQuery();
P         while(rs.next()) simgBlob = rs.getBlob("simage");
        }
Q       catch(SQLException e){
          msgDlg.setMessage("RowSet is wrong!" + e.getMessage());
          msgDlg.setVisible(true);
          System.exit( 1 );
        }
      }
R     else{
        msgDlg.setMessage("Only CachedRowSet Method is Available ");
        msgDlg.setVisible(true);
        return;
      }
S     try {
        if (!ShowStudent(simgBlob)){
          msgDlg.setMessage("No matched student image found!");
          msgDlg.setVisible(true);
        }
T     } catch (SQLException | IOException ex) {
        Logger.getLogger(FacultyFrame.class.getName()).log(Level.SEVERE, null, ex);
      }
  }
```

Fig. 6.56 The codes for the Select button Click event handler

B. One class-level, not class, variable is declared here since we need to use it in our whole class. The **msgDlg** is used to track and display any debug and warning information if any error is encountered during our project runs.

C. Two query methods are added into the Query Method combo box. In this application, we only use the second one, **CachedRowSet Method**.
D. Five students' names are added into the Student Name combo box.

Next, let's figure out the codes for the **Select** button Click event handler. When this button is clicked, the detailed information about the selected student should be displayed in both seven text fields and the Course Selected listbox.

6.3.7.5 Coding for the Select Button Event Handler to Query Data Using the CachedRowSet

Open this event handler and enter the codes that are shown in Fig. 6.56 into this event handler. Let's have a closer look at this new added piece of codes to see how it works.

A. Two local objects, **simgBlob** and **rowSet**, are declared first and the first one is used to hold the retrieved student image and the second is used to create a CachedRowSet object.
B. Then a new **CachedRowSet** object is created with the **RowSetFactory** class, **newFactory()**, which is created by a **RowSetProvider**. One point to be noted is that the old syntax used to create this CachedRowSet object, **CachedRowSet rowSet = new CachedRowSetImpl();**, is no longer available after JDBC 9.0. A **try-catch** block is used for this creation.
C. As we know, there is no **student_name** column available in the StudentCourse table, and the only relationship between a student and a course taken by that student is the **student_id**, which is a primary key in the **Student** table and a foreign key in the **StudentCourse** table. In order to pick up all courses taken by the selected student, we need to perform two queries: first we need to perform a query to the **Student** table to get a **student_id** based on the selected **student_name**, and then we can perform another query to the **StudentCourse** table based on the **student_id** to get all courses taken by the selected student. The first SQL query string, **strStudent**, is created here with a positional parameter, **student_name**.
D. The second SQL query string **strStudentCourse** is also created with another positional parameter, **student_id**.
E. If the user selected the CachedRowSet Method, a **try…catch** block is used to perform this query using the CachedRowSet implementation component. First, a database connection with some parameters, such as **url**, **username** and **password**, is setup since we are using a direct implementation with direct connection to our sample database. The **setCommand()** method is used to create an executable command with the first query string, **strStudent**, as the argument.
F. The **setString()** method is used to setup the real value for the positional parameter, **student_name**, which is obtained from the Student Name combo box, **ComboName**.

G. The query is actually executed by calling the **execute()** method to perform the first query using the CachedRowSet instance.
H. A **while** loop is used to repeatedly pick up all seven pieces of information related to the selected student. The **next()** method works as the loop condition and it returns a **true** as long as a valid row can be found from the returned data by the execution of the CachedRowSet object. The result of running this **next()** method is to move the cursor that points to the initial position to the first row in the returned data stored in the RowSet. In fact, only one row is returned and stored in the CachedRowSet object for the first query, and a sequence of **getXXX()** methods are used to pick up each column from the RowSet and assign each of them to the associated text field to be displayed on the StudentFrame Form.
I. To execute the second query, the **setCommand()** method is called again to create an executable Command object with the second query string as the argument. Then the **setString()** method is called to setup the positional parameter, **student_id**, for the second SQL query statement. The actual value for this parameter can be obtained from the Student ID text field and it has been retrieved and filled by the first query.
J. The query is executed by calling the **execute()** method to perform the second query using the CachedRowSet instance.
K. In order to pick up the second query result, which contains multiple rows with one column, we need to declare a String array **Result[]** and initialize it with a **null** value. This step is necessary, and otherwise a **NullPointer** exception may be encountered if this array has not been initialized as the project runs later.
L. A **while** loop is used with the **next()** method as the loop condition. Each time when the **next()** method is executed, the cursor in the CachedRowSet object is moved down one step to point to the next returned row. The **getString()** method is used to pick up that row and assign it to the local String variable **sResult**, and furthermore, to the String array **Result[]**. The index in the **getString()** method indicates the current column's number, and this process will be continued until all rows have been collected and assigned to the **Result[]** array.
M. All courses, exactly all **course_id**, collected and stored in the **Result[]** array are assigned to the Course Selected listbox to be displayed in there. The **setListData()** method is a very useful method and the argument of this method must be an array when this method is executed.
N. The CachedRowSet object must be closed when it finished its mission. A **close()** method is used to perform this job.
O. To retrieve the student's image, we still need to use the ResultSet object since the CachedRowSet cannot get any **Blob** from a database and it only can retrieve back an Object via **getObject()** method. An issue is that this Object data type cannot be converted to a Blob type, thus we cannot use the CachedRowSet to directly get any Blob. For that purpose, a ResultSet object **rs** is generated and the first query is executed to pick up all eight pieces of a student's information.

```
  private boolean ShowStudent(Blob bimg) throws SQLException, IOException{
A       Image img;
        int imgId = 1, timeout = 1000;
        FileOutputStream imgOutputStream = null;
        MediaTracker tracker = new MediaTracker(this);
B       String imgPath = System.getProperty("user.dir");
        String simgName = ComboName.getSelectedItem().toString() + ".jpg";
C       try {
            imgOutputStream = new FileOutputStream(imgPath + "/" + simgName);
          }catch (FileNotFoundException ex) {
              Logger.getLogger(StudentFrame.class.getName()).log(Level.SEVERE, null, ex);
        }
D       imgOutputStream.write(bimg.getBytes(1, (int)bimg.length()));
E       imgOutputStream.close();
F       img = this.getToolkit().getImage(simgName);
        Graphics g = ImageCanvas.getGraphics();
G       tracker.addImage(img, imgId);
H       try{
          if(!tracker.waitForID(imgId, timeout)){
             msgDlg.setMessage("Failed to load image");
             msgDlg.setVisible(true);
             return false;
          }
I       }catch(InterruptedException e){
           msgDlg.setMessage(e.toString());
           msgDlg.setVisible(true);
           return false;
        }
J       g.drawImage(img, 0, 0, ImageCanvas.getWidth(), ImageCanvas.getHeight(), this);
        return true;
  }
```

Fig. 6.57 The codes for the ShowStudent() method

```
private void BackButtonActionPerformed(java.awt.event.ActionEvent evt) {
     // TODO add your handling code here:
     this.setVisible(false);
     this.dispose();
}
```

Fig. 6.58 The codes for the Back button Click event handler

P. A **while()** loop is executed to pick up the selected student's image and it is assigned to our local Blob variable **simgBlob**, which will be used later by **ShowStudent()** method.
Q. The **catch** block is used to collect any possible exceptions and display them if they did occur.
R. If users selected another method, **Runtime Object Method**, to query to our **Student** and **StudentCourse** tables, a message is displayed to indicate that only one method is available for this application now.
S. A **try-catch** block is used to call our user-defined method **ShowStudent()**, whose codes will be shown later, to display the selected student's image in the Canvas in our StudentFrame Form.
T. Another **catch** block is used to collect any possible exceptions and display them if they did occur.

Next, let's build a user-defined method to display a student picture for the selected student.

6.3.7.6 Display a Student Picture for the Selected Student

As we did for the FacultyFrame class, we can display a student picture as a part of student information in the Canvas component. The codes are identical with those codes in our user-defined method **ShowFaculty()** in Sect. 6.3.5.3.2, and refer to that section to get more detailed information about this piece of codes. Fig. 6.57 shows the detailed codes for this method. Only one modification is made for this method, which is to change the **fimgName** to the **simgName**.

At this point, we have almost finished the coding for this StudentFrame class. Before we can run the project to test the function of this piece of codes, we need to finish the coding for the **Back** button, exactly for the **Back** button Click event handler. Open this event handler and enter the codes that are shown in Fig. 6.58 into this event handler.

The function of this piece of codes is very simple. The StudentFrame Form window will be closed and removed from the screen as this button is clicked by the user.

Before we can build and run our entire project to test this StudentFrame Form, one more job we need to do is to add some connection codes in the **SelectionFrame** Form class to enable a smooth transfer between the **SelectionFrame** Form and the **StudentFrame** Form, and to open

Our StudentFrame Form to allow users to perform desired queries to our database.

The exact coding modifications have happened in the OK Button Click event handler in the **SelectionFrame** Form. Open that event handler and make two modifications, as shown in Fig. 6.59, for this handler (both coding lines have been highlighted in bold):

```
package SQLSelectObjectPackage;
......
private void OKButtonActionPerformed(java.awt.event.ActionEvent evt) {
    // TODO add your handling code here:
    FacultyFrame facultyFrame = new FacultyFrame();
    CourseFrame courseFrame = new CourseFrame();
A   StudentFrame studentFrame = new StudentFrame();
    if (ComboSelection.getSelectedItem()== "Faculty Information"){
      facultyFrame.setVisible(true);
    } else if (ComboSelection.getSelectedItem()== "Course Information"){
      courseFrame.setVisible(true);
    } else {
      //dlg.setMessage("Student Information is selected\n");
      //dlg.setVisible(true);
B     studentFrame.setVisible(true);
    }
}
```

Fig. 6.59 The modified codes for the OK Button click event handler

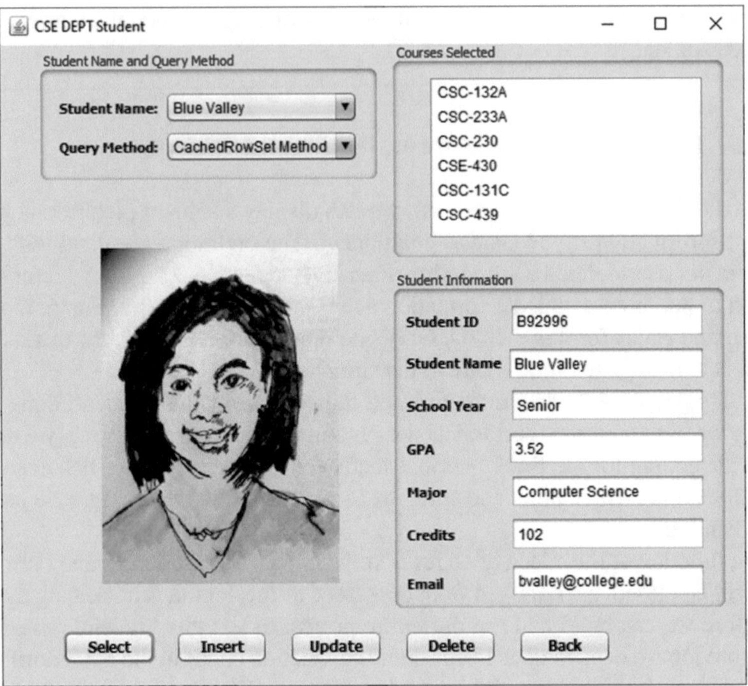

Fig. 6.60 A running sample of the StudentFrame Form window

A. Create a new instance for our **Studentframe** class **studentFrame**, which will be used later.
B. Comment-out two original coding lines, call and open this **StudentFrame** Form window by using **setVisible(true)** method.

Now we have completed all coding job for this StudentFrame class. Now let's build and run our project. Click on the **Clean and Build Main Project** button from the toolbar to build the project. Then click on the **Run Project** button (green arrow button) on the tool bar to run the project.

Complete the login process and select the **Student Information** item from the Selection combo box to open the StudentFrame Form, as shown in Fig. 6.60.

Select a student from the Student Name combo box and make sure to select the **CachedRowSet Method** from the Query Method combo box. Then click on the **Select** button to try to retrieve all pieces of information related to the selected student. A sample running result is shown in Fig. 6.60.

Click on the **Back** button to return to the **SelectionFrame** Form to allow users to perform some other queries from other Forms.

A complete project **SQLSelectObject** can be found from the folder **Class DB Projects\Chapter** 6 that is located under the **Students** folder at the Springer ftp site (see Fig. 1.2 in Chap. 1).

In the next section, we will discuss how to use JDBC API and the runtime object method to perform data query from Oracle databases.

6.4 Chapter Summary

A popular Java database programming method, runtime object method, is discussed in detail in this chapter with a Java Ant Application example project **SQLSelectObject**.

With a lot of coding developments and dynamic parameters setups, a completed set of techniques in Java database programming are discussed and analyzed, which include:

- How to perform a dynamic data query using standard JDBC drivers, such as
  1) Load and register database drivers
  2) Connect to databases and drivers
  3) Create and manage PreparedStatement object to perform dynamic query
  4) Use ResultSet object to pick up queried result
  5) Query data using JDBC MetaData interface
  6) The ParameterMetaData interface
  7) Use DatabaseMetaData interface
  8) Use ResultSetMetaData interface
  9) Query data using the CallableStatement method
- Query data using the Java RowSet object

The novel and key technique discussed in this part is the interface between a SQL stored procedure and a Java CallableStatement interface. Regularly, there is no mapped partner for the cursor data type in the JDBC data type; in other words, a cursor applied in the SQL Server stored procedure cannot be returned to a Java database application since the cursor cannot be mapped to a valid JDBC data type. In order to solve that problem, we developed a special SQL stored procedure to perform the conversion between a **VARCHAR** string and a cursor inside the SQL stored procedure, and returned a **VARCHAR** string to the Java database application.

Very detailed discussions in how to build SQL stored procedure are provided in this part, too, to give readers a full and clear picture in how to do a connection between a CallableStatement interface and a database stored procedure.

Homework

I. <u>True/False Selections</u>

____1. One does not need to change the TCP/IP port number when connecting to a SQL Server 2019 Express database since the default port number is 1434.

____2. The JDBC Drivers for SQL Server database, Microsoft SQL Server JDBC Driver 8.4, is a type IV driver.

____ 3. A static query is called a Named Query and it is defined statically with the help of annotation or XML before the entity class is created.

____ 4. Dynamic queries belong to queries in which the query strings are provided at run-time or created dynamically. All callings to EntityManager.createQuery(queryString) are actually creating dynamic query objects.

____ 5. Only one way can be used to load and register a JDBC Driver during a project runs, which is to use the Class.forName() method.

____ 6. When using the getConnection() method in the DriverManager class to perform a database connection, the connection is made as soon as this instruction runs.

____ 7. The executeQuery() method will definitely return a query result, but the executeUpdate() method will never returns any result.

____ 8. When a query is performed and a ResultSet is created, you need to retrieve the queried result from the ResultSet object by using a suitable getXXX() method.

____ 9. The advantage of using the getObject() method is that a returned datum, which is stored in a ResultSet object and its data type is unknown, can be automatically converted from its SQL data type to the ideal Java data type.

___10. The SQL92 syntax can only be used for calling a SQL stored procedure, not for an Oracle package or stored procedure.

___11. One has to use the registerOutParameter() method to register any output parameter in a SQL statement to allow the CallableStatement to know that there is an OUT parameter in that query and the returned value should be stored in that parameter.

___12. When using a Java RowSet object to query data, one has to create an instance of the RowSet Implementation class, not the RowSet class itself since all RowSet classes are abstract classes.

II. Multiple Choices

1. The sequence to perform a data query from a database using a JDBC driver is _____

    a. Connect to database, load JDBC driver, perform the query, get result from ResultSet
    b. Perform the query, connect to database, load JDBC driver, get result from ResultSet
    c. Get result from ResultSet, connect to database, load JDBC driver, perform the query
    d. load JDBC driver, connect to database, perform the query, get result from ResultSet

2. The difference between a JPQL and a standard SQL query string is that a(n) _______ is used and prefixed for each clause.

    a. Class name
    b. An abstract schema

c. Property name
d. A object schema

3. A named query can be considered as a ________ query.

a. Dynamic
b. Instance
c. Object
d. Static

4. One needs to use a _______ object as an image holder, a _______ object as a tool to display an image, and a ________ class as a monitor to coordinate the image processing.

a. Canvas, MediaTracker, Graphics
b. Graphics, MediaTracker, Canvas
c. Canvas, Graphics, MediaTracker
d. MediaTracker, Graphics, Canvas

5. Generally, a connection **url** contains three parts or three segments; __________, __________ and _________ for the database to be connected.

a. Subname, sub-protocol, sub-protocol name
b. Protocol name, sub-protocol, subname
c. Protocol name, sub-protocol name, subname
d. Protocol, sub-protocol, subname

6. The execute() method can _____________.

a. Not return any result
b. Return some results
c. Be used either to return a result or not return any result
d. None of above

7. To distinguish or identify the data type returned by the execute() method, one needs to __________________ .

a. Use the getResultSet() method
b. Use the getUpdateCount() method
c. Use either of them
d. Use both of them

8. The ResultSet object can be created by either executing the ___________ or __________ method, which means that the ResultSet instance cannot be created or used without executing a query operation first.

a. executeQuery(), getResultSet()
b. getResultSet(), execute()
c. createResultSet(), getResultSet()
d. buildResultSet(), executeQuery()

9. The cursor in a ResultSet object can be moved by executing the ____________ method.

   a. move()
   b. first()
   c. next()
   d. last()

10. A cursor in a SQL Server database can be mapped to an __________________ data type.

    a. jdbc.oracle.CURSOR
    b. oracle.jdbc.OracleTypes.CURSOR
    c. java.sql.ResultSet
    d. jdbc.CURSOR

11. A ____________ object, which contains all pieces of necessary information about the returned data stored in a ResultSet instance, is returned when the ___________ method is executed.

    a. getMetaData(), ResultSetMetaData
    b. ResultSet, getMetaData()
    c. getResultSet, ResultSet
    d. ResultSetMetaData, getMetaData()

12. A CallableStatement can either return a _________ object and multiple ResultSet objects by using executeQuery() method or return nothing by using _________ method.

    a. ResultSetMetaData, getResultSet()
    b. Cursor, getCursor()
    c. Object, getObject()
    d. ResultSet, execute()

III. Exercises

1. List 6 steps to build a data query from a Java database application project to a relational database using the Java runtime object method.
2. Using Java CallableStatement method to develop the data query from the Student and StudentCourse tables with the StudentFrame class in the **SQLSelectObject project (the project file can be found from the**

```
CREATE PROCEDURE [dbo].[StudentInfo]
     @sName VARCHAR(50)
AS
     SELECT student_id, student_name, gpa, credits, major, schoolYear, email, simage
     FROM Student WHERE student_name = @sName
RETURN 0
```

Fig. 6.61 The completed stored procedure dbo.StudentInfo

folder Class DB Projects\Chapter 6 that is located under the Students folder at the Springer ftp site (see Fig. 1.2 in Chap. 1). The procedures to develop this data query include the steps listed below:

a. Build a SQL Server stored procedure **[dbo].[StudentInfo]** using the Sever Explorer in Visual Studio.NET 2019.
b. Develop codes for the StudentFrame class to perform a data query to stored procedure (adding an **else if (ComboMethod.getSelectedItem()== "Java Callable Method")** block to the **Select** button Click event handler).

Hint:

1) Build a stored procedure **dbo.StudentInfo** with Visual Studio.NET 2019 as shown in Fig. 6.61. Only one input parameter, sName, which is the selected student name from the Student Name combo box, is applied to this procedure.
2) Call this procedure in Java Ant Application project with the **CallableStatement** method, exactly with the **executeQuery() method**, and retrieve the result with a **ResultSet object rs**. Then one can use a **while(rs.next())** loop to pick up each column and assign each of them to the related Text Field in the **StudentFrame** Form.

3. Based on Exercise 2, build another stored procedure, **dbo.StudentCourseInfo**, in the Visual Studio.NET 2019. Then in the same project **SQLSelectObject**, add some codes under the **Java Callable Method**, exactly under the codes to call the stored procedure, **dbo.StudentInfo** built in Exercise 2, to call the stored procedure, **dbo.StudentCourseInfo**, to get all courses, exactly **all course_id**, taken by the student based on the selected **student_id** from the student ID Text Field, and display them in **the CourseList** ListBox on the StudentFrame Form.

Hint:

1) Build a stored procedure **dbo.StudentCourseInfo** with Visual Studio.NET 2019 as shown in Fig. 6.62. Only one input parameter, sID, which is the selected **student_id** from the **Student ID** Text Field, is applied to this procedure.

```
CREATE PROCEDURE [dbo].[StudentCourseInfo]
      @sID VARCHAR(50)
AS
      SELECT course_id FROM StudentCourse WHERE student_id = @sID
RETURN 0
```

Fig. 6.62 The completed stored procedure dbo.StudentCourseInfo

2) Call this procedure in Java Ant Application project with the **CallableStatement** method, exactly with the **executeQuery() method**, and retrieve the result with a **ResultSet object rs**. Then one can use a **while(rs.next())** loop to pick up each row (**course_id**) and assign each of them to a String array, and then use the setListData() method to add them into the **CourseList** ListBox in the **StudentFrame** Form. Refer to the codes to get these **course_id** under the **CachedRowSet Method**, and they are similar.

4. Develop a method by adding some codes into the **LogIn** button. Click event handler in the **LogInFrame** class in the project **SQLSelectObject** to allow users to try the login process only 3 times. A warning message should be displayed and the project should be exited after 3 times of trying to login but all of them are failed. A project file **SQLSelectObject** can be found from the folder **Class DB Projects\Chapter 6** that is located under the Students folder at the Springer ftp site (see Fig. 1.2 in Chap. 1).

   Hint:

   1) Add a new class variable into the **LogInFrame** class constructor, **static int tryTimes = 0;**
   2) Inside the **LogInButtonActionPerformed()** event handler, increment **tryTimes** by 1 each time when this handler is triggered.
   3) Still inside that handler, using an **if** block to check whether the **tryTimes** is > 3? If it is, call the **CancelButton** Click event handler with **CancelButton.doClick()** method to stop this login process.
   4) Using a system method **System.exit(0);** to exit the project.

5. Adding a **Java Execute() Method** into the Query Method combo box on the StudentFrame Form via the constructor of the StudentFrame Form. Then build codes for this method to query student information from the **Student** table in our sample database. A project file **SQLSelectObject** can be found from the folder **Class DB Projects\Chapter 6** that is located under the **Students** folder at the Springer ftp site (see Fig. 1.2 in Chap. 1).
6. Figure 6.63 shows a stored procedure, **FacultyCourseInfo()**, which was built in the Visual Studio.NET 2019 and used to retrieve all course,

```
CREATE PROCEDURE [dbo].[FacultyCourseInfo]
    @fName VARCHAR(50)
AS
     DECLARE @facultyID AS VARCHAR(50)
     SET @facultyID = (SELECT faculty_id FROM Faculty WHERE faculty_name = @fName)
     SELECT course_id FROM Course WHERE faculty_id = @facultyID
RETURN 0
```

Fig. 6.63 The completed stored procedure dbo.FacultyCourseInfo

exactly all **course_id**, taught by the selected faculty member. Please develop your codes in the **CourseFrame** Form class in the **SQLSelectObject** project to use Java **Callable Method** to call this stored procedure to query all related **course_id** for the selected faculty member, and display them in the **CourseList** ListBox in the **CourseFrame** Form.

A project file **SQLSelectObject** can be found from the folder **Class DB Projects\Chapter 6** that is located under the Students folder at the Springer ftp site (see Fig. 1.2 in Chap. 1).

Hint:

1) Call this procedure in Java Ant Application project with the **CallableStatement** method in the **CourseFrame** class, exactly with the **execute() method**, and retrieve the result with a ResultSet object rs. Then one can use a **while(rs.next())** loop to pick up each row (**course_id**) and assign each of them to a String array, and then use the **setListData()** method to add them into the **CourseList** ListBox in the **CourseFrame** Form.
2) Develop your codes to replace the original codes inside the **Java Callable Method** to call this stored procedure. This stored procedure has only one input parameter, **facultyName**, which comes from the Faculty Name combo box.

Chapter 7
Insert, Update, and Delete Data from Databases

Similar to manipulating data in Visual Studio.NET, when manipulating data in the Java NetBeans IDE environment, a popular method is always utilized, the Java runtime object method. Java codes (SDK 1.x) enable users to access databases with a sequence of codes, starting from creating a DriverManager to load the database driver, setting up a connection using the Driver, creating a query statement object, running the **executeQuery** object, and processing the data using a ResultSet object. In this chapter, we introduce and use this method to perform the database manipulations to perform data insertions, data updating, and data deletion queries.

In the following sections, we will concentrate on inserting, updating, and deleting data against our sample database using Java runtime method.

7.1 Perform Data Manipulations to SQL Server Database Using Java Runtime Object

As we did for the data query operations, in this section we will discuss how to perform data manipulations using the Java runtime object method. Relatively speaking, there are some limitations in using the JAPI wizards to do the data manipulations. For instance, after the mapped entity has been built and the entity manager object has been created, the data manipulation can only be performed to that specified entity object or that data table. In other words, a defined or mapped entity object cannot perform data manipulations to any other entity object or data table.

A good solution to these limitations is to use the Java runtime object to perform the data manipulations, and this will provide much more flexibilities and

---

Supplementary Information The online version contains supplementary material available at [https://doi.org/10.1007/978-3-031-06553-8_7].

Y. Bai, *SQL Server Database Programming with Java*,
https://doi.org/10.1007/978-3-031-06553-8_7

controllabilities to the data manipulations against the database and allow a single object to perform multiple data manipulations against the target database.

Let's first concentrate on the data insertion to our SQL Server database using the Java runtime object method.

7.2 Perform Data Insertion to SQL Server Database Using Java Runtime Object

We have provided a very detailed and clear discussion about the Java runtime object method in Sect. 6.2 in Chap. 6. Refer to that section to get more details for this topic. Generally, to use Java runtime object to perform data manipulations against our target database, the following six steps should be adopted:

1) Load and register the database driver using DriverManager class and Driver methods.
2) Establish a database connection using the Connection object.
3) Create a data manipulation statement using the **createStatement()** method.
4) Execute the data manipulation statement using the **executeUpdate()** or **execute()** method.
5) Retrieve and check the execution result of the data manipulations.
6) Close the statement and connection using the **close()** method.

Generally, SQL Server database is a popular database system and has been widely implemented in most commercial and industrial applications. In this and the following sections in this chapter, we will concentrate on this database system to discuss how to perform data inserting, updating, and deleting operations.

To save time and space, we can use and modify a project **SQLSelectObject** we built in Chap. 6 to perform data manipulations against our target database. Perform the following operations to complete this project transferring:

1) Open the Windows Explorer, and create a new folder, such as **Class DB Project\Chapter 7**, in your root drive.
2) Open the Apache NetBeans 12, and one can find the project **SQLSelectObject** we built in Chap. 6 from the Projects window.
3) Right click on that project, and select the **Copy** item from the popup menu to open the **Copy Project** wizard.
4) Change the project name to **SQLInsertObject** in the Project Name box.
5) Browse to the folder, **Class DB Projects\Chapter 7**, which was created above in step 1, and click on the **OK** button to select this location as your project location.
6) Your finished **Copy Project** wizard should match one that is shown in Fig. 7.1.
7) Click on the **Copy** button to complete this copy process.

Now you can find this copied project **SQLInsertObject** from the Project window. With this project, we are ready to build our data insertion query to perform data manipulations to our SQL Server sample database **CSE_DEPT**.

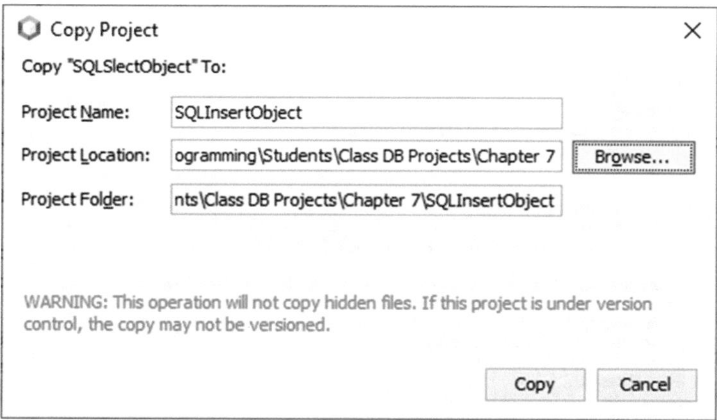

Fig. 7.1 The finished Copy Project wizard

In Sects. 6.3.1 and 6.3.3.2 in Chap. 6, we have created a **FacultyFrame** class and Faculty JFrame window FacultyFrame. Also the following components have been added into that project:

- A JDBC driver for SQL Server database has been loaded and registered.
- A valid database connection to that project has been established.
- A **PreparedStatement** instance has been created and implemented in the **Select** button click event handler to perform the data query.

In this section, we want to use the **Insert** button that has been built in the FacultyFrame window to perform this data insertion function. This data insertion action includes inserting a new faculty record with a new or a default faculty image.

7.2.1 Develop the Codes for the Insert Button Event Handler

In Sect. 6.3.3.5 in Chap. 6, we have given a detailed discussion about the dynamic data query using the PreparedStatement object method. Refer to that section to get more details about that method. In this section, we will use that object to perform a dynamic faculty member insertion to the Faculty table in our sample database.

Open the **Insert** button click event handler, and enter the codes that are shown in Fig. 7.2 into this handler. Let's have a close look at this piece of codes to see how it works.

A. Some local variables and objects are declared first, which include a local integer variable **numInsert** that is used to hold the returned number of inserted row as the data insert action is performed and a byte array **fImage** which is used to hold the selected faculty image to be inserted into the database later.

```
    private void InsertButtonActionPerformed(java.awt.event.ActionEvent evt) {
        // TODO add your handling code here:
A       int numInsert = 0;
        byte[] fImage;
B       if (!chkFaculty()) {
            msgDlg.setMessage("Fill all TextFields for a new record!");
            msgDlg.setVisible(true);
            return;
        }
C       fImage = getFacultyImage();
D       String InsertQuery = "INSERT INTO Faculty (faculty_id, faculty_name, title, office, phone, " +
                             "college, email, fimage) VALUES (?, ?, ?, ?, ?, ?, ?, ?)";
E       try {
            PreparedStatement pstmt = LogInFrame.con.prepareStatement(InsertQuery);
F           pstmt.setString(1, FacultyIDField.getText());
            pstmt.setString(2, FacultyNameField.getText());
            pstmt.setString(3, TitleField.getText());
            pstmt.setString(4, OfficeField.getText());
            pstmt.setString(5, PhoneField.getText());
            pstmt.setString(6, CollegeField.getText());
            pstmt.setString(7, EmailField.getText());
            pstmt.setBytes(8, fImage);
G           numInsert = pstmt.executeUpdate();
        }
H       catch (SQLException e) {
            msgDlg.setMessage("Error in Statement!" + e.getMessage());
            msgDlg.setVisible(true);
        }
I       System.out.println("The number of inserted row = " + numInsert);
J       ComboName.addItem(FacultyNameField.getText());
K       InsertButton.setEnabled(false);
L       clearFaculty();
    }
```

Fig. 7.2 The added codes to the Insert button click event handler

B. Prior to performing a data insertion, one needs to make sure that all TextFields that contained seven pieces of new faculty information must be filled. To do that, a user-defined method, **chkFaculty()**, is called to check all pieces of information to make sure that this insertion is a valid one. A warning message would be displayed if any field is empty.
C. Another user-defined method, **getFacultyImage()**, is executed to select and obtain a selected faculty image to be inserted into the **Faculty** table in our sample database.
D. An insert query string is created with eight positional dynamic parameters, which are associated with eight pieces of inserted faculty information. One point to be noted is that the order of these parameters must be identical with the order of columns defined in the **Faculty** table. Otherwise an exception may occur when this insertion is performed.
E. A **try…catch** block is used to initialize and execute the data insertion action. First a **PreparedStatement** instance is created using the **Connection** object that is located at the **LogInFrame** class with the insert query string as the argument.
F. The **setString()** method is used to initialize seven pieces of inserted faculty information, which are obtained from seven text fields and entered by the user as the project runs. Also the **setBytes()** method must be used to set the faculty image column, **fimage**, to insert a new selected faculty image into the database.

G. The data insertion function is performed by calling the **executeUpdate()** method. The running result of this method, which is an integer that equals to the number of rows that have been inserted into the database, is assigned to the local variable **numInsert**.
H. The **catch** block is used to track and collect any possible exception encountered when this data insertion is executed.
I. The running result is printed out as a debug purpose.
J. The new inserted faculty name is attached into the **Faculty Name** combo box to enable users to validate this data insertion later.
K. After this data insertion, the **Insert** button must be disabled to avoid any possible duplicated insertion operation to occur. To do that, a system method, **setEnable()**, with a **false** argument is used for that purpose.
L. Finally another user-defined method, **clearFaculty()**, is called to clean up all pieces of inserted information to make it ready for a validation of this insertion later.

Before we can build and run the project to test the data insertion function, we should first figure out how to check and validate this data insertion. First let's take care of the data checking to make sure that all pieces of new inserted faculty information are valid prior to this insertion.

7.2.2 Develop a Method for Data Checking Prior to Data Insertion

Create a new method named **chkFaculty(),** and enter the codes that are shown in Fig. 7.3 into this method. Let's take a closer look at this piece of codes to see how it works.

A. A Java TextField array, **f_field[]**, is declared and initialized with seven TextFields that will be filled by seven pieces of faculty information later. The purpose of this setting is to simplify this data checking process later.
B. A **for** loop is used to check all TextFields, exactly to use a system method **getText()**, to do this checking to make sure that all of them are filled without any

```
  private boolean chkFaculty() {
A   javax.swing.JTextField[] f_field = {FacultyIDField, FacultyNameField, TitleField, OfficeField, PhoneField,
                                        CollegeField, EmailField};

B   for (int loop = 0; loop <f_field.length; loop++) {
      if (f_field[loop].getText() == "") {
        return false;
      }
    }
    return true;
  }
```

Fig. 7.3 The detailed codes for the user-defined method chkFaculty()

empty one. A **false** would be returned if any of them is empty to indicate this error.

Next let's take care of how to get a selected faculty image to be inserted into the database.

7.2.3 Develop a Method for Selecting a Valid Faculty Image

When performing this data insertion, in addition to seven pieces of a new faculty information, a new or a default faculty image should also be involved to this action. It is crystal to get this image in a simple and easy way to speed up this insertion action. To that purpose, create another user-defined method **getFacultyImage(),** and enter the codes shown in Fig. 7.4 for this method.

Let's take a closer look at this piece of codes to see how it works.

A. Some local variables are declared first, which include a byte array **fimage** and a File object **imgFile**. The former is used to hold the selected faculty image, and the latter is used to keep the selected faculty image in a file format.
B. A **JFileChooser** object, **imgChooser**, is created, and it is used to assist users to select a desired faculty image via this kind of File Dialog.
C. To get and save a selected faculty image or a file, the current folder with the path is necessary, and this folder is our current project folder. The selected faculty image would be stored in that folder to enable system to pick it up later to get it to be displayed.
D. A **JFileChooser** dialog is opened to allow users to select a desired faculty image.
E. If this dialog is opened successfully, and a faculty image has been selected, a property **APPROVE_OPTION** is returned with a result whose value is non-zero. Then a system method **getSelectedFile()** is executed to return the

```
  private byte[] getFacultyImage() {
A     byte[] fimage = null;
      File imgFile = null;
B     JFileChooser imgChooser = new JFileChooser();
C     imgChooser.setCurrentDirectory(new File(System.getProperty("user.home")));
D     int result = imgChooser.showOpenDialog(this);
E     if (result == JFileChooser.APPROVE_OPTION) {
        imgFile = imgChooser.getSelectedFile();
F       System.out.println("Selected path: " + imgFile.getAbsolutePath());
        System.out.println("Selected file: " + imgFile.toString());
      }
G     try {
        fimage = Files.readAllBytes(imgFile.toPath());
H     } catch (IOException ex) {
        Logger.getLogger(FacultyFrame.class.getName()).log(Level.SEVERE, null, ex);
      }
I     return fimage;
  }
```

Fig. 7.4 The detailed codes for the user-defined method getFacultyImage()

selected image and assign it to the File object, **imgFile**, which is to be used in next step.

F. For the debug purpose, the file name and its path are displayed here.
G. A **try-catch** block is used to convert the image from the File format to the byte array format since this is the format to be allowed and to be used in the **fimage** column in the database. To do that, a system method **readAllBytes()** is used to do this kind of conversion. The argument of this method is the path of the selected image file.
H. A catch block is used to catch and report any possible exceptions if they occurred.
I. Finally the converted faculty image in the byte array format is returned.

Before we can handle the last user-defined method **clearFaculty()**, let's take a look at an issue related to the **Insert** button. As we know, this button is disabled after a data insertion is done to avoid any possible duplicated insertion in step **K** in Fig. 7.2. One question is: When should this button be enabled to allow users to begin a new insertion?

7.2.4 Find a Way to Enable the Insert Button to Begin a New Data Insertion

Now let's try to answer the above question, When should this **Insert** button be enabled again to allow users to insert another new record? Based on a fact, which is that when a new record is to be inserted into a database, the **Faculty ID** should be a new value, and it should not be identical with any current **faculty_id** in the database. This provided us with an idea, which is: as long as a new faculty record is to be inserted, the Faculty ID TextField, exactly its content, should be updated with a new value. Yes, that is true and a good solution to this question.

The answer is: the **Insert** button should be enabled again as long as the content of the Faculty ID TextField is changed, and this kind of changing can be reflected and triggered by a TextField event, **FacultyIDFieldKeyTyped**.

Perform the following operational steps to open this event handler:

1) Click on the **Design** tab on the top to open the Design View of the FacultyFrame Form.
2) Right click on the **Faculty ID** TextField, and select the item **Events > Key > keyTyped** to open this event handler.

Then enter the codes shown in Fig. 7.5 into this event handler.

Only one line of codes is built here, which is to call the system method **setEnabled()** with the **true** as an argument to enable this **Insert** button when the content of the Faculty ID TextField is changed. With this coding, we solved this issue, and let's continue to the next step.

```
  private void FacultyIDFieldKeyTyped(java.awt.event.KeyEvent evt) {
      // TODO add your handling code here:
A     InsertButton.setEnabled(true);
  }
```

Fig. 7.5 The codes inside the FacultyIDFieldKeyTyped event handler

```
  private void clearFaculty() {
A   javax.swing.JTextField[] f_field = {FacultyIDField, FacultyNameField, TitleField, OfficeField, PhoneField,
                                         CollegeField, EmailField};
B   for (int loop = 0; loop < f_field.length; loop++){
      f_field[loop].setText("");
    }
  }
```

Fig. 7.6 The codes in the method clearFaculty()

7.2.5 Develop a Method for Clearing Original Faculty Information

In order for us to perform a validation for this new inserted faculty record in the **Faculty** table in our sample database, we need to clean up all pieces of original faculty information stored in the seven TextFields in the FacultyFrame Form. To do that, we need to build another user-defined method, **clearFaculty()**, and enter the codes shown in Fig. 7.6 into this method.

Let's have a closer look at this piece of codes to see how it works.

A. A JTextField array is declared and initialized by adding seven TextFields into it. Each TextField in this array is associated with a TextField used to store and display a piece of selected faculty information. The purpose of using this array is to simplify this cleaning process with a for loop shown below.
B. A **for** loop is used to scroll all seven TextFields and to set empty strings to them to clean up each of them.

Next let's handle the validation process for this data insertion.

7.2.6 Develop the Codes for the Validation of the Data Insertion

To confirm and validate this data insertion, we can use the codes we built inside the **Select** button click event handler without any modifications.

Now we are ready to build and run the project to test the data insertion function.

7.2.7 Build and Run the Project to Test the Data Insertion

Click on the **Clean and Build Main Project** button from the toolbar to build the project. Make sure that our sample SQL Server database CSE_DEPT has been connected to our project.

Now click on the **Run Main Project** button to run the project. Enter suitable username and password, such as `jhenry` and `test`, to the **LogIn** frame form, and select the **Faculty Information** from the SelectFrame window to open the FacultyFrame form window. Make sure that the **Runtime Object Method** has been selected from the **Query Method** combo box. Then click on the **Select** button to query the default faculty information.

Modify the contents of seven text fields by entering the following credentials into these TextFields, which is equivalent to a new record of a faculty member:

- Faculty ID: **J28544**
- Faculty Name: **James Carson**
- Title: **Associate Professor**
- Office: **MTC-118**
- Phone: **750-378-1134**
- College: **University of Miami**
- Email: **jcarson@college.edu**

Then click on the **Insert** button to select a desired faculty image for this insertion.

The **JFileChooser** dialog appeared, as shown in Fig. 7.7. Browse to a desired folder on your computer, where all faculty images are stored, and click on the **Open** button to select that image. In our case, this folder is **C:\SQL Java DB Programming\Students\Images\Faculty**. You may select a default faculty image file, **Defaulty.**

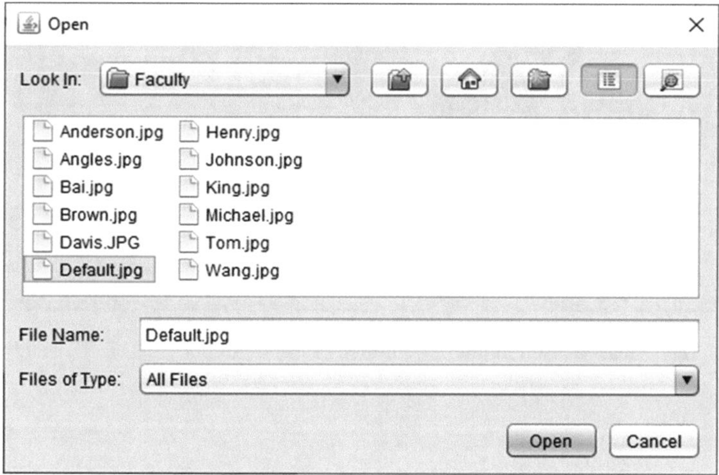

Fig. 7.7 The opened JFileChooser dialog

jpg, as we did in this example. All faculty images can be found from a folder **Students\Images\Faculty** at the Springer ftp site (refer to Fig. 1.2 in Chap. 1). You can copy and paste them in your desired folder in your computer.

Now all TextFields contained the original faculty information become blank. To confirm or validate this data insertion, just go to the **Faculty Name** combo box, and scroll down in that box and

you can find that our new inserted faculty member, **James Carson**, has been added there. Click

that faculty by clicking on it, and click on the **Select** button to try to retrieve back all pieces of information for this inserted faculty. Immediately you can find that all pieces of information for that inserted faculty are displayed in this FacultyFrame Form, as shown in Fig. 7.8.

Our data insertion action is successful!

It is recommended to remove this new inserted faculty from the **Faculty** table to keep our sample database neat and clean. Next let's perform the data updating action against our sample database using the Java runtime object method.

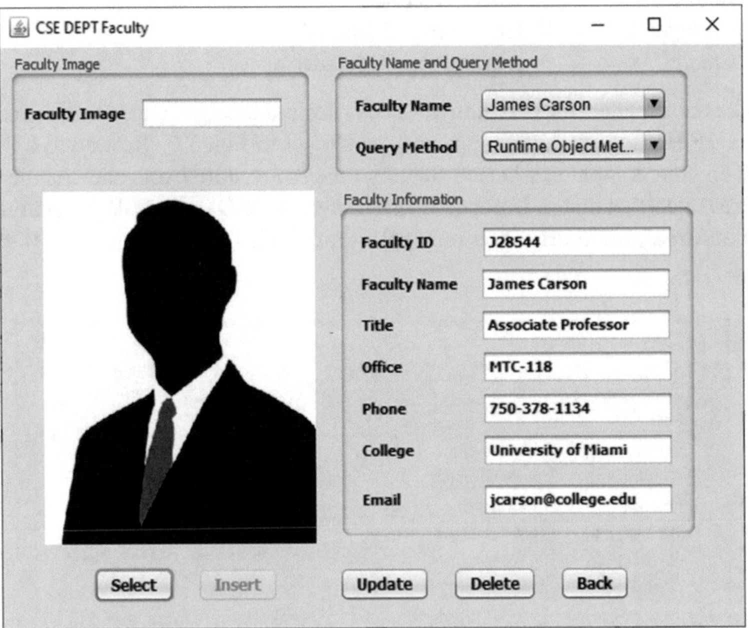

Fig. 7.8 The validation result for the new inserted faculty

7.3 Perform Data Updating to SQL Server Database Using Java Runtime Object

Regularly, we do not need to update a **faculty_id** when we update a faculty record since a better way to do that is to insert a new faculty record and delete the old one. The main reason for this is that a very complicated operational process would be performed if the **faculty_id** were updated since it is a primary key in the **Faculty** table and foreign keys in the **Course** and the **LogIn** tables. To update a primary key, one needs to update foreign keys first in the child tables and then update the primary key in the parent table. This will make our updating process very complicated and easy to be confused. In order to avoid this confusion, in this section, we will update a faculty record by changing any column except the **faculty_id**, and this is a popular way to update a table and widely implemented in most database applications.

We still want to work for the **Faculty** table in our sample database via the FacultyFrame Form; thus, we do not need to create a brand new project to perform this data updating action, instead we can use an existed project **SQLInsertObject** and add our codes to do this data updating action. Perform the following operations to make our new project based on that project:

1) Open the Windows Explorer and create a new folder, such as **Class DB Project\Chapter 7**, in your root drive if you did not do this.
2) Open the Apache NetBeans 12, and one can find the project **SQLInsertObject** we built in the last section from the **Projects** window.
3) Right click on that project, and select the **Copy** item from the popup menu to open the **Copy Project** wizard.
4) Change the project name to **SQLUpdateObject** in the Project Name box.
5) Browse to the folder, **Class DB Projects\Chapter 7**, which was created above in step 1, and click on the **OK** button to select this location as your project location.
6) Click on the **Copy** button to complete this copy process.

Before we can build codes for the **Update** button event handler, first let's perform some modifications for the codes in the **FacultyFrame** constructor.

7.3.1 Modify the Codes Inside the FacultyFrame Constructor

The reason we need to do this modification is that some faculty records in the **Faculty** table would be changed after this updating action. Thus we need to update the faculty members in the **Faculty Name** combobox, **ComboName**, to enable users to check and validate related updating action based on the updated faculty records. One of the most important updating is the faculty name stored in that combobox.

```
  public class FacultyFrame extends javax.swing.JFrame {
    MsgDialog msgDlg = new MsgDialog(new javax.swing.JFrame(), true);
    /**
     * Creates new form FacultyFrame
     */
    public FacultyFrame() {
      initComponents();
      this.setLocationRelativeTo(null);   // set the faculty Form at the center

      ComboMethod.addItem("Runtime Object Method");
      ComboMethod.addItem("Java execute() Method");
      ComboMethod.addItem("Java Callable Method");
A     CurrentFaculty();
    }
    ......
  }
```

Fig. 7.9 The modified codes in the FacultyFrame constructor

```
  private void CurrentFaculty() {
A     ResultSet rs;
B     try {
        PreparedStatement pstmt = LogInFrame.con.prepareStatement("SELECT faculty_name FROM Faculty");
C       rs = pstmt.executeQuery();
D       ComboName.removeAllItems();
E       while (rs.next()){
          ComboName.addItem(rs.getString(1));
        }
F       rs.close();
G     } catch (SQLException ex) {
        Logger.getLogger(FacultyFrame.class.getName()).log(Level.SEVERE, null, ex);
      }
  }
```

Fig. 7.10 The detailed codes in the user-defined method CurrentFaculty()

Open our new project **SQLUpdateObject** and the **FacultyFrame** Form, and enter the codes that are shown in Fig. 7.9 into the constructor of this class.

The only modification is to replace eight coding lines, which are used to add eight faculty members into this **Faculty Name** combobox **ComboName**, with a new user-defined method **CurrentFaculty()**, as shown in step **A** in Fig. 7.9.

The detailed codes for this method are shown in Fig. 7.10. Let's have a closer look at the codes in this method to see how it works.

A. A local **ResultSet** object, **rs**, is declared first since we need to use this object to hold our queried faculty members result.
B. A **try-catch** block is used to perform this data query. A database connection is established via the **LogInFrame** class, and a new **PreparedStatement** object, **pstmt**, is created with a query string to retrieve all faculty names from our **Faculty** table.
C. The query is executed by calling the **executeQuery**() method, and the query result is assigned to our local **ResultSet** object **rs**.
D. Prior to updating all faculty names in the **ComboName** box, it is cleared to make this updating action ready with a system method **removeAllItems**().

E. A **while()** loop is used to repeatedly pick up each faculty name with the **next()** method. The retrieved faculty name, **rs.getString(1)**, is added into the **ComboName** box by using a system method **addItem()**. Since only one column, **faculty_name**, is queried from the **Faculty** table, thus the column number is 1.
F. The **ResultSet** object is closed after this query.
G. A **catch** block is used to collect and report any possible exceptions during that query.

Now let's develop the codes for the **Update** button event handler to perform the data updating action to the **Faculty** table via the FacultyFrame Form in this project.

7.3.2 Develop the Codes for the Update Button Event Handler

We want to use the **Update** button built in the FacultyFrame form window to perform the faculty updating function, therefore no any modification to this FacultyFrame form window to be made. Now let's develop the codes for the **Update** button click event handler.

Open this event handler, and enter the codes that are shown in Fig. 7.11 into this event handler. Let's have a closer look at this piece of codes to see how it works.

A. A local variable, **numUpdated**, and a byte array object, **fImage**, are created first. The Integer variable is used to hold the running result of the data updating,

```
    private void UpdateButtonActionPerformed(java.awt.event.ActionEvent evt) {
      // TODO add your handling code here:
A     byte[] fImage;
      int numUpdated = 0;
B     fImage = getFacultyImage();
C     String query = "UPDATE Faculty SET faculty_name=?, title=?, office=?, phone=?, college=?, email=?, fimage=? " +
                     "WHERE faculty_id= ?";
D     try {
           PreparedStatement pstmt = LogInFrame.con.prepareStatement(query);
E          pstmt.setString(1, FacultyNameField.getText());
           pstmt.setString(2, TitleField.getText());
           pstmt.setString(3, OfficeField.getText());
           pstmt.setString(4, PhoneField.getText());
           pstmt.setString(5, CollegeField.getText());
           pstmt.setString(6, EmailField.getText());
F          pstmt.setBytes(7, fImage);
G          pstmt.setString(8, FacultyIDField.getText());
H          numUpdated = pstmt.executeUpdate();
      }
I     catch (SQLException e) {
             msgDlg.setMessage("Error in Statement!" + e.getMessage());
             msgDlg.setVisible(true);
      }
J     System.out.println("The number of updated row = " + numUpdated);
K     CurrentFaculty();
    }
```

Fig. 7.11 The developed codes for the Update button click event handler

and the byte array is used to hold a returned faculty image by calling the **getFacultyImage()** method later.

B. The user-defined method **getFacultyImage()** is executed to obtain an updated faculty image that can be selected by the user. The detailed codes and introductions to that user-defined method can be found in Sect. 7.2.3.
C. The updating query string is created with eight positional parameters. The query criterion is the faculty ID, which is the eighth parameter and placed after the **WHERE** clause.
D. A **try…catch** block is used to assist this data updating action. First a **PreparedStatement** instance is created using the **Connection** object that is located at the **LogInFrame** class with the updating query string as the argument.
E. A set of **setString()** methods is used to initialize six pieces of updated faculty information, which are obtained from six text fields and entered by the user as the project runs.
F. A **setBytes()** method is used to assign a byte array **fImage** to the **fimage** column in the **Faculty** table as an updated faculty image. This method is very important, and only a byte array can be used to hold an image to be stored to the related image column in database.
G. The eighth input parameter in the query string, **faculty_id**, is assigned to the query criterion that is located after the **WHERE** clause.
H. The data updating action is performed by calling the **executeUpdate()** method. The updating result, which is an integer number that is equal to the number of rows that have been updated by this data updating action, is returned and assigned to the local integer variable **numUpdated**.
I. The **catch** block is used to track and collect any possible exception encountered when this data updating is executed.
J. The running result is printed out as a debug purpose.
K. The user-defined method **CurrentFaculty()** is executed to retrieve all updated faculty name and add them into the Faculty Name combo box to enable the users to validate this data updating later.

Now let's build and run the project to test the data updating action.

7.3.3 Build and Run the Project to Test the Data Updating

Before you can run this project, the following conditions have to be met:

- The SQL Server sample database CSE_DEPT has been connected to this project.
- To check this connection, open the **Services** window and expand the **Databases** node to locate our sample database connection URL, **jdbc:sqlserver://localhost\SQL2019EXPRESS: 5000;databaseName=CSE_DEPT [SMART on dbo]**. Right click on this URL, and select the **Connect** item to do this connection.

Click on the **Clean and Build Main Project** button from the toolbar to build our project. Then click on the **Run Main Project** button to run the project.

Enter suitable username and password, such as **jhenry** and **test**, to complete the login process, and select the Faculty Information from the SelectFrame window to open the FacultyFrame window. Make sure that the **Runtime Object Method** has been selected from the **Query Method** combo box. Then click on the **Select** button to query any faculty information. As an example, here select the faculty member **Ying Bai** from the ComboName box, and display all pieces of information for this example faculty member.

To update this faculty record, enter the following information into six Text Fields (no **Faculty ID** Text Field) inside the Faculty Information panel as an updated faculty record.

- Faculty Name: **Susan Bai**
- Title: **Professor**
- Office: **MTC-215**
- Phone: **750-378-1348**
- College: **Duke University**
- Email: **sbai@college.com**

Click on the **Update** button to select a desired image for this updated faculty member, **White.jpg**. All example faculty image files, including this faculty image, can be found from a folder **Students\Images\Faculty** in the Springer ftp site (refer to Fig. 1.2 in Chap. 1). One can copy those image files from that folder and save them to your desired folder in your computer.

Now if one goes to the Faculty Name combobox, **ComboName**, and can find that the updated faculty name **Susan Bai** has been added into the Faculty Name combobox and the original faculty member **Ying Bai** has been removed from this box by clicking the drop-down arrow of that box.

One way to validate this data updating is to go to the **Output** window. You can find that a running successful message is displayed in that window, as shown in Fig. 7.12.

Similar to the data insertion action, here we have another two ways to validate this data updating. One way is to open our **Faculty** table in our sample database to confirm this data updating, and the other way is to use the **Select** button (exactly the codes inside that button's click event handler) to do this validation. We prefer to use

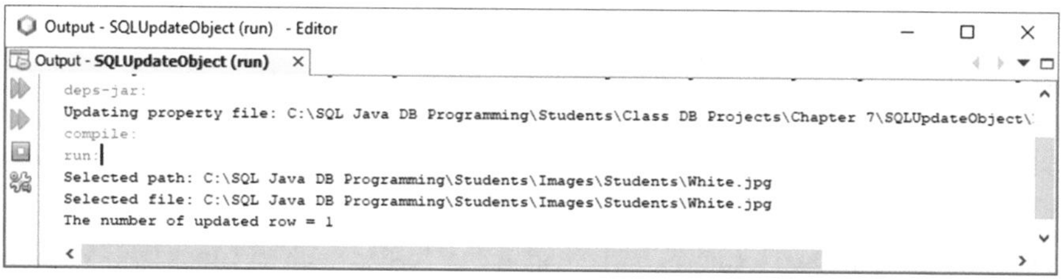

```
Output - SQLUpdateObject (run) - Editor
Output - SQLUpdateObject (run)
deps-jar:
Updating property file: C:\SQL Java DB Programming\Students\Class DB Projects\Chapter 7\SQLUpdateObject\
compile:
run:
Selected path: C:\SQL Java DB Programming\Students\Images\Students\White.jpg
Selected file: C:\SQL Java DB Programming\Students\Images\Students\White.jpg
The number of updated row = 1
```

Fig. 7.12 The successful data updating message

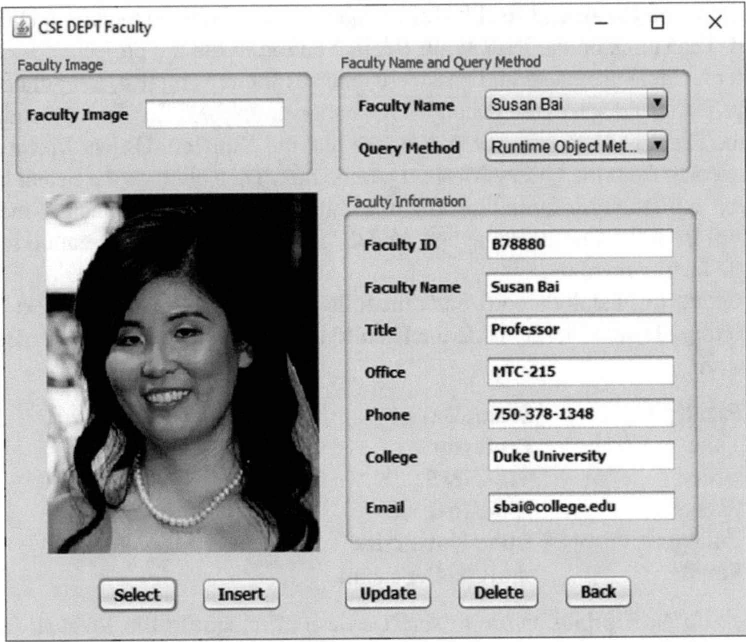

Fig. 7.13 The data updated result

the second way to do this validation. Click on the **Select** button to try to retrieve this updated faculty record, and the running result is shown in Fig. 7.13. Our data updating action is successful!

It is highly recommended to recover that updated faculty record to the original one to keep our database clean and neat. One can perform a similar updating action to do this recovery job. Of course, you can also perform this data recovering job using the Microsoft SQL Server Management Studio if you like.

Next let's handle the data deletion action against our sample database.

7.4 Perform Data Deleting to SQL Server Database Using Java Runtime Object

We still want to work for the **Faculty** table in our sample database via the FacultyFrame Form; thus, we do not need to create a brand new project to perform this data updating action; instead we can use an existed project **SQLUpdateObject** and add our codes to do this data deleting action. Perform the following operations to make our new project based on that project:

1) Open the Windows Explorer and create a new folder, such as **Class DB Project\Chapter 7**, in your root drive if you did not do this.

2) Open the Apache NetBeans 12, and one can find the project **SQLUpdateObject** we built in the last section from the **Projects** window.
3) Right click on that project, and select the **Copy** item from the popup menu to open the **Copy Project** wizard.
4) Change the project name to **SQLDeleteObject** in the Project Name box.
5) Browse to the folder, **Class DB Projects\Chapter 7**, which was created above in step 1, and click on the **OK** button to select this location as your project location.
6) Click on the **Copy** button to complete this copy process.

Basically, there is no significant difference between the data updating and deleting using Java runtime object method. In this section, we try to use the **Delete** button we built in the FacultyFrame Form window to perform this data deletion operation.

7.4.1 Develop the Codes for the Delete Button Event Handler

Open the **Delete** button click event handler, and enter the codes that are shown in Fig. 7.14 into this event handler. Let's have a closer look at this piece of codes to see how it works.

A. Two local variables, **numDeleted** and **cFacultyName**, are created first, and these two variables are used to hold the running result of the data deleting action and the current faculty name.
B. The deleting query string is created with one positional parameter. The query criterion is the faculty name that is placed after the WHERE clause.
C. A **try…catch** block is used to assist this data deleting action. First a `PreparedStatement` instance is created using the `Connection` object that is located at the LogInFrame class with the deleting query string as the argument.

```
  private void cmdDeleteActionPerformed(java.awt.event.ActionEvent evt) {
A     int numDeleted = 0;
      String cFacultyName = null;
B     String query = "DELETE FROM Faculty WHERE faculty_name = ?";
      try {
C         PreparedStatement  pstmt = LogInFrame.con.prepareStatement(query);
D         pstmt.setString(1, ComboName.getSelectedItem().toString());
E         cFacultyName = (String)ComboName.getSelectedItem();
F         numDeleted = pstmt.executeUpdate();
      }
G     catch (SQLException e) {
          msgDlg.setMessage("Error in Statement!" + e.getMessage());
          msgDlg.setVisible(true);
      }
H     System.out.println("The number of deleted row = " + numDeleted);
I     ComboName.removeItem(cFacultyName);
  }
```

Fig. 7.14 The developed codes for the Delete button click event handler

D. The **setString()** method is used to initialize the positional parameter, which is the faculty name to be deleted from the Faculty Name combo box.
E. After this faculty record has been deleted, we need to remove this faculty name from the Faculty Name combo box. In order to remember the current faculty name, we need to temporarily store it into our local string variable `cFacultyName`.
F. The data deleting action is performed by calling the **executeUpdate()** method. The deleting result, which is an integer number that is equal to the number of rows that have been deleted by this data deleting action, is returned and assigned to the local integer variable **numDeleted**.
G. The **catch** block is used to track and collect any possible exception encountered when this data deleting is executed.
H. The running result is printed out as a debug purpose.
I. The deleted faculty name is removed from this Faculty Name combo box.

Now we are ready to build and run the project to test the data deletion function.

7.4.2 Build and Run the Project to Test the Data Deleting

Make sure that our sample database **CSE_DEPT** has been connected to our project. To check this connection, open the **Services** window and expand the **Databases** node to locate our sample database connection URL, **jdbc:sqlserver://localhost\\SQL2019EXPRESS:5000;databaseName=CSE_DEPT [SMART on dbo]**. Right click on this URL, and select the **Connect** item to do this connection. You may need to use the password, **Happy2020**, to do this connection.

Now click on the **Clean and Build Main Project** button from the toolbar to build our project. Then click on the **Run Main Project** button to run the project.

Enter suitable username and password, such as **jhenry** and **test**, to complete the login process, and select the Faculty Information from the SelectFrame window to open the FacultyFrame window. Make sure that the **Runtime Object Method** has been selected from the **Query Method** combo box. Then click on the **Select** button to query the default faculty information. The default faculty information is displayed.

To test this data deletion function, we can try to delete one faculty member, such as **Ying Bai**, from our **Faculty** table. To do that, select this faculty member from the Faculty Name combo box, and click on the **Delete** button. Immediately you can find that this faculty name has been removed from the Faculty Name combo box. Also the running result is shown in the **Output** window, as shown in Fig. 7.15.

To confirm this data deletion, click on the **Back** and the **Exit** button to stop our project. Then open our **Faculty** table by going to the **Services** window, and expand the **Databases** node, and our connection URL, and finally our sample database **CSE_DEPT**. Expand our database schema **dbo**, and right click on the **Faculty** table. Select the **View Data** item from the popup menu to open our **Faculty** table.

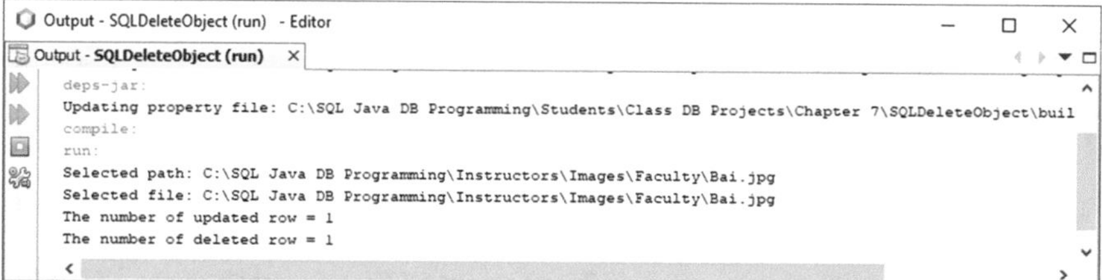

Fig. 7.15 The successful data deletion message

Table 7.1 The deleted faculty record in the Faculty table

faculty_ id	faculty_ name	title	office	phone	college	email	fimage
B78880	Ying Bai	Associate Professor	MTC-211	750-378-1148	Florida Atlantic University	ybai@college.edu	NULL

On the opened **Faculty** table, you can find that the faculty member **Ying Bai** has been removed from this table.

Our data deletion function is successful!

To make our database clean and neat, it is highly recommended to recover this deleted faculty member and related records in our **Faculty**, **LogIn**, **Course**, and **StudentCourse** tables. Refer to Tables 7.1, 7.2, 7.3 and 7.4 to complete these data recoveries.

An easy way to do this recovery job is to use the Microsoft SQL Server Management Studio. One can select and copy data with all rows from each table (Tables 7.1, 7.2, 7.3 and 7.4) and paste them at the bottom line on each opened Table with Microsoft SQL Management Studio.

Three points to be noted when recovering these data are:

1) The order to perform these rows' recovery. The faculty record in the parent table must be recovered first. In our case, the record in the **Faculty** table must be recovered first since it is a parent table. The records in the child tables can be recovered after the record in the parent table had been completed. Otherwise some error may be encountered.
2) The faculty image column, **fimage**. Now just enter a **NULL** to that column, and one can insert the actual image for that faculty when running one of our Visual Basic.NET projects, **SQL Image Project**, which was built in Sect. 2.9.5 in Chap. 2, to complete this recovery process later.
3) When you finished your copy-paste operations for all of those recovery rows, click **File > Save All** in Microsoft SQL Server Management Studio to save all of these additions.

Another way to do this recovery job is to run one of our projects, **SQLInsertObject**, to first insert the deleted faculty record into the **Faculty** table (parent table) with image, and then use the Microsoft SQL Server Management Studio to perform

Table 7.2 The deleted course records in the Course table

course_id	course	credit	classroom	schedule	enrollment	faculty_id
CSC-132B	Introduction to Programming	3	TC-302	T-H: 1:00-2:25 PM	21	B78880
CSC-234A	Data Structure & Algorithms	3	TC-302	M-W-F: 9:00-9:55 AM	25	B78880
CSE-434	Advanced Electronics Systems	3	TC-213	M-W-F: 1:00-1:55 PM	26	B78880
CSE-438	Advd Logic & Microprocessor	3	TC-213	M-W-F: 11:00-11:55 AM	35	B78880

Table 7.3 The deleted login records in the LogIn table

user_name	pass_word	faculty_id	student_id
ybai	come	B78880	NULL

Table 7.4 The deleted records in the StudentCourse table

s_course_id	student_id	course_id	credit	major
1005	T77896	CSC-234A	3	CS/IS
1009	A78835	CSE-434	3	CE
1014	A78835	CSE-438	3	CE
1016	A97850	CSC-132B	3	ISE
1017	A97850	CSC-234A	3	ISE

copy-paste operations to recovery all other records for the child tables (**LogIn**, **Course**, and **StudentCourse** tables).

As we discussed in Sect. 6.3.3.5 in Chap. 6, in addition to using the **executeUpdate()** method to perform data manipulations such as data insertion, updating, and deleting actions, one can use the **execute()** method to perform the similar data manipulations. It is preferred to leave this optional method as a home work and allow students to handle this issue.

A complete sample project **SQLDeleteObject** can be found from the folder **Class DB Projects\ Chapter 7** that is located under the **Students** folder at the Springer ftp site (refer to Fig. 1.2 in Chap. 1).

Next let's take care of the data manipulations against the SQL Server database using the Java Updatable ResultSet method.

7.5 Perform Data Manipulations Using Updatable ResultSet

As we discussed in Sect. 6.3.3.7 in Chap. 6, a ResultSet object can be considered as a table of data representing a database result set, which is usually generated by executing a statement that queries the database.

The **ResultSet** interface provides **getXXX()** methods for retrieving column values from the current row. Values can be retrieved using either the index number of the column or the name of the column. In general, using the column index will be more efficient. Columns are numbered from 1. For maximum portability, result set columns within each row should be read in left-to-right order, and each column should be read only once.

A default ResultSet object is not updatable with a cursor that moves forward only. Thus, it is possible to iterate through it only once and from the first row to the last row. New methods in the JDBC 4.0 API make it possible to produce ResultSet objects that are scrollable and/or updatable.

Before we can use the ResultSet object to perform data manipulations against our sample database, let's first have a clear picture about the ResultSet additional functionalities and categories supported in JDBC 4.0.

7.5.1 Introduction to ResultSet Enhanced Functionalities and Categories

ResultSet functionality in JDBC 4.0 includes enhancements for scrollability and positioning, sensitivity to changes by others, and updatability.

- **Scrollability**: the ability to move backward as well as forward through a ResultSet object. Associated with scrollability is the ability to move to any particular position in the ResultSet, through either relative positioning or absolute positioning.
- **Positioning**: the ability to move a specified number of rows forward or backward from the current row. Absolute positioning enables you to move to a specified row number, counting from either the beginning or the end of the ResultSet.
- **Sensitivity**: the ability to see changes made to the database while the ResultSet is open, providing a dynamic view of the underlying data. Changes made to the underlying columns values of rows in the ResultSet are visible.

Two parameters can be used to set up those properties of a ResultSet object when it is created: they are ResultSet type and Concurrency type of a ResultSet. Table 7.5 lists these types and their functions. Under JDBC 4.0, the **Connection** class has the following methods that take a ResultSet type and a concurrency type as input to define a new created ResultSet object:

- `Statement createStatement(int resultSetType, int resultSetConcurrency)`
- `PreparedStatement prepareStatement(String sql, int resultSetType, int resultSetConcurrency)`
- `CallableStatement prepareCall(String sql, int resultSetType, int resultSetConcurrency)`

Table 7.5 The ResultSet type and Concurrency type

ResultSet type	Functions
Forward-only	This is a JDBC 1.0 functionality. This type of ResultSet is not scrollable, not positionable, and not sensitive
Scroll-sensitive	This type of ResultSet is scrollable and positionable. It is also sensitive to underlying database changes
Scroll-insensitive	This type of result set is scrollable and positionable, but not sensitive to underlying database changes
Concurrency type	**Functions**
Updatable	Data updating, insertion, and deleting can be performed on the ResultSet and copied to the database
Read-only	The result set cannot be modified in any way

You can specify one of the following static constant values for ResultSet type:

- **ResultSet.TYPE_FORWARD_ONLY**
- **ResultSet.TYPE_SCROLL_INSENSITIVE**
- **ResultSet.TYPE_SCROLL_SENSITIVE**

And you can specify one of the following static constant values for concurrency type:

- **ResultSet.CONCUR_READ_ONLY**
- **ResultSet.CONCUR_UPDATABLE**

The following code fragment, in which **conn** is a valid Connection object and **sql** is a defined SQL query string, illustrates how to make a ResultSet that is scrollable and sensitive to updates by others and that is updatable.

```
PreparedStatement pstmt = conn.prepareStatement
                          (sql, ResultSet.TYPE_SCROLL_SENSITIVE,
                           ResultSet.CONCUR_UPDATABLE);
```

After we have a basic and fundamental understanding about the ResultSet and its enhanced functionalities, now we can go ahead to perform data manipulations against our sample database using the **Updatable ResultSet** object.

7.5.2 Perform Data Manipulations Using Updatable ResultSet Object

Generally, performing data manipulations using updatable ResultSet can be divided into the following three categories:

- Data insertion
- Data updating
- Data deleting

Table 7.6 The operational steps of data manipulations using updatable ResultSet

Manipulation type	Steps
Data deleting	Single step: Using the **deleteRow()** method of the ResultSet class.
Data updating	Two steps: 1. Update the data in the ResultSet using the associated **updateXXX()** methods. 2. Copy the changes to the database using the **updateRow()** method.
Data insertion	Three steps: 1. Move to the insert-row by calling the ResultSet **moveToInsertRow()** method. 2. Use the appropriate **updateXXX()** methods to update data in the insert-row. 3. Copy the changes to the database by calling the ResultSet **insertRow()** method.

Different data manipulations need different operational steps, and Table 7.6 lists the most popular operational steps for these data manipulations.

It can be found from Table 7.6 that the data deleting is the easiest way to remove a piece of data from the database since it only needs one step to delete the data from both the ResultSet and the database. The other two data manipulations, data updating and insertion, need at least two steps to complete that data manipulations.

The point to be noted is the data insertion action, in which the first step **moveToInsertRow()** is exactly moved to a blank row that is not a part of the ResultSet but related to the ResultSet. The data insertion exactly occurred when the **insertRow()** method is called and the next **commit** command is executed.

Let's start with the data insertion against our sample database first. Since there is no difference between data manipulation for SQL Server and Oracle database, in the following sections, we will use the SQL Server database as our target database, and the same codes can be used for the Oracle database as long as a valid database connection can be set up between our project and the target database.

7.5.2.1 Insert a New Row Using the Updatable ResultSet

To save time and space, we want to use and modify a project **SQLDeleteObject** we built in Sect. 7.4 to make it as our new project to perform this data insertion action. Perform the following operations to make it as our project:

1) Create a new folder **DB Projects\Chapter 7** in your computer if you did not do that and launch Apache NetBeans IDE 12 and open the **Projects** window.
2) Right click on the project **SQLDeleteObject** we built in Sect. 7.4, and select the **Copy** item from the popup menu to open the **Copy Project** wizard.
3) Change the project name to **SQLUpdatableInsert** in the Project Name box.
4) Browse to the folder, **Class DB Projects\Chapter 7**, which was created above in step 1, and click on the **OK** button to select this location as your project location.

5) Click on the **Copy** button to complete this copy process.

Perform the following coding modifications to the FacultyFrame Form:

1) Open the constructor of this class, and add one more statement into this constructor,

   ComboMethod.addItem("Java Updatable ResultSet");

   Your modified codes in this constructor should match one that is shown in Fig. 7.16. The modified part has been highlighted in bold.
2) Click on the **Design** button to switch back to the design view of the FacultyFrame form window, and double click on the **Insert** button to open its event handler. Enter the codes that are shown in Fig. 7.17 into this handler to perform data insertion action against our sample database.

Let's have a closer look at this piece of modified codes to see how it works.

A. First we add an **if** block to distinguish between the **Java Updatable ResultSet** method and other query methods to perform this data insertion.
B. An **else if** block is added with the same objective as step **A**.
C. The query string is created, and it is used to help to use the Updatable ResultSet object to do this data insertion action. One point to be noted is that because of the limitation for the Updatable ResultSet under JDBC 4.0, you cannot use a star (*) following the **SELECT** to query all columns from the target table; instead you have to explicitly list all columns for this query. An option is to use the table aliases such as **SELECT f.* FROM TABLE f** ...... to do this kind of query.
D. A **try…catch** block is used to perform this data insertion. A **PreparedStatement** is created with two ResultSet parameters, **TYPE_SCROLL_SENSITIVE** and **CONCUR_UPDATABLE**, to define the ResultSet object to enable it to be scrollable and updatable and enable it to perform data manipulations.
E. The **setString()** method is used to initialize the positional parameter in the query string.
F. The **executeQuery()** method is called to perform this query and return the query result to a new created ResultSet object.

```
public FacultyFrame() {
    initComponents();
    this.setLocationRelativeTo(null);   // set the faculty Form at the center

    ComboMethod.addItem("Java Updatable ResultSet");
    ComboMethod.addItem("Runtime Object Method");
    ComboMethod.addItem("Java execute() Method");
    ComboMethod.addItem("Java Callable Method");
    CurrentFaculty();
}
```

Fig. 7.16 The modified codes for the constructor of the FacultyFrame class

```
  private void InsertButtonActionPerformed(java.awt.event.ActionEvent evt) {
      int numInsert = 0;
      byte[] fImage;
      if (!chkFaculty()) {
         msgDlg.setMessage("Fill all TextFields for a new record!");
         msgDlg.setVisible(true);
         return;
      }
      fImage = getFacultyImage();
      String InsertQuery = "INSERT INTO Faculty (faculty_id, faculty_name, title, office, phone, " +
                           "college, email, fimage) VALUES (?, ?, ?, ?, ?, ?, ?, ?)";
A     if (ComboMethod.getSelectedItem()=="Runtime Object Method") {
      try {
           PreparedStatement pstmt = LogInFrame.con.prepareStatement(InsertQuery);
           pstmt.setString(1, FacultyIDField.getText());
           pstmt.setString(2, FacultyNameField.getText());
           pstmt.setString(3, TitleField.getText());
           pstmt.setString(4, OfficeField.getText());
           pstmt.setString(5, PhoneField.getText());
           pstmt.setString(6, CollegeField.getText());
           pstmt.setString(7, EmailField.getText());
           pstmt.setBytes(8, fImage);
           numInsert = pstmt.executeUpdate();
      }
      catch (SQLException e) {
           msgDlg.setMessage("Error in Statement!" + e.getMessage());
           msgDlg.setVisible(true);
      }
    }
B     else if (ComboMethod.getSelectedItem()=="Java Updatable ResultSet"){
C     String query = "SELECT faculty_id, faculty_name, title, office, phone, college, email, fimage " +
                     "FROM Faculty WHERE faculty_name = ?";
D     try {
           PreparedStatement pstmt = LogInFrame.con.prepareStatement(query,
                          ResultSet.TYPE_SCROLL_SENSITIVE, ResultSet.CONCUR_UPDATABLE);
E          pstmt.setString(1, ComboName.getSelectedItem().toString());
F          ResultSet rs = pstmt.executeQuery();
G          rs.moveToInsertRow();
H          rs.updateString(1, FacultyIDField.getText());
           rs.updateString(2, FacultyNameField.getText());
           rs.updateString(3, TitleField.getText());
           rs.updateString(4, OfficeField.getText());
           rs.updateString(5, PhoneField.getText());
           rs.updateString(6, CollegeField.getText());
           rs.updateString(7, EmailField.getText());
I          rs.updateBytes(8, fImage);
J          rs.insertRow();
K          rs.moveToCurrentRow(); // Go back to where we came from...
       }
L      catch (SQLException e){
         msgDlg.setMessage("Error in Updatable ResultSet! " + e.getMessage());
         msgDlg.setVisible(true);
       }
     }
     System.out.println("The number of inserted row = " + numInsert);
     ComboName.addItem(FacultyNameField.getText());
     InsertButton.setEnabled(false);
     clearFaculty();
  }
```

Fig. 7.17 The modified codes for the Insert button click event handler

G. In order to insert a new row into this ResultSet, the **moveToInsertRow()** method is executed to move the cursor of the ResultSet to a blank row that is not a part of the ResultSet but is related to that ResultSet.
H. A sequence of **updateString()** methods are executed to insert desired columns to the associated columns in the ResultSet. The point to be noted is that different **updateXXX()** methods should be used if the target columns have the different

data types, and the **XXX** indicate the associated data type, such as **Int**, **Float**, and **Double**.

I. For the image column, the system method **updateBytes()** must be used to insert or update a faculty image in the **Faculty** table.

J. The **insertRow()** method is executed to update this change to the database. Exactly, this data updating would not happen until the next Commit command is executed.

K. The **moveToCurrentRow()** method is optional, and it returns the cursor of the ResultSet to the original position before this data insertion is performed.

L. The **catch** block is used to track and collect any possible exception for this data insertion action.

Now let's build and run the project to test this data insertion.

Click on the **Clean and Build Main Project** button to build the project, and click on the **Run Main Project** button to run it.

Enter suitable username and password, such as **jhenry** and **test**, to complete the login process, and open the FacultyFrame form window. Make sure that the **Runtime Object Method** has been selected from the **Query Method** combo box. Then click on the **Select** button to query a faculty record. For example, select the faculty member, **Ying Bai**, to query and display this record.

Modify the content of seven text fields, as shown in Fig. 7.18, which is equivalent to a new faculty record:

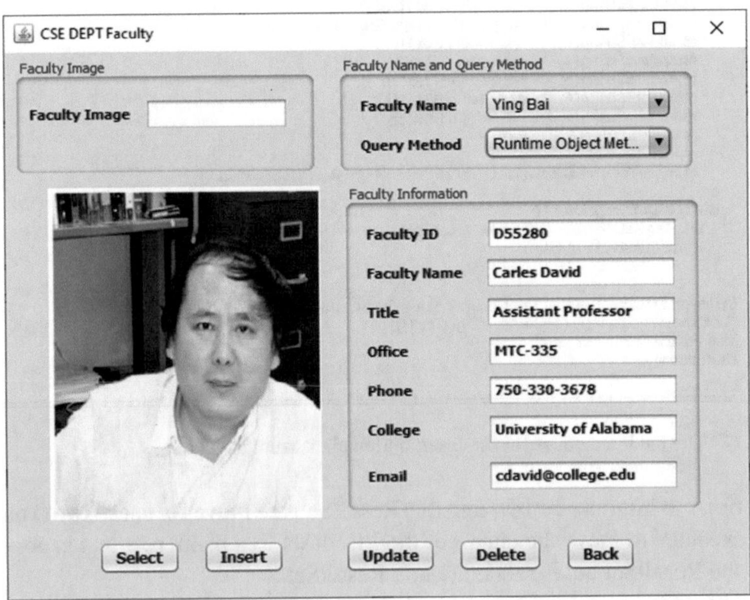

Fig. 7.18 The new inserted faculty record

- Faculty ID: **D55280**
- Faculty Name: **Charles David**
- Title: **Assistant Professor**
- Office: **MTC-335**
- Phone: **750-330-3678**
- College: **University of Alabama**
- Email: **cdavid@college.edu**
- fimage: **David.jpg**

To insert this new record using the **Java Updatable ResultSet** method, select the **Java Updatable ResultSet** from the Query Method combo box. Then click on the **Insert** button to perform this data insertion.

To confirm and validate this data insertion, the easiest way is to use this FacultyFrame form. Go to the Faculty Name combo box, and you will find that new inserted faculty name **Susan Bai** has been added into this box. Select this new inserted faculty member from that box, and select the **Runtime Object Method** from the Query Method combo box followed with a clicking on the

Select button to try to retrieve this new inserted faculty record. The returned faculty record is displayed, as shown in Fig. 7.19.

Another way to confirm this data insertion is to open the **Faculty** table in our sample database to confirm this data insertion. Open the **Services** window in the NetBeans IDE, and expand the **Databases** node and right click on our SQL Server database URL, **jdbc:sqlserver://localhost\SQL2019EXPRESS:**

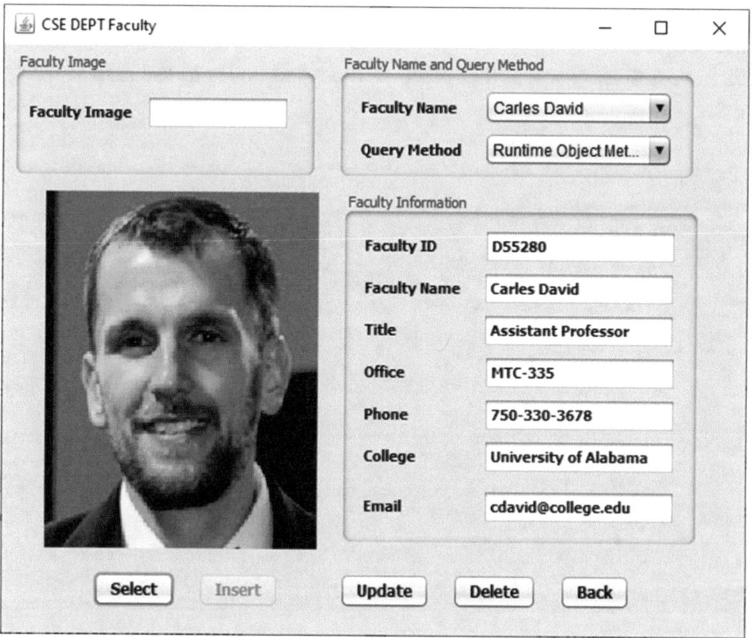

Fig. 7.19 The retrieved new inserted faculty record

5000;databaseName= CSE_DEPT [SMART on dbo]; select the **Connect** item to connect to our sample database. You may need to use our password **Happy2020** to do this connection. Then expand this connected database, **CSE_DEPT** and **dbo**, and the **Tables** node, and right click on the **Faculty** table and select the **View Data** to this table. On the opened **Faculty** table, you can find that the new inserted faculty member, **Charles David**, which is highlighted in the **Faculty** table, has been there as shown in Fig. 7.20.

Click on the **Back** and the **Exit** buttons to terminate our project, and our data insertion function is successful. It is highly recommended to remove this new inserted faculty record from our sample database to keep our database clean and neat.

Next let's take care of the data updating action using the Updatable ResultSet object.

As we did for the data insertion, we still want to use this FacultyFrame form window to update one of faculty members in the **Faculty** table in our sample database **CSE_DEPT**.

7.5.2.2 Update a Data Row Using the Updatable ResultSet

Copy the project **SQLUpdatableInsert** and change its name to **SQLUpdatableUpdate**, and save it to your default folder **DB Projects\Chapter 7**.

Then open this project and double click on the **Update** button from the FacultyFrame Form window to open its event handler, and modify the codes that are shown in Fig. 7.21 to perform the data updating function using the Updatable ResultSet object.

Let's have a closer look at this piece of modified codes to see how it works.

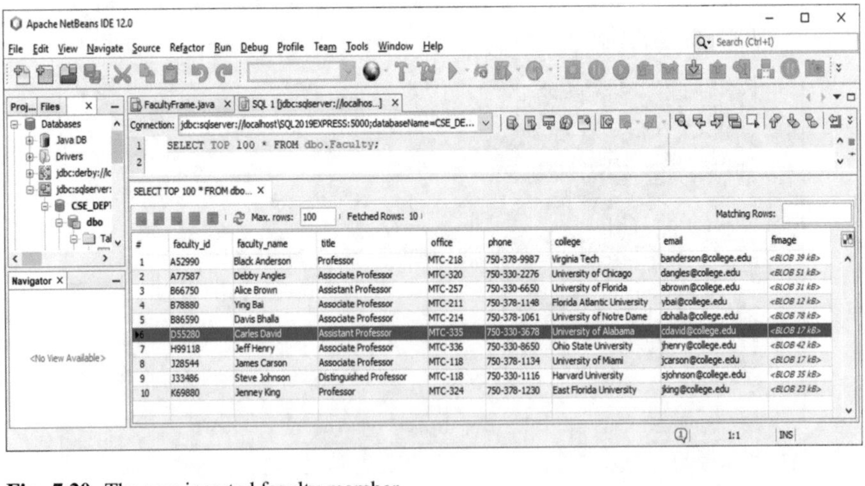

#	faculty_id	faculty_name	title	office	phone	college	email	fimage
1	A52990	Black Anderson	Professor	MTC-218	750-378-9987	Virginia Tech	banderson@college.edu	<BLOB 39 kB>
2	A77587	Debby Angles	Associate Professor	MTC-320	750-330-2276	University of Chicago	dangles@college.edu	<BLOB 51 kB>
3	B66750	Alice Brown	Assistant Professor	MTC-257	750-330-6650	University of Florida	abrown@college.edu	<BLOB 31 kB>
4	B78880	Ying Bai	Associate Professor	MTC-211	750-378-1148	Florida Atlantic University	ybai@college.edu	<BLOB 12 kB>
5	B86590	Davis Bhalla	Associate Professor	MTC-214	750-378-1061	University of Notre Dame	dbhalla@college.edu	<BLOB 78 kB>
6	D55280	Carles David	Assistant Professor	MTC-335	750-330-3678	University of Alabama	cdavid@college.edu	<BLOB 17 kB>
7	H99118	Jeff Henry	Associate Professor	MTC-336	750-330-8650	Ohio State University	jhenry@college.edu	<BLOB 42 kB>
8	J28544	James Carson	Associate Professor	MTC-118	750-378-1134	University of Miami	jcarson@college.edu	<BLOB 17 kB>
9	J33486	Steve Johnson	Distinguished Professor	MTC-118	750-330-1116	Harvard University	sjohnson@college.edu	<BLOB 35 kB>
10	K69880	Jenney King	Professor	MTC-324	750-378-1230	East Florida University	jking@college.edu	<BLOB 23 kB>

Fig. 7.20 The new inserted faculty member

```
   private void UpdateButtonActionPerformed(java.awt.event.ActionEvent evt) {
     byte[] fImage;
     int numUpdated = 0;

     fImage = getFacultyImage();
A    if (ComboMethod.getSelectedItem()=="Runtime Object Method") {
     String query = "UPDATE Faculty SET faculty_name=?, title=?, office=?, phone=?, college=?, email=?, fimage=? " +
                    "WHERE faculty_id= ?";
     try {
          PreparedStatement pstmt = LogInFrame.con.prepareStatement(query);
          pstmt.setString(1, FacultyNameField.getText());
          pstmt.setString(2, TitleField.getText());
          pstmt.setString(3, OfficeField.getText());
          pstmt.setString(4, PhoneField.getText());
          pstmt.setString(5, CollegeField.getText());
          pstmt.setString(6, EmailField.getText());
          pstmt.setBytes(7, fImage);
          pstmt.setString(8, FacultyIDField.getText());
          numUpdated = pstmt.executeUpdate();
      }
      catch (SQLException e) {
             msgDlg.setMessage("Error in Statement!" + e.getMessage());
             msgDlg.setVisible(true);
      }
      System.out.println("The number of updated row = " + numUpdated);
     }
B    else if (ComboMethod.getSelectedItem()=="Java Updatable ResultSet") {
C         String query = "SELECT faculty_name, title, office, phone, college, email, fimage " +
                         "FROM Faculty WHERE faculty_id = ?";
D         try {
             PreparedStatement pstmt = LogInFrame.con.prepareStatement(query,
                                  ResultSet.TYPE_SCROLL_SENSITIVE, ResultSet.CONCUR_UPDATABLE);
E            pstmt.setString(1, FacultyIDField.getText());
F            ResultSet rs = pstmt.executeQuery();
G            if (rs.absolute(1)) {
               rs.updateString(1, FacultyNameField.getText());
               rs.updateString(2, TitleField.getText());
               rs.updateString(3, OfficeField.getText());
               rs.updateString(4, PhoneField.getText());
               rs.updateString(5, CollegeField.getText());
               rs.updateString(6, EmailField.getText());
H              rs.updateBytes(7, fImage);
I              rs.updateRow();
             }
          }
J         catch (SQLException e){
             msgDlg.setMessage("Error in Updatable ResultSet! " + e.getMessage());
             msgDlg.setVisible(true);
          }
       }
          CurrentFaculty();
   }
```

Fig. 7.21 The modified codes for the Update button click event handler

A. First we add an **if** block to distinguish the **Runtime Object Method** and the **Java Updatable ResultSet** method to perform this data updating action.
B. An **else if** block is added with the same objective as step **A**.
C. The query string is created, and it is used to help to use the Updatable ResultSet object to do this data updating action.
D. A **try…catch** block is used to perform this data updating action. A **PreparedStatement** is created with two ResultSet parameters, `TYPE_SCROLL_SENSITIVE` and `CONCUR_UPDATABLE`, to define the ResultSet object to enable it to be scrollable and updatable and enable it to perform data manipulations.

E. The **setString()** method is used to initialize the positional parameter in the query string.
F. The **executeQuery()** method is called to perform this query and return the query result to a new created ResultSet object.
G. First we need to identify the location of the row to be updated. Exactly, there is only one row that has been retrieved from our Faculty table and saved in the ResultSet, which is the default faculty member **Ying Bai**, and this row will be updated in this data updating action. Therefore the absolute position for this row is 1. Then a sequence of **updateString()** methods are executed to update desired columns to the associated columns in the ResultSet. The point to be noted is that different **updateXXX()** methods should be used if the target columns have the different data types, and the **XXX** indicate the associated data type, such as **Int**, **Float**, and **Double**.
H. For the image column, the system method **updateBytes()** must be used to insert or update a faculty image in the **Faculty** table.
I. The **updateRow()** method is executed to update this change to the database. Exactly, this data updating would not happen until the next Commit command is executed. Be aware that by default, the auto-commit flag is set to **true** so that any operation run is committed immediately.
J. The **catch** block is used to track and collect any possible exception for this data updating action.

Now let's build and run the project to test this data updating function.

Click on the **Clean and Build Main Project** button to build the project, and click on the **Run Main Project** button to run it.

Enter suitable username and password, such as **jhenry** and **test**, to complete the login process, and open the FacultyFrame form window. Make sure that the **Runtime Object Method** has been selected from the **Query Method** combo box. Then click on the **Select** button to query any faculty information.

To perform updating action with the **Java Updatable ResultSet** method, select this method from the **Query Method** combo box, and change the content of six text fields (without the Faculty ID field), for example, update a faculty member **Ying Bai** to another faculty **Susan Bai**, as shown in Fig. 7.22, and click on the **Update** button to select her image file **White.jpg**. Your finished updating screen should match one that is shown in Fig. 7.22.

To confirm this data updating function using the Updatable ResultSet, select the **Runtime Object Method** from the Query Method combo box, and go to the **Faculty Name** combo box. You can find that the updated faculty member **Susan Bai** has been there. Select this faculty name and then click on the **Select** button to get this updated result back and displayed in this Form.

The returned faculty record is displayed, as shown in Fig. 7.23.

Click on the **Back** and the **Exit** buttons to terminate our project.

Now let's try to confirm this data updating in the second way, which is to open the **Faculty** table to confirm this data manipulation. Open the **Services** window in the NetBeans IDE, and expand the **Databases** node and right click on our sample

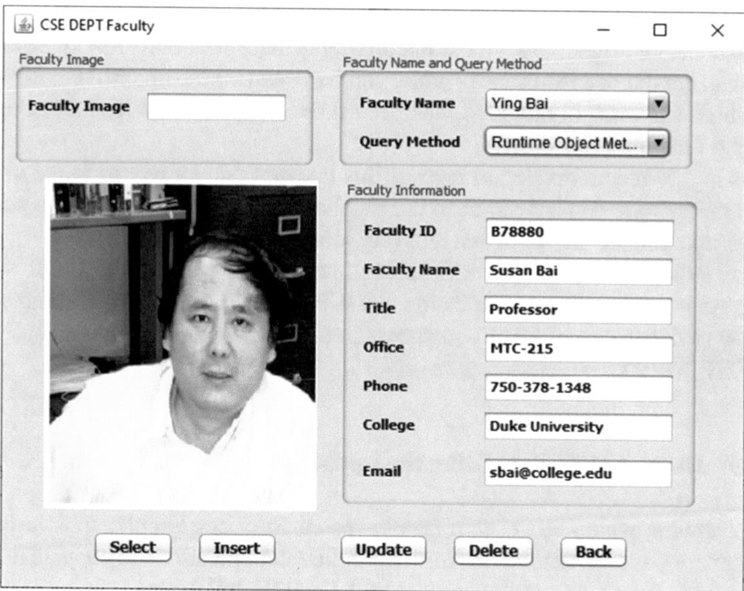

Fig. 7.22 The updated faculty information

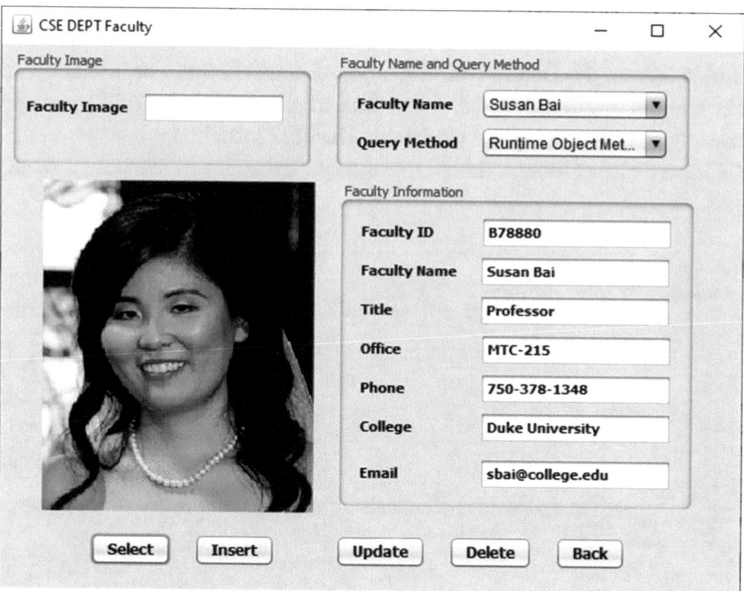

Fig. 7.23 The retrieved updated faculty record

database URL, **jdbc:sqlserver:// localhost\\SQL2019EXPRESS: 5000;databaseName= CSE_DEPT [SMART on dbo]**; select the **Connect** item to connect to our sample database. Then expand this connected database, **CSE_DEPT**, and the **Tables** node, and right click on the **Faculty** table and select the **View Data** to open this table. On the opened **Faculty** table, you can find that the updated faculty member, which has been highlighted, has been there as shown in Fig. 7.24. Our data updating function is successful.

It is highly recommended to recover this updated faculty record to the original one in our sample database to keep our database clean and neat. One can perform another updating action to do this recovery job.

Next let's take care of the data deletion action using the Updatable ResultSet object. As we did for the data updating, we still want to use this FacultyFrame form window to delete one of faculty members in the **Faculty** table in our sample database **CSE_DEPT**.

7.5.2.3 Delete a Data Row Using the Updatable ResultSet

In this section, we try to delete a faculty record from our **Faculty** table using the Updatable ResultSet method. Perform the following operations to copy an existing project, and make it as our new project **SQLUpdatableDelete**:

- Copy the project **SQLUpdatableUpdate**, and change its name to **SQLUpdatableDelete**.
- Save it to your default folder **DB Projects\Chapter 7**.

Double click on the **Delete** button from the FacultyFrame Form window to open its event handler, and modify the codes that are shown in Fig. 7.25 to perform the data deleting function using the Updatable ResultSet method.

Let's have a closer look at this piece of modified codes to see how it works.

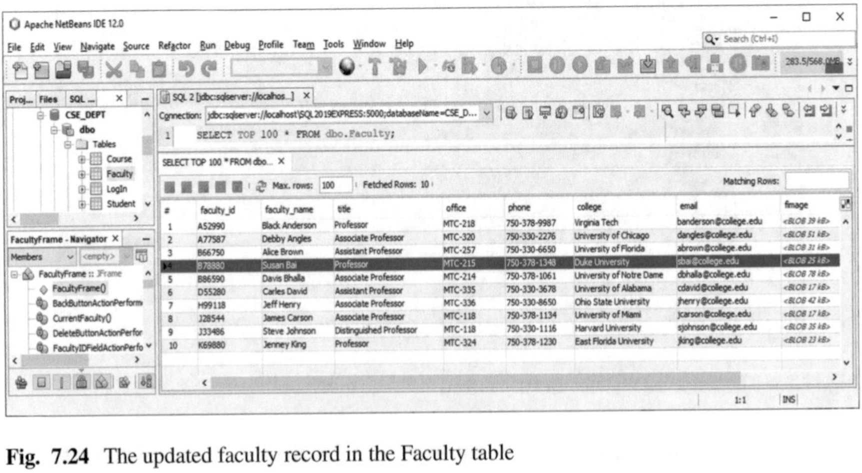

Fig. 7.24 The updated faculty record in the Faculty table

```
    private void DeleteButtonActionPerformed(java.awt.event.ActionEvent evt) {
      int numDeleted = 0;
A     if (ComboMethod.getSelectedItem()=="Runtime Object Method") {
      String query = "DELETE FROM Faculty WHERE faculty_name = ?";
      try {
          PreparedStatement  pstmt = LogInFrame.con.prepareStatement(query);
          pstmt.setString(1, ComboName.getSelectedItem().toString());
          numDeleted = pstmt.executeUpdate();
        }
        catch (SQLException e) {
          msgDlg.setMessage("Error in Statement!" + e.getMessage());
          msgDlg.setVisible(true);
        }
        System.out.println("The number of deleted row = " + numDeleted);
      }
B     else if (ComboMethod.getSelectedItem()=="Java Updatable ResultSet"){
C         String query = "SELECT f.* FROM Faculty f WHERE f.faculty_name = ?";
D         try {
            PreparedStatement pstmt = LogInFrame.con.prepareStatement(query,
                                    ResultSet.TYPE_SCROLL_SENSITIVE, ResultSet.CONCUR_UPDATABLE);
E           pstmt.setString(1, ComboName.getSelectedItem().toString());
F           ResultSet rs = pstmt.executeQuery();
G           rs.absolute(1);
H           rs.deleteRow();
            }
I         catch (SQLException e){
            msgDlg.setMessage("Error in Updatable ResultSet! " + e.getMessage());
            msgDlg.setVisible(true);
           }
        }
J     else {
          msgDlg.setMessage("Only Runtime & Updatable ResultSet methods available! ");
          msgDlg.setVisible(true);
        }
K       CurrentFaculty();
    }
```

Fig. 7.25 The modified codes for the Delete button click event handler

A. First we add an **if** block to distinguish the **Runtime Object Method** and the **Java Updatable ResultSet** method to perform this data deletion action.
B. An **else if** block is added with the same objective as step **A**.
C. The query string is created, and it is used to help the Updatable ResultSet object to do this data deleting action. The point to be noted here is that a table alias **f** is used to represent the **Faculty** table and enable this query to retrieve all columns from that table. You cannot directly use the star (*) to do this query since it is prohibited in this enhanced ResultSet.
D. A **try…catch** block is used to perform this data deleting action. A **PreparedStatement** is created with two ResultSet parameters, **TYPE_SCROLL_SENSITIVE** and **CONCUR_UPDATABLE**, to define the ResultSet object to enable it to be scrollable and updatable and furthermore enable it to perform data manipulations.
E. The **setString()** method is used to initialize the positional parameter in the query string.
F. The **executeQuery()** method is called to perform this query and return the query result to a new created ResultSet object.
G. We need first to identify the location of the row to be deleted. In fact, there is only one row that has been retrieved from our **Faculty** table and saved in the

ResultSet, which is the selected faculty member to be removed, and this row will be deleted from this data deleting action. Therefore the absolute position for this row is 1.

H. The **deleteRow()** method is executed to delete this record from the ResultSet and the database. In fact, this data deleting would not happen until the next Commit command is executed. Be aware that by default, the auto-commit flag is set to **true** so that any operational run is committed immediately.
I. The **catch** block is used to track and collect any possible exception for this data deletion.
J. Otherwise if some other methods are selected by the users, a warning message is displayed to remind users to select a valid method.
K. Finally the user-defined method, **CurrentFaculty()**, is called to update the Faculty Name combo box to enable users to confirm this deleting action later.

Now let's build and run the project to test this data deleting function.

Click on the **Clean and Build Main Project** button to build the project, and click on the **Run Main Project** button to run it.

Enter suitable username and password, such as **jhenry** and **test**, to complete the login process, and open the FacultyFrame form window. Make sure that the **Runtime Object Method** has been selected from the **Query Method** combo box. Then click on the **Select** button to query any faculty information, such as a faculty named **Charles David**.

To test this data deleting function using the Updatable ResultSet, select the **Java Updatable ResultSet** from the Query Method combo box. Then click on the **Delete** button to try to delete this selected faculty member from our sample database. To simplify this data deleting action and to avoid a completed recovery process, in this case, we try to delete a faculty member, **Charles David**, since this faculty is a new inserted one in Sect. 7.5.2.1 without other related records in any child tables. Select that faculty from the **Faculty Name** combo box, and click on the **Delete** button to remove this faculty from our sample database.

Click on the **Back** and the **Exit** button to terminate our project.

To confirm and validate this data deleting action, one can go to the Faculty Name combo box to check this member. It can be found that this faculty has been removed from the faculty name list.

Another way to confirm this data deleting is to open the **Faculty** table in our sample database **CSE_DEPT**. To do that, first open the **Services** window in the NetBeans IDE, and expand the **Databases** node and right click on our SQL Server database URL, **jdbc:sqlserver://localhost \\SQL2019EXPRESS: 5000;databaseName= CSE_DEPT [SMART on dbo]**; select the **Connect** item to connect to our sample database. You may need to use our password **Happy2020** to do this connection. Then expand this connected database, **CSE_DEPT** and **dbo**, and the **Tables** node, and right click on the **Faculty** table and select the **View Data** to this table. On the opened **Faculty** table, you can find that the faculty member, **Charles David**, has been deleted from the **Faculty** table.

Our data deleting function is successful.

A complete project **SQLUpdatableDelete** that contains the data insertion, updating, and deleting functions using the Updatable ResultSet object can be found from the folder **Class DB Projects \Chapter 7** located under the **Students** folder at the Springer ftp site (refer to Fig. 1.2 in Chap. 1).

Next let's discuss how to perform the data manipulations using the Callable statement.

7.6 Perform Data Manipulations Using Callable Statements

In Sects. 6.3.6 and 6.3.6.2 in Chap. 6, we have provided a very detailed discussion about the data query from the **Course** table in our sample database using the CallableStatement method. Some basic and fundamental ideas and techniques using the CallableStatement method and stored procedures have been given in detail with some real sample projects. Refer to those sections to get clear pictures and understanding about the CallableStatement object. In this section, we will use this method to perform data manipulations against the **Course** table in our sample database **CSE_DEPT**.

Since the similarity between data manipulations for the SQL Server and the Oracle databases, we start with the data manipulations against the SQL Server database. First let's take care of the data insertion to the **Course** table in our sample SQL Server database using the CallableStatement method.

7.6.1 Insert Data to the Course Table Using Callable Statements

In Sect. 6.3.1 in Chap. 6, we have built a project **SQLSelectObject** with some graphical user interface (GUI) including the CourseFrame Form window, and we want to use that CourseFrame Form window in that project with some modifications to make it as our new project. Copy that project and change its name to **SQLCallableInsert**, and save it to the folder **Class DB Projects\Chapter 7** on your computer. We will build the data insertion function with the CallableStatement method in the following procedures:

1) Build our stored procedure **dbo.InsertNewCourse** using the SQL Server Management Studio 18.
2) Develop the codes for the **Insert** button in the CourseFrame Form window to execute the CallableStatement method to call our stored procedure **dbo.InsertNewCourse** to insert this new course record into the **Course** table in our sample database.
3) Confirm and validate this new course insertion using the codes we built for the **Select** button event handler.

Now let's start from the first step.

7.6.1.1 Develop the Stored Procedure dbo.InsertNewCourse

Recall that when we built our sample database CSE_DEPT in Chap. 2, there is no faculty name column in the Course table, and the only relationship that existed between the **Faculty** and the **Course** tables is the **faculty_id**, which is a primary key in the **Faculty** table but a foreign key in the **Course** table. As the project runs, the user needs to insert new course record based on the faculty name, not the faculty ID. Therefore, for this new course data insertion, we need to perform two queries with two tables: first we need to make a query to the **Faculty** table to get the **faculty_id** based on the faculty name selected by the user, and second we can insert a new course record based on the **faculty_id** we obtained from our first query into the **Course** table. These two queries can be combined into a single stored procedure.

Launch the Microsoft SQL Server Management Studio by going to **Start > All Programs > Microsoft SQL Server Tools 18 > Microsoft SQL Server Management Studio**. Click the **Connect** button to open this studio server. On the opened studio, expand the **Databases** and our sample database **CSE_DEPT** nodes. Then expand the **Programmability** node, and right click on the **Stored Procedures** node; select the **Stored Procedure** from the popup menu to open a new stored procedure template, as shown in Fig. 7.26.

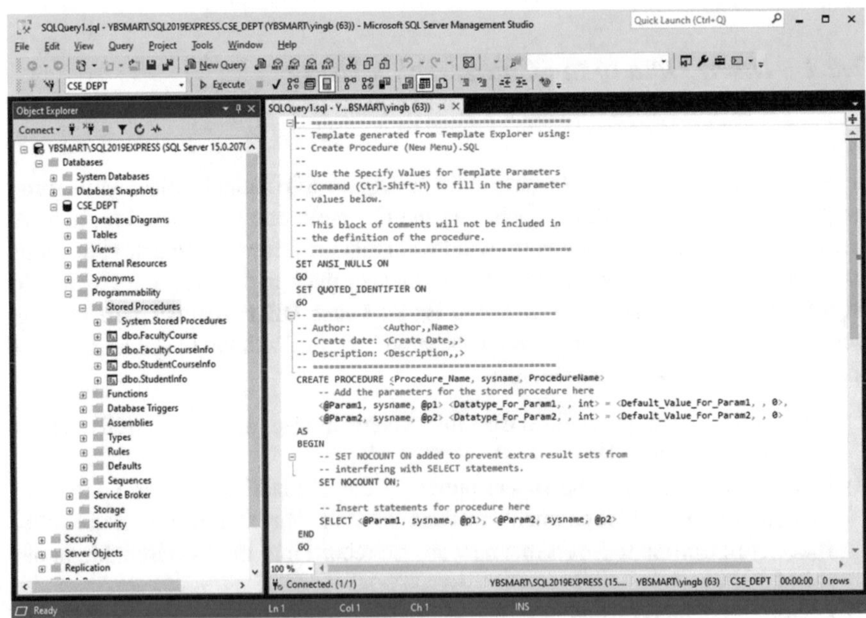

Fig. 7.26 The new stored procedure template

```
-- ================================================
SET ANSI_NULLS ON
GO
SET QUOTED_IDENTIFIER ON
GO
-- =============================================
-- Author:        Y. Bai
-- Create date:   Dec 23, 2020
-- Description:   SQL Server stored procedure
-- =============================================
A  CREATE PROCEDURE dbo.InsertNewCourse
   -- Add the parameters for the stored procedure here
B   @FacultyName VARCHAR(50),
    @CourseID VARCHAR(50),
    @Course text,
    @Schedule text,
    @Classroom text,
    @Credit int,
    @Enroll int
AS
BEGIN
  -- SET NOCOUNT ON added to prevent extra result sets from
  -- interfering with SELECT statements.
SET NOCOUNT ON;

   -- Insert statements for procedure here
C   DECLARE @FacultyID AS VARCHAR(50)
    SET @FacultyID = (SELECT faculty_id FROM Faculty WHERE (faculty_name = @FacultyName))
    INSERT INTO Course(course_id, course, credit, classroom, schedule, enrollment, faculty_id)
    VALUES (@CourseID, @Course, @Credit, @Classroom, @Schedule, @Enroll, @FacultyID)
END
GO
```

Fig. 7.27 The codes for our new stored procedure

You can use the **Ctrl-Shift-M** combination keys to enter all parameters for this stored procedure. However, an easy way to do that is to directly enter all parameters manually. On the opened new stored procedure template, enter the following codes that are shown in Fig. 7.27 into this stored procedure template as the body of our new stored procedure. The new added codes have been highlighted in bold and indicated in steps **A**, **B**, and **C**, respectively. The codes in green color are comments for this stored procedure.

Let's have a closer look at this piece of codes to see how it works.

A. First one needs to change the stored procedure's name to **dbo.InsertNewCourse**.
B. Seven input parameters to this procedure should be declared with the related data types.
C. The intermediate variable **FacultyID** is declared and queried from the **Faculty** table first. Then an Insert command is executed to insert these seven parameters into the **Course** table. One point to be noted is that the order of these parameters must be identical with the order of those data columns in the **Course** table.

Right click on any location inside our new stored procedure, and select the **Execute** item to try to build it. A successful query execution message should be displayed in the **Messages** box. Then right click on the **Stored Procedures** node from the Object Explorer window, and select the **Refresh** item to refresh it to get

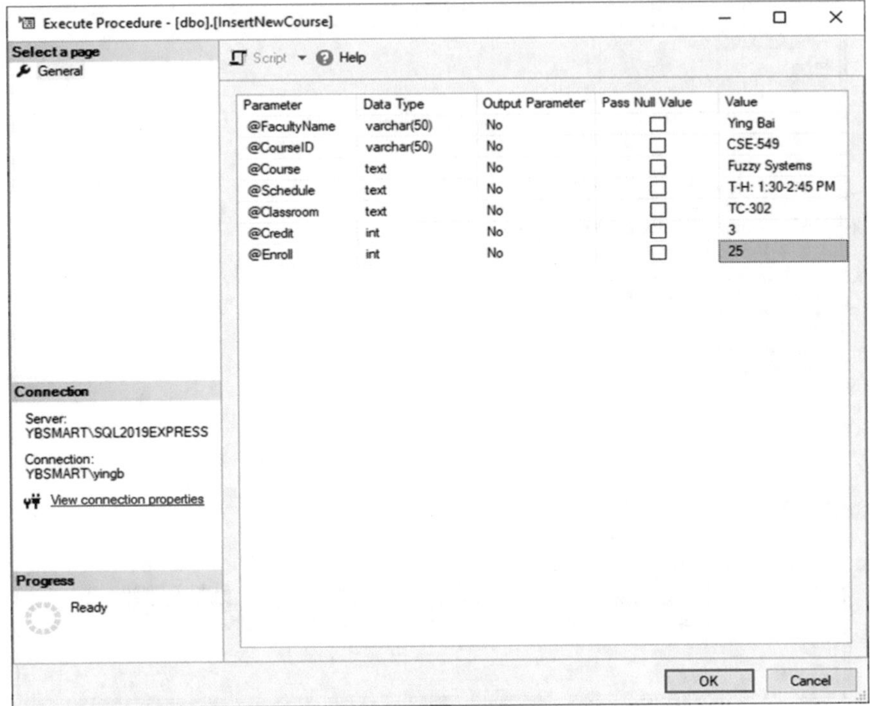

Fig. 7.28 The opened Execute Procedure wizard

our new created stored procedure **dbo.InsertNewCourse**. Right click on our new stored procedure, and select the **Execute Stored Procedure** to open the **Execute Procedure** wizard, which is shown in Fig. 7.28.

Enter a set of parameters shown in Fig. 7.28 into the associated **Value** columns as a new course record, and click on the **OK** button to run this stored procedure to test its functionality.

The test result is shown in Fig. 7.29. It can be found that a successful message, **1 row(s) affected**, is displayed in the **Messages** window. One can confirm this new course insertion by opening the **Course** table in this Microsoft SQL Server Management Studio.

It is highly recommended to delete this new inserted course record from our **Course** table since we need to keep our sample database clean and neat. Another point is that we need to call this stored procedure later from our project to perform this data insertion. In order to avoid a duplicated data insertion, we need to remove this course record now. You can do this data deletion by opening the **Course** in this Microsoft SQL Server Management Studio.

Now close the Microsoft SQL Server Management Studio, and we can continue to develop the codes for the CallableStatement method in our project to call this stored procedure to perform a new course insertion action against our sample

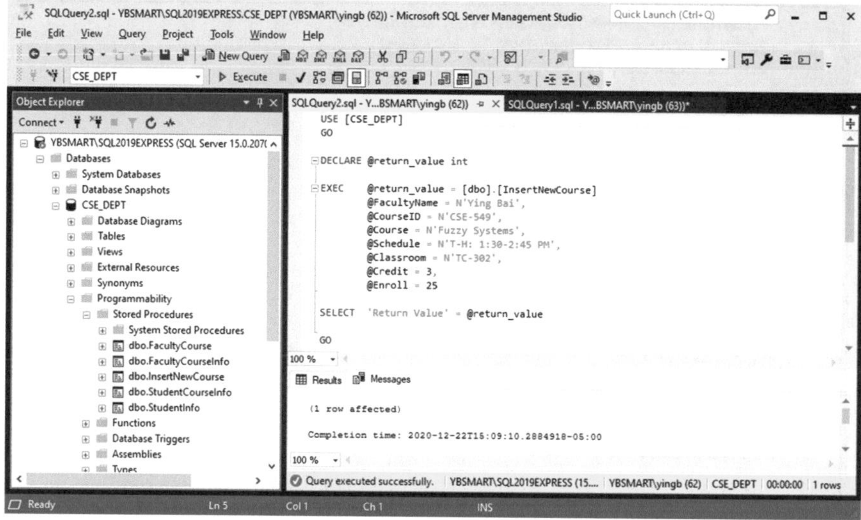

Fig. 7.29 The running result of the stored procedure

database. Click **No** for a message to ask you to save this procedure running script, **SQLQuery1.sql**, if it appeared.

7.6.1.2 Develop the Codes for the Insert Button Click Event Handler

The function of this piece of codes is to call the stored procedure we built in the last section to perform a new course insertion to the **Course** table in our sample database. The insertion criterion is the faculty member selected from the Faculty Name combo box. The new inserted course record can be retrieved and displayed in the CourseList listbox by clicking on the **Select** button to confirm this data insertion.

Generally, the sequence to run a CallableStatement to perform a stored procedure is:

1) Build and formulate the CallableStatement query string.
2) Create a CallableStatement object.
3) Set the input parameters.
4) Register the output parameters.
5) Execute CallableStatement.
6) Retrieve the running result by using different **getXXX()** method.

Since we do not have any output result to be returned from this stored procedure, therefore we can skip steps 4 and 6.

Now let's develop the codes for this event handler to perform the calling of the stored procedure we built in the last section to perform this data insertion function.

```
  private void InsertButtonActionPerformed(java.awt.event.ActionEvent evt) {
A   if (ComboMethod.getSelectedItem()=="Java Callable Method"){
B       CallableStatement cstmt = null;
      try{
C       String query = "{call dbo.InsertNewCourse(?, ?, ?, ?, ?, ?, ?)}";
D       cstmt = LogInFrame.con.prepareCall(query);
E       cstmt.setString(1, ComboName.getSelectedItem().toString());
        cstmt.setString(2, CourseIDField.getText());
        cstmt.setString(3, CourseField.getText());
        cstmt.setString(4, ScheduleField.getText());
        cstmt.setString(5, ClassRoomField.getText());
        cstmt.setInt(6, Integer.valueOf(CreditsField.getText()));
        cstmt.setInt(7, Integer.valueOf(EnrollField.getText()));
F       cstmt.execute();
        }
G     catch (SQLException e){
        msgDlg.setMessage("Error in CallableStatement! " + e.getMessage());
        msgDlg.setVisible(true);
        }
      }
H   else {
        msgDlg.setMessage("Only Java Callable Method is available!");
        msgDlg.setVisible(true);
    }
  }
```

Fig. 7.30 The codes for the Insert button click event handler

Double click on the **Insert** button on the CourseFrame form window to open its event handler, and enter the codes that are shown in Fig. 7.30 into this handler.

Let's have a closer look at this piece of codes to see how it works.

A. An **if** block is used to distinguish whether the **Java Callable Method** has been selected.
B. If it is, a new CallableStatement instance is declared.
C. A **try...catch** block is used to perform this data insertion using the CallableStatement method. The CallableStatement query string is created. Refer to Sect. 6.3.6.2.1 in Chap. 6 to get more detailed information about the structure and protocol of a CallableStatement query string. This is a dynamic query string with seven pieces of positional inserting information related to a new course; therefore, seven question marks are used as the position holders for those parameters.
D. A new CallableStatement instance is created by calling the **prepareCall()** method that is defined in the Connection class.
E. The dynamic query string is initialized with seven positional parameters, and the values of those parameters are entered by the user into the associated course-related text fields.
F. The CallableStatement instance is executed to call the stored procedure we built in the last section to insert a new course record into the **Course** table in our sample database.
G. The catch block is used to track and collect any possible exception for this data insertion process.
H. If some other method is selected by users, a warning message is displayed to remind this.

Two points to be noted are in step **E**, where all seven input parameters, including the **Credit** and **Enrollment**, are initialized and assigned to the stored procedure:

1) The order of these input parameters must be identical with that order used in the stored procedure **dbo.InsertNewCourse** exactly. Otherwise some data type mismatch errors may be encountered as the project runs.
2) For the last two parameters, **Credit** and **Enrollment**, both data types are **Integer**; thus, the collected contents from these two TextFields must be converted to integers, and then they can be assigned to the stored procedure. Both **parseInt()** and **valueOf()** methods, which belong to the Integer class, are available for this kind of conversion.

Now let's build and run the project to test this data insertion function. Click on the **Clean and Build Main Project** button to build the project, and click on the **Run Main Project** button to run the project.

Enter suitable username and password, such as **jhenry** and **test**, to the LogIn frame form, and select the **Course Information** from the SelectFrame window to open the CourseFrame form window. Make sure that the **Java Callable Method** has been selected from the **Query Method** combo box. Then click on the **Select** button to query the default course information for the selected faculty member **Ying Bai**.

Now enter the following data into seven text fields as a new course record for the selected faculty member:

Course ID: **CSE-549**
Course: **Fuzzy Systems**
Schedule: **T-H: 1:30 – 2:45 PM**
Classroom: **TC-302**
Credit: **3**
Enrollment: **25**

Then click on the **Insert** button to insert this course record into the **Course** table in our sample database.

To confirm and validate this data insertion, click on the **Select** button to try to retrieve all courses taught by the selected faculty member **Ying Bai**. The running result is shown in Fig. 7.31, and you can see that the new inserted course **CSE-549** is indeed added to the database and displayed in the **CourseList** Listbox.

Click on the **Back** and the **Exit** buttons to terminate our project.

Another way to confirm this data insertion is to open the **Course** table using the **Services** window in the Apache NetBeans IDE. To do that, follow the steps below:

1) Open the **Services** window and expand the **Databases** node and connect to our SQL Server database by right clicking on that URL **jdbc:sqlserver://localhost\\ SQL2019EXPRESS: 5000;databaseName= CSE_DEPT [SMART on dbo]**, and select the **Connect** item. You may need to use the password **Happy2020** to complete this connection process.
2) Then expand our **CSE_DEPT** database node, **dbo** schema, and **Tables** nodes.

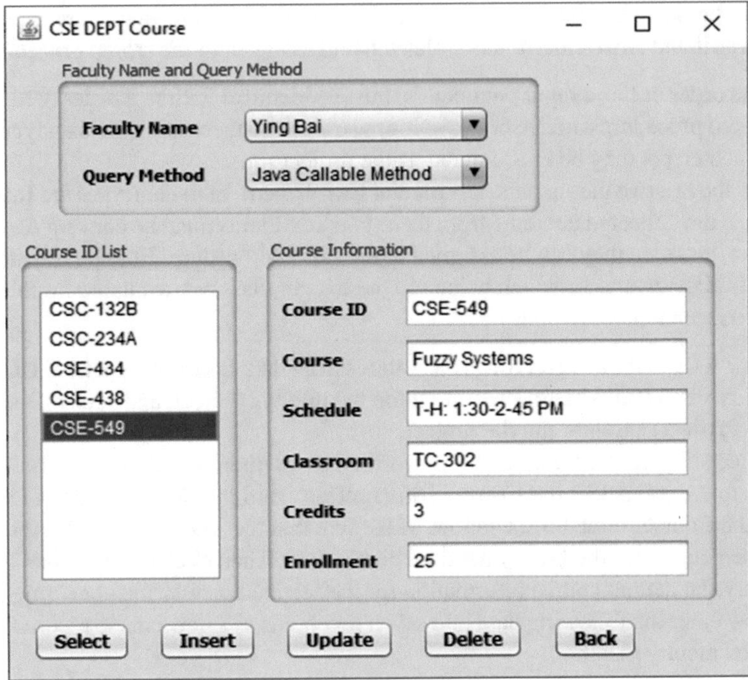

Fig. 7.31 The running result for the data insertion validation

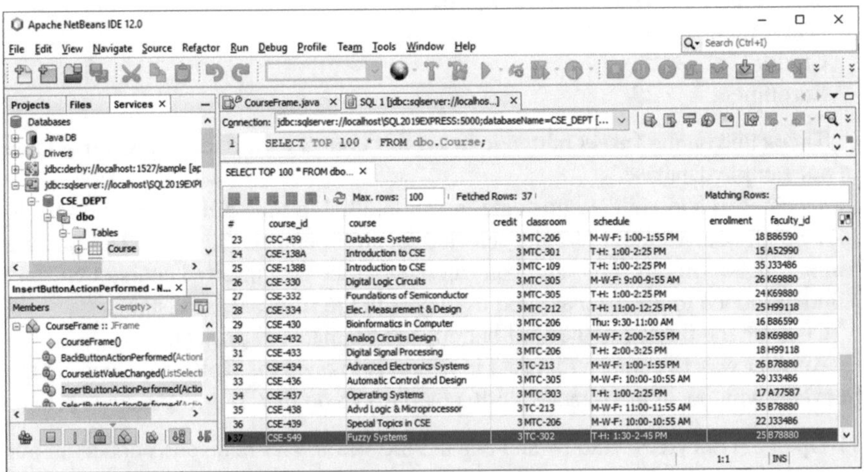

Fig. 7.32 The new inserted new course CSE-549

3) Right click on the **Course** table and select the **View Data** to open this table. Scroll down along this table, and you can find that the course CSE-549 has been inserted to the last line on this **Course** table, as shown in Fig. 7.32.

Our data insertion using the CallableStatement object is successful.
Next let's handle the data updating using the CallableStatement object method.

7.6.2 Update Data to the Course Table Using Callable Statements

Copy the project **SQLCallableInsert** and change its name to **SQLCallableUpdate**, and save it to the folder **Class DB Projects\Chapter 7** on your computer. We will build the data updating function with the CallableStatement method in the following procedures:

1) Build our stored procedure **dbo.UpdateCourse** using the SQL Server Management Studio.
2) Develop the codes for the **Update** button in the CourseFrame Form window to execute the CallableStatement method to call our stored procedure **dbo. UpdateCourse** to update a course record in the **Course** table in our sample database.
3) Confirm and validate this course updating action using the codes we built for the **Select** button event handler.

Now let's start from the first step.

7.6.2.1 Develop the Stored Procedure dbo.UpdateCourse

Generally, we do not need to update a **course_id** when we update a course record in the **Course** table since a better way to do that is to insert a new course record and delete the old one. The main reason for this is that a very complicated operation would be performed if the **course_id** were updated since it is a primary key in the **Course** table and foreign keys in the **StudentCourse** table. To update a primary key, one needs to update foreign keys first in the child tables and then update the primary key in the parent table. This will make our updating operation much more complicated and easy to be confused. In order to avoid this confusion, in this section, we will update a course record by changing any other columns except the **course_id**, and this is a popular way to update a table and widely implemented in most database applications.

Launch the Microsoft SQL Server Management Studio by going to **Start > All Programs > Microsoft SQL Server Tools 18 > Microsoft SQL Server Management Studio**. Click the **Connect** button to open this studio server. On the opened studio, expand the **Databases** and our sample database **CSE_DEPT** nodes. Then expand the **Programmability** node and right click on the **Stored Procedures** node; select the **Stored Procedure** from the popup menu to open a new stored procedure template.

```
-- =================================================
SET ANSI_NULLS ON
GO
SET QUOTED_IDENTIFIER ON
GO
-- ===============================================
-- Author:                    Y. Bai
-- ===============================================
CREATE PROCEDURE dbo.UpdateCourse
  -- Add the parameters for the stored procedure here
A  @CourseID VARCHAR(50),
   @Course text,
   @Schedule text,
   @Classroom text,
   @Credit int,
   @Enroll int
AS
BEGIN
 -- SET NOCOUNT ON added to prevent extra result sets from
 -- interfering with SELECT statements.
SET NOCOUNT ON;

  -- Insert statements for procedure here
B  UPDATE  Course
   SET course = @Course, schedule = @Schedule, classroom = @Classroom,
                credit = @Credit, enrollment = @Enroll
   WHERE  (course_id = @CourseID)
END
GO
```

Fig. 7.33 The codes for the dbo.UpdateCourse stored procedure

One way to do this coding is to directly enter all parameters manually. On the opened new stored procedure template, enter the codes that are shown in Fig. 7.33 into this stored procedure template as the body of our new stored procedure **dbo. UpdateCourse**.

Another way to do this **UPDATE** command (step **B** in Fig. 7.33) is to use the **Design Query in Editor** wizard. Here we try to use this wizard to build the **UPDATE** statement for this query.

First one needs to delete the default **SELECT** statement under the comment: **Insert statements for procedure here**, and move your cursor under this comment to locate the starting position of your **UPDATE** command.

To open this wizard, right click on any place inside our stored procedure template, and select the **Design Query in Editor** from the popup menu. Click on the **Close** button for the **Add Table** wizard to close this dialog. Perform the following operations to build this **UPDATE** statement.

1) Choose the **SELECT …FROM** codes from the bottom pane to delete them.
2) Right click on the bottom pane, and select the **Change Type** item and select the **Update** item from the popup menu.
3) Right click on the top pane and select the **Add Table** item. Select the **Course** table and click on the **Add** button. Click on the **Close** button to close this Add Table dialog.
4) Click on the row under the **Column** in the mid-pane, and select the **course** item.
5) In similar way, click on the row under the **course** item, and select the **schedule** item in the Column. Continue in this way to select all other items, **classroom**, **credit**, **enrollment**, and **course_id**.

6) Uncheck the check box for the row **course_id** in the **Set** column, and type a question mark '**?**' in the **Filter** column for the **course_id** row, and press the **Enter** key in your keyboard.
7) Modify the dynamic parameter's name from @**Param1** to @**CourseID**.
8) Enter the updated values to the associated **New Value** column in the bottom pane after the **SET** clause. The point to be noted is that all of these updated values' names must be identical with those input parameters to the stored procedure we built in step **A** in Fig. 7.33.

Your finished Query Designer wizard should match one that is shown in Fig. 7.34. Click on the **OK** button to create this **UPDATE** statement codes that have been highlighted in the background color at step **B** in Fig. 7.33.

Let's have a closer look at this piece of codes to see how it works.

A. Six input parameters to this stored procedure are declared first with the associated data types. These parameters must be identical with those parameters in the CallableStatement query string we will build later to enable the CallableStatement to recognize them when it is executed to perform the data updating action in our project.
B. The **UPDATE** statement we built using the Query Designer wizard is attached here, and the query criterion **course_id** is obtained from the **CourseList** Listbox.

Right click on any location inside our completed stored procedure, and select the **Execute** item to try to build it. A successful building result should be displayed in the **Messages** box if everything is fine. Then right click on the **Stored Procedures** node in the Object Explorer window, and select the **Refresh** item to show our new built stored procedure **dbo.UpdateCourse**.

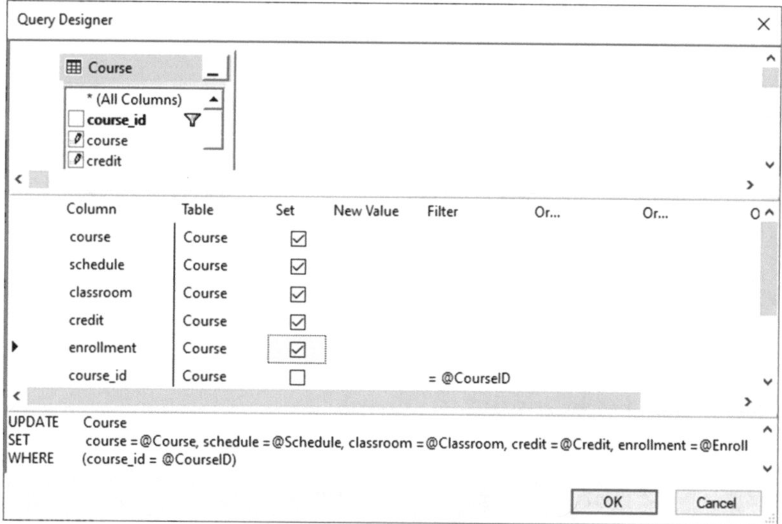

Fig. 7.34 The Finished Query Designer wizard

Now let's run this stored procedure to test its functionality. Right click on our new created stored procedure **dbo.UpdateCourse** from the Object Explorer window, and select the **Execute Stored Procedure** item to open the Execute Procedure wizard. Enter the following data into the associated **Value** columns to this wizard:

- @CourseID: **CSE-549**
- @Course: **Intelligent Controls**
- @Schedule: **M-W-F: 11:00 – 11:50 AM**
- @Classroom: **TC-303**
- @Credit: **3**
- @Enrollment: **28**

Click on the **OK** button to run this stored procedure. The running result is shown in Fig. 7.35. It can be found that a successful running message is displayed in the **Messages** windows (1 row(s) affected) and the **Query executed successfully** statement is also displayed in the status bar at the bottom of this window.

It is highly recommended to recover this updated course record to its original values since we need to call the CallableStatement object to run this stored procedure again when we test our project later. You can do this recovery job in two ways: (1) perform another updating action using this stored procedure or (2) use the Microsoft SQL Server Management Studio to open the **Course** table. Refer to Sect. 7.6.1.2 to get more details for this course to recover this course **CSE-549**.

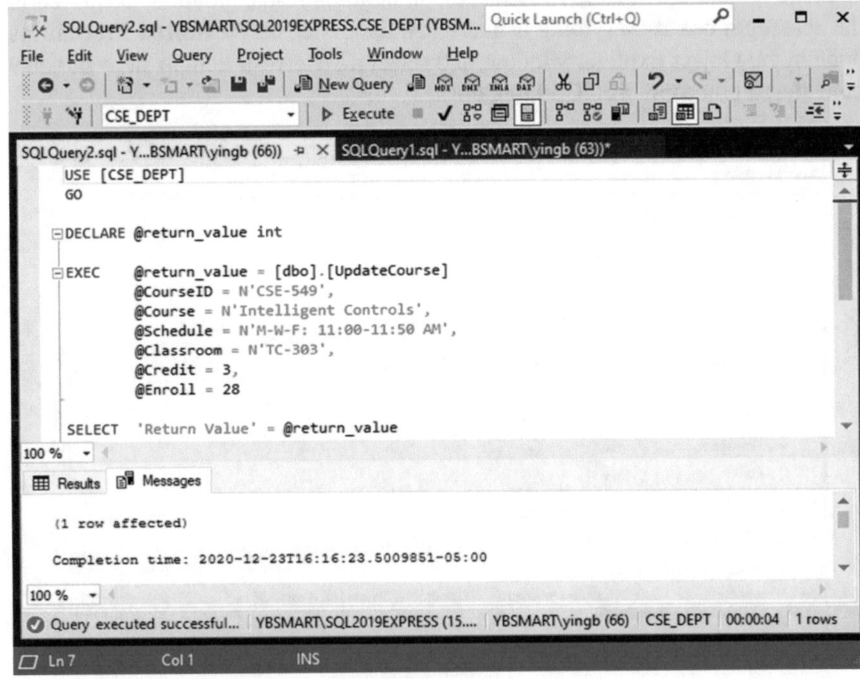

Fig. 7.35 The running result of the stored procedure dbo.UpdateCourse

Now Close the Microsoft SQL Server Management Studio since we have finished building and testing this stored procedure. Click **No** in the popup Messagebox since we do not need to save this running script **SQLQuery1.sql**.

Now let's build our codes for the **Update** button click event handler in the CourseFrame form to call this stored procedure to perform this data updating action.

7.6.2.2 Develop the Codes for the Update Button Click Event Handler

Open our project **SQLCallableUpdate** and the CourseFrame Form window in Design View, and double click on the **Update** button to open its event handler and enter the codes that are shown in Fig. 7.36 into this handler.

Let's have a close look at this piece of codes to see how it works.

A. An **if** block is used to distinguish whether the **Java Callable Method** has been selected.
B. If it is, a new CallableStatement instance is declared.
C. A **try…catch** block is used to perform this data updating action using the CallableStatement method. The CallableStatement query string is created. Refer to Sect. 6.3.6.2 in Chap. 6 to get more detailed information about the structure and protocol of a CallableStatement query string. This is a dynamic query string with six pieces of positional updating information related to a new course; therefore, six question marks are used as the position holders for those parameters.
D. A new CallableStatement instance is created by calling the **prepareCall()** method that is defined in the **Connection** class.
E. The dynamic query string is initialized with six positional parameters, and the values of those parameters are entered by the user into the associated course-related text fields. The point to be noted is the last two parameters, which are credits (**Integer**) and enrollment (**integer**), respectively. Therefore the associ-

```
  private void UpdateButtonActionPerformed(java.awt.event.ActionEvent evt) {
A     if (ComboMethod.getSelectedItem()=="Java Callable Method"){
B     CallableStatement cstmt;
      try{
C         String query = "{call dbo.UpdateCourse(?, ?, ?, ?, ?, ?)}";
D         cstmt = LogInFrame.con.prepareCall(query);
E         cstmt.setString(1, CourseList.getSelectedValue());
          cstmt.setString(2, CourseField.getText());
          cstmt.setString(3, ScheduleField.getText());
          cstmt.setString(4, ClassRoomField.getText());
          cstmt.setFloat(5, java.lang.Integer.valueOf(CreditsField.getText()));
          cstmt.setInt(6, java.lang.Integer.parseInt(EnrollField.getText()));
F         cstmt.execute();
        }
G     catch (SQLException e){
          msgDlg.setMessage("Error in CallableStatement! " + e.getMessage());
          msgDlg.setVisible(true);
        }
    }
H     CourseIDField.setText(CourseList.getSelectedValue());
  }
```

Fig. 7.36 The codes for the Update button click event handler

ated **setXXX()** methods need to be used to initialize these two parameters. Since the **Integer** class belongs to the **java.lang** package, here a full name is used for these classes. You can import this **Java.lang** package at the top of this coding window under the **Package** clause to remove those package names if you like.

F. The CallableStatement instance is executed to call the stored procedure to update the selected course record in the **Course** table in our sample database.
G. The **catch** block is used to collect any possible exception for this data updating process.
H. Finally the selected **course_id** from the **CourseList** Listbox is assigned to the **Course ID** field to indicate this updated course.

Now let's build and run the project to test the data updating function. Click on the **Clean and Build Main Project** button to build the project, and click the **Run Main Project** button to run the project.

Enter suitable username and password, such as **jhenry** and **test**, to the LogIn frame form, and select the **Course Information** from the SelectFrame window to open the CourseFrame form window. Make sure that the **Java Callable Method** has been selected from the **Query Method** combo box. Then click on the **Select** button to query the default course information for the selected faculty member **Ying Bai**.

Now select the course **CSE-549** from the CourseList listbox, and enter the following data into six text fields as an updated course record for the selected course **CSE-549**:

Course:	**Intelligent Controls**
Schedule:	**M-W-F: 11:00 – 11:50 AM**
Classroom:	**TC-303**
Credit:	**3**
Enrollment:	**28**

Then click on the **Update** button to update this course record in the **Course** table in our sample database. To confirm and validate this data updating, click on the **Select** button to try to retrieve all courses taught by the selected faculty **Ying Bai**. The running result is shown in Fig. 7.37.

Another way to confirm this data updating action is to open the **Course** table using the **Services** window in the NetBeans IDE. To do that, open the **Services** window and expand the **Databases** node, and connect to our SQL Server database by right clicking on that URL and select the **Connect** item. Then expand that connected URL and our **CSE_DEPT** database node, **dbo** schema, and **Tables** nodes. Right click on the **Course** table, and select the **View Data** to open this table. Scroll down along this table, and you can find that the course **CSE-549** has been updated and displayed at the last line on this **Course** table, as shown in Fig. 7.38.

It is highly recommended to recover this updated course record to its original values since we want to keep our database clean and neat. You can do this recovery job in two ways: (1) perform another updating action using this **Update** button

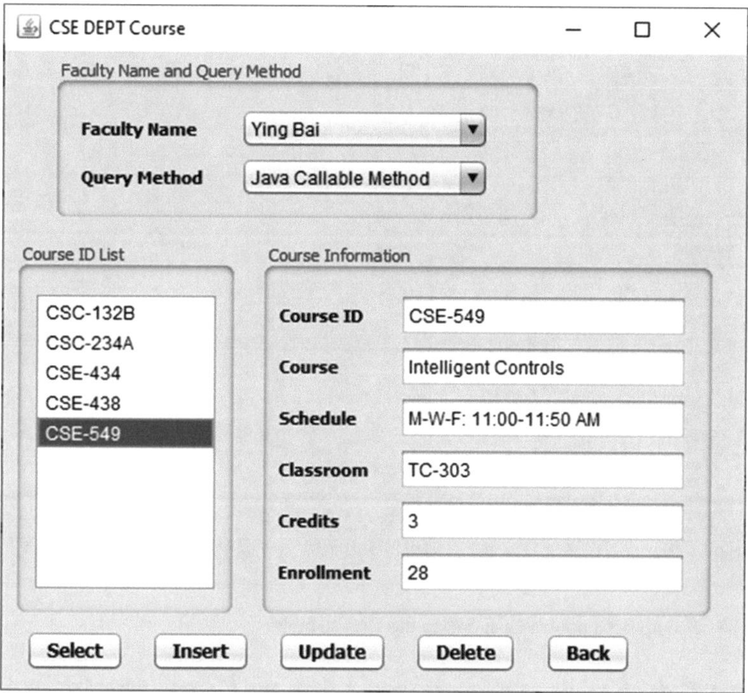

Fig. 7.37 The running result of the data updating action

event handler, or (2) use the Microsoft SQL Server Management Studio to open the **Course** table. Refer to Sect. 7.6.1.2 to get more details about this course to recover this course **CSE-549**.

Next let's handle the data deleting using the CallableStatement object method.

7.6.3 Delete Data from the Course Table Using Callable Statements

Copy the project **SQLCallableUpdate** and change its name to **SQLCallableDelete**, and save it to the folder **Class DB Projects\Chapter 7** on your computer. We will build the data deleting function with the CallableStatement method in the following procedures:

1) Build our stored procedure **dbo.DeleteCourse** using the SQL Server Management Studio.
2) Develop the codes for the **Delete** button in the CourseFrame Form window to execute the CallableStatement method to call our stored procedure **dbo.**

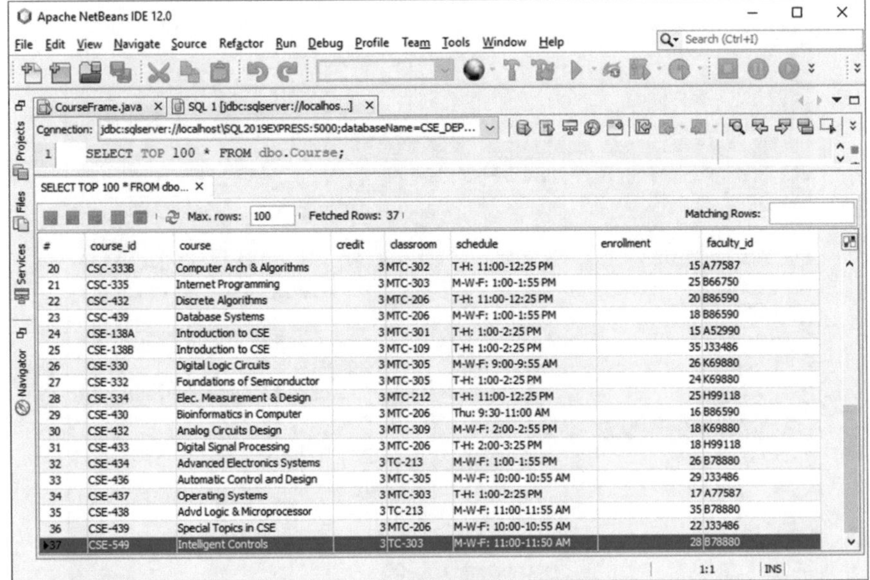

Fig. 7.38 The updated course CSE-549 in the Course table.

DeleteCourse to delete a course record from the **Course** table in our sample database.

3) Confirm and validate this course deleting action using the codes we built for the **Select** button event handler.

Now let's start from the first step.

7.6.3.1 Develop the Stored Procedure dbo.DeleteCourse

Launch the Microsoft SQL Server Management Studio by going to **Start > All Programs > Microsoft SQL Server Tools 18 > Microsoft SQL Server Management Studio**. Click the **Connect** button to open this studio server. On the opened studio, expand the **Databases** and our sample database **CSE_DEPT** nodes. Then expand the **Programmability** node, and right click on the **Stored Procedures** node; select the **Stored Procedure** from the popup menu to open a new stored procedure template.

You can use the **Ctrl-Shift-M** combination keys to enter all parameters for this stored procedure. However, an easy way to do that is to directly enter all parameters manually. On the opened new stored procedure template, enter the codes that are shown in Fig. 7.39 into this stored procedure template as the body of our new stored procedure **dbo.DeleteCourse**. You can create this piece of codes manually or using the Query Designer as we did in the last section for the stored procedure **dbo. UpdateCourse**.

```
-- ================================================
SET ANSI_NULLS ON
GO
SET QUOTED_IDENTIFIER ON
GO
-- ============================================
-- Author:          Y. Bai
-- Create date:     Dec 24, 2020
-- ============================================
CREATE PROCEDURE dbo.DeleteCourse
     -- Add the parameters for the stored procedure here
A    @CourseID VARCHAR(50)
AS
BEGIN
    -- SET NOCOUNT ON added to prevent extra result sets from
    -- interfering with SELECT statements.
    SET NOCOUNT ON;
   -- Insert statements for procedure here
B   DELETE FROM Course
    WHERE (course_id = @CourseID)
END
GO
```

Fig. 7.39 The codes for the stored procedure dbo.DeleteCourse

Let's have a closer look at this piece of codes to see how it works.

A. The only input to this stored procedure is the **course_id** that is a primary key to the **Course** table. Here we use **@CourseID** as a dynamic parameter for this stored procedure.
B. The **DELETE** statement is created with the **@CourseID** as this deleting criterion.

Right click on any location inside our new stored procedure, and select the **Execute** item to try to build and save this stored procedure. Then right click on the **Stored Procedures** node in the Object Explorer window, and select the **Refresh** item to show our new built stored procedure **dbo.DeleteCourse**.

Now let's run this stored procedure to test its functionality. Right click on our new created stored procedure **dbo.DeleteCourse** from the Object Explorer window, and select the **Execute Stored Procedure** item to open the Execute Procedure wizard. Enter the following data into the associated `Value` column to this wizard:

- @CourseID: **CSE-549**

Click on the **OK** button to run this stored procedure. The running result is shown in Fig. 7.40. It can be found that a successful running message is displayed in the **Messages** windows (**1 row affected**) and the **Query executed successfully** statement is also displayed in the status bar at the bottom of this window.

One can check and confirm this data deleting action by opening the **Course** table in this SQL Server Management Studio. Perform the following operations to open this table:

1) Expand our sample database **CSE_DEPT** and **Tables** folder in the Object Explorer.

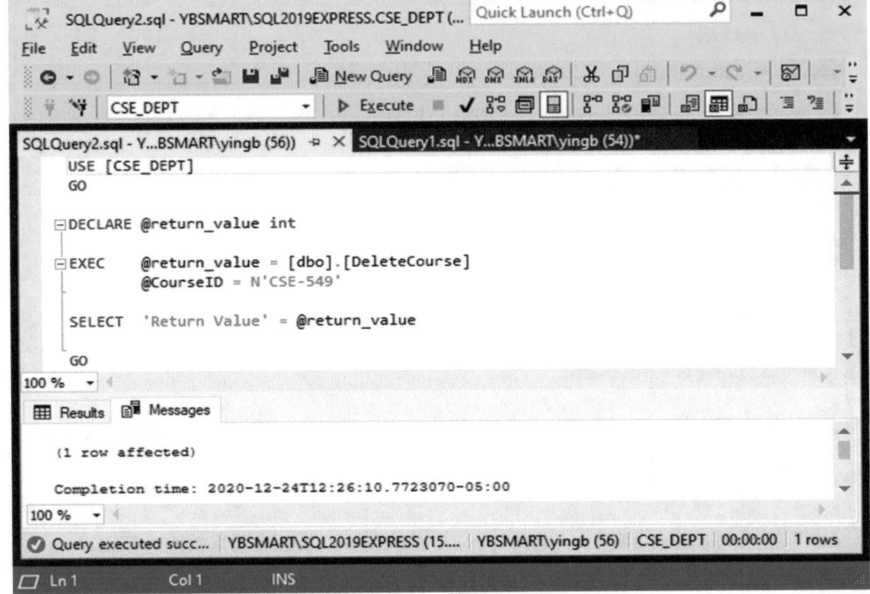

Fig. 7.40 The running result of the stored procedure dbo.DeleteCourse

Table 7.7 The deleted course record in the Course table

course_id	course	credit	classroom	schedule	enrollment	faculty_id
CSE-549	Fuzzy Systems	3	MTC-302	T-H: 1:30-2:45 PM	25	B78880

2) Right click on the **Course** table, **dbo.Course**, and select **Edit Top 200 Rows** item from the popup menu to open it.

One can find that the course, **CSE-549**, has been deleted from this table.

It is highly recommended to recover this deleted course record to its original values since we need to call the CallableStatement object to run this stored procedure again when we test our

project later. You can do this recovery job inside the Microsoft SQL Server Management Studio by opening the **Course** table and inserting this course record at the bottom line on this table. Refer to Table 7.7 to recover this deleted course record.

Before one can close this Microsoft SQL Server Management Studio, go to **File > Save All** to save this recovery job. Click on the **Cancel** and **No** buttons for some messages to ask us to save the procedure running script, **SQLQuery1.sql**, since we do not need to keep it.

Now close the Microsoft SQL Server Management Studio since we have finished building and testing the stored procedure.

Next we need to build our codes for the Delete button click event handler in the CourseFrame form to call this stored procedure to perform this data deleting action.

7.6.3.2 Develop the Codes for the Delete Button Click Event Handler

Open the Design View of our project **SQLCallableDelete**, and double click on the **Delete** button on the CourseFrame form window to open its event handler, and enter the codes that are shown in Fig. 7.41 into this handler. Let's have a close look at this piece of codes to see how it works.

A. An **if** block is used to distinguish whether the **Java Callable Method** has been selected.
B. If it is, a new **CallableStatement** instance is declared.
C. A **try…catch** block is used to perform this data deleting action using the CallableStatement method. The CallableStatement query string is created. Refer to Sect. 6.3.6.2 in Chap. 6 to get more detailed information about the structure and protocol of a CallableStatement query string. This is a dynamic query string with one positional parameter related to a new course; therefore, a question mark is used as the position holder for this parameter.
D. A new CallableStatement instance is created by calling the **prepareCall()** method that is defined in the **Connection** class.
E. The dynamic query string is initialized with a positional parameter, and the value of this parameter is selected by the user from the **CourseList** Listbox.
F. The CallableStatement instance is executed to call the stored procedure we built in the last section to delete the selected course record in the **Course** table from our sample database.
G. The **catch** block is used to track and collect any possible exception for this data deleting.
H. The deleted **course_id** is removed from the Course ID field to indicate this deleting action.

Now let's build and run the project to test this data deleting function. Click on the **Clean and Build Main Project** button to build the project, and click on the **Run Main Project** button to run the project.

```
  private void cmdDeleteActionPerformed(java.awt.event.ActionEvent evt) {
A     if (ComboMethod.getSelectedItem()=="Java Callable Method"){
B        CallableStatement cstmt;
         try{
C           String query = "{call dbo.DeleteCourse(?)}";
D           cstmt = LogInFrame.con.prepareCall(query);
E           cstmt.setString(1, CourseList.getSelectedValue());
F           cstmt.execute();
         }
G        catch (SQLException e){
            msgDlg.setMessage("Error in CallableStatement! " + e.getMessage());
            msgDlg.setVisible(true);
         }
      }
H     CourseIDField.setText(null);
  }
```

Fig. 7.41 The codes for the Delete button click event handler

Enter suitable username and password, such as **jhenry** and **test**, to the LogIn frame form, and select the **Course Information** from the SelectFrame window to open the CourseFrame form window. Make sure that the **Java Callable Method** has been selected from the **Query Method** combo box. Then click on the **Select** button to query the default course information for the selected faculty member **Ying Bai**.

Now select the course **CSE-549** from the **CourseList** Listbox, and click on the **Delete** button to try to delete this course from the **Course** table in our sample database.

To confirm and validate this data deletion action, click on the **Select** button again to try to retrieve all courses taught by the default faculty **Ying Bai**. It can be found that there is no **CSE-549** course in the **CourseList** Listbox, and this means that the course **CSE-549** has been deleted from the **Course** table. You can also confirm this data deleting action by opening the **Course** table using the **Services** window in the Apache NetBeans IDE.

At this point, we have finished developing and building data manipulations project using CallableStatement object method. A complete project **SQLCallableDelete** that contains all three data manipulation actions to SQL Server database can be found at the folder **Class DB Projects \Chapter 7** that is under the **Students** folder at the Springer ftp site (refer to Fig. 1.2 in Chap. 1).

7.7 Chapter Summary

Three popular data manipulation methods against the SQL Server database have been discussed and analyzed in detail with quite a few of real project examples in this chapter.

This chapter is divided into three parts based on three different data query methods: insert, update, and delete data to our sample database using the Java runtime object method. This method provides more flexibility and efficiency in data actions against different databases. Also in this chapter, two more data manipulation methods, Updatable ResultSet and CallableStatement, are discussed with real projects for the SQL Server database.

Detailed introductions and illustrations on building stored procedures under SQL Server database system are provided with real and step-by-step examples. After finishing this chapter, readers will be:

- Able to design and build professional data actions against SQL Server database system using the Java runtime objects.
- Able to design and build popular stored procedures for SQL Server database system.
- Able to design and build professional data actions against SQL Server database system using Updatable ResultSet methods.
- Able to design and build professional data actions against SQL Server database system using CallableStatement methods.

Starting from next chapter, we will discuss the database programming with Java Applet.

Homework

I. True/False Selections

____1. To use Java runtime method to insert an image into the SQL Server database, the **setString()** method should be used.

____2. When using **JFileChooser** object to select an image, the returned image is a Java File object, and one needs to convert it to a **Byte[]** array to be inserted into a column in a database table.

____3. When converting an image file to a **Byte[]** array, one can use a system method, **readAllBytes()**.

____4. To avoid possible duplicated record to be inserted into a database, the **Insert** button on a Frame Form should be enabled after a desired record has been inserted.

____5. By setting the Concurrency Type property as **Updatable** to a ResultSet object, that ResultSet object can be used to perform data insertion, updating, and deleting actions to a database.

____6. To use Updatable ResultSet object to delete a record from a database, only one step is enough, which is to use the **deleteRow()** method of the ResultSet class.

____7. When using Updatable ResultSet object to update a record in a database, only one step is good enough, which is to call the **updateXXX()** method.

____8. When performing data manipulations using Java runtime object method, one can use either **executeUpdate()** or **execute()** method.

____9. A default ResultSet object is updatable and has a cursor that can move either forwardly and backwardly.

___10. To insert a new record into a database using the Updatable ResultSet method, one needs first to move the cursor to an insert-row that is a blank row and it is not a part of the ResultSet but related to the ResultSet.

II. Multiple Choices

1. When using Updatable ResultSet object to update a record in a database, two steps are needed, and they are ________________.

   (a) Insert data in ResultSet, and update the data into database.
   (b) Update data in the ResultSet, and copy change to database.
   (c) Delete data from ResultSet, and copy change to database.
   (d) Select data in the ResultSet, and update the data in database.

2. When building a stored procedure with SQL Server Management Studio, one needs to build and save the procedure by _______________.

   (a) Going to File > Save All menu item
   (b) Building the procedure
   (c) Executing the procedure
   (d) Updating the procedure

3. When using an Updatable ResultSet to perform data manipulations, two parameters can be used to set up properties of a ResultSet object; they are ___________________.
   (a) Forward-only, Updatable
   (b) Scroll-sensitive, Read-only
   (c) ResultSet Type, Concurrency Type of a ResultSet
   (d) ResultSet Type, Updatable Type
4. Which of the following created ResultSet protocol is correct? __________
   (a) Statement createStatement(int resultSetType, int resultSetConcurrency)
   (b) PreparedStatement prepareStatement(String sql, int resultSetType, int resultSetConcurrency)
   (c) CallableStatement prepareCall(String sql, int resultSetType, int resultSetConcurrency)
   (d) All of them
5. To update a record using the Updatable ResultSet, one needs to use ______ steps and they are: ________________________.
   (a) 1, UpdateXXX()
   (b) 2, UpdateXXX() and UpdateRow()
   (c) 3, UpdateXXX(), UpdateCursor() and UpdateRow()
   (d) 4, MoveToRow(), UpdateXXX(), UpdateCursor() and UpdateRow()
6. To insert a new record using the Updatable ResultSet, one needs to use ______ steps and they are: ________________________ .
   (a) 1, insertRow()
   (b) 2, moveToInsertRow(), insertRow()
   (c) 3, moveToInsertRow(),updateXXX(), insertRow()
   (d) 4, moveToCursor(), moveToInsertRow(), updateXXX(), insertRow()
7. When building a stored procedure to perform data insertion action, the order of the input parameters must be __________ with the order of the related _________.
   (a) Identical, data column
   (b) Different, data column
   (c) Same or different, data row
   (d) Identical, data table
8. By using which of the following static constant values can we set an Updatable Result object that has a cursor that can move either forwardly and backwardly?
   (a) ResultSet.TYPE_FORWARD_ONLY
   (b) ResultSet.TYPE_SCROLL_INSENSITIVE

(c) ResultSet.CONCUR_UPDATABLE
(d) ResultSet.TYPE_SCROLL_SENSITIVE

9. By using which of the following static constant values can we set an Updatable Result object whose contents can be updated?

(a) ResultSet.TYPE_FORWARD_ONLY
(b) ResultSet.TYPE_SCROLL_INSENSITIVE
(c) ResultSet.CONCUR_UPDATABLE
(d) ResultSet.TYPE_SCROLL_SENSITIVE

10. When building a stored procedure, one can use two ways to build the query statement, and these two ways are ___________________.

(a) Manually write the statement, and run the stored procedure.
(b) Use the Designer Query in Editor, and run the stored procedure.
(c) Execute the procedure, and save the stored procedure.
(d) Manually write the statement, and use the Designer Query in Editor.

III. Exercises

1. List six steps to use Java runtime object to perform data manipulations against our target database.
2. List three steps to insert a new record into a target database using the Updatable ResultSet method. Convert the pseudo-codes shown below to the real Java codes (assume that a valid connection **conn** has been established).
3. Develop codes for the StudentFrame Form window to insert a new student record into the **Student** table in our sample database using the Java runtime object method. The new student's record is:

- Student ID: **F78569**
- Student Name: **Williams Ford**
- GPA: **3.42**
- Credits: **97**
- Major: **Computer Engineering**
- SchoolYear: **Junior**
- Email: **wford@college.edu**
- simage: **Any student image can be used**

Hint1
A sample project **SQLInsertObject**, which can be found from the folder **Class DB Projects \Chapter 7** under the **Students** folder in the Springer ftp site (refer to Fig. 1.2 in Chap. 1), is available. Based on that project, build your codes in the **Insert** button event handler on the StudentFrame Form.

Hint2
1) Add one more method, **Java Runtime Method**, into the StudentFrame constructor.

2) Add one **if** block in the **Insert** button event handler to identify the **Java Runtime Method**, and build and add your codes inside this block.
3) You may need to use three user-defined methods, **chkFaculty()**, **clearFaculty()**, and **getFacultyImage()**, which you can obtain from the **Insert** button event handler in the Facultyframe class in the same project. It is recommended to change their names to **chkStudent()**, **clearStudent()**, and **getStudent()**, respectively.

4. Figure 7.42 shows a stored procedure **dbo.UpdateFaculty**. Develop and build codes on the FacultyFrame form class to call this stored procedure to update a faculty record for the **Faculty** table in our sample SQL Server database using CallableStatement method. Any faculty's photo can be used for this updating action.

Hint1

A sample project **SQLCallableUpdate**, which can be found from the folder **Class DB Projects\Chapter 7** under the **Students** folder in the Springer ftp site (refer to Fig. 1.2 in Chap. 1), is available. Based on that project, build your codes in the **Update** button event handler on the FacultyFrame Form.

```
SET ANSI_NULLS ON
GO
SET QUOTED_IDENTIFIER ON
GO
-- ==============================================
CREATE PROCEDURE dbo.UpdateFaculty
    -- Add the parameters for the stored procedure here
    @FacultyID VARCHAR(50),
    @FacultyName VARCHAR(50),
    @Title text,
    @Office text,
    @Phone text,
    @College text,
    @Email text,
    @FImage Image
AS
BEGIN
   -- SET NOCOUNT ON added to prevent extra result sets from
   -- interfering with SELECT statements.
          SET NOCOUNT ON;
   -- Insert statements for procedure here
    UPDATE Faculty
    SET faculty_name = @FacultyName, title = @Title, office = @Office, phone = @Phone,
        college = @College, email = @Email, fimage = @FImage
    WHERE (faculty_id = @FacultyID)
END
GO
```

Fig. 7.42 A piece of codes used to insert some data into two tables

Hint2

Add one **if** block in the **Update** button event handler to identify the **Java Callable Method**, and build and add your codes inside this block.

Hint3

Refer to the codes in the **Update** button event handler in the sample project **SQLUpdateObject** located at the folder **Class DB Projects\Chapter 7** under the **Students** folder at the Springer ftp site (refer to Fig. 1.2 in Chap. 1). You may also need to use two user-defined methods, **getFacultyImage()** and **CurrentFaculty()**, developed in that project.

Part II
Building Three-Tier Client-Server Applications

Chapter 8
Developing Java Web Applications to Access Databases

As the rapid development of the Java Web application techniques, today the Java Web applications are closely related to Java Enterprise Edition platform, and the latter provides rich and powerful APIs to support developers to build and develop more efficient and productive Web applications with less complexity and developing efforts.

The Java EE platform uses a simplified programming model. XML deployment descriptors are optional. Instead, a developer can simply enter the information as an annotation directly into a Java source file, and the Java EE server will configure the component at deployment and runtime. These annotations are generally used to embed in a program data that would otherwise be furnished in a deployment descriptor. With annotations, the specification information is put directly in your code next to the program element that it affects.

In order to have a clear and understandable idea about Java Web applications and their developments, let's first have a quick historical review on this topic and this review is absolutely necessary for beginners who have never built and developed any Java Web application before. You are not required to understand all details on the codes in the following review sections, but we expect that you can understand them based on their functions.

8.1 A Historical Review About Java Web Application Development

Java Web applications are based on Servlet technique, and the Servlet works as a Web server that provides all supports such as receiving requests from the client and sending responses back to the client. Exactly a Servlet is a server class built in Java

Supplementary Information The online version contains supplementary material available at [https://doi.org/10.1007/978-3-031-06553-8_8].

Y. Bai, *SQL Server Database Programming with Java*,
https://doi.org/10.1007/978-3-031-06553-8_8

language with all functionalities of a server engine. A Servlet performs its job in the following ways:

- When a Servlet is created, the **init()** method is called to do the initialization jobs for the Web server.
- When a request is received by the Servlet, it creates two objects: request and response.
- Then the Servlet sends these two objects to the **service()** method.
- The request object encapsulates the information passed from the HTTP request coming from the client.
- The **service()** method is a main responding body and will be used to process the request and send the response that has been embedded into the response object back to the client.

The conventional Web applications are built with a Servlet as a Web container and HTML pages as Web clients.

8.1.1 Using Servlet and HTML Web Pages for Java Web Applications

The main purpose of using the Servlet is to compensate the shortcoming of using a Common Gateway Interface (CGI). Unlike the CGI, the Servlet can be used to create dynamic Web pages during the server-client communication processes. Two methods, **doGet()** and **doPost()**, are main channels to communicate between the server and clients.

General uses of Servlet include:

- Processing requests received from clients and responses back to clients
- Creating dynamic Web pages
- Managing state information for applications
- Storing data and information for clients

Generally, the client pages can be divided into two categories: reading-page and posting-page. The former is used to read data from the user, and the latter is used for displaying feedback from the server. To interface to the client to get user's data, in most time the server calls the **getParameter()** method that belongs to the **request** object to do this job. To send feedback to the client, in most time the server uses **println()** method that belongs to the **out** object. With this pair of methods, a server can easily communicate with the client and transfer data between them.

By using an example that utilizes these methods to transfer the login information between a Servlet and a client Web page, we can get a much clearer picture and deeper understanding for this topic.

Open a Notepad and enter the following codes that are shown in Fig. 8.1 to build the **Login.html** file. Save this file with the name of **"Login.html"** to make it an

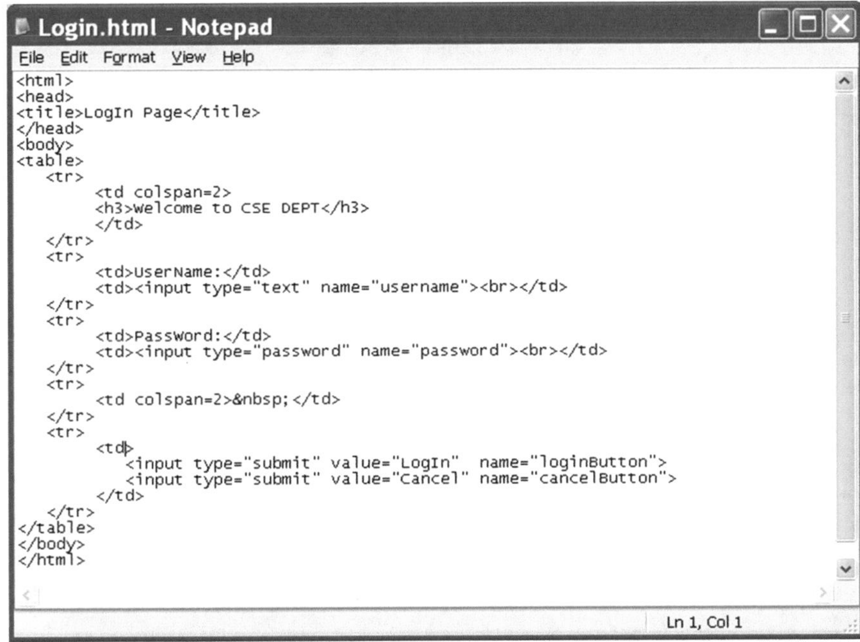


```
<html>
<head>
<title>LogIn Page</title>
</head>
<body>
<table>
   <tr>
        <td colspan=2>
        <h3>Welcome to CSE DEPT</h3>
        </td>
   </tr>
   <tr>
        <td>UserName:</td>
        <td><input type="text" name="username"><br></td>
   </tr>
   <tr>
        <td>Password:</td>
        <td><input type="password" name="password"><br></td>
   </tr>
   <tr>
        <td colspan=2> </td>
   </tr>
   <tr>
        <td>
          <input type="submit" value="LogIn"  name="loginButton">
          <input type="submit" value="Cancel" name="cancelButton">
        </td>
   </tr>
</table>
</body>
</html>
```

Fig. 8.1 The finished Login.html file

HTML file. You have to use double quotation marks to enclose this file name with the .html extension to let Notepad know that you want to save it as an HTML file.

Double click on this file to run it, and the running result is shown in Fig. 8.2.

Two input text fields are used by users to enable them to enter the desired username and password. The key is the identifier for both text fields, **username** and **password**, which is the name property or attribute of these two text fields. When a server needs these two pieces of login information, it uses the **getParameter()** method defined in the **request** object with the names of two text fields as identifiers to get them. Figure 8.3 shows a piece of codes developed in the server side to perform this login information picking up operation.

Two variables, **uname** and **pword**, are used in the server side to hold the picked up username and password entered by the user from the client Web page. The **getParameter()** method is used to do this picking up operation. The identifiers for these two parameters are the names of two text fields in the HTML page.

With this simple example, you can see how easy it is for server and client to communicate for each other. The server can send feedback or post any desired information in the client by using the **out** object that is obtained from creating a new **PrintWriter** instance at the first two coding lines in this piece of codes.

Ok, now we have a clear picture about the module of using a Servlet and a client to build and implement a Java Web application in the early days. To deploy this login Servlet, we need to locate the Servlet class file to the suitable directory.

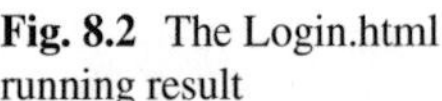

Fig. 8.2 The Login.html running result

```
public void doGet(HttpServletRequest request, HttpServletResponse response)
{
    response.setContentType("text/html");
    PrintWriter out = new PrintWriter(response.getWriter());
    String uname = request.getParameter("username");
    String pword = request.getParameter("password");
    // process the received uname and pword
```

Fig. 8.3 Using getParameter() method to get data from the client

One of shortcomings for this kind of application is that the server and the client use two different languages, and a converter or a render is necessary to perform this conversion between these two languages. This will reduce the running speed and efficiency of the Web application. A solution to this issue is the Java ServerPage (JSP) technique, which was developed by Sun. With the help of the JSP, parts of server codes can be extended and embedded into the client side to facilitate the communications between a server and a client.

8.1.2 Using JavaServer Pages Technology for Java Web Applications

In fact, JavaServer Pages technique provides a way of using Java code within an HTML page, which means that you can embed a piece of Java codes or a part of Servlet functions into the codes in the client side with appropriate tags. The embedded Java codes will be compiled and executed by the JSP engine in the server side as the application runs. From this point of view, the JavaServer Pages can be considered as a part of a Servlet or as an extension of an application server located at the client side. Although the JSP provides a lot of advantages over Servlets, it is actually a subclass of the Servlet class and built based on Servlets technology.

The JavaServer Pages can be implemented not only in the HTML files but also in the following files:

- Script language files, which allow you to specify a block of Java codes.
- JSP directives, which enable you to control the JSP structure and environment.
- Actions, which allow you to specify the executing commands such as loading a parameter from a client page.

The JSP provides some useful built-in or implicit objects to perform most interfacing functions with clients and server. The so-called implicit objects in JSP are objects that are automatically available in JSP. Implicit objects are Java objects that the JSP Container provides to a developer to access them in their applications using JavaBeans and Servlets. These objects are called implicit objects because they are automatically instantiated. Some popular implicit JSP objects include:

- request
- response
- out
- session
- application
- pageContext
- page
- exception

Among those objects, the **request**, **response**, and **session** are most popular objects and are often used in the interfacing between clients and servers. Some other objects such as **out** and **pageContext** are mainly used to write output to the client and to access most built-in objects.

Figure 8.4 shows an example of using the **out** and the **pageContext** objects to write some feedback to the client (the top section) and to get a session object (the bottom section).

Two popular tags used by JSP to distinguish with other languages are:

- *<% .... %>*

```
out.println("<HTML>");
out.println("<HEAD>Hello World</HEAD>");
out.println("</HTML>");
out.close();
```

```
HttpSession session = pageContext.getSession();
```

Fig. 8.4 An example of using the out and the pageContext objects

- **<jsp: .... />**

Between these two tags, you can put any Java codes as you want to improve the execution of the Servlet techniques for Java Web applications.

In fact, you can get a JSP file or page easily by just changing the extension of the **Login.html** file, such as from **Login.html** to **Login.jsp**. Yes, it is so easy to do this to get a JSP file.

An example of using a JSP file to display the received user login data is shown in Fig. 8.5.

Within the tags **<% ...%>**, two lines of Java codes are written, and they are used to call the **getParameter()** method to pick up the username and password entered by the user from the client Web page. You can directly display these received login data in the client side with the Java local variables **uname** and **pword** enclosed with the JSP tags.

In fact, the JavaServer Pages can handle more complicated jobs such as the business logic, JDBC-related database connections, data processing, and JSP pages switching. Generally, a main or controller JSP takes charge of passing parameters between the server and clients, forwarding the user to the other target JSP or Web pages based on the running result of Servlet.

A piece of example codes shown in Fig. 8.6 illustrate how to use a JSP to handle multiple jobs, including the parameters collections from the client page, database accessing, and data processing and forwarding from the current page to the target Java Server pages based on the running results of data processing. Let's have a closer look at these codes to see how they work.

A. The **getParameter()** method is called to pick up two pieces of login information, username and password, which are entered by the user from the client page and assigned to two local variables uname and pword in the Servlet.
B. These two picked up login data are displayed in the client side with the JSP tags.
C. Starting from the JSP tag <%, a piece of Java codes are developed. A SQL Server database driver is loaded, and this is a type IV JDBC driver.
D. The SQL Server JDBC URL is assigned to the local variable **url**.

```
<HTML>
<HEAD>
<TITLE>Welcome to CSE DEPT LogIn Page</TITLE>
</HEAD>
<BODY>
<%@ Page language="java" %>
<%
    String uname = request.getParameter("username");
    String pword = request.getParameter("password");
%>
User Name = <%=uname%><br>
Pass Word  = <%=pword%><br>
</BODY>
</HTML>
```

Fig. 8.5 An example of Java Server Page file

```
  <HTML>
  <HEAD>
  <TITLE>Welcome to CSE DEPT LogIn Page</TITLE></HEAD>
  <BODY>
  <%@ Page language="java" %>
  <%
A     String uname = request.getParameter("username");
      String pword = request.getParameter("password");
  %>
B User Name = <%=uname%><br>
  Pass Word  = <%=pword%><br>
  <%
      try {
C          Class.forName("com.microsoft.sqlserver.jdbc.SQLServerDriver");
      }
      catch (Exception e) {
         msgDlg.setMessage("Class not found exception!" + e.getMessage());
         msgDlg.setVisible(true);
      }
D     String url = "jdbc:sqlserver://localhost\\SQL2019EXPRESS: 5000;databaseName=
                                                CSE_DEPT;";
      try {
E     con = DriverManager.getConnection(url,"SMART","Happy2020");
      }
      catch (SQLException e) {
         msgDlg.setMessage("Could not connect!" + e.getMessage());
         msgDlg.setVisible(true);
         e.printStackTrace();
      }
      Statement  stmt = null;
      ResultSet  rs = null;
F     String query = "SELECT user_name, pass_word FROM LogIn " +
                     "WHERE user_name = '" + uname + "' " + " AND pass_word = '"+pword+"';";
G     stmt = con.createStatement();
H     rs = stmt.executeQuery(query);
I     while (rs.next()) {
         String c_uname = rs.getString("user_name");
         String c_pword = rs.getString("pass_word");
      }
J     if (c_uname.equals(uname) && c_pword.equals(pword)) {
         String  nextPage = "Selection.jsp";
      }
K     else {
         String  nextPage = "LoginError.jsp";
      }
  %>
L <jsp:forward  page = "<%=nextPage%>" />
```

Fig. 8.6 A piece of example codes

E. The **getConnection()** method is executed to establish this database connection.
F. A query string is created, and it is used to query a matched username and password from the LogIn table.
G. The **createStatement()** method is called to create a Statement object.
H. The **executeQuery()** method is executed to perform this query, and the returned result is assigned to the ResultSet object **rs**.
I. A **while** loop is used to pick up any possible matched username and password. In fact, only one row is returned, and therefore this loop can run only one time.
J. If a matched username and password pair is found, the **nextPage** is assigned to the **Selection.jsp**.
K. Otherwise the **nextPage** is assigned to the **LoginError.jsp**.

L. The **<jsp:forward />** is used to direct the page to an appropriate page based on the matching result.

A good point of using this JSP technique to handle a lot of JDBC-related codes or business logics in this JavaServer Page is that the Servlet processing speed and efficiency can be improved. However, you can find that at the same time a shortcoming is also coming up with this benefit, which is relatively complex in the coding development. Quite a few codes for the JDBC database accessing and data processing as well as the business logics are involved into this JSP and therefore make it a big mess during the coding development.

To solve this mess problem and separate the business logics and JDBC-related database processing from the result displaying in Web pages and make our coding process easy and clear, three possible ways can be used:

1) Using a Java help class to handle all business logics and database-related processing. In this way, we can separate this login process into two different parts: the data displaying Web page and JDBC-related database processing or business logics to make this process more objective and clear based on its functionality. This Java help class file works just like a bridge or an intermediate layer to help the JavaServer Pages to perform business-related jobs in a separate file to allow the JSP to concentrate on the data displaying process. You will see that this Java help class file can be translated to a Java Bean later.
2) Using the session implicit object provided by JSP to store and transfer data between clients and server. This method still belongs to the Java help class category. Exactly, the session objects are used in the Java help class to help the data storage and retrieving between clients and clients and between clients and the server.
3) Using Java Beans techniques to cover and handle the JDBC-related database accessing, data processing, and business logics such as data matching and comparison process. The main role of JavaServer Pages is to provide a view to display the results. A JSP can also need to load the Java Beans, pass the necessary parameters between Servlet and clients, and forward users to the different targeting pages based on the running result.

Let's have a detailed discussion about these methods one by one.

8.1.3 Using Java Help Class Files for Java Web Applications

To distinguish between the database-related data processing and running results displaying, we can separate a Java Web application into two parts: the JDBC-related database processing and the business logics such as checking and confirming a pair of matched username and password located at a Java help class file and the data and running results displaying at a Web or a JavaServer page.

Take a look at the codes in Fig. 8.6; you can find that about 80% of those codes are JDBC-related database processing codes, and 10% are about the data processing codes. Totally about 90% codes are used to access the database and query for the data and perform data matching functions. Only 10% codes are HTML codes.

To separate these two kinds of codes into two different files, we can pick up all JDBC-related codes and put them in a Java help class file, **LogInQuery.java**, as shown in Fig. 8.7.

Let's have a closer look at this piece of codes to see how it works.

A. Some member data or attributes are defined first inside this class, which include two private String member data **user_name** and **pass_word**, a class level

```
   import java.sql.*;
   public class LogInQuery {
A     private String user_name = null;
      private String pass_word = null;
      static Connection con;
      MsgDialog msgDlg = new MsgDialog(new javax.swing.JFrame(), true);
      public LogInQuery() {
         try {
B           Class.forName("com.microsoft.sqlserver.jdbc.SQLServerDriver");
         }
         catch (Exception e) {
            msgDlg.setMessage("Class not found exception!" + e.getMessage());
            msgDlg.setVisible(true);
         }
C        String url = "jdbc:sqlserver://localhost\\SQL2019EXPRESS: 5000;databaseName=
                                                   CSE_DEPT [SMART on dbo]";
         try {
D           con = DriverManager.getConnection(url,"SMART","Happy2020");
         }
         catch (SQLException e) {
            msgDlg.setMessage("Could not connect!" + e.getMessage());
            msgDlg.setVisible(true);
            e.printStackTrace();
         }
      }
E     public String checkLogIn(String uname, String pword) {
F        String c_uname = null, c_pword = null;
         Statement stmt = null;
         ResultSet rs = null;
G        String query = "SELECT user_name, pass_word FROM LogIn " +
                        "WHERE user_name = '" + uname + "' " + " AND pass_word = '"+pword+"';";
H        stmt = con.createStatement();
I        rs = stmt.executeQuery(query);
J        while (rs.next()) {
            c_uname = rs.getString("user_name");
            c_pword = rs.getString("pass_word");
         }
K        if (c_uname.equals(uname) && c_pword.equals(pword)) {
            user_name = c_uname;
            pass_word = c_pword;
            return "Matched";
         }
L        else {
            return "UnMatched";
         }
      }
   }
```

Fig. 8.7 The codes for the Java Web help class LogInQuery.java

connection variable **con**, and a dialog box that is used to display some debug information.

B. Inside the class constructor, a SQL Server database driver is loaded, and this is a type IV JDBC driver.
C. The SQL Server JDBC URL is assigned to the local variable **url**.
D. The **getConnection()** method is executed to establish this database connection.
E. The Java help method **checkLogIn()** is declared inside this help class. This method is a main function to perform the JDBC-related data query and data matching operations.
F. Some local variables used in this method are defined first, which include the Statement and the ResultSet objects.
G. A query string is created, and it is used to query a matched username and password from the LogIn table.
H. The **createStatement()** method is called to create a Statement object.
I. The **executeQuery()** method is executed to perform this query, and the returned result is assigned to the ResultSet object **rs**.
J. A **while** loop is used to pick up any possible matched username and password. In fact, only one row is returned, and thus this loop can run only one time. The **getString()** method is used to pick up the queried username and password. A point to be noted is that the arguments of this method, **user_name** and **pass_word**, are both column names in the LogIn table in our database **CSE_DEPT**, and they are different with those member data declared at the beginning of this class even though they have the same names. The retuned username and password are assigned to two local variables **c_uname** and **c_pword**, respectively.
K. If a pair of matched username and password is found, they are assigned to two member data **user_name** and **pass_word**, and return a "**Matched**" string to indicate that this **checkLogIn()** method is successful and the matched results are found.
L. Otherwise an "**UnMatched**" string is returned to indicate that no matched login information can be found.

Now let's do a little modification to our **Login.html** file and break this file into two JSP files: **index.jsp** and **LogInQuery.jsp**. The reason for us to make it into two JSP files is that we want to process and display data in two separate files to make it clear and easy. Generally the **index.jsp** can be considered as a starting or a home page as a Web application runs. Figure 8.8 lists the modified codes for our original **Login.html** file that will be renamed to **index.jsp**, and the modified parts have been highlighted in bold.

Let's have a closer look at this piece of modified codes to see how it works.

A. The first modification is that a Form tag is added into this page with a **POST** method and an **action** attribute. Generally a Form tag is used to create a HTML form to collect user information and send all pieces of those collected information to the server when a submit button on this Form is clicked. Therefore a Form and all submitting buttons on that Form have a coordinate relationship. If a button is defined as a **submit** button by its **type** attribute, all Form data will be

```
  <html>
   <head>
        <meta http-equiv="Content-Type" content="text/html; charset=UTF-8">
        <title>LogIn Page</title>
   </head>
    <body>
    <%@page language="java" %>
A   <form method="POST" action=".\LogInQuery.jsp">
    <table>
      <tr>
            <td colspan=2>
            <h3>Welcome to CSE DEPT</h3>
            </td>
      </tr>
      <tr>
            <td>UserName:</td>
            <td><input type="text" name="username"><br></td>
      </tr>
      <tr>
            <td>PassWord:</td>
            <td><input type="password" name="password"><br></td>
      </tr>
      <tr>
            <td colspan=2> </td>
      </tr>
      <tr>
            <td>
              <input type="submit" value="LogIn"  name="loginButton">
B             <input type="button" value="Cancel" name="cancelButton" onclick="self.close()">
            </td>
      </tr>
    </table>
C   </form>
    </body>
  </html>
```

Fig. 8.8 The modified Login.html file (now it is index.jsp)

sent to the server whose URL is defined in the **action** attribute on the Form tag when this submitting button is clicked by the user. Here we use a Java Server Page, **.\LogInQuery.jsp**, as the URL for our target page. Exactly this target page is used to access our Java help class file to handle all JDBC and data-related processing and business logics. The **.** symbol is used to indicate that our JSP file is located at the relatively current folder since this page is a part of the server functions and will be run at the server side as the whole project runs.

B. The second modification is to change the **type** of our Cancel button from **submit** to **button** and add one more attribute **onclick** for this button. The reason for us to do this modification is that we want to close our **Login.jsp** page when this Cancel button is clicked as the project runs, but we do not want to forward this button-click event to the server to allow the server to do this close action. Therefore we have to change the type of this button to **button** (not **submit**) to avoid triggering the **action** attribute in the Form tag. We also need to add a **self.close()** method to the **onclick** attribute of this button to call the system **close()** method to terminate our application. The **self** means the current page.

C. The Form close tag is also added when the form arrived to its bottom.

Now let's build our **LogInQuery.jsp** page, which works as a part of server, to receive and handle the Form data including the login information sent by the **index.jsp** page. Figure 8.9 shows the codes for this page. Let's have a closer look at this piece of codes to see how it works.

A. A JSP directive tag is to indicate that this page uses the Java language, and it is a JSP file.
B. Some local variable and object are declared first. The string variable **nextPage** is used to hold the URL of the next page, and the **lquery** is a new instance of our Java help class LogInQuery we built at the beginning of this section.
C. The **getParameter()** method is used to pick up the login information entered by the user in the **index.jsp** page. The collected login information including the username and password is assigned to two local string variables **u_name** and **p_word**, respectively.
D. The **checkLogIn()** method defined in our Java help class file is called to perform the database query and the login matching processing. The collected login information is used as arguments and passed into this method. The running result of this method is a string, and it is assigned to the local string variable **result**.
E. An **if** block is used to check the running result of the **checkLogIn()** method. The program will be forwarded to a successful page (**Selection.jsp**) if the login process is successful.
F. Otherwise an error message is printed to indicate that this login process failed.
G. A JSP forward directive is used to direct the program to the next page.

In summary, to use a JavaServer Page to assist a Java Web application, the following components should be considered and adopted:

```
  <html>
    <head>
      <meta http-equiv="Content-Type" content="text/html; charset=UTF-8">
      <title>LogIn Query Page</title>
    </head>
    <body>
A     <%@page language="java" %>
      <%
B       String  nextPage = null;
        LogInQuery  lquery = new  LogInQuery();
C       String u_name = request.getParameter("username");
        String p_word = request.getParameter("password");
D       String result = lquery.checkLogIn(u_name, p_word);
E       if (result.equals("Matched")) {
          nextPage = "Selection.jsp";
          }
F       else { out.println("LogIn is failed"); }
      %>
G     <jsp:forward  page = "<%=nextPage%>" />
    </body>
  </html>
```

Fig. 8.9 The codes for the LogInUuery.jsp page

1) The whole Web application can be divided into two parts:

   (a) The JDBC and database processing-related functions and business logics – Java help class file (**LogInQuery.java**).
   (b) The user data input and running result output functions – HTML or JavaServer Pages (**index.jsp** and **LogInQuery.jsp**).

2) The relationships between these three pages are:

   (a) The **index.jsp**, which runs on the client side, works as a starting or a home page as the Web application runs, and it is used to collect the user information and sends it to the Web server.
   (b) The **LogInQuery.jsp**, which can be considered as a part of the application server and runs at the server side, provides the information passing or transformation functions between the home page and other target pages to collect the user information, call the Java help class to perform the data and business logic processing, and direct the program to the different target pages based on the data processing results.
   (c) The Java help class file **LogInQuery.java**, which provides the JDBC and database processing functions and business logics processing abilities, works as an intermediate layer between the server and clients to support above two JSP files. Since this help class file will be called by the **LogInQuery.jsp**, it also belongs to the server-side software.

These components and their relationships can be expressed and illustrated in Fig. 8.10.

Compared with our first Java Web application that utilized the Java Servlet and HTML page, the Web application that used the JavaServer Pages techniques has a great improvement on simplification of data collection and processing by using different function-related pages and help class file. However, one defect is that the JDBC- and database-related functions make the Java help class file LogInQuery.java very complicated because too many database-related functions must be involved and executed, such as loading database driver, connecting to the database, creating query-related objects, building the data query, and collecting the queried results, all of these operations make this file longer and increase the complex in operations. A good solution to this is to use the Java persistence API to simplify these operations and make the file short and simple.

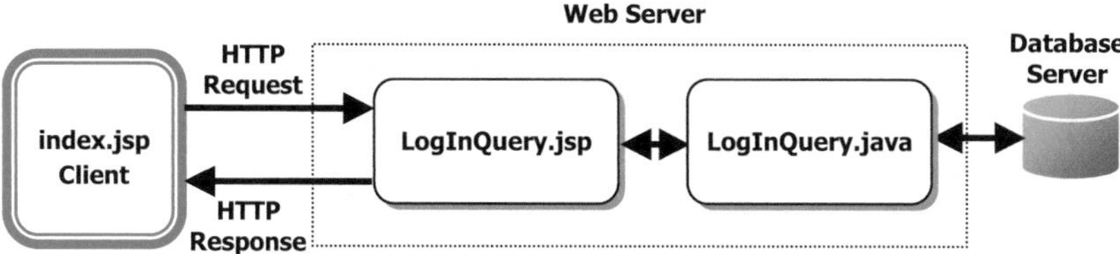

Fig. 8.10 The components and their relationships in a JSP Web application

8.1.4 Using the JSP Implicit Object Session for Java Web Applications

As we mentioned in Sect. 8.1.2, the session is a JSP implicit object used to facilitate developers to build professional Java Web applications. The implicit means that those objects, including the session object, can be created automatically as a new JSP is executed. The specific property of using a session object is that you can save user data in some Web pages and retrieve them from other Web pages. This provides a great and convenient way to transfer data between clients and clients and also between clients and a server.

In this section, we will use this session object to help us to build our Faculty page to query and display the desired faculty information from the Faculty table in our sample database. The structure or architecture of using the session object to coordinate the data query from the Faculty table is shown in Fig. 8.11.

Basically this structure is identical with that we discussed in the last section, and the only difference is that we use a new Java help class file **FacultyBean.java** that is not a real Java Bean class but is very similar to one JavaBean. The reason we did this is that we do not want to have a big jump between the help class and JavaBean to make this design difficult.

The **FacultyPage.jsp** that is our Web client page is shown in Fig. 8.12. Because of its complexity in HTML and JSP codes, we will leave the building and coding of this page in our real project later. In fact, we need to use Microsoft Office Publisher 2007 to build a **FacultyPage.html** file first and then convert it to a **FacultyPage.jsp** file. Now we just assume that we have built this page and want to use it in our Faculty table query process.

Now let's modify this **FacultyPage.jsp** to use session object to perform data storage and retrieving functions between this page and the help class file **FacultyQuery.jsp**.

8.1.4.1 Modify the FacultyPage JSP File to Use the Session Object

Perform the modifications shown in Fig. 8.13 to this **FacultyPage.jsp** file to use the session object to store and pick up data between client pages. All modified codes have been highlighted in bold.

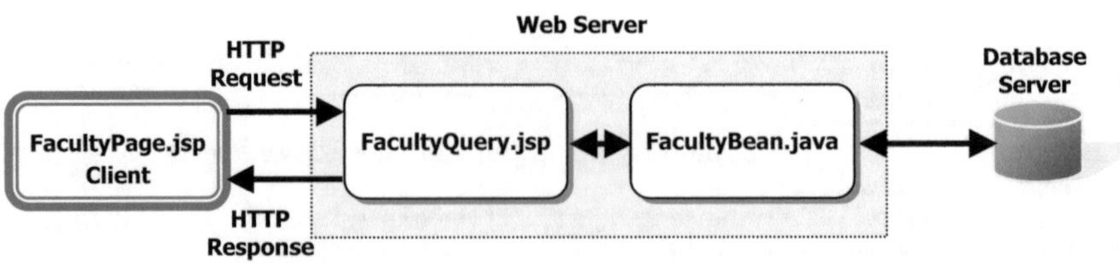

Fig. 8.11 The architecture of using session object in Web applications

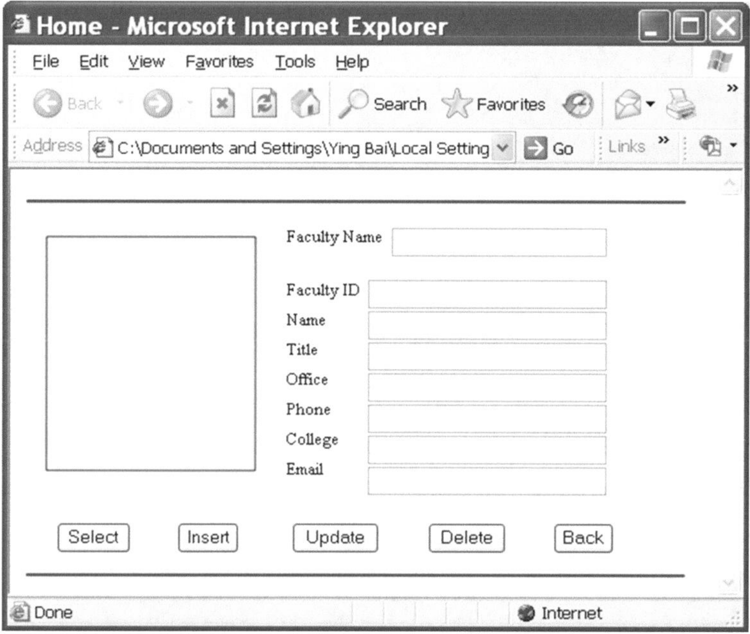

Fig. 8.12 The preview of the FacultyPage.jsp page

In step **A**, we add an `action` attribute to forward all information collected from this page to our model and controller page **FcaultyQuery.jsp** that will call our FacultyBean file to perform the faculty data query process.

Starting from step **B** until step **H**, we use the embedded JSP codes to assign the real queried faculty columns from our Faculty table to the `value` tag of each text field in the **Facultypage.jsp** using the **getAttribute()** method of the session class. In this way, as long as the queried faculty row has any change, this modification will be immediately updated and reflected to each text field in our **FacultyPage.jsp** page. In this way, a direct connection or binding between the text fields in our **Facultypage.jsp** page and the queried Faculty columns in our help class is established.

Now let's take a look at our model and controller page **FacultyQuery.jsp**.

8.1.4.2 Build the Transaction JSP File FacultyQuery.jsp

The purpose of this file is to transfer data and information between our main displaying page **FacultyPage.jsp** and our working help class file FacultyBean that performs all JDBC- and database-related operations and business logics. The codes for this file are shown in Fig. 8.14.

Let's take a closer look at this piece of codes to see how it works.

```
  <html>
    <head>
      <meta http-equiv="Content-Type" content="text/html; charset=UTF-8">
      <title>LogIn Query Page</title>
    </head>
    <body>
    <%@page language="java" %>
A   <form method=post action=".\FacultyQuery.jsp">
    <input name=FacultyNameField maxlength=255 size=24
B    value="<%=session.getAttribute("facultyName") %>" type=text v:shapes="_x0000_s1109">
    .........
    <input name=FacultyIDField maxlength=255 size=26
C    value="<%=session.getAttribute("facultyId") %>" type=text  v:shapes="_x0000_s1110">
    .........
    <input name=NameField maxlength=255 size=26
D    value="<%=session.getAttribute("facultyName") %>" type=text  v:shapes="_x0000_s1106">
    .........
    <input name=OfficeField maxlength=255 size=26
E    value="<%=session.getAttribute("office") %>"  type=text  v:shapes="_x0000_s1104">
    .........
    <input name=PhoneField maxlength=255 size=26
F    value="<%=session.getAttribute("phone") %>"  type=text  v:shapes="_x0000_s1116">
    .........
    <input name=CollegeField maxlength=255 size=26
G    value="<%=session.getAttribute("college") %>" type=text  v:shapes="_x0000_s1117">
    .........
    <input name=EmailField maxlength=255 size=26
H    value="<%=session.getAttribute("email") %>" type=text  v:shapes="_x0000_s1118">
    .........
    </body>
  </html>
```

Fig. 8.13 The modifications to the FacultyPage.jsp file

```
A <%@ page  import="java.util.*" %>
  <%@ page  import="JavaWebHibDBOraclePackage.*" %>
  <html>
    <head>
      <meta http-equiv="Content-Type" content="text/html; charset=UTF-8">
      <title>FacultyQuery JSP Page</title>
    </head>
    <body>
      <h1>This is the FaculrtQuery JSP Page!</h1>
      <%
B     String  fname = request.getParameter("FacultyNameField");
C     FacultyBean  fBean = new  FacultyBean();
D     List  fList = fBean.QueryFaculty(fname);
E     session.setAttribute("facultyId", fBean.getFacultyID());
      session.setAttribute("facultyName", fBean.getFacultyName());
      session.setAttribute("office", fBean.getOffice());
      session.setAttribute("title", fBean.getTitle());
      session.setAttribute("college", fBean.getCollege());
      session.setAttribute("phone", fBean.getPhone());
      session.setAttribute("email", fBean.getEmail());
F     response.sendRedirect("FacultyPage.jsp");
      %>
    </body>
  </html>
```

Fig. 8.14 The codes for the model and controller page FacultyQuery.jsp

A. You can embed any import directory using the JSP directive in a HTML or a JSP file. The format is **<%@ page import="java package" %>**. In this page, we embed two packages: one is **java.util.*** since we need to use the List class and **JavaWebHibDBOraclePackage.*** since we build our FacultyBean help class in that package.

B. The **getParameter()** method is executed to get the faculty name entered by the user to the Faculty Name text field in the **FacultyPage.jsp** page, and this faculty name is assigned to a local String variable **fname**.
C. A new instance of our help class FacultyBean is created.
D. The main help method **QueryFaculty()** we built in the FacultyBean is called to query a faculty record based on the faculty name we obtained from step **B**.
E. The **setAttribute()** method in the session class is executed to store each column of queried faculty row from the Faculty table with a given name. The **getter()** methods defined in the FacultyBean class are executed to pick up each queried column. The point to be noted is that later on when we need to pick up these queried columns from the session object in other pages, we need to use the identical names we used here for each column, such as `facultyId`, `facultyName`, title, and so on.
F. Finally since we need to display all queried columns to the associated text field in the **FacultyPage.jsp** page, we use the **sendRedirect()** method to return to that page.

Finally let's take care of the help class file **FacultyBean**.

8.1.4.3 Build the Help Class FacultyBean

This class is a help class but is very similar to a real Java bean class. The codes of this class are shown in Fig. 8.15.

Let's have a closer look at this piece of codes to see how it works.

A. At the beginning of this class, seven member data or properties of this class are defined. This is very important in a Java bean class since all data-related transactions between the client pages and Java bean are dependent on these properties. In other words, all clients could pick up data from a Java bean using those properties, and a one-to-one relationship existed between each property in the Java bean class and each queried column in the data table. According to the convention, all of these properties should be defined in private data type and can be accessed by using the **getter()** methods provided in this Java bean class.
B. A new instance of the Hibernate session class is created and initialized. The point to be noted is that this Hibernate session object is different with that JSP implicit session object.
C. The **getCurrentSession()** method is executed to get the default Hibernate session object.
D. The detailed definition of the **QueryFcaulty()** method starts from here with the method header.
E. A new **java.util.List** instance is created and initialized since we need this object to pick up and hold our queried faculty result. The MsgDislog instance is used

```
  @Stateless
  public class FacultyBean {
A   private String facultyID;
    private String facultyName;
    private String office;
    private String title;
    private String phone;
    private String college;
    private String email;
B   public Session session = null;
    public FacultyBean() {
C     this.session = HibernateUtil.getSessionFactory().getCurrentSession();
    }
D   public List QueryFaculty(String fname) {
E     List<Faculty> facultyList = null;
      MsgDialog msgDlg = new MsgDialog(new javax.swing.JFrame(), true);
      try {
F       org.hibernate.Transaction tx = session.beginTransaction();
G       Query f = session.createQuery ("from Faculty as f where f.facultyName like '"+fname+"'");
H       facultyList = (List<Faculty>) f.list();
I     } catch (Exception e) {
        msgDlg.setMessage("Query is failed and no matched found!");
        msgDlg.setVisible(true);
        e.printStackTrace();
      }
J     facultyID = facultyList.get(0).getFacultyId();
      facultyName = facultyList.get(0).getFacultyName();
      office = facultyList.get(0).getOffice();
      title = facultyList.get(0).getTitle();
      phone = facultyList.get(0).getPhone();
      college = facultyList.get(0).getCollege();
      email = facultyList.get(0).getEmail();
      return facultyList;
    }
K   public String getFacultyID() {
      return this.facultyID;
    }
    public String getFacultyName() {
      return this.facultyName;
    }
    public String getOffice() {
      return this.office;
    }
    public String getTitle() {
      return this.title;
    }
    public String getPhone() {
      return this.phone;
    }
    public String getCollege() {
      return this.college;
    }
    public String getEmail() {
      return this.email;
    }
  }
```

Fig. 8.15 The codes for the FacultyBean help class

to display error information in case any exception was encountered during this query operation.

F. A **try…catch** block is used to perform our data query. First a new Transaction instance **tx** is created with the **beginTransaction()** method being executed.

G. Then a query string built with the Hibernate Query Language (HQL) is created, and this query string will be used to perform the faculty information query later.
H. The **list()** method is executed to perform a query to the Faculty table in our sample database to try to retrieve a matched faculty record based on the selected faculty name **fname**. The query result is assigned to and held in a local variable **facultyList** that has a **List<Faculty>** data type.
I. The **catch** block is used to track and collect any possible exception during this query process. An error message will be displayed if this query encountered any problem.
J. The **facultyList.get(0)** method is used to retrieve the first matched row from the query result. In fact, only one faculty row should be queried and retrieved since all faculty names are unique in our sample database. A sequence of **getter()** methods is used to pick up the associated columns and assign them to the associated properties in this FacultyBean class. Finally the query result is returned to the **FacultyQuery.jsp** page.
K. Seven **getter()** methods are defined at the bottom of this class, and they can be used to pick up all properties defined in this class.

An operational sequence and data transformation structure of the Faculty Name is shown in Fig. 8.16. In Fig. 8.16, the faculty name is used as an example to illustrate how to transfer this data between client and the help class. The operational sequence is:

1) First a desired faculty name is entered by the user into the Faculty Name text field in the **FacultyPage.jsp** page. This piece of data will be transferred to the **FacultyQuery.jsp** page as the Select button is clicked by the user.
2) In the **FcaultyQuery.jsp** page, the **getParameter()** method is used to pick up this transferred Faculty Name.

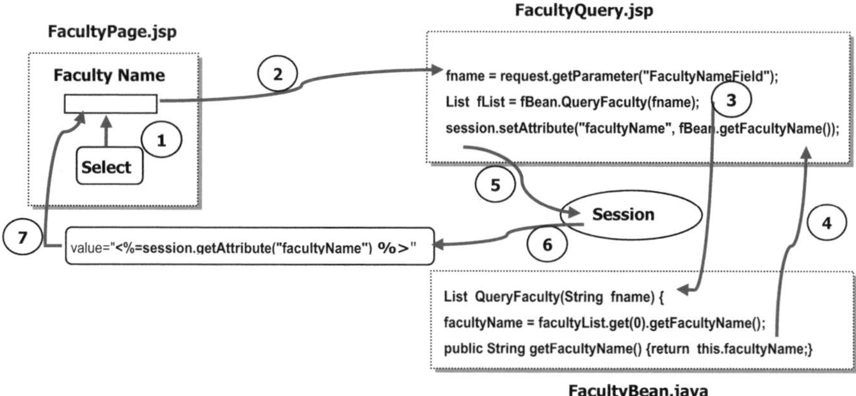

Fig. 8.16 The operational sequence and data transfer structure using the session object

3) Then the help method **QueryFaculty()** in the help class FacultyBean is called to query a matched faculty record from the **Faculty** table based on the transferred faculty name **fname**.
4) When the **getter()** method in the FacultyBean class is executed, the queried faculty name is returned to the **FacultyQuery.jsp** page.
5) One of session methods, **setAttribute()**, is called to store this queried faculty name into the JSP implicit object session.
6) The **getAttribute("facultyName")** method that is assigned to the `value` tag of the `FacultyName` text field will pick up the queried faculty name and display in this text field in step 7.

By referring to Fig. 8.16, we can get a clear and complete picture about the data storage and transferring between different pages.

Now if you compile and run these three files, **FacultyPage.jsp**, **FacultyQuery.jsp** and **FacultyBean.java**, you can get the start page shown in Fig. 8.17. Enter a desired faculty name such as **Ying Bai** into the Faculty Name text field, and click on the **Select** button; the running result is shown in Fig. 8.18.

As we mentioned at the beginning of this chapter, Java EE provides a set of powerful tools and supports to Java Web applications to access and manipulate databases. One of the most important components provided by Java EE is the Java bean that works as a separate component to perform database-related operations and business logics. By combining the JavaServer Faces techniques and Java beans, a professional Java Web database application can be divided into two separate parts:

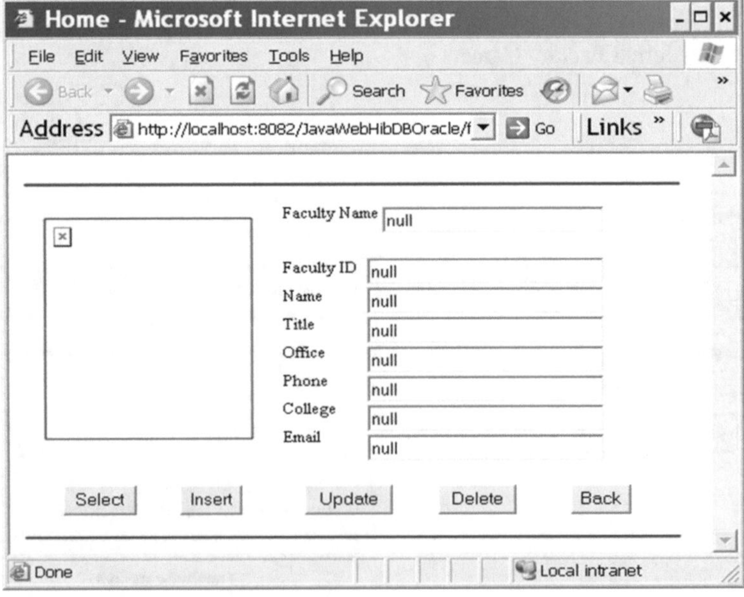

Fig. 8.17 The running status of the FacultyPage.jsp

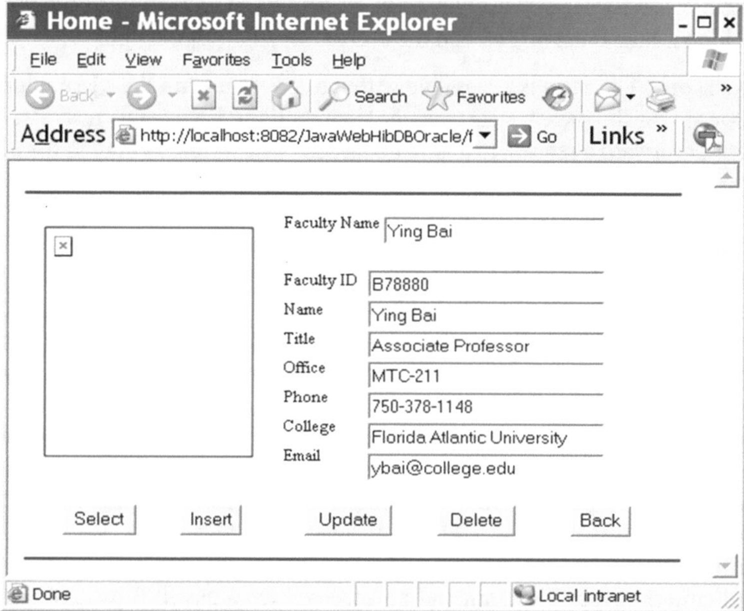

Fig. 8.18 The running result of the FacultyPage.jsp

the GUIs that are built with JSF tags in JavaServer Pages that are used for data presentations and results displaying and Java managed beans used for database-related operations and business logics. By dividing a Web application into these two sections, it greatly reduces the development efforts and complexities in the coding development and organizations of the whole application.

Now let's take care of using Java beans technology for Java Web applications.

8.1.5 *Using Java Beans Technology for Java Web Applications*

In recent years, the Java bean technique has been widely applied in Java Web applications. In fact, a Java bean can be considered as an extended Java help class as we discussed in the previous sections, and the main purpose of a Java bean is to handle the JDBC- and database-related operations as well as business logics in a Web application.

In fact, Java beans are reusable components, and the main purpose of using Java beans is to separate business logics from the presentations. Exactly, a Java bean is just an instance of a class.

Once a JavaBean is created and loaded, it can be used by all parts of your applications based on its scope. The so-called scope defined the section or part of you applications can access and use this bean. Generally, there are four popular scopes available to a Java Bean object, and the default scope is **page** scope.

- **page scope**: The bean is accessible within a JSP page with the **<jsp: useBean>** tag or any of the page's static include files until the page sends response to the client or forward a request to another page. In other words, as long as the process happened in the current page, the bean can be accessed and used until the process has been transferred to other pages.
- **request scope**: The bean is accessible from any JSP page as long as the same request is processed in that page until a JSP page sends a response to the client or forward the request to another page. In other words, the bean can be used until a different request has been forwarded or a response for that request has been received, which means that the life time or the scope of that request has been completed.
- **session scope**: The bean is accessible from any JSP page in the same session as the JSP page that creates the bean. A session can be considered as commonplace where many JSP pages can exist and share. The JSP page in which you create the Java bean must have a JSP page directive <%@ page % > with the session = true.
- **application scope**: The bean can be accessed from any JSP page in the same application as the JSP page that creates the bean. In other words, any JSP page can use the bean as long as that page is included in the application in which the JSP page that creates the bean is included.

It is no difference between creating a help class and creating a Java bean class. In fact, the help class **FacultyBean.java** we created in the last section is exactly a Java bean class.

To use a Java bean, the JSP provide three basic tags for working with beans.

```
<jsp:useBean id="bean name" class="bean class" scope = "page | request
| session |application "/>
```

The definitions for these three tags are:

1) The **bean name** is just a given name to refer to the used Java bean. You can use any valid name for this tag.
2) The **bean class** is a full name of the Java bean class you created. The so-called full name means that you need to use both the bean class's name and the package's name in which the bean is located. For example, this bean class should be: **mypackage.mybeanclass** if the bean class named **mybeanclass** is located at the package **mypackage**.
3) The **scope** indicates the range or the life time the bean can be used. Refer to those four scopes we discussed above to get more detailed information about them.

A very useful JSP directive used for Java bean class is **<jsp:setProperty />**. The protocol of this directive is:

```
<jsp:setProperty name = "id" property = "someProperty" value = "someValue" />
```

Three arguments for this directive are:

1) The **id** is the bean name as we discussed in step 1 above.
2) The **someProeprty** is exactly the property's name defined inside the Java bean class, such as **facultyId** and **facultyName** we defined in our **FacultyBean.java** class in the last section.
3) The **someValue** is the initialized value assigned to a property in the bean class.

A variant for this tag is the property attribute can be replaced by an " * ". What this does is that it accepts all the form parameters and thus reduces the need for writing multiple **setProperty** tags. The only point to be remembered when you using this variant is that the form parameters' names must be the same as those of the bean properties' names.

An example of using this **setProperty** tag is:

```
<jsp:setProperty name = "dbFaculty" property = "*" />
```

In this **setProperty** tag, the **id** of the Java bean class is **dbFaculty**. The * in the property value means that all parameters transferred from another page can be assigned to the associated properties in the Java bean class.

Now let's modify the **FacultyBean.java** to make it a Java bean class to replace the help class file **FacultyBean.java** we built in the last section.

8.1.5.1 Modify the Help Class FacultyBean to Make It a Java Bean Class

First we need to create a new Java Session Bean class named FacultyBean in the NetBeans IDE. Then we need to add seven **setter()** methods into this bean class. Your finished Java bean class **FacultyBean.java** is shown in Fig. 8.19. All modified codes have been highlighted in bold.

Let's have a closer look at this piece of modified codes to see how it works.

Starting from step **A** until step **G**, seven **setter()** methods are added into this Java bean class. All of these **setter()** methods are used to set up the initial values for seven properties in this bean.

Next we need to create a new transaction JSP page **FacultyBeanQuery.jsp** to make it to transfer data between our new starting page **FacultyBeanPage.jsp** and our Java bean class **FacultyBean.java**. Basically this **FacultyBeanQuery.jsp** file has no significant difference with the **FacultyQuery.jsp** we built in the last section. The only different part is the way to execute the JDBC- and database-related queries or business logics. In **FacultyQuery.jsp** file, we called a Java help class **FacultyBean.java** to do those functions. However, in **FacultyBeanQuery.jsp**, we will call a modified help class that has been converted to a Java bean **FacultyBean.java** to perform these functions.

The codes of the **FacultyBeanQuery.jsp** file are shown in Fig. 8.20.

Now let's have a closer look at this piece of codes to see how it works.

Some system-related or user-related packages are imported at the beginning of this page. The JSP directive <%@ page /> is used to convert those packages and

```
  @Stateless
  public class FacultyBean {
      private String facultyID;
      private String facultyName;
      private String office;
      private String title;
      private String phone;
      private String college;
      private String email;
      public Session session = null;
      public FacultyBean() {
          this.session = HibernateUtil.getSessionFactory().getCurrentSession();
      }
      public List QueryFaculty(String fname) {
          List<Faculty> facultyList = null;
          MsgDialog msgDlg = new MsgDialog(new javax.swing.JFrame(), true);
          .........
          return facultyList;
      }
      public String getFacultyID() {
          return this.facultyID;
      }
      .........
A     public void setFacultyID(String facultyID) {
          this.facultyID = facultyID;
      }
B     public void setFacultyName(String facultyName) {
          this.facultyName = facultyName;
      }
C     public void setOffice(String office) {
          this.office = office;
      }
D     public void setTitle(String title) {
          this.title = title;
      }
E     public void setPhone(String phone) {
          this.phone = phone;
      }
F     public void setCollege(String college) {
          this.college = college;
      }
G     public void setEmail(String email) {
          this.email = email;
      }
  }
```

Fig. 8.19 The modified help class – now it is a Java bean class

embedded into this page. Three packages are imported here: the **java.util.*** package contains the List class, the **JavaWebHibDBOraclePackage** contains our Java bean class FacultyBean, and the **csedept.entity.Faculty** is a Hibernate class mapping for the Faculty table in our sample database **CSE_DEPT**.

A. The Java bean class is declared with the JSP tag **<jsp:useBean />** with three tags we discussed at the beginning of this section. The referenced name for this bean is **dbFaculty**, which is assigned to the **id** of the bean. The scope of this bean is **session**, and the full name of this bean class is **JavaWebHibDBOraclePackage.FacultyBean**.

```
  <%@ page import="java.util.*" %>
  <%@ page import="JavaWebHibDBOraclePackage.*" %>
  <%@ page import="csedept.entity.Faculty" %>
  <html>
    <head>
      <meta http-equiv="Content-Type" content="text/html; charset=UTF-8">
      <title>FacultyBeanQuery Page</title>
    </head>
    <body>
      <h1>This is the FacultyBeanQuery Page</h1>
A     <jsp:useBean id="dbFaculty" scope="session" class="JavaWebHibDBOraclePackage.FacultyBean" />
B     <jsp:setProperty name="dbFaculty" property="*" />
      <%
C       String fname = request.getParameter("FacultyNameField");
D       List<Faculty> facultyList = dbFaculty.QueryFaculty(fname);
E       response.sendRedirect("FacultyBeanPage.jsp");
      %>
    </body>
  </html>
```

Fig. 8.20 The codes for the FacultyBeanQuery.jsp page

B. The **setProperty** tag is used to set up all parameters passed from the **FacultyBeanPage.jsp** page to the associated properties in the bean class FacultyBean.
C. The Java codes are starting from a JSP tag, and the faculty name parameter is retrieved by using the **getParanmeter()** method and assigned to a local String variable **fname**.
D. The main bean method **QueryFaculty()** is executed to query a faculty record based on the retrieved faculty name from the FacultyBeanPage.jsp page. The result is assigned to a local List variable. In fact, this result is not important in this application since the columns in the query result have been assigned to the associated properties in the bean class, and later on we can pick up those columns by calling the **getter()** methods in the bean class.
E. Since we want to fill those text fields in our starting page **FacultyBeanPage.jsp** with the queried result, we used the **sendRedirect()** method to return the process back to that page.

Now let's take a look at a new starting page **FacultyBeanPage.jsp** that will be used to call the transaction JSP page and Java bean to perform the faculty data query and display query result in this page. Because of the complexity in building this page with HTML codes, we leave this coding job to our project development stage later.

8.1.5.2 Build a New Starting Web Page FacultyBeanPage

The preview of this page is shown in Fig. 8.21.

The difference between this starting page and the starting page **FacultyPage.jsp** we built in the last section is in the **FcaultyPage.jsp**, we used a JSP built-in or implicit object session to transfer data between this page and the help class.

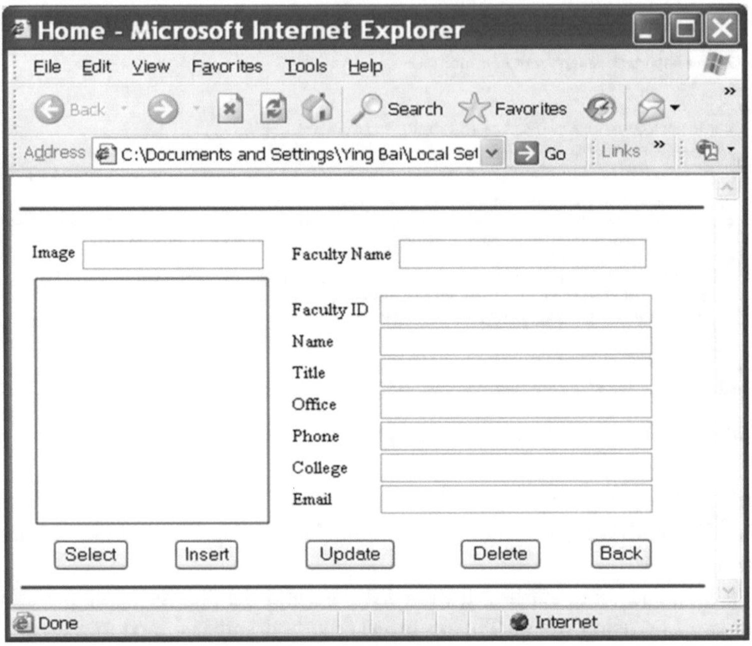

Fig. 8.21 The new starting Web page FacultyBeanPage.jsp

However, in the new starting page **FacultyBeanPage.jsp**, we need to use the properties defined in the Java bean class to do this data transferring jobs.

Exactly, we need to use the Java bean's **getter()** method to replace those **session.getAttribute()** methods embedded in the `value` tag of each text field to retrieve and display the associated column queried from the Faculty table in our sample database in each text field in this new starting page.

The codes for this new starting page are shown in Fig. 8.22. The modified parts have been highlighted in bold.

Let's have a closer look at this piece of codes to see how it works.

A. A JSP tag that declared to use a Java bean is put in the beginning of this page to indicate that a Java bean will be called to perform JDBC- and database-related queries or business logics, and the result will be retrieved and reflected in this starting page.
B. The next page is changed to **FacultyBeanQuery.jsp** in the `action` tag of the form, which means that the page and all data in this starting page will be forwarded to the next page if any submit button is clicked by the user from this page.
C. Start from step **C** until step **I**; the different Java bean's **getter()** methods are executed to retrieve the matched columns from the queried result and display them one by one in each associated text field.

```
A <jsp:useBean id="dbFaculty" scope="session" class="JavaWebHibDBOraclePackage.FacultyBean" />
  <html>
    <head>
      <meta http-equiv="Content-Type" content="text/html; charset=UTF-8">
      <title>Faculty Query Page</title>
    </head>
    <body>
    <%@page language="java" %>
B   <form method=post action=".\FacultyBeanQuery.jsp">
    <input name=FacultyNameField maxlength=255 size=24
C    value="<%=dbFaculty.getFacultyName() %>" type=text v:shapes="_x0000_s1109">
    .........
    <input name=FacultyIDField maxlength=255 size=26
D    value="<%=dbFaculty.getFacultyID() %>" type=text  v:shapes="_x0000_s1110">
    .........
    <input name=NameField maxlength=255 size=26
E    value="<%=dbFaculty.getFacultyName() %>" type=text  v:shapes="_x0000_s1106">
    .........
    <input name=OfficeField maxlength=255 size=26
F    value="<%=dbFaculty.getOffice() %>"  type=text  v:shapes="_x0000_s1104">
    .........
    <input name=PhoneField maxlength=255 size=26
G    value="<%=dbFaculty.getPhone() %>"  type=text  v:shapes="_x0000_s1116">
    .........
    <input name=CollegeField maxlength=255 size=26
H    value="<%=dbFaculty.getCollege() %>" type=text  v:shapes="_x0000_s1117">
    .........
    <input name=EmailField maxlength=255 size=26
I    value="<%=dbFaculty.getEmail() %>" type=text  v:shapes="_x0000_s1118">
    .........
    </body>
  </html>
```

Fig. 8.22 The new starting page FacultyBeanPage.jsp

From this piece of codes, you can find how easy it is to transfer data between the starting Web page written in either HTML or JSP and Java bean class by using the Java bean's properties.

From examples discussed above, it can be found that the JavaServer Pages technology did provide a good communication and data passing ways between the Servlet and client Web pages; however, they did not provide a direct binding and mapping between the Web page's components and the server-side codes. This kind of binding and mapping plays more important roles in today's complicated and multitier Web applications. To meet this need, a new technology has been introduced in recent years, which is the JavaServer Faces (JSF) technology.

With this new technology, all Web components can be installed and distributed in a Web page by using the JSF tags. Also, more important, all of these components can be bound to the server-side properties and functions using the so-called backing beans or Java managed beans. By using a Unified Expression Language (EL) value expression, the value of the property of a mapped or bound Web component can be easily picked up from a backing bean in the server side.

8.1.6 Using JavaServer Faces Technology for Java Web Applications

JavaServer Faces (JSF) provides new techniques and components for building User Interfaces (UI) for server-side applications. In fact, JSF is a server-side technology for developing Web applications with rich user interfaces. Before JavaServer Faces, developers who built Web applications had to rely on building HTML user interface components with Servlets or JavaServer Pages (JSP pages). This is mainly because HTML user interface components are the lowest common denominator that Web browsers support. One of defects of using HTML or JSP techniques to build Web applications is that such Web applications do not have rich user interfaces, compared with stand-alone fat clients, and therefore less functionality and/or poor usability is involved in those Web applications. One of possible solutions is to use Applets to develop rich user interfaces; however, in most cases Web application developers do not always know whether those Applets are signed or unsigned applets and whether they can access the local database files or not. This will greatly limit the roles and implementations of Applets in Java Web database applications.

A good solution is to use JavaServer Face technique that provides a set of rich GUI components and can be installed and run in the server side. The GUI components provided by JSF are represented by a collection of component tags. All component tags are defined and stored in the `UIComponent` class. A Model-View-Controller mode is applied to the JSF technique.

The JSF technology consists of following main components:

- JSF APIs used to represent UI components, manage state, handle events, and validate input. The UI components are represented and implemented using JSF tags. The API has support for internationalization and accessibility.
- A special Servlet class `FacesServlet` that is located at the server side and works as a controller to handle all JSF-related events.
- JSP pages that contain rich user interface components represented by customer tags and work as views. The GUI of a JSF page is one or more JSP pages that contain JSF component tags.
- Two JSP custom tag libraries used for expressing the JSF user interface (UI) components within a JSP page and for wiring components to server-side objects. Page authors can easily add UI components to their pages.

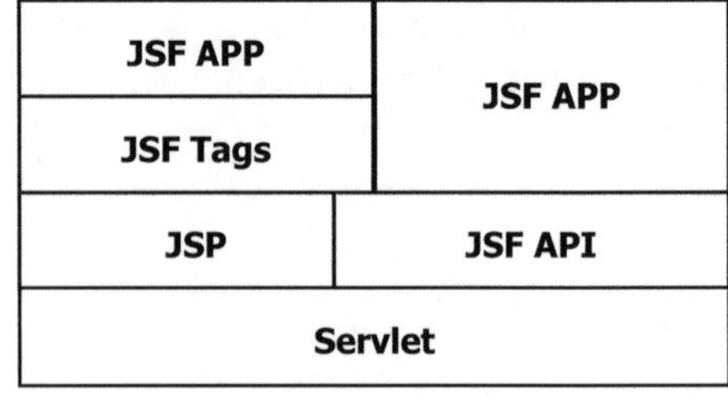

Fig. 8.23 High-level architecture of JSF

- Java bean components used to work as model objects.
- Application configuration resource file **faces-config.xml** used to define the navigation rules between JSP pages and register the Java backing beans.
- Web deployment descriptor file **web.xml** used to define the FaceServlet and its mapping.

JavaServer Face technology is basically built based on JavaServer Page and Servlet techniques. It uses JSP pages as the GUI and FacesServlet as the Web container. A high-level architecture of JSF is shown in Fig. 8.23.

It can be found from Fig. 8.23 that a JSF Web application is composed of JSP pages representing the user interface components using the JSF custom tag library and FacesServlet Web container that can be considered as a part of Servlet class and takes care of the JSF-related events.

JSF defines two standard tag libraries (Core and HTML) that you have to declare in your JSP pages with the **<%@taglib%>** directive. Two tag libraries are:

- **html_basic.tld**: A JSP custom tag library for building JSF applications that render to an HTML client.
- **jsf_core.tld**: A JSP custom tag library for representing core actions independent of a particular render kit.

The JSF core library contains tags that do not depend on any markup language, while the JSF HTML library was designed for pages that are viewed in a Web browser. The standard prefixes of the two tag libraries are **f** for the JSF Core and **h** for the JSF HTML. All JSF tags must be nested inside a **< f:view>** element. The **<f:view>** tag allows the JSF framework to save the state of the UI components as part of the response to a HTTP request.

To use these customer tags to represent JSF components in JSP pages, one needs to indicate them by using the following two `taglib` directives on the top of each JSF file:

- **<%@ taglib uri="http://java.sun.com/jsf/html" prefix="h" %>**
- **<%@ taglib uri="http://java.sun.com/jsf/core" prefix="f" %>**

The **uri** is used to indicate the locations of the customer tag libraries.

JavaServer Face (JSF) pages are just regular JSP pages that use the standard JSF tag libraries or other libraries based on the JSF API. When using JSF tag components to build a JavaServer Page, a component tree or a view is created in the server-side memory, and this tree will be used by the JSF frameworks to handle the requests coming from the clients and send responses to the clients. Each JSF tag component is mapped to a component class defined in the `UIComponent` class. In fact, each tag is an instance of the mapped class in the `UIComponent`.

JSF utilized a Model-View-Controller (MVC) architecture, which means that it uses Java beans as models to stored application data and JSF GUI as the view and the Servlet as the controller.

8.1.6.1 The Application Configuration Resource File faces-config.xml

The navigation from one page to another can be done in two ways. One way is directly to use the codes by writing the JSP tag such as **<jsp:forward />** or the HTML hyperlink in the JSF file. Another way that is provided by JSF is to use the application configuration resource file `faces-config.xml` to build these navigation rules. The task of defining navigation rules involves defining which page is to be displayed after the user clicks on a button or a hyperlink. Each **<navigation-rule>** element defines how to get from one page as defined by the **<form-view-id>** to the other pages of the application. A **< navigation-rule>** element can contain any number of **<navigation-case>** elements that define the page to open next using the **<to-view-id>** based on a logical outcome defined by the **<from-outcome>**. This outcome is defined by the **action** attribute of the component that submits the form (such as the commandButton).

An application configuration resource file, `faces-config.xml`, is used to define your Java managed beans, validators, converters, and navigation rules.

Figure 8.24 shows a part of an example of an application configuration resource file. The configuration resource file is composed of a sequence tag listed below:

Starting from **<navigation-rule>** tag, a new navigation rule is defined. The **<from-view-id>** tag is used to define the navigation source, which is the current page (**Current.jsp**). The **<navigation-case>** tag is used to define one of the navigation destinations defined by the **<to-view-id>** tag based on the output of some clicked buttons or links triggered by the **action** tag in the current page. Those outputs are defined by the **<from-outcome>** tag.

You can use the design tools such as `PageFlow` to do this navigation plan graphically and directly. Refer to Sect. 5.3.5.12 in Chap. 5 to get more detailed information about using the design tools to build this configuration file graphically.

8.1.6.2 Sample JavaServer Face Page Files

Two JSF files are shown in Figs. 8.25 and 8.26. In Fig. 8.25, a **Current.jsp** page that works as a receiving page to get the username is shown and in Fig. 8.26, a **Next.jsp** that works as a responding page to select and return a matched password based on the username to the **Current.jsp** page.

The function of the **Current.jsp** page is:

```
<navigation-rule>
<from-view-id>/Current.jsp</from-view-id>
   <navigation-case>
   <from-outcome>clickAction</from-outcome>
   <to-view-id>/Next.jsp</to-view-id>
   </navigation-case>
</navigation-rule>
```

Fig. 8.24 A part of application configuration resource file

```
  <html>
    <head>
      <title>Current Page</title>
    </head>
A   <%@ taglib uri="http://java.sun.com/jsf/html" prefix="h" %>
    <%@ taglib uri="http://java.sun.com/jsf/core" prefix="f" %>
B   <body bgcolor="white">
C       <f:view>
D       <h:form id="QueryForm" >
E       <h:inputText id="userName" value="#{QueryBean.userName}"
            validator="#{ QueryBean.validate}"/>
F       <h:commandButton id="Query"  action="success"
            value="Query" />
G       <h:message style="color: red; font-family: 'New Century Schoolbook',
            serif; font-style: oblique; text-decoration: overline"
            id="QueryError" for="userName"/>
        </h:form>
       </f:view>
    </body>
  </html>
```

Fig. 8.25 The codes for the Current.jsp page

```
  <html>
    <head>
      <title>Next Page</title>
    </head>
    <%@ taglib uri="http://java.sun.com/jsf/html" prefix="h" %>
    <%@ taglib uri="http://java.sun.com/jsf/core" prefix="f" %>
    <body bgcolor="white">
        <f:view>
A       <h:form id="ResponseForm" >
B       <h:graphicImage id="ResponseImg" url="/Response.jpg" />
C       <h:outputText  id="QueryResult"  value="#{QueryBean.passWord}" />
D       <h:commandButton id="Back"  action="success"
          value="Back" />
        </h:form>
       </f:view>
    </body>
  </html>
```

Fig. 8.26 The codes for the Next.jsp page

A. In order to use JSF tags, you need to include the **taglib** directives to the html and core tag libraries that refer to the standard HTML renderkit tag library and the JSF core tag library, respectively.
B. A **body** tag with the **bgcolor** attribute is defined.
C. A page containing JSF tags is represented by a tree of components whose root is the **UIViewRoot**, which is represented by the **view** tag. All component tags must be enclosed in the **view** tag. Other contents such as HTML and other JSP pages can be enclosed within that tag.

D. A typical JSP page includes a **form**, which is submitted to the next page when a button is clicked. The tags representing the form components (such as textfields and buttons) must be nested inside the **form** tag.
E. The **inputText** tag represents an input text field component. The **id** attribute represents the ID of the component object represented by this tag, and if it is missing, then the implementation will generate one. The **validator** attribute refers to a method-binding expression pointing to a Java backing bean method that performs validation on the component's data. The Java backing bean's property **userName** is bound to the **value** attribute by using the Unified Expression Language (EL) value expression.
F. The **commandButton** tag represents the button used to submit the data entered in the text field. The **action** attribute helps the navigation mechanism to decide which page to open next. Exactly, the next page has been defined in the application configuration resource file `faces-config.xml` using the <to-view-id> tag above, which is the **Next.jsp**.
G. The **message** tag displays an error message if the data entered is not valid. The **for** attribute refers to the component whose value failed validation.

An interesting thing in step **E** in this piece of sample codes is that an embedded backing bean property **userName** has been bound to the **value** attribute of the **inputText** tag. Recall that we used either the **getAttribute()** method of a JSP implicit object **session (session.getAttribute())** or the **getProperty()** method of a Java bean to hook to the **value** attribute of this text field tag in the previous sample codes to enable this text field's value to be updated automatically. However, in this JSF file, we directly bind one of backing bean's properties, **userName**, with the **value** attribute of this text field by using the `value-binding` expressions that is called expression language (EL) and have the syntax **#{bean-managed-property}** to do this data updating job. One point to be noted is that the JSF EL bindings are bidirectional when it makes sense. For example, the UI component represented by the **inputText** tag can get the value of a bean property **userName** and present it to the user as a default value. When the user submits the **QueryForm** data, the UI component can automatically update the bean property **userName** so that the application logic can process the new value. You can see how easy it is now to set up a connection between a component in a JSF page and the related property in the backing bean object when using this binding for a JSF file. In fact, you can bind not only the bean's properties but also the bean's methods, to certain UI components in the JSP pages.

The codes for the **Next.jsp** file are shown in Fig. 8.26. The detailed function of this piece of codes is:

A. The form **id** is defined as a ResponseForm.
B. An image is added into this page with the image id and the image URL. The forward slash "/" before the image name **Response.jpg** indicates that this image is located at the current project folder.
C. An **outputText** tag is equivalent to a label in a Web page. The selected password is assigned to the **value** attribute using the value-binding expressions that have

the syntax `#{bean-managed-property}`. In fact, this value has been bound with a property password in the backing bean QueryBean class.

D. The commandButton **Back** is used to direct the page to return to the **Current.jsp** page as it is clicked by the user. This returning function has been defined in the application configuration source file `faces-config.xml` we discussed above.

The real tracking issue is that there is no username-password matching process that occurred in either of these two pages. Yes, that is true! All of those data matching processes or we called them business logics occurred in the backing Java bean QueryBean class.

When user entered a valid username into the input textbox and clicked the **Submit** button in the **Current.jsp** page, all input data are sent to the next page **Next.jsp**. Of course, you can handle this data matching in the **Next.jsp** page based on the passed username. However, in order to separate the presentations from business logics, JSF uses JSF pages as views and assigns the business logics to the Java beans who work as controllers to handle those data matching jobs. In fact, since the **userName** has been bound to the **value** attribute of the inputText tag by using the `value-binding` expressions that have the syntax **#{bean-managed-property}**, any change of this data item will be immediately reflected to the associated property **userName** defined in the Java bean QueryBean class. The Java bean will perform the password matching process based on that username and send the matched password to the **passWord** property in that bean class. As soon as the Java bean finished the password matching processing and sent the matched password to the **passWord** property, it can be immediately updated and displayed in the outputText **QueryResult** in the **Next.jsp** page using the `value-binding` expressions **#{QueryBean.passWord}**.

8.1.6.3 The Java Bean Class File

The java bean class used in JSF pages is very similar to the **FacultyBean** class we built in Sect. 8.1.5.1. Like most Java bean classes, it should contain setter and getter methods as well as some special methods to process the business logics.

In addition, the Java beans need to be configured in the application configuration resource file **faces-config.xml** so that the implementation can automatically create new instances of the beans as needed. The **<managed-bean>** element is used to create a mapping between a bean name and class. The first time the QueryBean is

```
<managed-bean-name>QueryBean</managed-bean-name>
<managed-bean-class>LogInQuery.QueryBean</managed-bean-class>
<managed-bean-scope>session</managed-bean-scope>
```

Fig. 8.27 A piece of sample codes to register a Java bean

```
<managed-property>
<property-name>userName</property-name>
<property-class>string</property-class>
<value>null</value>
</managed-property>
<managed-property>
<property-name>passWord</property-name>
<property-class>string</property-class>
<value>null</value>
</managed-property>
```

Fig. 8.28 A piece of codes to define all properties in a Java bean class

```
<web-app>
<display-name>JSF LogIn Application</display-name>
<description>JSF LogIn Application</description>
<!-- Faces Servlet -->
<servlet>
<servlet-name>Faces Servlet</servlet-name>
<servlet-class>javax.faces.webapp.FacesServlet</servlet-class>
<load-on-startup> 1 </load-on-startup>
</servlet>
<!-- Faces Servlet Mapping -->
<servlet-mapping>
<servlet-name>Faces Servlet</servlet-name>
<url-pattern>/login/*</url-pattern>
</servlet-mapping>
```

Fig. 8.29 An example coding for the Web deployment descriptor file

referenced, the object is created and stored in the appropriate scope. You can use the code elements shown in Fig. 8.27 to register a Java bean in the **faces-config.xml** file:

Besides to register the Java bean class, you also need to use this configuration file to configure and define all properties created inside this Java bean. In this example, only two properties, **userName** and **passWord**, have been defined in this Java bean. Therefore you need to use the **<managed-property>** element to do this configuration, as shown in Fig. 8.28.

In fact, you do not need to worry about these configurations if you are using an IDE such as the NetBeans IDE, and the NetBeans IDE can do these configurations automatically for you as you built the Java bean class file.

Next let's take a look at the Web deployment descriptor file.

8.1.6.4 The Web Deployment Descriptor File web.xml

Before you can use and access a Servlet such as FacesServlet in the server side from a Web browser, you need to map the **FacesServlet** to a path in your deployment descriptor file **web.xml**. By using this deployment descriptor file, you can register Servlet and FacesServlet, register listeners, and map resources to URLs. Figure 8.29 shows a piece of example codes used in the **web.xml** file for the **FacesServlet** class.

Most codes in this file will be created automatically if you are using the NetBeans IDE to build your Web applications.

As we discussed in Sect. 8.1.6.1, regularly JSP pages use the **<jsp:useBean>** tag to instantiate JavaBeans. When using the JSF framework, you do not have to specify the Java bean class names in your Web pages anymore. Instead, you can configure your bean instances in the application configuration resource file **faces-config.xml** using the **<managed-bean>** element. You may use multiple configuration files if you develop a large application. In that case, you must add a **javax.faces.CONFIG_FILES** parameter in the deployment descriptor file **web.xml**.

Now that we have worked through all main techniques of JSF, now let's have a full picture about the complete running procedure of JSF Web applications.

8.1.6.5 A Complete Running Procedure of JSF Web Applications

As we mentioned, a UI component represented by a JSF tag in a JSP page can be bound to a Java bean's property or a Java bean's method. To separate the presentations and business logics, we can use JSP pages to present our GUI and the Java beans to store our data to perform business-related logics. Therefore, we can divide methods into two categories: data access methods (business methods) and action methods. The data access methods should be located at the Java bean side, and the action methods should be located at the JSF page side. Each data access method defined in the Java bean can be called by an associated action method defined in an **action** attribute of a submit button tag in the JSP page if that submit button has been bound to the **action** attribute.

Here we use a login process to illustrate the operational procedure using the JSF technique. Two JSP pages, the **LogIn.jsp** and **Selection.jsp**, and a Java bean class, **LogInBean.java**, are involved in this procedure. Two JSP pages work as views and are used to display the input and output login information, and the Java bean works as a model to handle the database-related processing and business logics. The functional procedure of this example application is:

1) When the user entered a username/password pair into the Username/Password input text fields in the **LogIn.jsp** page and clicked on the LogIn button, a query request is sent to the Web server with all form data (Username and Password) for processing.
2) After the server received the request, if the validation is passed, all form data (Username and Password) will be stored into the associated properties of the Java bean.

Table 8.1 The relationship between the data access method and the action method

Data access method	Action method	JSF page
LogInQuery()	LogInBean.LogInAction()	LogIn.jsp

3) The action method that is bound to the LogIn button will call the data access method defined in the Java bean to perform the database query to find the matched login information in the LogIn table.
4) If the data access method is successful, the next page, Selection.jsp, should be displayed.

To run this procedure using JSF technique, we need to have a clear picture between the JSF pages and Java beans and the page-to-page navigation schedule.

8.1.6.5.1 The Java Bean-JSF Page Relationship and Page Navigations

Table 8.1 lists all data access methods and action methods used in this example.

A Java bean can be connected to a JSF page by using the **value** attribute of an UI component represented by a JSF tag in that page. Exactly, a property or a method defined in a Java bean class can be mapped to a **value** attribute of a UI component in a JSF page. This relationship can be triggered and set up when a submit button in the JSF page is clicked by the user and all form data will be sent to the Web server. Refer to Fig. 8.30: the operational procedure of executing a request is:

1) The data access method **LogInQuery()** is defined in the Java bean class LogInBean and will be called by the action method **LogInBean.LogInAction()** defined in the JSF page **LogIn.jsp** as the user clicks the **LogIn** button. Since the action method **LogInBean.LogInAction()** has been bound to the **LogIn** command button, all form data including the Username and Password entered by the user to the JSF page will be submitted to the FacesServlet as the **LogIn** button is clicked by the user.

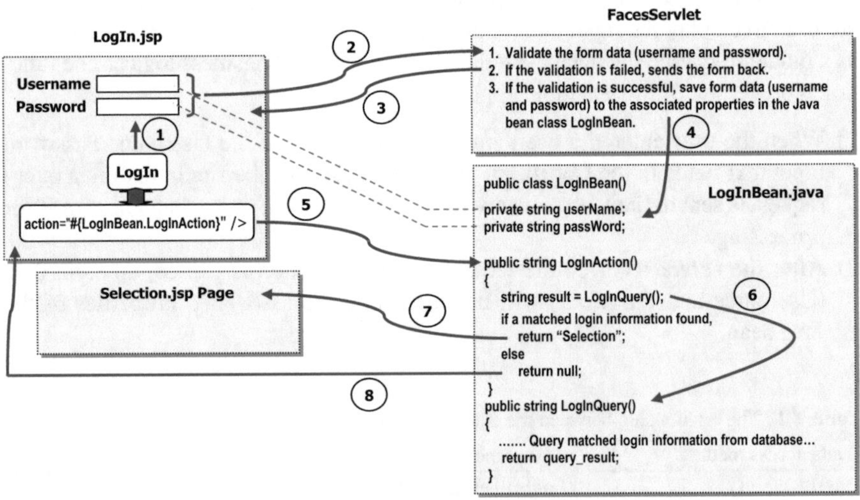

Fig. 8.30 The operational procedure of executing a request using JSF

2) After the FacesServlet received the form data, it will validate them and return the form back to the client if any error is encountered.
3) Otherwise the validated form data including the Username and Password will be stored to the associated properties in the Java bean class. Then JSF engine will call the action method **LogInBean.LogInAction()** that has been bound to the LogIn button and, in turn, call the data access method **LogInQuery()** to perform database-related query to find matched login information.
4) After a piece of matched login information has been found, the associated properties, **userName** and **passWord**, which are defined inside the Java bean class, will be updated by assigning the matched username and password to them. These updating that occurred in the Java bean side will be immediately reflected to the **value** attributes of the Username and Password inputText fields in the JSF page since they have been bound together. Therefore the content of each inputText tag will also be updated.
5) The action method **LogInAction()** defined in the `LogInBean` class will also be called when the `LogIn` button is clicked by the user since it is bound to the `LogIn` button.
6) The data access method **LogInQuery()** will be executed to perform database-related queries and business logics.
7) Each action method returns a string called "outcome." JSF uses a navigation handler to determine what it is supposed to do for each outcome string. If an action method returns a **null**, which means that the execution of that method encountered some problems and the same page must be redisplayed. Otherwise, the desired next page should be displayed, depending on the returned outcome string. The default JSF navigation handler uses a set of navigation rules that are specified in the JSF application configuration file **faces-config.xml**, which is shown in Fig. 8.31. In this example, if a piece of matched login information is found, the action method will return an outcome string "**SELECTION**", and the next page, **Selection.jsp**, should be displayed.

```
  <faces-config version="2.0"
  <managed-bean>
A     <managed-bean-name>LogInBean</managed-bean-name>
B     <managed-bean-class>JavaWebDBApp. LogInBean</managed-bean-class>
C     <managed-bean-scope>session</managed-bean-scope>
  </managed-bean>
  <navigation-rule>
D     <from-view-id>/LogIn.jsp</from-view-id>
      <navigation-case>
E        <from-outcome>SELECTION</from-outcome>
F        <to-view-id>/Selection.jsp</to-view-id>
      </navigation-case>
   </navigation-rule>
  </faces-config>
```

Fig. 8.31 The application configuration resource file faces-config.xml

8) Otherwise, the query failed, and no matched login user information can be found. The **LogInAction()** method returns a **null** to the JSF engine to redisplay the LogIn page.

The detailed explanation on the codes shown in Fig. 8.31 is listed below:

A. Our Java managed bean **LogInBean** is defined using the `<managed-bean-name>` tag.
B. The full class name, including the package name and the bean class name, is defined by the `<managed-bean-class>` tag.
C. The scope of this Java bean is defined by using the `<managed-bean-scope>` tag.
D. The current JSF page **LogIn.jsp** is defined by using the `<from-view-id>` tag.
E. The outcome string **SELECTION**, which is mapped to the next page **Selection.jsp**, is defined by using the `<from-outcome>` tag and should be returned by the action method **LogInAction()** if a matched login user has been found.
F. The name of the next page, **Selection.jsp**, is defined by using the `<to-view-id>` tag.

The points to be noted for this configuration file are:

1) Both outcome string and the next page should be defined inside the `<navigation-case>` tag, and all navigation pages should be defined inside the `<navigation-rule>` tag.
2) The forward-slash symbol "/" before each page name is used to indicate that those pages are located at the current location as the JSF project is located.
3) You can create and edit this configuration file using either the XML editor or the PageFlow design tool.

In order to use the PageFlow design tool to build the navigation rules in the faces-config.xml file, sometimes you need to close and reopen the NetBeans IDE to do this.

The codes for a sample **LogIn.jsp** page are shown in Fig. 8.32. Let's ave a closer look at this piece of codes to see how it works.

A. Two JSF standard customer tag libraries, one is for building JSF applications that render to an HTML client and another is for representing core actions independent of a particular render kit, are declared first at this page using the **<%@ taglib% >** directive. The **uri** is used to indicate the valid sites where both libraries are located.
B. All of **JSF** tag components are represented by a tree of components whose root is the **UIViewRoot**, which is represented by the **<f:view>** tag. All JSF component tags must be enclosed in this **<f: view>** tag.
C. A JSP **form**, which is submitted to the Web server when a button is clicked, is represented by the **<h:form>** tag. The tags representing the form components,

```
  <html>
    <head>
      <meta http-equiv="Content-Type" content="text/html; charset=UTF-8">
      <title>LogIn Page</title>
    </head>
A   <%@ taglib uri="http://java.sun.com/jsf/html" prefix="h" %>
    <%@ taglib uri="http://java.sun.com/jsf/core" prefix="f" %>
    <body>
B     <f:view>
C       <h:form id="LogInForm">
D         <h:inputText id="userName" required="true" value="#{LogInBean.userName}"
          size="10" maxlength="40">
E         <f:validateLength minimum="1" maximum="40"/>
          </h:inputText>
F         <h:inputSecret id="passWord" required="true" value="#{LogInBean.passWord}"
          size="10" maxlength="20">
G         <f:validateLength minimum="6" maximum="20"/>
           </h:inputSecret>
H         <h:commandButton id="LogIn" action="#{LogInBean.LogInAction}"
          value="LogIn" />
        </h:form>
      </f:view>
    </body>
  </html>
```

Fig. 8.32 The codes of a sample LogIn.jsp page

such as textfields and buttons, must be nested inside this **form** tag. The form is identified by its **id**; here it is a LogInForm.

D. An inputText tag is used to represent an input field to allow user to enter one line of text string, such as a username in this example. This inputText tag is identified by its **id**, and the **required** attribute is set to true. This means that this inputText cannot be empty and must be filled something by user as the project runs. The **value** attribute of this inputText tag is bound to the property **userName** in the Java bean class, LogInBean, by using the EL value expression. Two points to be noted for this tag are (1) the value of this tag's **id** must be identical with the property name **userName** defined in the Java managed bean LogInBean and (2) the **value** attribute of this tag must be bound to the same property **userName** defined in the Java managed bean LogInBean class, too. In this way, any updating made to this property **userName** in the Java bean can be immediately reflected to the **value** of this inputText tag and, furthermore, displayed in this input field.

E. A **< f:validateLength>** tag is used to make sure that the length of this username is in the range defined by the **minimum** and **maximum** attributes.

F. A similar tag is used for the `passWord` inputText, and it is bound to the **passWord** property defined in the Java managed bean LogInBean class. The only difference between this tag and the `userName` inputText tag is that a **< h:inputSecret>** tag is used to replace the **<h:inputText>** tag since this is a way to present a password input style.

G. A **< f:validateLength>** tag is also used to validate the length of the `passWord` to make sure that it is in the required range.

H. A **< h:commandButton>** tag is used to present a submit button component, and its **action** attribute is bound to the action method defined in the Java managed bean LogInBean using the EL value expression **"#{LogInBean.LogInAction}"**.

```
  @ManagedBean(name="LogInBean")
  @SessionScoped
  public class LogInBean {

     /** Creates a new instance of LogInBean */
     public LogInBean() {
     }
A    private String userName;
     private String passWord;

B    public String getPassWord() {
        return passWord;
     }
C    public void setPassWord(String passWord) {
        this.passWord = passWord;
     }
D    public String getUserName() {
        return userName;
     }
E    public void setUserName(String userName) {
        this.userName = userName;
     }
F    public String LogInAction()
     {
        String result=null;
        result = LogInQuery();
        return result;
     }
G    public String LogInQuery()
     {
        // query username from database and assign the queried value to the userName property
        // query password from database and assign the queried value to the passWord property
        return "SELECTION";
     }
  }
```

Fig. 8.33 The codes for the Java bean class LogInBean

Next let's have a closer look at the codes for our Java Bean class.

8.1.6.5.2 The Detailed Codes for the Java Bean Class

The codes for the Java bean class **LogInBean.java** are shown in Fig. 8.33. The functionality of each part of these codes is illustrated below.

A. Two properties, **userName** and **passWord**, are defined first, and these two properties must be identical with the **id** attributes defined in the inputText and inputSecret tags in the JSF page **LogIn.jsp** we discussed above.
B. The associated getter methods for these two properties are declared and defined in steps **B** and **D**, respectively.
C. The associated setter methods for these two properties are defined in steps **C** and **E**.
F. The action method **LogInAction()** is defined, and this method has been bound with the **action** attribute of the LogIn `commandButton` tag in the **LogIn.jsp** page. This method will be executed as the LogIn button is clicked by the user.

G. The data access method **LogInQuery()** is defined, and this method is used to perform the database-related query and business logics and return a outcome string to the JSF page. The JSF page will use its handler to search the returned outcome string to determine the next page to navigate.

So far, we have provided a very detailed introduction and review about the development history of Java Web applications using different components, such as Java Servlet and HTML pages, JavaServer Pages and help classes, JavaServer Pages and Java beans, as well as JavaServer Faces and Java bean techniques. In the following sections, we will provide more detailed discussion for each component and techniques. Following these discussions, we will begin to build and develop real Java Web application projects to perform data actions against our sample databases.

8.2 Java EE Web Application Model

The Java EE application model begins with the Java programming language and the Java virtual machine. The proven portability, security, and developer productivity they provide form the basis of the application model. Java EE is designed to support applications that implement enterprise services for customers, employees, suppliers, partners, and others who make demands on or contributions to the enterprise. Such applications are inherently complex, potentially accessing data from a variety of sources and distributing applications to a variety of clients.

The Java EE application model defines an architecture for implementing services as multitier applications that deliver the scalability, accessibility, and manageability needed by enterprise-level applications. This model partitions the work needed to implement a multitier service into two parts: the business and presentation logic to be implemented by the developer and the standard system services provided by the Java EE platform. The developer can rely on the platform to provide solutions for the hard systems-level problems of developing a multitier service.

The Java EE platform uses a distributed multitiered application model for enterprise applications. Application logic is divided into components according to function, and the various application components that make up a Java EE application are installed on different machines depending on the tier in the multitiered Java EE environment to which the application component belongs.

Most Java Web database applications are three-tier client-server applications, which means that this kind of application can be built in three tiers or three containers: client container, Web server container, and database server container. Java Enterprise Java Beans or EJB plays an additional role in business data management and processing in this three-tier architecture. However in recent years, because of its complexity and time-consuming development cycles as well as undesired output performances, some researchers recommend to use Java EE without EJB.

In order to get a clearer picture about these two kinds of architectures, let's first concentrate on the difference between them.

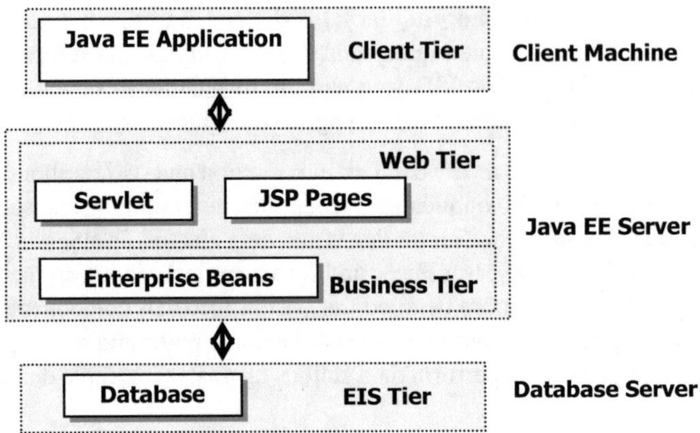

Fig. 8.34 An illustration of Java EE three-tier application with EJB

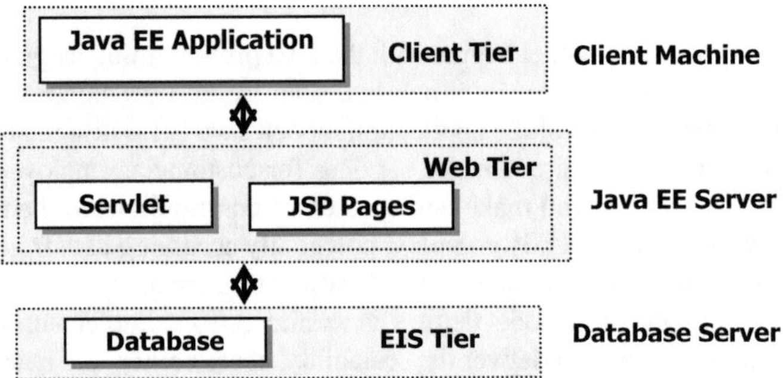

Fig. 8.35 An illustration of Java EE three-tier application without EJB

8.2.1 Java EE Web Applications with and Without EJB

Most Java Web applications can be divided into three tiers: client tier composed of client machines, Web tier consists of Java EE Server, and EIS tier made of Database server. The Java Enterprise Java Bean (EJB) also works as a business tier attached with the Java server layer. This relationship can be represented by different tiers shown in Fig. 8.34.

In fact in recent years, because of undesired output results and complicated developing processes, some developers have changed their mind and moved to Java EE without EJB. This simplification can be illustrated by an architecture shown in Fig. 8.35.

Compare two architectures shown in Figs. 8.34 and 8.35; it can be found that the business tier, Enterprise Java Bean, has been removed from the Web layer, and this greatly simplifies the communications and data transformations between those related tiers. From the point of practical application view, this will also significantly reduce the coding development cycles and improve the efficiency of the program's executions in real time.

As we know, the popular Java EE components are:

- Application clients and Applets are components that run on the client machine.
- Java Servlet, JavaServer Faces, and JavaServer Pages (JSP) technology components are web components that run on the server.
- Enterprise JavaBeans (EJB) components are business components that run on the server.

As we build a Java Web application using the architecture shown in Fig. 8.35, the third component, EJB, can be removed from this three-tier architecture.

When building a Java Web application, different modules can be adopted based on the different applications. A Java EE module consists of one or more Java EE components for the same container type and, optionally, one component deployment descriptor of that type. An enterprise bean module deployment descriptor, for example, declares transaction attributes and security authorizations for an enterprise bean. A Java EE module can be deployed as a stand-alone module.

The four types of Java EE modules are:

1) EJB modules, which contain class files for enterprise beans and an EJB deployment descriptor. EJB modules are packaged as JAR files with a **.jar** extension.
2) Web modules, which contain Servlet class files, Web files, supporting class files, GIF and HTML files, and a Web application deployment descriptor. Web modules are packaged as JAR files with a **.war** (Web ARchive) extension.
3) Application client modules, which contain class files and an application client deployment descriptor. Application client modules are packaged as JAR files with a **.jar** extension.
4) Resource adapter modules, which contain all Java interfaces, classes, native libraries, and other documentation, along with the resource adapter deployment descriptor. Together, these implement the Connector architecture for a particular EIS. Resource adapter modules are packaged as JAR files with a **.rar** (resource adapter archive) extension.

We will concentrate on more deep discussions about Java EE Web application in the following sections.

8.3 The Architecture and Components of Java Web Applications

A Web application is a dynamic extension of a web or application server. There are two types of Web applications:

- **Presentation-Oriented**: A presentation-oriented Web application generates interactive Web pages containing various types of markup language (HTML,

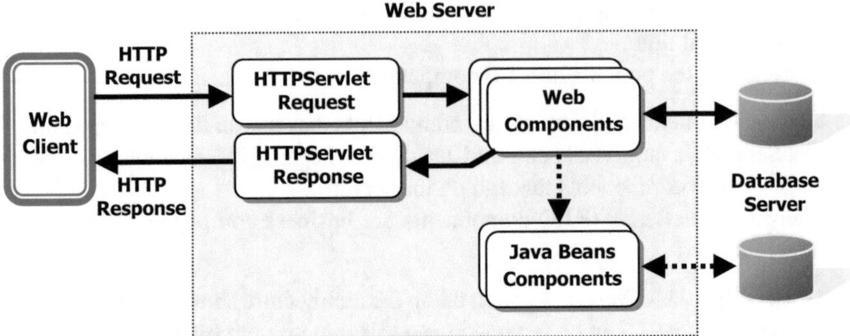

Fig. 8.36 An illustration of the Java Web application

XHTML, XML, and so on) and dynamic content in response to requests. We will cover how to develop presentation-oriented Web applications in this chapter.

- **Service-Oriented**: A service-oriented Web application implements the endpoint of a Web service. Presentation-oriented applications are often clients of service-oriented Web applications. We will discuss how to develop service-oriented Web applications in the next chapter.

In the Java EE platform, Web components provide the dynamic extension capabilities for a Web server. Web components can be either Java Servlets, Web pages, Web service endpoints, or JSP pages. The interaction between a Web client and a Web application is illustrated in Fig. 8.36.

Based on Fig. 8.36, a complete request-response message transformation for a Java Web application between a client and a Web server can be illustrated as below:

1) The client sends an HTTP request to the Web server.
2) A Web server that implements Java Servlet and JavaServer Pages technology converts the request into an HTTPServletRequest object.
3) The Web component can then generate an HTTPServletResponse or it can pass the request to another Web component.
4) Eventually a Web component generates an HTTPServletResponse object.
5) The Web server converts this object to an HTTP response and returns it to the client.

The dash lines between the Web components and Java Beans components, between Java Beans components and Database, are alternative ways to interact with database via business layer that is supported by the Java Beans components.

In order to get a clear and complete picture about how to control and transmit these request and response messages between Java EE Web Components, we need first to have a basic understanding about the Java EE Containers.

8.3.1 *Java EE Containers*

Java EE containers are the interfaces between a component and the low-level platform-specific functionality that supports the component. Before a Web, enterprise bean, or application client component can be executed, it must be assembled into a Java EE module and deployed into its container. Refer to Sect. 8.2 for a detailed discussion about four types of Java EE modules.

The assembly process involves specifying container settings for each component in the Java EE application and for the Java EE application itself. Container settings customize the underlying support provided by the Java EE server, including services such as security, transaction management, JavaNaming and Directory Interface (JNDI) lookups, and remote connectivity.

The deployment process installs Java EE application components in the Java EE containers as illustrated in Fig. 8.37.

The function of each container is listed below:

- **Java EE server**: The runtime portion of a Java EE product. A Java EE server provides EJB and web containers.
- **Enterprise JavaBeans (EJB) container**: Manages the execution of enterprise beans for Java EE applications. Enterprise beans and their container run on the Java EE server.
- **Web container**: Manages the execution of Web pages, Servlets, and some EJB components for Java EE applications. Web components and their containers run on the Java EE server.
- **Application client container**: Manages the execution of application client components. Application clients and their container run on the client.

All Web components are under the control of the associated containers, and the containers take charge of collecting, organizing, and transmitting requests and

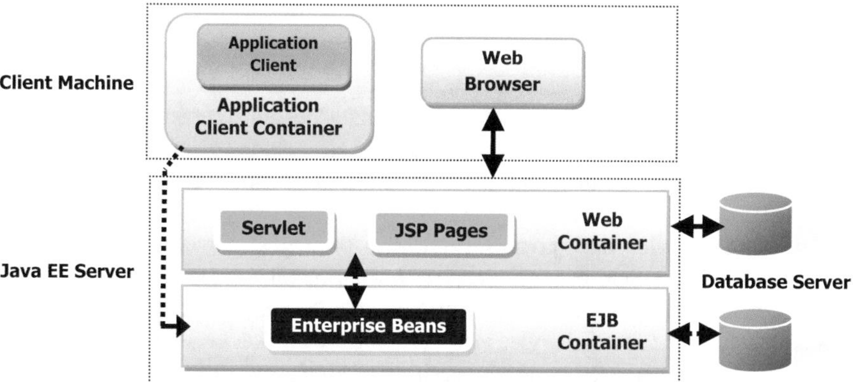

Fig. 8.37 Java EE server and containers

responses between those components. Java EE Web components can be implemented with multiple APIs. Let's have a brief review about these APIs.

8.3.2 *Java EE 8 APIs*

In this section, we will give a brief summary of the most popular technologies required by the Java EE platform and the APIs used in Java EE applications.

8.3.2.1 Enterprise Java Beans API Technology

An Enterprise Java Beans (EJB) component, or enterprise bean, is a body of code having fields and methods to implement modules of business logic. You can think of an enterprise bean as a building block that can be used alone or with other enterprise beans to execute business logic on the Java EE server.

There are two kinds of enterprise beans: *session beans* and *message-driven beans*. A *session bean* represents a transient conversation with a client. When the client finishes executing, the *session bean* and its data are gone. A *message-driven bean* combines features of a *session bean* and a message listener, allowing a business component to receive messages asynchronously. Commonly, these are JavaMessage Service (JMS) messages. Refer to Fig. 5.58 in Chap. 5 to get more detailed information about the EJB.

In the Java EE 8 platform, new enterprise bean features include the following:

1) The ability to package local enterprise beans in a. WAR file.
2) Singleton session beans, which provide easy access to shared state.
3) A lightweight subset of Enterprise Java Beans functionality that can be provided within Java EE Profiles such as the Java EE Web Profile.

8.3.2.2 Java Servlet API Technology

A Servlet is a class defined in Java programming language, and it is used to extend the capabilities of servers that host applications accessed by means of a request-response programming model. Although Servlets can respond to any type of request, they are commonly used to extend the applications hosted by Web servers. For such applications, Java Servlet API technology defines HTTP-specific Servlet classes.

The **javax.servlet** and **javax.servlet.http** packages provide interfaces and classes for writing Servlets. All Servlets must implement the Servlet interface, which defines life-cycle methods. When implementing a generic service, you can use or extend the GenericServlet class provided with the Java Servlet API. The HttpServlet class provides methods, such as **doGet()** and **doPost()**, for handling HTTP-specific services.

The life cycle of a Servlet is controlled by the container in which the Servlet has been deployed. When a request is mapped to a Servlet, the container performs the following steps.

1) If an instance of the Servlet does not exist, the Web container.

   (a) Loads the Servlet class.
   (b) Creates an instance of the Servlet class.
   (c) Initializes the Servlet instance by calling the **init()** method.

2) Invokes the service method, passing request and response objects.

If the container needs to remove the Servlet, it finalizes the Servlet by calling the Servlet's **destroy()** method.

You can monitor and react to events in a Servlet's life cycle by defining listener objects whose methods get invoked when life-cycle events occur. To use these listener objects, you must define and specify the listener class.

8.3.2.3 JavaServer Pages API Technology

JavaServer Pages (JSP) is a Java technology that helps software developers serve dynamically generated web pages based on HTML, XML, or other document types. Released in 1999 as Sun's answer to ASP and PHP, JSP was designed to address the perception that the Java programming environment didn't provide developers with enough support for the Web.

Architecturally, JSP may be considered as a high-level abstraction of Java Servlets. JSP pages are loaded in the server and operated from a structured special installed Java server packet called a Java EE Web Application, often packaged as a **.war** or **.ear** file archive.

JSP allows Java code and certain pre-defined actions to be interleaved with static Web markup content, with the resulting page being compiled and executed on the server to deliver an HTML or XML document. The compiled pages and any dependent Java libraries use Java byte-code rather than a native software format and must therefore be executed within a Java Virtual Machine (JVM) that integrates with the host operating system to provide an abstract platform-neutral environment.

JSP syntax is a fluid mix of two basic content forms: *scriptlet elements* and *markup*. Markup is typically standard HTML or XML, while scriptlet elements are delimited blocks of Java code which may be intermixed with the markup. When the page is requested, the Java code is executed, and its output is added, in situ, with the surrounding markup to create the final page. Because Java is a compiled language, not a scripting language, JSP pages must be compiled to Java byte-code classes before they can be executed, but such compilation is needed only when a change to the source JSP file has occurred.

Java code is not required to be complete (self-contained) within its scriptlet element block, but can straddle markup content provided the page as a whole is syntactically correct (e.g., any Java **if/for/while** blocks opened in one scriptlet element must be correctly closed in a later element for the page to successfully compile). This system of split inline coding sections is called *step over scripting* because it can wrap around the static markup by stepping over it. Markup which falls inside a split block of code is subject to that code, so markup inside an *if* block will only appear in the output when the *if* condition evaluates to true; likewise markup inside a loop construct may appear multiple times in the output depending upon how many times the loop body runs.

The JSP syntax adds additional XML-like tags, called JSP actions, to invoke built-in functionality. Additionally, the technology allows for the creation of JSP tag libraries that act as extensions to the standard HTML or XML tags. JVM operated tag libraries provide a platform independent way of extending the capabilities of a Web server. Note that not all commercial Java servers are Java EE specification compliant.

JavaServer Pages (JSP) technology lets you put snippets of Servlet code directly into a text-based document. A JSP page is a text-based document that contains two types of text: static data (which can be expressed in any text-based format such as HTML, WML, and XML) and JSP elements, which determine how the page constructs dynamic content.

The JavaServer Pages Standard Tag Library (JSTL) encapsulates core functionality common to many JSP applications. Instead of mixing tags from numerous vendors in your JSP applications, you employ a single, standard set of tags. This standardization allows you to deploy your applications on any JSP container that supports JSTL and makes it more likely that the implementation of the tags is optimized.

JSTL has an iterator and conditional tags for handling flow control, tags for manipulating XML documents, internationalization tags, tags for accessing databases using SQL, and commonly used functions.

JSP pages are compiled into Servlets by a JSP compiler. The compiler either generates a Servlet in Java code that is then compiled by the Java compiler, or it may compile the Servlet to byte code which is directly executable. JSPs can also be interpreted on-the-fly, reducing the time taken to reload changes.

JSP simply puts Java inside HTML pages using JSP tags. You can take any existing HTML page and change its extension to **.jsp** instead of **.html**.

Regardless of whether the JSP compiler generates Java source code for a Servlet or emits the byte code directly, it is helpful to understand how the JSP compiler

```
A  <%@ page myPage="mypage.jsp" %>
   <%@ page import="com.foo.bar" %>

   <html>
   <head>
B  <%! int serverInstanceVariable = 1;%>

   <% int localStackBasedVariable = 1; %>
   <table>
   <tr><td><%= toStringOrBlank( "expanded inline data " + 1 ) %></td></tr>
```

Fig. 8.38 An example of JSP pages

transforms the page into a Java Servlet. For example, consider an input JSP page shown in Fig. 8.38, and this JSP page can be compiled to create its resulting generated Java Servlet. The JSP tags **<% ... % >** or **<jsp ... />** enclose Java expressions, which are evaluated at the run time by JVM.

Refer to Fig. 8.38. In step **A**, two JSP coding lines are created to declare a JSP page and an import component. Then in step **B**, two Java integer variables are created: one is an instance variable and the other one is the Stack-based variable.

8.3.2.4 JavaServer Faces API Technology

JavaServer Faces technology is a server-side component framework for building Java technology-based Web applications. JavaServer Faces technology consists of the following:

- An API for representing components and managing their state; handling events, server-side validation, and data conversion; defining page navigation; supporting internationalization and accessibility; and providing extensibility for all these features
- Tag libraries for adding components to Web pages and for connecting components to server-side objects

JavaServer Faces technology provides a well-defined programming model and various tag libraries. These features significantly ease the burden of building and maintaining Web applications with server-side UIs. With minimal effort, you can complete the following tasks:

1) Create a Web page
2) Drop components onto a Web page by adding component tags
3) Bind components on a page to server-side data
4) Wire component-generated events to server-side application code
5) Save and restore application state beyond the life of server requests
6) Reuse and extend components through customization

The functionality provided by a JavaServer Faces application is similar to that of any other Java Web application. A typical JavaServer Faces application includes the following parts:

- A set of Web pages in which components are laid out.
- A set of tags to add components to the Web page.
- A set of *backing beans* which are JavaBeans components that define properties and functions for components on a page.
- A Web deployment descriptor (**web.xml** file).
- Optionally, one or more application configuration resource files such as a **faces-config.xml** file, which can be used to define page navigation rules and configure beans and other custom objects such as custom components.

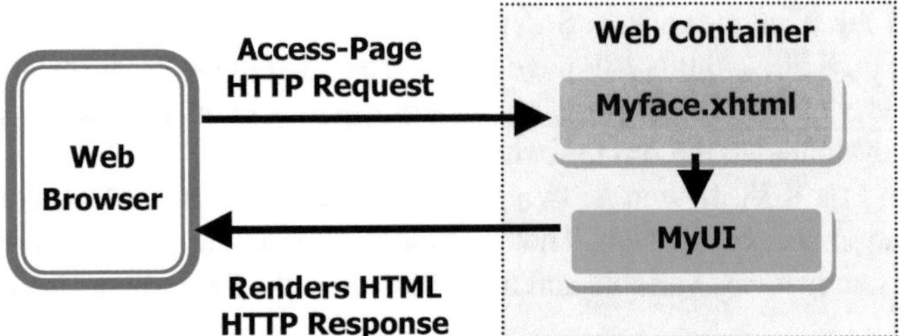

Fig. 8.39 Responding to a client request for a JavaServer Faces page

- Optionally, a set of custom objects created by the application developer. These objects can include custom components, validators, converters, or listeners.
- A set of custom tags for representing custom objects on the page.

Figure 8.39 describes the interaction between client and server in a typical JavaServer Faces application. In response to a client request, a Web page is rendered by the Web container that implements JavaServer Faces technology.

The Web page, **Myface.xhtml**, is built using JavaServer Faces component tags. Component tags are used to add components to the view (represented by **MyUI** in the diagram), which is the server-side representation of the page. In addition to components, the Web page can also reference objects such as the following:

1) Any event listeners, validators, and converters that are registered on the components
2) The JavaBeans components that capture the data and process the application-specific functionality of the components

On request from the client, the view is rendered as a response. Rendering is the process whereby, based on the server-side view, the Web container generates output such as HTML or XHTML that can be read by the browser.

8.3.2.5 Java Transaction API

The Java Transaction API (JTA) provides a standard interface for demarcating transactions.

The Java EE architecture provides a default auto commit to handle transaction commits and rollbacks. An **auto commit** means that any other applications that are viewing data will see the updated data after each database reads or writes operation. However, if your application performs two separate database access operations that depend on each other, you will want to use the JTA API to demarcate where the entire transaction, including both operations, begins, rolls back, and commits.

In Sect. 7.1 in Chap. 7, we have provided a very detailed discussion about the Java Persistence API on Transaction mechanism and its implementation with some data manipulations in real projects, such as data inserting, updating, and deleting, using the JPA wizard. Refer to those parts to get more information for this API.

8.3.2.6 Java Message Service API

The JavaMessage Service (JMS) API is a messaging standard that allows Java EE application components to create, send, receive, and read messages. It enables distributed communication that is loosely coupled, reliable, and asynchronous.

Now that we have a basic and clear understanding about the Java EE architecture and components, now let's take a look at the Java Web application life cycle.

8.3.3 Java Web Application Life Cycle

A Web application consists of Web components, static resource files such as images, and helper classes and libraries. The Web container provides many supporting services that enhance the capabilities of Web components and make them easier to develop. However, because a Web application must take these services into account, the process for creating and running a Web application is different from that of traditional stand-alone Java classes.

The process for creating, deploying, and executing a Web application can be summarized as follows:

1) Develop the Web component code.
2) Develop the Web application deployment descriptor.
3) Compile the Web application components and helper classes referenced by the components.
4) Optionally package the application into a deployable unit.
5) Deploy the application into a Web container.
6) Access a URL that references the Web application.

We will illustrate how to use this life-cycle module to develop and build some professional Java Web applications in Sect. 8.4.

8.3.4 Java Web Modules

As we discussed in Sect. 8.2.1, four Java EE Web modules are available, and the Web module is one of them. In the Java EE architecture, Web components and static Web content files such as images are called **web resources**. A **web module** is the smallest deployable and usable unit of Web resources. A Java EE Web module corresponds to a Web application as defined in the Java Servlet specification.

In addition to Web components and Web resources, a Web module can contain other files:

- Server-side utility classes (database beans, shopping carts, and so on). Often these classes conform to the JavaBeans component architecture.
- Client-side classes (applets and utility classes).

A Web module has a specific structure. The top-level directory of a Web module is the **document root** of the application. The document root is where XHTML pages, client-side classes and archives, and static Web resources, such as images, are stored.

The document root contains a subdirectory named WEB-INF, which contains the following files and directories:

- **web.xml**: The Web application deployment descriptor
- Tag library descriptor files
- **classes**: A directory that contains server-side classes: Servlets, utility classes, and JavaBeans components
- **tags**: A directory that contains tag files, which are implementations of tag libraries
- **lib**: A directory that contains JAR archives of libraries called by server-side classes

If your Web module does not contain any Servlets, filter, or listener components, then it does not need a Web application deployment descriptor. In other words, if your Web module only contains XHTML pages and static files, you are not required to include a **web.xml** file.

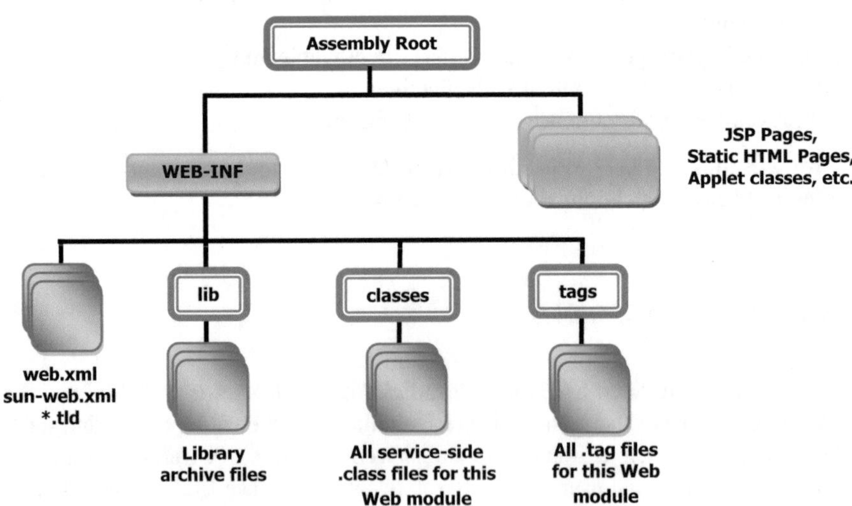

Fig. 8.40 A Web module structure

You can also create application-specific subdirectories (i.e., package directories) in either the document root or the WEB-INF/classes/directory.

A Web module can be deployed as an unpacked file structure or can be packaged in a JAR file known as a Web archive (WAR) file. Because the contents and use of WAR files differ from those of JAR files, WAR file names use a **.war** extension. The Web module just described is portable; you can deploy it into any Web container that conforms to the Java Servlet Specification.

To deploy a WAR on the Enterprise Server, the file must also contain a runtime deployment descriptor. The runtime deployment descriptor is an XML file that contains information such as the context root of the Web application and the mapping of the portable names of an application's resources to the Enterprise Server's resources. The Enterprise Server Web application runtime DD is named **sun-web.xml** and is located in the WEB-INF directory along with the Web application DD. The structure of a Web module that can be deployed on the Enterprise Server is shown in Fig. 8.40.

To successfully build and implement a Java Web application, one needs to perform the following operations to make it a distributable application:

- Packaging Web modules
- Deploying a WAR file
- Testing deployed Web modules
- Listing deployed Web modules
- Updating Web modules
- Undeploying Web modules

We will discuss these operations with more details in the following sections with some real Java Web application projects.

8.3.5 Java Web Frameworks

A Web application framework is a software framework that is designed to support the development of dynamic websites, Web applications, and Web services. The framework aims to alleviate the overhead associated with common activities performed in Web development. For example, many frameworks provide libraries for database access, template frameworks, and session management, and they often promote code reuse, too.

As we know, all Web components such as Java Servlets, Web pages, or JSP pages, are under the control of the associated Web containers. The question is: who controls those Web containers? The answer is the Web frameworks. A Web framework is a software framework that provides all supports to develop and organize dynamic sites. Some main features provided by a Web framework include:

- Provide user-friendly graphical user interfaces (GUIs) to Web applications

- Provide managements to Web containers to coordinate requests and responses transmission between Web server and clients
- Provide security supports to Web servers
- Provide supports to database accessing and mapping
- Provide supports to URL mapping
- Provide supports to update Web templates

Almost all modern Web-development frameworks follow the Model-View-Controller (MVC) design. Business logic and presentation are separated, and a controller of logic flow coordinates requests from clients and actions taken on the server. This approach has become a popular style of Web development.

All frameworks use different techniques to coordinate the navigation within the Web application, such as the XML configuration file, java property files, or custom properties. All frameworks also differ in the way the controller module is implemented. For instance, EJBs may instantiate classes needed in each request, or Java reflection can be used to dynamically invoke appropriate action classes. Also, frameworks may differ conceptually.

Java frameworks are similar in the way they structure data flow. After request, some action takes place on the application server, and some data populated objects are always sent to the JSP layer with the response. Data is then extracted from those objects, which could be simple classes with setter and getter methods, java beans, value objects, or some collection objects. Modern Java frameworks also simplify a developer's tasks by providing automatic Session tracking with easy APIs, database connection pools, and even database call wrappers. Some frameworks either provide hooks into other J2EE technologies, such as JMS (Java Messaging Service) or JMX, or have these technologies integrated. Server data persistence and logging also could be part of a framework.

The most popular Web frameworks include:

- JavaServer Faces (JSF)
- Apache Wicket
- JBoss Seam
- Spring MVC & WebFlow
- Adobe Flex
- Hibernate
- PHP
- Perl
- Ruby
- ASP.NET
- Struts 2

Two popular Java frameworks used in NetBeans IDE are JavaServer Faces and Hibernate.

Now that we have both a historical review and detailed discussion for each part of Java Web applications, let's concentrate on building and developing real Java Web database application projects starting from the next section.

8.4 Build Java Web Project to Query SQL Server Database

It is the time for us to do some practical works to build our Web application projects to show users how to use knowledge we discussed above to apply them in real applications. First let's build some useful Web pages to begin our developments.

8.4.1 Create Five Web Pages Using Microsoft Office Publisher 2007

In this section, we will create five Web pages, LogIn, Selection, Faculty, Course, and Student, as the GUIs to access and manipulate our sample database via Web server.

When a Web application starts, the default starting page is **index.jsp**. However, in this application, we want to use the **LogIn.jsp** page as our starting page. Because of the relative complexity in our five pages, we need to use Microsoft Office Publisher 2007 as a tool to help us to do this job.

Let's first handle the LogIn page.

8.4.1.1 Create the LogIn Page

The purpose of this page is to allow users to login to our sample SQL Server database to perform data actions to five tables in our sample database. Exactly this page is related to the LogIn table to enable users to log in and enter this database.

Launch Microsoft Office Publisher 2007, and click on the **Web Sites** icon to open the **Web Sites** wizard. Scroll down to the bottom of this wizard, and double click on the **Web 984 × 4608px** item under the **Blank Sizes** category as the template of this page. Perform the following operations to build this page:

1) Go to **Insert > Text Box** menu item to add a textbox to the top of this page. Enter **Welcome to CSE DEPT LogIn Page** into this textbox as a label for this page.
2) Highlight the text of the label, and select the **Arial Black** as the font type and **12** as the font size.
3) Perform the similar operation as step 1 to create another two textboxes, and enter **User Name** and **Pass Word** as another two labels. Locate these two labels just under the top label as we did in step 1 above.
4) Go to **Insert > Form Control > TextBox** menu item to add two textboxes, and align each of them after each of two labels, **User Name** and **Pass Word**, respectively.
5) Right click on the first textbox we added in step 4 above, and select **Format Form Properties** item. Enter **UserNameField** into the text field under the

Return data with this label as the name of this textbox. Click on the OK button to complete this naming process.

6) Perform the similar operation to the second textbox we added in step 4 above, and name it as **PassWordField**.
7) Go to **Insert > Form Control > Submit** menu item to add a command button into this page. Uncheck the **Button text is same as button type** checkbox, and enter **LogIn** into the **Button text** field. Locate this button under two textboxes we added in steps 4 through 6. Click on the OK button to close this dialog box.
8) Perform similar operation to add another button, and use **Cancel** as the button text for this button.
9) Go to **File > Save As** item to save this page as an HTML file. On the opened **Save As** dialog, select the **Web Page, Filtered (*.htm, *.html)** from the **Save as type** combo box, and enter **LogIn.html** to the **File name** field. Click on the **Save** button to save this HTML file to certain location in your root driver, such as **C:\Temp**. Click **Yes** to the message box and **OK** to the **Form Properties** dialog to complete this saving process.

Now go to **File > Web Page Preview** menu item, and select a browser, such as Internet Explorer or Microsoft Edges, to take a look at this LogIn page. Your finished LogIn page should match one that is shown in Fig. 8.41. To convert this HTML page to a JSP page, open the Notepad, and perform the following operations:

1) On the opened Notepad, go to **File > Open** menu item to open the Open dialog box. Make sure to select **All Files** from the **Files of type** combo box at the bottom of this dialog.
2) Browse to the folder where you saved the **LogIn.html** file, such as **C:\Temp**, select it, and click on the **Open** button to open this file.

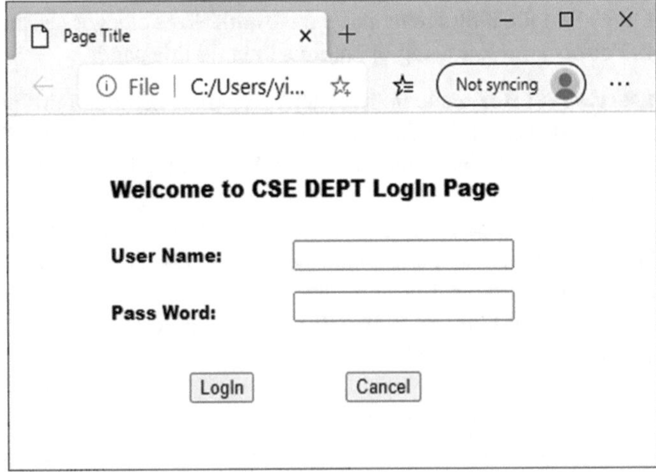

Fig. 8.41 The finished LogIn page

3) Go to **File > Save As** menu item to open the **Save As** dialog box. Then enter **"LogIn.jsp"** into the **File name** field as the name of this page. The point to be noted is that you must use the double quotation marks to cover this file name to enable the Notepad to save it as a JSP file. Click on the **Save** button to save this JSP file to your desired folder, such as **C:\Temp**.
4) Close the Notepad, and we have completed creating our **LogIn.jsp** file.

Next let's handle to create our Selection JSP file.

8.4.1.2 Create the Selection Page

The purpose of this page is to allow users to choose other Web pages to perform the related data actions with the different data tables in our sample database. Therefore this page can be considered as a main or control page to enable users to browse to other pages to perform data actions against the related data table in our sample database.

Launch Microsoft Office Publisher 2007, and click on the **Web Sites** icon to open the **Web Sites** wizard. Scroll down to the bottom of this wizard, and double click on the **Web 984 × 4608px** item under the **Blank Sizes** category as the template of this page. Click on the **Change Page Size** button under the **Web Site Options** tab if you cannot find this item. Perform the following operations to build this page:

1) Go to **Insert > Text Box** menu item to add a textbox to the top of this page. Enter **Make Your Selection** into this textbox as a label for this page.
2) Highlight the text of the label, and select the **Arial Black** as the font type and **12** as the font size.
3) Go to **Insert > Form Control > List Box** menu item to add a listbox control. Locate this listbox just under the top label as we did in step 1 above.
4) Right click on the new added listbox, and select **Format Form Properties** item to open **List Box Properties** dialog. Enter **ListSelection** into the **Return data with this label** field as the name of this listbox.
5) In the **Appearance** list, click on the **Remove** buttons three times to delete all default items from this list.
6) Click on the **Add** button to add the first item to this list. On the opened dialog, enter the **Faculty Information** into the **Item** field, and check the **Selected** radio button. Make sure that the **Item value is same as item text** checkbox is checked. Your finished **Add/Modify List Box Item** dialog should match one that is shown in Fig. 8.42. Click on the **OK** button to close this dialog box.
7) Click on the **Add** button to add our second item into this listbox. On the opened **Add/Modify List Box Item** dialog, enter **Course Information** into the **Item** field, and make sure that both **Not selected** radio button and the **Item value is same as item text** checkbox are checked. Click on the **OK** button to close this dialog box.
8) Perform the similar operations as we did in step 7 above to add the third item, **Student Information**, into this listbox.

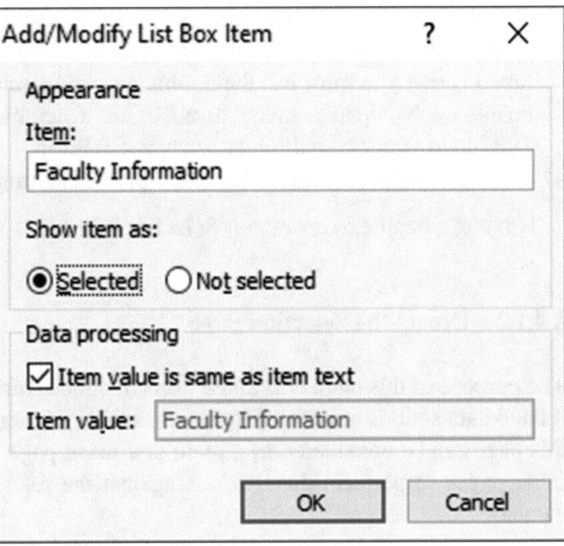

Fig. 8.42 The finished Add/Modify List Box Item dialog box

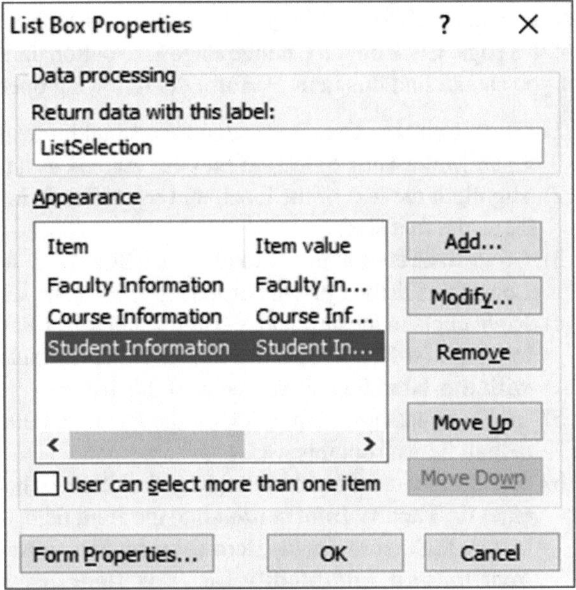

Fig. 8.43 The finished List Box Properties dialog box

9) Your finished **List Box Properties** dialog should match one that is shown in Fig. 8.43. Click on the **OK** button to complete this listbox setup process.
10) Go to **Insert > Form Control > Submit** menu item to add a command button into this page. Uncheck the **Button text is same as button type** checkbox, and enter **OK** into the **Button text** field. Locate this button under the listbox we added above. Click on the **OK** button to close this dialog box.

11) Perform the similar operation to add another button, and use **Exit** as the button text for this button.
12) Go to **File > Save As** item to save this page as an HTML file. On the opened **Save As** dialog, select the **Web Page, Filtered (*.htm, *.html)** from the **Save as type** combo box, and enter **Selection.html** to the **File name** field. Click on the **Save** button to save this HTML file to certain location in your root driver, such as **C:\Temp**. Click **Yes** to the message box and **OK** to the **Form Properties** dialog to complete this saving process.
13) Now go to **File > Web Page Preview** menu item to take a look at this Selection page. Your finished Selection page should match one that is shown in Fig. 8.44.

To convert this HTML page to a JSP page, open the Notepad, and perform the following operations:

1) On the opened Notepad, go to **File > Open** menu item to open the **Open** dialog box. Make sure to select **All Files** from the **Files of type** combo box at the bottom of this dialog.
2) Browse to the folder where you saved the **Selection.html** file, such as **C:\Temp**, select it, and click on the **Open** button to open this file.
3) Go to **File > Save As** menu item to open the **Save As** dialog box. Enter **"Selection.jsp"** into the **File name** field as the name of this page. The point to be noted is that you must use the double quotation marks to cover this file name to enable the Notepad to save it as a JSP file. Click on the **Save** button to save this JSP file to your desired folder, such as **C:\Temp**.
4) Close the Notepad, and we have completed creating our **Selection.jsp** file.

Next let's handle to create our Faculty JSP file.

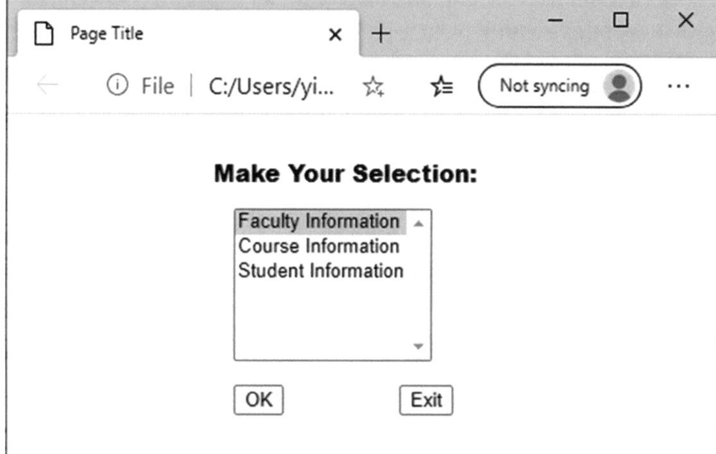

Fig. 8.44 The preview of the Selection page

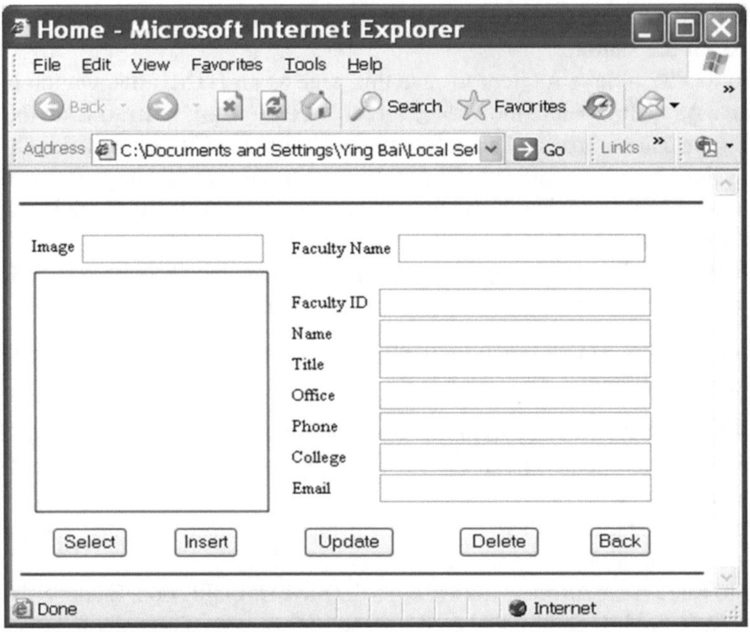

Fig. 8.45 The preview of the Faculty page

8.4.1.3 Create the Faculty Page

The purpose of this page is to allow users to access the Faculty table in our sample database to perform data actions via this page, such as data query, new faculty records insertion, and faculty member updating and deleting. Because the HTML and JSP did not provide any combo box control, in this application, we have to use text box control to replace the combo box control and apply it in this page.

The preview of this Faculty page is shown in Fig. 8.45.

Now let's start to build this page using Microsoft Office Publisher 2007.

Launch Microsoft Office Publisher 2007, and click on the **Web Sites** icon to open the **Web Sites** wizard. Scroll down to the bottom of this wizard, and double click on the **Web 984 × 4608px** item under the **Blank Sizes** category as the template of this page. Perform the following operations to build this page:

1) Go to **Insert > Text Box** menu item to insert a textbox into this page, and enter **Image** into this textbox as an image label.
2) Go to **Insert > Form Control > Textbox** menu item to insert a Textbox into this page, and locate this textbox just to the right of the **Image** label we added in step 1 above.
3) Right click on this inserted Textbox, and select the **Format Form Properties** item to open the **Text Box Properties** dialog, as shown in Fig. 8.46a. Then enter **FacultyImageField** into the **Return data with this label** field, as shown in Fig. 8.46a. Click on the **OK** button to close this dialog.

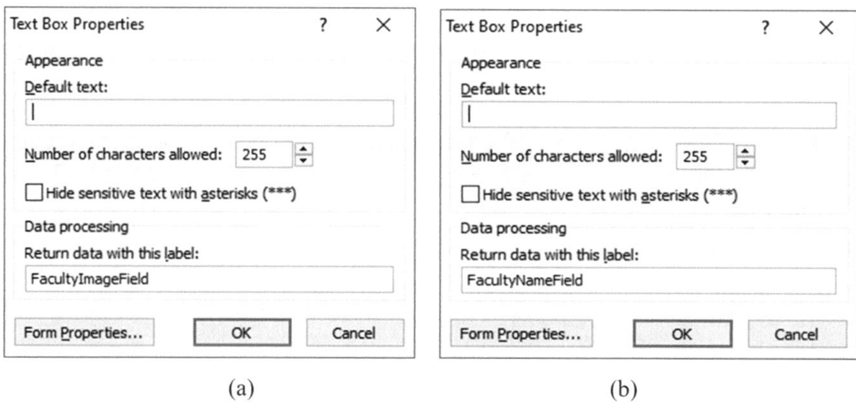

Fig. 8.46 The FacultyImageField and FacultyNameField textboxes

4) Go to **Insert > Picture > Empty Picture Frame** menu item to insert a blank picture to this page. Locate this picture under the **FacultyImageField** textbox we added in step 2.
5) Go to **Insert > Text Box** to insert a new TextBox, and move it to the right of the picture. Type **Faculty Name** in this inserted TextBox as the **Faculty Name** label.
6) Go to **Insert > Form Control > Textbox** menu item to insert a Textbox into this page, and locate this textbox to the right of the **Faculty Name** label.
7) Right click on this inserted Textbox, and select the **Format Form Properties** item to open the **Text Box Properties** dialog. Enter **FacultyNameField** into the **Return data with this label** field, as shown in Fig. 8.46b. Click on the **OK** button to close this dialog.
8) Go to **Insert > Text Box** menu item again to insert another TextBox, and move it to the right of the picture under the **Faculty Name** TextBox. Type **Faculty ID** into this TextBox, and use it as the **Faculty ID** label.
9) Go to **Insert > Form Control > Textbox** menu item to insert a Textbox into this page, and move this Textbox to the right of the **Faculty ID** label.
10) Change this Textbox's name to **FacultyIDField** as we did in step 7 above.
11) In a similar way, you can finish adding another six Textboxes and the associated labels, as shown in Fig. 8.45. Use step 7 above to change these six Textboxes' names to:

    (a) NameField
    (b) TitleField
    (c) OfficeField
    (d) PhoneField
    (e) CollegeField
    (f) EmailField

12) You can use **Format > Paragraph > Line spacing > Between lines** menu property to modify the vertical distances between each label. In this application, set this distance to 0.6sp.
13) Go to **Insert > Form Control > Submit** menu item to insert five buttons at the bottom of this page. In the opened `Command Button Properties` dialog, uncheck the `Button text is same as button type` checkbox, and enter

    (a) Select
    (b) Insert
    (c) Update
    (d) Delete
    (e) Back

    into the `Button text` field for these five buttons one by one. Click on the **OK** button to complete these five-button creation process.
14) Your finished Faculty page in Microsoft Publisher 2007 should match one that is shown in Fig. 8.47.
15) Go to **File > Save As** item to save this page as an HTML file. On the opened `Save As` dialog, select the **Web Page, Filtered (*.htm, *.html)** from the **Save as type** combo box, and enter **Faculty.html** to the **File name** field. Click on the **Save** button to save this HTML file to certain location in your root driver, such as **C:\Temp**. Click **Yes** to the message box and **OK** to the **Form Properties** dialog to complete this saving process.

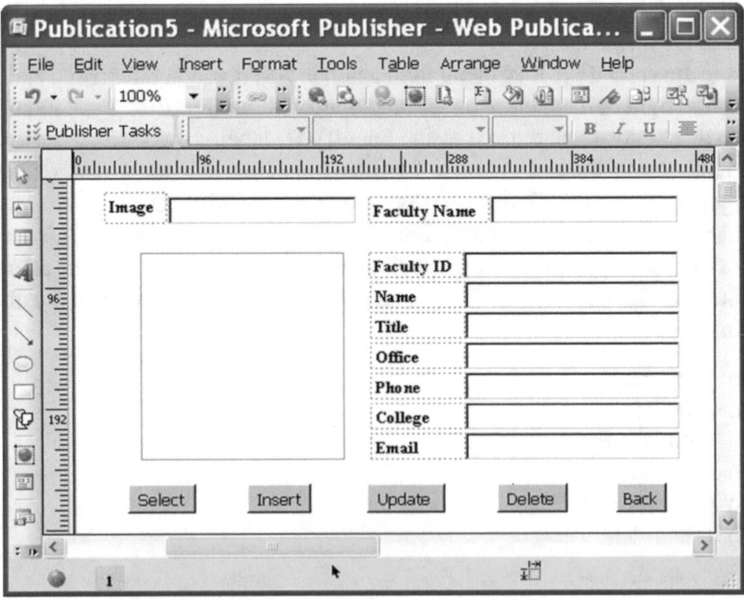

Fig. 8.47 The finished Faculty page

To convert this HTML page to a JSP page, open the Notepad, and perform the following operations:

1) On the opened Notepad, go to **File > Open** menu item to open the `Open` dialog box. Make sure to select **All Files** from the **Files of type** combo box at the bottom of this dialog.
2) Browse to the folder where you saved the **Faculty.html** file, such as **C:\Temp**, select it, and click on the **Open** button to open this file.
3) Go to **File > Save As** menu item to open the **Save As** dialog box. Enter **"Faculty.jsp"** into the **File name** field as the name of this page. The point to be noted is that you must use the double quotation marks to cover this file name to enable the Notepad to save it as a JSP file. Click on the **Save** button to save this JSP file to your desired folder, such as **C:\Temp**.
4) Close the Notepad, and we have completed creating our **Faculty.jsp** file.

Next let's handle to create our Course JSP file.

8.4.1.4 Create the Course Page

The purpose of using this page is to allow users to access and manipulate data in the Course table in our sample database via the Web server, such as course query, new course insertion, and course updating and deleting, based on the selected faculty member from the Faculty Name textbox.

The finished Course page is shown in Fig. 8.48.

Now let's start to build this page using Microsoft Office Publisher 2007.

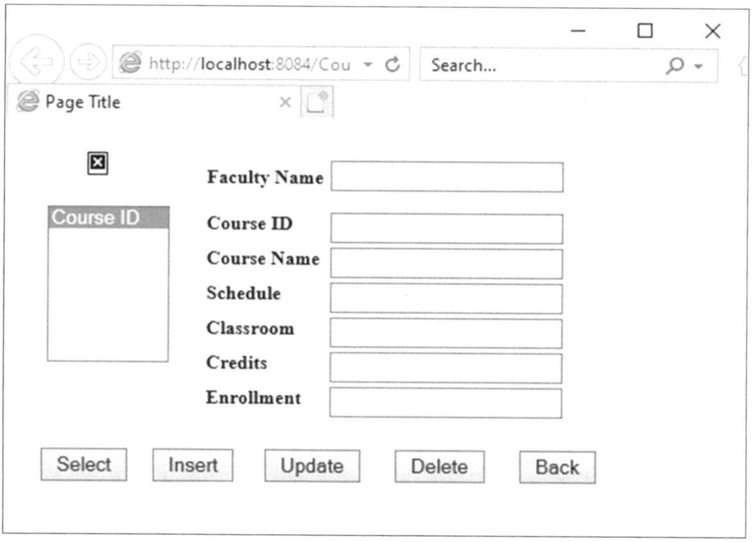

Fig. 8.48 The preview of the Course page

Launch Microsoft Office Publisher 2007, and click on the **Web Sites** icon to open the **Web Sites** wizard. Scroll down to the bottom of this wizard, and double click on the **Web 984 × 4608px** item under the **Blank Sizes** category as the template of this page. Perform the following operations to build this page:

1) Go to **Insert > Picture > Clip Art** menu item to open the **Clip Art** dialog box. Make sure to select the **geometry** in the **Search for** field, and click on the **Go** button to display all clip arts related to geometry. Click on the first one, and add it into the upper left corner of this page.
2) Go to **Insert > Text Box** menu item to insert a textbox into this page, and enter **Faculty Name** into this textbox as the **Faculty Name** label.
3) Go to **Insert > Form Control > Textbox** menu item to insert a Textbox into this page, and locate this textbox just to the right of the **Faculty Name** label we added in step 1 above.
4) Right click on this inserted Textbox, and select the **Format Form Properties** item to open the **Text Box Properties** dialog. Then enter **FacultyNameField** into the **Return data with this label** field. Click on the **OK** button to close this dialog.
5) Go to **Insert > Form Control > List Box** menu item to add a listbox control. Locate this listbox just under the top label as we did in step 1 above.
6) Right click on the new added listbox, and select **Format Form Properties** item to open **List Box Properties** dialog. Enter **CourseList** into the **Return data with this label** field as the name of this listbox.
7) In the **Appearance** list, click on the **Remove** buttons three times to delete all default items from this list.
8) Right click on the new added listbox **CourseList** and select **Format Form Properties** item to open **List Box Properties** dialog. Click on the **Add** button to open the **Add/Modify List Box Item** dialog box. Enter **Course ID** into the `Item` field and check the **Selected** radio button, and click on the **OK** button.
9) Go to **Insert > Text Box** to insert a new TextBox, and move it to the right of the listbox. Type **Course ID** in this TextBox as the **Course ID** label.
10) Go to **Insert > Form Control > Textbox** menu item to insert a Textbox into this page, and locate this textbox to the right of the **Course ID** label.
11) Right click on this inserted Textbox, and select the **Format Form Properties** item to open the **Text Box Properties** dialog. Enter **CourseIDField** into the **Return data with this label** field. Click on the **OK** button to close this dialog.
12) In a similar way, you can finish adding another four Textboxes and the associated labels, as shown in Fig. 8.48. Use step 10 above to change these four Textboxes' names to:

    (a) CourseNameField
    (b) ScheduleField
    (c) ClassroomField
    (d) CreditField
    (e) EnrollmentField

13) You can use **Format > Paragraph > Line spacing > Between lines** menu property to modify the vertical distances between each label. In this application, set this distance to 0.6sp.
14) Go to **Insert > Form Control > Submit** menu item to insert five buttons at the bottom of this page. In the opened **Command Button Properties** dialog, uncheck the **Button text is same as button type** checkbox, and enter

    (a) Select
    (b) Insert
    (c) Update
    (d) Delete
    (e) Back

    into the **Button text** field for these five buttons one by one. Click on the **OK** button to complete these five button creation process.
15) Your finished Faculty page in Microsoft Publisher 2007 is shown in Fig. 8.49.

To convert this HTML page to a JSP page, open the Notepad and perform the following operations:

1) On the opened Notepad, go to **File > Open** menu item to open the `Open` dialog box. Make sure to select **All Files** from the **Files of type** combo box at the bottom of this dialog.

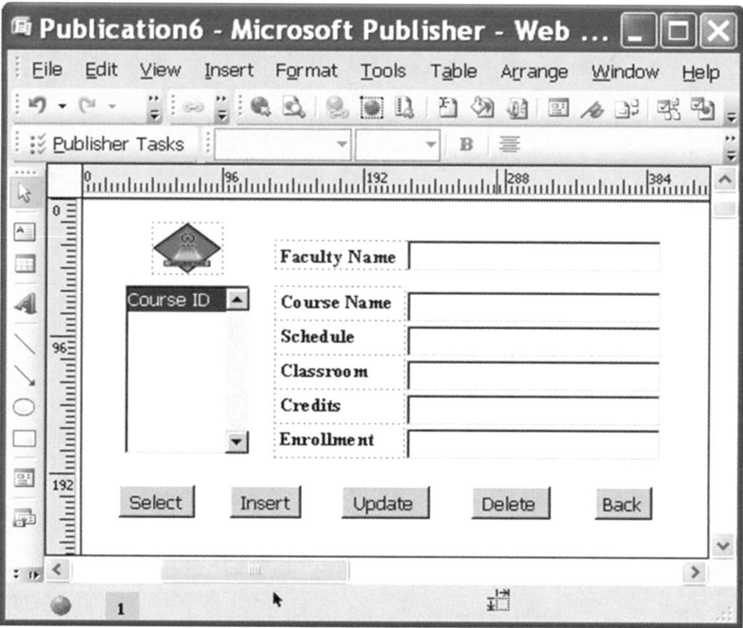

Fig. 8.49 The finished Course page

2) Browse to the folder where you saved the **Course.html** file, such as **C:\Temp**, select it and click on the **Open** button to open this file.
3) Go to **File > Save As** menu item to open the `Save As` dialog box. Enter **"Course.jsp"** into the **File name** field as the name of this page. The point to be noted is that you must use the double quotation marks to cover this file name to enable the Notepad to save it as a JSP file. Click on the **Save** button to save this JSP file to your desired folder, such as **C:\Temp**.
4) Close the Notepad, and we have completed creating our **Course.jsp** file.

Next let's handle to create our last page, Student JSP file.

8.4.1.5 Create the Student Page

Because of the similarity between the Student page and all other pages we discussed above, here we only provide the necessary information for the names of those controls to be added to this page. A preview of this Student page is shown in Fig. 8.50.

Table 8.2 lists the name of each control in the Student page.

Refer to discussions we made in the previous sections to build this Student page, and convert it to the **Student.jsp** page.

At this point, we have finished all five Web pages design and building process. Next we will begin to code these Web pages and the associated help class or Session object to perform data queries against our database.

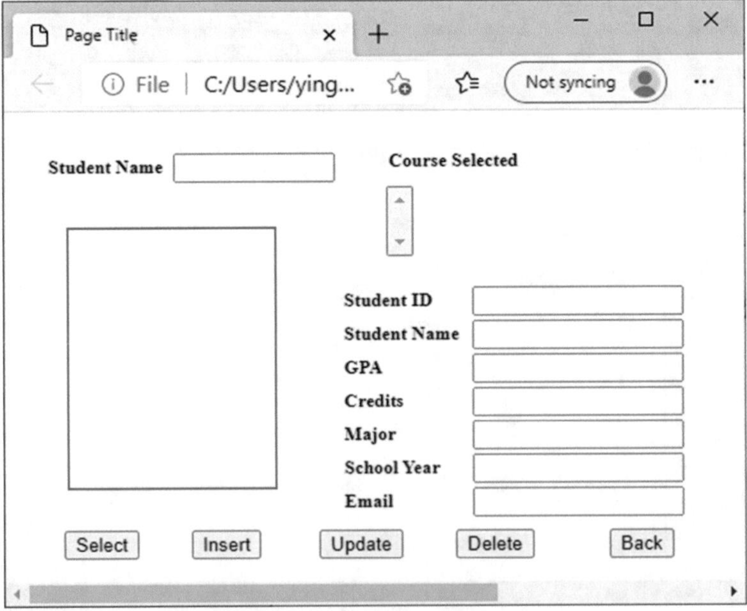

Fig. 8.50 The preview of the Student page

Table 8.2 All controls in the Student page

Control	Name
Student Name Textbox	StudentNameField
Course Selected Listbox	CourseList
The Item in the Course Selected Listbox	Course ID
Student ID Textbox	StudentIDField
Student Name Textbox	NameField
GPA Textbox	GPAField
Credits Textbox	CreditsField
Major Textbox	MajorField
School Year Textbox	SchoolYearField
Email Textbox	EmailField
Select Button	Select
Insert Button	Insert
Update Button	Update
Delete Button	Delete
Back Button	Back

8.4.2 Setup Environments for NetBeans IDE to Build Java Web Applications

To build Java Web application projects, some basic components are required, and these components include:

1) Basic NetBeans IDE
2) Web server
3) Java SE JDK
4) Database drive JDBC

Because of some compatibility issues, the following facts with special attentions must be paid and emphasized:

1) Starting Apache NetBeans IDE 9, no any supports are provided or continued for building any Web-related projects, including Java EE. In order to build any Web applications, additional Web server and components must be installed and configured by users.
2) In Apache NetBeans IDE 12, which is the latest version of the IDE, only GlassFish server is bundled with this IDE, but the latest version of this server is GlassFish 5, which only supports JDK 8, not the current JDK 14, which was installed and added into the NetBeans 12 and used by us to build all projects in the previous Chapters.
3) A possible solution to that GlassFish server is to use another popular server, Tomcat. But the issue is that the Apache NetBeans 12 only bundled the GlassFish

server with it, and the users must try to download, install, and configure this Tomcat server under the NetBeans 12 environment if they want to use this server with NetBeans 12. Those are very challenging jobs to general users as students and beyond the scope of this book.

4) Another problem is the JDK and JDBC driver compatibility issue. For JDK 14, it supports JDBC 8, but for JDK 8, it does not support JDBC 8; instead it supports JDBC 4.

Based on all of these facts above, we have to perform the following configurations to our NetBeans IDE with related components to meet the needs to build our Web applications:

1) Use NetBeans 8.2 IDE, instead of using Apache NetBeans 12 IDE, since the former bundled both GlassFish and Tomcat servers into the IDE to facilitate users to save a lot of trouble workings on installing and configuring the Tomcat server on the IDE.
2) To match to the requirements of NetBeans 8.2, the JDK 8, instead of JDK 14, is used as a Standard Edition (SE) of Java Development Kits (JDK).
3) To match to the JDK 8, the JDBC 4.2, not JDBC 8, is used to work as a Java Database Connection (JDBC) component.

As for the compatibility between the JDBC 4.2 and the Microsoft SQL Server 2019 Express database, the good news is that fortunately this JDBC is compatible with that database.

Thus starting from this Chapter, Chap. 8, we will change our development environments, including the NetBeans IDE, Java JDK, and JDBC driver, to those components we mentioned above, which can be summarized as:

- Use NetBeans 8.2 IDE to replace the Apache NetBeans 12 IDE.
- Use JDK 8 to replace JDK 14.
- Use JDBC 4.2 to replace JDBC 8.

Now let's begin our setup process to download, install, and configure those components one by one.

8.4.2.1 Download and Install Required Components

As we did for the Apache NetBeans 12 IDE, prior to downloading and installing NetBeans 8.2 IDE, we need first to download and install JDK 8. Refer to Appendix F to complete this downloading and installing process for JDK 8.

Refer to Appendix G to download and install JDBC 4.2, and refer to Appendix H to complete the downloading and installing process for NetBeans 8.2 IDE.

Now we have completed the downloading and installing process for all our required components; we are ready to build our Web application projects. However, before we can continue, we need to first configure our NetBeans 8.2 IDE to make it ready for us to start our project development process.

8.4.2.2 Configure NetBeans IDE 8.2 and Create Our First Web Application Project

On the desktop, double click on the NetBeans IDE 8.2 icon to open it.

1) On the opened IDE, three tabs are displayed on the left, **Projects**, **Files**, and **Services**. Click on the **Services** tab to open the **Services** pane.
2) Expand the **Servers** folder, and you can find two Web servers, Tomcat and GlassFish, have been installed. Right click on the **GlassFish Server**, and click on the **Remove** item from the popup menu to delete this server since we need to use the Tomcat server for all our projects. Click on the **Yes** button to confirm this deletion.

In order to configure the IDE to meet our requirements to build our Java Web applications, we need to first create a new Web project. We can start creating our first Web application project as this new project. Perform the following steps to create our first Web application project, **JavaWebDBJSPSQL** in the default folder **C:\Class DB Projects\Chapter 8**:

1) On the opened NetBeans IDE, go to **File\New Project** item to open **New Project** wizard.
2) On the opened **New Project wizard**, select **Java Web** from the Categories list and **Web Application** from the Projects list, as shown in Fig. 8.51. Click on the **Next** button.

Enter **JavaWebDBJSPSQL** into the **Project Name** box, as shown in Fig. 8.52, and click on the **Next** button.

On the next wizard, **Server and Settings**, which is shown in Fig. 8.53, keep the default Web server, **Apache Tomcat 8.0.27.0**, and click on the **Next** button. The

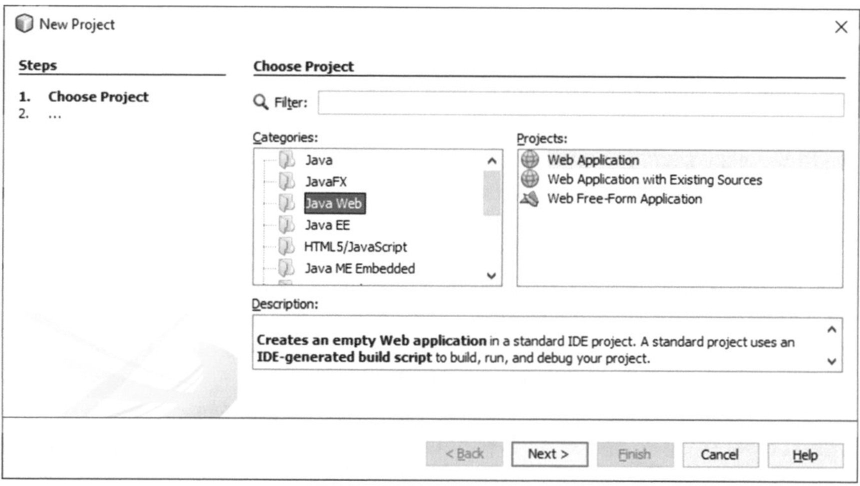

Fig. 8.51 The opened New Project wizard

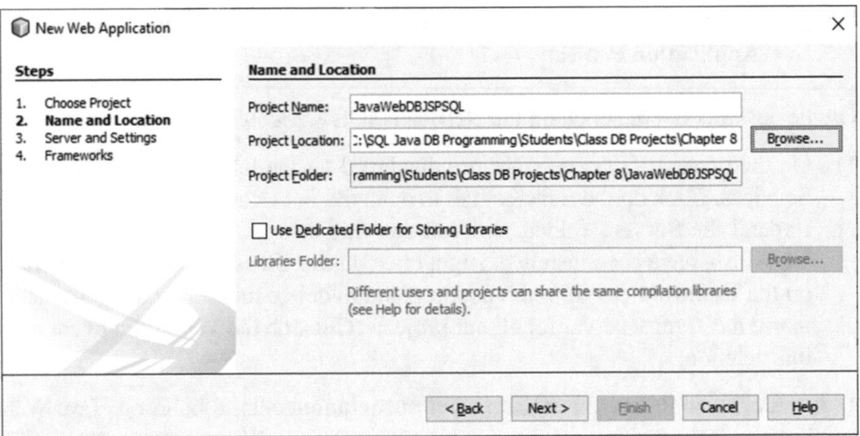

Fig. 8.52 The finished Name and Location wizard

New Web Application
Steps
1. Choose Project
2. Name and Location
3. Server and Settings
4. Frameworks
Server and Settings
Add to Enterprise Application: <None>
Server: Apache Tomcat 8.0.27.0
Add...
Java EE Version: Java EE 7 Web
Context Path: /JavaWebTest
< Back
Next >
Finish
Cancel
Help

Fig. 8.53 The opened Server and Settings wizard

reason why this server is selected as a default one is because we deleted the GlassFish server and only one server is available now.

On the next wizard, **Frameworks**, just click on the **Finish** button to complete this creating Web application process since we do not need to use any framework on this project.

Next let's add the JDBC Driver to access our SQL Server 2019 database. Right click on our project **JavaWebDBJSPSQL** from the **Projects** window, and select the **Properties** item to open the project properties wizard, as shown in Fig. 8.54.

Click on the **Libraries** node, and click on the **Add JAR/Folder** button to open the Windows Explorer to locate our installed JDBC Driver.

On the opened Windows Explorer, browse to the location where we installed the JDBC Driver (refer to Appendix G to download and install this driver). In our case, it is **C:\Program Files\sqljdbc_4.2\enu\jre7\sqljdbc41.jar**. Click on this JAR file to select it, and click on the **Open** button to add it into our project.

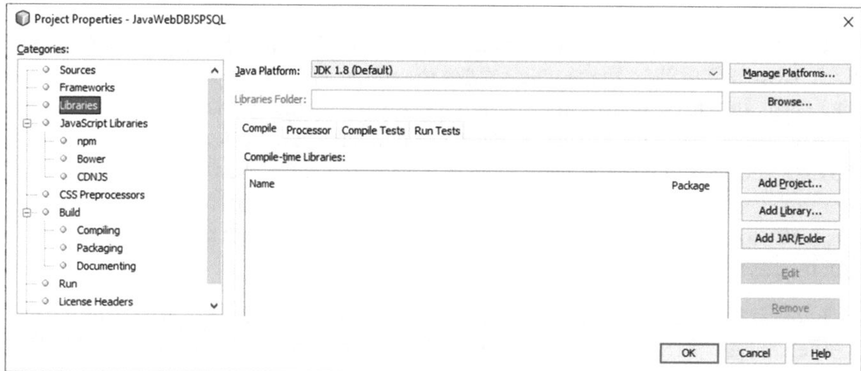

Fig. 8.54 The opened Project Properties wizard

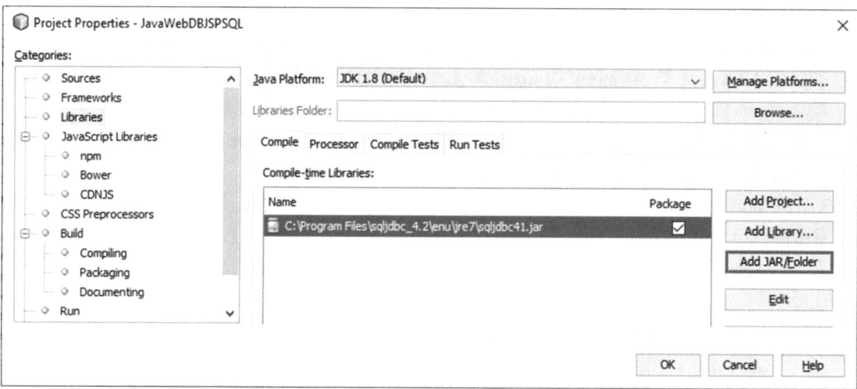

Fig. 8.55 The finished Adding JDBC Driver wizard

Your finished **Project Properties** wizard should match one that is shown in Fig. 8.55.

Click on the **OK** button to complete this JDBC driver addition operation.

Now we can continue to build our first Web application project by adding other required components.

8.4.3 Access and Query the LogIn Table Using JavaServer Pages and Help Class Files

First let's use JavaServer Pages and help class file to access and query data from the LogIn table in our sample SQL Server database **CSE_DEPT** via the **LogIn.jsp** page we built in Sect. 8.4.1.1 in this chapter.

We have provided a very detailed discussion about building and developing Java Web applications using JavaServer Pages and Java help class file in Sects. 8.1.2 and 8.1.3. Now let's follow those discussions to coding the LogIn page and creating the Java help class file **LogInQuery.java** to perform data query from the LogIn table.

Now we will use this project to build our database application project to perform the data actions against our sample SQL Server database. Next we need to add all five Web pages we built in Sects .8.4.1.1, 8.4.1.2, 8.4.1.3, 8.4.1.4 and 8.4.1.5 into this new project. Perform the following operations to complete this Web pages addition process:

1) Launch the Windows Explorer, and go to the folder where we stored those five Web pages; in this application, it is **C:\Temp**. Copy all five pages including **LogIn.jsp**, **Selection.jsp**, **Faculty.jsp**, **Course.jsp**, and **Student.jsp**, and then paste them to our new Web project folder, which is **Class DB Projects\Chapter 8\JavaWebDBJSPSQL** in this application.
2) Launch the NetBeans IDE, and open our new Web project **JavaWebDBJSPSQL**. Click on the **Files** tab to open the **Files** window, and browse to our Web project folder **JavaWebDBJSPSQL**. You can find that all five Web pages have been added into this project. Select all of these five pages using the **Shift** key, right click on these five selected pages, and click on the **Copy** item from the popup menu.
3) Click on the **Projects** tab to open the **Projects** window, browse to our project folder and then the **Web Pages** folder, right click on this folder, and select the **Paste** item to paste these five Web Pages to this **Web Pages** folder.

Next we need to do a little modification to our **LogIn.jsp** file and break this file into two JSP files: **LogIn.jsp** and **LogInQuery.jsp**. The reason for us to make it into two JSP files is that we want to process and display data in two separate files to make these operations clear and easy.

8.4.3.1 Modify the LogIn.jsp Page and Create LogInQuery.jsp File

Now let's first modify the **LogIn.jsp** page by double clicking on the **LogIn.jsp** to open it and perform the following modifications to this page. The modified parts have been highlighted in bold and are shown in Fig. 8.56.

Let's have a closer look at these modifications to see how they work.

A. The first modification is to the `form` tag, and an **action** attribute has been added into this tag. Generally a `form` tag is used to create a HTML form to collect user information and send all pieces of those collected information to the server when a submit button on this Form is clicked. Therefore a `form` and all submitting buttons on that `form` have a coordinate relationship. If a button is defined as a **submit** button by its **type** attribute, all Form data will be sent to the server whose URL is defined in the **action** attribute on the `form` tag when this submitting button is clicked by the user. Here we use a Java Server Page, **.\LogInQuery.**

```
  <html xmlns:v="urn:schemas-microsoft-com:vml"
  .........
  <body style='margin:0'>
  <div style='position:absolute;width:10.-2040in;height:1.-1423in'>
  <![if !pub]>
A <form method=post action=".\LogInQuery.jsp">
  .........
  <input name=UserNameField maxlength=255 size=21 value="" type=text
   v:shapes="_x0000_s1028">
  .........
  <input name=PassWordField maxlength=255 size=21 value="" type=text
   v:shapes="_x0000_s1029">
  .........
B <input type=submit value=LogIn name="LogInButton" v:shapes="_x0000_s1030">
C <input type=button value=Cancel name="cancelButton" onclick="self.close()" v:shapes="_x0000_s1031">
  .........
  </form>
  </body>
  </html>
```

Fig. 8.56 The modifications to the LogIn.jsp page

jsp, as the URL for our target page. Exactly this target page is used to access our Java help class file to handle all JDBC- and database-related processing and business logics. The **.** symbol is used to indicate that our next JSP file is located at the relatively current folder since this page is a part of the server functions and will be run at the server side as the whole project runs.

B. The second modification is to add a **name** attribute to the LogIn button in order for it to be identified in the server side later.
C. The third modification is to change the **type** of our Cancel button from **submit** to **button**, and add a **name** and an **onclick** attribute for this button. The reason for us to do these modifications is that we want to close our **LogIn.jsp** page when this Cancel button is clicked as the project runs, but we do not want to forward this button-click event to the server to allow the server to do this close action. Therefore we have to change the type of this button to **button** (not **submit**) to avoid triggering the **action** attribute in the Form tag. We also need to add a **self.close()** method to the **onclick** attribute of this button to call the system **close()** method to terminate our application. The **self** means the current page.

Go to **File > Save** item to save these modifications.

Now let's create and build our **LogInQuery.jsp** page, which works as a part of server, to receive and handle the Form data including the login information sent by the **LogIn.jsp** page. Right click on our project **JavaWebDBJSPSQL** from the **Projects** window, and select the **New > JSP** item from the popup menu to open the **New JSP File** wizard. If you cannot find the **JSP** item under the **New** menu item, go to **Other** item and select the **Web** from the **Categories** list and the **JSP** item from the **File Types** list. Click on the **Next** button to open this wizard.

Enter **LogInQuery** to the **File Name** field in the opened **New JSP File** wizard, and keep all other default settings unchanged. Then click on the **Finish** button to create this JSP file. Enter the codes that are shown in Fig. 8.57 into the **<body> … </body>** tags in this page.

```
  <html>
    <head>
      <meta http-equiv="Content-Type" content="text/html; charset=UTF-8">
      <title>LogIn Query Page</title>
    </head>
    <body>
A   <%@page language="java" %>
    <%
B     String nextPage = null;
      LogInQuery lquery = new LogInQuery();
C     String u_name = request.getParameter("UserNameField");
      String p_word = request.getParameter("PassWordField");
D     String result = lquery.checkLogIn(u_name, p_word);
E     if (result.equals("Matched"))
          nextPage = "Selection.jsp";
F     else
          out.println("LogIn is failed");
G     lquery.CloseDBConnection();
    %>
H   <jsp:forward page = "<%=nextPage%>" />
    </body>
  </html>
```

Fig. 8.57 The codes for the LogInQuery.jsp page

Let's have a closer look at this piece of codes to see how it works.

A. A JSP directive tag is used to indicate that this page uses Java language in this JSP page.
B. Some local variables and objects are declared first. The string variable **nextPage** is used to hold the URL of the next page, and the **lquery** is a new instance of our Java help class **LogInQuery.java** we will build in the next section.
C. The **getParameter()** method is used to pick up the login information entered by the user in the **LogIn.jsp** page. The collected login information including the username and password is assigned to two local string variables **u_name** and **p_word**, respectively.
D. The **checkLogIn()** method defined in our Java help class file is called to perform the database query and the login matching processing. The collected login information is used as arguments and passed into this method. The running result of this method is a string, and it is assigned to the local string variable **result**.
E. An **if** block is used to check the running result of the **checkLogIn()** method. The program will be directed to a successful page (**Selection.jsp**) if a matched login record is found.
F. Otherwise an error message is printed out to indicate that this login process failed.
G. The **CloseDBConnection()** method defined in the help class is called to disconnect the connection to our sample database.
H. A JSP forward directive is used to direct the program to the next page.

Next let's create and build our Java help class file **LogInQuery.java** to perform JDBC- and database-related operations and actions.

8.4.3.2 Create the Java Help Class File LogInQuery.java

The purpose of this help class file is to handle the JDBC-related operations and database-related actions. As we discussed in Sect. 8.1.3, to distinguish between the database-related data processing and running results displaying, we can separate a Java Web application into two parts: the JDBC-related database processing and the business logics such as checking and confirming a pair of matched username and password located at a Java help class file and the data and running results displaying at a Web or a JavaServer page.

It looks like that we can use the Java persistence API to perform the database accessing and query to our LogIn table. However, because the Java persistence API can only be implemented in a limited number of Java EE containers that provide the Resource Injection function, we cannot inject the Java persistence API into our normal Java help class file. Therefore in this part, we have to use the Java runtime object method to perform database-related actions to check matched username and password from the LogIn table in our sample database. We can include these database-related actions into this Java help class file.

Right click on our project **JavaWebDBJSPSQL** from the **Projects** window, and select the **New > Java Class** item from the popup menu to open the `New Java Class` wizard. If you cannot find the **Java Class** item under the **New** menu item, go to **Other** item and select the **Java** item from the `Categories` list and the **Java Class** item from the `File Types` list. Click on the **Next** button to open this wizard. On the opened wizard, enter **LogInQuery** into the `Class Name` field, and select **JavaWebDBJSPSQLPackage** from the `Package` combo box, as shown in Fig. 8.58. Click on the **Finish** button to create this help class file.

Before we can do the coding for this help class, we need first to create a dialog box in this project. This dialog box works as a message box to provide possible debug information during the project runs.

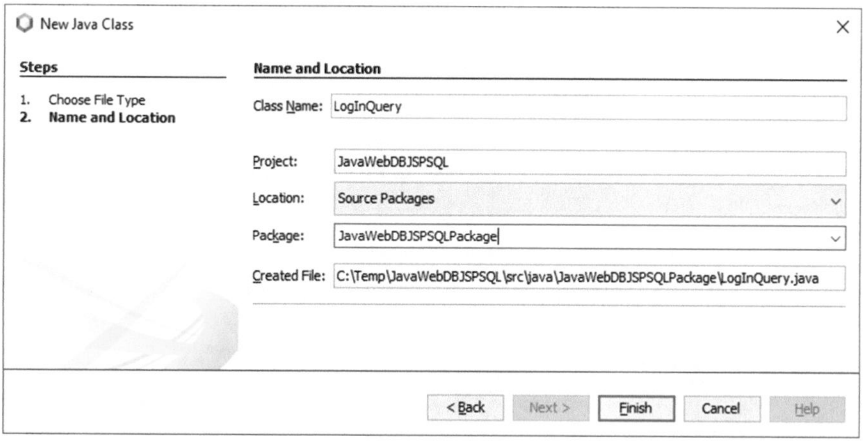

New Java Class

Steps
1. Choose File Type
2. Name and Location

Name and Location
Class Name: LogInQuery
Project: JavaWebDBJSPSQL
Location: Source Packages
Package: JavaWebDBJSPSQLPackage
Created File: C:\Temp\JavaWebDBJSPSQL\src\java\JavaWebDBJSPSQLPackage\LogInQuery.java

< Back | Next > | Finish | Cancel | Help

Fig. 8.58 The completed New Java Class wizard

8.4.3.3 Create a Dialog Box as the Message Box

To create a new dialog box form window, perform the following operations:

1) Right click on our project **JavaWebDBJSPSQL** from the Projects window, and select the **New > Other** item from the popup menu to open the **New File** wizard. Select the **Swing GUI Forms** from the `Categories` list and **OK/Cancel Dialog Sample Form** item from the `File Types` list. Click on the **Next** button to open a new dialog box form.
2) Enter **MsgDialog** into the `Class Name` field, and select the **JavaWebDBJSPSQLPackage** from the `Package` field. Your finished **New Dialog Form** wizard should match one that is shown in Fig. 8.59. Click on the **Finish** button to create this new dialog box.
3) A new Java dialog box class file **MsgDialog.java** is created and located under the **JavaWebDBJSPSQLPackage** folder in the **Projects** window. Click on the **Design** button to open its dialog form window. Add a label to this dialog form window by dragging a Label control from the Palette window, exactly from the AWT sub-window, and placing it to the dialog form window.
4) Resize this label to an appropriate size, as shown in Fig. 8.60. Right click on this label and select the **Change Variable Name** item from the popup menu to open the `Rename` dialog. Enter **MsgLabel** into the `New Name` field, and click on the **OK** button.
5) Go to the **text** property and remove the default text **label1** for this label.

Now click on the **Source** button to open the code window for this dialog box, and we need to add some codes to this class to enable it to display some necessary messages as the project runs.

On the opened code window, add the codes that are highlighted in bold and shown in Fig. 8.61.

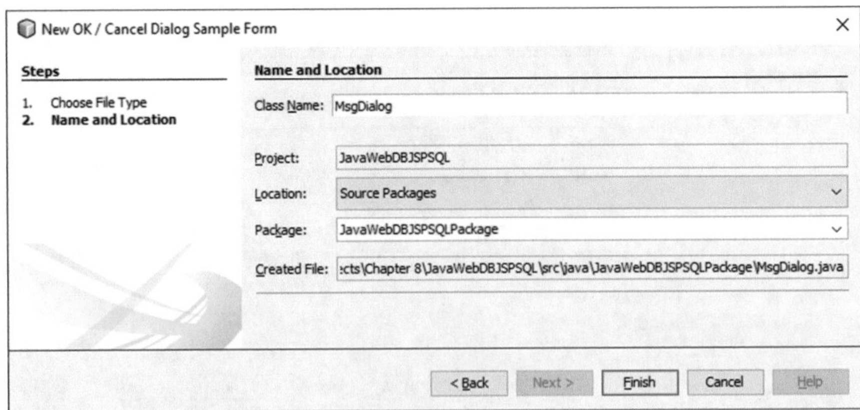

Fig. 8.59 The finished New OK/Cancel Dialog Form wizard

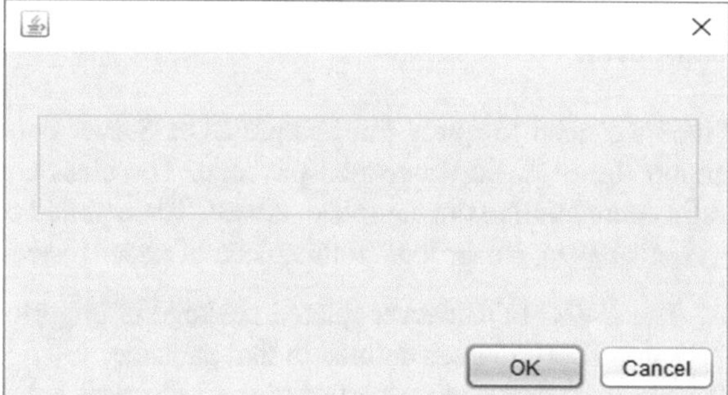

Fig. 8.60 The preview of the dialog box

```
public MsgDialog(java.awt.Frame parent, boolean modal) {
        super(parent, modal);
        initComponents();
        this.setLocationRelativeTo(null);
 }
public void setMessage(String  msg){
    MsgLabel.setText(msg);
}
```

Fig. 8.61 The added codes to the MsgDialog.java class

The **setLocationRelativeTo(null)** instruction is used to set this dialog box at the center of the screen as the project runs. The method **setMessage()** is used to set up a user message by calling the **setText()** method.

Now we have finished creating and building our dialog box form, and let's begin to do the coding for our help class file.

8.4.3.4 Develop the Codes for the Help Class File

Double click on this help class **LogInQuery.java** from the **Projects** window to open its code window. Perform the following operations to complete the coding process for this class:

1) Import the SQL Server-related package, and create the constructor of this class.
2) Build the codes for the **checkLogIn()** method to access and query the LogIn table.
3) Build the codes for the **CloseDBConnection()** method to close the connection to our sample database when this login query is complete.

Let's do these one by one.

8.4.3.4.1 Import SQL Server-Related Package and Create the Class Constructor

Since we need to query our sample SQL Server database, therefore we need to import the SQL Server-related package. The class constructor is used to build a valid connection to our sample database. The detailed codes are shown in Fig. 8.62.

Let's have a closer look at this piece of codes to see how it works.

A. The JDBC SQL Server-related package is imported first since we need to use some JDBC classes defined in that package.
B. Some attributes or properties of this help class are defined first inside this class, which include two private String properties **user_name** and **pass_word**, a class level connection variable **con**, and a dialog box that is used to display some debug information.
C. Inside the class constructor, a **try….catch** block is used to load the JDBC SQL Server driver, which is a type IV JDBC driver. Refer to Sect. 6.3.3.3 in Chap. 6 to get more detailed information about this driver name.
D. The **catch** block is used to collect any possible exceptions that occurred during this driver loading process.
E. The JDBC SQL Server URL is assigned to the local variable **url**. Refer to Sect. 6.3.3.3.1 in Chap. 6 to get more detailed information about this URL.
F. The **getConnection()** method that is embedded in a **try** block is executed to establish this database connection.
G. The **catch** block is used to collect any possible exceptions that occurred during this database connection process.

```
  package JavaWebDBJSPSQLPackage;
A import java.sql.*;
  public class LogInQuery {
B    String user_name;
     String pass_word;
     static Connection con;
     MsgDialog msgDlg = new MsgDialog(new javax.swing.JFrame(), true);
     public LogInQuery() {
C       try {
              Class.forName("com.microsoft.sqlserver.jdbc.SQLServerDriver");
          }
D         catch (Exception e) {
              msgDlg.setMessage("Class not found exception!" + e.getMessage());
              msgDlg.setVisible(true);
          }
E         String url = "jdbc:sqlserver://localhost\\SQL2019EXPRESS:5000;databaseName=CSE_DEPT;";
F         try {
                con = DriverManager.getConnection(url,"SMART","Happy2020");
          }
G         catch (SQLException e) {
              msgDlg.setMessage("Could not connect!" + e.getMessage());
              msgDlg.setVisible(true);
              e.printStackTrace();
          }
     }
     .........
```

Fig. 8.62 The codes of the class constructor

Now let's build the codes for our two user-defined methods, the **checkLogIn()** and **CloseDBConnection()**. First let's start with the **checkLogIn()** method to try to query the LogIn table to find a match username and password pair.

8.4.3.4.2 Build the Codes for the checkLogIn() Method

The function of this method is to query the LogIn table in our sample database to try to find a matched username and password pair based on the username and password entered by the user from the **LogIn.jsp** page. A "**Matched**" string will be returned to the **LogInQuery.jsp** page if a matched username and password pair is found. Otherwise, an "**Unmatched**" string is returned. Based on this returned string, the **LogInQuery.jsp** will determine the next page to be opened. If a matched pair has been found, the **Selection.jsp** page will be displayed to allow users to select different information item to access and query different table in our sample database. Otherwise, an error message will be displayed to indicate that this login process failed since no matched login information can be found from our sample database.

In the opened code window of the help class **LogInQuery.java**, enter the codes that are shown in Fig. 8.63 under the class constructor, and make it the body of our **checkLogIn()** method.

Let's have a closer look at this piece of codes to see how it works.

A. The query string, which is a standard SQL statement, is created first with the actual column names as the query columns. The positional parameters are used for both username and password dynamic inputs.
B. Starting from a **try** block, the **prepareStatement()** method is called to create a PreparedStatement object **pstmt**.
C. The setter method is used to set two positional parameters in the positional order.

```
    public String checkLogIn(String uname, String pword) {
A       String query = "SELECT user_name, pass_word FROM LogIn " +
                       "WHERE user_name = ? AND pass_word = ?";
        try{
B           PreparedStatement pstmt = con.prepareStatement(query);
C           pstmt.setString(1, uname);
            pstmt.setString(2, pword);

D           ResultSet rs = pstmt.executeQuery();
E           while (rs.next()){
              user_name = rs.getString(1);
              pass_word = rs.getString(2);
            }
        }
F       catch (SQLException e) {
          msgDlg.setMessage("Error in Statement! " + e.getMessage());
          msgDlg.setVisible(true);
        }
G       if (user_name.equals(uname) && pass_word.equals(pword))
           return "Matched";
H       else
           return "Nomatched";
    }
```

Fig. 8.63 The codes for the checkLogIn() method

D. The **executeQuery()** method is executed to perform this query, and the returned result is assigned to the ResultSet object **rs**.
E. A **while** loop is used to pick up any possible matched username and password. In fact, only one row is returned, and therefore this loop can run only one time. The **getString()** method is used to pick up the queried username and password. The retuned username and password are assigned to two properties, **user_name** and **pass_word**, respectively.
F. The **catch** block is used to collect any possible exceptions that occurred during this database query process.
G. If a matched username/password pair is found, a "**Matched**" string will be returned to the **LogInQuery.jsp** page.
H. Otherwise, an "**Unmatched**" string is returned to indicate that this login query failed.

Next let's build the codes for the **CloseDBConnection()** method.

8.4.3.4.3 Build the Codes for the CloseDBConnection() Method

This method is necessary when a data query is finished and no more data actions are needed for a database application. A possible running error may be encountered if one did not disconnect the established connection to a target database and exit the project.

On the opened code window of the help class **LogInQuery.java**, enter the codes that are shown in Fig. 8.64 under the **checkLogIn()** method to create our **CloseDBConnection()** method.

Let's have a closer look at this piece of codes to see how it works.

A. A **try** block is used to handle this database disconnection function. First we need to check whether a valid connection object existed, which means that the database is still being connected. The **isClosed()** method is executed to do this

```
  public void CloseDBConnection()
  {
A       try{
           if (con != null)
              con.close();
B       }catch (SQLException e) {
           msgDlg.setMessage("Error in close the DB! " + e.getMessage());
           msgDlg.setVisible(true);
        }
  }
```

Fig. 8.64 The codes for the CloseDBConnection() method

checking. A `false` will be returned if a valid connection object existed, which means that the database is still being connected. In that case, the **close()** method is called to disconnect this connection.

B. The **catch** block is used to collect any possible exceptions that occurred during this disconnection process.

Now we have finished all coding development for this login process.

Now we are ready to build and run our Web project to test the login function using the **LogIn.jsp**, **LogInQuery.jsp** and the help class file **LogInQuery.java**.

Click on the **Clean and Build Main Project** button to build our project. Then right click on the **LogIn.jsp** file from the **Projects** window, and select **Compile File** item from the popup menu to compile our Web pages. Right click on the **LogIn.jsp** page again, and select the **Run File** item from the popup menu to run our project.

If the HTTP Port of the Tomcat server **8080** has been occupied by some other devices and the page cannot be opened, refer to Appendix I to fix this Port number issue.

As the **LogIn.jsp** is displayed, enter a valid username and password, such as **jhenry** and **test**, into the associated fields, as shown in Fig. 8.65.

Click on the **LogIn** button to call the **checkLogIn()** method to perform the login query to find a matched username and password pair. The **Selection.jsp** page is displayed to indicate that this login process is successful and a matched username and password has been found, as shown in Fig. 8.66.

Our login process using the JSP and help class file is successful.

When you run this **LogIn.jsp** file, a possible bug you may encounter is the database connection error. In that case, you need to open the **SQL Server 2019 Configuration Manager** and open the **SQL Server Services** wizard to start the

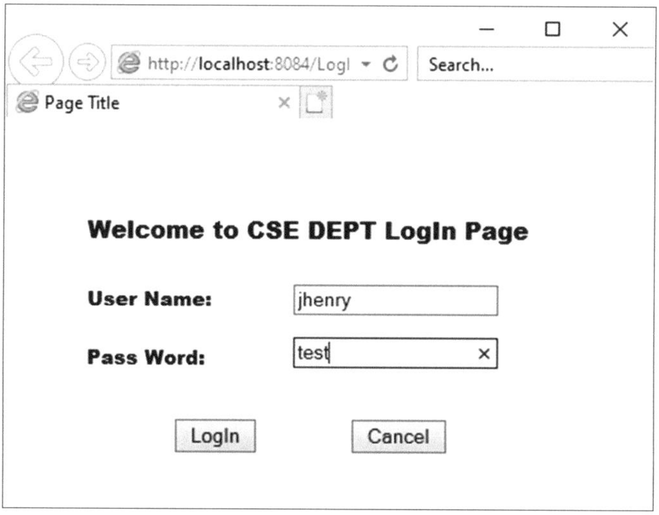

Fig. 8.65 The displayed LogIn.jsp page

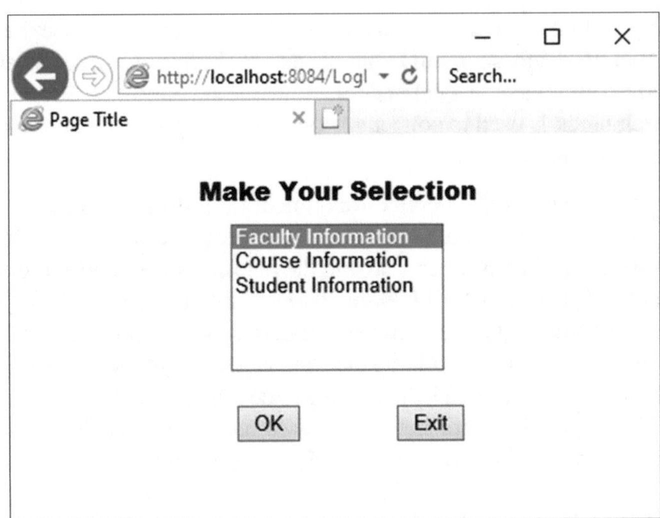

Fig. 8.66 The successful page – Selection.jsp page

server **SQL2019EXPRESS** if it is stopped. Go to **Start > All Programs > Microsoft SQL Server 2019** to find and open that Manager.

Next let's build and code for the Selection.jsp page. As we mentioned, this page can be considered as the control page, and it will direct users to the different pages to perform the different database query functions based on the users' choices.

8.4.4 Develop the Codes for the Selection Page

To handle the users' input and direct to the different target pages based on the users' input, we still want to use the Model-View-Controller (MVC) mode to build this page. We can use the **Selection.jsp** page as a **view** to display the input and output and create another JSP page **SelectionProcess.jsp** as the **Model** and **Controller** to process the users' input and direct to the target page.

Of course, you can combine the MVC mode together to perform displaying and processing page at a single JSP page file. However, you need to add a hidden field to the page and use that hidden field as an identifier to indicate whether the page has been submitted or not. That will make the **Selection.jsp** page complex in the coding process. We divide this page building process into two steps: modify the **Selection.jsp** page and create the **SelectionProcess.jsp** page. Let's first perform some necessary modifications to the **Selection.jsp** page.

Launch the NetBeans IDE, and open the **Selection.jsp** page by double clicking on it from the **Projects** window, and perform the modifications shown in Fig. 8.67 to this page. All modifications have been highlighted in bold.

Let's have a closer look at these modifications to see how they work.

```
  .........
  <div style='position:absolute;width:10.-2040in;height:2.047in'>
  <![if !pub]>
A <form method=post action=".\SelectionProcess.jsp">
  .........
  <input type=submit value=OK v:shapes="_x0000_s1028">
  .........
B <input type=button value=Exit onclick="self.close()"  v:shapes="_x0000_s1029">
  <![if !pub]></span><![endif]><![if !pub]>
  </form>
  .........
```

Fig. 8.67 The coding modifications to the Selection.jsp page

```
  <html>
    <head>
      <meta http-equiv="Content-Type" content="text/html; charset=UTF-8">
      <title>Selection Process Page</title>
    </head>
    <body>
A    <%@page language="java" %>
     <%
B     String nextPage = null;
C     String userSel = request.getParameter("ListSelection");
D     if (userSel.equals("Faculty Information"))
        nextPage = "Faculty.jsp";
      else if (userSel.equals("Course Information"))
        nextPage = "Course.jsp";
      else
        nextPage = "Student.jsp";
     %>
E    <jsp:forward  page = "<%=nextPage%>" />
    </body>
  </html>
```

Fig. 8.68 The codes for the SelectionProcess.jsp page

A. An **action** attribute is added to the `Form` tag, and the destination of this action is the **SelectionProcess.jsp** page. The '.\' operator is used to indicate to the Web controller that the next page, **SelectionProcess.jsp**, is located at the current folder.
B. The type of the second button, **Exit**, is changed from the **submit** to the **button** since we do not want to submit any form data to the next page when this button is clicked. Instead, we want a system method, **self.close()**, to be executed as this button is clicked to exit our project. Therefore an **onclick** attribute is used to direct the control to this method when this button is clicked.

Now let's create the selection process page **SelectionProcess.jsp**.

Open our project **JavaWebDBJSPSQL** from the **Projects** window. Perform the following operations to create this page:

1) Right click on our project **JavaWebDBJSPSQL** from the **Projects** window, and select the **New > JSP** item from the popup menu. If you cannot find the **JSP** item from the popup menu, go to the **Other** item to open the **New File** wizard. Select the **Web** from the **Categories** list and **JSP** from the **File Types** list to do this.

2) On the opened **New JSP File** wizard, enter **SelectionProcess** into the **File Name** field, and click on the **Finish** button.

Now let's develop the codes for this page. Double click on our new created page **SelectionProcess.jsp** from the **Projects** window to open its code window. On the opened code window, perform the modifications shown in Fig. 8.68 to this page. All modification parts have been highlighted in bold.

Let's have a closer look at this piece of codes to see how it works.

A. A JSP directive tag is used to indicate that this page uses the Java language, and it is a JSP file.
B. A local string variable **nextPage** is declared first. This variable is used to hold the URL of the next page, which we will use later to direct the control to the associated page.
C. The **getParameter()** method is used to pick up the selected item by the user from the selection list in the **Selection.jsp** page. The argument of the **getParameter()** method is the name of the selection list in the **Selection.jsp** page. The selected item is then assigned to another local string variable **userSel**.
D. An **if** selection structure is used to check the user's selection and assign the associated next page to the local variable **nextPage**.
E. Finally a JSP forward directive is used to direct the program to the next page.

Now we can build and run this page to test its function.

Click on the **Clean and Build Main Project** button to compile and build our project. First right click on the **Selection.jsp** page from the **Projects** window, and select the **Compile File** item to compile it, and then right click on the **Selection.jsp**

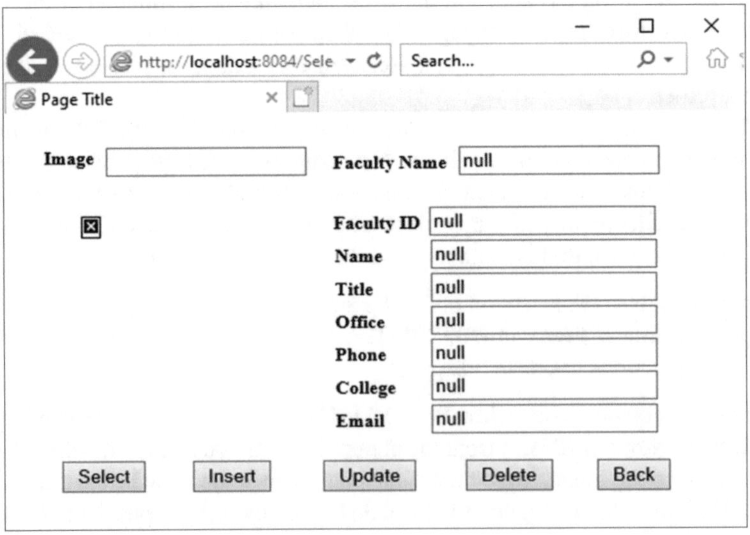

Fig. 8.69 The running status of the Faculty.jsp page

page again to select the **Run File** item from the popup menu to run the project. The **Selection.jsp** is displayed, as shown in Fig. 8.66, when the project runs.

Select a desired item, such as **Faculty Information**, from the Selection listbox, and click on the **OK** button. You can find that the **Faculty.jsp** page is displayed as shown in Fig. 8.69. You can try to select other item from the listbox to open other related pages.

Click on the **Exit** button to terminate our project.

Our Selection page is successful!

8.4.5 Query the Faculty Table Using JavaServer Pages and JSP Implicit Session Object

In this section, we will discuss how to access and query data from the **Faculty** table in our sample database using the JavaServer Pages and JSP implicit session object.

In Sect. 8.1.4, we have provided a detailed discussion about how to use the JSP implicit session object to query our **Faculty** table. In this part, we will build a real project to perform this data query using this object. We divide this discussion into the following three parts:

1) Modify the **Faculty.jsp** page, and use it as a view.
2) Create a new **FacultyProcess.jsp** page, and use it as a model and controller page.
3) Create a help class file **FacultyQuery.java** to handle data query and related business logics.

First let's modify our view class, **Fcaulty.jsp** page.

8.4.5.1 Modify the Faculty.jsp Page

The **Faculty.jsp** page works as a view to provide the displaying function for input and output. We need to modify this page to enable it to forward the user's inputs to the model and controller page and, furthermore, to call the help class to process our data query. Also this page needs to return to the **Selection.jsp** page if the user clicks on the **Back** button on this page.

Open this page by double clicking on it from the **Projects** window, and perform the modifications shown in Fig. 8.70 to this page. All modified coding parts have been highlighted in bold.

Let's have a closer look at this piece of modified codes to see how it works.

A. An **action** attribute is added to the Form tag to forward all information collected from this page to the model and controller page **FcaultyProcess.jsp** that will call our help class file **FacultyQuery.java** to perform the faculty data query process.

```
A  <form method=post action=".\FacultyProcess.jsp">
   .........
   <v:imagedata src="" o:title="&lt;EMPTY&gt;"/><v:shadow color="#ccc [4]"/>
   .........
   left:47px;top:67px;width:154px;height:166px'><img width=154 height=166
B  src="<%=session.getAttribute("facultyImage") %>" v:shapes="_x0000_s1027"></span><![endif]>
   ..........
   <input name=FacultyNameField maxlength=255 size=18
C   value="<%=session.getAttribute("facultyName") %>" type=text v:shapes="_x0000_s1029">
   .........
   <input name=FacultyIDField maxlength=255 size=21
D   value="<%=session.getAttribute("facultyId") %>"  type=text v:shapes="_x0000_s1031">
   .........
   <input name=NameField maxlength=255 size=21
E   value="<%=session.getAttribute("facultyName") %>"  type=text v:shapes="_x0000_s1033">
   .........
   <input name=TitleField maxlength=255 size=21
F   value="<%=session.getAttribute("title") %>"   type=text v:shapes="_x0000_s1035">
   .........
   <input name=OfficeField maxlength=255 size=21
G   value="<%=session.getAttribute("office") %>"   type=text v:shapes="_x0000_s1037">
   .........
   <input name=PhoneField maxlength=255 size=21
H   value="<%=session.getAttribute("phone") %>"  type=text v:shapes="_x0000_s1039">
   .........
   <input name=CollegeField maxlength=255 size=21
I   value="<%=session.getAttribute("college") %>"  type=text v:shapes="_x0000_s1041">
   .........
   <input name=EmailField maxlength=255 size=21
J   value="<%=session.getAttribute("email") %>"  type=text v:shapes="_x0000_s1043">
   .........
K  <input type=submit value=Select name="Select" v:shapes="_x0000_s1044">
   .........
L  <input type=submit value=Insert name="Insert" v:shapes="_x0000_s1045">
   .........
M  <input type=submit value=Update name="Update" v:shapes="_x0000_s1046">
   .........
N  <input type=submit value=Delete name="Delete" v:shapes="_x0000_s1047">
   .........
O  <input type=submit value=Back name="Back" v:shapes="_x0000_s1048">
   .........
```

Fig. 8.70 The modified codes for the Faculty.jsp page

B. In order to select the correct faculty image based on the faculty member selected by the user, we need to assign the **session.getAttribute()** method to the **src** attribute under the **imagedata** tag. The argument of this method should be defined as a property in our help class file, and a method, **getFacultyImage()** defined in that help class file, will be used to select the appropriate faculty image and assign it to this property.

C. Starting from step **C** until step **J**, we use the embedded JSP codes to assign the selected faculty image and queried faculty columns from our **Faculty** table to the **src** and the **value** tags of the associated text field in this **Faculty.jsp** using the **getAttribute()** method of the session class. In this way, as long as the queried faculty row has any change, this modification will be immediately updated and reflected to each text field in our **Faculty.jsp** page. Thus, a direct connection or binding between the text fields in our **Faculty.jsp** page and the queried Faculty columns in our help class is established.

K. From steps **K** to **O**, a **name** attribute is added into each **Submit** button tag. This attribute is very important since we need to use it to identify each submit button in the next page, our model and controller page, **FacultyProcess.jsp**, using the **getParameter()** method of the **request** object to direct the control to the different pages to handle different data query and data manipulation actions to the **Faculty** table in our sample SQL Server database **CSE_DEPT**.

Now let's take a look at our model and controller page **FacultyProcess.jsp**.

8.4.5.2 Create the FacultyProcess.jsp Page

The purpose of this page is to direct the control to the different help class files based on the button clicked by the user from the **Faculty.jsp** page. The following help class files will be triggered and executed based on the button clicked by the user from the **Faculty.jsp** page:

1) If the user selected and clicked the **Select** button, the control will be directed to the faculty data query help class file **FacultyQuery.java** to perform the faculty record query function.
2) If the user clicked the **Insert** button, the control will be directed to the faculty data insertion help class file **FacultyInsertBean.java** to do the faculty record insertion.
3) If the user clicked the **Update** or **Delete** button, the control will be directed to the faculty record updating and deleting help class file **FacultyUpdateDeleteBean.java** to perform the associated data manipulations.
4) If the user selected and clicked the **Back** button, the control will be returned to the **Selection.jsp** page to enable users to perform other information query operations.

Now let's create this **FacultyProcess.jsp** page.

Right click on our project **JavaWebDBJSPSQL** from the **Projects** window, and select the **New > JSP** item from the popup menu to open the **New JSP File** wizard. Enter **FacultyProcess** into the **File Name** field, and click on the **Finish** button.

Double click on our new created **FacultyProcess.jsp** page from the **Projects** window, exactly under the **Web Pages** folder, to open this page. Enter the codes shown in Fig. 8.71 into this page. The new entered codes have been highlighted in bold.

Now let's have a close look at these codes to see how they work.

A. You can embed any import directory using the JSP directive in a HTML or a JSP file. The format is **<%@ page import="java package" %>**. In this page, we embed one package, **JavaWebDBJSPSQLPackage.*** since we will build our Java help class file **FacultyQuery.java** under that package in the next section.
B. A new instance of our help class **FacultyQuery** that will be created in the next section, **fQuery**, is created since we need to use properties and methods defined in that class to perform faculty record query and faculty image selection functions.

```
A  <%@ page import="JavaWebDBJSPSQLPackage.*" %>
   <html>
     <head>
       <meta http-equiv="Content-Type" content="text/html; charset=UTF-8">
       <title>Faculty Process Page</title>
     </head>
     <body>
      <%
B       FacultyQuery fQuery = new FacultyQuery();
C       if (request.getParameter("Select")!= null) {
          //process the faculty record query
D         String imgPath = "FImages\\";
E         String fname = request.getParameter("FacultyNameField");
F         boolean res = fQuery.QueryFaculty(fname);
          if (!res)
G           response.sendRedirect("Faculty.jsp");
          else {
H           session.setAttribute("facultyId", fQuery.getFacultyID());
            session.setAttribute("facultyName", fQuery.getFacultyName());
            session.setAttribute("office", fQuery.getOffice());
            session.setAttribute("title", fQuery.getTitle());
            session.setAttribute("college", fQuery.getCollege());
            session.setAttribute("phone", fQuery.getPhone());
            session.setAttribute("email", fQuery.getEmail());
          }
I         String fimg = fQuery.getFacultyImage();
J         if (fimg == null) {
            if (request.getParameter("FacultyImageField")!= null)
              session.setAttribute("facultyImage", imgPath + request.getParameter("FacultyImageField"));
K           else
            session.setAttribute("facultyImage", "Default.jpg");
            }
L         else
            session.setAttribute("facultyImage", imgPath + fimg);
M         fQuery.setFacultyImage(null);
N         response.sendRedirect("Faculty.jsp");
          }
O       else if (request.getParameter("Insert")!= null) {
          //process the faculty record insertion
          }
P       else if (request.getParameter("Update")!= null) {
          //process the faculty record updating
          }
Q       else if (request.getParameter("Delete")!= null) {
          //process the faculty record deleting
          }
R       else if (request.getParameter("Back") != null) {
          fQuery.CloseDBConnection();
          response.sendRedirect("Selection.jsp");
          }
      %>
     </body>
   </html>
```

Fig. 8.71 The codes for the FacultyProcess.jsp page

C. The **getParameter()** method defined in the session class is executed to identify which submit button has been clicked by the user in the **Faculty.jsp** page. As you know, totally we have five buttons in the **Faculty.jsp** page. All **Faculty.jsp** form data, including all text fields, image box, and submit buttons, will be submitted to this **FacultyProcess.jsp** page when any of five buttons is clicked. If a button is clicked, the **getParameter()** method with the name of that clicked button as the argument of this method will return a non-null value. In this way, we can identify which button has been clicked. We use a sequence of **if … else if** selection structures to check all five buttons to identify the clicked button.

D. A local folder, **FImages**, is created, and it is used to hold all faculty images to be queried later. This folder is just under our **Web Pages** folder in our project. The purpose of using this folder is to store all faculty image files and make our projects clean and neat.
E. If the **Select** button is clicked by the user, the **getParameter()** method with this button's name as argument will return a non-null value. This means that the user wants to perform a faculty record query from the Faculty table in our sample database. Again, the **getParameter()** method with the name of the faculty name field, **FacultyNameField**, is used to pick up a desired faculty name that is entered by the user from the **Faculty.jsp** page. The picked up faculty name is assigned to a local String variable **fname**.
F. Then the method **QueryFaculty()** defined in the help class file **FacultyQuery.java** will be called to execute this faculty data query based on the selected faculty name **fname** obtained from step **E** above.
G. If the **QueryFaculty()** method is executed unsuccessfully, which means that no matched faculty record has been found, a false is returned to indicate this situation. In this case, we need to re-open the **Faculty.jsp** page to enable the user to re-enter new faculty data to do another query using the **sendRedirect()** method defined in the `response` class.
H. Otherwise a matched faculty record has been found, and the query is successful. The **setAttribute()** method defined in the session class is used to set up all properties defined in the help class file using the associated getter methods in that class.
I. The **getFacultyImage()** method, which is defined in the help class file **FacultyQuery.java** that will be developed in the next section, is executed to pick up the correct faculty image file, exactly the correct name of the faculty image file.
J. If the **getFacultyImage()** method returns a null, which means that no matched faculty image has been found, then we will continue to check whether the user has entered a new faculty image in the **FacultyImageField** textbox in the **Faculty.jsp** page, and this is a normal case if the user wants to insert a new faculty record into the Faculty table with a new faculty image. If the **getParameter()** method returns a non-null value, which means that the user did enter a new faculty image, exactly the name of a new faculty image, into that field, in that case, we need to set up the **facultyImage** property with that name and later on display that new faculty image based on that property.
K. Otherwise, it means that no matched faculty image has been found and the user did not want to enter a new faculty image. In that case, we need to display a default faculty image by assigning the name of that default faculty image to the **facultyImage** property.
L. If the **getFacultyImage()** method returns a non-null value, which means that a matched faculty image's name has been found, the **setAttribute()** method is executed to set up the **facultyImage** property with that faculty image's name attached with the image path, **FImages**, which is declared in step **D**, to get a complete faculty image name.

M. The **setFacultyImage()** method is executed to clean up the content of the property of the help class, **facultyImage**, which is a static String variable and works as a global variable to store the current faculty image's name. When a new faculty image is inserted or updated with a faculty record insertion or updating, the name of that new faculty image will be assigned to the global variable facultyImage. To avoid displaying the same new faculty image in multiple times, we need to clean up this global variable each time when a faculty record has been retrieved and displayed.
N. The **sendRedirect()** method defined in the **response** class is executed to redisplay the **Fcaulty.jsp** page with the queried result on that page.
O. If the **getParameter("Insert")** method returns a non-null value, which means that the **Insert** button has been clicked by the user in the **Faculty.jsp** page and the user wants to insert a new faculty record into the Faculty table in our sample database, we will build a Java bean class to handle this faculty data insertion later.
P. Similarly, if the **getParameter("Update")** method returns a non-null value, which means that the **Update** button has been clicked by the user in the **Faculty.jsp** page and the user wants to update an existing faculty record in the Faculty table in our sample database, we will build a Java bean class to handle this faculty data updating action later.
Q. If the **getParameter("Delete")** method returns a non-null value, which means that the **Delete** button has been clicked by the user in the **Faculty.jsp** page and the user wants to delete an existing faculty record from the Faculty table in our sample database, we will build a Java bean class to handle this faculty data deleting action later.
R. If the **getParameter("Back")** method returns a non-null value, which means that the **Back** button has been clicked by the user in the **Faculty.jsp** page and the user wants to return to the **Selection.jsp** page to perform other data query operations, the **CloseDBConnection()** method is firstly executed to close the connection to our sample database, and then the **sendRedirect()** method is called to do this returning function.

Now let's build our Java help class file **FacultyQuery.java** to handle all data query actions, getter methods, class properties, and related business logics.

8.4.5.3 Create the Help Class File FacultyQuery.java

To create our Java help class file **FacultyQuery.java** to handle the faculty record query, right click on our project **JavaWebDBJSPSQL** from the **Projects** window, and select the **New > Java Class** item from the popup menu to open the **New Java Class** wizard. Enter **FacultyQuery** into the **Class Name** field, and select the **JavaWebDBJSPSQLPackage** from the **Package** combo box. Your finished **New Java Class** wizard should match one that is shown in Fig. 8.72. Click on the **Finish** button to create this new Java help class file.

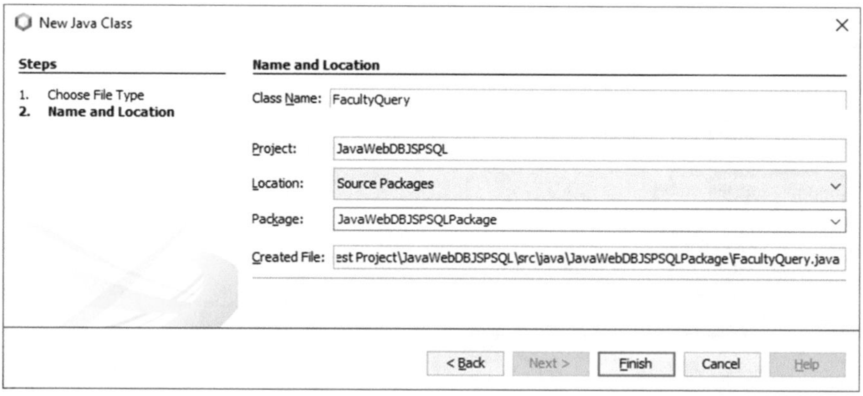

Fig. 8.72 The finished New Java Class wizard

Now let's develop the codes for this new Java help class file. Double click on our new created Java help class file **FacultyQuery.java** from the **Projects** window to open this file, and enter the codes that are shown in Fig. 8.73 into this file. Because of the large size of this piece of codes, we divide this coding process into two parts. The first part is shown in Fig. 8.73, and the second part is shown in Fig. 8.74. The new entered codes have been highlighted in bold.

Let's have a close look at these new added codes in Fig. 8.73 to see how they work.

A. The **java.sql.*** package is imported first since all SQL Server database-related classes and methods are defined in that package.
B. Eight class properties related to the associated columns in the Faculty table in our sample database are declared first. These properties are very important since they are directly mapped to the associated columns in the Faculty table. All of these properties can be accessed by using the associated getter method defined at the bottom of this class.
C. A class-level database connection object is created, and a Dialog object is also created. We will use the latter as a message box to display some debug information during the project runs.
D. A **try…catch** block is used to load the database JDBC driver. The **catch** block is used to track and collect any possible exception during this database driver loading process.
E. The database connection URL is defined. Refer to Sect. 6.3.3.3.1 in Chap. 6 to get more detailed information about this URL definition.
F. Another **try…catch** block is used to connect to our sample SQL Server database with desired username and password. The **catch** block is used to track and collect any possible exception that occurred during this database connection process.
G. The main query method, **QueryFaculty()**, is defined with the selected faculty name as the argument. The SQL query statement is firstly created with the faculty name as the positional dynamic parameter.

```
  package JavaWebDBJSPSQLPackage;
A import java.sql.*;
  public class FacultyQuery {
B    private static String facultyImage = null;
     private String facultyID;
     private String facultyName;
     private String office;
     private String title;
     private String phone;
     private String college;
     private String email;
C    static Connection con;
     MsgDialog msgDlg = new MsgDialog(new javax.swing.JFrame(), true);
  public FacultyQuery() {
D      try {
               Class.forName("com.microsoft.sqlserver.jdbc.SQLServerDriver");
          }
          catch (Exception e) {
              msgDlg.setMessage("Class not found exception!" + e.getMessage());
              msgDlg.setVisible(true);
          }
E        String url = "jdbc:sqlserver://localhost\\SQL2019EXPRESS:5000;databaseName=CSE_DEPT;";
F        try {
              con = DriverManager.getConnection(url,"SMART","Happy2020");
         }
         catch (SQLException e) {
              msgDlg.setMessage("Could not connect!" + e.getMessage());
              msgDlg.setVisible(true);
              e.printStackTrace();
         }
     }
G  public boolean QueryFaculty(String  fname) {
       String query = "SELECT faculty_id, faculty_name, title, office, phone, college, email  FROM Faculty " +
                      "WHERE faculty_name = ?";
H      try{
           PreparedStatement pstmt = con.prepareStatement(query);
I          pstmt.setString(1, fname);
J          ResultSet rs = pstmt.executeQuery();
K          while (rs.next()){
              facultyID = rs.getString(1);
              facultyName = rs.getString(2);
              title = rs.getString(3);
              office = rs.getString(4);
              phone = rs.getString(5);
              college = rs.getString(6);
              email = rs.getString(7);
           }
L          return true;
       }
M      catch (SQLException e) {
          msgDlg.setMessage("Error in Statement! " + e.getMessage());
          msgDlg.setVisible(true);
N         return false;
       }
   }
```

Fig. 8.73 The first part of the codes for the Java help class file

H. Starting from a **try** block, the **prepareStatement()** method is called to create a PreparedStatement object **pstmt**.

I. The setter method is used to set the positional parameter in the positional order.

J. The **executeQuery()** method is executed to perform this query, and the returned result is assigned to the ResultSet object **rs**.

K. A **while** loop is used to pick up a matched faculty record. In fact, only one row is returned, and therefore this loop can run only one time. The **getString()** method is used to pick up each queried column and assign the associated prop-

```
     public String getImage(String f_name) {
A        int maxNumber = 7;
         String  fImage = null;
         String[] fname = { "Ying Bai", "Black Anderson", "Davis Bhalla", "Steve Johnson",
                            "Jenney King", "Alice Brown", "Debby Angles", "Jeff Henry"};
         String[] fimage = { "Bai.jpg", "Anderson.jpg", "Davis.jpg", "Johnson.jpg",
                             "King.jpg", "Brown.jpg", "Angles.jpg", "Henry.jpg"};
B        if (facultyImage != null)
            return  facultyImage;
         else {
C           for (int i=0; i<=maxNumber; i++){
               if (fname[i].equals(f_name)){
                  fImage = fimage[i];
                  break;
               }
            }
D           facultyImage = fImage;
E           return fImage;
         }
      }
F     public void setFacultyImage(String img) {
         facultyImage = img;
      }
G     public void CloseDBConnection()
      {
         try{
            if (con != null)
               con.close();
         }catch (SQLException e)  {
            msgDlg.setMessage("Error in close the DB! " + e.getMessage());
            msgDlg.setVisible(true);
         }
      }
H     public String getFacultyID() {
         return  this.facultyID;
      }
I     public String getFacultyName() {
         return  this.facultyName;
      }
J     public String getOffice() {
         return  this.office;
      }
K     public String getTitle() {
         return  this.title;
      }
L     public String getPhone() {
         return  this.phone;
      }
M     public String getCollege() {
         return  this.college;
      }
N     public String getEmail() {
         return  this.email;
      }
O     public String getFacultyImage() {
         String result = getImage(facultyName);
         if (result != null)
            return this.facultyImage;
         else
            return null;
      }
   }
```

Fig. 8.74 The second part of the codes for the Java help class file

erty defined at the beginning of this help class. The index used for this **getString()** method should be matched to the order of the queried columns in the SQL query statement built in step **G**.

L. A **true** is returned to the **FacultyProcess.jsp** page to indicate that the execution of this query method is successful.
M. The **catch** block is used to collect any possible exception that occurred during this query process.
N. A **false** is returned to the **FacultyProcess.jsp** page to indicate that this query failed.

Now let's handle the second part of the codes of this help class file, which is shown in Fig. 8.74. Let's have a closer look at these codes to see how they work.

A. A local method **getImage()** is defined inside the class file, and it is used to select the matched faculty image and returns the name of the matched faculty image. Some local variables are defined at the beginning of this method, such as the maximum number of faculty images **maxNumber**, the string variable **fImage** that is used to return the faculty image's name, and two string arrays, **fname[]** and **fimage[]**, which contain all eight faculty members and the associated faculty images' names.
B. If the global variable **facultyImage** is not null, which means that a new faculty image has been assigned to this global variable when an insertion or an updating of a new faculty record has been executed, this new image's name will be returned.
C. Otherwise a **for** loop is used to check all eight faculty members to try to find the matched faculty name and the associated faculty image's name. If a matched faculty name were found, the loop is broken, and the associated faculty image's name is assigned to the variable **fImage**.
D. Then the matched faculty image's name is assigned to the global variable **facultyImage**, which is a property defined at the beginning of this class.
E. The matched faculty image's name is returned to the calling method.
F. The setter method, **setFacultyImage()**, is used to assign a new faculty image's name to the global variable **facultyImage**. Since we are working in the Web server environment, we need to use this global variable to keep a record for our current faculty image's name.
G. The codes for the **CloseDBConnection()** method are identical with those we discussed in step **Q** in the last section.
H. Starting from step **H**, including steps **I** through **O**, all getter methods are defined, and they are used to pick up all related properties defined at the beginning of this class. A null will be returned from the method **getFacultyImage()** if no matched faculty image's name can be found.

Now we have finished all coding process for the Faculty Information query operations. Before we can run the project to test the function of these codes, we need to store all faculty image files to our project. You can find all faculty image files at the folder **Images\Faculty** under the **Students** folder that is located at the Springer ftp site (refer to Fig. 1.2 in Chap. 1). Perform the following operations to complete this image storage process:

1) Open the Windows Explorer, and locate our project folder **JavaWebDBJSPSQL\web**.
2) Create a new folder **FImages** under above folder, like **JavaWebDBJSPSQL\web**.
3) Go to the Springer ftp site shown above, and copy all faculty images from the **Images\Faculty** folder and paste them into our created folder **FImages**.

The reason we store all faculty files in this **FImages** folder is that we can directly use those images' names to access and pick them up as the project runs. Also we can separate all project files under the **web** folder from those image files to keep our project clean and neat.

Now we can build and run our project to test its functions. Click on the **Clean and Build Main Project** button to build our project. Then right click on the **LogIn.jsp** file from the **Projects** window, and select the **Run File** item to run our project.

In the opened **LogIn** page, enter an appropriate username and password, such as **jhenry** and **test**, and click on the **LogIn** button to perform the login process. If the login process is successful, select the **Faculty Information** from the **Selection.jsp** page to open the **Faculty.jsp** page. On the opened **Faculty.jsp** page, enter a desired faculty name, such as **Ying Bai**, into the **Faculty Name** field, and click on the **Select** button to try to query the detailed information for the selected faculty member.

If a matched faculty record is found, the detailed information about that faculty with a faculty image is displayed in seven fields and the Image box, as shown in Fig. 8.75.

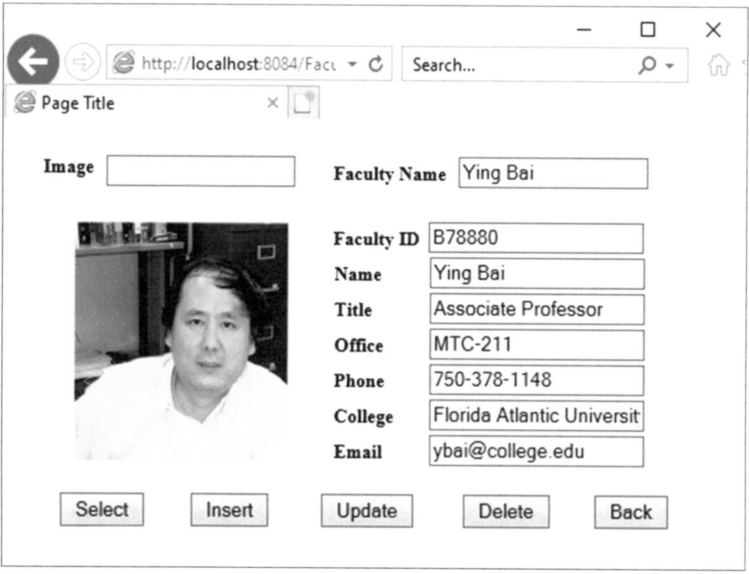

Fig. 8.75 The running result of the Faculty.jsp page

You can try to enter other desired faculty names, such as **Jenney King** or **Davis Bhalla**, into the **Faculty Name** field to query the information related to those faculty members.

Click on the **Back** and then **Exit** button on the **Selection.jsp** page to terminate our Web project.

Our Web project and faculty information query are successful!

A complete Web application project **JavaWebDBJSPSQL** that includes the login, selection, and faculty information query processes can be found at the folder **Class DB Projects\Chapter 8** under the **Students** folder in the Springer ftp site (refer to Fig. 1.2 in Chap. 1).

Next let's handle to insert new records into the **Faculty** table using JavaServer Pages and Java beans technologies.

8.5 Build Java Web Project to Manipulate SQL Server Database

Now let's take care of manipulating data against our SQL Server database by using different methodologies, which include inserting, updating, and deleting records from our sample database **CSE_DEPT** via our Web application project.

First let's take care of inserting a new record into our **Faculty** table in our sample database **CSE_DEPT**. To do that, we need to create a new Web project **JavaWebDBJSPSQL_Insert**. In order to save time and space, we can copy and modify our current project **JavaWebDBJSPSQL** to make it as our new project.

Perform the following operational steps to create this new project:

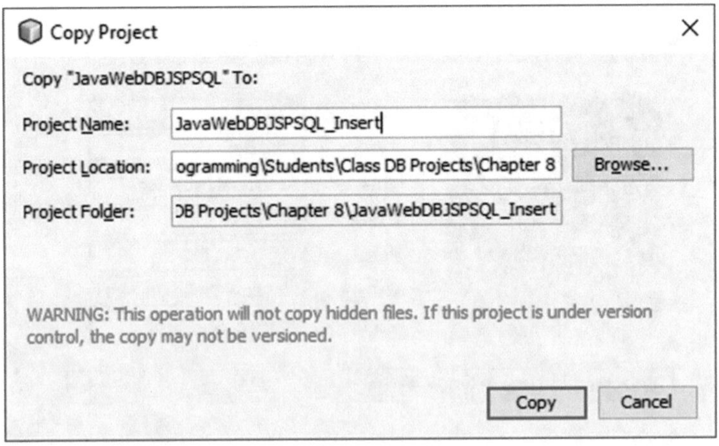

Fig. 8.76 The opened Copy Project wizard

1) In the **Projects** window, right click on our project **JavaWebDBJSPSQL**, and select the **Copy** item from the popup menu to open the **Copy Project** wizard, as shown in Fig. 8.76.
2) Enter our new project name, **JavaWebDBJSPSQL_Insert**, into the **Project Name** box, and browse to the default project folder, **C:\Class DB Projects\Chapter 8**, as the **Project Location**, which is shown in Fig. 8.76, and click on the **Copy** button.

A new project **JavaWebDBJSPSQL_Insert** is generated and added into our **Projects** window. Next let's build the codes for the related pages to insert some new records into our database.

8.5.1 Modify the Faculty.jsp Page by Adding A File Selection Function

In order to insert a new faculty record, especially to insert a new faculty image, into our sample database, a File Selection function should be added into this **Faculty.jsp** page to provide a way to enable users to select a desired faculty image for the new inserted faculty member. Perform the following operational steps to add this function:

1) **On the opened Faculty.jsp page, scroll down along this file until one of input tags,**

```
<input name=FacultyImageField maxlength=255 size=18 value="" type=text
v:shapes="_x0000_s1026">
```

is **found**, which should be around line 384.

2) **Enter the following tag located just above the tag shown above.**

```
<input name=Faculty_Image maxlength=50 size=4 value="" type=file
v:shapes="_x0000_s1026">
```

Your modified **Faculty.jsp** page should match one that is shown in Fig. 8.77. The new added tag part has been highlighted in bold.

```
<form method=post action=".\FacultyProcess.jsp">
.........
</span><![endif]><!--[if gte vml 1]><v:shapetype id="_x0000_t201" coordsize="21600,21600"
 o:spt="201" path="m,l,21600r21600,l21600,xe">
 <span style='position:absolute;top:18.0pt; left:54.0pt;z-index:2'><![endif]>

A  <input name=Faculty_Image maxlength=50 size=4 value="" type=file
   v:shapes="_x0000_s1026">

<input name=FacultyImageField maxlength=255 size=18 value="" type=text
v:shapes="_x0000_s1026">
............
```

Fig. 8.77 The modified codes for the Faculty.jsp page

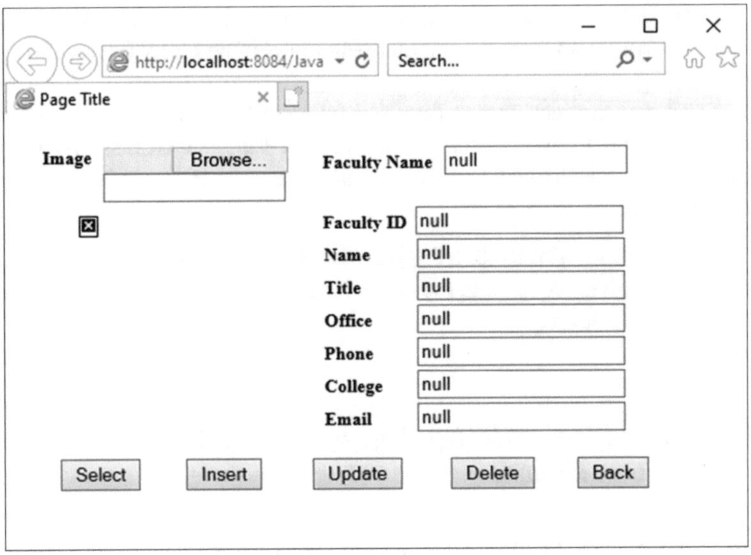

Fig. 8.78 The running result of modified Faculty.jsp page

Now go to the **Projects** window and right click on our modified **Faculty.jsp** file, and click on the **Compile File** item to compile this file. Then right click on this file, and select the **Run File** item to run this page. The running result is shown in Fig. 8.78. One File Selection tag is added on the top of **Faculty Image** TextField, which can be used to select a faculty image to be inserted.

Next we can begin our code developments for this data insertion action.

8.5.2 Insert New Records to the Faculty Table Using JavaServer Pages and Java Beans

To use the JavaServer Pages and Java bean techniques to perform inserting new record into the Faculty table, we need to perform the following operations:

1) Modify the Java help class file **FacultyQuery.java** to make it our Java bean file **FacultyInsertBean.java** to handle the new faculty record insertion actions.
2) Modify the model controller page **FacultyProcess.jsp** to handle the faculty data collection and insertion operations.

First let's modify the Java help class file **FacultyQuery.java** to make it our new Java bean class **FacultyInsertBean.java** to handle the new faculty record insertion actions.

8.5.2.1 Create a New Java Help Class File FacultyInsertBean.java

To save time and space, we can modify an existing class file **FacultyQuery.java** and make it as our new class file **FacultyInsertBean.java**. Perform the following operational steps to complete this modification and creation:

1) Open the Windows Explorer, and browse to our new project **JavaWebDBJSPSQL_Insert**, which is located at the folder **C:\Class DB Projects\Chapter 8**.
2) Expand this project subfolder to **src > java>JavaWebDBJSPSQLPackage**, and then you can find our class file **FacultyQuery.java**.
3) Copy and paste this file in the same folder, and rename the copied file to our new class file **FacultyInsertBean.java**.

Now open the NetBeans IDE and our new project **JavaWebDBJSPSQL_Insert** as well as our class file **FacultyInsertBean.java** from the **Projects** window, exactly from our package **JavaWebDBJSPSQLPackage**. Perform the following modifications to this file to make it our new Java bean class:

```
A   package JavaWebDBJSPSQLPackage;
    import java.io.File;
    import java.io.FileInputStream;
    import java.io.FileNotFoundException;
    import java.io.InputStream;
    import java.sql.*;
    import java.util.logging.Level;
    import java.util.logging.Logger;
B   public int InsertFaculty(String[]  newFaculty) {
C         int  numInsert = 0;
          FileInputStream fis = null;
          File fimage= new File(newFaculty[7]);

D         String  InsertQuery = "INSERT  INTO  Faculty (faculty_id,  faculty_name,  title,  office,  phone, " +
                                "college,  email,  fimage)  VALUES  (?, ?, ?, ?, ?, ?, ?, ?)";
E         try{
              PreparedStatement pstmt = con.prepareStatement(InsertQuery);
F             pstmt.setString(1, newFaculty[0]);
              pstmt.setString(2, newFaculty[1]);
              pstmt.setString(3, newFaculty[2]);
              pstmt.setString(4, newFaculty[3]);
              pstmt.setString(5, newFaculty[4]);
              pstmt.setString(6, newFaculty[5]);
              pstmt.setString(7, newFaculty[6]);
G             try {
                    fis = new FileInputStream(fimage);
            } catch (FileNotFoundException ex) {
               Logger.getLogger(FacultyInsertBean.class.getName()).log(Level.SEVERE, null, ex);
            }
H             pstmt.setBinaryStream(8, (InputStream)fis, (int)(fimage.length()));
I             numInsert = pstmt.executeUpdate();
          }
J         catch (SQLException e) {
             msgDlg.setMessage("Error in Insert Statement! " + e.getMessage());
             msgDlg.setVisible(true);
          }
K         return numInsert;
    }
```

Fig. 8.79 The codes for the new created method InsertFaculty()

1) Change the class name and the constructor's name from the **FacultyQuery** to the **FacultyInsertBean**.
2) Remove the **QueryFaculty()** method and the **getImage()** method.
3) Remove the **getFacultyImage()**, **setFacultyImage()** method and the **facultyImage** property.
4) Create a new method **InsertFaculty()**, and enter the codes shown in Fig. 8.79 into this method.

Let's have a close look at the codes for this method to see how they work.

A. Some useful Java libraries are imported at the top of this class since we need to use some components defined in those libraries.
B. A new **InsertFaculty()** method is created with a String array as the argument of this method. The String array contains all eight pieces of new faculty information.
C. A local integer variable **numInsert** is used to hold the returned data insertion result, and regularly it is equal to the number of records that have been inserted into the Faculty table. A FileInputStream object, **fis**, is also created, and it works as a handler of converting our faculty image to a FileInputStream before it can be written or inserted into our database. A new File object, **fimage**, is declared with the name of our faculty image file as the target for this File object since the String variable, **newFaculty[7]**, contained the name of a selected faculty image to be inserted into the database.
D. The insert string is created with eight positional parameters represented by the question marks in the query string.
E. A **try…catch** block is used to perform this faculty record insertion action. First a PreparedStatement object is created with the query string as the argument.
F. Then seven elements in the String array **newFaculty[]**, which are equivalent to seven pieces of new faculty information, are assigned to seven positional parameters. The point to be noted is that the order of those seven elements must be identical with the order of columns represented in the query string and in the **Faculty** table in our sample database.
G. Another **try…catch** block is used to create a new handler for the converted FileInputStream object with our faculty image as the input.
H. The faculty image is inserted by calling the **setBinaryStream()** method with the handler of our FileInputStream as the source.
I. The **executeUpdate()** method is executed to perform this new record insertion action. The running result, which is equal to the number of records that have been successfully inserted into the Faculty table, is returned and assigned to the local integer variable **numInsert**.
J. The **catch** block is used to track and collect any possible exceptions during this data insertion action.
K. Finally the running result is returned to the calling method in the **FacultyProcess.jsp** page.

Next let's modify the model controller page **FacultyProcess.jsp** to handle the faculty data collection and insertion operations.

8.5.2.2 Modify the FacultyProcess.jsp Page to Handle Faculty Data Collection and Insertion

Double click on the **FacultyProcess.jsp** page from the **Projects** window in our new project, and perform the following modifications to this page to use Java bean **FacultyInsertBean.java** to perform new faculty record insertion actions:

1) Move cursor to the **else if (request.getParameter("Insert")!= null)** block, then type a JSP ending tag, % > under the **else if** statement, and click on the **Enter** key from the keyboard to get a new line under the **else if** block.
2) Open the **Palette** window by going to **Window > IDE Tools > Palette** item. In the opened **Palette** window, browse to the **JSP** tab, drag the **Use Bean** icon, and place it under the JSP ending tag % > .
3) On the opened **Insert Use Bean** dialog, and enter **InsertFaculty** into the **ID** field and **JavaWebDBJSPSQLPackage.FacultyInsertBean** into the **Class** filed. Select the **session** from the **Scope** combo box. Your finished **Insert Use Bean** dialog should match one that is shown in Fig. 8.80. Click on the **OK** button to close this dialog box. A JSP directive that contains the bean id, bean scope, and class is added to this block.
4) Add a JSP directive to set up all properties on the Java bean class **FacultyInsertBean.java** shown below:

```
<jsp:setProperty name="InsertFaculty" property="*" />
```

5) Add an opening JSP directive to start our Java codes to be built below.

The codes related to steps 1–5 above are shown in the top on Fig. 8.81. Add the Java codes shown in steps **A–G** in Fig. 8.81 into this block.

Let's have a closer look at these codes to see how they work.

A. A local integer variable **res** is created, and it is used to hold the running result of executing the **InsertFaculty()** method in the Java bean class **FacultyInsertBean** with the bean id of **InsertFaculty**.

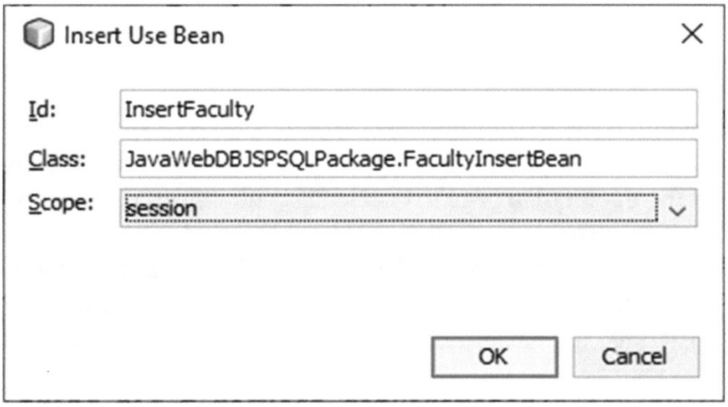

Fig. 8.80 The finished Insert Use Bean dialog box

```
  else if (request.getParameter("Insert")!= null) {
        //process the faculty record insertion
1    %>
2       <jsp:useBean id="InsertFaculty" scope="session"
3                    class="JavaWebDBJSPSQLPackage.FacultyInsertBean" />
4       <jsp:setProperty name="InsertFaculty" property="*" />
5    <%
A      int res = 0;
B      String fid = request.getParameter("FacultyIDField");
       String fname = request.getParameter("NameField");
       String office = request.getParameter("OfficeField");
       String phone = request.getParameter("PhoneField");
       String college = request.getParameter("CollegeField");
       String title = request.getParameter("TitleField");
       String email = request.getParameter("EmailField");
       String fImage = request.getParameter("Faculty_Image");
C      String[] fnew = {fid, fname, title, office, phone, college, email, fImage };
D      res = InsertFaculty.InsertFaculty(fnew);
E      if (res == 0) {
          response.sendRedirect("Faculty.jsp");
         }
F      else {
          request.setAttribute("FacultyIDField", null);
          request.setAttribute("NameField", null);
          request.setAttribute("OfficeField", null);
          request.setAttribute("PhoneField", null);
          request.setAttribute("CollegeField", null);
          request.setAttribute("TitleField", null);
          request.setAttribute("EmailField", null);
G         response.sendRedirect("Faculty.jsp");
         }
H      InsertFaculty.CloseDBConnection();
     }
     %>
```

Fig. 8.81 The modified codes for the Insert block in the FacultyProcess.jsp

B. Eight **getParameter()** methods are used to pick up eight pieces of new inserted faculty information stored in the eight fields in the **Faculty.jsp** page. The collected eight pieces of new faculty information are assigned to eight local String variables.
C. A new String array **fnew** is created, and it is used to hold eight pieces of new faculty information stored in the eight local String variables.
D. The **InsertFaculty()** method defined in our Java bean is executed to insert these eight pieces of faculty information as a new faculty record into the Faculty table. The eight pieces of new faculty information are stored in the String array **fnew** that works as the argument for this method. The running result of this method is returned and assigned to the local integer variable **res**.
E. If the running result is 0, which means that no any record has been inserted into the **Faculty** table and this data insertion action failed, in that case, we need to redisplay the **Faculty.jsp** page to enable users to reinsert that faculty record.
F. If the running result is non-zero, which means that at least one new faculty record has been inserted into the **Faculty** table. We need to clean up all seven fields that contain seven pieces of new inserted faculty information in the **Faculty.jsp** page to enable users to either test this insertion or insert the next faculty record.

G. Also we need to redisplay the **Faculty.jsp** page to enable users to perform the next action.
H. Finally the **CloseDBConnection()** method is called to disconnect to our database.

Prior to building and running this Web application, make sure that the new faculty image to be selected and inserted into our database has been stored in our default project image folder; in this case, it is **C:\Class DB Projects\Chapter 8\JavaWebDBJSPSQL_Insert\web\FImages**.

Now we can build and run our project to test this new faculty record insertion function. Click on the **Clean and Build Main Project** button to perform cleaning up and building our project. Then right click on the **LogIn.jsp** page from the **Projects** window to run our project. Enter the appropriate username and password to finish the login process, and select the **Faculty Information** item from the **Selection.jsp** page to open the **Fcaulty.jsp** page.

First enter a faculty member, such as **Ying Bai**, into the **Faculty Name** box, and click on the **Select** button to query the record for this faculty, then enter seven pieces of information into the associated seven fields as a new faculty record, and click on the **Browse** button on the File Selection box (above the **Image** TextField) to select a desired faculty image, **White.jpg**, which is located at our default project image folder and belongs to the new inserted faculty member, **Susan Bai**. The finished new faculty record is shown in Fig. 8.82.

Click on the **Insert** button to try to insert this new faculty record into the **Faculty** table in our sample database. Immediately you can find that the original faculty information is displayed, which means that this data insertion is successful.

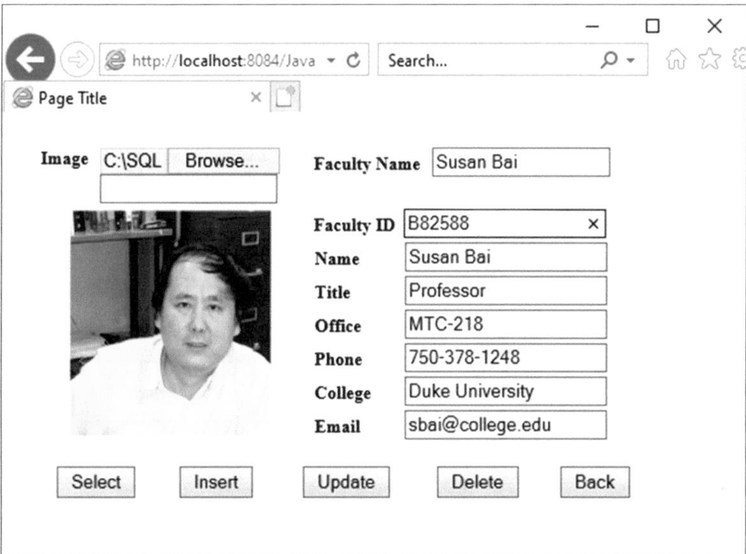

Fig. 8.82 The entered new faculty information

To confirm this insertion, two ways could be used. The first way is to use the **Select** button in the **Faculty.jsp** page to retrieve this new inserted record from the **Faculty** table. To do that, enter **Susan Bai** to the **Faculty Name** field and **White.jpg** into the **Image** TextField, and then click on the **Select** button. You can find that the new inserted record is retrieved and displayed in the seven fields with the new faculty image, as shown in Fig. 8.83. Now click on the **Back** and **Exit** button to terminate our project.

The second way to confirm this data insertion is to open the **Faculty** table by using either the Microsoft SQL Server Management Studio 18 or our connected database **CSE_DEPT** under the **Services** window in the NetBeans IDE. Here we prefer to use the second way to confirm this insertion action.

To use the second way to check this data insertion, first we need to connect to our database. Perform the following operations to do this connection.

1) In the NetBeans IDE with our project opened, open the **Services** window.
2) Right click on the **Databases** folder and select the **New Connection** item.
3) On the opened New Connection Wizard, click on drop-down arrow from the **Driver** combo box, and select the **New Driver** item to open the New JDBC Driver wizard.
4) Click on the **Add** button and browse to our JDBC driver, **sqljdbc41.jar**, which is located at the folder **C:\Program Files\sqljdbc_4.2\enu\jre7**. Select this driver, and click on the **Open** button to return to the New JDBC Driver wizard.

Fig. 8.83 The retrieved new inserted faculty record

5) You can select a desired name for this driver by entering it into the **Name** box, such as **SQL Server 2019**, and click on the **OK** button to return to the New Connection Wizard. Click on the **Next** button to continue.
6) On the opened New Connection Wizard, enter the following credentials into the related boxes as the connection parameters:

   (a) Host: **localhost**
   (b) Port: **5000**
   (c) Database: **CSE_DEPT**
   (d) Instance Name: **SQL2019EXPRESS**
   (e) User Name: **SMART**
   (f) Password: **Happy2020**

Your finished New Connection Wizard should match one that is shown in Fig. 8.84.

Pay special attention to the content on the **JDBC URL** box, which is our completed connection URL, and click on the **Test Connection** button to make and check this connection.

A **Connection Succeeded** message is displayed if this connection is successful. Click on the **Next** button to select the database schema. Click on the drop-down arrow on the **Select schema** combo box and select the **dbo** as the schema, and click on the **Next** button.

Modify our connection name by cutting off the attached **[SMART on Default schema]** to get our final Input connection name as: **jdbc:sqlserver://localhost**

New Connection Wizard

Customize Connection

Driver Name: Microsoft SQL Server 2005 on Microsoft SQL Server 2019
Host: localhost Port: 5000
Database: CSE_DEPT
Instance Name: SQL2019EXPRESS
User Name: SMART
Password: ••••••••••
Remember password
Connection Properties Test Connection
JDBC URL: jdbc:sqlserver://localhost\SQL2019EXPRESS:5000;databaseName=CSE_DEPT
< Back Next > Finish Cancel Help

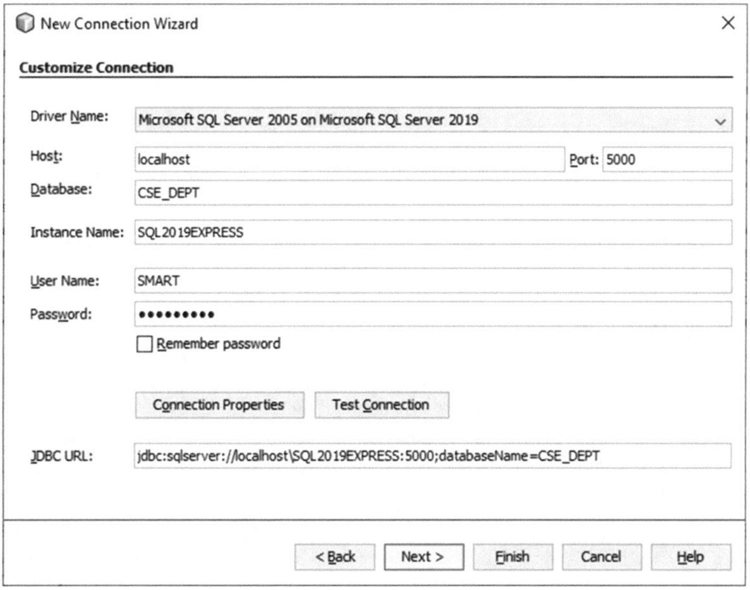

Fig. 8.84 The finished New Connection Wizard

SQL2019EXPRESS:5000; databaseName =CSE_DEPT, and click on the **Finish** button to complete this database connection job.

Now that our database is connected, we can open it to check our data insertion action.

On the opened **Services** window, expand each of the following folders: our database URL, our database **CSE_DEPT**, the **dbo** schema, and the **Tables** folder. Now right click on our **Faculty** table, and select the **View Data** item to open this table. The opened **Faculty** table is shown in Fig. 8.85.

You can find that the new inserted faculty member, **Susan Bai**, has been inserted to this table, and this record has been highlighted in Fig. 8.85. Our data insertion using the JavaServer Pages and Java bean is successful! To keep our database clean and neat, it is recommended to delete this inserted new faculty member from the **Faculty** table in our sample database.

8.5.3 Update and Delete Data from the Faculty Table Using JSP and Java Beans Techniques

To use the JavaServer Pages and Java bean techniques to perform data updating and deleting actions against the Faculty table, we need to perform the following operations:

1) Create a new Java Session bean class **FacultyUpdateDeleteBean.java** to handle the data updating and deleting actions.
2) Modify the model controller page **FacultyProcess.jsp** to handle the faculty data collection and manipulations.

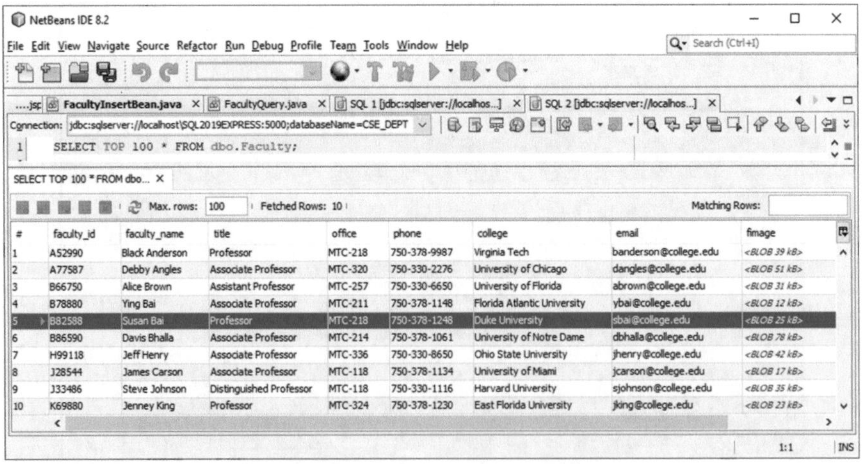

#	faculty_id	faculty_name	title	office	phone	college	email	fimage
1	A52990	Black Anderson	Professor	MTC-218	750-378-9987	Virginia Tech	banderson@college.edu	<BLOB 39 kB>
2	A77587	Debby Angles	Associate Professor	MTC-320	750-330-2276	University of Chicago	dangles@college.edu	<BLOB 51 kB>
3	B66750	Alice Brown	Assistant Professor	MTC-257	750-330-6650	University of Florida	abrown@college.edu	<BLOB 31 kB>
4	B78880	Ying Bai	Associate Professor	MTC-211	750-378-1148	Florida Atlantic University	ybai@college.edu	<BLOB 12 kB>
5	B82588	Susan Bai	Professor	MTC-218	750-378-1248	Duke University	sbai@college.edu	<BLOB 25 kB>
6	B86590	Davis Bhalla	Associate Professor	MTC-214	750-378-1061	University of Notre Dame	dbhalla@college.edu	<BLOB 78 kB>
7	H99118	Jeff Henry	Associate Professor	MTC-336	750-330-8650	Ohio State University	jhenry@college.edu	<BLOB 42 kB>
8	J28544	James Carson	Associate Professor	MTC-118	750-378-1134	University of Miami	jcarson@college.edu	<BLOB 17 kB>
9	J33486	Steve Johnson	Distinguished Professor	MTC-118	750-330-1116	Harvard University	sjohnson@college.edu	<BLOB 35 kB>
10	K69880	Jenney King	Professor	MTC-324	750-378-1230	East Florida University	jking@college.edu	<BLOB 23 kB>

Fig. 8.85 The opened Faculty table with new inserted faculty record

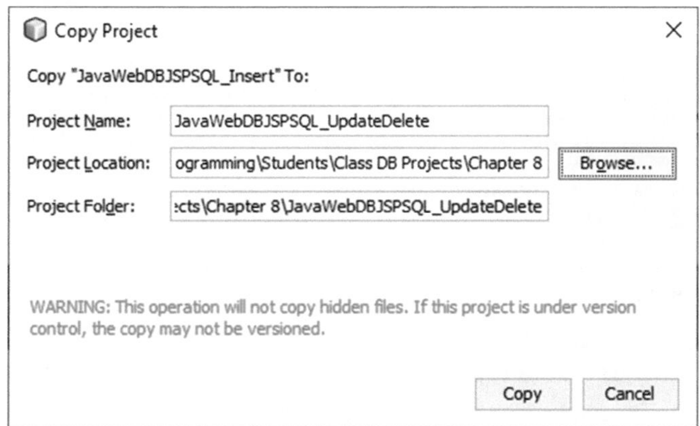

Fig. 8.86 The copied project JavaWebDBJSPSQL_UpdateDelete

Now let's create a new project **JavaWebDBJSPSQL_UpdateDelete** based on our existing project **JavaWebDBJSPSQL_Insert**. Perform the following operations to complete this creation:

1) In the **Projects** window, right click on the project **JavaWebDBJSPSQL_Insert**, and select the **Copy** item from the popup menu to open the **Copy Project** wizard, as shown in Fig. 8.86.
2) Enter our new project name, **JavaWebDBJSPSQL_UpdateDelete**, into the **Project Name** box, and browse to the default project folder, **C:\Class DB Projects\Chapter 8**, as the **Project Location**, which is shown in Fig. 8.86, and click on the **Copy** button.

A new project **JavaWebDBJSPSQL_UpdateDelete** is generated and added into our **Projects** window. Next let's build the codes for the related pages to update or delete some records in the **Faculty** table in our database.

First let's create our Java session bean class **FacultyUpdateDeleteBean.java** to handle the data updating and deleting actions.

8.5.3.1 Create a New Java Session Bean Class

Perform the following operations to create a new Java session bean class:

1) Right click on our project **JavaWebDBJSPSQL_UpdateDelete** from the **Projects** window, and select the **New > Java Class** item from the popup menu to open the **New Java Class** wizard.
2) Enter **FacultyUpdateDeleteBean** into the **Class Name** field, and select the **JavaWebDBJSPSQL Package** from the **Package** combo box.
3) Keep all other default settings and click on the **Finish** button.

```
  package JavaWebDBJSPSQLPackage;
A import java.sql.*;
  import java.io.File;
  import java.io.FileInputStream;
  import java.io.FileNotFoundException;
  import java.io.InputStream;
  import java.util.logging.Level;
  import java.util.logging.Logger;

  public class FacultyUpdateDeleteBean {
B    private String facultyID;
     private String facultyName;
     private String office;
     private String title;
     private String phone;
     private String college;
     private String email;
     static Connection con;

     public FacultyUpdateDeleteBean() {
C       try {
             Class.forName("com.microsoft.sqlserver.jdbc.SQLServerDriver");
          }
          catch (Exception e) {
             System.out.println("Class not found exception!" + e.getMessage());
          }
D         String url = "jdbc:sqlserver://localhost\\SQL2019EXPRESS:5000;databaseName=CSE_DEPT;";
E         try {
             con = DriverManager.getConnection(url,"SMART","Happy2020");
          }
          catch (SQLException e) {
             System.out.println ("Could not connect!" + e.getMessage());
             e.printStackTrace();
          }
     }
F    public int UpdateFaculty(String[] upFaculty) {
        int  numUpdated = 0;
G       FileInputStream fis = null;
H       File fimage= new File(upFaculty[6]);

I       String query = "UPDATE  Faculty SET faculty_name=?, title=?, office=?, phone=?, college=?," +
                     "email=?, fimage=? " + "WHERE faculty_id= ?";
J    try {
          PreparedStatement pstmt = con.prepareStatement(query);
K         pstmt.setString(1, upFaculty[0]);          // FacultyNameField
          pstmt.setString(2, upFaculty[1]);          // TitleField
          pstmt.setString(3, upFaculty[2]);          // OfficeField
          pstmt.setString(4, upFaculty[3]);          // PhoneField
          pstmt.setString(5, upFaculty[4]);          // CollegeField
          pstmt.setString(6, upFaculty[5]);          // EmailField
L         try {
              fis = new FileInputStream(fimage);
          } catch (FileNotFoundException ex) {
             Logger.getLogger(FacultyInsertBean.class.getName()).log(Level.SEVERE, null, ex);
          }
M           pstmt.setBinaryStream(7, (InputStream)fis, (int)(fimage.length()));
N           pstmt.setString(8, upFaculty[7]);          // FacultyIDField
O           numUpdated = pstmt.executeUpdate();
        }
P     catch (SQLException e) {
             System.out.println("Error in Statement!" + e.getMessage());
        }
Q       return numUpdated;
     }
     .........
```

Fig. 8.87 The first part of the codes of the Java bean class file

On the created **FacultyUpdateDeleteBean.java** class, we need to create two new methods **UpdateFaculty()** and **DeleteFaculty()**. These two methods are used to perform the data updating and deleting operations against our sample database. Figure 8.87 shows the first part of the codes.

Let's have a closer look at the codes for these two methods to see how they work.

A. Some useful packages are imported first since all SQL Server database-related classes and other components are defined in those packages.
B. Seven class properties related to the associated columns in the **Faculty** table are declared first. These properties are very important since they are directly mapped to the associated columns in the **Faculty** table. All of these properties can be accessed by using the associated **getter()** method defined in the second coding part of this class. A class-level database connection object is created.
C. In the constructor of this class, a **try…catch** block is used to load the database JDBC driver. The **catch** block is used to track and collect any possible exception during this database driver loading process.
D. The database connection URL is defined. Refer to Sect. 6.3.3.3.1 in Chap. 6 to get more detailed information about this URL definition.
E. Another **try…catch** block is used to connect to our sample SQL Server database with desired username and password. The **catch** block is used to track and collect any possible exception that occurred during this database connection process.
F. The main data updating method, **UpdateFaculty()**, is defined with the selected faculty updating information as the argument. This argument is exactly a String array that contains all seven pieces of updating faculty information. A local integer variable **numUpdated** and the SQL updating statement are firstly created with the faculty ID as the positional dynamic parameter.
G. A FileInputStream object, **fis**, is created, and it works as a handler of the InputStream for the updated faculty image later.
H. A new File object, **fimage**, is also generated to convert the updated faculty image that is stored in a string variable, **upFaculty[6]**, to a file object, and it will be further converted to an InputStream object later to be written into the **Faculty** table.
I. The updated query string is generated with eight positional parameters to make this updating action ready.
J. Starting from a **try** block, the **prepareStatement()** method is called to create a PreparedStatement object **pstmt**.
K. Six setter methods are used to set the positional parameters in the SQL updating statement with the positional order. This order must be identical with that defined in the input argument **upFaculty[]**, which is a String array.
L. With another **try…catch** block, a new FileInputStream object, **fis**, is generated with the File **fimage** as the argument to convert that File to a FileInputStream object and assign it to that new created object. The **catch** block is used to check and inspect any possible exception for this File if it cannot be found.
M. Then the **setBinaryStream()** method is executed to assign this faculty image file as a binary stream sequence to the seventh input position parameter, **fimage**, to the Update query statement.

N. The **setString()** method is executed to set up the eighth input positional parameter, **faculty_id**, to the query **WHERE** clause in the Update query statement.
O. The **executeUpdate()** method is executed to perform this data updating action, and the returned result, which is the number of the rows that have been successfully updated in the **Faculty** table, is assigned to the local integer variable **numUpdated**.
P. The **catch** block is used to track and collect any exceptions during this data updating operation.
Q. The data updating result is returned to the calling method.

The second part of the codes for this Java bean class is shown in Fig. 8.88. Let's have a closer look at this piece of codes to see how it works.

A. The codes for the **CloseDBConnection()** method are identical with those we discussed in the last section, and the purpose of this method is to close the connection between our Web application and our sample database.
B. Starting from step **B**, including steps **C** through **H**, seven getter methods are defined, and they are used to pick up all seven properties defined at the beginning of this class.

In fact, the codes for this Java bean class file are basically identical with those we built in our Java help class file, which include the loading JDBC driver, defining the

```
A   public void CloseDBConnection()
    {
      try{
        if (!con.isClosed())
          con.close();
      }catch (SQLException e) {
        System.out.println("Error in close the DB! " + e.getMessage());
      }
    }
B   public String getFacultyID() {
      return this.facultyID;
    }
C   public String getFacultyName() {
      return this.facultyName;
    }
D   public String getOffice() {
      return this.office;
    }
E   public String getTitle() {
      return this.title;
    }
F   public String getPhone() {
      return this.phone;
    }
G   public String getCollege() {
      return this.college;
    }
H   public String getEmail() {
      return this.email;
    }
  }
```

Fig. 8.88 The second part of the codes of the Java bean class file

database connection URL, connecting to database, and executing the appropriate method to perform related data actions against our database.

Next let's modify the **FacultyProcess.jsp** page to handle the faculty data collection and manipulation.

8.5.3.2 Modify the FacultyProcess Page to Handle Faculty Data Updating

Double click on the **FacultyProcess.jsp** page from the **Projects** window, and perform the following modifications to this page to use Java bean **FacultyUpdateDeleteBean.java** to perform the faculty record updating actions:

1) Move to the **else if (request.getParameter("Update")!= null)** block, and then open the **Palette** window by going to **Window > IDE Tools > Palette** menu item. In the opened **Palette** window, browse to the **JSP** tab, drag the **Use Bean** icon, and place it inside the **else if** block.
2) On the opened **Insert Use Bean** dialog, enter **UpdateFaculty** into the **ID** field and **JavaWebDBJSPSQLPackage.FacultyUpdateDeleteBean** into the **Class** filed. Select the **session** from the **Scope** combo box, and then click on the **OK**

```
    else if (request.getParameter("Update")!= null) {
       //process the faculty record updating
       %>
1          <jsp:useBean id="UpdateFaculty" scope="session"
2                              class="JavaWebDBJSPSQLPackage.FacultyUpdateDeleteBean" />
3          <jsp:setProperty name="UpdateFaculty" property="*" />
4      <%
A          int update = 0;
B          String fname = request.getParameter("NameField");
           String office = request.getParameter("OfficeField");
           String phone = request.getParameter("PhoneField");
           String college = request.getParameter("CollegeField");
           String title = request.getParameter("TitleField");
           String email = request.getParameter("EmailField");
           String f_id = request.getParameter("FacultyIDField");
           String fImage = request.getParameter("Faculty_Image");
C          String[] upf = {fname, title, office, phone, college, email, fImage, f_id };
D          update = UpdateFaculty.UpdateFaculty(upf);
E          if (update == 0)
             response.sendRedirect("Faculty.jsp");
F          else {
             session.setAttribute("FacultyIDField", null);
             session.setAttribute("NameField", null);
             session.setAttribute("OfficeField", null);
             session.setAttribute("PhoneField", null);
             session.setAttribute("CollegeField", null);
             session.setAttribute("TitleField", null);
             session.setAttribute("EmailField", null);
G            response.sendRedirect("Faculty.jsp");
             }
H          UpdateFaculty.CloseDBConnection();
           }
           .........
```

Fig. 8.89 The modified codes for the Update block

button. A JSP directive that contains the bean id, bean scope, and class is added to this block.

3) Add a JSP directive to the Java bean class **FacultyUpdateDeleteBean.java** shown below:

```
<jsp:setProperty name = "UpdateFaculty" property = "*" />
```

4) Add the opening and ending JSP directives to enclose those two JSP directives we added above.

The codes related to steps 1~4 above are shown in the top on Fig. 8.89. Add the codes shown in steps **A~I** in Fig. 8.89 into this block.

Let's have a closer look at these codes to see how they work.

A. A local integer variable **update** is created, and it is used to hold the running result of executing the **UpdateFaculty()** method in the Java bean class **FacultyUpdateDeleteBean** with the bean id of **UpdateFaculty**.
B. Eight **getParameter()** methods are used to pick up eight pieces of updating faculty information stored in the eight fields in the **Faculty.jsp** page. The collected eight pieces of new faculty information are assigned to eight local String variables.
C. A new String array **upf[]** is created, and it is used to hold eight pieces of updating faculty information stored in the eight local String variables.
D. The **UpdateFaculty()** method in our Java bean is executed to update a faculty record with these eight pieces of faculty information in the Faculty table. The eight pieces of updating faculty information are stored in the String array **upf[]** that works as the argument for this method. The running result of this method is returned and assigned to the local integer variable **update**.
E. If the running result is 0, which means that no any record has been updated in the **Faculty** table and this data updating action failed, in that case, we need to redisplay the **Faculty.jsp** page to enable users to re-update that faculty record.
F. If the running result is non-zero, which means that at least one faculty record has been updated in the **Faculty** table, we may clean up all seven fields that contain seven pieces of updated faculty information in the **Faculty.jsp** page to enable users to either test this updating or update another faculty record.
G. We need to redisplay the **Faculty.jsp** page to enable users to perform the next action.
H. Finally the **CloseDBConnection()** method is called to disconnect the connection to our database.

Prior to building and running this Web application, make sure that the faculty image to be selected and updated, in this case, it is **White.jpg**, has been stored in our default project image folder; in this case, it is **C:\Class DB Projects\Chapter 8\JavaWebDBJSPSQL_UpdateDelete\web\ FImages**.

Now we can build and run our project to test this faculty record updating function. Click on the **Clean and Build Main Project** button to perform cleaning up and building our project. Then right click on the **LogIn.jsp** page from the **Projects**

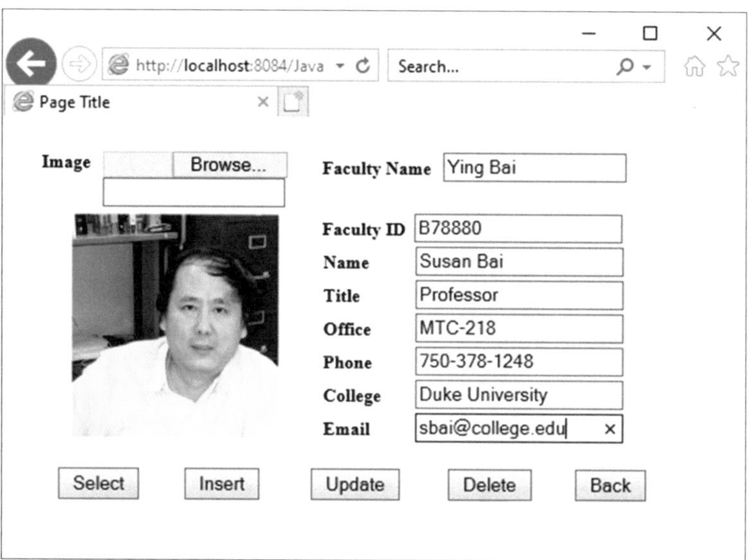

Fig. 8.90 The entered faculty updating information

window to run our project. Enter the appropriate username and password, such as **jhenry** and **test**, to finish the login process, and select the **Faculty Information** item from the **Selection.jsp** page to open the **Fcaulty.jsp** page.

To update a faculty record, first let's perform a query operation to retrieve and display that faculty record. Enter a faculty name, such as **Ying Bai**, into the **Faculty Name** field, and click on the **Select** button. All seven pieces of information related to that faculty are retrieved and displayed in this page. Now enter six pieces of updating information into the associated six fields without **Faculty ID** field, as shown in Fig. 8.90, and click on the **Browse** button on the File Selector box to browse and select that updating faculty image, **White.jpg**, as our updating faculty image. The finished faculty updating record is shown in Fig. 8.90.

Click on the **Update** button to try to update this faculty record in the **Faculty** table in our sample database. Immediately you can find that the original faculty information is displayed, which means that this data updating is successful.

To confirm this data updating action, two ways could be used. The first way is to use the **Select** button in the **Faculty.jsp** page to retrieve this updated faculty record from the **Faculty** table. To do that, enter **Susan Bai** to the **Faculty Name** field and **White.jpg** into the **Image** TextField, and then click on the **Select** button. You can find that the updated record is retrieved and displayed in the seven fields with the updated faculty image, as shown in Fig. 8.91. Now click on the **Back** and **Exit** button to terminate our project.

The second way to confirm this data updating is to open the Faculty table. Open the **Services** window, and expand the **Databases** node and our SQL Server database URL: **jdbc:sqlserver://localhost\SQL2019EXPRESS:5000;**

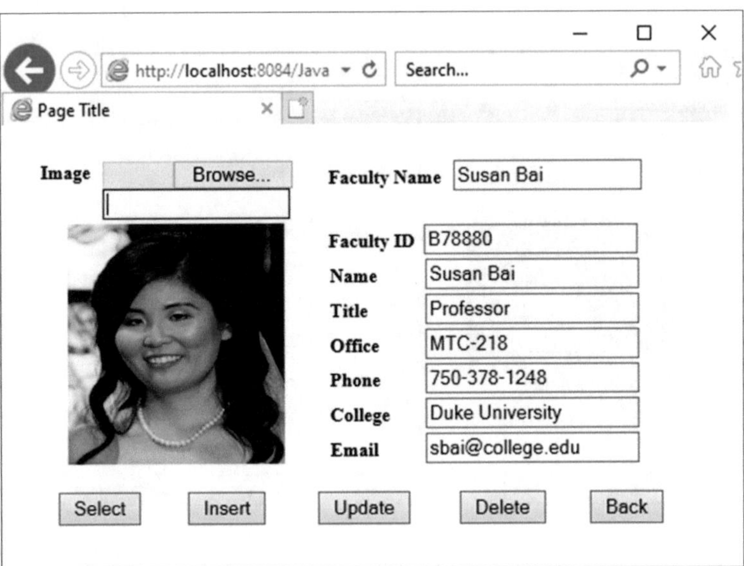

Fig. 8.91 The running result of confirming the data updating action

Table 8.3 The original data for faculty member Ying Bai

faculty_ id	faculty_ name	office	phone	college	title	email	fimage
B78880	Ying Bai	MTC-211	750-378-1148	Florida Atlantic University	Associate Professor	ybai@ college.edu	Bai. jpg

databaseName=CSE_DEPT. Right click on this URL, and select the **Connect** item to connect to our sample database. Then expand our database **CSE_DEPT**, **dbo** and **Tables**. Right click on the **Faculty** table, and select the **View Data** item to open this table. You can find that the faculty record with the **faculty_id** of **B78880** has been updated.

Our data updating action using the JavaServer Pages and Java bean is successful!

It is highly recommended to recover this updated faculty record in the **Faculty** table since we want to keep our database neat and clean. Apply the data shown in Table 8.3 to recover this faculty record with a faculty image file **Bai.jpg** that can be found from the folder **Images\Faculty** under the **Students** folder in the Springer ftp site (refer to Fig. 1.2 in Chap. 1). You can do this data recovery by using this project to do another Updating action or the Microsoft SQL Server Management Studio to open the Faculty table.

```
  .........
  public int DeleteFaculty(String fname) {
A     int numDeleted = 0;
B     String query = "DELETE FROM Faculty WHERE faculty_name = ?";
      try {
C        PreparedStatement pstmt = con.prepareStatement(query);
D        pstmt.setString(1, fname);
E         numDeleted = pstmt.executeUpdate();
      }
F     catch (SQLException e) {
         System.out.println("Error in Statement!" + e.getMessage());
      }
G     return numDeleted;
  }
  .........
```

Fig. 8.92 The codes for the DeleteFaculty() method

8.5.3.3 Add a Method to the Java Bean to Perform Faculty Data Deleting

To perform the faculty record deleting action, we need to perform the following operations:

1) Add a new method to the Java session bean **FacultyUpdateDeleteBean** to handle the faculty record deleting actions.
2) Modify the **FacultyProcess.jsp** page to handle the faculty data collection and manipulations.

Let's first add a new method **DeleteFaculty()** into our Java session bean class **FacultyUpdateDeleteBean** to handle the faculty record deleting actions. Create a new method **DeleteFaculty()**, and enter the codes shown in Fig. 8.92 into this Java Bean class file.

Let's have a closer look at this piece of codes to see how it works.

A. A local integer variable **numDeleted** is created, and it is used to hold the running result of executing the **DeleteFaculty()** method in the Java bean class **FacultyUpdateDeleteBean.java** with the bean id as **DeleteFaculty**.
B. The SQL deleting statement is created with the **faculty_name** as the positional dynamic parameter.
C. A **try…catch** block is used to perform this data deleting action. The **prepareStatement()** method is called to create a PreparedStatement object **pstmt**.
D. The setter method is used to set up the positional dynamic parameter **faculty_name**.
E. The **executeUpdate()** method is executed to perform this data deleting action, and the running result, which is the number of the rows that have been successfully deleted from the **Faculty** table, is assigned to the local integer variable **numDeleted**.
F. The **catch** block is used to track and collect any exceptions during this data deleting operation.
G. The data deleting result is returned to the calling method.

Now let's modify the **FacultyProcess.jsp** page to handle the faculty data collection and manipulations.

8.5.3.4 Modify the FacultyProcess Page to Handle Faculty Data Deleting

Double click on the **FacultyProcess.jsp** page from the **Projects** window to open this page, and perform the following modifications to this page to use Java bean **FacultyUpdateDeleteBean.java** to perform the faculty record deleting actions:

1) Move to the **else if (request.getParameter("Delete")!= null)** block, and then open the **Palette** window by going to **Window > IDE Tools > Palette** menu item. In the opened **Palette** window, browse to the **JSP** tab, drag the **Use Bean** icon, and place it inside the **else if** block.
2) On the opened **Insert Use Bean** dialog, enter **DeleteFaculty** into the **ID** field and **JavaWebDBJSPSQLPackage.FacultyUpdateDeleteBean** into the **Class** field. Select the **session** from the **Scope** combo box. Click on the **OK** button, and a JSP directive that contains the bean id, bean scope, and class is added to this block.
3) Add a JSP directive to the Java bean class **FacultyUpdateDeleteBean.java** shown below:

```
<jsp:setProperty name="DeleteFaculty" property="*" />
```

4) Add the opening and ending JSP directives to enclose those two JSP directives we added above.

The codes related to steps 1~4 above are shown in the top on Fig. 8.93. Add the codes shown in steps **A~E** in Fig. 8.93 into this block.

Let's have a closer look at these codes to see how they work.

A. A local integer variable **delete** is created, and it is used to hold the running result of executing the **DeleteFaculty()** method in the Java bean class **FacultyUpdateDeleteBean** with the bean id of **DeleteFaculty**.

```
  .........
  else if (request.getParameter("Delete")!= null) {
      //process the faculty record deleting
1     %>
2         <jsp:useBean id="DeleteFaculty" scope="session"
3                        class="JavaWebDBJSPSQLPackage.FacultyUpdateDeleteBean" />
4         <jsp:setProperty name="DeleteFaculty" property="*" />
      <%
A         int delete = 0;
B         String fname = request.getParameter("FacultyNameField");
C         delete = DeleteFaculty.DeleteFaculty(fname);
D         response.sendRedirect("Faculty.jsp");
E         DeleteFaculty.CloseDBConnection();
    }
  .........
```

Fig. 8.93 The modified codes for the Delete block

B. The **getParameter()** method is used to pick up the name of the faculty to be deleted from the **Faculty** table. The retrieved faculty name is assigned to the local variable **fname**.
C. The **DeleteFaculty()** method in our Java bean is executed to delete a faculty record based on the selected faculty name from the **Faculty** table. The running result of this method is returned and assigned to the local integer variable **delete**.
D. We need to redisplay the **Faculty.jsp** page to enable users to perform the next action.
E. Finally the **CloseDBConnection()** method is called to disconnect the connection to our database.

Now we can build and run our project to test this faculty record deleting function. Click on the **Clean and Build Main Project** button to perform cleaning up and building our project. Then right click on the **LogIn.jsp** page from the **Projects** window to run our project. Enter the appropriate username and password, such as **jhenry** and **test**, to finish the login process, and select the **Faculty Information** item from the **Selection.jsp** page to open the **Fcaulty.jsp** page.

To delete a faculty record, first let's perform a query operation to retrieve and display that faculty record. Enter a faculty name, such as **Ying Bai**, into the **Faculty Name** field, and click on the **Select** button. All seven pieces of information related to that faculty are retrieved and displayed in this page. Now click on the **Delete** button to try to delete this record from our **Faculty** table.

To confirm this data deleting action, two ways could be used. The first way is to use the **Select** button in the **Faculty.jsp** page to try to retrieve this deleted record from the **Faculty** table. To do that, enter the deleted faculty name **Ying Bai** to the

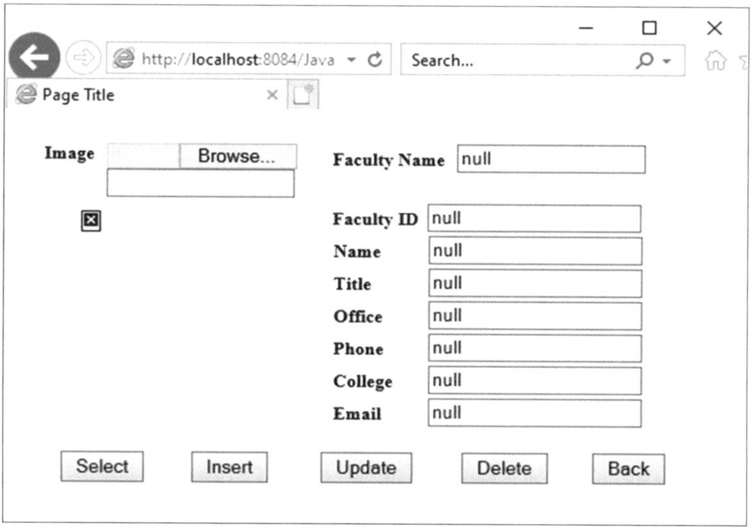

Fig. 8.94 The confirmation of the faculty data deletion action

Faculty Name field, and click on the **Select** button. You can find that all seven fields are displayed with nulls, as shown in Fig. 8.94, which means that the faculty member **Ying Bai** has been deleted from the **Faculty** table. Now click on the **Back** and **Exit** button to terminate our project.

The second way to confirm this data deleting is to open the **Faculty** table in the NetBeans IDE environment. Open the **Services** window, and expand the **Databases** node to find our SQL Server database URL: **jdbc:sqlserver://localhost\SQL2019EXPRESS:5000; databaseName = CSE_DEPT**. Right click on this URL, and select the **Connect** item to connect to our sample database. Then expand our database **CSE_DEPT**, **dbo**, and **Tables**. Right click on the **Faculty** table, and select the **View Data** item to open this table. You can find that the faculty record with the **faculty_id** of B78880 has been deleted.

Our data deleting action using the JavaServer Pages and Java bean is successful!

It is highly recommended to recover this deleted faculty record in the **Faculty** table since we want to keep our database neat and clean.

One point to be noted is that when we delete a faculty member from the **Faculty** table, which is a parent table relative to the child tables, the **Course** and **LogIn** tables, the related records to that deleted faculty in those child tables will also be deleted since a cascaded deleting relationship has been set up between the parent and child tables when we built this database in Chap. 2. Therefore the faculty login record in the **LogIn** table and all courses taught by that faculty in the **Course** table will be deleted when the faculty member is deleted from the **Faculty** table. Also because the **Course** table is a parent table relative to the **StudentCourse** table, all courses taken by students and taught by the deleted faculty will be deleted from the **StudentCourse** table. To recover these deleted records, one needs to recover all of those deleted records related to the deleted faculty in those four tables. An easy way to do this recovery job is to use the Microsoft SQL Server Management Studio. For your convenience, we show these original records in Tables 8.4, 8.5, 8.6 and 8.7 again, and you can add or insert them back to those four tables to complete this data recovery.

Another point to be noted is that you must recover the **Faculty** table first, and then you can recover other records in other tables since the **faculty_id** is a primary key in the **Faculty** table. An easy way to do this recovery is to use the **Insert** button with its method in this project to insert that deleted faculty record based on data in Table 8.4. Then you can exit our project and use Microsoft SQL Management Studio to add all other data items for other tables by hand based on data in Tables 8.5, 8.6 and 8.7.

Table 8.4 The deleted faculty record in the Faculty table

faculty_id	faculty_name	title	office	phone	college	email	fimage
B78880	Ying Bai	Associate Professor	MTC-211	750-378-1148	Florida Atlantic University	ybai@college.edu	Bai.jpg

Table 8.5 The deleted course records in the Course table

course_ id	course	credit	classroom	schedule	enrollment	faculty_ id
CSC-132B	Introduction to Programming	3	MTC-302	T-H: 1:00-2:25 PM	21	B78880
CSC-234A	Data Structure & Algorithms	3	MTC-302	M-W-F: 9:00-9:55 AM	25	B78880
CSE-434	Advanced Electronics Systems	3	MTC-213	M-W-F: 1:00-1:55 PM	26	B78880
CSE-438	Advd Logic & Microprocessor	3	MTC-213	M-W-F: 11:00-11:55 AM	35	B78880

Table 8.6 The deleted login records in the LogIn table

user_name	pass_word	faculty_id	student_id
ybai	come	B78880	NULL

Table 8.7 The deleted student course records in the StudentCourse table

s_course_id	student_id	course_id	credit	major
1005	T77896	CSC-234A	3	CS/IS
1009	A78835	CSE-434	3	CE
1014	A78835	CSE-438	3	CE
1016	A97850	CSC-132B	3	ISE
1017	A97850	CSC-234A	3	ISE

8.6 Chapter Summary

Most key techniques and knowledge in Java Web database programming are fully discussed and analyzed in this chapter with real project examples. The most popular and important techniques in Java Web database programming, such as JavaServer Pages (JSP), JavaServer Faces (JSF), and Enterprise Java Beans (EJB), are introduced and discussed in detail in different sections in this chapter.

Starting from an introduction to the fundamental Java Web server Servlets and HTML Web pages, a comprehensive historical review about Java Web application development and implementations are provided with some example codes. Then an introduction about the development of JavaServer Pages and Java help classes to improve the Java Web database applications are given with some pieces of coding examples.

To effectively improve and enhance the efficiency and quality of Java Web database applications, the Java core techniques, Java beans and Java enterprise edition (Java EE 7), are discussed and analyzed in detail with a few of coding examples.

Following a quick introduction to the Java EE Web application models, three actual Java Web database projects are introduced and discussed in detail.

The first project **JavaWebDBJSPSQL**, which is built based on the different techniques listed above, is used to access the SQL Server 2019 database with the help of runtime object method. Four popular Web pages, **LogInPage.jsp**, **SelectionPage.jsp**, **FacultyPage.jsp**, and **CoursePage.jsp**, which work as Web views, are built and developed with JSP techniques. The Glassfish v4 that works as a Web server and the Java help classes and Java beans that work as models are developed and implemented to provide users a global and detailed picture in the process of Java Web database application building and development.

The second project **JavaWebDBJSPSQL_Insert**, which is built based on the JSP pages and Java EJB techniques, is used to insert new records into the SQL Server database with the help of Java Beans techniques. The binding relationships between each attribute of tags in the JSP pages and the associated property in the Java bean class are built and illustrated in detail with actual example codes and step-by-step explanations in the coding process.

The third project **JavaWebDBJSPSQL_UpdateDelete**, which is built based on the JSP pages and Java EJB techniques, is used to manipulate the SQL Server database.

Some important techniques and points in developing and building a successful Web database application are emphasized and highlighted as below:

- Different data actions are performed and illustrated by using the coding process and line by line explanations, which include the data query, data insertion, and data updating and deleting.
- The Web project structure and navigation process are developed with the help of the Web configuration file, **faces-config.xml**, with actual examples and step-by-step illustrations.
- The relationships between the Java managed beans and the Java session beans are fully discussed and analyzed using the actual example codes and line by line explanations.
- The mapping relationships between each attribute in the tags on our JSP pages and the associated property in the Java managed beans are explicitly illustrated with the real coding process.

After finishing this chapter, readers can have a solid understanding and a clear and a full picture about the Java Web database application, including the Web structures, components, navigation, and mapping relationships between different objects, as well as the connections among those components.

It is hard to find a similar book that contains so much details and so clear illustrations on these topics about the Java Web applications from the current market.

Homework

I. True/False Selections.

___ 1. When a Servlet is created, the **init()** method is called to do the initialization jobs for the Web server.

___ 2. When a request is received by the Servlet, it creates two objects: request and response. Then the Servlet sends these two objects to the **service()** method, in which these two objects are further to be processed.

___ 3. The conventional Web applications are built with a Servlet as a Web container and JSF pages as Web clients.

___ 4. Unlike a Common Gateway Interface (CGI), a Servlet can be used to create dynamic Web pages during the server-client communication processes.

___ 5. To interface to the client to get user's data, in most time the Web server calls the **getParameter()** method that belongs to the **request** object to do this job.

___ 6. The so-called implicit objects in JSP are objects that are automatically available in JSP because they are automatically instantiated as the project runs.

___ 7. Among those implicit objects, the **request**, **response**, and **session** are most popular objects and are often used in the interfacing between clients and servers.

___ 8. To use a Java bean, the JSP provide three basic tags for working with beans,
<jsp:useBean id="**bean name**" class="**bean class**" scope = "page|request|session|application"/>

___ 9. To embed any Java codes into a HTML page, the JSP directive <%@ page /> must be used.

___10. The navigation from one page to another can be done in two ways. One way is directly to use the codes by writing the JSP tag such as <jsp:forward /> or the HTML hyperlink in the JSF file. Another way that is provided by JSF is to use the application configuration resource file faces-config.xml to build these navigation rules.

II. Multipe Choices.

1. The <from-view-id> tag is used to define a navigation ______________.

   (a) Source
   (b) Terminal
   (c) Destination
   (d) None of above

2. To bind a Java bean's property to an associated attribute of a tag in the JSF page, one needs to use the ________________.

   (a) Expression language (EL) with the syntax #(managedbean.property)
   (b) Expression language (EL) with the syntax #{managedbean.property}
   (c) Expression language (EL) with the syntax #[managedbean.property]
   (d) Expression language (EL) with the syntax ${managedbean.property}

3. A typical Java bean class should contain ________________.

   (a) All properties
   (b) All properties, setter methods
   (c) All properties, setter and getter methods
   (d) All properties, setter and getter methods as well as user-defined methods

4. Java beans need to be configured in the Web configuration file faces-config.xml so that the implementation can automatically create new ________ of the beans as needed.

   (a) Statement
   (b) Method
   (c) Instance
   (d) Project

5. Before you can use a Servlet such as FacesServlet in the server side from a Web browser, you need to map the FacesServlet to a path in your deployment descriptor file ________.

   (a) Web pages
   (b) WEB INF file
   (c) Web configuration file
   (d) web.xml

6. To separate the presentations and business logics, we can use ________ pages to present our GUI and the ___________ to store our data to perform business-related logics.

   (a) HTML, Java help class
   (b) XML, JSF pages
   (c) JSP, Java beans
   (d) JSF, JSP pages

7. All JSF tag components are represented by a tree of components whose root is the UIViewRoot, which is represented by the ________ tag. All JSF component tags must be enclosed in this ________ tag.

   (a) UIComponent
   (b) UITree
   (c) <h:form>
   (d) <f:view>

8. A JSP form, which is submitted to the Web server when a button is clicked, is represented by the ________ tag. The tags representing the form components, such as textfields and buttons, must be nested inside this tag.

   (a) <f:form>
   (b) <h:form>
   (c) <h:view>
   (d) <f:view>

9. If the required attribute is set to true, this means that the inputText _______________.

   (a) Cannot be empty
   (b) Must be filled something by the user
   (c) Both of above
   (d) Neither of above

10. A Web application is a dynamic extension of a web or application server. There are two types of Web applications: ______________ and ______________.

    (a) Dynamic, static
    (b) Single-tier, multitier
    (c) Web server, web client
    (d) Presentation-oriented, service-oriented

III. Exercises.

1. Provide a brief description about the Java EE three-tier Web application with EJB.
2. What is the difference between a Java EE with EJB and a Java EE without EJB?
3. What are popular Java EE components?
4. Provide a brief description to illustrate the interaction between a Web client and a Web application.
5. Provide a brief description about the Java EE containers.
6. Refer to Sect. 8.4.5 to develop a Java Web application **WebDBJSPSQL_Student** to query the **Student** table in our sample SQL Server database **CSE_DEPT** using JavaServer pages and JSP implicit session object.

   Hint 1: Use an existing **Student.jsp** page located under the folder **HTML and JSP Pages** in the Springer ftp site (refer to Fig. 1.2 in Chap. 1) under the **Students** folder. Modify that page based on Sect. 8.4.5.1 to make it a desired **Student.jsp** page.
   Hint 2: Create a **StudentProcess.jsp** page based on Sect. 8.4.5.2.
   Hint 3: Create a Help or Java Bean class **StudentQuery.java** based on Sect. 8.4.5.3.
   Hint 4: Create a new folder **SImages** under the project folder, **WebDBJSPSQL_Student\web**.
   Go to Springer ftp site, and copy all student images from the folder **Images\Students** under the **Students** folder and paste them into our created folder **SImages**.
   Hint 5: In the NetBeans IDE, open the project **Properties** wizard, click on the **Libraries** node and add the JDBC 4.2 driver by clicking on the **Add JAR/Folder** button, and browse to **C:\Program Files\sqljdbc_4.2\enu\jre7\sqljdbc41.jar**, select it, and click on the **Open** button.

Chapter 9
Developing Java Web Services to Access Databases

We provided a very detailed discussion about the Java Web applications in the last chapter. In this chapter, we will concentrate on another Java Web-related topic—Java Web Services.

Unlike Java Web applications in which the user needs to access the Web server through the client browser by sending requests to the server to obtain the desired information, the Java Web Services provide an automatic way to search, identify, and return the desired information required by the user through a set of methods installed in the Web server, and those methods can be accessed by a computer program, not the user, via the Internet. Another important difference between the Java Web applications and Java Web services is that the latter do not provide any graphic user interfaces (GUIs) and users need to create those GUIs themselves to access the Web services via the Internet.

When finishing this chapter, you will

- Understand the basic and popular Java Web services models
- Understand the structure and components of SOAP/WSDL-based Java Web Services, such as Simple Object Access Protocol (SOAP), Web Services Description Language (WSDL), and Universal Description, Discovery and Integration (UDDI)
- Create correct SOAP Namespaces for the Web Services to make used names and identifiers unique in the user's document
- Create suitable security components to protect the Web methods
- Build the professional Java Web Service projects to access our sample database to obtain required information
- Build client applications to provide GUIs to consume a Web Service
- Build the professional Java Web Service projects to access our sample database to insert new information into that database

---

Supplementary Information The online version contains supplementary material available at [https://doi.org/10.1007/978-3-031-06553-8_9].

Y. Bai, *SQL Server Database Programming with Java*,
https://doi.org/10.1007/978-3-031-06553-8_9

- Build the professional Java Web Service projects to access our sample database to update and delete information against that database

In order to help readers to successfully complete this chapter, first we need to provide a detailed discussion about the Java Web Services and their components.

9.1 Introduction to Java Web Services

Web services are distributed application components that are externally available. You can use them to integrate computer applications that are written in different languages and run on different platforms. Web services are language and platform independent because vendors have agreed on common Web service standards.

Essentially Web Services can be considered as a set of methods installed in a Web server and can be called by computer programs installed on the clients through the Internet. Those methods can be used to locate and return the target information required by the computer programs. Web Services do not require the use of browsers or HTML, and therefore Web Services are sometimes called *application services*.

A complete Web services stack Metro, which is developed by the Sun Microsystems, covers all of a developer's needs from simple Java Web services demonstrations to reliable, secured, and transacted web services. Metro includes Web Services Interoperability Technologies (WSIT). WSIT supports enterprise features such as security, reliability, and message optimization. WSIT ensures that Metro services with these features are interoperable with Microsoft .NET services. Within Metro, Project Tango develops and evolves the codebase for WSIT.

Several programming models are available to Web service developers. These models can be categorized into two groups, and both are supported by the NetBeans IDE:

- **REST-based: RE**presentational **S**tate **T**ransfer is a new way to create and communicate with Web services. In REST, resources have Uniform Resource Identifiers (URIs) and are manipulated through HTTP header operations.
- **SOAP/WSDL-based:** In traditional Web service models, Web service interfaces are exposed through Web Services Description Language (WSDL) documents (a type of XML), which have URLs. Subsequent message exchange is in Simple Object Access Protocol (SOAP), another type of XML document.

Let's have a little more discussion about these two kinds of Web services.

9.1.1 REST-Based Web Services

REST-based or RESTful Web services are collections of Web resources identified by URIs. Every document and every process is modeled as a Web resource with a unique URI. These Web resources are manipulated by the actions that can be specified in an HTTP header. Neither SOAP, nor WSDL, nor WS-* standards are used. Instead, message exchange can be conducted in any format—XML, JavaScript Object Notation (JSON), HTML, etc. In many cases a Web browser can serve as the client.

HTTP is the protocol in REST. Only four methods are available: GET, PUT, POST, and DELETE. Requests can be bookmarked and responses can be cached. A network administrator can easily follow what is going on with a RESTful service just by looking at the HTTP headers.

REST is a suitable technology for applications that do not require security beyond what is available in the HTTP infrastructure and where HTTP is the appropriate protocol. REST services can still deliver sophisticated functionality. NetBeans IDE Software as a Service (SaaS) functionality lets you use Facebook, Zillow, and other third-party-provided services in your own applications.

Project Jersey is the open source reference implementation for building RESTful Web services. The Jersey APIs are available as the **RESTful Web Services** plug-in for NetBeans IDE.

RESTful Web services are services built using the RESTful architectural style. Building Web services using the RESTful approach is emerging as a popular alternative to using SOAP-based technologies for deploying services on the Internet, due to its lightweight nature and the ability to transmit data directly over HTTP.

The NetBeans IDE supports rapid development of RESTful Web services using Java Specification Requests (JSR 311), a Java API for RESTful Web Services (JAX-RS) and Jersey, the reference implementation for JAX-RS.

In addition to building RESTful Web services, the NetBeans IDE also supports testing, building client applications that access RESTful Web services, and generating code for invoking Web services (both RESTful and SOAP-based).

Here is the list of RESTful features provided by the NetBeans IDE:

1) Rapid creation of RESTful Web services from JPA entity classes and patterns
2) Rapid code generation for invoking Web services such as Google Map, Yahoo News Search, and StrikeIron Web services by drag-and-dropping components from the RESTful component palette
3) Generation of JavaScript client stubs from RESTful Web services for building RESTful client applications
4) Test client generation for testing RESTful Web services
5) Logical view for easy navigation of RESTful Web service implementation classes in the project
6) Fully integrated Spring framework, providing Spring transaction handling

A structure and architecture of using RESTful model to build a Web service is shown in Fig. 9.1.

Next let's take a look at the SOAP-based Web services.

9.1.2 SOAP-Based Web Services

In SOAP-based Web services, Java utilities create a WSDL file based on the Java code in the Web service. The WSDL is exposed on the net. Parties interested in using the Web service create a Java client based on the WSDL. Messages are exchanged in SOAP format. The range of operations that can be passed in SOAP is much broader than what is available in REST, especially in security.

SOAP-based Web services are suitable for heavyweight applications using complicated operations and for applications requiring sophisticated security, reliability, or other WS-* standards-supported features. They are also suitable when a transport protocol other than HTTP has to be used. Many of Amazon's Web services, particularly those involving commercial transactions, and the Web services used by banks and government agencies are SOAP-based.

The Java API for XML Web Services (JAX-WS) is the current model for SOAP-based Web services in Metro. JAX-WS is built on the earlier Java API for XML Remote Procedure Call (JAX-RPC) model but uses specific Java EE 5 features, such as annotations, to simplify the task of developing Web services. Because it uses SOAP for messaging, JAX-WS is transport neutral. It also supports a wide range of modular WS-* specifications, such as WS-Security and WS-ReliableMessaging.

When you create a Web service client, you have the option of using either the JAX-WS or JAX-RPC model. This is because some older JAX-RPC services use a binding style that is not supported by JAX-WS. These services can only be consumed by JAX-RPC clients.

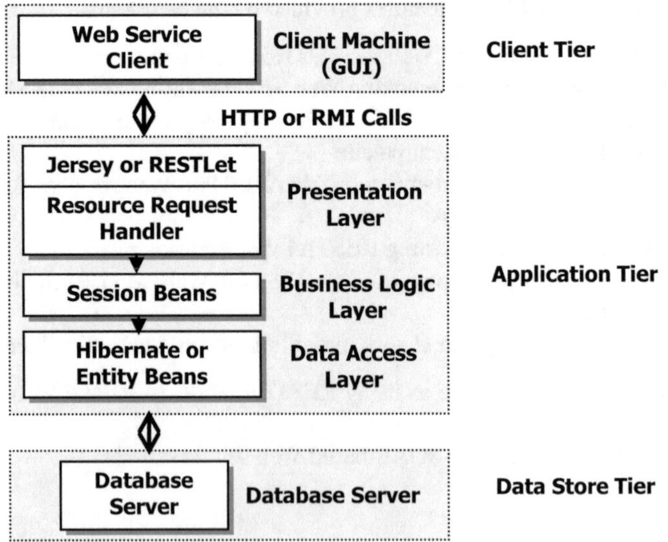

Fig. 9.1 The architecture of a multitier Web services

Metro Web services are interoperable with Apache Axis2 Web services. Apache Axis2 is an open-source implementation of the SOAP submission to the W3C. Two popular implementations of the Apache Axis2 Web services engine are Apache Axis2/Java and Apache Axis2/C. In addition, Axis2 not only supports SOAP 1.1 and SOAP 1.2, but it also has integrated support for RESTful Web services.

Because the SOAP-based Web services are suitable for heavyweight applications using complicated operations and for applications requiring sophisticated security and reliability, in this chapter, we will concentrate on this kind of Web services.

9.2 The Structure and Components of SOAP-Based Web Services

To effectively find, identify, and return the target information required by computer programs, a SOAP-based Web Service needs the following components:

1) XML (Extensible Markup Language)
2) SOAP (Simple Object Access Protocol)
3) UDDI (Universal Description, Discovery and Integration)
4) WSDL (Web Services Description Language)

The functionality of each component is listed below:

XML is a text-based data storage language, and it uses a series of tags to define and store data. Exactly the so-called tags are used to "mark up" data to be exchanged between applications. The "marked up" data then can be recognized and used by different applications without any problem. As you know, the Web Services platform is XML + HTTP (Hypertext Transfer Protocol), and the HTTP protocol is the most popular Internet protocol. However, the XML provides a kind of language that can be used between different platforms and programming languages to express complex messages and functions. In order to make the codes used in the Web Services to be recognized by applications developed in different platforms and programming languages, the XML is used for the coding in the Web Services to make them up line by line.

SOAP is a communication protocol used for communications between applications. Essentially SOAP is a simple XML-based protocol to help applications developed in different platforms and languages to exchange information over HTTP. Therefore, SOAP is a platform-independent and language-independent protocol, which means that it can be run at any operating systems with any programming languages. Exactly SOAP works as a carrier to transfer data or requests between applications. Whenever a request is made to the Web server to request a Web Service ,that request is first wrapped into a SOAP message and sent over the Internet to the Web server. Similarly, as the Web Service returns the target information to the client, the returned information is also wrapped into a SOAP message and sent over the Internet to the client browser.

WSDL is an XML-based language for describing Web Services and how to access them. In WSDL terminology, each Web Service is defined as an abstract endpoint or a Port, and each Web method is defined as an abstract operation. Each operation or method can contain some SOAP messages to be transferred between applications. Each message is constructed by using the SOAP protocol as a request is made from the client. WSDL defines two styles for how a Web Service method can be formatted in a SOAP message: Remote Procedure Call (RPC) and Document. Both RPC and Document style messages can be used to communicate with a Web Service using a RPC.

A single endpoint can contain a group of Web methods, and that group of methods can be defined as an abstract set of operations called a Port Type. Therefore, WSDL is an XML format for describing network services as a set of endpoints operating on SOAP messages containing either document-oriented or procedure-oriented information. The operations and messages are described abstractly and then bound to a concrete network protocol and message format to define an endpoint.

UDDI is an XML-based directory for businesses to list themselves on the Internet, and the goal of this directory is to enable companies to find one another on the Web and make their systems interoperable for e-commerce. UDDI is often considered as a telephone book's yellow and white pages. By using those pages, it allows businesses to list themselves by name, products, locations, or the Web services they offer.

Summarily, based on these components and their roles discussed above, we can conclude:

- The XML is used to tag the data to be transferred between applications.
- SOAP is used to wrap and pack the data tagged in the XML format into the messages represented in the SOAP protocol.
- WSDL is used to map a concrete network protocol and message format to an abstract endpoint and describe the Web services available in an WSDL document format.
- UDDI is used to list all Web Services that are available to users and businesses.

Figure 9.2 shows a diagram to illustrate these components and their roles in a Java Web Service process.

By now we have obtained the fundamental knowledge about the SOAP-based Web Services and their components; next let's see how to build a Web Service project.

9.3 The Procedure of Building a Typical SOAP-Based Web Service Project

Different methods and languages can be used to develop Web Services such as the C# Web Services, Java Web Services, and Perl Web Services. In this section we only concentrate on the Java Web Services using the NetBeans IDE. Before we can start

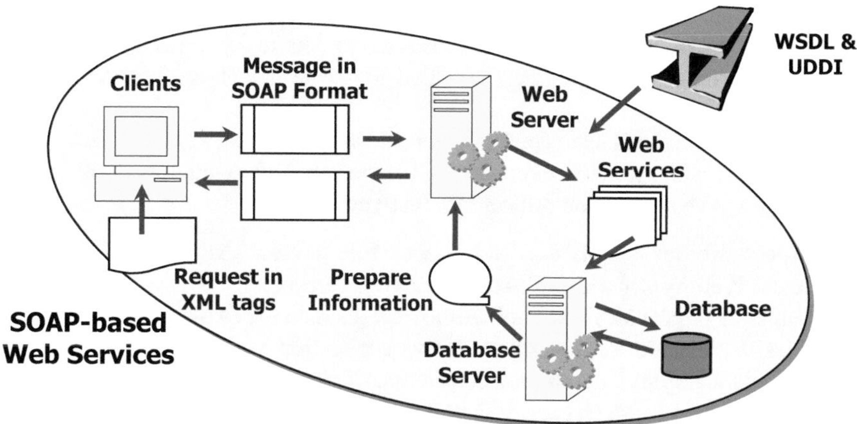

Fig. 9.2 A typical process of a SOAP-based Web Service

to build a real Web Service project, let's first take a closer look at the procedure of building a Java Web Service project.

Unlike ASP.NET Web services applications, a Java SOAP-based Web service project is involved in a Java Web application project in which the Web service can be deployed based on an appropriate container. Once a Java Web application project has been created with a desired container, you can create a new Java Web service project in that Web application project.

Regularly, to build and implement a Java SOAP-based Web service project, you need to follow the procedures listed below:

1) Create a new Java Web application project with an appropriate container.
2) Create a new Java SOAP-based Web service project.
3) Add desired operations (methods) to the Web service to build the desired functions for the Web service.
4) Deploy and test the Web service on the selected container.
5) Create Web service clients to consume the developed Java Web service.

Next let's use a real simple Web service example **WSTestApplication** to illustrate these steps.

9.3.1 Create a New Java Web Application Project WSTestApplication

Before we can create a new Web service application project, we need to select our desired container to deploy our Web service. Generally we can either deploy our Web service in a Web container or in an EJB container. This depends on our choice of implementation. If we are creating a Java EE 7 application, we had better used a

Web container in any case since we can put EJBs directly in a Web application. However, if we plan to deploy our Web service project to the Tomcat Web Server, which only has a Web container, we need to create a Web application, not an EJB module.

After a container has been determined, next we can create a new Java Web application project with the selected container. Perform the following operations to create this new Web application project **WSTestApplication**:

1) Launch NetBeans IDE 8.2, and choose **File > New Project** (Ctrl-Shift-N). Select **Web Application** from the **Java Web** category.
2) Name the project **WSTestApplication**, and click on the **Browse** button to select a desired location for the project. In this application, we used the **C:\Class DB Projects\Chapter 9** as our project location. Click on the **Next** button to continue.
3) On the next wizard, **Server and Settings**, click on the **Add** button to add the GlassFish 4.1 server since it was deleted from our previous project developments in Chap. 8.
4) In the opened **Add Server Instance** wizard, select the **GlassFish Server** from the Server List, and click on the **Next** button to open the Server Location wizard, as shown in Fig. 9.3.
5) Browse to the location where our installed GlassFish server is located by clicking the **Browse** button, as shown in Fig. 9.3. Check **I have read and accent the license agreement** checkbox, and click on the **Next** button to create a user domain.
6) On the opened **Domain Location** wizard, as shown in Fig. 9.4, keep the default user domain location as shown in Fig. 9.4, and then click on the **Finish** button to complete this adding server operation. You can add your username and password if you like to add some additional security function to access this server.
7) A **Domain creation successful** message is displayed if this process is fine. Click on the **No** button to skip the viewing of the result step, and continue to the next step.

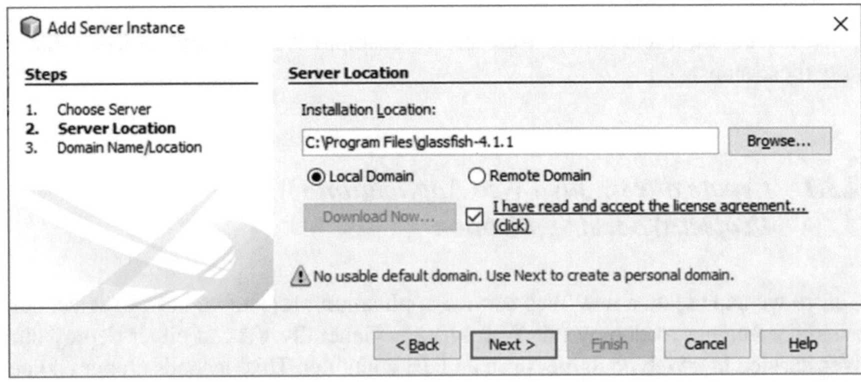

Fig. 9.3 The opened Server Location wizard

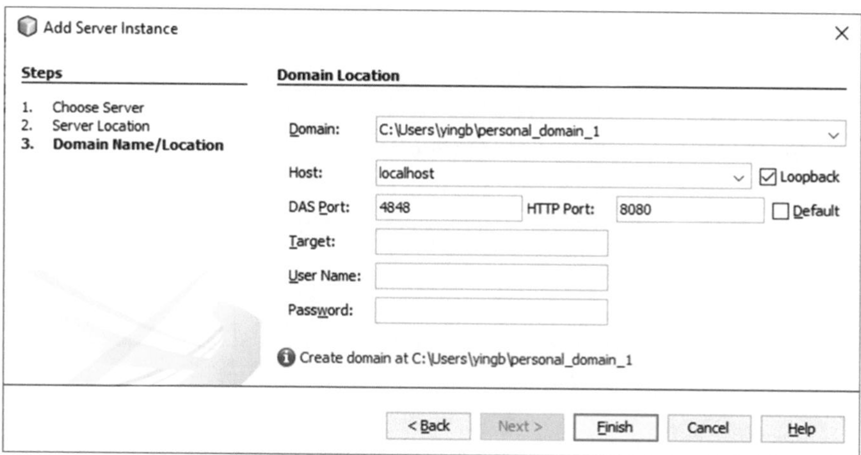

Fig. 9.4 The opened Domain Location wizard

8) On the **Server and Settings** wizard, select **Java EE 7 Web** as the Java EE version, and your finished **Server and Settings** wizard should match one that is shown in Fig. 9.5. Click on the **Next** button to continue.
9) On the next wizard, **Framework**, just click on the **Finish** button to complete this new application creation process since we do not need to use any framework.

Now that a Web application has been created with a selected Web container; next we can create our new Web service project **WSTest**.

9.3.2 *Create a New Java SOAP-Based Web Service Project WSTest*

The function of this Web service is to add two integers together and return the result. Perform the following operations to create this new Web service project **WSTest**:

1) In the opened **Projects** window, right click on our new created project **WSTestApplication**, and select the **New > Other** menu item to open the **New File** wizard.
2) Select **Web Services** from the **Categories** list and **Web Service** from the **File Types** list, and click on the **Next** button.
3) Name the Web service **WSTest** and type **org.wstest** into the **Package** field. Leave **Create Web Service from Scratch** selected.
4) Check the **Implement Web Service as Stateless Session Bean** checkbox if we want to use Java beans in this Web service.

Your finished **Name and Location** wizard should match one that is shown in Fig. 9.6. Click on the **Finish** button to complete this process.

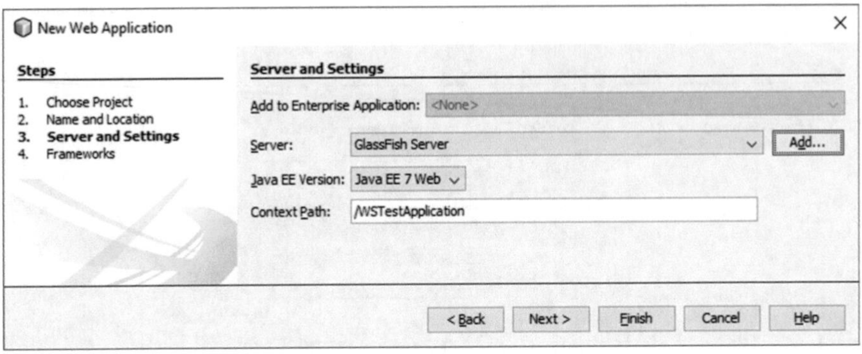

Fig. 9.5 The finished Server and Settings wizard

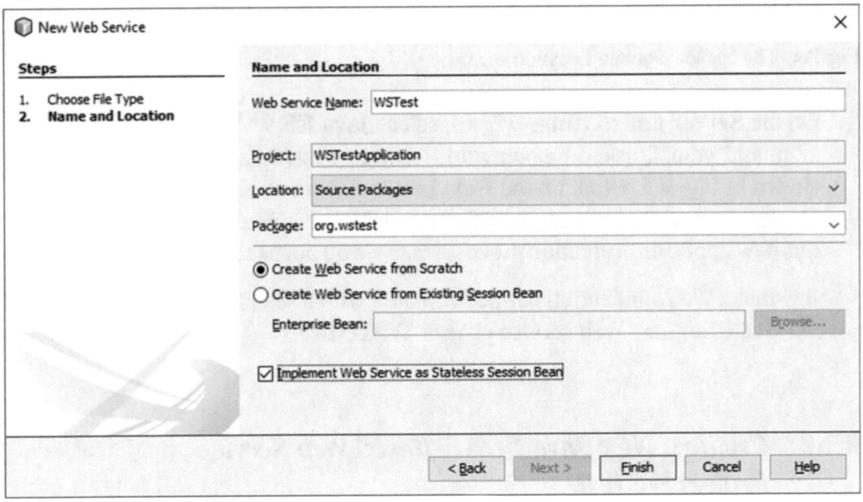

Fig. 9.6 The finished Name and Location wizard

After a new Web service project **WSTest** is created, the following components are added into our Web application **WSTestApplication**:

1) A new node named **org.wstest** with a new Java class **WSTest.java** has been added to the **Source Packages** node in our application. This Java class file **WSTest.java** is the main body of this Web service, and all functions of this Web service should be performed by adding operations or methods into this class.
2) A new node named **Web Services** with a new icon **WSTest** has been added into our Web application. This **WSTest** icon is our target Web service output file that can be tested later when it is built.
3) A new file named **web.xml** has been added into the **Configuration Files** node in our project. This file is called the Web deployment descriptor file, and it is used to define and describe how to deploy our Web service on a server.

4) Some Metro Web service libraries have also been added into the **Libraries** node in our project to provide all supports and assistances to our Web service developments.
5) A new node named **Enterprise Beans** with a new added bean class **WSTest** has been added into our project, and this enables us to use any Java beans in our Web service project.

All of these new added components are shown in Fig. 9.7.

Now we can add new operations or methods into our main body class **WSTest.java** to build our Web service to perform the addition function for two integers input by users via a client.

9.3.3 Add Desired Operations to the Web Service

The goal of this project is to add to the Web service an operation that adds two integer numbers received from a client. The NetBeans IDE provides a dialog for adding an operation or a method to a Web service. You can open this dialog either in the Web service visual designer or in the Web service context menu.

To open this dialog using the Web service visual designer,

- Open our Web service main body file **WSTest.java** by double clicking on it from the Projects window.
- Click on the **Design** button on the top of this window.

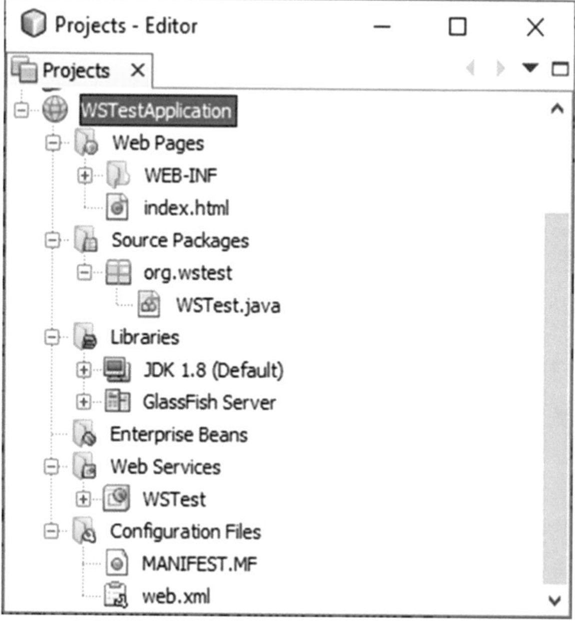

Fig. 9.7 New added components for our new Web service project

To open this dialog using the Web service context menu,

- Find our target Web service output file **WSTest** from the **Web Services** node in the **Projects** window.
- Right click on that node to open the context menu.

Click on **Add Operation** menu item in either the visual designer or the context menu. A dialog box appears where you can define the new operation.

Perform the following operations to add a new addition operation or new method:

1) In the upper part of the **Add Operation** dialog box, type **Add** into the **Name** field and type **int** into the **Return Type** drop-down list. In the lower part of the **Add Operation** dialog box, click on the **Add** button, and create a parameter of type **int** named **input1**. Then click on the **Add** button again, and create the second parameter of type **int** called **input2**. Your finished **Add Operation** dialog should match one that is shown in Fig. 9.8.
2) Click on the **OK** button to close this dialog. The new added operation is displayed in the visual designer if the **Design** tab is clicked for this service.
3) Click on the **Source** button on the top of this window to open the code window of this Web service main body file, and you can find that our new Web operation or method **Add()** has been added into this class, as shown in Fig. 9.9.
4) In the opened WebMethod **Add()**, enter the codes shown below into this method:

```
int  result = input1 + input2;
return  result;
```

5) Your finished codes for this new operation method, which have been highlighted, are shown in Fig. 9.10. The function of this operation is simple, and it only adds two input numbers entered by users via a client and returns the result to the client.

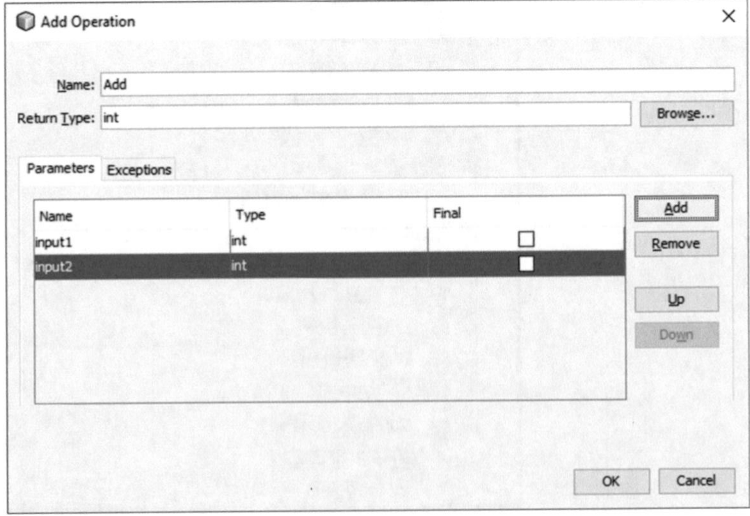

Fig. 9.8 The finished Add Operation dialog

6) If you like, you can delete the default Web Method **Hello** from this service. Click on the **Design** tab on the top to open the Design View for this service, and right click on the **hello** icon, and select the **Remove Operation** item, and click on the **Yes** button.

At this point, we have finished developing our Web service project, and next we need to deploy it to the selected Web container and test it with some consuming projects.

9.3.4 Deploy and Test the Web Service on the Selected Container

The NetBeans IDE provides a server's test client to assist us to test our Web service after it has been successfully deployed. Perform the following operations to deploy our Web service to our Web container GlassFish:

1) Right click on our project **WSTestApplication** from the **Projects** window, and choose the **Deploy** item. The NetBeans IDE will start the application server, build the application, and deploy the application to the server. You can follow the progress of these operations in the **WSTestApplication** (run-deploy) and the GlassFish Server in the Output window view.

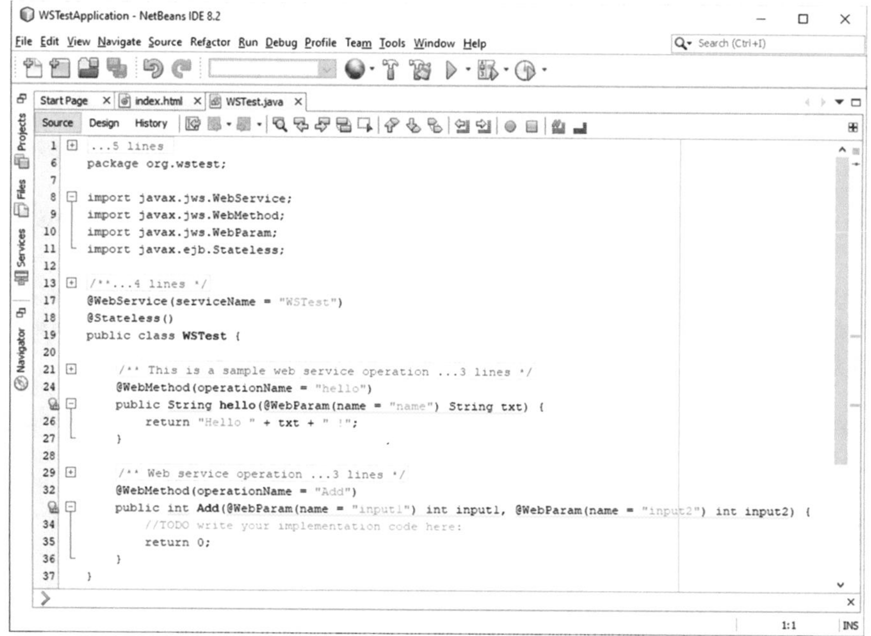

Fig. 9.9 The codes created for the new added operation

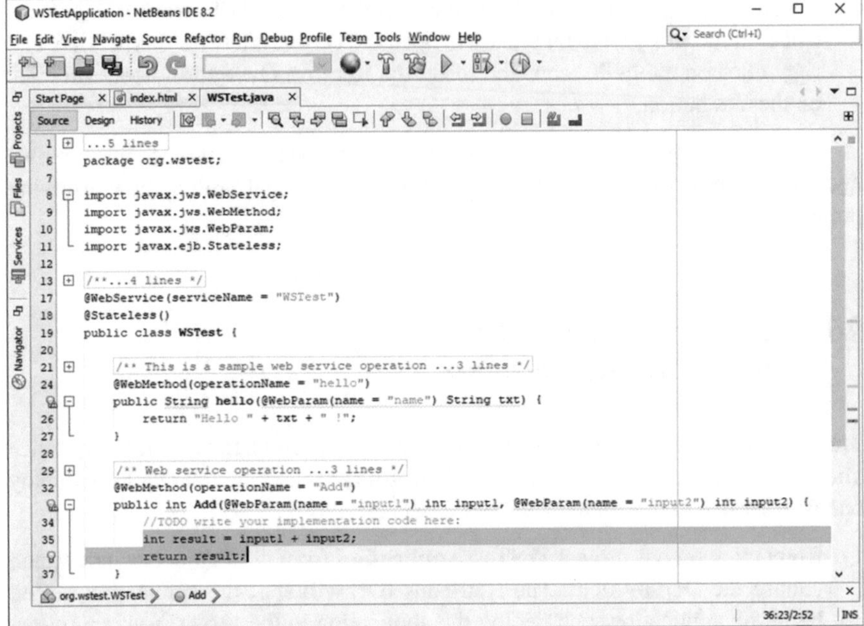

Fig. 9.10 The finished codes for the new operation method

2) If everything is fine, a successful deploy result should be obtained and displayed in the Output window at the bottom.

To test our Web service, perform the following operations:

1) In the opened **Projects** window, expand the **Web Services** node of our project and right click on our target Web service output file **WSTest**, and choose the **Test Web Service** item.
2) The NetBeans IDE will display a tester page in your browser if everything is fine, which is shown in Fig. 9.11.

To test our Web service project, enter **5** and **3** to the two input boxes, and click on the **add** button. You can find that a successful running result of our Web service is displayed with an addition result of 8, which is shown in Fig. 9.12.

One point to be noted is that if you are using the Tomcat Web Server as your application server, you would not find this tester page, and only a testing successful page is displayed without the page testing ability available. Also if you are deploying a Web service built with EJB module, you cannot find this tester page, neither since the NetBeans IDE will not support this testing function to any EJB module.

Next let's build a Web service consuming project to consume our Web service.

Fig. 9.11 The Web Service testing page

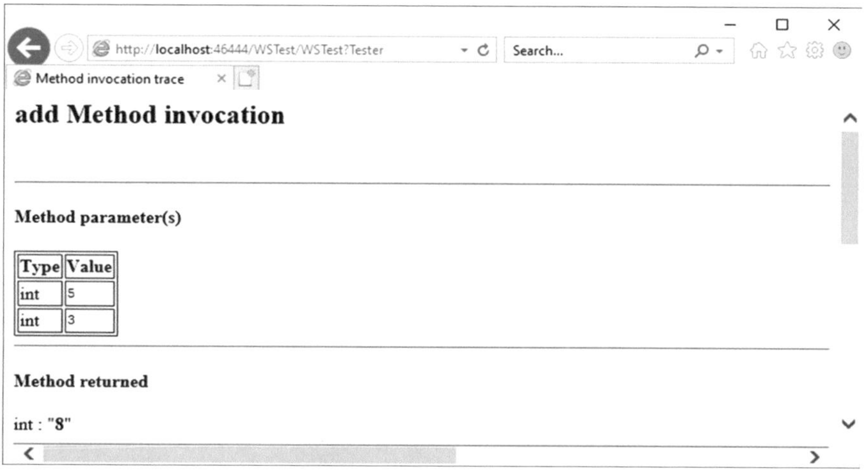

Fig. 9.12 The Web Service testing result

9.3.5 *Create Web Service Clients to Consume the Web Service*

In fact, you can develop any kind of Java applications as a consuming project to consume a Web service, such as a general desktop Java application project, a Java servlet, or a JSP page in a Web application.

To make this client project simple, we prefer to build a simple Java desktop application project **WSTestClient** to consume this Web service.

Perform the following operations to create our client project:

1) Choose **File > New Project** menu item to open **New Project** wizard. Select **Java** from the **Categories** list and **Java Application** from the **Projects** list, and click on the **Next** button.
2) Name the project **WSTestClient**, and select an appropriate location for this client project. Leave **Create Main Class** checkbox checked, and accept all other default settings. Your finished **Name and Location** wizard should match one that is shown in Fig. 9.13. Click on the **Finish** button to complete this new project creation process.
3) Right click on our new client project **WSTestClient** node from the **Projects** window, and choose **New > Web Service Client** item to open the **New Web Service Client** wizard.
4) Click on the **Browse** button that is next to the **Project** radio button to browse to our Web service project **WSTest**, as shown in Fig. 9.14. Click on our Web service **WSTest** and click on the **OK** button.
5) Your finished **New Web Service Client** wizard should match one that is shown in Fig. 9.15. Click on the **Finish** button to complete this new consuming project creation process.

Two issues need to be noticed if some errors occurred for this WSDL Location mapping process: (1) The GlassFish Server must be run first, (2) The Web Service project WSTest **must be deployed first. Complete these two steps before you can locate this WSDL.**

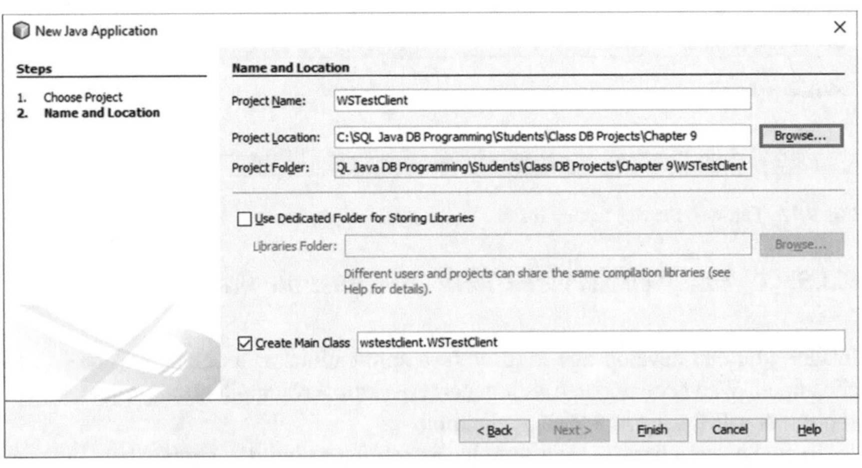

Fig. 9.13 The finished Name and Location wizard

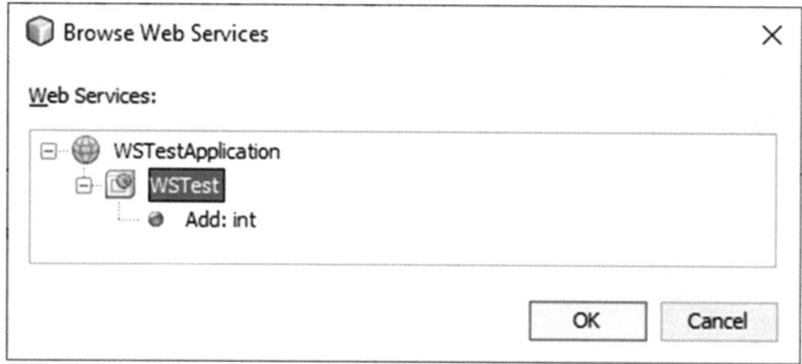

Fig. 9.14 The Web service browse wizard

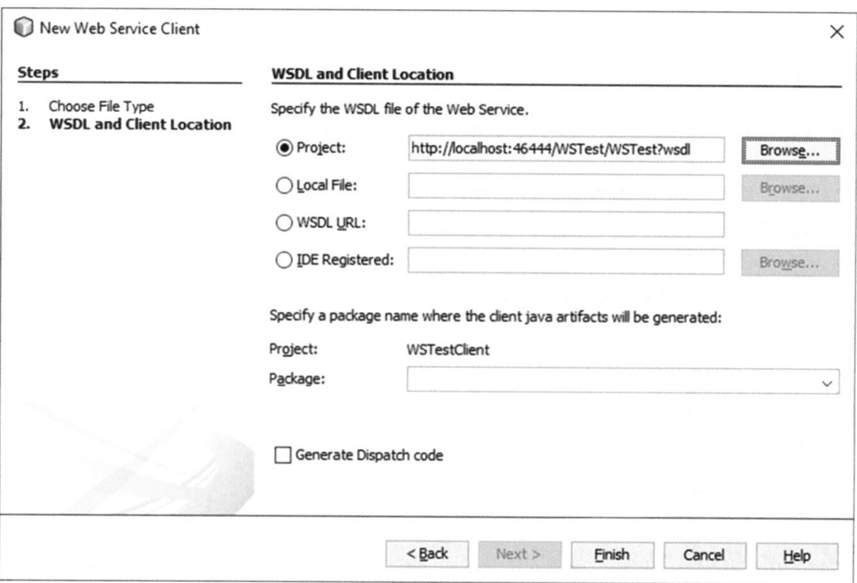

Fig. 9.15 The finished New Web Service Client wizard

6) A new node named **Web Service References** with the following components has been added into our client project **WSTestClient**, as shown in Fig. 9.16:

   (a) Our target Web service output file **WSTest**
   (b) Our Web service port file **WSTestPort**
   (c) Our operation **Add()** method

Now let's build the codes for this consuming project to consume our Web service. Perform the following operations to build the codes for this consuming project:

1) Double click on our main Java file **WSTestClient.java** that is located at the **Source Packages\wstestclient** node to open the code window of this file.
2) Enter the codes that are shown in Fig. 9.17 into the **main()** method on this file.

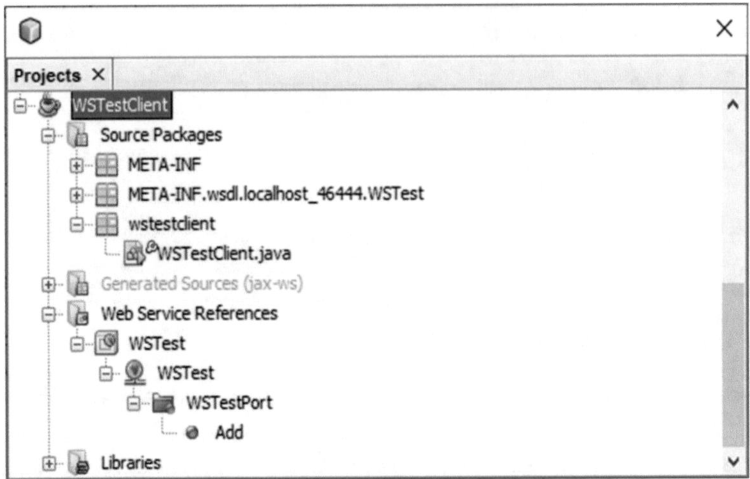

Fig. 9.16 The new added Web Service References node and components

```
  public class Main {
      /**
       * @param args the command line arguments
       */
      public static void main(String[] args) {
      // TODO code application logic here
A     try {
B         org.wstest.WSTest_Service service = new org.wstest.WSTest_Service();
C         org.wstest.WSTest port = service.getWSTestPort();
D         int a = 5, b = 7;
E         int result = port.add(a, b);
F         System.out.println("Result = " + result);
      }
G     catch (Exception ex){
        System.out.println("exception" + ex);
      }
    }
  }
```

Fig. 9.17 The codes for the main() method

Let's have a closer look at this piece of codes to see how it works.

A. A **try … catch** block is used to call our Web service to perform a two-integer addition operation.
B. A new Web service instance **service** is created based on our Web service class **WSTestService**.
C. The **getWSTestPort()** method is executed to get the current port used by our Web service. This port is returned and assigned to a new Port instance **port**.
D. Two testing integers are created and initialized with 5 and 7, respectively.
E. The operation method **Add()** in our Web service is called to perform this addition operation. The running result of this method is assigned to a local variable named **result**.

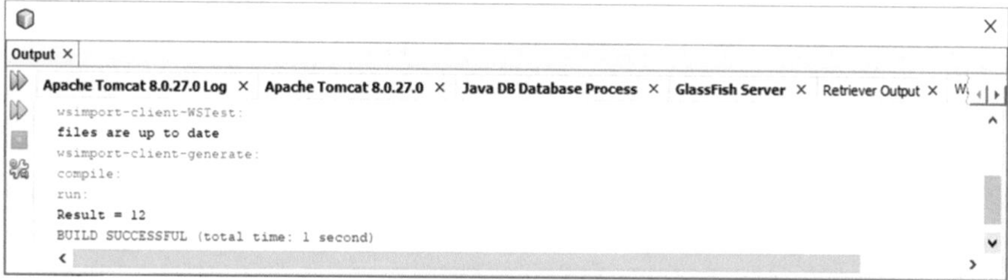

Fig. 9.18 The running result of calling our Web service

F. The result is displayed on the **Output** window.
G. Any exception during this Web service calling process will be tracked and displayed on the **Output** window, too.

Now let's build and run our client project to call the **Add()** method built in our Web service to perform this two-integer addition operation.

Click on the **Clean and Build Main Project** button to build our client project. Then right click on our project **WSTestClient**, and select the **Run** menu item from the popup menu. The running result is shown in Fig. 9.18.

It can be found that the calling of our Web service is successful and the addition result of 12 has been returned. Our first Web service project is successful.

At this point, we have gotten a fundamental knowledge and basic understanding about Java Web services. Now let's start building some real Java Web services projects to perform database query and manipulation operations against our sample database.

9.4 Getting Started with Java Web Services Using NetBeans IDE

In the following sections, we will develop and build different Java Web services projects based on the database system, SQL Server 2019 Express, and different database operations.

A sequence of real Java Web service projects will be developed and built, such as Web services project, to access and manipulate data against the SQL Server database by adding the different operations or methods to those Web service projects, respectively. Due to the space limitations, we will concentrate on accessing and manipulating data against the Faculty table and accessing and manipulating data against the Course table in our sample SQL Server 2019 database:

1) Query data from the SQL Server 2019 database with **QueryFaculty()** operation.
2) Insert data into the SQL Server 2019 database with **InsertFaculty()** operation.

3) Update and delete data against the SQL Server 2019 database with **UpdateFaculty()** and **DeleteFaculty()** operations.
4) Query data from the SQL Server 2019 database with **QueryCourse()** operation.
5) Query detailed course information from the SQL Server 2019 database with **DetailCourse()** operation.
6) Update and delete data against the SQL Server 2019 database with **UpdateCourse()** and **DeleteCourse()** operations.

For each Web services project, we need to build an associated Web client project to consume the Web services project to test its function. The following client projects will be built:

1) Web client project to consume the Web service to access the SQL Server database
2) Web client project to consume the Web service to insert data into the SQL Server database
3) Web client project to consume the Web service to update and delete data against the SQL Server database
4) Web client project to consume the Web service to query course information from the SQL Server database
5) Web client project to consume the Web service to query course details from the SQL Server database
6) Web client project to consume the Web service to update and delete course data against the SQL Server database

As we know, we can develop any kind of client project to consume a Web service, either a standard Java desktop application, a JSP page, or a JSF page. We will develop and build different client projects to consume our Web services to enable our projects to meet the actual needs in our real world.

9.5 Build Java Web Service Projects to Access SQL Server Database

In this section, we will discuss how to access and perform queries and manipulations against SQL Server 2019 database using Java Web services. To make our Web Services project simple, we will use the following components to fulfill this query and manipulation:

- Build different operations or methods in our Web services as interfaces to communicate with Web clients that will be built in the future to perform desired data actions.
- Use runtime object method to actually access and query our sample SQL Server 2019 database.

The structure and components used in our Web services are shown in Fig. 9.19.

Now let's create our first Web service project **WebServiceSQLApp** to perform data query and manipulation against our sample database.

9.5.1 Create a New Java Web Application Project WebServiceSQLApp

When creating a new Web service application project, we need to select a desired container to deploy our Web service. Generally we can either deploy our Web service in a Web container or in an EJB container. In this application we prefer to use a Web container since we are creating a Java EE 7 application.

Perform the following operations to create our Web application project **WebServiceSQLApp**:

1) Launch NetBeans IDE 8.2, and choose **File > New Project** (Ctrl-Shift-N). Select **Web Application** from the **Java Web** category, and click on the **Next** button.
2) Name the project **WebServiceSQLApp**, and click on the **Browse** button to select a desired location for the project. In this application, we used the **C:\Class DB Projects\Chapter 9** as our project location. Click on the **Next** button to continue.
3) Select **GlassFish Server** as our Web container and **Java EE 7 Web** as the Java EE version; your finished **Server and Settings** wizard should match one that is shown in Fig. 9.20. Click on the **Finish** button to complete this new application creation process.

Now that a Web application has been created with a selected Web container, next we can create our new Web service project **WebServiceSelect**.

9.5.2 Create a New Java SOAP-Based Web Service Project WebServiceSelect

The function of this Web service is to perform data queries and manipulations to our sample SQL Server 2019 database and return the result. Perform the following operations to create this new Web service project **WebServiceSelect**:

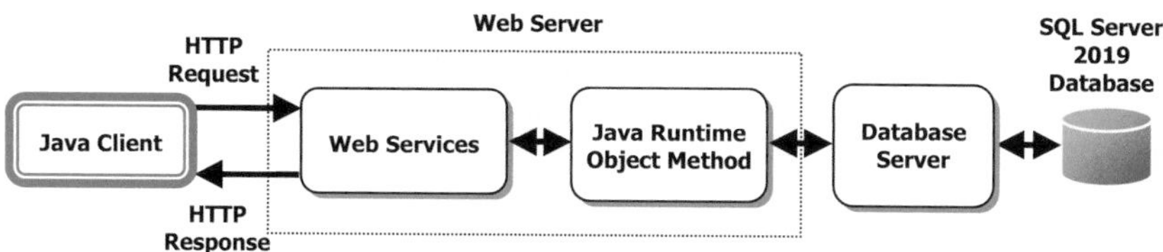

Fig. 9.19 The structure and components used in our Web services

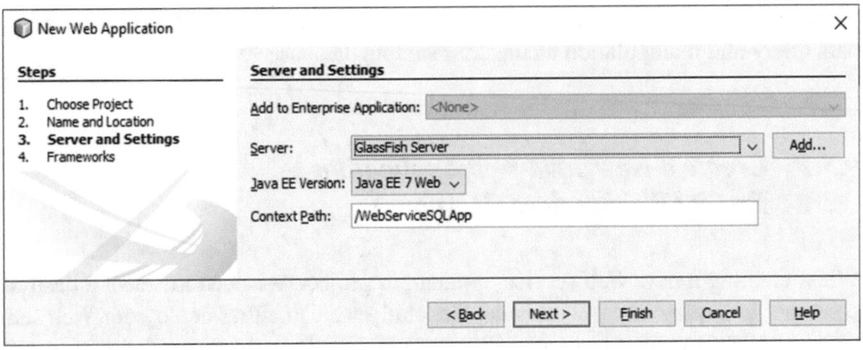

Fig. 9.20 The finished Server and Settings wizard

1) In the opened **Projects** window, right click on our new created project **WebServiceSQLApp**, and select the **New > Other** menu item to open the **New File** wizard.
2) Select **Web Services** from the **Categories** list and **Web Service** from the **File Types** list, and click on the **Next** button.
3) Name the Web service **WebServiceSelect** and type **org.ws.sql** into the **Package** field. Leave **Create Web Service from Scratch** selected.

Your finished **Name and Location** wizard should match one that is shown in Fig. 9.21. Click on the **Finish** button to complete this process.

Before we can add any operation to this Web service project, we need first to add a JDialog class into our project, and we need to use this component to display the debug information during the testing process for our Web service project.

Next let's handle the adding new operations and coding for the new added operations or methods in our Web service.

9.5.3 Add New Operations to Our Web Services to Perform Data Query

The main purpose of using the Web service in this section is to query data from the **Faculty** table in our sample database; therefore, we need to add one new operation **QueryFaculty()** to the Web service project.

Perform the following operations to add a new operation **QueryFaculty()** into our Web service:

1) Double click our project source file **WebServiceSelect.java** from the **Projects** window under the **Source Packages\org.ws.sql** folder to open it, and click on the **Design** button on the top of the window to open the **Design View** of our Web service project.

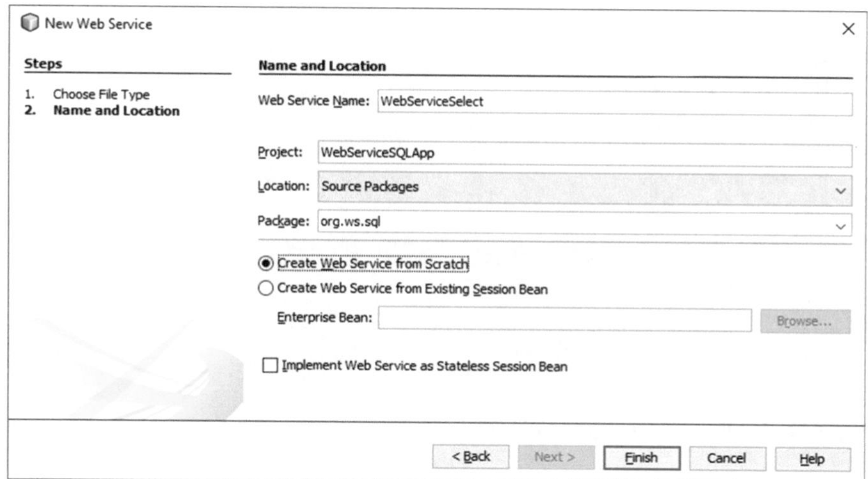

Fig. 9.21 The finished Name and Location wizard

2) Right click on the default operation **hello**, and click on the **Remove Operation** item from the popup menu to delete this operation.
3) Click on the **Add Operation** button to open the **Add Operation** wizard.
4) Enter **QueryFaculty** into the **Name** field, and click on the **Browse** button that is next to the **Return Type** combo box. Type **ArrayList** into the **Type Name** field and select the item **ArrayList (java.util)** from the list, and click on the **OK** button.
5) Click on the **Add** button, and enter **fname** into the **Name** parameter field. Keep the default type **java.lang.String** unchanged, and click on the **OK** button.

Your finished **Add Operation** wizard should match one that is shown in Fig. 9.22. Click on the **OK** button again to complete this add operation process.

Click on the **Source** button on the top of this window to open the code window of our Web service project. On the opened code window, enter the codes that are shown in Fig. 9.23 into this new added operation.

Let's have a closer look at this piece of codes to see how it works.

A. First the **java.sql.*** package should be imported since we need to use SQL components and all components are prototyped and declared in that package.
B. Then two class-level variables, **con** and **msgDlg**, are created. The first variable is used to hold the connection instance to our sample database, and the second is used to track and display the debug information when this Web service project is tested later.
C. An **ArrayList** instance **result** is created, and this is an array list instance used to collect and store our query result and return to the consuming project. The reason we used this ArrayList and not List is that the former is a concrete class but the latter is an abstract class,

Fig. 9.22 The finished Add Operation wizard

```
A  import java.sql.*;
   @WebService(serviceName = "WebServiceSelect")
   public class WebServiceSelect {
B     Connection con = null;
      public class WebServiceSQL {
      @WebMethod(operationName = "QueryFaculty")
      public ArrayList QueryFaculty(@WebParam(name = "fname") String fname) {
         //TODO write your implementation code here:
C        ArrayList<String> result = new ArrayList<String>();
D        String query = "SELECT * FROM Faculty WHERE faculty_name = ?";
         try {
E           con = DBConnection(con);
F           PreparedStatement pstmt =con.prepareStatement(query);
G           pstmt.setString(1, fname);
H           ResultSet rs = pstmt.executeQuery();
I           ResultSetMetaData rsmd = rs.getMetaData();
J           while (rs.next()){
               for (int colNum = 1; colNum <= rsmd.getColumnCount() - 1; colNum++)
                  result.add(rs.getString(colNum));
            }
K           con.close();
L           return result;
         }
M        catch (Exception ex) {
            System.out.println("exception is: " + ex);
            return null;
         }
      }
   }
```

Fig. 9.23 The codes for the new operation QueryFaculty()

and a runtime exception may be encountered if an abstract class is used as a returned object to the calling method.

D. The SQL query statement is created with a positional parameter as the dynamic parameter for the query criterion **faculty_name**.

E. The user-defined method **DBConnection()** that will be built later is called to set up a connection between our Web service and our sample database. A connection instance **con** is returned after the execution of this method.

F. A new PreparedStatement instance **pstmt** is declared and created to perform the query.
G. The **setString()** method is used to set up the actual value that is our input faculty name for the positional parameter **faculty_name**.
H. The query is performed by calling the **executeQuery()** method, and the query result is returned and stored in a ResultSet object **rs**.
I. To get more related information about the queried database, the **getMetaData()** method is executed, and the result is stored in a ResultSetMetaData instance **rsmd**.
J. A **while** and a **for** loop are used to pick up each column from the queried result that is stored in the ResultSet object **rs**. In fact, the **while** loop only runs one time since only one matched faculty row will be returned. The **getColumnCount()** method is used as the upper-bound of the for loop, but this upper bound must be decreased by 1 since totally there are eight (8) columns in the Faculty table, but we only need to query and pick the first seven (7) columns and the last column is the faculty image object but it cannot be added into the ArrayList as a String object. Thus this query only returns the first seven columns in the matched faculty row.
K. The **close()** method is executed to disconnect the connection to our database.
L. The queried result is returned.
M. The **catch** block is used to track and display any exception that occurred during this data query process, and a null will be returned if this situation really happened.

During the coding process, you may encounter some in-time compiling errors. The main reason for those errors is that some packages are missed. To fix these errors, just right click on any space inside this code window, and select the **Fix Imports** item to find and add those missed packages, such as **java.sql.***.

Next let's add another operation to our Web Service project to query and get the faculty image for the selected faculty member.

9.5.4 Add Another Operation to Our Web Service to Query Faculty Image

Perform the following operations to add a new operation **QueryImage()** into our Web service:

1) Click on the **Design** button on the top of the window to open the **Design View** of our Web service project file **WebServiceSelect.java**.
2) Click on the **Add Operation** button to open the **Add Operation** wizard.
3) Enter **QueryImage** into the **Name** field, and click on the **Browse** button that is next to the **Return Type** combo box. Type **Image** into the **Type Name** field, and select the item **Image (java.awt)** from the list, and click on the **OK** button.

4) Click on the **Add** button, and enter **fname** into the **Name** parameter field. Keep the default type **java.lang.String** unchanged, and click on the **OK** button.

Your finished **Add Operation** wizard should match one that is shown in Fig. 9.24. Click on the **OK** button again to complete this second add operation process.

Click on the **Source** button on the top of this window to open the code window of our Web service project. On the opened code window, enter the codes that are shown in Fig. 9.25 into this new added operation.

Let's have a closer look at this piece of codes to see how it works.

A. Some useful packages are first imported into this source window for this operation. You can right click on this code window and select **Fix Imports** item from the popup menu if you do not want to declare these packages yourself.
B. Some local objects and variables are declared here: the **bimg** is a **Blob** object since we need to retrieve a desired faculty image from the **Faculty** table and the image is a Blob format in our database column. The **fimg** is a type of **Image** object since this type of object can be used as a returned object from the Web Service project. Since this object belongs to the **java.awt.Image** class, thus a full package name is used.
C. The SQL query string is declared with the **faculty_name** as an input position parameter.
D. A **try-catch** block is used to perform this image query operation. First a connection method **DBConnection()**, which will be built in the next section, is executed to connect to our sample database **CSE_DEPT**.
E. A new PreparedStatement instance **pstmt** is declared and created to perform the query.

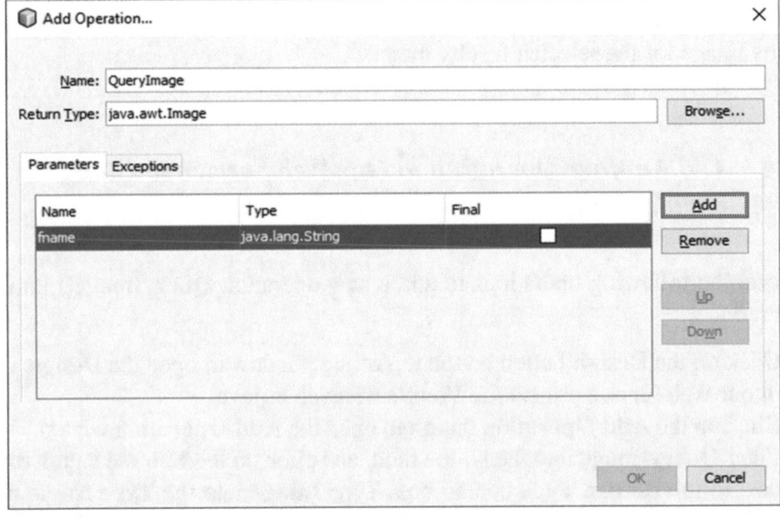

Fig. 9.24 The finished Add Operation wizard

```
  package org.ws.sql;
A import java.awt.Image;
  import java.io.InputStream;
  import java.util.ArrayList;
  import javax.jws.WebService;
  import javax.jws.WebMethod;
  import javax.jws.WebParam;
  import java.sql.*;
  import javax.imageio.ImageIO;

  @WebMethod(operationName = "QueryImage")
    public Image QueryImage(@WebParam(name = "fname") String fname) {
      //TODO write your implementation code here:
B     Blob bimg = null;
      java.awt.Image fimg = null;
C     String query = "SELECT fimage FROM Faculty WHERE faculty_name = ?";
      try {
D       con = DBConnection(con);
E       PreparedStatement pstmt =con.prepareStatement(query);
F       pstmt.setString(1, fname);
G       ResultSet rs = pstmt.executeQuery();
H       ResultSetMetaData rsmd = rs.getMetaData();
I       while (rs.next()){
          for (int i = 1; i <=rsmd.getColumnCount(); i++) {
J           if (i == rsmd.getColumnCount()){
              bimg = rs.getBlob("fimage");
K             InputStream in = bimg.getBinaryStream();
              fimg = ImageIO.read(in);
L             break;
            }
          }
        }
M       con.close();
        rs.close();
        pstmt.close();
        return fimg;
      }
N     catch (Exception ex) {
        System.out.println("exception is: " + ex);
        return null;
      }
    }
  }
```

Fig. 9.25 The codes for the second operation QueryImage()

F. The **setString()** method is used to set up the actual value that is our input faculty name for the positional parameter **faculty_name**.
G. The query is performed by calling the **executeQuery()** method, and the query result is returned and stored in a ResultSet object **rs**.
H. To get more detailed information about the queried database, the **getMetaData()** method is executed, and the result is stored in a ResultSetMetaData instance **rsmd**.
I. A **while** and a **for** loop are used to pick up the queried faculty image stored in the ResultSet object **rs**. In fact, the **while** loop only runs one time since only one matched faculty row will be returned. The **getColumnCount()** method is used as the upper-bound of the for loop, and it should be equal to eight (8) since the 8th column in the Faculty table stored the desired faculty image.
J. An **if** selection structure is used to check if the 8th column has been retrieved. If it is, the **getBlob()** method is executed to pick up the image in that column and assigned to the local object **bimg**, which is Blob type object.

K. The system method **getBinaryStream()** is used to convert this Blob object to an **Image** object **fimg** with another system method **read()** that belongs to the **ImageIO** class.
L. Then a **break** instruction skips out and terminates this **for** loop.
M. A sequence of cleaning jobs is performed to close all used objects, and the queried faculty image is returned.
N. The **catch** block is used to catch and display any possible error during this image query.

Now let's build our user-defined method **DBConnection()** to set up a connection to our sample database from our Web service project.

9.5.5 Build the User-Defined Method DBConnection()

To make our Web service project simple, we will use the Java runtime object method to perform this database connection function. In the opened code window of our Web service project file WebServiceSelect.java, add the codes that are shown in Fig. 9.26 into this service to create and define this connection method **DBConnection()**.

Let's have a closer look at this piece of codes to see how it works.

A. A **try catch** block is used to perform this database connection function. First the SQL Server JDBC driver is loaded using the **forName()** method.
B. The **catch** block is used to track and detect any possible exception for this JDBC driver loading process. The debug information will be displayed using the **msgDlg** object if any exception occurred.

```
  private Connection DBConnection(Connection conn) {
A      try
       {
          //Load and register SQL Server driver
          Class.forName("com.microsoft.sqlserver.jdbc.SQLServerDriver");
       }
B      catch (Exception e) {
          System.out.println ("Class not found exception!" + e.getMessage());
       }
C      String url = "jdbc:sqlserver://localhost\\SQL2019EXPRESS:5000;databaseName=CSE_DEPT;";
D      try {
          conn = DriverManager.getConnection(url,"SMART","Happy2020");
       }
E      catch (SQLException e) {
          System.out.println ("Could not connect! " + e.getMessage());
          e.printStackTrace();
       }
F      return conn;
  }
```

Fig. 9.26 The codes for the user-defined method DBConnection()

C. Our sample SQL Server database connection URL is defined, and it is used to set up a connection to our sample database. Refer to Sect. 6.3.3.3.1 in Chap. 6 to get more details about this connection URL.
D. Another **try** block is used to set up a connection to our sample database using the **getConnection()** method that belongs to the DriverManager class with the username and password as arguments.
E. The **catch** block is used to detect and display any possible exception during this connection process.
F. The established connection object is returned to the calling method.

At this point, we have finished all coding development for our Web service used to perform queries to our Faculty table. Now let's build and deploy our Web service project.

9.5.6 Deploy the Web Service Project and Test the Data Query Function

Perform the following operations to build and deploy our Web service project:

1) Click on the **Clean and Build Main Project** button to build our Web service.
2) Right click on our Web application **WebServiceSQLApp**, and select the **Deploy** item to deploy our Web service. If everything is fine, a successful deployment result should be displayed, as shown in Fig. 9.27.
3) To test this Web service, right click on our target service output file **WebServiceSelect** under the **Web Services** node in our project, and select the **Test Web Service** item.
4) The tested page is opened and displayed as shown in Fig. 9.28.
5) Enter a desired faculty name such as **Ying Bai** into the text field, and click on the **queryImage** button. The selected faculty image is returned as [B : **"[B@6a225a6f"**. Click on the **Back** button to return the testing page again for the next testing.

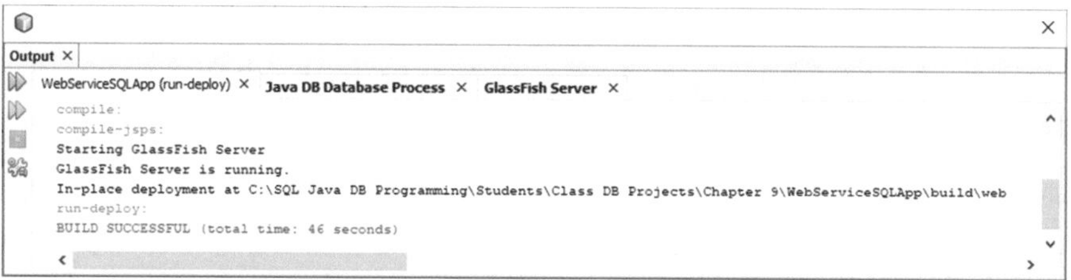

Fig. 9.27 The deployment result of our Web service project

http://localhost:46444/Web Search...

WebServiceSelect Web Serv...

WebServiceSelect Web Service Tester

This form will allow you to test your web service implementation (WSDL File)

To invoke an operation, fill the method parameter(s) input boxes and click on the button labeled with the method name.

Methods :

public abstract byte[] org.ws.sql.WebServiceSelect.queryImage(java.lang.String)

queryImage ( )

public abstract java.util.List org.ws.sql.WebServiceSelect.queryFaculty(java.lang.String)

queryFaculty ( )

Fig. 9.28 The tested page for our Web service

6) Enter a desired faculty name such as **Ying Bai** into the text field, and click on the **queryFaculty** button to call our Web service. The running result is shown in Fig. 9.29.

It can be found that all seven pieces of queried faculty information for the selected faculty member have been retrieved and the data query for our **Faculty** table is successful.

Two issues need to be noticed if some errors occurred for this Testing:

1) **The JDBC Driver 4.2 must be added into this project. By checking the** Properties **of this project and cli cking on the** Libraries **node. If not, click on the** Add JAR/Folder **button and browse to the location the** sqljdbc41.jar **is downloaded to add it.**
2) **The GlassFish Server must be in the running status. Go to** Services **window and** Servers **folder to confirm this.**

Next we can develop some Web client projects to consume this Web service to perform data query from the Faculty table in our sample database. In fact, as we discussed in Sect. 9.3.5, we can develop different kinds of Web client projects to consume a Web service. In the following sections, we will discuss two popular client projects, Window-based and Web-based clients, to consume our Web service to perform queries to our Faculty table.

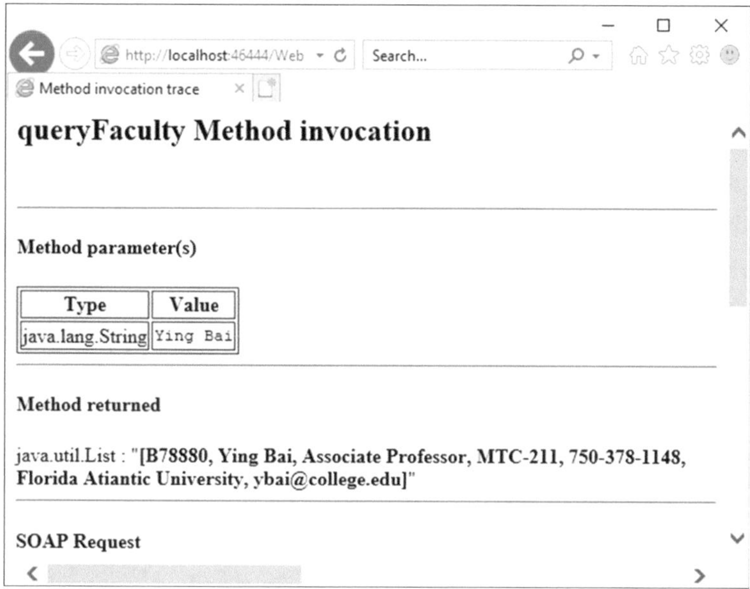

Fig. 9.29 The testing result of our Web service project

First let's discuss how to build a Window-based client project to consume our Web service.

9.6 Build a Window-Based Client Project to Consume the Web Service

To save time and space, we can use a Window-based project **SQLSelectObject** we developed in Sect. 6.3 in Chap. 6 to build this client project. The project can be found from the folder **Class DB Projects\Chapter 6** that is located under the **Students** folder at the Springer ftp site (refer to Fig. 1.2 in Chap. 1).

9.6.1 Copy the FacultyFrame and MsgDislog Components as GUIs

Perform the following operations to create a GUI for our Window-based client project **WinClientSelect** to consume our Web service:

1) Launch NetBeans IDE 8.2, and choose **File > New Project** item.

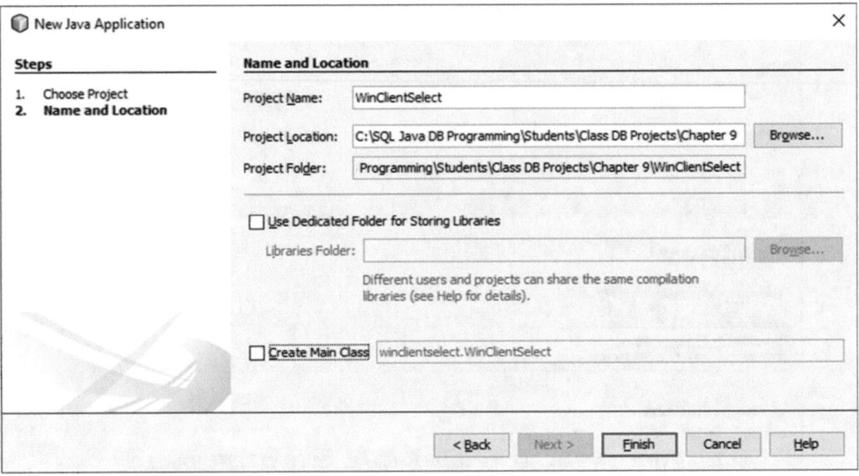

Fig. 9.30 The finished Name and Location wizard

Copy Class
New Name: FacultyFrame
Project: WinClientSelect
Location: Source Packages
To Package:
Preview Refactor Cancel Help

Fig. 9.31 The finished Copy Class wizard

2) Select **Java** and **Java Application** from the **Categories** and the **Projects** lists, respectively. Click on the **Next** button.
3) Name the project as **WinClientSelect**, and select a desired folder to save this project. Uncheck the **Create Main Class** checkbox. Your finished **Name and Location** wizard should match one that is shown in Fig. 9.30. Click on the **Finish** button to create this new project.
4) Go to the **Students** folder in the Springer ftp site, and load and open the project **SQLSelectObject** from the folder **Class DB Projects\Chapter 6**.
5) On the opened project, right click on the Faculty Frame file **FacultyFrame.java** under the project package node, and select the **Refactor > Copy** item to copy this form file.
6) On the opened **Copy Class – FacultyFrame** wizard, select our new project **WinClientSelect** from the **Project** combo box, and remove the **1** after the **FacultyFrame** from the **New Name** field. Your finished **Copy Class – FacultyFrame** wizard is shown in Fig. 9.31.

7) Click on the **Refactor** button to make a refactoring copy for this frame file.
8) Return to our new project **WinClientSelect**, and you can find that a copied **FacultyFrame.java** file has been pasted in the default package in our project.

Perform a similar **Refactor** operation to copy the **MsgDialog.java** file, and paste it into our new client project. Next let's develop the codes to call our Web service to perform this faculty data query. However, before we can begin the coding process, we must first set up or create a Web service reference for our **WinClientSelect** project to enable our project to recognize that Web service and to call it when it is instructed to do that.

9.6.2 Create a Web Service Reference for Our Window-Based Client Project

Perform the following operations to set up a Web service reference for our client project:

1) First our Web Service project **WebServiceSQLApp** must be deployed to make the GlassFish Server to run. To do that, right click on our service project **WebServiceSQLApp**, and select the **Deploy** item from the popup menu to start deploying it.
2) Right click on our client project **WinClientSelect** from the **Projects** window, and select the **New > Other** item to open the **New File** wizard.
3) On the opened **New File** wizard, select **Web Services** from the **Categories** and **Web Service Client** from the **File Types** list, respectively. Click on the **Next** button to continue.
4) Click on the **Browse** button for the **Project** field, and expand our Web application project **WebServiceSQLApp**, and click on our Web service project **WebServiceSelect** to select it. Then click on the **OK** button to select this Web service. Your finished Web Service Client wizard should match one that is shown in Fig. 9.32.
5) Click on the **Finish** button to complete this Web service reference setup process.

Immediately you can find a new node named **Web Service References** has been created and added into our client project. Expand this node, and you can find the associated Web service port and our Web service operations **QueryFaculty()** and **QueryImage()** under that node.

Now let's develop the codes for this project to call the Web service to perform the data query from the **Faculty** table in our sample database.

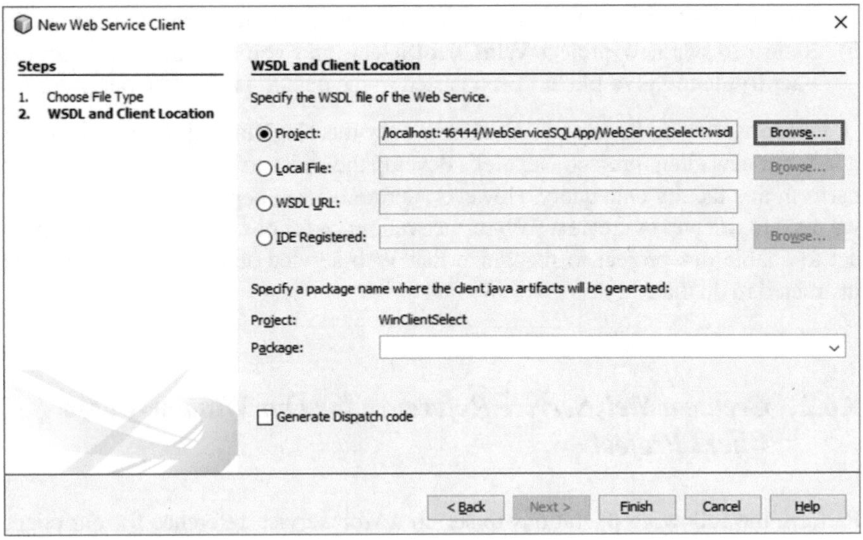

Fig. 9.32 The finished New Web Service Client wizard

9.6.3 Develop the Codes to Call Our Web Service Project

The coding process is divided into two parts: modify the original codes and add new codes. First let's do some modifications to the original codes in this FacultyFrame class. Perform the following code modifications to make this project as our Web consuming project:

1) Double click on our new copied **FacultyFrame.java** file from our project to open it.
2) Click on the **Source** button on the top to open the code window.
3) Open the **SelectButtonActionPerformed()** method, and remove all codes inside this method except the first or top two coding lines and the codes in the last **try-catch** block.

Now let's develop codes to perform the faculty data query by calling our Web service.

On the **Design** view of the FacultyFrame form window, double click on the **Select** button to open its event method **SelectButtonActionPerformed()**. Then enter the codes that are shown in Fig. 9.33 into this method. The new added and modified codes have been highlighted in bold.

Let's have a closer look at this piece of codes to see how it works.

A. A java TextField array, **JTextField[]**, is declared first, and all seven related TextFields used to store a faculty record are initialized to this TextField. The order of these TextFields must be identical with the order of the columns in our **Faculty** table. One point to be noticed is that all of these TextFields must be in

```
  private void SelectButtonActionPerformed(java.awt.event.ActionEvent evt) {
    // TODO add your handling code here:
A   javax.swing.JTextField[] f_field = {FacultyIDField,FacultyNameField,TitleField,OfficeField,PhoneField,
                                                                  CollegeField,EmailField};
B   ArrayList al = new ArrayList();
    try {
C       org.ws.sql.WebServiceSelect_Service service = new org.ws.sql.WebServiceSelect_Service();
D       org.ws.sql.WebServiceSelect port = service.getWebServiceSelectPort();
E       al.clear();
F       al = (ArrayList)port.queryFaculty(ComboName.getSelectedItem().toString());
G       for (int col = 0; col < al.size(); col++)
           f_field[col].setText(al.get(col).toString());
    }
H   catch (Exception ex){
       System.out.println("exception: " + ex);
    }
    try {
I        if (!ShowFaculty()){
            System.out.println.setMessage("No matched faculty image found!");
         }
      } catch (SQLException | IOException ex) {
         Logger.getLogger(FacultyFrame.class.getName()).log(Level.SEVERE, null, ex);
      }
  }
```

Fig. 9.33 The modified codes for the SelectButtonActionPerformed() method

a single line in the real code window; otherwise an error may be displayed if you arrange these TextFields in a way that is shown in here. Due to the space limitations, here it separates into two lines.

B. A new ArrayList instance **al** is created to receive and hold the query result.

C. A **try catch** block is used to call our Web service to perform the faculty data query operation. First a new Web service instance **service** is created based on our Web service class **WebServiceSelect_Service**. Starting NetBeans IDE 7, a keyword **_Service** must be appended after the Web Service name to create a new service object.

D. The **getWebServiceSelectPort()** method is executed to get the current port used by our Web service. This port is returned and assigned to a new Port instance **port**.

E. Before we can call our Web service, make sure that our ArrayList object **al** is empty by executing the **clear()** method.

F. The **queryFaculty()** method defined in our Web service is called to perform this faculty data query. Two points to be noted are:

   1) The argument of this method is a selected faculty name obtained from the **getSelectedItem()** method from the Faculty Name combo box **ComboName**. Since this method returns an object, a **toString()** method must be attached to convert it to a string.
   2) An ArrayList cast must be used to make sure that the returned query result is in this ArrayList type since an **ArrayList<String>** type is used in our Web service project. The query result is assigned to our ArrayList instance **al**.

G. A **for** loop is used to pick up each column from the query result using the **get()** method. Two points to be noted are:

1) The argument of the **get()** method indicates the index of each column in the returned query result that is a single row, and the data type of this method is an object. Therefore a **toString()** method must be attached to convert it to a string.
2) To assign each column to each item in the **f_field** array, the **setText()** method must be used.

H. The **catch** block is used to track and display any possible exception during this Web service calling process.
I. The user-defined method **ShowFaculty()** is modified by removing its argument. The codes for this method will be built later.

During the coding process, you may encounter some real-time compiling errors. Most of these errors are introduced by missing some packages that contain classes or components used in this file. To fix these errors, just right click on this code window, and select the **Fix Imports** item to load and import those missed packages to the top of this code window.

Now let's build the codes for our user-defined method **ShowFaculty()** to get and display a selected faculty image by calling another operation, **QueryImage()**, built in our Web Service.

```
    private boolean ShowFaculty() throws SQLException, IOException{
A       byte[] bimg = null;
        Image img = null;
        int imgId = 1, timeout = 1000;
        MediaTracker tracker = new MediaTracker(this);
        try {
B         org.ws.sql.WebServiceSelect_Service service = new org.ws.sql.WebServiceSelect_Service();
C         org.ws.sql.WebServiceSelect port = service.getWebServiceSelectPort();
D         bimg = port.queryImage(ComboName.getSelectedItem().toString());
E         ByteArrayInputStream binput = new ByteArrayInputStream(bimg);
          img = ImageIO.read(binput);
      }
F     catch (Exception ex){
         System.out.println("exception: " + ex);
      }
G       String imgPath = System.getProperty("user.dir");
H       String fimgName = ComboName.getSelectedItem().toString() + ".jpg";
I       File outfile = new File(imgPath + "/" + fimgName);
        ImageIO.write((RenderedImage) img, "jpg", outfile);
J       img = this.getToolkit().getImage(fimgName);
        Graphics g = ImageCanvas.getGraphics();
K       tracker.addImage(img, imgId);
L       try{
            if(!tracker.waitForID(imgId, timeout)){
               msgDlg.setMessage("Failed to load image");
               msgDlg.setVisible(true);
               return false;
            }
M           }catch(InterruptedException e){
              msgDlg.setMessage(e.toString());
              msgDlg.setVisible(true);
              return false;
            }
N           g.drawImage(img, 0, 0, ImageCanvas.getWidth(), ImageCanvas.getHeight(), this);
            return true;
    }
```

Fig. 9.34 The modified codes for the cmdSelectActionPerformed() method

In the opened **FacultyFrame.java** file, browse to this **ShowFaculty()** method, and replace all original codes with those codes shown in Fig. 9.34.

Let's have a closer look at these modified codes to see how they work.

A. Some local objects are declared first, which include a byte[] array object **bimg** and an Image object **img**, and both objects are used to hold the created **byte[]** image array and converted Image object. Both integer variables, **imgId** and **timeout**, are used to keep the image ID and timeout value when displaying this image in the Canvas object in our client.
B. A **try catch** block is used to call our Web service to perform the faculty data query operation. First a new Web service instance **service** is created based on our Web service class **WebServiceSelect_Service**. Starting NetBeans IDE 7, a keyword **_Service** must be appended after the Web Service name to create a new service object.
C. The **getWebServiceSelectPort()** method is executed to get the current port used by our Web service. This port is returned and assigned to a new Port instance **port**.
D. Now our Web Service operation, **QueryImage()**, is called with the selected faculty name as the argument to retrieve the selected faculty image from our sample database and assign it to our local variable **bimg**. One issue is that this returned object is an Image type when it is defined in our Web Service, but now we are using **byte[]** array data type to hold this image. The reason for that is due to the default conversion by NetBeans IDE.
E. Two coding lines in this section are used to convert the data type of this returned image from the **byte[]** to Image. A **ByteArrayInputStream** object and **ImageIO.read()** method must be used for this conversion.
F. A **catch** block is used to detect and report any error for this conversion process.
G. In order to store our retrieved faculty image into our current project folder, the system method, **getProperty()** with our current directory (**user.dir**), is used, and this current folder is assigned to a local string variable **imgPath**.
H. To get the selected faculty image, we need to get the current selected or queried faculty name from the Faculty Name combo box, and convert this item to a string and attach a "**.jpg**" to the image file name. We need to use the name of this faculty image later to store and display this selected faculty image in the Canvas.
I. To save this converted faculty image into our current project folder, a new File object is generated with the image path and image name. A system method, **ImageIO.write()**, is used to complete this image saving job.
J. To display the selected faculty image, the **getImage()** method that belongs to the abstract class **Toolkit** is executed to load the selected image. Since the Toolkit class is an abstract class, we used a method **getToolkit()** to create it instead of generating it by invoking its constructor. The **getGraphics()** method is called to get a Graphics context, and our **ImageCanvas** works as an image holder for this faculty image.
K. The **addImage()** method that belongs to the MediaTracker class is called to add our image with its ID into the tracking system.

L. A **try catch** block is used to begin this tracking process, and the **waitForID()** method is called to execute this tracking. If a timeout occurred for this tracking process, which means that the selected faculty image has not been loaded into the project, a warning message is displayed using our **MsgDialog** object, and a False is returned to indicate this error.
M. Any other possible exception or error will be caught by the **catch** block and to be displayed in our **msgDlg** dialog.
N. If no timeout error happened, which means that the selected faculty image has been loaded into our project and ready to be displayed, the **drawImage()** method is executed to display it in the **FacultyFrame** Form window. We want to display this image starting from the origin of the Canvas object, which is the upper-left corner of the canvas (0, 0), with a width and height that are identical with those of the canvas. Therefore, the **getWidth()** and **getHeight()** methods are called to get both of them from the canvas object. A **true** is returned to the main program to indicate that the execution of this method is successful.

Before we can build and run our client project to test this faculty query, add one more coding line, **System.exit(0);**, to the bottom of the **BackButtonActionPerformed()** handler or method on the Source window of this **FacultyFrame** class to terminate our project if the **Back** button is clicked.

9.6.4 Build and Run Our Client Project to Query Faculty Data via Web Service

Click on the **Clean and Build Main Project** button to build our client project. If everything is fine, click on the **Run Main Project** button to run our client project.

A message box may pop up to ask the main starting class, which is shown in Fig. 9.35. Select our **FacultyFrame** class as the starting class, and click on the **OK**

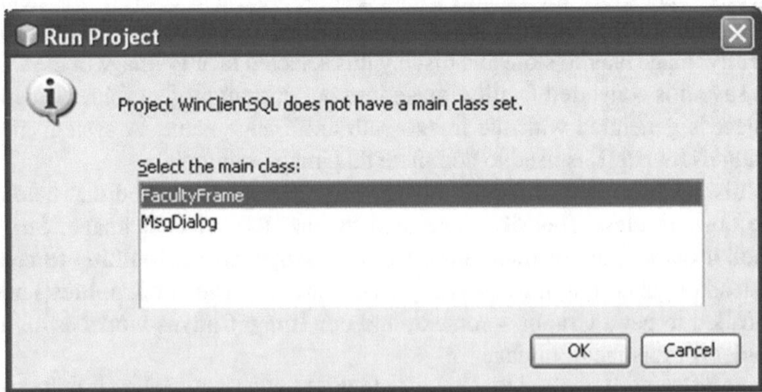

Fig. 9.35 The Run Project dialog

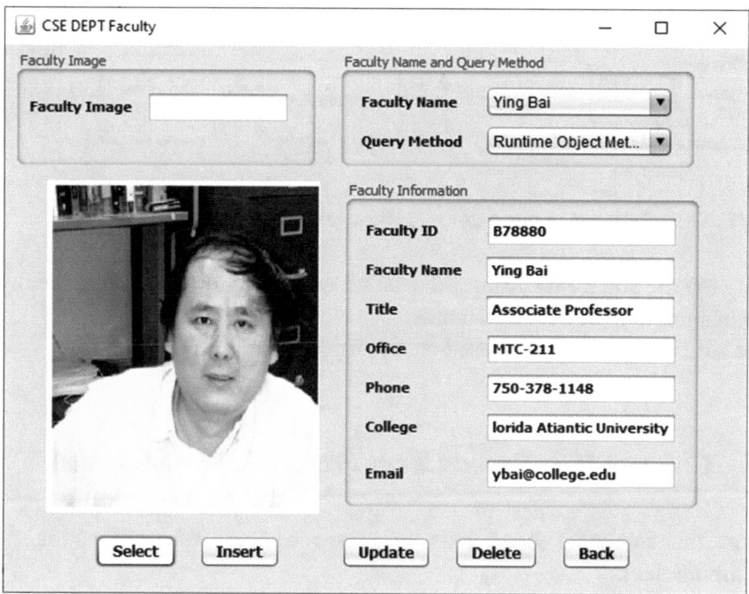

Fig. 9.36 The running result of our client project

button to run the project. The FacultyFrame form window is displayed, as shown in Fig. 9.36.

Select a desired faculty member, such as **Ying Bai**, from the Faculty Name combo box, and click on the **Select** button to query the detailed information for this faculty via our Web service. The queried result is displayed in this form, as shown in Fig. 9.36.

Our Web service and client projects are very successful!

One important point to be noted is that the Web Service project **WebServiceSQLApp** must be deployed first before our Windows Client project **WinClientSelect** can be run. Otherwise a dynamic error may be encountered.

A complete Window Client project **WinClientSelect** can be found from a folder **Class DB Projects\Chapter 9** that is under the **Students** folder at the Springer ftp site (refer to Fig. 1.2 in Chap. 1). Next let's build a Web-based client project to consume our Web service **WebServiceSelect** to perform the faculty data query action.

9.7 Build a Web-Based Client Project to Consume the Web Service

To save time and space, we can use some components and frames in a Web application project **JavaWebDBJSPSQL** we developed in Chap. 8 to build our Web-based client consuming project **WebClientSelect** in this section. In fact, we will use the

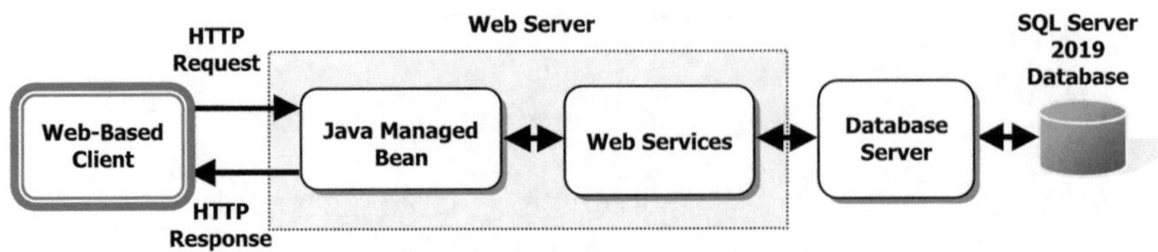

Fig. 9.37 The architecture of our Web-based client project

Faculty.jsp file and a Java managed bean class in that project to query faculty data from our sample SQL Server database.

The structure of this Web-based client project is shown in Fig. 9.37.

9.7.1 Create a Web-Based Client Project WebClientSelect

Perform the following operations to create a new Web application project **WebClientSelect**:

1) Launch NetBeans IDE 8.2, and go to **File > New Project** item to open the **New Project** wizard. Select the **Java Web** from the **Categories** list and **Web Application** from the **Projects** list, and then click on the **Next** button to go to the next wizard.
2) Enter **WebClientSelct** into the **Project Name** field as this new project's name. Make sure that the desired folder in which you want to save this project is included in the **Project Location** field, and then click on the **Next** button.
3) In the opened **Server and Settings** wizard, make sure that the **GlassFish Server** has been selected as the Web server for this Web application and the **Java EE 7 Web** has been selected for this application. Click on the **Next** button to continue.
4) On the next wizard, Frameworks, just click on the **Finish** button to complete this new Web application creation process.

Since we need a Faculty page as a view to query data from the Faculty table in our sample database, thus we need to add the **Faculty.jsp** and **FacultyProcess.jsp** files we built in the project **JavaWebDBJSPSQL** in Chap. 8 into our current project. Perform the following operations to complete this Web pages addition process:

1) Open the NetBeans IDE 8.2 and our project **JavaWebDBJSPSQL** that is located at the **Class DB Projects\Chapter 8** folder under the **Students** folder at the Springer ftp site, and copy two files, **Faculty.jsp** and **FacultyProcess.jsp**, from the **Web Pages** folder.
2) In the NetBeans IDE, open our new project **WebClientSelect**, and paste two copied files in step 1 into the folder **Web Pages** under our new project **WebClientSelect** project.

Next we need to create a Java managed bean class **FacultyBean.java** and copy the codes from the managed bean **FacultyQuery.java** we built in the Web application project **JavaWebDBJSPSQL** and paste them into our managed bean class **FacultyBean.java** in our Web-based client project.

9.7.2 Create a Java Managed Bean FacultyBean

Perform the following operations to create this Java managed bean into our current project:

1) Right click on our Web-based client project **WebClientSelect** from the **Projects** window, and select **New > Java Class** item to open the **New Java Class** wizard.
2) On the opened wizard, enter **FacultyBean** into the **Class Name** field, and enter **webclient** into the **Package** field.
3) Then click on the **Finish** button to complete this Java managed bean creation process.
4) Double click on our new created managed bean **FacultyBean.java** to open its code window.
5) Now open the Web application project **JavaWebDBJSPSQL** we built in Chap. 8. You can find and download this project from the folder **Class DB Projects\Chapter 8** under the **Students** folder at the Springer ftp site (refer to Fig. 1.2 in Chap. 1).
6) Expand the package **JavaWebDBJSPSQL**, and copy all codes inside the managed bean class **FacultyQuery.java** (exclude the imported packages at the top of this file).
7) In our opened managed bean **FacultyBean.java**, paste all copied codes inside this class.

Let's first modify the **FacultyBean.java** class file to make it as our new Java Bean class:

1) Change the class name from **FacultyQuery** to **FacultyBean**. Change the constructor's name from **FacultyQuery()** to **FacultyBean()**.
2) Remove the class **MsgDialog** and its object **msgDlg** coding line since we like to use **System.out.println()** to replace it.
3) Replace all **msgDlg.setMessage()** and **msgDlg.setVisible()** with **System.out.println()** method.
4) Remove all original codes inside the FacultyBean constructor.

Now let's modify the **FacultyProcess.jsp** file to make it as our new process page class:

1) Replace the import package name **<%@ page import="JavaWebDBJSPSQL Package.*" %>** with our new package **<%@ page import="webclient.*" %>** in coding line 10.

2) Replace the original constructor coding line (line 19), **FacultyQuery fQuery = new FacultyQuery();**, with our new Java Bean class **FacultyBean fQuery = new FacultyBean();**.
3) Click on the **Clean and Build Main Project** button to compile the project.

Before we can modify and develop the codes for the Java managed bean to perform faculty data query, we need first to add a Web reference to our current Web-based client project to enable our client to recognize our Web service and its operations.

9.7.3 Create a Web Service Reference for Our Web-Based Client Project

Perform the following operations to set up a Web service reference for our client project:

1) Open and deploy our Web Service project **WebServiceSQLApp** built in Sect. 9.5.
2) Right click on our client project **WebClientSelect** from the **Projects** window, and select the **New > Other** item to open the **New File** wizard.
3) On the opened **New File** wizard, select **Web Services** from the **Categories** and **Web Service Client** from the **File Types** list, respectively. Click on the **Next** button to continue.

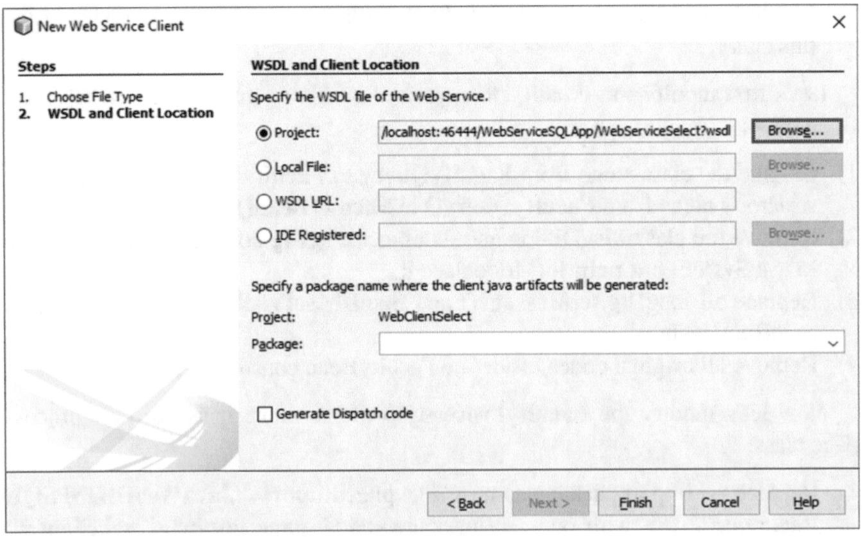

Fig. 9.38 The finished New Web Service Client wizard

4) Click on the **Browse** button for the **Project** field, and expand our Web application project **WebServiceSQLApp**, and click on our Web service project **WebServiceSelect** to select it. Then click on the **OK** button to select this Web service. Your finished Web Service Client wizard should match one that is shown in Fig. 9.38.
5) Click on the **Finish** button to complete this Web service reference setup process.

Immediately you can find a new node named **Web Service References** has been created and added into our client project. Expand this node, and you can find the associated Web service port and our Web service operations **QueryFaculty()** and **QueryImage()** under that node.

A point to be noted is that you must deploy our Web service project first before you can add this Web Reference to any client project.

Now let's modify and develop the codes to the different methods defined in the Java managed bean **FacultyBean** one by one to perform data actions against the Faculty table in our sample database by calling the associated operations defined in our Web service project.

9.7.4 Build the Codes to Call the Web Service to Perform Data Query

First let's concentrate on the **QueryFaculty()** method. The function of this method is to:

1) Call our Web service operation **QueryFaculty()** to pick up a matched faculty record from the Faculty table in our sample database.
2) Assign each queried column to the associated property defined in our Java managed bean class **FacultyBean.java**.

There are two ways to develop the codes inside the **QueryFaculty()** method to call our Web service operation **QueryFaculty()** to perform the faculty data query: (1) drag the Web service operation node from the **Projects** window, and drop it to inside the **QueryFaculty()** method and (2) right click on any place inside the **QueryFaculty()** method, and select the **Insert Code** item and choose the **Call Web Service Operation** item from the popup menu.

Let's use the first method as an example to add the codes to call our Web service operation.

```
  private static java.util.List<java.lang.Object> queryFaculty(java.lang.String fname) {
A     org.ws.sql.WebServiceSelect_Service service = new org.ws.sql.WebServiceSelect_Service();
B     org.ws.sql.WebServiceSelect port = service.getWebServiceSelectPort();
C     return port.queryFaculty(fname);
  }
```

Fig. 9.39 The automatically added codes by dragging the operation node

```
  public boolean QueryFaculty(String fname) {
A     org.ws.sql.WebServiceSelect_Service service = new org.ws.sql.WebServiceSelect_Service();
      org.ws.sql.WebServiceSelect port = service.getWebServiceSelectPort();
B     java.util.List<java.lang.Object> result = port.queryFaculty(fname);
C     System.out.println("Result = " + result);
D     return true;
  }
```

Fig. 9.40 The created codes for the QueryFaculty() method

1) Remove all original codes inside this **FacultyQuery()** method.
2) Expand the **Web Service References** node under our Web-based client project **WebClientSelect**, and continue to expand the sub-service port until our operation **QueryFaculty** node.
3) Open the code window of our Java managed bean class **FacultyBean.java**, and browse to the **QueryFaculty()** method.
4) Drag our Web service operation **QueryFaculty** node, and place it inside the **QueryFaculty()** method in our managed bean.

A piece of codes is automatically created and added into the bottom on this class, which has been highlighted in bold and shown in Fig. 9.39.

It is unnecessary to explain the function of this piece of codes line by line since all of coding lines are used to create a new instance of our Web Service class.

Now let's do some modifications to this piece of codes and add some codes to meet our data query requirements. Perform the following operations to make this piece of codes to perform our desired faculty data query:

A. Copy top two coding lines **A** and **B**, as shown in Fig. 9.39, and paste them into the top of inside the **QueryFaculty()** method, as shown in Fig. 9.40.
B. Create a new instance of **Java.util.List**, **result**, to call our Web Service operation **queryFaculty()** to get a selected faculty record in a List format.
C. For the debug purpose, the queried record can be printed and displayed in the Output window to track this query operation.
D. Return a true to indicate the success of this query operation.

Now let's add more codes to this method to complete this query and display action. Prior to doing this, delete those auto-created codes shown in Fig. 9.39 from the bottom of this method.

The Completed codes for the **QueryFaculty()** method are shown in Fig. 9.41. All new added codes have been highlighted in bold. Let's have a closer look at this piece of codes to see how they work.

```
    public boolean QueryFaculty(String  fname) {
A        ArrayList al = new ArrayList();
         try { // Call Web Service Operation
B           org.ws.sql.WebServiceSelect_Service service = new org.ws.sql.WebServiceSelect_Service();
            org.ws.sql.WebServiceSelect port = service.getWebServiceSelectPort();
            // TODO process result here
C           al = (ArrayList)port.queryFaculty(fname);
D           facultyID = al.get(0).toString();
            facultyName = al.get(1).toString();
            title = al.get(2).toString();
            office = al.get(3).toString();
            phone = al.get(4).toString();
            college = al.get(5).toString();
            email = al.get(6).toString();
E           facultyImage = getFacultyImage();
F        } catch (Exception ex) {
            // TODO handle custom exceptions here
            System.out.println("Exception in Query Faculty Table: " + ex);
            return false;
         }
G        return true;
    }
```

Fig. 9.41 The completed codes for the QueryFaculty() method

A. An **ArrayList** instance **al** is created first. This local variable **al** is used to hold the returned query record in a List format during the project runs.
B. Two auto-generated coding lines shown in Fig. 9.39, which are illustrated in steps **B** and **C** here, are used to create a new instance of our Web Service class and a new port instance, and both are used to access to our Web Service to perform data query operations later. Starting NetBeans IDE 8.0, a new instance generation format as shown here must be used to replace the original format.
C. A try-catch block is used to perform this data query via our Web Service. First the **queryFaculty()** operation in our Web service is executed to perform the faculty data query, and the result is returned and assigned to the local variable **al**. One point to be noted is that this returned result must be casted with **ArrayList** class since the **ArrayList<String>** data type is used for this query result in our Web service operation.
D. Seven returned columns are assigned to the associated properties defined in this managed bean **FacultyBean.java** class and will be displayed in the associated text field in our JSP page **Faculty.jsp** since each of those tags has been bound to each associated property. The **get()** method is used to pick up each column from the returned query result and a **toString()** method is used to convert each column to a String and assigned each of them to the associated property.
E. The getter method **getFacultyImage()** is executed to pick up a matched faculty image and display it in the faculty image box in our JSP page **Faculty.jsp**. Refer to that getter method to get the detailed codes for this method defined in this Java managed bean.
F. The **catch** block is used to track and display any possible exception during this Web service operation. A **false** is returned if any error was occurred to indicate this situation.

G. Otherwise a **true** is returned to indicate the successful execution of this method.

During the coding process, you may encounter some real-time compiling errors. Most of these errors are introduced by missing some packages that contain classes or components used in this file. To fix these errors, just right click on this code window, and select the **Fix Imports** item to load and import those missed packages to the top of this code window.

The last coding job is to modify one coding line in the bottom of the JSP file, **Faculty.jsp,** to safely terminate and exit our Web consume client project.

Open this JSP file **Faculty.jsp**, and browse to the bottom of that file, exactly in the coding line 520. Replace the original coding line:

```
<input type=submit value=Back name="Back" v:shapes="_x0000_s1048">
```

with the following coding line:

```
<input type=button value=Back onclick="self.close()" v:shapes="_x0000_s1048">
```

The reason for this changing is because the **Faculty.jsp** page in our previous projects will be returned to the **Selection.jsp** page if this **Back** button is clicked by the user, and the **Exit** button in the **Selection.jsp** page can be triggered to terminate our projects. But in this Web Client project, **WebClientSelect**, we only rebuild and use the **Faculty.jsp** page without using any other pages; thus, we need to modify the code in the **Back** button event handler to terminate and exit this project.

Now we have finished all coding process for this faculty data query action. Before we can build and run our project to test its function, we need to copy and save all images used in this project, including both faculty and students' image files, to our current project folder. Perform the following actions to finish this image file processing:

1) Open the **Images\Faculty** folder that is located under the **Students** folder at the Springer ftp site (refer to Fig. 1.2 in Chap. 1), and copy all faculty image files from this folder.
2) In the NetBeans IDE 8.2, open our project **WebClientSelect**, and click on the **Files** button on the top to open the **Files** window.
3) Then right click on the **web** node under our project **WebClientSelect**, and select the **New → Folder** item to open a New Folder wizard.
4) Enter **FImages** into the **Folder Name** box, and click on the **Finish** button to create this new folder.
5) Then paste all image files into this new added folder **FImages** under our current project node **WebClientSelect**.

Now we are ready to build and run our client project to test its function.

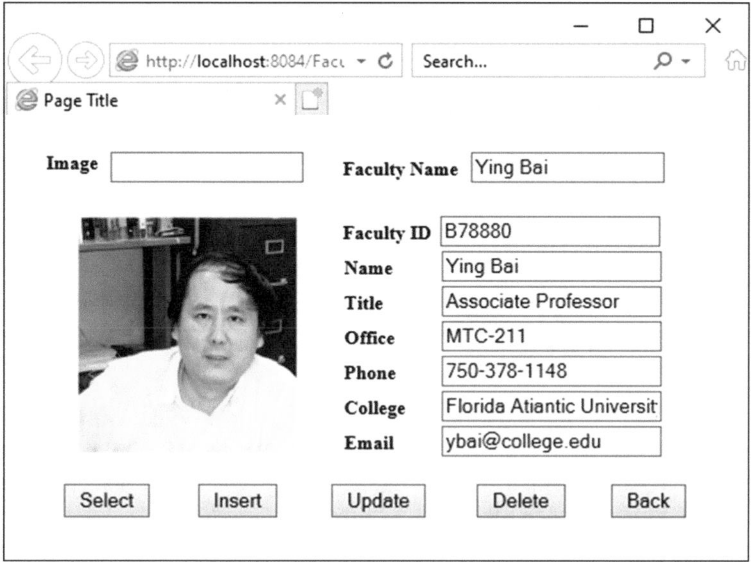

Fig. 9.42 The testing result for our Web client project

9.7.5 Build and Run Our Client Project to Query Faculty Data via Web Service

Click on the **Clean and Build Main Project** button to build our client project. If everything is fine, right click on our JSP page **Faculty.jsp** from the **Projects** window and choose the **Compile File** item, and then **Run File** item to run our client project.

On the opened JSP page, enter a desired faculty name such as **Ying Bai** into the **Faculty Name** field. Then click the **Select** button to perform a query for this selected faculty member. The query result is returned and displayed in this page, as shown in Fig. 9.42.

Our Web client project **WebClientSelect** used to consume our Web service is successful! A complete Web client project **WebClientSelect** can be found from a folder **Class DB Projects\Chapter 9** that is located under the **Students** folder at the Springer ftp site (refer to Fig. 1.2 in Chap. 1).

Next let's discuss how to build a Web service to perform data insertion into our sample SQL Server database.

9.8 Build Java Web Service to Insert Data into the SQL Server Database

To perform a faculty record insertion action using our Web service, we need to add another operation or method called **InsertFaculty()** into our Web service project **WebServiceSQLApp**.

9.8.1 Add a New Operation InsertFaculty() into Our Web Service Project

First let's perform a Refactor operation to copy our original Web Service file **WebServiceSelect.java** and paste it into the same Web Service project **WebServiceSQLApp** with a different name, **WebServiceInsert.java**, and we need to use this modified service file as our data insertion service.

Perform the following operational steps to do this refactor function:

1) Launch NetBeans IDE 8.2 and open our Web service project **WebServiceSQLApp**, and select our Web service main class file **WebServiceSelect.java** from the **Projects** window, which is located under the **Source Packages\org.ws.sql** folder.
2) Right click on our main class file **WebServiceSelect.java**, and select **Refactor\Copy** item from the popup menu to open the **Copy Class** wizard, as shown in Fig. 9.43.
3) Change the class name to **WebServiceInsert** by modifying it in the **New Name** box.
4) Your finished **Copy Class** wizard should match one that is shown in Fig. 9.43. Click on the **Refactor** button to complete this copy class function.
5) Now you can find that a new copied class file **WebServiceInsert.java** has been added into this project under the **Source Packages\org.ws.sql** folder. Double

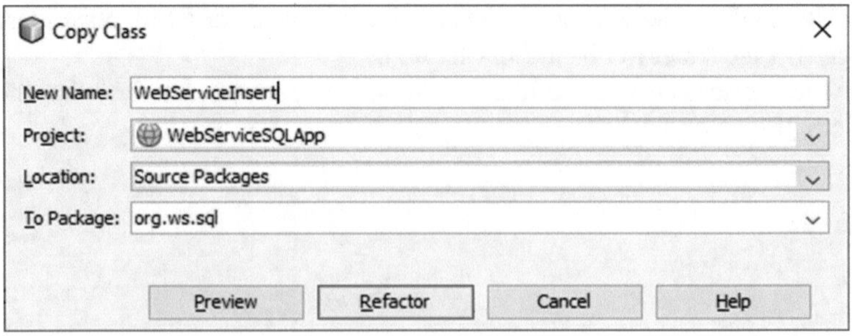

Fig. 9.43 The opened Copy Class wizard

click on this class file to open it, and click on the **Source** button on the top to open its code window.

6) Change the coding line 20 from **@WebService(serviceName = "WebServiceSelect")** to **@WebService(serviceName = "WebServiceInsert")**.
7) Now you can clean and build the project to update this copied class file.

Next we need to add a new operation or method to this class file to perform data insertion function. Perform the following operations to add this operation into our Web service:

1) Launch NetBeans IDE 8.2 and open our Web service project **WebServiceSQLApp**, and select our Web service class file **WebServiceInsert.java** from the **Projects** window.
2) Click on the **Design** button on the top of the window to open the Design View of our Web service project **WebServiceInsert**.
3) Click on the **Add Operation** button on the upper-right to open the **Add Operation** wizard.
4) Enter **InsertFaculty** into the **Name** field, and click on the **Browse** button that is next to the **Return Type** combo box. Type **boolean** into the **Type Name** field and select the item **Boolean (java.lang)** from the list, and click on the **OK** button.
5) Click on the **Add** button, and enter **fdata** into the **Name** parameter field. Then click on the drop-down arrow of the **Type** combo box, and select the **Choose** item to open the **Find Type** wizard. Type **arraylist** into the top field and select the **ArrayList (java.util)** data type, and click on the **OK** button to select an ArrayList as the data type for the input parameter.

Your finished **Add Operation** wizard should match one that is shown in Fig. 9.44. Click on the **OK** button to complete this new operation creation process.

Click on the **Source** button on the top of this window to open the code window of our Web service project. Let's perform the coding development for this new added operation. On the opened code window, enter the codes that are shown in

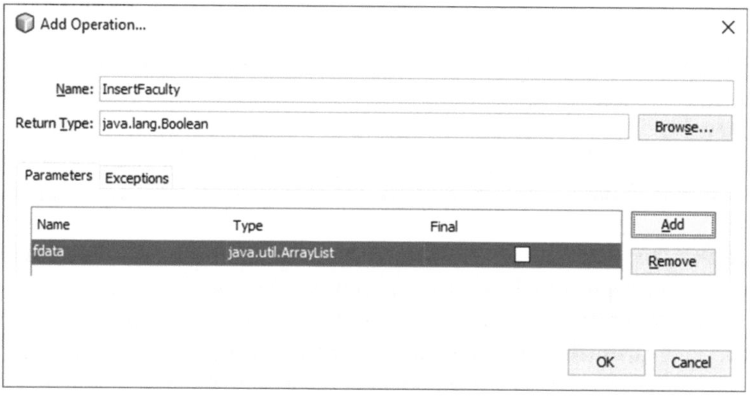

Fig. 9.44 The complete Add Operation wizard

```
  @WebMethod(operationName = "InsertFaculty")
    public Boolean InsertFaculty(@WebParam(name = "fdata") ArrayList fdata) {
      //TODO write your implementation code here:
A     int numInsert = 0;
B     FileInputStream fis = null;
C     File fimage= new File(fdata.get(7).toString());
D     String query = "INSERT INTO Faculty (faculty_id, faculty_name, title, office, " +
                     "phone, college, email, fimage) VALUES (?, ?, ?, ?, ?, ?, ?, ?)";
      try {
E       con = DBConnection(con);
F       PreparedStatement pstmt =con.prepareStatement(query);
        pstmt.setString(1, fdata.get(0).toString());
        pstmt.setString(2, fdata.get(1).toString());
        pstmt.setString(3, fdata.get(2).toString());
        pstmt.setString(4, fdata.get(3).toString());
        pstmt.setString(5, fdata.get(4).toString());
        pstmt.setString(6, fdata.get(5).toString());
        pstmt.setString(7, fdata.get(6).toString());
G       try {
            fis = new FileInputStream(fimage);
H       } catch (FileNotFoundException ex) {
I         Logger.getLogger(WebServiceInsert.class.getName()).log(Level.SEVERE, null, ex);
        }
J       pstmt.setBinaryStream(8, (InputStream)fis, (int)(fimage.length()));
K       numInsert = pstmt.executeUpdate();
L       pstmt.close();
        con.close();
M       if (numInsert != 0)
          return true;
N       else
          return false;
      }
O     catch (Exception ex) {
        System.out.println("exception is: " + ex);
        return false;
      }
    }
  }
```

Fig. 9.45 The codes for the new operation InsertFaculty()

Fig. 9.45 into this new added operation **InsertFaculty()**. Let's have a closer look at this piece of codes to see how it works.

A. First a local integer variable **numInsert** is created, and it is used to hold the running result of inserting a new faculty record into our sample database.
B. An instance of the FileInputStream class, **fis**, is generated, and it is used to convert the inserting faculty image to a FileInputStream format and inserted into the database later.
C. A new File instance **fimage** is also declared and initialized with the path or location of the inserting faculty image, which is located at the eighth position with an index of 7 on the input **arrayList** that contained all eight pieces of inserted faculty information.
D. The SQL **INSERT** command is generated with eight pieces of inserted faculty information represented by eight position parameters.
E. A try-catch block is used to start this insertion action. First a valid database connection is established by calling a user-defined method **DBConnection()**.
F. A new instance of PreparedStatement class, **pstmt**, is declared with seven **setString()** methods to set up the actual values for seven positional dynamic

parameters in the inserting query statement. One point to be noted is that the order of these **setString()** methods must be identical with the order of columns in our **Faculty** table.

G. Another try-catch block is used to convert the inserted faculty image to the FileInputStream format and make it ready to be written into the database.
H. The catch block is used to check any possible exception for this conversion.
I. The exception information will be recorded into a system log file if it occurred.
J. The converted faculty image is written into the eighth positional dynamic parameter via a **setBinaryStream()** system method.
K. The inserting action is performed by calling the **executeUpdate()** method, and the inserting result is returned and stored in the local integer variable **numInsert**.
L. Some used instances, including the PreparedStatement and Connection classes, are closed since we have completed our data insertion action and need to disconnect with our database.
M. The **executeUpdate()** method will return an integer to indicate whether this data insertion is successful or not. If a non-zero value is returned, which means that at least one row has been inserted into our Faculty table and this data inserting action is successful, a **true** is returned to the client project.
N. Otherwise, no any row has been inserted into our sample database and this data insertion failed. A **false** is returned for this situation.
O. The **catch** block is used to track and display any exception that occurred during this data inserting operation, and a **false** will be returned if this situation is really happened.

You may experience some compiling errors during this coding process, which is normal, and all of these errors are due to some missed imports packages. To fix them up, just right click on any place inside the code window, and select the **Fix Imports** item from the popup menu.

At this point, we have completed all coding development for the data insertion action. Now let's build and run our Web service project to test its function.

9.8.2 Deploy the Web Service Project

Perform the following operations to build and deploy our Web service project:

1) Click on the **Clean and Build Main Project** button to build our Web service.
2) Right click on our Web application **WebServiceSQLApp**, and select the **Deploy** item to deploy our Web service. If everything is fine, a successful deployment result should be displayed, as shown in Fig. 9.46.

A problem arises when testing this Web service project using the tester page, which is the input parameter array **fdata**. As we know, the **fdata** has a data type of ArrayList, and it needs to (1) create an ArrayList instance and then and (2) assign a group of faculty information to that ArrayList object to call this Web service

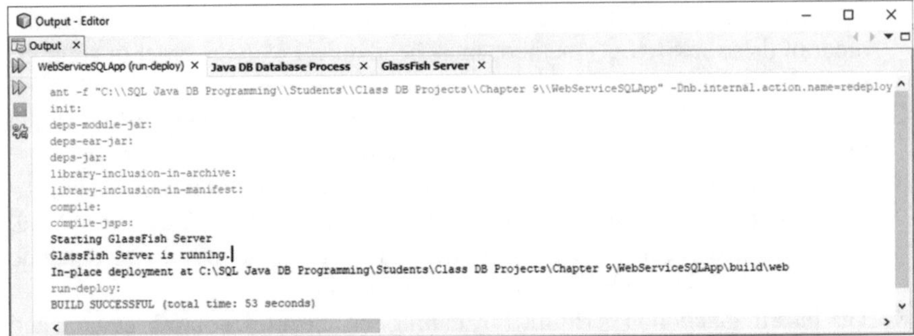

Fig. 9.46 The deployment result of our Web service project

operation **InsertFaculty()** to perform the faculty data insertion. However, it is difficult to do those two operations manually by using this tester page. Therefore we need to create some Web client projects to consume and test this Web service project.

When testing or running a Web project, the default Web browser may not be available. In that case, go to Tools|Options **menu and select the** Internet Explorer **as the Web Browser, and** No Proxy **for the Proxy Settings under the** General **tab in NetBeans IDE.**

Next we can develop some Web client projects to consume this Web service to perform data insertion to the Faculty table in our sample database. First let's discuss how to build a Window-based client project to consume our Web service.

9.9 Build a Window-Based Client Project to Consume the Web Service

We can still use the Window-based client project **WinClientSelect** we built in Sect. 9.6 to consume the Web service to perform faculty data inserting action. One point to be noted is that although a Web reference to our Web service has been established in Sect. 9.6, we still need to refresh this Web reference since our Web service project has been modified by adding one more operation **InsertFaculty()** in our Web service. Otherwise we would still use the original Web service that does not include this **InsertFaculty()** operation.

To make things clear, we can copy the project **WinClientSelect** and rename it as our new Windows-based client project **WinClientInsert** and use this project to consume our Web Service project to insert a new faculty record into the Faculty table in our sample database.

Perform the following operations to complete this renaming project process:

1) Right click on our original Windows-based client project **WinClientSelect**, and select the **Copy** item from the popup menu to open the **Copy Project** wizard.
2) Change the project name to **WinClientInsert** in the **Project Name** box, and click on the **Copy** button to complete this project copy operation.

Now you may find that our copied project contained some errors with red-color error indicators. The reason for that is because of our Web Service since we need to update our Web Service Reference for this new project **WinClientInsert**.

9.9.1 Refresh the Web Service Reference for Our Window-Based Client Project

In order to call this **InsertFaculty()** operation in our Web service project **WebServiceSQLApp**, we need to refresh the Web reference in our Window-based client project to use the updated Web service project. Perform the following operations to refresh the Web service reference:

1) Open our Window-based client project **WinClientInsert**, and expand the **Web Service References** node.
2) Right click on our Web service **WebServiceSelect**, and choose the **Delete** item to remove this old Web reference. Click on the **Yes** button to confirm this deletion.
3) Right click on our Window-based client project **WinClientInsert**, and select the **New > Web Service Client** item to open the **New Web Service Client** wizard.
4) On the opened wizard, click on the **Browse** button that is next to the **Project** field, and expand our Web application **WebServiceSQLApp**. Then choose our Web service **WebServiceInsert** by clicking on it, and click on the **OK** button.
5) Click on the **Finish** button to complete this Web service reference refreshing process.

Now some errors occurred on four coding lines in the main Source file **FacultyFrame.java**; two of them are in the **SelectButtonActionPerformed()** event method (coding lines 359–360), and another two are in the **ShowFaculty()** user-defined method (coding lines 399–400). To fix them, just change the Web Service name for coding lines 359 and 399 from:

```
org.ws.sql.WebServiceSelect_Service service = new org.ws.sql.
WebServiceSelect_Service();
to: org.ws.sql.WebServiceInsert_Service service = new org.ws.
sql.WebServiceInsert_Service();
```

and change coding lines 360 and 400 from:

```
org.ws.sql.WebServiceSelect port = service.getWebServiceSelect
Port();
to:org.ws.sql.WebServiceInsert port = service.getWebServiceInsert
Port();
```

If you rebuild the project now, those errors would be removed.

Now that we have refreshed or updated the Web service reference for our Window-based client project **WinClientInsert**, next let's develop the codes in our client project to call that Web service operation **InsertFaculty()** to perform faculty data insertion.

```
  private void InsertButtonActionPerformed(java.awt.event.ActionEvent evt) {
        // TODO add your handling code here:
A       File imgFile = null;
        ArrayList al = new ArrayList();
B       JFileChooser imgChooser = new JFileChooser();
C       imgChooser.setCurrentDirectory(new File(System.getProperty("user.home")));
D       int result = imgChooser.showOpenDialog(this);
E       if (result == JFileChooser.APPROVE_OPTION) {
          imgFile = imgChooser.getSelectedFile();
F         System.out.println("Selected path: " + imgFile.getAbsolutePath());
          System.out.println("Selected file: " + imgFile.toString());
        }
G       al.clear();
H       al.add(0, FacultyIDField.getText().toString());
        al.add(1, FacultyNameField.getText().toString());
        al.add(2, TitleField.getText().toString());
        al.add(3, OfficeField.getText().toString());
        al.add(4, PhoneField.getText().toString());
        al.add(5, CollegeField.getText().toString());
        al.add(6, EmailField.getText().toString());
        al.add(7, imgFile.toString());
I       try {
           org.ws.sql.WebServiceInsert_Service service = new org.ws.sql.WebServiceInsert_Service();
           org.ws.sql.WebServiceInsert port = service.getWebServiceInsertPort();
J          Boolean insert = port.insertFaculty(al);
K          if (!insert) {
              msgDlg.setMessage("The data insertion is failed!");
              msgDlg.setVisible(true);
           }
L          else
              ComboName.addItem(FacultyNameField.getText());
         }
M        catch (Exception ex){
            System.out.println("exception: " + ex);
         }
  }
```

Fig. 9.47 The codes for the Insert button event method

9.9.2 Modify the Design View and Develop the Codes to Call Our Web Service Project

Open the Window-based client project **WinClientInsert**, and double click on our main class **FacultyFrame.java** to open it. Click on the **Design** button to open the graphic user interface. In this client project, we want to use the **Insert** button in this form as a trigger to start the faculty data insertion action. Therefore double click on the **Insert** button to open its event handler or method **InsertButtonActionPerformed()**, and enter the codes that are shown in Fig. 9.47 into this method. Since we need to allow users to select a desired faculty image to be inserted into our sample database with a new insertion action, thus a new component, **File Chooser**, should be added into this handler. Let's have a closer look at this piece of codes to see how it works.

A. Some local objects are first declared, which include a File object, **imgFile**, which is used to hold the selected image file, and a new ArrayList instance **al**, which is used to pick up and reserve the input new faculty data array.
B. A Java File Chooser instance, **imgChooser**, is generated, and it provides a File Interface GUI to allow users to select a desired faculty image to be inserted into our database later.
C. The current directory, which is exactly the folder of our current project, is selected, and this location will work as a default folder to store all selected faculty image files later.
D. The system method, **showOpenDialog()**, is executed to display this Chooser GUI to enable users to browse and select a desired faculty image to be inserted into our database later.
E. By checking one property, **APPROVE_OPTION**, one can confirm whether this GUI's operation is successful or not. If it is opened and an image has been selected, a true is returned. Then the selected image can be retrieved by calling a method, **getSelectedFile()**.
F. These two coding lines are used to display the path and directory for the selected faculty image, and they are used for the debugging purpose.
G. The **clear()** method is executed to make sure that the ArrayList instance is clean before a new faculty record is collected.
H. The **add()** method is used to pick up and add eight pieces of new faculty information into this new ArrayList instance **al**. These eight pieces of new faculty information are entered by the user and stored in seven text fields and the File Chooser in this FacultyFrame window form. The **toString()** method is used to convert each piece of new faculty information obtained using the **getText()** method that returns an object data type to a String. The index is necessary since it is used to indicate the position of each parameter in this ArrayList. One point to be noted is the order of adding these text fields, which must be identical with order of columns in our **Faculty** table.
I. A **try catch** block is used to perform the calling of our Web service operation **InsertFaculty()** to perform this faculty data inserting action. First a new Web

service instance **service** is created based on our Web service class **WebServiceInsert_Service**. Then the **getWebServiceInsertPort()** method is executed to get the current port used by our Web service. This port is returned and assigned to a new Port instance **port**.

J. The Web service operation **InsertFaculty()** is executed with the ArrayList instance **al** that has been filled with eight pieces of new faculty information as the argument of this method. The running result of that operation is returned and assigned to a Boolean variable **insert**.
K. If the value of the variable **insert** is **false**, which means that no any row has been inserted into our **Faculty** table and this insertion has been failed, the **msgDlg** instance is used to show this situation.
L. Otherwise if the value of the **insert** variable is true, which means that this data insertion is successful, the new inserted faculty name will be added into the Faculty Name combo box **ComboName** using the **addItem()** method.
M. The **catch** block is used to track and display any possible exception during this Web service operation execution.

Now let's build and run our client project to call and test our Web service to perform faculty data inserting action. However, prior to running our client project, one needs to deploy our Web Service project **WebServiceSQLApp** to activate our new operation or Web method **InsertFaculty()**.

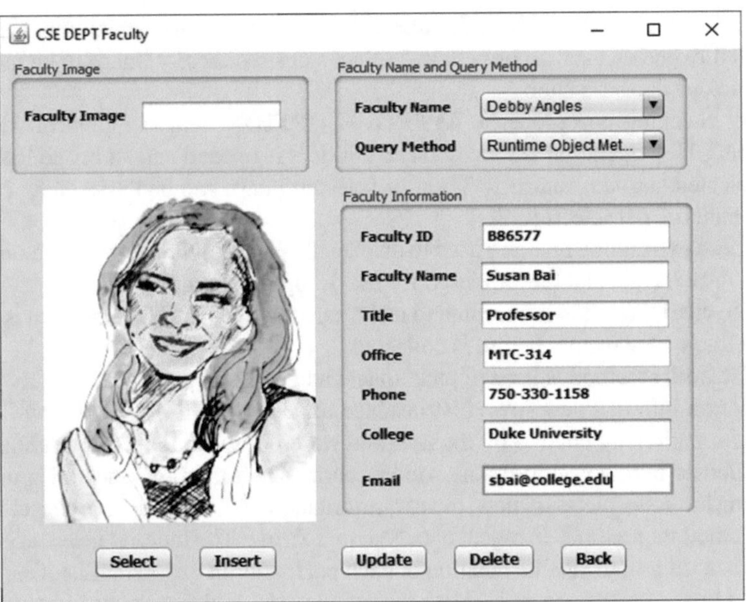

Fig. 9.48 The seven pieces of new inserted faculty information

9.9.3 Build and Run Our Client Project to Insert Faculty Data via Web Service

Click on the **Clean and Build Main Project** button to build our client project. If everything is fine, click on the **Run Main Project** button to run our client project.

The FacultyFrame form window is displayed. First let's perform a faculty query action. Select a desired faculty member, such as **Debby Angles**, from the **Faculty Name** combo box, and click on the **Select** button to query the detailed information for this faculty via our Web service **WebServiceApp**. The queried result is displayed in seven text fields.

Now enter a new faculty record with seven pieces of new faculty information shown below into seven text fields, which is shown in Fig. 9.48.

- Faculty ID: **B86577**
- Name: **Susan Bai**
- Title: **Professor**
- Office: **MTC-314**
- Phone: **750-330-1158**
- College: **Duke University**
- Email: **sbai@college.edu**

Click on the **Insert** button to open the **File Chooser** wizard. On the opened **File Chooser** wizard, browse to the location where all faculty image files are located; in this case, it is **C:\Images\Faculty**, and select the desired image, **White.jpg**, and click on the **Open** button to select this faculty image and insert it into the **Faculty** table in our sample database.

To confirm this data insertion, two methods can be used. First we can open our **Faculty** table using either the **Services** window in the NetBeans IDE or the Microsoft SQL Server Management Studio 2018 to check whether this new faculty record has been inserted. To do that by using the **Services** window in the NetBeans IDE, perform the following operations:

1) Open the **Services** window, and expand the **Databases** node.
2) Right click on our SQL Server database URL: **jdbc:sqlserver://localhost\SQL2019EXPRESS: 5000; databaseName=CSE_DEPT**, and select the **Connect** item to try to connect to our database. Enter **Happy2020** as password into the **Password** box, and click on the **OK** button.
3) If one encountered a connection problem due to TCP/IP issue, open the **SQL Server 2019 Configuration Manager** to make sure that the SQL Server 2019 Express Server is running. If it is stopped, select the **SQL Server Services** icon on the left, and right click on the **SQL Server (SQL2019EXPRESS)** item on the right, and select **Start** item to run this server. You may need to try one more time to make it running.
4) After our database has been connected, expand our sample database **CSE_DEPT**, **dbo**, and **Tables**.

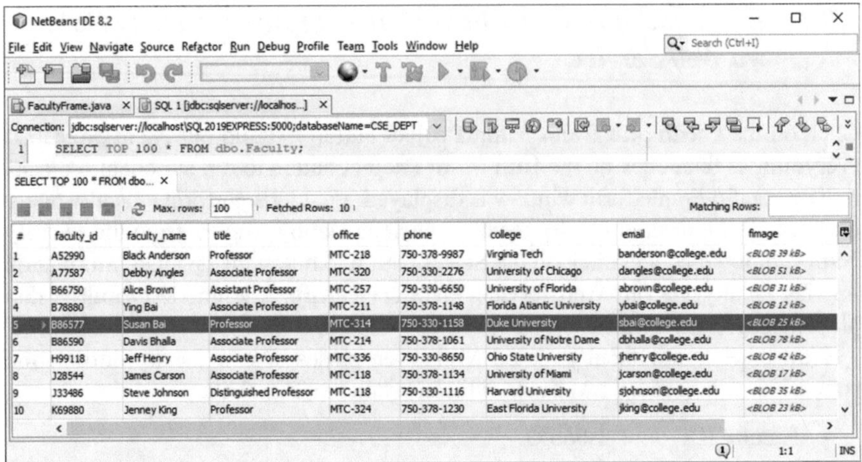

Fig. 9.49 The opened Faculty table in the NetBeans IDE

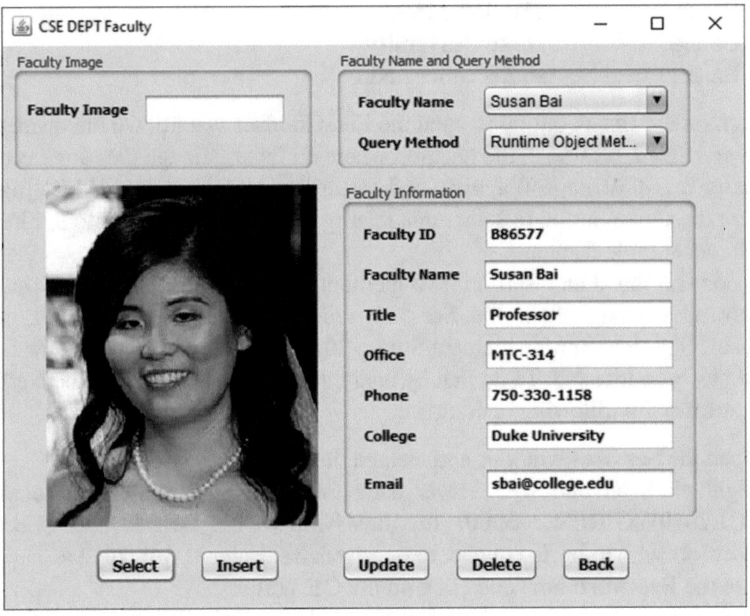

Fig. 9.50 The confirmation of new inserted faculty record

5) Right click on the **Faculty** table, and select the **View Data** item.

Your opened **Faculty** table is shown in Fig. 9.49.

It can be found that the new faculty record with the **faculty_id** of **B86577**, which is highlighted in dark color, has been successfully inserted into our database.

The second way to confirm this data insertion, which is simpler, is to use the **Select** button in this form to perform a query to try to retrieve the inserted faculty record.

To do this checking in second way, go to the Faculty Name combo box, and you can find that the new faculty name **Susan Bai** has been added into this box. Click it to select it and click on the **Select** button, and you can find that seven pieces of new inserted faculty information with the selected faculty image have been retrieved and displayed in this form window, as shown in Fig. 9.50. Our data insertion is successful!

It is highly recommended to remove this new inserted faculty record from our database since we want to keep our database clean. You can delete this record by opening and using the Microsoft SQL Server Management Studio 2018.

A complete Windows client project **WinClientInsert** used to consume our Web Service to insert a new faculty record into our sample database can be found from a folder **Class DB Projects\Chapter 9**, which is located under the **Students** folder at the Springer ftp site (refer to Fig. 1.2 in Chap. 1).

Next let's build a Web-based client project to consume our Web service to insert a new faculty record into the Faculty table in our sample database.

9.10 Build a Web-Based Client Project to Consume the Web Service

We can modify a Web-based project **JavaWebDBJSPSQL_Insert** we built in Sect. 8.5 in Chap. 8 to consume our Web service to perform the faculty data insertion action.

Perform the following operational steps to create our new project **WebClientInsert**:

1) In the **Projects** window, right click on the project **JavaWebDBJSPSQL_Insert**, and select the **Copy** item from the popup menu to open the **Copy Project** wizard.
2) Enter our new project name, **WebClientInsert**, into the **Project Name** box, and browse to the default project folder, **C:\Class DB Projects\Chapter 9**, as the **Project Location**, and click on the **Copy** button.

A new project **WebClientInsert** is generated and added into our **Projects** window.

First let's add a Web service reference to our Web-based client project to allow it to use our Web service operations.

9.10.1 Add a Web Service Reference to Our Web-Based Client Project

In order to call the **InsertFaculty()** operation in our Web service project **WebServiceSQLApp**, we need to add the Web reference to our Web-based client project **WebClientInsert** to use the updated Web service project. Perform the following operations to add this Web service reference:

1) Right click on our Web-based client project **WebClientInsert**, and select the **New > Web Service Client** item to open the **New Web Service Client** wizard.
2) On the opened wizard, click on the **Browse** button that is next to the **Project** field, and expand our Web application **WebServiceSQLApp**. Then choose our Web service **WebServiceInsert** by clicking on it, and click on the **OK** button.
3) Click on the **Finish** button to complete this Web service reference refreshing process.

Next let's develop the codes in our client project to call that Web service operation **InsertFaculty()** to perform faculty data insertion.

```
    public FacultyInsertBean() {
A
    }
    public int InsertFaculty(String[]  newFaculty) {
B       int numInsert = 1;
        ArrayList al = new ArrayList();
        MsgDialog msgDlg = new MsgDialog(new javax.swing.JFrame(), true);
C       al.clear();
D       al.add(0, newFaculty[0]);
        al.add(1, newFaculty[1]);
        al.add(2, newFaculty[2]);
        al.add(3, newFaculty[3]);
        al.add(4, newFaculty[4]);
        al.add(5, newFaculty[5]);
        al.add(6, newFaculty[6]);
        al.add(7, newFaculty[7]);
        try{
E         org.ws.sql.WebServiceInsert_Service service = new org.ws.sql.WebServiceInsert_Service();
          org.ws.sql.WebServiceInsert port = service.getWebServiceInsertPort();
F         Boolean insert = port.insertFaculty(al);
G         if (!insert) {
            msgDlg.setMessage("The data insertion is failed!");
            msgDlg.setVisible(true);
            return 0;
          }
        }
H       catch (Exception e) {
          msgDlg.setMessage("Error in Insert Statement! " + e.getMessage());
          msgDlg.setVisible(true);
          return 0;
        }
I       return numInsert;
    }
```

Fig. 9.51 The modified codes for the constructor and InsertFaculty() method

9.10.2 Develop the Codes to Call Our Web Service Project

The main coding process is in the Java managed bean class **FacultyInsertBean.java** and some modifications in the **FacultyProcess.jsp** file.

First let's take care of the coding development for the managed bean **FacultyInsertBean.java** class file. Open our Web-based client project **WebClientInsert**, and double click on the **FacultyInsertBean.java** from the **Projects** window to open this managed bean class file. Let's first do the coding modifications for this **FacultyInsertBean.java** class file.

1) Remove all original codes inside the constructor of this class file, **public FacultyInsertBean()**.
2) Add some new codes shown in Fig. 9.51 into the method **InsertFaculty()**.

Let's have a closer look at this piece of new added codes to see how it works.

A. The original codes inside the constructor **public FacultyInsertBean()** are totally removed.
B. Inside the Web method, **InsertFaculty()**, some local objects and variables are first declared. An integer variable, **numInsert**, is generated and initialized to 1. This variable is used to hold the data insertion result later. Then a new **ArrayList** instance **al** is created and initialized. This variable is used to pick up and reserve the input new faculty data array. A **MsgDialog** object is also created, and it is used to display some debugging information.
C. The **clear()** method is executed to make sure that the ArrayList instance is clean before a new faculty record is collected.
D. The **add()** method is used to pick up and add eight pieces of new faculty information into this new ArrayList instance **al**. These eight pieces of new faculty information are entered by the user in the JSP page **FacultyPage.jsp** and stored in eight properties defined in this managed bean.
E. A try-catch block is used to perform the calling of our Web method to insert this new faculty record into our sample database. First a new Web service instance **service** is created based on our Web service class **WebServiceInsert_Service**. Then a system method **getWebServiceInsertPort()** is executed to get the current port used by our Web service. This port is returned and assigned to a new Port instance **port**.
F. The **InsertFaculty()** operation in our Web service is called with the ArrayList instance that contains eight pieces of new faculty information as the argument. The execution result of this faculty data insertion is returned and assigned to the local Boolean variable **insert**.
G. If the returned Boolean variable **insert** is false, which means that this data insertion failed, the **msgDlg** instance is used to indicate this situation. A 0 is returned to the calling method in our **FacultyProcess.jsp** file to indicate this situation.
H. The **catch** block is used to catch any possible exception during this data insertion process. If any error occurred, a 0 is returned to our **FacultyProcess.jsp** file to feedback this error.

```
else if (request.getParameter("Insert")!= null) {
        //process the faculty record insertion
        %>
        <jsp:useBean id="InsertFaculty" scope="session" class="JavaWebDBJSPSQLPackage.FacultyInsertBean" />
        <jsp:setProperty name="InsertFaculty" property="*" />
        <%
        int res = 0;
        String fid = request.getParameter("FacultyIDField");
        String fname = request.getParameter("NameField");
        String office = request.getParameter("OfficeField");
        String phone = request.getParameter("PhoneField");
        String college = request.getParameter("CollegeField");
        String title = request.getParameter("TitleField");
        String email = request.getParameter("EmailField");
        String fImage = request.getParameter("Faculty_Image");
        String[] fnew = {fid, fname, title, office, phone, college, email, fImage };
A       res = InsertFaculty.InsertFaculty(fnew);
        if (res == 0) {
           response.sendRedirect("Faculty.jsp");
           }
        else {
           session.setAttribute("FacultyIDField", null);
           request.setAttribute("NameField", null);
           request.setAttribute("OfficeField", null);
           request.setAttribute("PhoneField", null);
           request.setAttribute("CollegeField", null);
           request.setAttribute("TitleField", null);
           request.setAttribute("EmailField", null);
           response.sendRedirect("Faculty.jsp");

           }
        InsertFaculty.CloseDBConnection();
   }
```

Fig. 9.52 The modified codes for the Insert section on the FacultyProcess.jsp file

I. Finally the local variable **numInsert** whose value is set to 1 is returned to our **FacultyProcess.jsp** file to indicate a success of this data insertion action.

Next let's handle the coding modifications to our **FacultyProcess.jsp** file.

In fact, the only modification is to remove a comment-out symbol for the calling our **InsertFaculty()** method in this file. As you may remember, when testing our data query function by using the **Select** button and its method in this file, we comment out this data insertion calling function to make our query easier. Now we need to use this function; thus, just remove this comment-out symbol. Your modified codes for the data insertion section on this FacultyProcess.jsp file are shown in Fig. 9.52.

The only modification is to remove the comment-out symbol, as shown in **A** in Fig. 9.52, which has been highlighted in bold.

Now let's build and run our Web client project to call our Web service operation to perform the faculty data inserting action.

However, prior to building and running our client project to call Web Service project **WebServiceSQLApp** to insert any new record into our database, our Web Service project needs to be built and deployed first. Perform building and deploying operations to our Web Service project first to make sure that our Web Service is running and ready to be called.

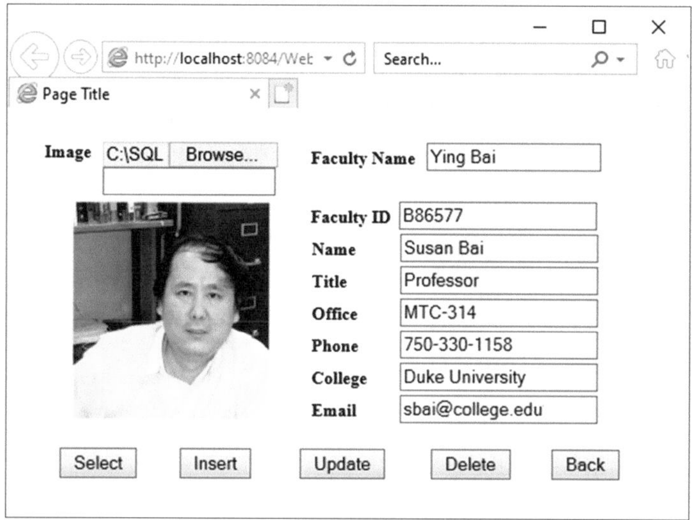

Fig. 9.53 The information for a new inserted faculty member

9.10.3 Build and Run Our Client Project to Insert Faculty Data via Web Service

Click on the **Clean and Build Main Project** button to build our client project. If everything is fine, right click on our JSP page **FacultyPage.jsp** from the **Projects** window, and choose the **Run File** item to run our client project.

On the opened JSP page, first let's perform a faculty record query by entering a desired faculty name such as **Ying Bai** into the **Faculty Name** field, and then click on the **Select** button to get details for this faculty member. To insert a new faculty record, enter seven pieces of new faculty information shown below into the associated seven text fields, as shown in Fig. 9.53.

- Faculty ID: **B86577**
- Name: **Susan Bai**
- Title: **Professor**
- Office: **MTC-314**
- Phone: **750-330-1158**
- College: **Duke University**
- Email: **sbai@college.edu**

Click on the **Browse** button to open a **File Selection** dialog to select the desired faculty image file, **White.jpg** for this case, and click on the **Insert** button to call our Web service operation **InsertFaculty()** to insert this new faculty record into the **Faculty** table in our sample database. Now you can find that the information for

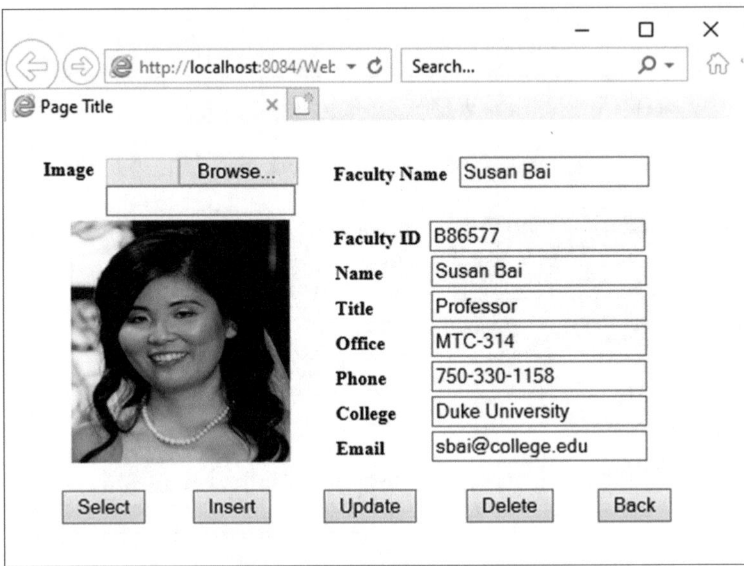

Fig. 9.54 The confirmation of a new faculty record insertion

original faculty member is displayed again, which means that our data insertion is successful.

To confirm this data insertion, one way is to perform another query for the new inserted faculty member, **Susan Bai**. Perform the following operations to do this confirming query:

1) Enter the inserted faculty name, **Susan Bai**, into the **Faculty Name** TextField.
2) Go to the **File Chooser**, which is shown as a textbox under the **Image** and **Browse** button, and enter **White.jpg** into that box as the faculty image's name.
3) Click on the **Select** button to try to retrieve that inserted record.

Now you can find that seven pieces of new inserted faculty information with the selected faculty image have been retrieved and displayed in this page, as shown in Fig. 9.54.

To do this checking in second way, one can open our **Faculty** table using either the **Services** window in the NetBeans IDE or the Microsoft SQL Server Management Studio 18 to check whether this new faculty record has been inserted. To do that by using the **Services** window in the NetBeans IDE, perform the following operations:

1) Open the **Services** window, and expand the **Databases** node.
2) Right click on our SQL Server database URL: **jdbc:sqlserver://localhost\SQL2019EXPRESS: 5000; databaseName=CSE_DEPT**, and select the **Connect** item to connect to our database. Enter **Happy2020** as password into the **Password** box, and click on the **OK** button.
3) If one encountered a connection problem due to TCP/IP issue, open the **SQL Server 2019 Configuration Manager** to make sure that the SQL Server 2019

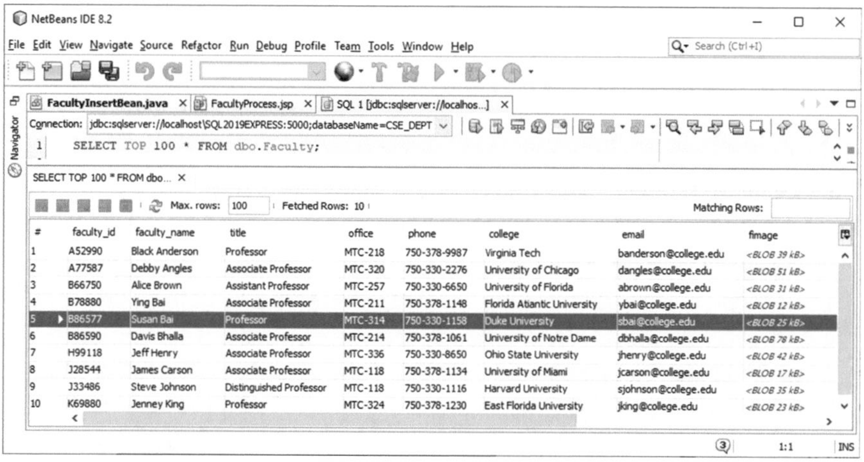

Fig. 9.55 The opened Faculty table with the new inserted faculty record

Express Server is running. If it is stopped, select the **SQL Server Services** icon on the left, and right click on the **SQL Server (SQL2019EXPRESS)** item on the right and select **Start** item to run this server. You may need to try one more time to make it running.

4) After our database has been connected, expand our sample database **CSE_DEPT**, **dbo**, and **Tables**. Right click on the **Faculty** table, and select the **View Data** item.
5) Your opened **Faculty** table is shown in Fig. 9.55.

You can find that the new inserted faculty record has been there.

One point to be noted to make this confirmation query successful is to make sure that all faculty image files, including the new faculty image to be inserted to our database, have been stored in a default folder under our project folder. In this case, it is: **C:\...\WebClientInert\web\ FImages**.

Regularly it is recommended to remove this new inserted faculty record to keep our database clean. But now we need to keep this new inserted faculty record since we can delete it in the next (Sect. 9.11.3) when we test our Web Service project via Web method **DeleteFaculty()**.

Our Web client project used to consume our Web service **WebServiceSQLApp** to insert a new faculty record is successful! A complete Web client project **WebClientInsert** can be found from a folder **Class DB Projects\Chapter 9** that is located under the **Students** folder at the Springer ftp site (refer to Fig. 1.2 in Chap. 1).

Next let's discuss how to build a Web service to perform data updating and deleting against our sample SQL Server database.

9.11 Build Java Web Service to Update and Delete Data from the SQL Server Database

To perform data updating and deleting actions against our sample SQL Server database via Web service is straightforward, and we can add two more new operations, **UpdateFaculty()** and **DeleteFaculty()**, into our Web service project **WebServiceSQLApp** we built in the previous sections. First let's concentrate on the faculty data updating action.

As we discussed in the previous sections, the key point to perform a faculty data updating is that in most real applications, all pieces of faculty information should be updated except the **faculty_id** since it is much easier to insert a new faculty record with a new **faculty_id** than updating a record with an updated **faculty_id** because of the complexity in cascaded updating relationships we built in Chap. 2 when we create our sample database. Therefore in this section, we will concentrate on the updating a faculty record based on an existing **faculty_id**.

9.11.1 Add a New Operation UpdateFaculty() to Perform Faculty Data Updating

First let's perform a Refactor operation to copy one of our original Web Service files, **WebServiceInsert.java**, and paste it into the same Web Service project **WebServiceSQLApp** with a different name, **WebServiceUpdtDelt.java**, and we need to use this modified service file as our data updating and deleting services.

Perform the following operational steps to do this refactor function:

1) Launch NetBeans IDE 8.2 and open our Web service project **WebServiceSQLApp**, and select one of our Web service class files, **WebServiceInsert.java**, from the **Projects** window, which is located under the **Source Packages\org.ws.sql** folder.
2) Right click on our class file **WebServiceInsert.java**, and select **Refactor\Copy** item from the popup menu to open the **Copy Class** wizard, as shown in Fig. 9.56.

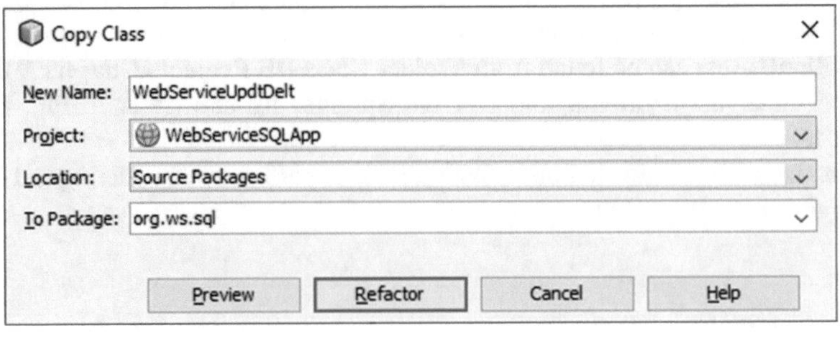

Fig. 9.56 The opened Copy Class wizard

3) Change the class name to **WebServiceUpdtDelt** by modifying it in the **New Name** box.
4) Your finished **Copy Class** wizard is shown in Fig. 9.56. Click on the **Refactor** button to complete this copy class function.
5) Now you can find that a new copied class file **WebServiceUpdtDelt.java** has been added into this project under the **Source Packages\org.ws.sql** folder.
6) Double click on this class file to open it, and click on the **Source** button on the top to open its code window. Change the coding line 25 from **@WebService (serviceName = "WebServiceInsert")** to **@WebService(serviceName = "WebServiceUpdtDelt")**.
7) Now you can clean and build the project to update this copied class file.

Next we need to add a new operation or method to this class file to perform data insertion function. Perform the following operations to add a new operation **UpdateFaculty()** into our Web service project **WebServiceSQLApp**:

1) Launch NetBeans IDE 8.2 and open our Web service project **WebServiceSQLApp**, and select our Web service class file, **WebServiceUpdtDelt.java**, from the **Projects** window.
2) Click on the **Design** button on the top of the window to open the Design View of our Web service file **WebServiceUpdeDelt.java**.
3) Click on the **Add Operation** button to open the **Add Operation** wizard.
4) Enter **UpdateFaculty** into the **Name** field (Fig. 9.57), and click on the **Browse** button that is next to the **Return Type** combo box. Type **boolean** into the **Type Name** field and select the item **Boolean (java.lang)** from the list, and click on the **OK** button.
5) Click on the **Add** button, and enter **fdata** into the **Name** parameter field. Then click on the drop-down arrow of the **Type** combo box, and select the **Choose** item to open the **Find Type** wizard. Type **arrayList** into the top field, and select the **ArrayList (java.util)** data type, and click on the **OK** button to select an ArrayList as the data type for the input parameter.

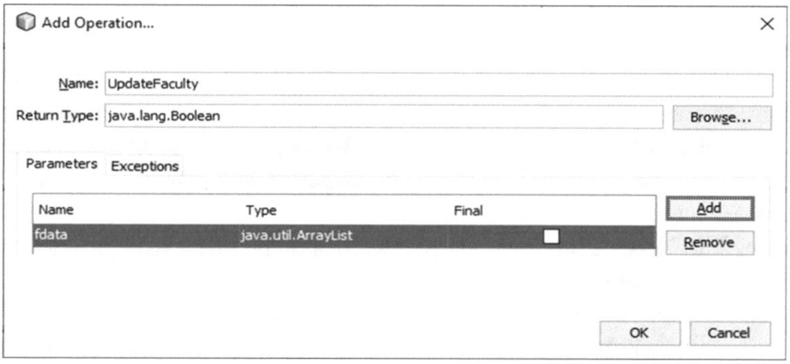

Fig. 9.57 The complete Add Operation wizard

```
  @WebMethod(operationName = "UpdateFaculty")
  public Boolean UpdateFaculty(@WebParam(name = "fdata") ArrayList fdata) {
  //TODO write your implementation code here:
A int numUpdated = 0;
B FileInputStream fis = null;
C File fimage= new File(fdata.get(6).toString());
D String query = "UPDATE  Faculty SET faculty_name=?, title=?, office=?, phone=?, college=?," +
                   "email=?, fimage=? " + "WHERE faculty_id= ?";
  try {
E     con = DBConnection(con);
F     PreparedStatement pstmt =con.prepareStatement(query);
G     pstmt.setString(1, fdata.get(0).toString());
      pstmt.setString(2, fdata.get(1).toString());
      pstmt.setString(3, fdata.get(2).toString());
      pstmt.setString(4, fdata.get(3).toString());
      pstmt.setString(5, fdata.get(4).toString());
      pstmt.setString(6, fdata.get(5).toString());
      pstmt.setString(8, fdata.get(7).toString());      // faculty_id
      try {
H         fis = new FileInputStream(fimage);
I     } catch (FileNotFoundException ex) {
        Logger.getLogger(WebServiceUpdtDelt.class.getName()).log(Level.SEVERE, null, ex);
      }
J     pstmt.setBinaryStream(7, (InputStream)fis, (int)(fimage.length()));
K     numUpdated = pstmt.executeUpdate();
L     con.close();
M     if (numUpdated != 0)
        return true;
N     else
        return false;
  }
O catch (Exception ex) {
      System.out.println("exception is: " + ex);
      return false;
  }
  }
}
```

Fig. 9.58 The codes for the new operation UpdateFaculty()

Your finished **Add Operation** wizard should match one that is shown in Fig. 9.57. Click on the **OK** button to complete this new operation creation process.

Click on the **Source** button on the top of this window to open the code window of our Web service project. Let's perform the coding developments for this new added operation.

On the opened code window, enter the codes that are shown in Fig. 9.58 into this new added operation **UpdateFaculty()**.

Let's have a closer look at this piece of codes to see how it works.

A. A local integer variable **numUpdated** is created first, and this variable is used to hold the running result of execution of the data updating operation.
B. An instance of the FileInputStream class, **fis**, is generated, and it is used to convert the updating faculty image to a FileInputStream format and update to the database later.
C. A new File instance **fimage** is also declared and initialized with the path or location of the updating faculty image, which is located at the sixth position with an index of 6 on the input **arrayList** that contained all eight pieces of updated faculty information. A point to be noted is that the seventh position (7) on the input array is the **faculty_id** value.

D. The updating query string is created with eight positional parameters. The query criterion is the **faculty_id** that is the eighth positional parameter and placed after the **WHERE** clause.
E. A try-catch block is used to perform this data updating action. First a user-defined method **DBConnection()** is called to set up a connection between our Web service and our sample database. A connection instance **con** is returned after the execution of this method.
F. A new PreparedStatement instance **pstmt** is created to perform this updating query.
G. Seven **setString()** methods are used to set up the actual values for seven positional dynamic updated parameters in the updating query statement. One point to be noted is that the order of these **setString()** methods is not continuous from 1 to 8 because the seventh positional parameter is the updated faculty image, which will be processed separately, and the eighth positional parameter is the **faculty_id**.
H. Another try-catch block is used to convert the updating faculty image to the FileInputStream format and make it ready to be written into the database.
I. The catch block is used to check any possible exception for this conversion. The exception information will be recorded into a system log file if it occurred.
J. The converted faculty image is written into the seventh positional dynamic parameter via a **setBinaryStream()** system method.
K. The updating action is performed by calling the **executeUpdate()** method, and the updating result is returned and stored in the local integer variable **numUpdated**.
L. The database connection is closed by executing the **close()** method since we have completed our data updating action and need to disconnect with our database.
M. The **executeUpdate()** method will return an integer to indicate whether this data updating is successful or not. If a non-zero value is returned, which means that at least one row has been updated in our **Faculty** table and this data updating action is successful, a **true** is returned to the client project.
N. Otherwise, no any row has been updated in our sample database, and this data updating failed. A **false** is returned for this situation.
O. The **catch** block is used to track and display any exception that occurred during this data updating process, and a **false** will be returned if this situation really happened.

Next let's take care of the data deleting action against our sample database using Web service operation **DeleteFaculty()**.

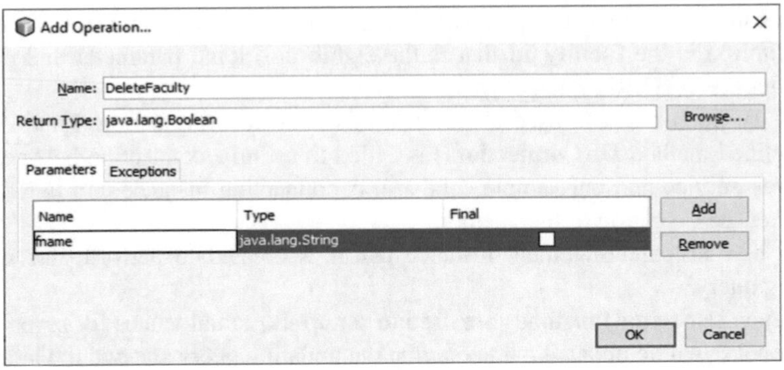

Add Operation...

Name: DeleteFaculty

Return Type: java.lang.Boolean Browse...

Parameters | Exceptions

Name	Type	Final
fname	java.lang.String	☐

Add Remove

OK Cancel

Fig. 9.59 The complete Add Operation wizard

```
  @WebMethod(operationName = "DeleteFaculty")
    public Boolean DeleteFaculty(@WebParam(name = "fname")  String fname) {
        //TODO write your implementation code here:
A       int numDeleted = 0;
B       String query = "DELETE FROM Faculty WHERE faculty_name = ?";
        try {
C         con = DBConnection(con);
D         PreparedStatement pstmt =con.prepareStatement(query);
E         pstmt.setString(1, fname);
F         numDeleted = pstmt.executeUpdate();
G         con.close();
H         if (numDeleted != 0)
            return true;
I         else
            return false;
        }
J       catch (Exception ex) {
          System.out.println("exception is: " + ex);
          return false;
        }
  }
```

Fig. 9.60 The codes for the new operation DeleteFaculty()

9.11.2 Add a New Operation DeleteFaculty() to Perform Faculty Data Deleting Action

Perform the following operations to add a new operation **DeleteFaculty()** into our Web service project **WebServiceSQLApp**:

1) Launch NetBeans IDE 8.2 and open our Web Service project **WebServiceSQLApp**, and select our Web service class file **WebService UpdtDelt.java** from the **Projects** window.
2) Click on the **Design** button on the top of the window to open the Design View of our Web service class file **WebServiceUpdtDelt.java**.
3) Click on the **Add Operation** button to open the **Add Operation** wizard.

4) Enter **DeleteFaculty** into the **Name** field, and click on the **Browse** button that is next to the **Return Type** combo box. Type **boolean** into the **Type Name** field and select the item **Boolean (java.lang)** from the list, and click on the **OK** button.
5) Click on the **Add** button, and enter **fname** into the **Name** parameter field to add a new parameter for this operation. Keep the default data type **java.lang.String** unchanged for this new added parameter **fname**.

Your finished **Add Operation** wizard should match one that is shown in Fig. 9.59. Click on the **OK** button to complete this new operation creation process.

Click on the **Source** button on the top of this window to open the code window of our Web service project. Let's perform the coding developments for this new added operation.

On the opened code window, enter the codes that are shown in Fig. 9.60 into this new added operation **DeleteFaculty()**.

Let's have a closer look at this piece of codes to see how it works.

A. A local integer variable **numDeleted** is created first, and this variable is used to hold the running result of execution of the data deleting operation.
B. The deleting query string is created with one positional parameter, which is the original faculty name that works as the query criterion and is placed after the **WHERE** clause.
C. A **try-catch** block is used for this data deleting action. First the user-defined method **DBConnection()** is called to set up a connection between our Web service and our sample database. A connection instance **con** is returned after the execution of this method.
D. A new PreparedStatement instance **pstmt** is created to perform this deleting query.
E. The **setString()** method is used to set up the actual value for the positional dynamic parameter in the deleting query statement.
F. The deleting action is performed by calling the **executeUpdate()** method, and the deleting result is returned and stored in the local integer variable **numDeleted**.
G. The database connection is closed by executing the **close()** method since we have completed our data deleting action and need to disconnect with our database.
H. The **executeUpdate()** method will return an integer to indicate whether this data deleting is successful or not. If a non-zero value is returned, which means that at least one row has been deleted from our **Faculty** table and this data deleting action is successful, a **true** is returned to the client project.
I. Otherwise, no any row has been deleted from our sample database, and this data deleting failed. A **false** is returned for this situation.
J. The **catch** block is used to track and display any exception that occurred during this data deleting process, and a **false** will be returned if this situation really happened.

At this point, we have completed all coding developments for the data updating and deleting actions. Now let's build and run our Web service project to test its functions.

9.11.3 Deploy and Test the Web Service Project

Perform the following operations to build and deploy our Web service project:

1) Click on the **Clean and Build Main Project** button to build our Web service.
2) Right click on our Web application **WebServiceSQLApp**, and select the **Deploy** item to deploy our Web service. If everything is fine, a successful deployment result should be displayed.

A problem arises when testing the **UpdateFaculty()** operation of this Web service using the tester page, which is the input parameter array **fdata**. As we know, the **fdata** has a data type of ArrayList, and it needs to (1) create an ArrayList instance and then (2) assign a group of updated faculty information to that ArrayList object to call this Web service operation **UpdateFaculty()** to perform the faculty data updating. However, it is difficult to do those two operations manually by using this

Fig. 9.61 The tester page for our Web service project WebServiceSQL

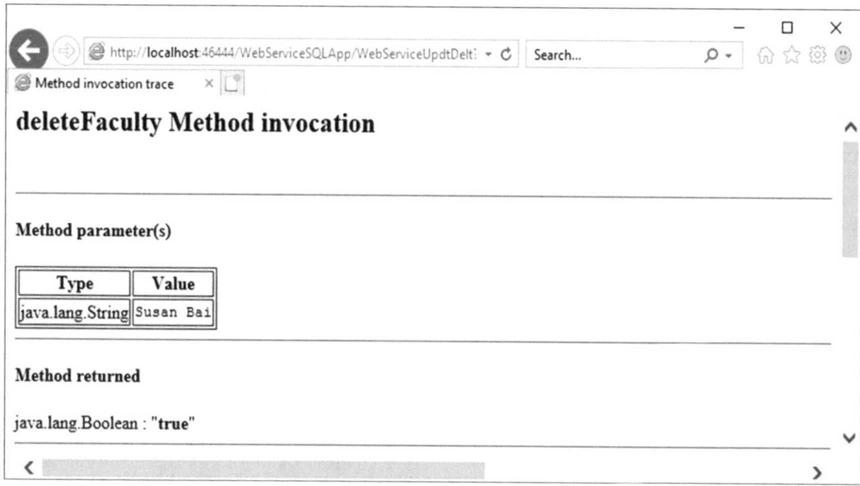

Fig. 9.62 The testing result of the deleting operation

tester page. Therefore we need to create some Web client projects to consume and test this updating operation later.

To test the **DeleteFaculty()** operation, just right click on our Web service output file **WebServiceUpdtDelt** under the **Web Services** node from the **Projects** window, and choose the **Test Web Service** item to open the tester page, which is shown in Fig. 9.61.

Enter a desired faculty name to be deleted from the **Faculty** table in our sample database, such as **Susan Bai**, into the text field that is next to the **deleteFaculty** button, and click on the **deleteFaculty** button to perform this faculty data deleting action.

The testing result is shown in Fig. 9.62. A **true** is returned, and this indicates that our data deleting action is successful.

To confirm this data deleting action, open our **Faculty** table by going to the **Services** window, and expand the **Databases** node, and our connection URL, and finally our sample database **CSE_DEPT**. Expand our database schema **dbo**, and right click on the **Faculty** table. Select the **View Data** item from the popup menu to open our **Faculty** table. On the opened **Faculty** table, you can find that the faculty record with the faculty name of **Susan Bai** has been removed from this table.

Our data deleting action is successful!

But the story is not finished yet. The deleting action for this faculty member, **Susan Bai**, who is not an original faculty record in our sample database, is not a real deleting action. This means that this faculty record is not an original record when we built our sample database in Chap. 2, but it is inserted later when we testing our data insertion action in the last section, Sect. 9.10.3. Therefore this faculty member has no any relational data columns in any other tables in our sample database.

Recall that when we built our sample SQL Server database **CSE_DEPT** in Chap. 2, we set up different columns in different tables for an original faculty record. For

Table 9.1 The deleted record in the Faculty table

faculty_ id	faculty_ name	office	phone	college	title	email	fimage
B78880	Ying Bai	MTC-211	750-378-1148	Florida Atlantic University	Associate Professor	ybai@college.edu	Bai.jpg

Table 9.2 The deleted records in the Course table

course_ id	course	credit	classroom	schedule	enrollment	faculty_ id
CSC-132B	Introduction to Programming	3	MTC-302	T-H: 1:00-2:25 PM	21	B78880
CSC-234A	Data Structure & Algorithms	3	MTC-302	M-W-F: 9:00-9:55 AM	25	B78880
CSE-434	Advanced Electronics Systems	3	MTC-213	M-W-F: 1:00-1:55 PM	26	B78880
CSE-438	Advd Logic & Microprocessor	3	MTC-213	M-W-F: 11:00-11:55 AM	35	B78880

Table 9.3 The deleted records in the LogIn table

user_name	pass_word	faculty_id	student_id
ybai	come	B78880	NULL

Table 9.4 The deleted records in the StudentCourse table

s_course_id	student_id	course_id	credit	major
1005	T77896	CSC-234A	3	CS/IS
1009	A78835	CSE-434	3	CE
1014	A78835	CSE-438	3	CE
1016	A97850	CSC-132B	3	ISE
1017	A97850	CSC-234A	3	ISE

example, for an original faculty member, **Ying Bai**, we set up a **faculty_id** related to that member in the **LogIn** table, detailed information with 8 columns in the **Faculty** table, some columns in the **Course** table, and some courses in the **StudentCourse** table. These columns made some relationships via some primary or foreign keys. If this kind of faculty record was deleted from the **Faculty** table, all other related columns in other tables would also be deleted.

Recalled that cascaded updating and deleting relationships among our five tables are set up in Chap. 2 when we built our sample database. Therefore if an original faculty record, such as **Ying Bai**, was deleted from the **Faculty** table, not only that single faculty record whose name is **Ying Bai** has been deleted from the **Faculty** table when we perform this data deleting action, but also all columns related to this faculty member in other tables, such as the **LogIn, Course**, and **StudentCourse**, have also been deleted because of this cascaded relationship.

If one of the original faculty records, such as **Ying Bai**, was deleted by this Web Service tester, it is highly recommended to recover this deleted faculty member and related records in our **Faculty, LogIn, Course**, and **StudentCourse** tables. An easy way to do this recovery is to use the Microsoft SQL Server Management Studio. For your convenience, we show these deleted records in Tables 9.1, 9.2, 9.3 and 9.4, and you can add or insert them back to the related tables to complete this data recovery.

Next we can develop some Web client projects to consume this Web service to perform data updating and deleting actions to the **Faculty** table in our sample database. First let's discuss how to build a Window-based client project to consume our Web service.

9.12 Build a Window-Based Client Project to Consume the Web Service

We can use one Window-based client project **WinClientInsert** we built in Sect. 9.8 to consume the Web service to perform faculty data updating action. One point to be noted is that although a Web reference to our Web service has been established in Sect. 9.8, we still need to refresh this Web reference since our Web service project has been modified by adding two more operations, **UpdateFaculty()** and **DeleteFaculty()**, in our Web service. Otherwise we would still use the original Web service that does not include these added operations.

To make things clear, we can copy the project **WinClientInsert** and rename it as our new Windows-based client project **WinClientUpdtDelt** and use this project to consume our Web Service to perform data updating and deleting actions to the **Faculty** table in our sample database.

Perform the following operations to complete this renaming project process:

1) Right click on our original Windows-based client project **WinClientInsert**, and select the **Copy** item from the popup menu to open the **Copy Project** wizard.
2) Change the project name to **WinClientUpdtDelt** in the **Project Name** box, and click on the **Copy** button to complete this project copy operation.

Now you may find that our copied project contained some errors with red-color error indicators. The reason for that is because of our Web Service since we need to update our Web Service Reference for this new project **WinClientUpdtDelt**.

9.12.1 *Refresh the Web Service Reference for Our Window-Based Client Project*

In order to call those Web operations, such as **UpdateFaculty()** and **DeleteFaculty()**, in our Web service project **WebServiceSQLApp**, we need to refresh the Web reference in our Window-based client project to use the updated Web service project.

However, prior to do this refreshing action, our Web Service project **WebServiceSQLApp** should be deployed first. Only after our Web Service project is successfully deployed, perform the following operations to refresh the Web service reference:

1) Open our Window-based client project **WinClientUpdtDelt**, and expand the **Web Service References** node.
2) Right click on our Web service **WebServiceInsert**, and choose the **Delete** item to remove this old Web reference. Click on the **Yes** button to confirm this deletion.
3) Right click on our Window-based client project **WinClientUpdtDelt**, and select the **New > Web Service Client** item to open the **New Web Service Client** wizard.
4) On the opened wizard, click on the **Browse** button that is next to the **Project** field, and expand our Web application **WebServiceSQLApp**. Then choose our Web service **WebServiceUpdtDelt** by clicking on it, and click on the **OK** button.
5) Click on the **Finish** button to complete this Web service reference refreshing process.

Now some errors occurred on six coding lines in the main Source file **FacultyFrame.java**; two of them are in the **SelectButtonActionPerformed()** event method (coding lines 360 ~ 361), and two of them are in the InsertButtonActionPerformed() event handler (coding lines 406 ~ 407), and another two are in the **ShowFaculty()** user-defined method (coding lines 435 ~ 436). To fix them, just change the Web Service name for coding lines 360, 406, and 435 from:

```
org.ws.sql.WebServiceInsert_Service service = new org.ws.sql.
WebServiceInsert_Service();
```

```
to:org.ws.sql.WebServiceUpdtDelt_Service service = new org.ws.
sql.WebServiceUpdtDelt_Service();
```

and change coding lines 361, 407, and 436 from:

```
org.ws.sql.WebServiceInsert port = service.getWebServiceInsert
Port();
to:org.ws.sql.WebServiceUpdtDelt port = service.getWebServiceUpdt
DeltPort();
```

If you rebuild the project now, those errors would be removed.

```
  private void UpdateButtonActionPerformed(java.awt.event.ActionEvent evt) {
      // TODO add your handling code here:
A     File imgFile = null;
      ArrayList al = new ArrayList();
B     JFileChooser imgChooser = new JFileChooser();
C     imgChooser.setCurrentDirectory(new File(System.getProperty("user.home")));
D     int result = imgChooser.showOpenDialog(this);
E     if (result == JFileChooser.APPROVE_OPTION) {
         imgFile = imgChooser.getSelectedFile();
F        System.out.println("Selected path: " + imgFile.getAbsolutePath());
         System.out.println("Selected file: " + imgFile.toString());
      }
G     al.clear();
H     al.add(0, FacultyNameField.getText());
      al.add(1, TitleField.getText());
      al.add(2, OfficeField.getText());
      al.add(3, PhoneField.getText());
      al.add(4, CollegeField.getText());
      al.add(5, EmailField.getText());
      al.add(6, imgFile.toString());
      al.add(7, FacultyIDField.getText());
I     try {
         org.ws.sql.WebServiceUpdtDelt_Service service = new org.ws.sql.WebServiceUpdtDelt_Service();
         org.ws.sql.WebServiceUpdtDelt port = service.getWebServiceUpdtDeltPort();
J        Boolean update = port.updateFaculty(al);
K        if (!update) {
            msgDlg.setMessage("The data updating is failed!");
            msgDlg.setVisible(true);
         }
L        else
            ComboName.addItem(FacultyNameField.getText());
      }
M     catch (Exception ex){
         System.out.println("exception: " + ex);
      }
  }
```

Fig. 9.63 The complete codes for the UpdateButtonActionPerformed() method

Now that we have refreshed or updated the Web service reference for our Window-based client project **WinClientUpdtDelt**, next let's develop the codes in our client project to call that Web service operations, **UpdateFaculty()** and **DeleteFaculty()**, to perform faculty data updating and deleting actions. First let's concentrate on the data updating action.

9.12.2 Build the Codes to Call the UpdateFaculty() Operation

Open our Window-based client project **WinClientUpdtDelt**, and double click on our main class **FacultyFrame.java** to open it. Click on the **Design** button to open the graphic user interface. In this client project, we want to use the **Update** button in this form as a trigger to start the faculty data updating action. Therefore double click on the **Update** button to open its event method **UpdateButtonActionPerformed()**, and enter the codes that are shown in Fig. 9.63 into this method.

Let's have a closer look at this piece of codes to see how it works.

A. Some local objects are first declared, which include a File object, **imgFile**, which is used to hold the selected image file, and a new ArrayList instance **al**, which is used to pick up and reserve the input new faculty data array.
B. A Java File Chooser instance, **imgChooser**, is generated, and it provides a File Interface GUI to allow users to select a desired faculty image to be updated to our database later.
C. The current directory, which is exactly the folder of our current project, is selected, and this location will work as a default folder to store all selected faculty image files later.
D. The system method, **showOpenDialog()**, is executed to display this Chooser GUI to enable users to browse and select a desired faculty image to be updated to our database later.
E. By checking one property, **APPROVE_OPTION**, one can confirm whether this GUI's operation is successful or not. If it is opened and an image has been selected, a true is returned. Then the selected image can be retrieved by calling a method, **getSelectedFile()**.
F. These two coding lines are used to display the path and directory for the selected faculty image, and they are used for the debugging purpose.
G. The **clear()** method is executed to make sure that the ArrayList instance is clean before a new faculty record is collected.
H. The **add()** method is used to pick up and add eight pieces of updated faculty information into this new ArrayList instance **al**. These eight pieces of new faculty information are entered by the user and stored in seven text fields and the File Chooser in this FacultyFrame window form. The **toString()** method is used to convert some piece of new faculty information obtained using the **getText()** method that returns an object data type to a String. The index is necessary since it is used to indicate the position of each parameter in this ArrayList. One point to be noted is the order of adding these text fields, which must be identical with order of columns in our **Faculty** table.
I. A **try catch** block is used to perform the calling of our Web service operation **UpdateFaculty()** to perform this faculty data updating action. First a new Web service instance **service** is created based on our Web service class

```
  private void DeleteButtonActionPerformed(java.awt.event.ActionEvent evt) {
      // TODO add your handling code here:
      try {
A         org.ws.sql.WebServiceUpdtDelt_Service service = new org.ws.sql.WebServiceUpdtDelt_Service();
          org.ws.sql.WebServiceUpdtDelt port = service.getWebServiceUpdtDeltPort();
B         Boolean delete = port.deleteFaculty(ComboName.getSelectedItem().toString());
C          if (!delete) {
             msgDlg.setMessage("The data deleting is failed!");
             msgDlg.setVisible(true);
          }
      }
D     catch (Exception ex){
         System.out.println("exception: " + ex);
      }
  }
```

Fig. 9.64 The automatically created codes by NetBeans IDE

WebServiceUpdtDelt_Service. Then the **getWebServiceUpdtDeltPort()** method is executed to get the current port used by our Web service. This port is returned and assigned to a new Port instance **port**.

J. The Web service operation **updateFaculty()** is executed with the ArrayList instance **al** that has been filled with eight pieces of updated faculty information as the argument of this method. The running result of that operation is returned and assigned to a Boolean variable **update**.
K. If the value of the variable **update** is **false**, which means that no any row has been updated in our **Faculty** table and this updating action has been failed, the **msgDlg** instance is used to show this situation.
L. Otherwise if the value of the **update** variable is true, which means that this data updating action is successful, the new updated faculty name will be added into the Faculty Name combo box **ComboName** using the **addItem()** method.
M. The **catch** block is used to track and display any possible exception during this Web service operation execution.

Next let's build the codes to perform the faculty data deleting action.

9.12.3 Build the Codes to Call the DeleteFaculty() Operation

Open our Window-based client project **WinClientUpdtDelt**, and double click on our main class **FacultyFrame.java** to open it. Click on the **Design** button to open the graphic user interface. In this client project, we want to use the **Delete** button in this form as a trigger to start the faculty data deleting action. Therefore double click on the **Delete** button to open its event method **DeleteButtonActionPerformed()**.

Enter the codes that are shown in Fig. 9.64 into this **DeleteButtonActionPerformed()** event handler. Let's have a closer look at this piece of codes to see how it works.

A. A **try catch** block is used to perform the calling of our Web service method **DeleteFaculty()** to perform this faculty data deleting action. First a new Web service instance **service** is created based on our Web service class **WebServiceUpdtDelt_Service**. Then the method **getWebServiceUpdtDelt-Port()** is executed to get the current port used by our Web service.
   This port is returned and assigned to a new Port instance **port**.
B. The Web service operation **DeleteFaculty()** is executed with the selected faculty name as the argument of this method. The running result of that operation is returned and assigned to a Boolean variable **delete**.
C. If the value of the variable **delete** is **false**, which means that no any row has been deleted from our **Faculty** table and this data deleting has been failed, the **msgDlg** instance is used to show this situation.
D. The **catch** block is used to track and display any possible exception during this Web service operation execution.

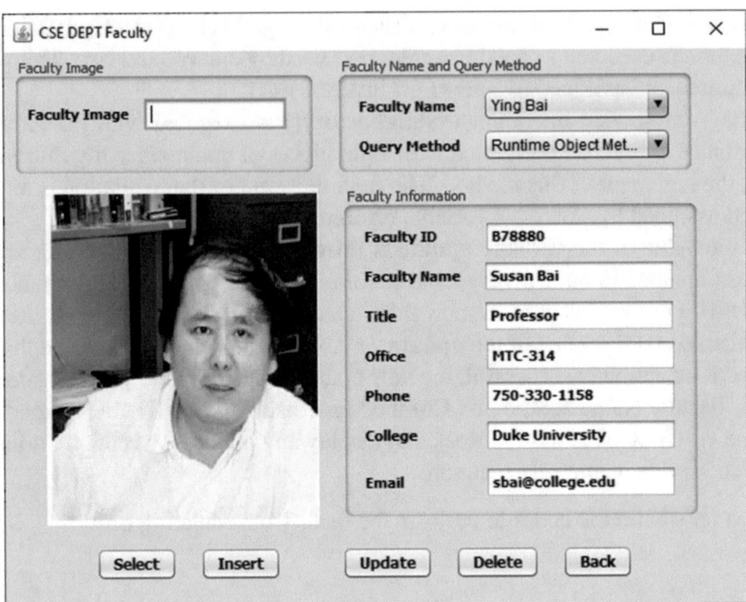

Fig. 9.65 Six pieces of updated faculty information

At this point, we have completed all coding development for our Window-based client project for the data updating and deleting actions. Now let's build and run our client project to call and test our Web service to perform faculty data updating and deleting actions.

9.12.4 Build and Run Our Client Project to Update and Delete Faculty Record via Web Service

Make sure to deploy our Web Service project prior to running our Windows client project to call our Web Service project; otherwise, you may encounter some errors.

Now click on the **Clean and Build Main Project** button to build our client project. If everything is fine, click on the **Run Main Project** button to run our client project.

The FacultyFrame form window is displayed. First let's perform a faculty query action. Select a desired faculty member, such as **Ying Bai**, from the Faculty Name combo box, and click on the **Select** button to query the detailed information for this faculty via our Web service **WebServiceApp**. The queried result is displayed in seven text fields.

Now enter an updating faculty record with six pieces of updated faculty information shown below into six text fields, which is shown in Fig. 9.65.

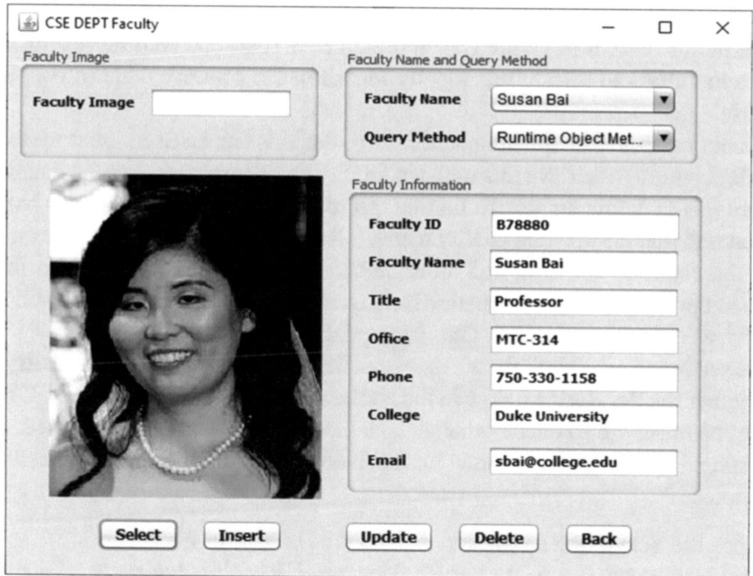

Fig. 9.66 The updated faculty information

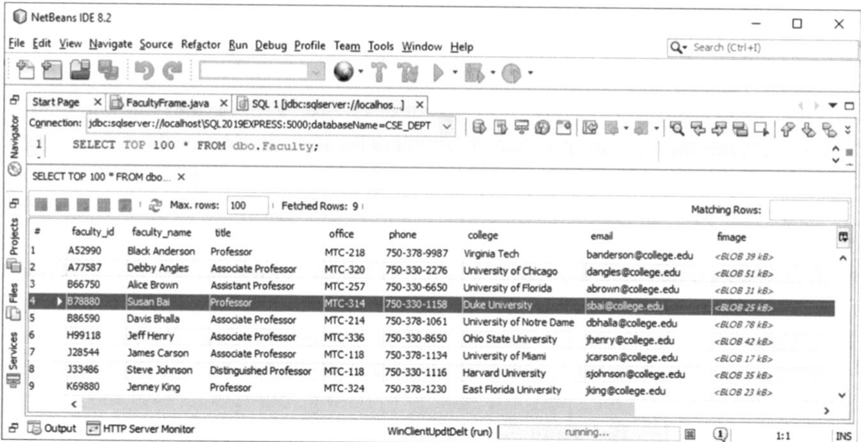

Fig. 9.67 The opened Faculty table in the NetBeans IDE

- Name: **Susan Bai**
- Title: **Professor**
- Office: **MTC-314**
- Phone: **750-330-1158**
- College: **Duke University**
- Email: **sbai@college.edu**

Click on the **Update** button to browse and select the desired updating faculty image; in this case, it is **White.jpg**, and then try to call our Web service operation **UpdateFaculty()** to update this faculty record in the **Faculty** table in our sample database.

To confirm this data updating action, two methods can be used. First we can use the **Select** button to retrieve this updated faculty record from our sample database to confirm this updating action. To do that, go to the **Faculty Name** combo box, and you can find that the updated faculty name, **Susan Bai**, has been added into this box. Click this name to select it, and click on the **Select** button. You can find that six pieces of updated faculty information have been retrieved and displayed in this form window, as shown in Fig. 9.66. Our data updating is successful!

The second way to confirm this data updating action is to open our **Faculty** table using either the **Services** window in the NetBeans IDE or the Microsoft SQL Server Management Studio to check whether this faculty record has been updated. To do that using the **Services** window in the NetBeans IDE, perform the following operations:

1) Open the **Services** window and expand the **Databases** node.
2) Right click on our SQL Server database URL: **jdbc:sqlserver://localhost\SQL2019EXPRESS: 5000; databaseName=CSE_DEPT**, and select the **Connect** item to try to connect to our database. Enter **Happy2020** into the Password box and click on the **OK** button.
3) Expand our sample database **CSE_DEPT**, **dbo**, and **Tables**.
4) Right click on the **Faculty** table and select the **View Data** item.

Your opened Faculty table is shown in Fig. 9.67. It can be found that the faculty record with the **faculty_id** of **B78880**, which is located at row 4 and has been highlighted in dark color, has been successfully updated in our database.

However, it is highly recommended to recover this updated faculty record to the original one to keep our database clean and neat. Refer to Table 9.5 to perform another data updating action by using the **Update** button on this FacultyFrame Form to recover this faculty record to the original one with the faculty name as **Ying Bai**.

Next let's test the faculty record deleting action via our Web service operation **DeleteFaculty()**. First let's perform another updating action to recover the updated faculty member **Ying Bai** using the data shown in Table 9.5. Enter these six pieces of original faculty information into those six text fields and click on the **Update** button.

Then keep the faculty member **Ying Bai** selected in the Faculty Name combo box, and click on the **Delete** button to try to call our Web service operation **DeleteFaculty()** to delete this faculty record from our sample database.

Table 9.5 The original faculty record in the Faculty table

faculty_id	faculty_name	office	phone	college	title	email	fimage
B78880	Ying Bai	MTC-211	750-378-1148	Florida Atlantic University	Associate Professor	ybai@college.edu	Bai.jpg

To confirm this data deleting action, two ways can be used. First you can perform a faculty data query operation by selecting the deleted faculty member **Ying Bai** from the **Faculty Name** combo box, and click on the **Select** button to try to retrieve this faculty record from our database. You can find that the querying faculty record cannot be found from our sample database and an error information with a **null** is displayed, and this means that our data deleting is successful.

Another way to confirm this data deleting is to open the Faculty table in our sample database.

To make our sample database clean and neat, it is highly recommended to recover this deleted faculty member and related records in our **Faculty, LogIn, Course**, and **StudentCourse** tables. Perform the following operational steps to recover this faculty record:

1) Perform a data insertion operation by using the **Insert** button on this FacultyFrame Form to insert a new faculty record with faculty name as **Ying Bai**. Refer to Table 9.5 to perform this data insertion action.
2) Open and use the Microsoft SQL Server Management Studio 18 to perform recovery jobs for all other Tables, such as **LogIn, Course**, and **StudentCourse**. You can copy all records and then paste them into the related Tables in Microsoft SQL Server Management Studio. Refer to original records shown in Tables 9.2, 9.3 and 9.4 in Sect. 9.11.3 to add or insert them to the related tables to complete this data recovery.

A point to be noted is that as you perform data recovery, the recovery order is very important. It means that you have to first recovery the faculty data in the Faculty table, and then the data in other tables since the Faculty table is a primary table.

A complete Window-based client project **WinClientUpdtDelt** can be found from the folder **Class DB Projects\Chapter 9** that is located under a folder **Students** at the Springer ftp site (refer to Fig. 1.2 in Chap. 1).

Next let's build a Web-based client project to consume our Web service to insert a new faculty record into the Faculty table in our sample database.

9.13 Build a Web-Based Client Project to Consume the Web Service

We can modify a Web-based project **JavaWebDBJSPSQL_UpdateDelete** we built in Sect. 8.5.3 in Chap. 8 to make it as our new Web client project to consume our Web service to perform the faculty data updating and deleting actions.

Perform the following operational steps to create our new project **WebClientUpdtDelt**:

1) In the **Projects** window, right click on the project **JavaWebDBJSPSQL_UpdateDelete**, and select the **Copy** item from the popup menu to open the **Copy Project** wizard.
2) Enter our new project name, **WebClientUpdtDelt**, into the **Project Name** box, and browse to the default project folder, **C:\Class DB Projects\Chapter 9**, as the **Project Location**, and click on the **Copy** button.

A new project **WebClientUpdtDelt** is generated and added into our **Projects** window.

First let's add a Web Service reference to our Web-based client project to allow it to use our Web service operations.

9.13.1 Add a Web Service Reference to Our Web-Based Client Project

In order to call the **UpdateFaculty()** and **DeleteFaculty()** operations in our Web service project **WebServiceSQLApp**, we need to add a Web reference to our Web-based client project **WebClientUpdtDelt** to use the updated Web service project. Perform the following operations to add this Web service reference:

1) Deploy our Web Service project **WebServiceSQLApp** prior to adding it into our project.
2) Right click on our Web-based client project **WebClientUpdtDelt**, and select the **New > Web Service Client** item to open the **New Web Service Client** wizard.
3) On the opened wizard, click on the **Browse** button that is next to the **Project** field, and expand our Web application **WebServiceSQLApp**. Then choose our Web service class **WebServiceUpdtDelt** by clicking on it, and click on the **OK** button.
4) Click on the **Finish** button to complete this adding Web service reference process.

Now that we have added a Web service reference to our Web-based client project **WebClientUpdtDelt**, next let's develop the codes in our client project to call that Web service operations, **UpdateFaculty()** and **DeleteFaculty()**, to perform faculty data updating and deleting actions. The main coding job is inside the Java Bean class file, **FacultyUpdateDeleteBean.java**.

First let's take care of the data updating operation **UpdateFaculty()**.

```
  public FacultyUpdateDeleteBean() {
A
  }
B   public int UpdateFaculty(String[] upFaculty) {
C     int numUpdated = 1;
      ArrayList al = new ArrayList();
      MsgDialog msgDlg = new MsgDialog(new javax.swing.JFrame(), true);
D     al.clear();
E     al.add(0, upFaculty[0]);      // faculty_name
      al.add(1, upFaculty[1]);      // title
      al.add(2, upFaculty[2]);      // office
      al.add(3, upFaculty[3]);      // phone
      al.add(4, upFaculty[4]);      // college
      al.add(5, upFaculty[5]);      // email
      al.add(6, upFaculty[6]);      // fimage
      al.add(7, upFaculty[7]);      // faculty_id
    try{
F       org.ws.sql.WebServiceUpdtDelt_Service service = new org.ws.sql.WebServiceUpdtDelt_Service();
        org.ws.sql.WebServiceUpdtDelt port = service.getWebServiceUpdtDeltPort();
G       Boolean update = port.updateFaculty(al);
H       if (!update) {
          msgDlg.setMessage("The data updating is failed!");
          msgDlg.setVisible(true);
          return 0;
        }
      }
I     catch (Exception e) {
        msgDlg.setMessage("Error in Update Statement! " + e.getMessage());
        msgDlg.setVisible(true);
        return 0;
      }
J     return numUpdated;
  }
```

Fig. 9.68 The modified codes for the Update() method

9.13.2 Develop the Codes to Call Our Web Service Operation UpdateFaculty()

To make things simple and easy, we can use and modify one of our Java Bean class files, **FacultyUpdateDelete.java**, and use it to access our Web Service operational methods to perform faculty data updating and deleting actions.

Open our Web-based client project **WebClientUpdtDelt**, and double click on the **FacultyUpdateDelete.java** from the **Projects** window to open this managed bean class file. The main modification jobs are performed in this class file. Perform the following operations to complete these modifications:

1) Remove all codes inside the constructor, **FacultyUpdateDeleteBean()**, to make it empty.
2) Add the codes shown in Fig. 9.68 into the **UpdateFaculty()** method.

Let's have a closer look at this piece of new added codes to see how it works.

A. The codes inside the constructor of this Java Bean class have been removed.
B. The **UpdateFaculty()** method is declared with a string array, **upFaculty**, as the argument to be passed into this method, in which all eight pieces of updated information are involved.

C. Some local variables are declared, including an integer variable **numUpdated** that will hold the data updating result later and a new ArrayList instance **al** that is used to pick up and reserve the input updating faculty data array.
D. The **clear()** method is executed to make sure that the ArrayList instance is clean before a updating faculty record is collected.
E. A sequence of **add()** method is used to pick up and add all pieces of updating faculty information into this new ArrayList instance **al**. Seven pieces of updating faculty information are entered by the user in the JSP page **FacultyPage.jsp** and stored in seven properties defined in this managed bean. The last parameter, the eighth one, is the original faculty ID.
F. A **try catch** block is used to perform the calling of our Web service operation **UpdateFaculty()** to perform this faculty data updating action. First a new Web service instance **service** is created based on our Web service class **WebServiceUpdtDelt_Service**. Then the **getWebServiceUpdtDeltPort()** method is executed to get the current port used by our Web service. This port is returned and assigned to a new Port instance **port**.
G. The **UpdateFaculty()** operation in our Web service is called with the ArrayList instance that contains all pieces of updated faculty information as the argument. The execution result of this faculty data updating is returned and assigned to the local Boolean variable **update**.
H. If the returned Boolean variable **update** is false, which means that this data updating failed, the **msgDlg** instance is used to indicate this situation.
I. The **catch** block is used to catch any possible exception during this data updating process.
J. Finally the local variable **numUpdated** is returned to indicate that this data updating action is successful.

Next let's build the codes for the **Delete()** method in this Java bean to call our Web service operation **DeleteFaculty()** to perform the faculty data deleting action.

9.13.3 Develop the Codes to Call Our Web Service Operation DeleteFaculty()

On the opened Java bean class file **FacultyUpdateDeleteBean.java** under the **Projects** window, enter the codes shown in Fig. 9.69 into the **Delete()** method in this class to fulfill this data deleting function.

Let's have a closer look at this piece of new added codes to see how it works.

A. First a local integer variable, **numDeleted**, is declared, and this variable is used to hold our data deleting operation result later.
B. A **try catch** block is used to perform the calling of our Web service operation **DeleteFaculty()** to perform this faculty data deleting action. First a new Web service instance **service** is created based on our Web service class **WebServiceUpdtDelt_Service**.

```
  public int DeleteFaculty(String fname) {
A    int numDeleted = 0;
     try{
B        org.ws.sql.WebServiceUpdtDelt_Service service = new org.ws.sql.WebServiceUpdtDelt_Service();
         org.ws.sql.WebServiceUpdtDelt port = service.getWebServiceUpdtDeltPort();
C        Boolean delete = port.deleteFaculty(fname);
D        if (!delete) {
            System.out.println("The data deleting is failed!");
            return 0;
         }
      }
E     catch (Exception e) {
         System.out.println("Error in Delete Statement! " + e.getMessage());
         return 0;
      }
F     return numDeleted;
  }
```

Fig. 9.69 The completed codes for the DeleteFaculty() method

Then the **getWebServiceUpdtDeltPort()** method is executed to get the current port used by our Web service. This port is returned and assigned to a new Port instance **port**.

C. The **deleteFaculty()** operation in our Web service is called with the original faculty name as the argument. The execution result of this faculty data deleting is returned and assigned to the local Boolean variable **delete**.
D. If the returned Boolean variable **delete** is false, which means that this data deleting failed, a **System.out.println()** method is used to indicate this situation.
E. The **catch** block is used to catch any possible exception during this data deleting process.
F. Finally the local variable, **numDeleted**, is returned to indicate a success of this data deleting operation.

Before we can build and run our Web client project to call our Web Service to perform data updating and deleting actions, we need to modify some codes, exactly two coding lines, in our **FacultyProcess.jsp** page to allow it to work properly.

Open this File, and browse to coding lines 111 and 124, and comment out these two lines:

```
//UpdateFaculty.CloseDBConnection();
//DeleteFaculty.CloseDBConnection();
```

The reason for this comment-out is that we do not need to call this method to close our database; instead this database closing job has been handled in our Web Service project.

Now let's build and run our Web client project to call our Web service operations to perform the faculty data updating and deleting actions. One point to be noted is that our Web Service project **WebServiceSQLApp** must be deployed first before we can run our client project.

Fig. 9.70 Six pieces of updated faculty information

9.13.4 Build and Run Our Client Project to Update and Delete Faculty Record via Web Service

First right click on our Web Service **WebServiceSQLApp**, and select the **Deploy** to make it active. Then click the **Clean and Build Main Project** button to build our client project. Right click on our **FacultyPage.jsp** from the **Projects** window, and choose the **Run File** item to run our client project.

On the opened JSP page, first let's perform a faculty record query by entering a desired faculty name, such as **Ying Bai**, into the **Faculty Name** field, and then click on the **Select** button to get details for this faculty member. To update this faculty record, enter six pieces of updating faculty information shown below into the associated six text fields, as shown in Fig. 9.70.

- Name: **Susan Bai**
- Title: **Professor**
- Office: **MTC-314**
- Phone: **750-330-1158**
- College: **Duke University**
- Email: **sbai@college.edu**

Then click on the **Browse** button that is on the right of the **Image** box, and browse to our desired faculty image folder, in this case, it is **C:\...**

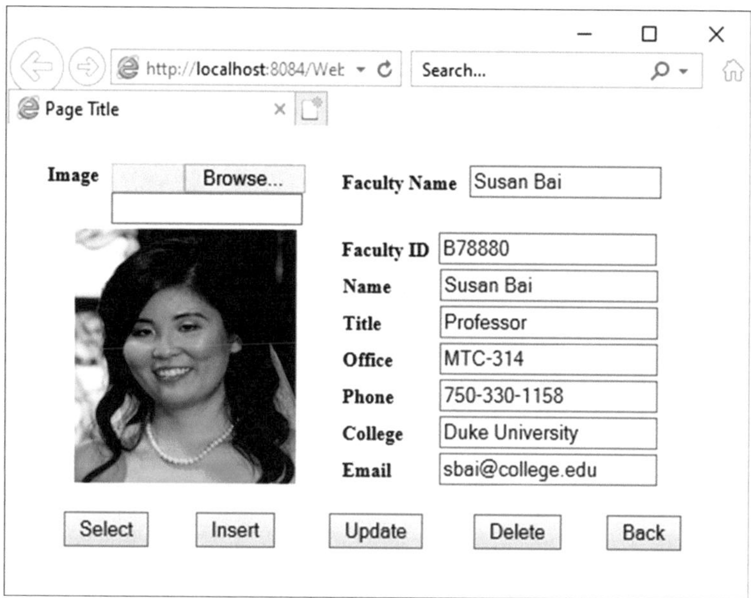

Fig. 9.71 The confirmation of an updated faculty record

WebClientUpdtDelt\web\FImages. Then select the desired faculty image, **White.jpg**, and click on the **Open** button to select this image.

You may need to create this folder under this project and copy all faculty image files from the Springer ftp site (refer to Fig. 1.2 in Chap. 1) and paste them into this folder.

Now click on the **Update** button to try to call our Web service operation **UpdateFaculty()** to update this faculty record in the **Faculty** table in our sample database.

To confirm this data updating action, two methods can be used. First we can use the **Select** button to query this updated faculty record. To do that, enter the updated faculty image name, **White.jpg**, into the **Image** box, which is under the **Browse** button, and enter the updated faculty name, **Susan Bai**, into the **Faculty Name** box on the top, and then click on the **Select** button to try to retrieve back this updated faculty record from our sample database. Immediately you can find that the updated faculty record is retrieved and displayed, as shown in Fig. 9.71.

To use the second way to check this updating action, we can open our **Faculty** table using either the **Services** window in the NetBeans IDE or the Microsoft SQL Server Management Studio to check whether this faculty record has been updated.

To use the second way in the NetBeans IDE, perform the following operations:

1) Open the **Services** window and expand the **Databases** node.
2) Right click on our SQL Server database URL: **jdbc:sqlserver://localhost\SQL2019EXPRESS: 5000; databaseName=CSE_DEPT**, and select the

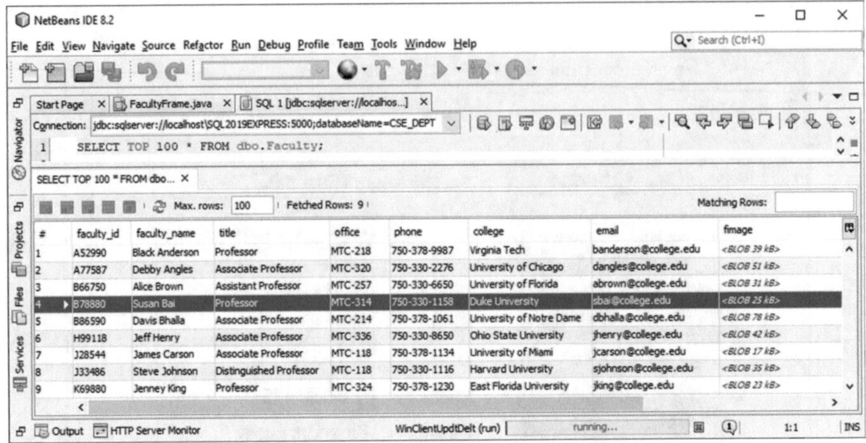

Fig. 9.72 The opened Faculty table in the NetBeans IDE

Table 9.6 The original faculty record in the Faculty table

faculty_id	faculty_name	office	phone	college	title	email	fimage
B78880	Ying Bai	MTC-211	750-378-1148	Florida Atlantic University	Associate Professor	ybai@college.edu	Bai.jpg

Connect item to try to connect to our database. Enter **Happy2020** into the Password box, and click on the **OK** button.

3) Expand our sample database **CSE_DEPT**, **dbo**, and **Tables**.
4) Right click on the **Faculty** table and select the **View Data** item.

Your opened Faculty table is shown in Fig. 9.72. It can be found that the faculty record with the **faculty_id** of **B78880**, which is located at row 4 and has been highlighted in dark color, has been successfully updated in our database.

It is highly recommended to recover this updated faculty record back to the original one to keep our database clean and neat. Refer to Table 9.6 to perform another data updating action by using the **Update** button to recover this faculty record with the faculty name as **Ying Bai**.

Next let's test the faculty deleting action by calling our Web service operation **DeleteFaculty()**. Suppose another faculty updating action has been performed to recover the faculty member **Ying Bai** to its original record.

Now type the original faculty name **Ying Bai** into the **Faculty Name** field, and click on the **Select** button to retrieve this faculty record. Then click on the **Delete** button to try to delete this faculty record. To confirm this data deleting action, click on the **Select** button again to try to retrieve this faculty record from our sample database. A null record is returned and displayed in all related TextFields, which means that the queried faculty record did not exist. Our data deleting is successful!

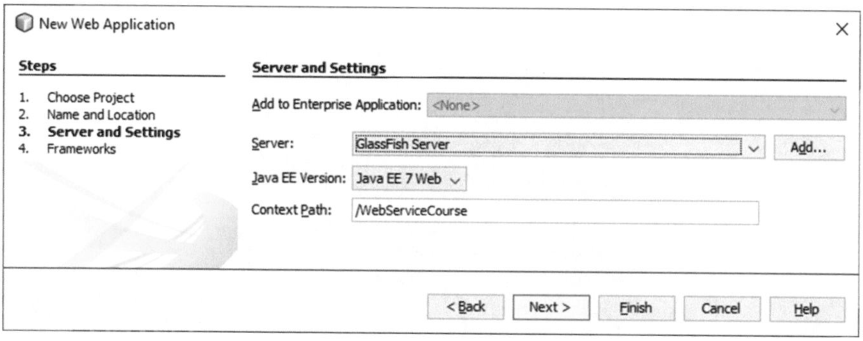

New Web Application

Steps
1. Choose Project
2. Name and Location
3. Server and Settings
4. Frameworks

Server and Settings
Add to Enterprise Application: <None>
Server: GlassFish Server
Java EE Version: Java EE 7 Web
Context Path: /WebServiceCourse

< Back | Next > | Finish | Cancel | Help

Fig. 9.73 The finished Server and Settings wizard

You can also try to open the **Faculty** table in our sample database by using the **Services** window in the NetBeans IDE. The faculty record with faculty name **Ying Bai** cannot be found from this table, which means that the queried faculty record has been deleted from our database.

To make our sample database clean and neat, it is highly recommended to recover this deleted faculty member and related records in our **Faculty, LogIn, Course,** and **StudentCourse** tables. An easy way to do this recovery is to use our Windows-based client project **WinClientUpdtDelt** and the Microsoft SQL Server Management Studio. Refer to Sect. 9.12.4 to complete this data recovery job.

A complete Web client project **WebClientUpdtDelt** can be found from a folder **Class DB Projects\Chapter 9** that is located under the **Students** folder at the Springer ftp site (refer to Fig. 1.2 in Chap. 1).

9.14 Build Java Web Service Projects to Access Course Table in Our Sample Database

We have provided very detailed discussions and analyses on accessing and manipulating **Faculty** table in our sample SQL Server database. Starting from this section, we will concentrate on accessing and manipulating data in the **Course** table in our sample database.

9.14.1 Create a New Java Web Application Project WebServiceCourseApp

First let's create a new Java Web Application project. Perform the following operations to create our new Web application **WebServiceCourse**:

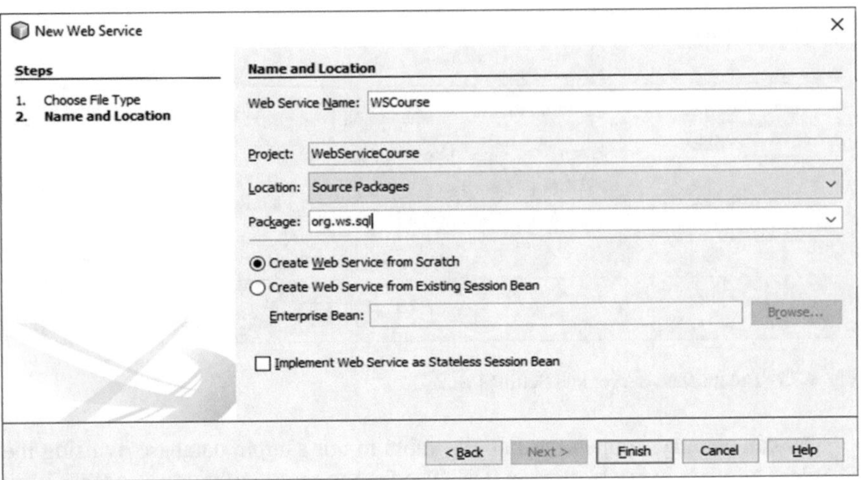

Fig. 9.74 The finished Name and Location wizard

1) Launch NetBeans IDE 8.2, and choose **File > New Project** (Ctrl-Shift-N). Select **Web Application** from the **Java Web** category, and click on the **Next** button.
2) Name the project **WebServiceCourse**, and click on the **Browse** button to select a desired location for the project. In this application, we used the **C:\Class DB Projects\Chapter 9** as our project location. Click on the **Next** button to continue.
3) Select **GlassFish Server** as our Web container and **Java EE 7 Web** as the Java EE version; your finished **Server and Settings** wizard should match one that is shown in Fig. 9.73. Click on the **Next** button to go to the next wizard.
4) In the opened Frameworks wizard, click on the **Finish** button to complete this new application creation process.

Now that a Web application has been created with a selected Web container, next we can create our new Web service project **WSCourse**.

9.14.2 Create a New Java SOAP-Based Web Service Project WebServiceCourse

The function of this Web service is to execute related operations in this Web service and furthermore to call the associated methods defined in our Java session beans to perform data queries and manipulations to the **Course** table in our sample database.

Perform the following operations to create this new Web service project **WSCourse**:

1) In the **Projects** window, right click on our new created project **WebService Course**, and select the **New > Other** menu item to open the **New File** wizard.

2) Select **Web Services** from the **Categories** list and **Web Service** from the **File Types** list, and click on the **Next** button.
3) Name the Web service **WSCourse** and type **org.ws.sql** into the **Package** field. Leave **Create Web Service from Scratch** selected.

Your finished **Name and Location** wizard should match one that is shown in Fig. 9.74. Click on the **Finish** button to complete this process.

9.14.3 The Organization of Web Service Operations

The main purpose of using our Web service is to query and manipulate data from the **Course** table in our sample database. Therefore we need to add some new operations to the Web service project. We will add five new operations based on the sequence of five operational tasks on the **Course** table. This means that we will add the following five operations into this Web service project to perform related Course information query and manipulations:

- **QueryCourseID()**: Query all **course_id** taught by the selected faculty member.
- **QueryCourse()**: Query detailed information for selected **course_id**.
- **InsertCourse()**: Insert a new course record into the **Course** table.
- **UpdateCourse()**: Update an existing course record in the **Course** table.
- **DeleteCourse()**: Delete a course record from the **Course** table.

Next let's start to build these five Web operations in our Web Service project one by one. Unlike those operations we built in the last section, here we combined all operations in one Web Service class file, **WSCourse.java**.

9.14.4 Create and Build Web Service Operations

Let's start to create each Web operation and develop the codes for each of them. First let's start from the **QueryCourseID()** method.

Recall that when we built our sample database in Chap. 2, especially when we built the **Course** table, there is no **faculty_name** column available in the **Course** table and the only relationship between each **course_id** and each faculty member is the **faculty_id** column in the **Course** table. This is a many-to-one relationship between the **course_id** and the **faculty_id** in this table, which means that many courses (**course_id**) can be taught by a single faculty (**faculty_id**). However, in the **Faculty** table, there is a one-to-one relationship between each **faculty_name** and each **faculty_id** column.

Therefore, in order to query all courses, exactly all **course_id**, taught by the selected faculty member, exactly the **faculty_name**, we need to perform two queries from two tables.

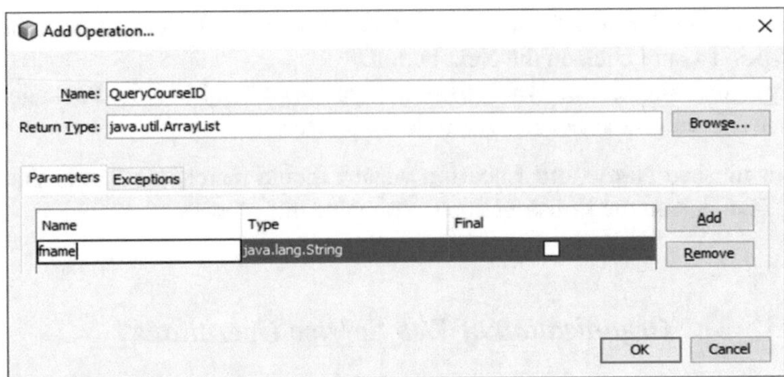

Fig. 9.75 The finished Add Operation wizard

- First we need to perform a query to the **Faculty** table to get a matched **faculty_id** based on the selected faculty member (**faculty_name**).
- Then we need to perform another query to the **Course** table to get all **course_id** taught by the selected **faculty_id** that is obtained from the first query.

In fact, we can combine these two queries into a single JOIN query to simplify this process.

Based on this discussion, now let's perform the following operations to add a new operation **QueryCourseID()** into our main class file **WSCourse.java** to perform this **course_id** query.

9.14.4.1 Create and Build the Web Operation QueryCourseID()

Perform the following operations to create a new operation **QueryCourseID()** in our main class file **WSCourse.java**:

1) Double click on our Web service class file **WSCourse.java** from the **Projects** window to open it.
2) Click on the **Design** button on the top of the window to open the Design View of our Web service project **WebServiceCourse**.
3) Click on the **Add Operation** button to open the **Add Operation** wizard.
4) Enter **QueryCourseID** into the **Name** field, and click on the **Browse** button that is next to the **Return Type** combo box. Type **arrayList** into the **Type Name** field and select the item **ArrayList (java.util)** from the list, and click on the **OK** button.
5) Click on the **Add** button and enter **fname** into the **Name** parameter field. Keep the default type **java.lang.String** unchanged.
6) Your finished **Add Operation** wizard should match one that is shown in Fig. 9.75.
7) Click on the **OK** button to complete this new operation creation process.

```
  package org.ws.sql;
  import java.sql.*;
  import java.sql.SQLException;
  import java.util.ArrayList;
  import javax.jws.WebService;
  import javax.jws.WebMethod;
  import javax.jws.WebParam;
  @WebService(serviceName = "WSCourse")
   public class WSCourse {
A   Connection con = null;
    private Connection DBConnection(Connection conn) {
B       try
        {
          //Load and register SQL Server driver
C         Class.forName("com.microsoft.sqlserver.jdbc.SQLServerDriver");
        }
D       catch (Exception e) {
          System.out.println("Class not found exception!" + e.getMessage());
        }
E       String url = "jdbc:sqlserver://localhost\\SQL2019EXPRESS:5000;databaseName=CSE_DEPT;";
F       try {
          conn = DriverManager.getConnection(url,"SMART","Happy2020");
        }
G       catch (SQLException e) {
          System.out.println("Could not connect! " + e.getMessage());
          e.printStackTrace();
        }
H       return conn;
    }
I @WebMethod(operationName = "QueryCourseID")
    public ArrayList QueryCourseID(@WebParam(name = "fname") String fname) {
        //TODO write your implementation code here:
J       ArrayList<String> result = new ArrayList<String>();
K       String query = "SELECT Course.course_id, course FROM Course JOIN Faculty " +
                   "ON (Course.faculty_id = Faculty.faculty_id) AND (Faculty.faculty_name = ?)";
L   try {
          con = DBConnection(con);
M         PreparedStatement pstmt =con.prepareStatement(query);
N         pstmt.setString(1, fname);
O         ResultSet rs = pstmt.executeQuery();
P         ResultSetMetaData rsmd = rs.getMetaData();
Q         while (rs.next()){
            for (int colNum = 1; colNum <= rsmd.getColumnCount() - 1; colNum++)
              result.add(rs.getString(colNum));
          }
R         con.close();
          rs.close();
          pstmt.close();
S         return result;
        }
T       catch (Exception ex) {
          System.out.println("exception is: " + ex);
          return null;
        }
    }
  }
```

Fig. 9.76 The codes for the Web service operation QueryCourseID()

Now let's develop the codes for this operation.

Click on the **Source** button on the top of this window to open the code window of our Web service project **WSCourse.java**. On the opened code window, enter the codes that are shown in Fig. 9.76 into this code window.

Let's have a closer look at this piece of codes to see how it works.

A. A class level variable, **con**, which is our database connection object, is declared first since we need it to work as our database connection object for all of operations later.
B. A user-defined method, **DBConnection()**, is executed to try to connect to our sample database. Exactly a **try-catch** block is used to help in performing this connection process.
C. First the SQL Server JDBC driver is loaded using the **forName()** method.
D. The **catch** block is used to track and detect any possible exception for this JDBC driver loading process. The debug information will be displayed using the **System.out.println()** method if any exception occurred.
E. Our sample SQL Server database connection URL is defined, and it is used to set up a connection to our sample database. Refer to Sect. 6.3.3.3.1 in Chap. 6 to get more details about this connection URL.
F. Another **try** block is used to set up a connection to our sample database using the **getConnection()** method that belongs to the DriverManager class with the username and password as arguments.
G. The **catch** block is used to detect and display any possible exception during this connection process.
H. The established connection object is returned to the calling method.
I. Our Web operation method, **QueryCourseID()**, is declared and defined with a selected faculty name as the argument.
J. An ArrayList instance **result** is created, and this variable is an array list instance used to collect and store our query result and return to the consuming project.
K. A Joined query statement that combined the first query to the **Faculty** table and the second query to the **Course** table is declared with one position parameter faculty_name. This definition is a so-called **ANSI 92 Standard** and used to simplify multiple query statements.
L. Another **try-catch** block is used to perform this query job. First our user-defined method **DBConnection()** is called to set up a valid database connection to our sample database.
M. A new PreparedStatement instance **pstmt** is created to perform this query.
N. The **setString()** method is used to set up the actual value for the positional dynamic parameter in the query statement.
O. The query is performed by calling the **executeQuery()** method, and the query result is returned and stored in a ResultSet object **rs**.
P. To get more detailed information about the queried database, the **getMetaData()** method is executed, and the result is stored in a ResultSetMetaData instance **rsmd**.
Q. A **while** and a **for** loop are used to pick up all queried **course_id** stored in the ResultSet object **rs**. A **for** loop is used to pick up each queried **course_id** and add it into the ArrayList instance **result**. The reason we used an ArrayList, not a List instance, as the returned object is that the former is a concrete class but the latter is an abstract class, and a runtime exception may be encountered if an abstract class is used as a returned object to the calling method.
R. A sequence of cleaning jobs is performed to close all used objects.

S. The queried result stored in the local variable **result** is returned to the calling method.
T. The **catch** block is used to catch and display any possible error during this query

During the coding process, you may encounter some in-time compiling errors. The main reason for those errors is that some packages are missed. To fix these errors, just right click on any space inside this code window, and select the **Fix Imports** item to find and add those missed packages.

At this point, we have finished all coding process for the **course_id** query. Now let's build and test our Web service to test this **course_id** query function.

9.14.4.2 Build and Run the Web Service to Test the CourseID Query Function

Click on the **Clean and Build Main Project** button on the top of the window to build our Web service project. Then right click on our Web service application project **WebServiceCourse**, and choose the **Deploy** item to deploy our Web service.

If everything is fine, expand the **Web Services** node under our Web service project, and right click on our Web service target file **WSCourse**, and choose the **Test Web Service** item to run our Web service project. The running status of our Web service is shown in Fig. 9.77.

Enter a desired faculty name, such as **Jenney King**, into the text field, and click on the **queryCourseID** button to test this query function. The testing result is shown in Fig. 9.78.

It can be found from Fig. 9.78 that all **course_id** taught by the selected faculty member **Jenney King** have been retrieved and displayed at the bottom of this page, and our **course_id** query via Web service is successful!

Next let's handle creating and coding process for the second Web service operation **QueryCourse()** to query details for the selected **course_id**.

9.14.4.3 Create and Build the Web Operation QueryCourse()

Perform the following operations to add a new operation **QueryCourse()** into our Web service project to perform this course details query:

1) Double click on our Web service main class file **WSCourse.java** from the **Projects** window to open it.
2) Click on the **Design** button on the top of the window to open the Design View of our Web service project **WSCourse**.
3) Click on the **Add Operation** button to open the **Add Operation** wizard.
4) Enter **QueryCourse** into the **Name** field, and click on the **Browse** button that is next to the **Return Type** combo box. Type **arraylist** into the **Type Name** field, and select the item **ArrayList (java.util)** from the list, and click on the **OK** button.

Fig. 9.77 The testing status of our Web Service project

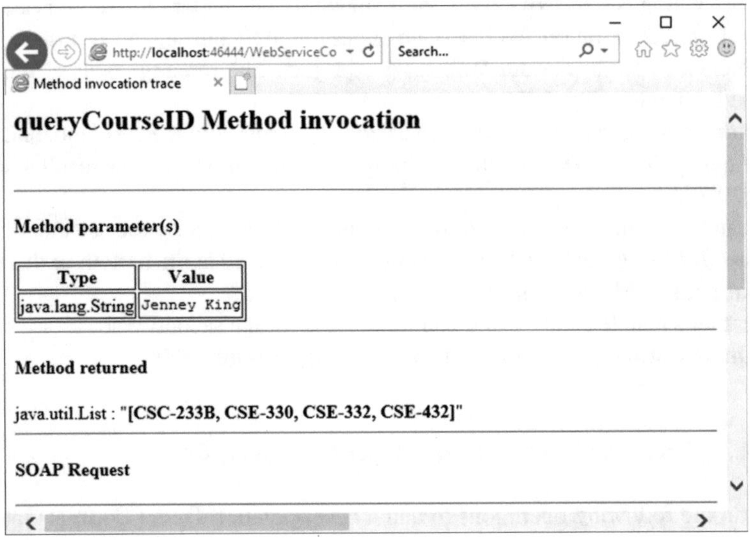

Fig. 9.78 The testing results of our Web Service project

5) Click on the **Add** button and enter **courseID** into the **Name** parameter field. Keep the default type **java.lang.String** unchanged, and click on the **OK** button to complete this new operation creation process.

Your finished **Add Operation** wizard should match one that is shown in Fig. 9.79.

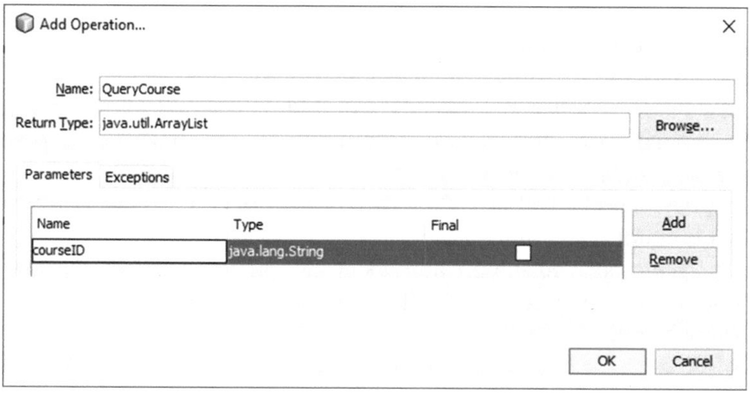

Add Operation...

Name: QueryCourse
Return Type: java.util.ArrayList Browse...

Parameters Exceptions

Name	Type	Final
courseID	java.lang.String	☐

Add Remove OK Cancel

Fig. 9.79 The completed Add Operation wizard

```
  @WebMethod(operationName = "QueryCourse")
    public ArrayList QueryCourse(@WebParam(name = "courseID") String courseID) {
      //TODO write your implementation code here:
A     ArrayList<String> result = new ArrayList<String>();
B     String query = "SELECT * FROM Course WHERE course_id = ?";
    try {
C       con = DBConnection(con);
D       PreparedStatement pstmt =con.prepareStatement(query);
E       pstmt.setString(1, courseID);
F       ResultSet rs = pstmt.executeQuery();
G       ResultSetMetaData rsmd = rs.getMetaData();
H       while (rs.next()){
          for (int colNum = 1; colNum <= rsmd.getColumnCount() - 1; colNum++)
            result.add(rs.getString(colNum));
        }
I       con.close();
        rs.close();
        pstmt.close();
J       return result;
      }
K     catch (Exception ex) {
        System.out.println("exception is: " + ex);
        return null;
      }
  }
```

Fig. 9.80 The codes for the Web service operation QueryCourse()

Click on the **Source** button on the top of this window to open the code window of our Web service project. Let's perform the coding for this new added operation.

On the opened code window, enter the codes that are shown in Fig. 9.80 into this new added operation. Let's have a closer look at this piece of codes to see how it works.

A. An ArrayList instance **result** is created, and this variable is an array list instance used to collect and store our query result and return to the consuming project.
B. A single query statement is declared with one dynamic position parameter **course_id**. This statement is used to query all course details related to the selected **course_id**.

C. A **try-catch** block is used to perform this query job. First our user-defined method **DBConnection()** is called to set up a valid database connection to our sample database.
D. A new PreparedStatement instance **pstmt** is created to perform this query.
E. The **setString()** method is used to set up the actual value for the positional dynamic parameter in the query statement.
F. The query is performed by calling the **executeQuery()** method, and the query result is returned and stored in a ResultSet object **rs**.
G. To get more detailed information about the queried database, the **getMetaData()** method is executed and the result is stored in a ResultSetMetaData instance **rsmd**.
H. A **while** and a **for** loop are used to pick up all pieces of queried course information stored in the ResultSet object **rs**. The **for** loop is used to pick up each piece of detailed course information and add it into the ArrayList instance **result**. One issue to be noted is the upper bound of the loop count for this **for** loop. Here we did not collect all pieces of detailed course information since the last column in the **Course** table is the **faculty_id**, and we do not need this piece of information to be displayed in our Course Form when we consume this service later. Thus the count for the last column is **getColumnCount() – 1**.
I. A sequence of cleaning jobs is performed to close all used objects.
J. The queried result stored in the local variable **result** is returned to the calling method.
K. The **catch** block is used to catch and display any possible error during this query, and a **null** is returned to indicate this situation if any of errors really occurred.

Now let's build and test this Web Service operation by using the Web Service Tester.

Click on the **Clean and Build Main Project** button on the top of the window to build our Web service project. Then right click on our Web service application project **WebServiceCourse**, and choose the **Deploy** item to deploy our Web service.

If everything is fine, expand the **Web Services** node under our Web service project, and right click on our Web service target file **WSCourse**, and choose the **Test Web Service** item to run our Web service project. Enter a desired **course_id**, such as **CSE-434**, into the text field, and click on the **queryCourse** button to test this query function. The testing result is shown in Fig. 9.81.

It can be found from Fig. 9.81 that all six pieces of detailed course information related to the selected **course_id**, except the **faculty_id**, have been retrieved and displayed at the bottom of this page, and our course query via Web service is successful!

Next let's handle creating and building of our third Web service operation **InsertCourse()** to insert a new course record into the **Course** table in our sample database.

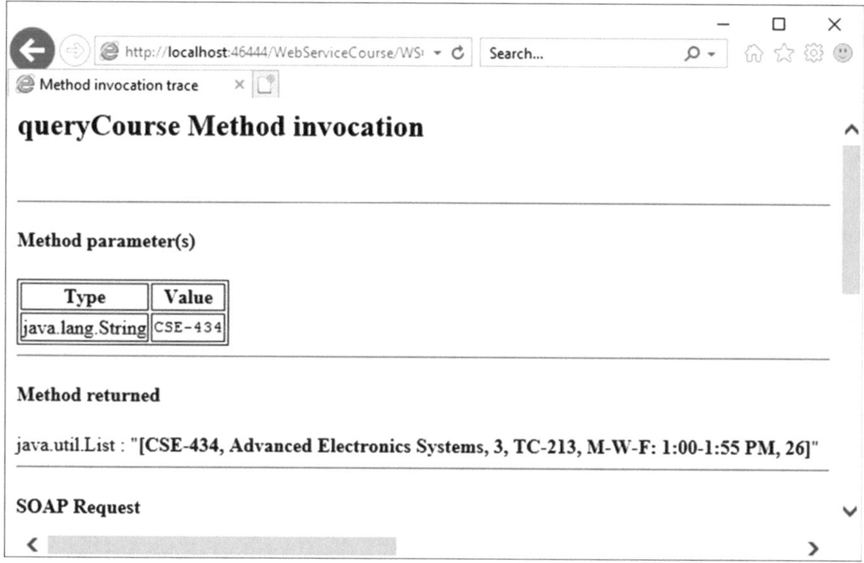

Fig. 9.81 The testing result for our Web Service operation QueryCourse()

9.14.4.4 Create and Build the Web Operation InsertCourse()

One issue to be noted to perform this new course insertion action against our sample database is that two queries will be performed: (1) query the **Faculty** table to get the desired **faculty_id** based on the input **faculty_name** and (2) insert a new course record based on the queried **faculty_id** from (1). The reason for that is because there is no **faculty_name** column available in the **Course** table and the only foreign key connecting the **Faculty** with the **Course** tables is the **faculty_id**.

Keep this fact in mind, and let's start to build this operation. First perform the following operations to add a new operation **InsertCourse()** into our Web service project to perform this course details query:

1) Double click on our Web service main class file **WSCourse.java** from the **Projects** window to open it.
2) Click on the **Design** button on the top of the window to open the Design View of our Web service project **WSCourse**.
3) Click on the **Add Operation** button to open the **Add Operation** wizard.
4) Enter **InsertCourse** into the **Name** field, and click on the **Browse** button that is next to the **Return Type** combo box. Type **boolean** into the **Type Name** field, and select the item **Boolean (java.lang)** from the list, and click on the **OK** button.
5) Click on the **Add** button and enter **cdata** into the **Name** parameter field. Then click on the drop-down arrow of the **Type** combo box, and select the **Choose** item to open the **Find Type** wizard. Type **arrayList** into the top field and select

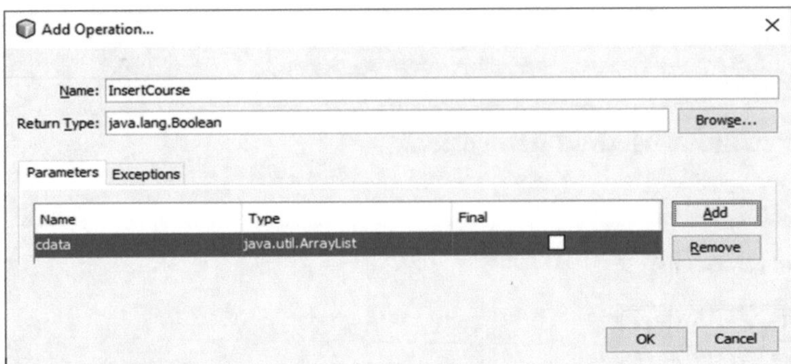

Fig. 9.82 The completed Add Operation wizard

the **ArrayList (java.util)** data type, and click on the **OK** button to select an ArrayList as the data type for the input parameter.

Your finished **Add Operation** wizard should match one that is shown in Fig. 9.82. Click on the **OK** button to complete this new operation creation process. Next let's build the codes for this operation.

Click on the **Source** button on the top of this window to open the code window of our Web service project. On the opened code window, enter the codes that are shown in Fig. 9.83 into this new added operation **InsertCourse()**.

Let's have a closer look at this piece of new added codes to see how it works.

A. First some local variables, such as an instance of ResultSet **rs**, a blank **faculty_id** string **fid**, and an integer variable **numInsert**, are declared since we need to use them to hold some of our query results.
B. A try-catch block is used to do our first query for the **Faculty** table to get a desired **faculty_id** based on the selected **faculty_name**. First a valid database connection is established by calling our user-defined method **DBConnection()**.
C. A PreparedStatement object, **pstfid**, is generated with a connection object **con** and query statement to get the desired **faculty_id** based on the selected **faculty_name**, and the latter is a positional dynamic input parameter.
D. A system method **setString()** is executed to set up the input positional dynamic parameter that is stored in the input arrayList instance, **cdata**, and exactly it is located at the first position on that list; thus another system method **get(0).toString()** is used to pick it up.
E. The first query is executed by calling the system method **executeQuery()**, and the returned query result is stored in the instance of ResultSet class, **rs**.
F. A **while()** loop with its condition, **rs.next()**, is executed to pick up the selected **faculty_id** by calling another system method **getString()**. The argument of that method is the column name of the **fculty_id**.
G. The second query statement is created with a standard SQL statement format with seven input positional dynamic parameters. One point to be noted is that

```
   @WebMethod(operationName = "InsertCourse")
    public Boolean InsertCourse(@WebParam(name = "cdata") ArrayList cdata) {
    //TODO write your implementation code here:
A   ResultSet rs;
    String fid = null;
    int  numInsert = 0;
    try {
B       con = DBConnection(con);
C       PreparedStatement pstfid =con.prepareStatement("SELECT faculty_id FROM Faculty WHERE faculty_name = ?");
D       pstfid.setString(1, cdata.get(0).toString());        // set faculty_name; cdata(0) = faculty_name
E       rs = pstfid.executeQuery();
F       while (rs.next()) {
           fid = rs.getString("faculty_id");
          }
G       String query = "INSERT INTO Course (course_id, course, credit, classroom, schedule, " +
                          "enrollment, faculty_id) VALUES (?, ?, ?, ?, ?, ?, ?)";
H       PreparedStatement pstmt =con.prepareStatement(query);  // cdata(0) = faculty_name
I       pstmt.setString(1, cdata.get(1).toString());            // cdata(1) = course_id
        pstmt.setString(2, cdata.get(2).toString());            // cdata(2) = course
        pstmt.setString(3, cdata.get(3).toString());            // cdata(3) = credit
        pstmt.setString(4, cdata.get(4).toString());            // cdata(4) = classroom
        pstmt.setString(5, cdata.get(5).toString());            // cdata(5) = schedule
        pstmt.setString(6, cdata.get(6).toString());            // cdata(6) = enrollment
J       pstmt.setString(7, fid);
K       numInsert = pstmt.executeUpdate();
L       con.close();
        rs.close();
M       if (numInsert != 0)
           return true;
N       else
           return false;
O       } catch (SQLException ex) {
           Logger.getLogger(WSCourse.class.getName()).log(Level.SEVERE, null, ex);
           return false;
        }
   }
```

Fig. 9.83 The detailed codes for the operation InsertCourse()

the order of those input positional parameters must be pre-defined with the input **faculty_name** as the first one, followed by six pieces of new inserted course information.

H. Another PreparedStatement object, **pstmt**, is declared with the second query statement.
I. A sequence of **setString()** methods is executed to set up and initialize all seven input positional parameters, which include a new inserted course record and the selected **faculty_name**.
J. The seventh positional dynamic parameter to the second query is the **faculty_id**, which is obtained from the first query, not from the input arrayList variable, **cdata**.
K. The second query is executed by calling another **executeUpdate()** method, and the running result is returned and assigned to the integer variable **numInsert**.
L. A sequence of cleaning jobs is performed to close all objects we used for these queries.
M. If this data insertion is successful, a non-zero integer value would be returned, and a **true** is also returned to the calling method to indicate this situation.

N. Otherwise if a zero is returned, which means that this data insertion failed and no any record has been inserted into our database, a **false** is returned to indicate this error.
O. The **catch** block is used to monitor and track these query operations. A **false** would be returned if any exception occurred.

Now one can click on the **Clean and Build Project** button to build our Web Service project to compile and update this new operation. Next let's build our Web operation, **UpdateCourse()**.

9.14.4.5 Create and Build the Web Operation UpdateCourse()

Perform the following operations to add a new operation **UpdateCourse()** into our Web service project to perform this course updating query:

1) Double click on our Web service main class file **WSCourse.java** from the **Projects** window to open it.
2) Click on the **Design** button on the top of the window to open the Design View of our Web service project **WSCourse**.
3) Click on the **Add Operation** button to open the **Add Operation** wizard.
4) Enter **UpdateCourse** into the **Name** field, and click on the **Browse** button that is next to the **Return Type** combo box. Type **boolean** into the **Type Name** field, and select the item **Boolean (java.lang)** from the list, and click on the **OK** button.
5) Click on the **Add** button and enter **cdata** into the **Name** parameter field. Then click on the drop-down arrow of the **Type** combo box, and select the **Choose** item to open the **Find Type** wizard. Type **arrayList** into the top field and select the **ArrayList (java.util)** data type, and click on the **OK** button to select an ArrayList as the data type for the input parameter.

Your finished **Add Operation** wizard should match one that is shown in Fig. 9.84. Next let's build the codes for this operation.

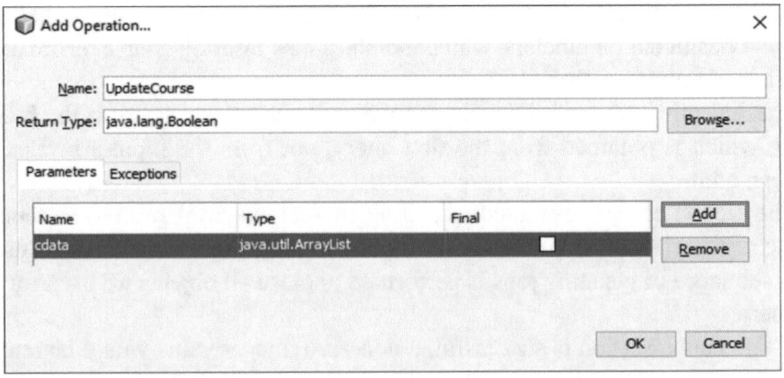

Fig. 9.84 The completed Add Operation wizard

```
  @WebMethod(operationName = "UpdateCourse")
    public Boolean UpdateCourse(@WebParam(name = "cdata") ArrayList cdata) {
    //TODO write your implementation code here:
A   ResultSet rs;
    String fid = null;
    int numUpdate = 0;
    try {
B       con = DBConnection(con);
C       PreparedStatement pstfid =con.prepareStatement("SELECT faculty_id FROM Faculty WHERE faculty_name = ?");
D       pstfid.setString(1, cdata.get(0).toString());        // set faculty_name; cdata(0) = faculty_name
E       rs = pstfid.executeQuery();
F       while (rs.next()) {
          fid = rs.getString("faculty_id");
        }
G       String query = "UPDATE Course SET course = ?, credit = ?, classroom = ?, schedule = ?, " +
                     "enrollment = ?, faculty_id = ? WHERE course_id = ?";
H         PreparedStatement pstmt =con.prepareStatement(query);  // cdata(0) = faculty_name
I         pstmt.setString(1, cdata.get(1).toString());           // cdata(1) = course
          pstmt.setString(2, cdata.get(2).toString());           // cdata(2) = creit
          pstmt.setString(3, cdata.get(3).toString());           // cdata(3) = classroom
          pstmt.setString(4, cdata.get(4).toString());           // cdata(4) = schedule
          pstmt.setString(5, cdata.get(5).toString());           // cdata(5) = enrollment
          pstmt.setString(7, cdata.get(6).toString());           // cdata(6) = course_id
          pstmt.setString(6, fid);
J         numUpdate = pstmt.executeUpdate();
K         con.close();
          rs.close();
L         if (numUpdate != 0)
             return true;
M         else
             return false;
N     } catch (SQLException ex) {
          Logger.getLogger(WSCourse.class.getName()).log(Level.SEVERE, null, ex);
          return false;
      }
  }
```

Fig. 9.85 Detailed codes for the operation UpdateCourse()

As we discussed in the previous chapters, to update a record in the **Course** table, regularly one does not need to update the primary key, **course_id**; instead one can insert a new course record with a new **course_id** into the **Course** table to simplify this kind of updating action. The reason for that is because of the cascaded updating actions. The **course_id** is a primary key in the **Course** table, but a foreign key in the **StudentCourse** table. Multiple updating actions must be performed in certain order if this **course_id** is updated. To make things simple and easy, here we would not update any **course_id** when we update a course record, and we only update all other columns in the **Course** table based on the original **course_id**.

Based on the discussion and analysis above, now let's build the codes for this operation.

Click on the **Source** button on the top of this window to open the code window of our Web service project. On the opened code window, enter the codes that are shown in Fig. 9.85 into this new added operation **UpdateCourse()**.

Let's have a closer look at this piece of new added codes to see how it works.

A. First some local variables, such as an instance of ResultSet **rs**, a blank **faculty_id** string **fid**, and an integer variable **numUpdate**, are declared since we need to use them to hold some of our query results.

B. A try-catch block is used to do our first query for the **Faculty** table to get a desired **faculty_id** based on the selected **faculty_name**. First a valid database connection is established by calling our user-defined method **DBConnection()**.
C. A PreparedStatement object, **pstfid**, is generated with a connection object **con** and query statement to get the desired **faculty_id** based on the selected **faculty_name**, and the latter is a positional dynamic input parameter.
D. A system method **setString()** is executed to set up the input positional dynamic parameter that is stored in the input arrayList instance, **cdata**, and exactly it is located at the first position on that list; thus, another system method **get(0).toString()** is used to pick it up.
E. The first query is executed by calling the system method **executeQuery()**, and the returned query result is stored in the instance of ResultSet class, **rs**.
F. A **while()** loop with its condition, **rs.next()**, is executed to pick up the selected **faculty_id** by calling another system method **getString()**. The argument of that method is the column name of the **fculty_id**.
G. The second query statement is created with a standard SQL statement format with seven input positional dynamic parameters. One point to be noted is that the order of those input positional parameters must be pre-defined with the input **faculty_name** as the first one, followed by six pieces of updated course information.
H. Another PreparedStatement object, **pstmt**, is declared with the second query statement.
I. A sequence of **setString()** methods is executed to set up and initialize all seven input positional parameters, which include an updated course record and the selected **faculty_name**.
J. The second query is executed by calling a system method **executeUpdate()**, and the running result is returned and assigned to the integer variable **numUpdate**.
K. A sequence of cleaning jobs is performed to close all objects we used for these queries.
L. If this course updating is successful, a non-zero integer value would be returned, and a **true** is also returned to the calling method to indicate this situation.
M. Otherwise if a zero is returned, which means that this data updating failed and no any record has been updated in our database, a **false** is returned to indicate this error.
N. The **catch** block is used to monitor and track these query operations. A **false** would be returned if any exception occurred.

Now one can click on the **Clean and Build Project** button to build our Web Service project to compile and update this new operation. Finally let's build our Web operation, **DeleteCourse()**.

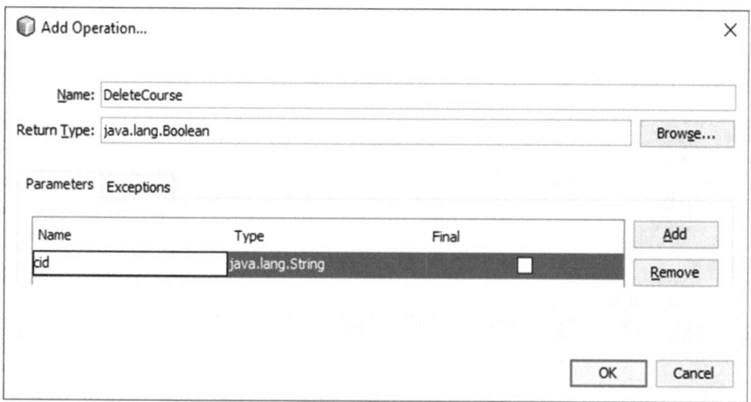

Fig. 9.86 The completed Add Operation wizard

9.14.4.6 Create and Build the Web Operation DeleteCourse()

Perform the following operations to add a new operation **DeleteCourse()** into our Web service project to perform this course updating query:

1) Double click on our Web service main class file **WSCourse.java** from the **Projects** window to open it.
2) Click on the **Design** button on the top of the window to open the Design View of our Web service project **WSCourse**.
3) Click on the **Add Operation** button to open the **Add Operation** wizard.
4) Enter **DeleteCourse** into the **Name** field, and click on the **Browse** button that is next to the **Return Type** combo box. Type **boolean** into the **Type Name** field and select the item **Boolean (java.lang)** from the list, and click on the **OK** button.
5) Click on the **Add** button and enter **cid** into the **Name** parameter field. Keep the default type, **java.lang.String**, as the data type for this input parameter. Your finished **Add Operation** wizard should match one that is shown in Fig. 9.86.
6) Click on the **OK** button to create this new operation.

Next let's build the codes for this operation.

Click on the **Source** button on the top of this window to open the code window of our Web service project. On the opened code window, enter the codes that are shown in Fig. 9.87 into this new added operation **UpdateCourse()**.

Let's have a closer look at this piece of new added codes to see how it works.

A. A local integer variable, **numDelete**, is declared since we need to use it to hold our query result.
B. A try-catch block is used to do our deleting query for the **Course** table to remove the desired course record based on the selected **course_id**. First a valid database connection is established by calling our user-defined method **DBConnection()**.

```
  @WebMethod(operationName = "DeleteCourse")
  public Boolean DeleteCourse(@WebParam(name = "cid") String cid) {
     //TODO write your implementation code here:
A    int numDelete = 0;
     try {
B         con = DBConnection(con);
C         PreparedStatement pstmt =con.prepareStatement("DELETE FROM Course WHERE course_id = ?");
D         pstmt.setString(1, cid);                    // set course_id
E         numDelete = pstmt.executeUpdate();
F         con.close();
G         if (numDelete != 0)
             return true;
H         else
             return false;
I     } catch (SQLException ex) {
         Logger.getLogger(WSCourse.class.getName()).log(Level.SEVERE, null, ex);
         return false;
      }
  }
```

Fig. 9.87 Detailed codes for the operation DeleteCourse()

C. A PreparedStatement object, **pstmt**, is generated with a connection object **con** and the deleting statement with a selected **course_id** as a positional dynamic input parameter.
D. A system method **setString()** is executed to set up the input positional dynamic parameter **cid**, which is a desired **course_id** and works as a query criterion for this deleting action.
E. The deleting action is then executed by calling a system method **executeUpdate()**, and the running result of this action is returned and assigned to our local variable **intDelete**.
F. A cleaning job is performed to close the connection object we used for this query.
G. If this course deleting is successful, a non-zero integer value would be returned, and a **true** is also returned to the calling method to indicate this situation.
H. Otherwise if a zero is returned, which means that this data deleting failed and no any record has been deleted from our database, a **false** is returned to indicate this error.
I. The **catch** block is used to monitor and track this query operation. A **false** would be returned if any exception is occurred.

Now one can click on the **Clean and Build Project** button to build our Web Service project to compile and update this new operation.

At this point, we have completed all developments for our Web Service project. Next we like to build some Windows-based or Web-based projects to consume or test these operations to perform related database actions to query, insert, and update and delete desired records from our sample database. First let's start from the Windows-based consuming projects.

9.15 Build Windows-Based Project to Consume the Web Service Project

To consume our Web Service project, we need to build some Windows-based projects to call different operations to perform related actions to our database.

To save time and space, we can modify one of our projects, **WinClientSelect**, and make it as our new project. Perform the following operational steps to build our new Windows-based project, **WinClientCourse** project, to call the related Web operations to perform appropriate query to the **Course** table in our sample database.

1) Open the NetBeans IDE 8.2, and browse to our project **WinClientSelect** (one can find and copy this project from a folder **Class DB Projects\Chapter 9** under the **Students** folder in the Springer ftp site (refer to Fig. 1.2 in Chap. 1)).
2) Right click on this project **WinClientSelect**, and select the **Copy** item from the popup menu.
3) On the opened **Copy Project** wizard, change the project name to **WinClientCourse** in the **Project Name** box, select your desired location from the **Project Location** box, and click on the **Copy** button.
4) Now expand our new project **WinClientCourse** from the **Projects** window in the NetBeans, which is **WinClientCourse→Source Packages→<default package>**, and one can find the **FacultyFrame.java** main class file. Right click on this file, and select **Delete** item to remove this file since we do not need this file in this project. Make sure to check the **Safely delete** checkbox, and click on the **Refactor** button.
5) Now we need to create our **CourseFrame** GUI and class file to perform this course query action. To make it easy, we can use a **CourseForm** we built in one of our previous projects, **SQLSelectObject**, which was built in Chap. 6. One can find this project from a folder **Class DB Projects\Chapter 6** under the **Students** folder in the Springer ftp site.
6) Open the Windows Explorer, and browse and expand that project **SQLSelectObject**, which is **SQLSelectObject→src→SQLSelectObjectPackage**. Click the folder **SQLSelectObjectPackage**, and one can find our class file **CourseFrame.form**. Copy that file and paste it to our new project **WinClientCourse**, exactly under the **WinClientCourse→Source Packages→<default package>** folder in the NetBeans IDE 8.2.
7) Double click on our pasted **CourseFrame.java** to open it, and perform the following operations to make it as our new class file:

   (a) Remove the top coding line: **package SQLSelectObjectPackage;**.
   (b) Remove all codes from the **SelectButtonActionPerformed()** event handler.
   (c) Remove all codes from the **CourseListValueChanged()** event handler.

Now build our new project by clicking on the **Clean and Built Project** button on the top. Next let's develop the codes for these event handlers to access our Web operations to perform related queries to the **Course** table in our sample database.

Table 9.7 The relationship between each button's method and each operation

Client button and method	Web service operation	Function
Select SelectButtonActionPerformed()	QueryCourseID()	Query all **course_id** taught by the selected faculty
CourseListValueChanged()	QueryCourse()	Query detailed information for selected **course_id**
Insert InsertButtonActionPerformed()	InsertCourse()	Insert a new course record into the Course table
Update UpdateButtonActionPerformed()	UpdateCourse()	Update an existing course record in the Course table
Delete DeleteButtonActionPerformed()	DeleteCourse()	Delete a course record from the Course table

9.15.1 Develop the Codes to Query Course Information from our Web Service Project

In our Web service project **WebServiceCourse**, we built five operations with five different data actions against the **Course** table in our database. Now we need to develop the codes in our client project to call those five operations to access and query the **Course** table in our sample database via five buttons in our client project **WinClientCouse**, exactly in this **CourseFrame.java** class file. Each button has a one-to-one relationship with the related operation, as shown in Table 9.7.

Let's start our coding process from the **Select** button, exactly with its event handler or method **SelectButtonActionPerformed()**, in our client project.

9.15.2 Build Codes for the Select Button Event Handler to Query CourseIDs

The function of this method is to query all **course_id** taught by the selected faculty member as the **Select** button is clicked by the user. The queried result will be added and displayed in the Course ID List box in this CourseFrame form.

On the opened **Design** view of the CourseFrame form window, double click on the **Select** button to open this method or event handler. Enter the codes shown in Fig. 9.88 into this event handler. Let's have a closer look at this piece of new added codes to see how it works.

```
  private void SelectButtonActionPerformed(java.awt.event.ActionEvent evt) {
      // TODO add your handling code here:
A     ArrayList<String> al = new ArrayList();

      try {
B     org.ws.sql.WSCourse_Service service = new org.ws.sql.WSCourse_Service();
      org.ws.sql.WSCourse port = service.getWSCoursePort();
C     al.clear();
D     al = (ArrayList)port.queryCourseID(ComboName.getSelectedItem().toString());
E     String[] alArray = al.toArray(new String[al.size()]);
F     CourseList.setListData(alArray);

G     }catch (Exception ex) {
        System.out.println("exception: " + ex);
      }
  }
```

Fig. 9.88 The complete codes for the SelectButtonActionPerformed() event handler

A. A local variable, **al**, is created first, and it is an ArrayList instance, and it can be used to hold the query result, in which all selected **course_id** is stored.
B. A **try-catch** block is used to call our Web service operation **QueryCourseID()** to perform this query action. First a new Web service instance **service** is created based on our Web service class **WSCourse_Service**. Then the **getWSCoursePort()** method is executed to get the current port used by our Web service. This port is returned and assigned to a new Port instance **port**.
C. The ArrayLit instance **al** is first cleaned to make it ready to store all queried **course_id**.
D. The Web service operation **QueryCourseID()** is called to perform this course data query to collect all **course_id** taught by the selected faculty member that is obtained from the **ComboName** combo box. The query result is returned and assigned to the local ArrayList instance **al**.
E. A conversion between an ArrayList object and a standard String array object is performed since we need to add this query result into the **CourseList**, but the latter can only accept a String array, not an ArrayList, as an argument to be added into this list.
F. The converted query results are sent to the Course ID List variable, **CourseList**, to have them displayed in there using the **setListData()** method.
G. The **catch** block is used to track and display any possible exception during this **course_id** query process.

Now we have finished all coding process for calling one of our Web service operations, **QueryCourseID()**, to query all **course_id** based on the selected faculty member. Click on the **Clean and Build Project** button to build our project.

Before we can run and test our client project, make sure that our Web Service project **WebServiceCourse** has been built and deployed successfully.

Click on the **Run Main Project** button to run our client project to test this **course_id** query function. Select the **CourseFrame** as our main class, and click on the **OK** button to the **Run Project** dialog to run our project.

On the opened client project, keep the default faculty member **Ying Bai** unchanged, and click on the **Select** button to query all **course_id** taught by this

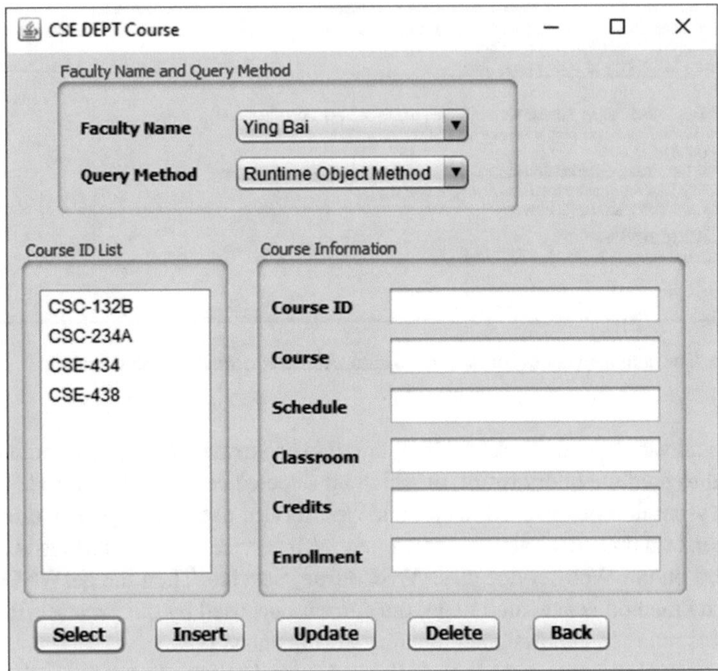

Fig. 9.89 The running result of calling the Web operation QueryCourseID()

selected faculty. Immediately you can find that all four courses or four **course_id** taught by this faculty have been returned and displayed in the Course ID List box, as shown in Fig. 9.89.

You can also try to query **course_id** for other faculty members by selecting other faculty member from the Faculty Name combo box. Our client project in querying **course_id** is successful.

Next let's take care of the coding for the **CourseListValueChanged()** method to query the detailed course information for a selected **course_id** from the Course ID List.

9.15.3 Build Codes for the CourseListValueChanged() Method to Get Course Details

The function of this method is that when users click a **course_id** from the Course ID List box, the detailed course information, including the course title, credit, classroom, schedule, and enrollment for the selected **course_id**, will be retrieved and displayed in six text fields in this CourseFrame Form window.

```
  private void CourseListValueChanged(javax.swing.event.ListSelectionEvent evt) {
    // TODO add your handling code here:
A   ArrayList<String> al = new ArrayList();
B   javax.swing.JTextField[] cfield = {CourseIDField, CourseField, CreditsField, ClassRoomField, ScheduleField, EnrollField};
C   if(!CourseList.getValueIsAdjusting() ){
      String courseid = (String)CourseList.getSelectedValue();
D     if (courseid != null){
        try {
E           org.ws.sql.WSCourse_Service service = new org.ws.sql.WSCourse_Service();
            org.ws.sql.WSCourse port = service.getWSCoursePort();
F           al.clear();
G           al = (ArrayList)port.queryCourse(courseid);
H           for (int i = 0; i < al.size(); i++)
              cfield[i].setText(al.get(i));
I       }catch (Exception ex) {
          System.out.println("exception: " + ex);
        }
      }
    }
  }
```

Fig. 9.90 The completed codes for the CourseListValueChanged() event handler

Perform the following operations to build the codes for this method to perform this function:

1) Open our client project **WinClientCourse** if it has not been opened, and open our main GUI **CourseFrame.java** by double clicking on it.
2) Click on the **Design** button on the top of the window to open the GUI window, and right click on our **Course ID List** Listbox and select **Events > ListSelection > valueChanged** item to open this method or event handler.
3) Enter the codes shown in Fig. 9.90 into this event handler.

Let's have a closer look at this piece of new added codes to see how it works.

A. An ArrayList instance **al** is created first, and it is used to collect the queried course details stored in an ArrayList object that will be returned from the execution of the Web service operation **QueryCourse()**.
B. A JTextField array **cField[]** is created and initialized with six text fields in this CourseFrame Form. The purpose of this array is to store queried course details and display them in these six text fields.
C. Since the JList component belongs to the **javax.swing** package, not **java.awt** package, therefore a clicking on an entry in the CourseList box causes the **itemStateChanged()** method to fire twice. The first time is when the mouse button is depressed, and the second time is when it is released. Therefore, the selected **course_id** will appear twice when it is selected. To prevent this from occurring, the **getValueIsAdjusting()** method is used to make sure that no any item has been adjusted to be displayed twice. Then the selected **course_id** is assigned to a local String variable **courseid** by calling the **getSelectedValue()** method of the CourseList Box class.

D. Before we can proceed to the course query operation, first we need to confirm that the selected **courseid** is not a null value. A null value would be returned if the user did not select any **course_id** from the CourseList box, but the user just clicked on the **Select** button to try to find all courses taught by a faculty member. Even the user only clicked on the **Select** button without touching any **course_id** in the CourseList box; however, the system still considers that a null **course_id** has been selected, and thus a null value will be returned. To avoid that situation from occurring, an **if** selection structure is used to make sure that no null value has been returned from the CourseList box.
E. A **try-catch** block is used to perform the calling to our Web service operation **QueryCourse()** to get detailed course information. First a new Web service instance **service** is created based on our Web service class **WSCourse_Service**. Then the **getWSCoursePort()** method is executed to get the current port used by our Web service. This port is returned and assigned to a new Port instance **port**.
F. The ArrayList instance **al** is first cleaned up to make it ready to hold the retrieved course details in the next step.
G. The Web service operation **QueryCourse()** is called to perform this course data query to collect detailed course information for the selected **course_id**. The query result is returned and assigned to the local ArrayList instance **al**. A cast (ArrayList) is necessary for this assignment since the data type of **al** is an ArrayList<String> in this method.
H. A **for** loop is used to pick up each piece of detailed course information and assign it to each text field in the **cField[]** array using the **setText()** method.
I. The **catch** block is used to track and display any possible exception during this course details query process.

At this point, we have finished all coding process for calling to our Web service operation, **QueryCourse()**, to query detailed information for a selected **course_id**. Click on the **Clean and Build Project** button to build our project.

Before we can run and test our client project, make sure that our Web Service project **WebServiceCourse** has been built and deployed successfully.

Click on the **Run Main Project** button to run our client project to test this course details query function.

On the opened client project, keep the default faculty member **Ying Bai** unchanged, and click on the **Select** button to query all **course_id** taught by this selected faculty. Immediately you can find that all four courses or four **course_id** taught by this faculty have been returned and displayed in the Course ID List box. Then click on any **course_id** for which you want to get detailed information from the CourseList Listbox. The detailed course information for the selected **course_id** is retrieved and displayed in five inputText fields, as shown in Fig. 9.91. Figure 9.91 shows an example of course details for a **course_id** that is CSE-434.

You can try to click the different **course_id** to get related detailed course information. Our client project in querying detailed course information is successful.

Next let's take care of the coding for the **InsertButtonActionPerformed()** method to call our Web Service to insert a new course record into the Course table in our sample database.

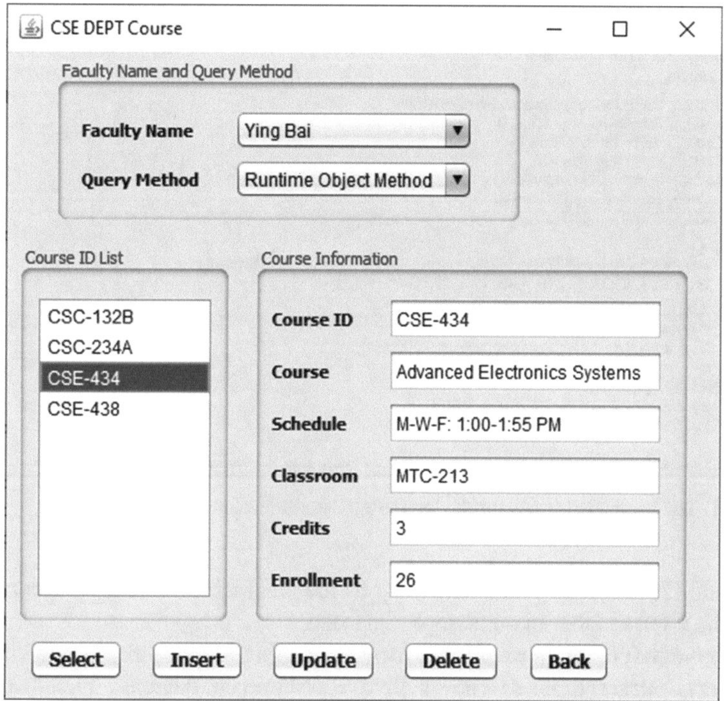

Fig. 9.91 The running result of calling the Web operation QueryCourse()

9.15.4 Build Codes for the Insert Button Event Handler to Insert a New Course

The function of this method is to insert a new course record into the **Course** table in our sample database as the **Insert** button is clicked by the user. A new course record will be inserted into our sample database when this method is complete.

On the opened **Design** view of the CourseFrame form window, double click on the **Insert** button to open this method or event handler. Enter the codes shown in Fig. 9.92 into this event handler. Let's have a closer look at this piece of codes to see how it works.

A. A local variable, **al**, is created first. This is a Boolean variable used to hold the running result of the execution of the Web service operation **InsertCourse()** to insert a new course record into the **Course** table in our sample database.
B. The ArrayList instance **al** is cleaned up by using the **clear()** method to make sure that the **al** is empty before it can be used to store any data.
C. A group of **add()** methods are used to add seven pieces of new course information into the ArrayList instance. One point to be noted is that the order in which

```
  private void InsertButtonActionPerformed(java.awt.event.ActionEvent evt) {
      // TODO add your handling code here:
A     ArrayList al = new ArrayList();
B     al.clear();
C     al.add(0, ComboName.getSelectedItem().toString());      // faculty_name
      al.add(1, CourseIDField.getText());
      al.add(2, CourseField.getText());
      al.add(3, CreditsField.getText());
      al.add(4, ClassRoomField.getText());
      al.add(5, ScheduleField.getText());
      al.add(6, EnrollField.getText());
      try {
D        org.ws.sql.WSCourse_Service service = new org.ws.sql.WSCourse_Service();
         org.ws.sql.WSCourse port = service.getWSCoursePort();
E        Boolean insert = port.insertCourse(al);
F        if (!insert)
            System.out.println("The data insertion is failed!");
      }
G     catch (Exception ex){
         System.out.println("exception: " + ex);
      }
  }
```

Fig. 9.92 The completed codes for the InsertButtonActionPerformed() event handler

to add these course parameters must be identical with the order of the columns in the **Course** table in our sample database.

D. A **try-catch** block is used to perform the calling to our Web service operation **InsertCourse()** to insert a new course record into our database. First a new Web service instance **service** is created based on our Web service class **WSCourse_Service**. Then the **getWSCoursePort()** method is executed to get the current port used by our Web service. This port is returned and assigned to a new Port instance **port**.
E. The Web operation **InsertCourse()** is called to insert this new course record stored in the argument **al** into the **Course** table via our Web service. The execution result that is a Boolean variable is returned and assigned to the local variable **insert**.
F. If a **false** is returned, which means that this course data insertion has been failed, the system **println()** method is used to indicate this situation. Otherwise our data insertion action is successful.
G. The **catch** block is used to track and display any possible exception during this data insertion process.

Now we have finished the coding process to call our Web service operation **InsertCourse()** to insert a new course record into the **Course** table based on the selected faculty member. Click on the **Clean and Build Main Project** button to build our project. Before running and testing our client project, make sure that our Web Service project **WebServiceCourse** has been built and deployed successfully. Now click on the **Run Main Project** button to run our client project to test this course data insertion function.

On the opened client project, keep the default faculty member **Ying Bai** unchanged, and click on the **Select** button to query all **course_id** taught by this

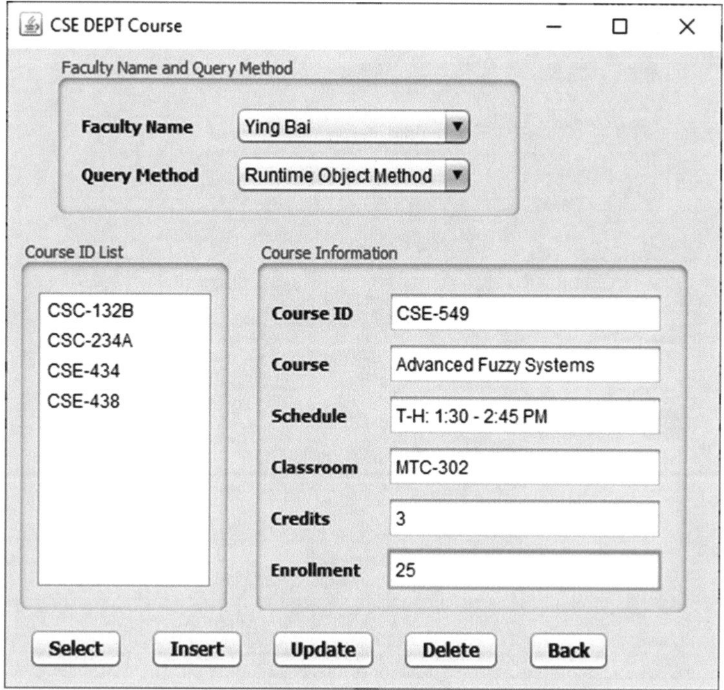

Fig. 9.93 The new course record to be inserted into our database

selected faculty. Immediately you can find that all four courses or four **course_id** taught by this faculty have been returned and displayed in the Course ID List box. To insert a new course, enter six pieces of new course information shown below into six text fields.

- Course ID: **CSE-549**
- Course: **Advanced Fuzzy Systems**
- Schedule: **T-H: 1:30 – 2:45 PM**
- Classroom: **MTC-302**
- Credit: **3**
- Enrollment: **25**

Your finished CourseFrame window should match one that is shown in Fig. 9.93. Click on the **Insert** button to insert this new course record into the **Course** table in our sample database.

To check or confirm this new course insertion action, two ways can be used. The easy way is to use the **Select** button, exactly the codes inside the event handler of this button, to try to retrieve back all courses, exactly all **course_id**, taught by the selected faculty member, **Ying Bai**. To do this, just click on the **Select** button to perform a query to get all **course_id** taught by that faculty member. The running result is shown in Fig. 9.94.

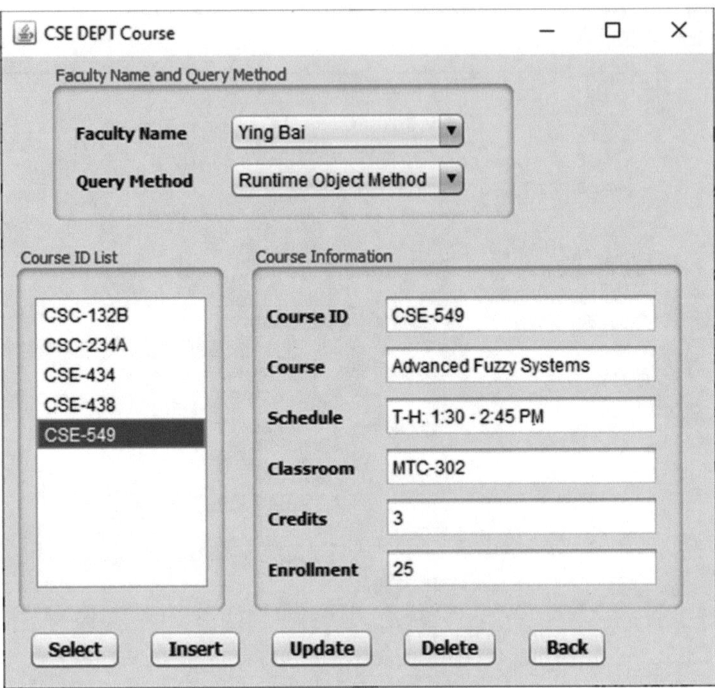

Fig. 9.94 The checking result for our new inserted course record

As shown in Fig. 9.94, one can find that the new inserted course, **CSE-549**, has been retrieved and displayed in the Course ListBox. Click on that new **course_id** from that Course

ListBox; the details about that course are displayed in six TextFields, as shown in Fig. 9.94. This confirmed that our data insertion action is successful!

The second way is to open the **Course** table in our sample database to do this checking. One can use the **Databases** icon inside the **Services** window on the NetBeans IDE to connect to our sample database CSE_DEPT.

Then expand the connected URL, **jdbc:sqlserver://localhost\SQL2019EXPRESS: 5000; database Name=CSE_DEPT → CSE_DEPT → dbo → Tables → Course**, right click on the **Course** table, and select the **View Data** item to open the **Course** table. Browse to the bottom of this table, and one can find that our new inserted course, **CSE-549**, has been added there, as shown in Fig. 9.95.

Next let's discuss how to perform a course updating action to update an existing course in our sample database via Web service.

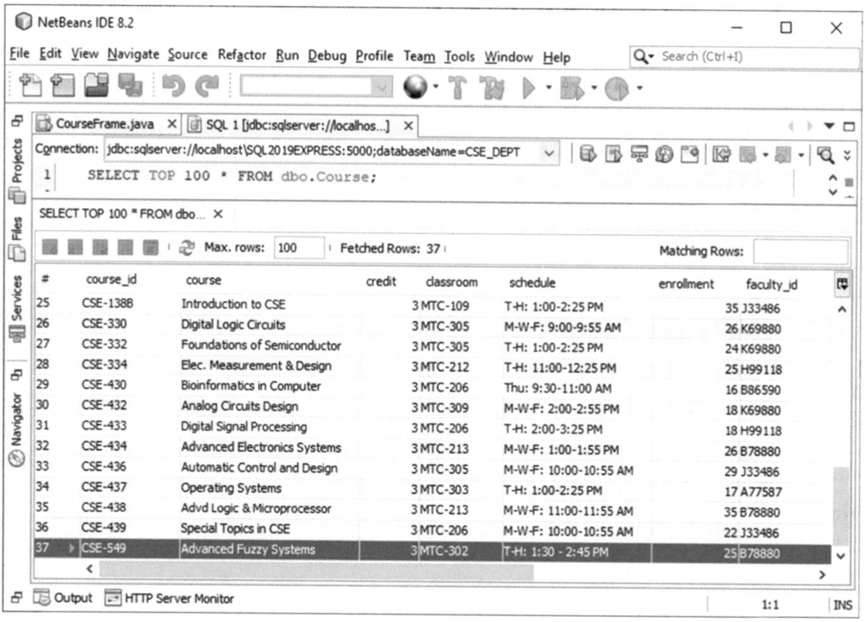

#	course_id	course	credit	classroom	schedule	enrollment	faculty_id
25	CSE-138B	Introduction to CSE	3	MTC-109	T-H: 1:00-2:25 PM	35	J33486
26	CSE-330	Digital Logic Circuits	3	MTC-305	M-W-F: 9:00-9:55 AM	26	K69880
27	CSE-332	Foundations of Semiconductor	3	MTC-305	T-H: 1:00-2:25 PM	24	K69880
28	CSE-334	Elec. Measurement & Design	3	MTC-212	T-H: 11:00-12:25 PM	25	H99118
29	CSE-430	Bioinformatics in Computer	3	MTC-206	Thu: 9:30-11:00 AM	16	B86590
30	CSE-432	Analog Circuits Design	3	MTC-309	M-W-F: 2:00-2:55 PM	18	K69880
31	CSE-433	Digital Signal Processing	3	MTC-206	T-H: 2:00-3:25 PM	18	H99118
32	CSE-434	Advanced Electronics Systems	3	MTC-213	M-W-F: 1:00-1:55 PM	26	B78880
33	CSE-436	Automatic Control and Design	3	MTC-305	M-W-F: 10:00-10:55 AM	29	J33486
34	CSE-437	Operating Systems	3	MTC-303	T-H: 1:00-2:25 PM	17	A77587
35	CSE-438	Advd Logic & Microprocessor	3	MTC-213	M-W-F: 11:00-11:55 AM	35	B78880
36	CSE-439	Special Topics in CSE	3	MTC-206	M-W-F: 10:00-10:55 AM	22	J33486
37	CSE-549	Advanced Fuzzy Systems	3	MTC-302	T-H: 1:30 - 2:45 PM	25	B78880

Fig. 9.95 The new inserted course record in our sample database

9.15.5 *Build Codes for the Update Button Method to Update Course Records*

The function of this method is to update an existing course record as the **Update** button is clicked by the user. The existing course record will be updated in the **Course** table in our sample Oracle database when this method is complete.

On the opened **Design** view of the CourseFrame form window, double click on the **Update** button to open its event handler. Enter the codes shown in Fig. 9.96 into this event handler. Let's have a closer look at this piece of codes to see how it works.

A. Two local variables, **update** and **al**, are created first. The first is a Boolean variable used to hold the running result of execution of the Web service operation **UpdateCourse()**, and the second is an ArrayList instance used to store an updating course record to be updated in the **Course** table in our sample database later.
B. The ArrayList instance **al** is cleaned up by using the **clear()** method to make sure that the **al** is empty before it can store any data.
C. A group of **add()** methods are used to add six pieces of updated course information into the ArrayList instance. The first parameter is a **faculty_name** for whom a course record will be updated, and the seventh parameter is a **course_id** that will work as a query criterion and will not be changed. One point to be noted is that the order in which to add these course parameters must be identical with the

```
  private void UpdateButtonActionPerformed(java.awt.event.ActionEvent evt) {
      // TODO add your handling code here:
A     Boolean update = false;
      ArrayList al = new ArrayList();
B     al.clear();
C     al.add(0, ComboName.getSelectedItem().toString());
      al.add(1, CourseField.getText());
      al.add(2, CreditsField.getText());
      al.add(3, ClassRoomField.getText());
      al.add(4, ScheduleField.getText());
      al.add(5, EnrollField.getText());
      al.add(6, CourseIDField.getText());
      try { // Call Web Service Operation
D        org.ws.sql.WSCourse_Service service = new org.ws.sql.WSCourse_Service();
         org.ws.sql.WSCourse port = service.getWSCoursePort();
E        update = port.updateCourse(al);
F         if (!update)
             System.out.println("Error in course updating...");
G     } catch (Exception ex) {
         System.out.println("exception is: " + ex);
      }
  }
```

Fig. 9.96 The completed codes for the UpdateButtonActionPerformed() event handler

order of assigning these parameters to the ArrayList object **cdata** in our Web service operation **UpdateCourse()**. Refer to that operation to make sure that both orders are identical.

D. A **try-catch** block is used to call our Web operation **UpdateCourse()** to update an existing course record via our Web service. First a new Web service instance **service** is created based on our Web service class **WSCourse_Service**. Then the **getWSCoursePort()** method is executed to get the current port used by our Web service. This port is returned and assigned to a new Port instance **port**.
E. Our Web Service operation **UpdateCourse()** is executed to try to update the selected course based on six pieces of updated information. The execution result that is a Boolean variable is returned and assigned to the local variable **update**.
F. If a **false** is returned, which means that this course data updating failed, the system **println()** method is used to indicate this situation.
G. The **catch** block is used to track and display any possible exception during this data updating process.

Now we have finished the coding process for calling one of our Web service operations, **UpdateCourse()**, to update an existing course record in the **Course** table based on the selected faculty member. Click on the **Clean and Build Main Project** button to build our project. Make sure that our Web Service project **WebServiceCourse** has been built and deployed before our client project can be run. Then click on the **Run Main Project** button to run our client project to test this course data updating function.

On the opened client project, keep the default faculty member **Ying Bai** unchanged, and click on the **Select** button to query all **course_id** taught by this selected faculty. Immediately you can find that all four courses or four **course_id**

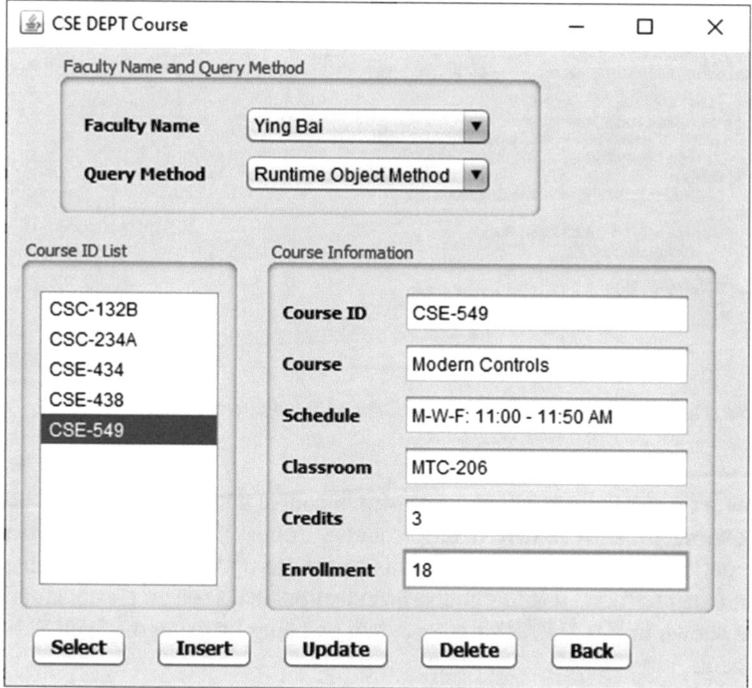

Fig. 9.97 The updated course information for the course CSE-549

taught by this faculty have been returned and displayed in the Course ID List box. To update an existing course **CSE-549**, enter six pieces of updated course information shown below into six text fields.

- Course ID: **CSE-549**
- Course: **Modern Controls**
- Schedule: **M-W-F: 11:00 – 11:50 AM**
- Classroom: **MTC-206**
- Credit: **3**
- Enrollment: **18**

Your finished CourseFrame window is shown in Fig. 9.97. Click on the **Update** button to update this course record in the **Course** table in our sample database.

To test this course record updating action, there are more than one way that can be used. The first way is to connect to our sample database **CSE_DEPT** and open the **Course** table by using the **Databases** icon in the **Services** window inside the NetBeeans IDE to confirm that this course has been updated. But the second way, which is to select the **course_id** whose course details have been updated from the Course ID List Listbox to get course details, is an easier way to confirm this course data updating.

```
  private void DeleteButtonActionPerformed(java.awt.event.ActionEvent evt) {
     // TODO add your handling code here:
A    Boolean delete = false;
     javax.swing.JTextField[] cfield = {CourseIDField, CourseField, CreditsField, ClassRoomField, ScheduleField, EnrollField};
     try { // Call Web Service Operation
B       org.ws.sql.WSCourse_Service service = new org.ws.sql.WSCourse_Service();
        org.ws.sql.WSCourse port = service.getWSCoursePort();
C       delete = port.deleteCourse(CourseIDField.getText());
D       if (!delete)
           System.out.println("Error in course deleting...");
E       else {
           for (int i = 0; i < cfield.length; i++)
               cfield[i].setText("");
        }
F    } catch (Exception ex) {
          System.out.println("exception is: " + ex);
     }
  }
```

Fig. 9.98 The completed codes for the DeleteButtonActionPerformed() event handler

Now let's use the second way to test this course data updating. Just click any other **course_id**, such as **CSC-132B**, from the Course ID List Listbox. Then click on the **course_id CSE-549** whose details have been updated, to retrieve all course details. It can be found that this course is really updated based on the updating information shown in Fig. 9.97. Our course data updating by using our Web Service is successful.

Generally it is recommended to recover this updated course in the **Course** table in our sample database to keep our database neat and clean. However, we will keep this course right now since we need to use this record to perform the course deleting action in the following section.

9.15.6 Build Codes for the Delete Button Method to Delete Course Records

The function of this method is to delete an existing course record from our **Course** table as the **Delete** button is clicked by the user. The existing course record will be permanently deleted from the **Course** table in our sample Oracle database when this method is complete.

On the opened **Design** view of the CourseFrame form window, double click on the **Delete** button to open this event handler. Enter the codes shown in Fig. 9.98 into this event handler. Let's have a closer look at this piece of codes to see how it works.

A. Two local variables, **delete** and **cfield[]**, are created first. The former is a Boolean variable used to hold the running result of execution of the Web service operation **DeleteCourse()**, and the latter is a JTextField array used to hold all TextFields in our CourseFrame Form. The purpose of using this JTextField array is to make it easier to clear all TextFields when this deleting action is executed.

B. A **try-catch** block is used to call our Web operation **DeleteCourse()** to delete an existing course record via our Web service. First a new Web service instance **service** is created based on our Web service class **WSCourse_Service**. Then the **getWSCoursePort()** method is executed to get the current port used by our Web service. This port is returned and assigned to a new Port instance **port**.
C. The Web service operation **DeleteCourse()** is called to delete an existing course record from our **Course** table based on the selected **course_id**. The running result is returned and assigned to the local variable **delete**.
D. If a **false** is returned, which means that this course data deleting has been failed, the system **println()** method is used to indicate this situation.
E. Otherwise this data deleting is successful. A **for** loop is used to clean up all six TextFields to indicate this situation, too.
F. The **catch** block is used to track and display any possible exception during this data deleting process.

Now we have finished the coding process for calling and executing our last Web service operation **DeleteCourse()** to delete an existing course record from the **Course** table based on the selected **course_id**. Click on the **Clean and Build Main Project** button to build our project. Click on the **Run Main Project** button to run our client project to test this course data deleting function.

On the opened client project, keep the default faculty member **Ying Bai** unchanged, and click on the **Select** button to query all **course_id** taught by this selected faculty. Immediately you can find that all four courses or four **course_id** taught by this faculty have been returned and displayed in the Course ID List box. To delete an existing course **CSE-549**, just click on this **course_id** from the Course ID List Listbox, and click on the **Delete** button.

To confirm this course deleting action, two ways can be utilized. First you can open our **Course** table to check whether this course has been deleted from our database. Another way, it is easier, is to use the **Select** button to try to retrieve this deleted course from our database. To do that, just keep the selected faculty member **Ying Bai** in the **Faculty Name** combo box unchanged, and click on the **Select** button. It can be found from the returned courses, exactly all **course_id** taught by the selected faculty are displayed but without **CSE-549**. Our course record deleting using Web service is successful.

At this point, we have finished building and developing a Windows-based project to consume our Web Service project for the **Course** table in our sample database. A complete Window-based client project that is used to consume our Web service to query and manipulate data against our sample database, **WinClientCourse**, can be found from the folder **Class DB Projects\Chapter 9** that is under the **Students** folder at the Springer ftp site (refer to Fig. 1.2 in Chap. 1).

Next let's build a Web-based client project to consume this Web service.

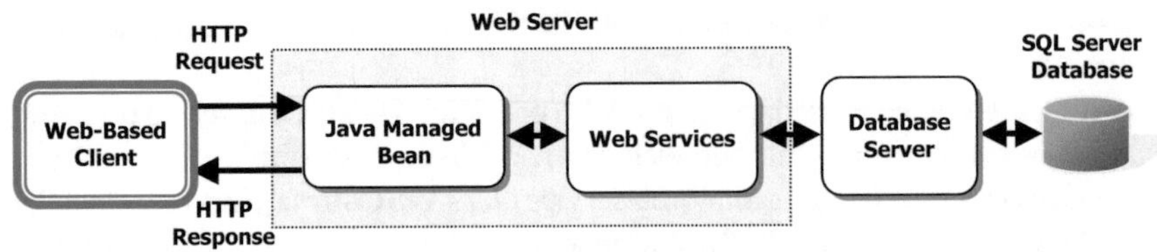

Fig. 9.99 The architecture of our Web-based client project

9.16 Build a Web-Based Project to Consume the Web Service Project WebServiceCourse

To consume our Web Service project, we can also build some Web-based projects to call different operations to perform related actions to our database. The structure of this Web-based client project is shown in Fig. 9.99.

The Java Managed bean works as an interface to talk to Web Service to perform physical query operations to our **Course** table in our sample database.

9.16.1 Create a Web-Based Client Project WebClientCourse

To save time and space, we can modify one of our projects, **WebClientUpdtDelt**, we built in the previous section in this Chapter and make it as our new project. One can find this project from the Springer ftp site, exactly in the folder **Students\Class DB Projects\Chapter 9** in that site. One can copy and paste that project to your local drive. Perform the following operational steps to build our new Web-based project, **WebClientCourse**.

1) Open NetBean IDE 8.2 and **Projects** window, right click on the copied project **WebClient-UpdtDelt**, and select the **Copy** item from the popup menu to open the **Copy Project** wizard.
2) Enter our new project name, **WebClientCourse**, into the **Project Name** box, and browse to the default project folder, **C:\Class DB Projects\Chapter 9**, as the **Project Location**, and click on the **Copy** button.

A new project **WebClientCourse** is generated and added into our **Projects** window.

First let's delete one Java bean class file, **FacultyUpdateDeleteBean.java**, which is located under the folder, **Source Packages|JavaWebDBJSPSQLPackag e**, since we do not need this file.

Then let's add a Web Service reference to our Web-based client project to allow it to use our Web service operations.

9.16.2 Add a Web Service Reference to Our Web-Based Client Project

In order to call any operation in our Web service project **WebServiceCourse**, we need to update the Web reference in our Web-based client project **WebClientCourse** to direct all calls to our Web service project. Perform the following operations to update this Web service reference:

1) Expand our **Web Service References** folder under our client project, and right click on the original Web Service project **WebServiceUpdtDelt**, and select **Delete** item to remove it.
2) Build and deploy our Web Service project **WebServiceCourse** to make it ready.
3) Right click on our Web-based client project **WebClientCourse**, and select the **New > Web Service Client** item to open the **New Web Service Client** wizard.
4) On the opened wizard, click on the **Browse** button that is next to the **Project** field, and expand our Web application **WebServiceCourse**. Then choose our Web service class **WSCourse** by clicking on it, and click on the **OK** button.
5) Click on the **Finish** button to complete this Web service reference addition process.

Now that we have added a Web service reference to our Web-based client project **WebClientCourse**, next let's develop the codes in our client project to call that Web service operations to perform related course data query actions. The main coding jobs are concentrated on building the transaction JSP file, **CourseProcess.jsp**, and Java Managed Bean class file, **CourseQuery.java**. First let's do some modifications to our **Course.jsp** page.

9.16.3 Modify the Course.jsp Page

The **Course.jsp** page works as a view to provide the displaying function for input and output. We need to modify this page to enable it to forward the user's inputs to the model and controller page and, furthermore, to call the Java bean class to process our data query.

Open this page by double clicking on it from the **Projects** window, and perform the modifications shown in Fig. 9.100 to this page. All modified coding parts have been highlighted in bold. Let's have a closer look at this piece of modified codes to see how it works.

A. Some JSP tags are first declared at the top of this page, including the package name, Java bean, session, class, and property or method used in this page. The name of our Java bean class file, **CourseQuery.java**, and one of methods, **getCourseID()**, are declared, and both of them will be built later.

```
A   <%@ page import="JavaWebDBJSPSQLPackage.*" %>
    <jsp:useBean id="CourseQuery" scope="session" class="JavaWebDBJSPSQLPackage.CourseQuery" />
    <jsp:setProperty name="getCourseID" property="*" />
B   <% String[] al = null; %>
    .........
C   <form method=post action=".\CourseProcess.jsp">
    .........
    <%
D     CourseQuery cQuery = new CourseQuery();
E     String fname = request.getParameter("FacultyNameField");
F     boolean res = cQuery.Query_CourseID(fname);
G     if (!res)
        response.sendRedirect("Course.jsp");
H     else {
        al = cQuery.getCourseID();
I       session.setAttribute("FacultyName", request.getParameter("FacultyNameField"));
      }
    %>
    <select name="CourseList" size=7 v:shapes="_x0000_s1027">
J   <% for (int i = 0; i < al.length; i++) { %>
K   <option value="<%=al[i] %>"><%=al[i]%></option>
L   <%}%>
    </select>
    .........
M   <input name=CourseIDField maxlength=255 size=22 value="<%=session.getAttribute("CourseID") %>"
    type=text v:shapes="_x0000_s1029">
    .........
N   <input name=CourseNameField maxlength=255 size=22 value="<%=session.getAttribute("CourseName") %>"
    type=text v:shapes="_x0000_s1031">
    .........
O   <input name=ScheduleField maxlength=255 size=22 value="<%=session.getAttribute("Schedule") %>"
    type=text v:shapes="_x0000_s1033">
    .........
P   <input name=ClassroomField maxlength=255 size=22 value="<%=session.getAttribute("ClassRoom") %>"
    type=text v:shapes="_x0000_s1035">
    .........
Q   <input name=CreditField maxlength=255 size=22 value="<%=session.getAttribute("Credit") %>" type=text
    v:shapes="_x0000_s1037">
    .........
R   <input name=EnrollmentField maxlength=255 size=22 value="<%=session.getAttribute("Enrollment") %>"
    type=text v:shapes="_x0000_s1039">
    .........
S   <input type=submit value=Select name="Select" v:shapes="_x0000_s1040">
    .........
U   <input type=submit value=Insert name="Insert" v:shapes="_x0000_s1041">
    .........
V   <input type=submit value=Update name="Update" v:shapes="_x0000_s1042">
    .........
W   <input type=submit value=Delete name="Delete" v:shapes="_x0000_s1043">
    .........
X   <input type=button value=Back name="Back" onclick="self.close()" v:shapes="_x0000_s1044">
    .........
Y   <input name=FacultyNameField maxlength=255 size=22 value="<%=session.getAttribute("FacultyName") %>"
    type=text v:shapes="_x0000_s1045">
    .........
```

Fig. 9.100 The modified codes for the Course.jsp page

B. A page-level variable **al**, which is a string array, is also declared and initialized here. This array variable will be used to hold the queried **course_id** later.
C. An **action** attribute is added to the Form tag to forward all information collected from this page to the model and controller page **CourseProcess.jsp** that will call our Java bean class file **CourseQuery.java** to perform the course data query process.

D. Starting from section **D**, a piece of Java codes is embedded into this JSP file to speed up the querying process for all collected **course_id** and display them in our CourseList box. A symbol pair **<%...%>** must be used to indicate the starting and the ending of this piece of embedded Java codes. First an instance of our Java bean class, **cQuery**, is created.

E. The selected faculty name, which is stored in the TextField **FacultyNameField** in our **Course.jsp** page, is retrieved by using a system method **getParameter()** and assigned to a String variable, **fname**, which will be used for the next query.

F. A user-defined method, **Query_CourseID()**, which will be built later in our Java bean, is called with the retrieved faculty name as the argument, to query all **course_id** for the selected faculty member.

G. If this query is not successful, the JSP page, **Course.jsp**, is refreshed and redisplayed.

H. Otherwise, all queried **course_id** is collected by using one user-defined method, **getCourseID()**, which will be built in our Java bean class later and stored into **al** array.

I. The selected faculty name is refreshed by calling the system method, **setAttribute()**.

J. A Java **for** loop is embedded here to select each **course_id** from the **al** array and display each of them in the CourseList box via the **<option>** tag. One point to be noted is that a pair of <%...%> tag must be used to cover this **for** loop, including the opening brace (**{**).

K. The **value** option property is used to add and display each **course_id** in our CourseList box. Similarly, a pair of <%...%> tag is used to cover the actual assignment value of the embedded Java code variable **=al[i]**. The first value is a label, and the second one is the actual value of **course_id**.

L. The ending brace (**}**) of this **for** loop is also covered by a pair of <%...%> tag.

M. Starting from step **M** until step **R**, we use the embedded JSP codes to assign the queried course columns from our **Course** table to the **value** tags of the associated text field in this **Course.jsp** using the **getAttribute()** method of the session class. In this way, as long as the queried course row has any change, this modification will be immediately updated and reflected to each text field in our **Course.jsp** page. Thus, a direct connection or binding between the text fields in our **Course.jsp** page and the queried course columns in our Java bean class is established.

S. From steps **S** to **W**, a **name** attribute is added into each **Submit** button tag. This attribute is very important since we need to use it to identify each submit button in the next page, our model and controller page, **CourseProcess.jsp**, by using the **getParameter()** method of the **request** object to direct the control to handle different actions to the **Course** table in our sample SQL Server database.

X. The type of the **Back** button is changed to **button**, and an **onclick="self.close()"** tag is added with this button. The purpose of this changing is to use this button's action to close our client page in this client page without forwarding this action to the next page.

Y. Finally the **FacultyNameField** is also set to be connected to the **faculty_name** column in the **Faculty** table. The reason for this setup is that there is no **faculty_name** column in the **Course** table, and the only connection between a course and a faculty is **faculty_id**.

Now let's take a look at our model and controller page **CourseProcess.jsp**.

9.16.4 Build the Transaction JSP File CourseProcess.jsp

The purpose of this file is to transfer data and information between our main displaying page **Course.jsp** and our Java bean class file **CourseQuery.java** that calls related Web Service operations to perform all JDBC- and database-related operations and business logics. Perform the following operations to create this page:

Right click on our project **WebClientCourse** from the **Projects** window, and select the **New > JSP** item from the popup menu to open the **New JSP File** wizard. Enter **CourseProcess** into the **File Name** field, keep the default **JSP File** selection unchanged, and click on the **Finish** button.

Double click on our new created **CourseProcess.jsp** page from the **Projects** window, exactly under the **Web Pages** folder, to open this page. Enter the codes shown in Fig. 9.101 into this page. The new entered codes have been highlighted in bold.

Now let's have a close look at these codes to see how they work.

A. You can embed any import directory using the JSP directive in a HTML or a JSP file. The format is **<%@ page import="java package" %>**. In this page, we embed one package, **JavaWebDBJSPSQLPackage.*** since we will build our Java bean class file **CourseQuery.java** under that package in the next section.
B. Some JSP directives are declared first, and they are used to set up the Java bean, session, class, and property used on this JSP page.
C. To prepare to perform a query to get course details, an instance of our Java bean class, **cQuery**, is created first.
D. An instance of the RequestDispatcher class, **dpt**, is declared here, and it is used to set up a communication channel between the client and the server, exactly between the **Course.jsp** page and the Java bean class file **CourseQuery.java** to be installed and run in a Web server.
E. After an instance of the RequestDispatcher class is generated, a system method, **forward()**, is used to dispatch all requests from the client and responses from the server between the client and the server.
F. If the **Select** button in the **Course.jsp** page is clicked and a **course_id** has been selected by the user, the system method **getParameter()** will return a value "**Select**" since we defined its value in that page. Then this action will be processed. First the selected **course_id** is retrieved by calling the system method **getParameter()** with the CourseList that is the name of our CourseList defined in the **Course.jsp page** as an argument.

```
A  <%@ page import="JavaWebDBJSPSQLPackage.*" %>
   <html>
     <head>
       <meta http-equiv="Content-Type" content="text/html; charset=UTF-8">
       <title>Faculty Process Page</title>
     </head>
    <body>
B   <jsp:useBean id="getCourseID" scope="session" class="JavaWebDBJSPSQLPackage.CourseQuery" />
    <jsp:setProperty name="getCourseID" property="*" />
    <%
C      CourseQuery cQuery = new CourseQuery();
D      RequestDispatcher dpt = request.getRequestDispatcher("Course.jsp");
E      dpt.forward(request, response);
F      if (request.getParameter("Select")!= null) {
          //process the course record query
          String c_id = request.getParameter("CourseList");
G         boolean res = cQuery.QueryCourse(c_id);
H         if (!res)
             response.sendRedirect("Course.jsp");
I         else {
             session.setAttribute("CourseID", cQuery.getCID());
             session.setAttribute("CourseName", cQuery.getCourseName());
             session.setAttribute("Credit", cQuery.getCredit());
             session.setAttribute("ClassRoom", cQuery.getClassRoom());
             session.setAttribute("Schedule", cQuery.getSchedule());
             session.setAttribute("Enrollment", cQuery.getEnrollment());
          }
       }
J      else if (request.getParameter("Insert")!= null) {
          //process the course record insertion
          }
K      else if (request.getParameter("Update")!= null) {
          //process the course record updating
          }
L      else if (request.getParameter("Delete")!= null) {
          //process the course record deleting
          }
M      else if (request.getParameter("Back") != null) {
          //cQuery.CloseDBConnection();
          response.sendRedirect("Selection.jsp");
         }
    %>
     </body>
   </html>
```

Fig. 9.101 The codes for the CourseProcess.jsp page

G. With the retrieved **course_id** as argument, our user-defined method, **QueryCourse()**, which will be built in our Java bean class file **CourseQuery.java**, is executed to get course details.
H. If this execution returns a false, it means that that query failed, and our client page, **Course.jsp**, is refreshed and redisplayed to enable users to perform next actions.
I. Otherwise, that query is successful, and a sequence of **setAttribute()** methods is used to set all six TextFields in our client page with queried course detailed information. All query methods, such as **getCID(), getCourseName(), getCredit(),** …will be built in our Java bean class file **CourseQuery.java** later.
J. From steps **J** to **M**, four **else if** blocks are used for all other query actions, such as **Inserting**, **Updating**, and **Deleting** a course record. Those actions are reserved for future developments.

One important point for this piece of codes is: any clicking on this **Select** button triggers two actions: (1) query and retrieve all **course_id** based on the selected faculty name, and display them in the CourseList box, and (2) query the course details based on a selected **course_id** from the CourseList box and display them in six TextFields. Due to this dual function of this **Select** button, when a user performs a course query, the following actions should be adopted:

1) When querying, retrieving, and displaying all **course_id** taught by a selected faculty member represented by a faculty name, one needs to click on the **Select** button by one time.
2) When querying, retrieving, and displaying all course details based on a selected **course_id** in the CourseList box, one needs to click on the **Select** button by two times.

The reason for that is because we used only one button to handle two actions to simplify our GUI design for our Web page; we therefore need to pay something for that simplification to keep a balance in this world.

In fact, the first single clicking is used to get all **course_id** based on the selected faculty member, and the second two-time clicking is used to get all course details based on the selected **course_id** on the CourseList box.

Due to the communications between the server and the client, each time when the server responds to the client, it will first refresh the client page and then sends the queried information to the client. To avoid a possible responded data losing because of that refreshing, a two-time clicking on the **Select** button is a good solution since it can first trigger the **Select** button to get all **course_id**, and immediately the details for a selected **course_id** can be retrieved and displayed in six TextFields after the second clicking for that button prior to a refreshing coming.

Next let's take care of our Java bean class file CourseQuery.java.

9.16.5 Build the Java Bean Class File CourseQuery.java

To create our Java bean class file **CourseQuery.java** to handle the course record query, right click on our project **WebClientCourse** from the **Projects** window, and select the **New > Java Class** item from the popup menu to open the **New Java Class** wizard. Enter **CourseQuery** into the **Class Name** field, and select the **JavaWebDBJSPSQLPackage** from the **Package** combo box. Your finished **New Java Class** wizard should match one that is shown in Fig. 9.102. Click on the **Finish** button to create this new Java bean class file.

Now let's develop the codes for this new Java bean class file.

Double click on our new created Java help class file **CourseQuery.java** from the **Projects** window to open this file, and enter the codes that are shown in Fig. 9.103 into this file. Because of the large size of this piece of codes, we divide this coding process into two parts. The first part is shown in Fig. 9.103, and the second part is shown in Fig. 9.104. The new entered codes have been highlighted in bold.

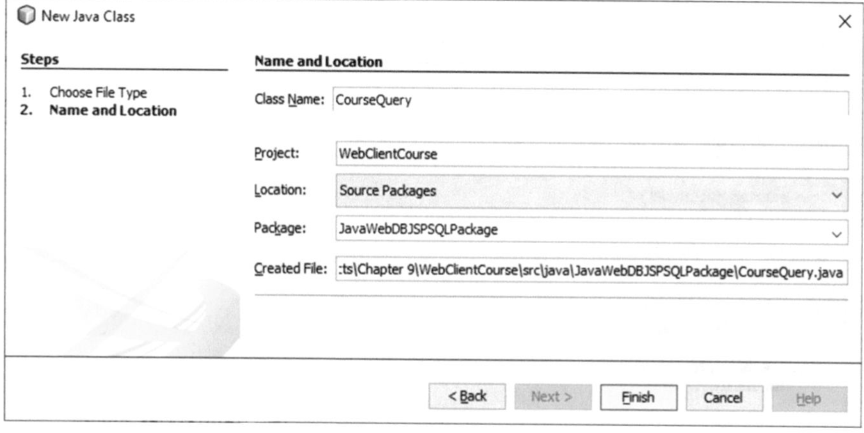

Fig. 9.102 The new created CourseQuery.java class file

```
  package JavaWebDBJSPSQLPackage;
A import java.util.ArrayList;
B public class CourseQuery {
    private String CourseID;
    private String CourseName;
    private String Credit;
    private String ClassRoom;
    private String Schedule;
    private String Enrollment;
    private String[] alArray;
C   public CourseQuery() { }
D   public boolean Query_CourseID(String f_name){
E     ArrayList<String> al = new ArrayList();
F     try {
        org.ws.sql.WSCourse_Service service = new org.ws.sql.WSCourse_Service();
        org.ws.sql.WSCourse port = service.getWSCoursePort();
G       al.clear();
H       al = (ArrayList)port.queryCourseID(f_name);
I       alArray = al.toArray(new String[al.size()]);
J     }catch (Exception ex) {
        System.out.println("exception: " + ex);
        return false;
      }
K     return true;
    }
L   public String[] getCourseID() {
      return alArray;
    }
M   public boolean QueryCourse(String cid){
      ArrayList<String> al = new ArrayList();
N     try {
        org.ws.sql.WSCourse_Service service = new org.ws.sql.WSCourse_Service();
        org.ws.sql.WSCourse port = service.getWSCoursePort();
O       al.clear();
P       al = (ArrayList)port.queryCourse(cid);
Q       CourseID = al.get(0);
        CourseName = al.get(1);
        Credit = al.get(2);
        ClassRoom = al.get(3);
        Schedule = al.get(4);
        Enrollment = al.get(5);
R       return true;
S     }catch (Exception ex) {
        System.out.println("exception: " + ex);
        return false;
      }
    }
```

Fig. 9.103 The first part of the codes for the Java bean file CourseQuery.java

```
A  public String getCID() {
       return this.CourseID;
   }
B  public String getCourseName() {
       return this.CourseName;
   }
C  public String getCredit() {
       return this.Credit;
   }
D  public String getClassRoom() {
       return this.ClassRoom;
   }
E  public String getSchedule() {
       return this.Schedule;
   }
F  public String getEnrollment() {
       return this.Enrollment;
   }
}
```

Fig. 9.104 The second part of the codes for the Java bean file CourseQuery.java

Let's have a close look at these new added codes in Fig. 9.103 to see how they work.

A. A Java class, **java.util.ArrayList** that is included in the **java.util** package, is imported into this file since we need to use this component to store collected course details later.
B. Our Java bean class is declared with seven member data: the top six are private String variables with each being mapped to the related TextField in the **Course.jsp** page, and the bottom one is a private String[] array, **alArray**, and it is used by this file to collect the queried course details and send them back to the **CourseProcess.jsp** page later.
C. Keep the constructor of this Java bean as empty since we do not need to use it now.
D. The first course query method, **Query_CourseID()**, is declared with a selected faculty name as the argument. The added underscore between the **Query** and **CourseID** is to distinguish this method with an operation, **QueryCourseID()**, in our Web Service.
E. An ArrayList instance, al, is generated, and it is used to store the queried **course_id** later.
F. A **try-catch** block is used to call our Web operation **QueryCourseID()** to get all **course_id** via our Web service. First a new Web service instance **service** is created based on our Web service class **WSCourse_Service**. Then the **getWSCoursePort()** method is executed to get the current port used by our Web service. This port is returned and assigned to a new Port instance **port**.
G. The ArrayList instance **al** is cleaned up by using the **clear()** method to make sure that the **al** is empty before it can be used to store any data.
H. Our Web Service operation **QueryCourseID()** is executed with a selected faculty name as the argument, and the query results are assigned to our ArrayList object **al**.

I. Since we want to use a String[] array to transfer this **course_id** collection, thus this ArrayList data type is converted to that String[] array type with a system method **toArray()**.
J. The **catch** block is used to track and detect any possible exception during this query process, and a **false** would be returned if any error occurred.
K. Otherwise this query is successful, and a **true** is returned.
L. The user-defined method, **getCourseID()**, which is equivalent to a getting method, is executed to return the class-level variable **alArray** that contains all queried **course_id** to our **CourseProcess.jsp** page for the further process.
M. Another user-defined method, **QueryCourse()**, which is used to query the details for a selected CourseID, is declared with an argument **cid**, which is an input **course_id**. Also an ArrayList instance, **al**, is generated, and it is used to store the queried course details later.
N. A **try-catch** block is used to call our Web operation **QueryCourse()** to get all details for a selected course via our Web service. First a new Web service instance **service** is created based on our Web service class **WSCourse_Service**. Then the **getWSCoursePort()** method is executed to get the current port used by our Web service. This port is returned and assigned to a new Port instance **port**.
O. The ArrayList instance **al** is cleaned up by using the **clear()** method to make sure that the **al** is empty before it can be used to store any data.
P. Our Web Service operation **QueryCourse()** is executed with a selected **course_id** as the argument, and the query results are assigned to our ArrayList object **al**.
Q. A sequence of system methods, **get()**, is used to pick up each item of the queried course details in **al** and assign each of them to the related class variable. One point to be noted is the order of these assignments, and it must be identical with the column order in our **Course** Table in our sample database **CSE_DEPT**.
R. A true is returned to indicate that this query is successful.
S. The **catch** block is used to track and detect any possible exception during this query process, and a **false** would be returned if any error occurred.

Let's continue to take care of the second part of codes for this Java bean class file **CourseQuery.java**. The second part of codes is shown in Fig. 9.104. Let's have a close look at these new added codes in Fig. 9.104 to see how they work.

Basically six getting methods are shown here, from steps **A** to **F**, and each of them allows one piece of queried course details, which is stored in each related class-level variable, such as **CourseID**, **CourseName**, **Credit**, and so on, to be used by the **CourseProcess.jsp** page to get and set them on the related TextFields in the **Course.jsp** page. Where **this** is the current class followed by the related class variable separated with a dot operator. Refer to step **I** in Fig. 9.101, where all of these six methods are used to set up six related TextFields in the **Course.jsp** page by using six system methods **setAttribute()**.

Now we have completed all coding developments for our Web client page, transaction JSP page, and Java bean class file. Next let's build and run our client project to consume our Web Service to query the **Course** table in our sample database.

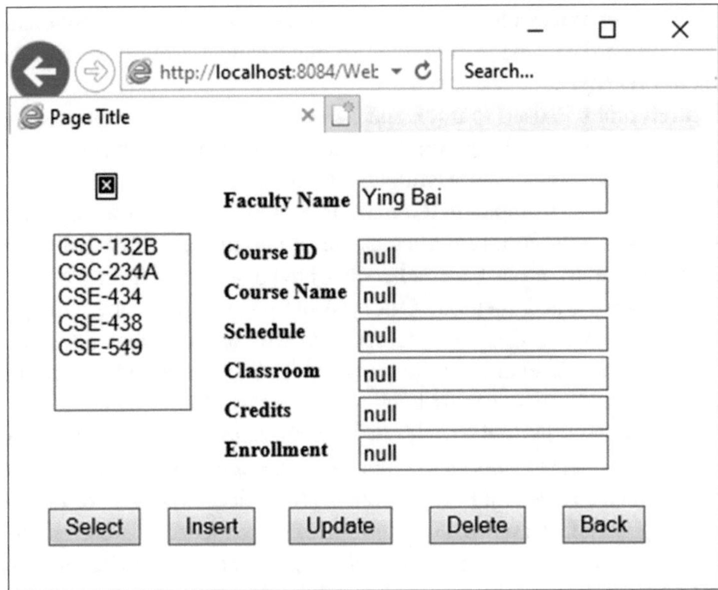

Fig. 9.105 The running status of our client project

9.16.6 Build and Run Our Client Project to Query Course Record via Our Web Service

Prior to building and running our client project, make sure that our Web Service project **WebServiceCourse** has been built and deployed successfully.

Perform the following operations to build and run our client project **WebClientCourse**:

1) Click on the **Clean and Build Main Project** button to build our project, and exactly build our Java bean class file **CourseQuery.java**.
2) Right click on our client page **Course.jsp** from the **Projects** window, and select the **Compile File** item to compile this page.
3) Right click on our transaction page **CourseProcess.jsp** from the **Projects** window, and select the **Compile File** item to compile this page.
4) Right click on our client page **Course.jsp** from the **Projects** window, and select the **Run File** item to run our client project.

The running status of our client project is shown in Fig. 9.105.

Enter a valid faculty name, such as **Ying Bai**, into the Faculty Name box, and then click on the **Select** button to query all courses (**course_id**) taught by this faculty. All five courses (**course_id**) are retrieved from our database and displayed in the CourseList box, as shown in Fig. 9.105.

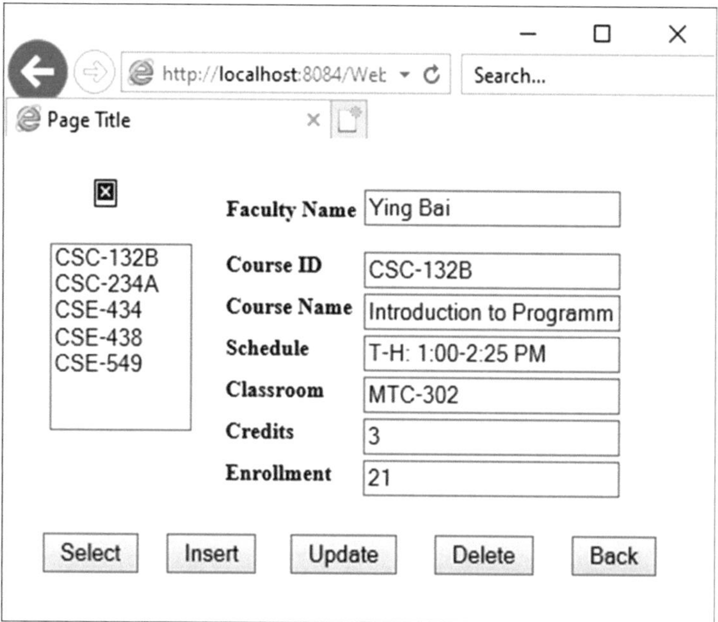

Fig. 9.106 The query result for the course details

Now select one **course_id** from the CourseList box, such as **CSC-132B**, by clicking on it, and then click on the **Select** button by two times; all course details related to this **course_id** are displayed in the six TextFields on the right, as shown in Fig. 9.106.

One can try to check other **course_id** to get course details for the selected **course_id**. Our Web-based client project used to consume our Web Service to query course information is successful. Click on the **Back** button to close our project.

Next let's concentrate on how to insert a new course record into the **Course** table in our sample database via our Web-based client project.

9.16.7 Build Our Client Project to Insert New Course Records via Our Web Service

The main coding jobs for inserting a new course record are concentrated on our transaction JSP pages **CourseProcess.jsp** and Java bean class file **CourseQuery.java**. Let's first take care of the coding development for the transaction page **CourseProcess.jsp**.

```
.........
else if (request.getParameter("Insert")!= null) {
    //process the course record insertion
    %>
A   <jsp:useBean id="Insert_Course" scope="session" class="JavaWebDBJSPSQLPackage.CourseQuery" />
    <jsp:setProperty name="Insert_Course" property="*" />
    <%
B   boolean res = false;
C   String cid = request.getParameter("CourseIDField");
    String cname = request.getParameter("CourseNameField");
    String credit = request.getParameter("CreditField");
    String classroom = request.getParameter("ClassroomField");
    String schedule = request.getParameter("ScheduleField");
    String enroll = request.getParameter("EnrollmentField");
    String fname = request.getParameter("FacultyNameField");
D   String[] cnew = {fname, cid, cname, credit, classroom, schedule, enroll};
E   res = cQuery.Insert_Course(cnew);
F   if (!res)
         response.sendRedirect("Course.jsp");
G   else {
         session.setAttribute("CourseIDField", null);
         request.setAttribute("CourseNameField", null);
         request.setAttribute("CreditField", null);
         request.setAttribute("ClassroomField", null);
         request.setAttribute("ScheduleField", null);
         request.setAttribute("EnrollmentField", null);
       }
    }
else if (request.getParameter("Update")!= null) {
    //process the course record updating
    }
.........
```

Fig. 9.107 The codes for the Insert Course block in the CourseProcess.jsp page

Double click on this page from the **Projects** window to open it, and enter the codes shown in Fig. 9.107 into this page, exactly into the **else if (request.getParameter("Insert")!= null)** block.

Let's have a closer look at this piece of codes to see how it works.

A. Two JSP directives are declared first, and they are used to set up the Java bean, session, class, and property used on this JSP page. The **Insert_Course()** method will be built in our Java bean class later, and the underscore between the **Insert** and the **Course** is to distinguish this method with a similar operation, **InsertCourse()**, in our Web Service. These two directives must not be enclosed by a pair of <%...%> symbols.
B. Starting from step **B**, the following codes will be Java codes to be embedded into this page; thus an opening symbol **<%** is used to start this part. Since the Web operation **InsertCourse()** in our Service returns a Boolean result, to hold it, a Boolean variable **res** is created first.
C. To set up a new course record that contains seven pieces of new course information, seven system methods, **getParameter()**, are used to pick up each piece of new course information from the related TextField in our client page, **Course.jsp**, and assign each of them to a local String variable.
D. Then a String[] array is created and initialized with those seven local variables to make a new course record ready to be sent to the Java bean class.

```
  ........
  public boolean Insert_Course(String[] newCourse){
A     boolean insert = false;
      ArrayList al = new ArrayList();
B     al.clear();
C     al.add(0, newCourse[0]);
      al.add(1, newCourse[1]);
      al.add(2, newCourse[2]);
      al.add(3, newCourse[3]);
      al.add(4, newCourse[4]);
      al.add(5, newCourse[5]);
      al.add(6, newCourse[6]);
D     try{
        org.ws.sql.WSCourse_Service service = new org.ws.sql.WSCourse_Service();
        org.ws.sql.WSCourse port = service.getWSCoursePort();
E       insert = port.insertCourse(al);
F       if (!insert) {
          System.out.println("The data insertion is failed!");
        }
      }
G     catch (Exception e) {
        System.out.println("Error in Insert Statement! " + e.getMessage());
        return false;
      }
H     return insert;
    }
  }
```

Fig. 9.108 The added codes for the Insert_Course() method in the Java bean

E. The **Insert_Course()** method that will be defined in our Java bean class is executed with the initialized String[] as the argument. The running result of this method is returned and assigned to our local Boolean variable **res**.
F. If a **false** is returned, which means that the execution of this method failed, then the client page, **Course.jsp**, is refreshed to make it ready for the next operation.
G. Otherwise the running of that method is successful, and a new course record has been inserted into the **Course** table in our sample database; thus, all TextFields in the client page will be reset to null to recover them to show the original record.

Next let's handle the coding process in our Java bean class file **CourseQuery.java**. Double click on this file from the **Projects** window, exactly under the folder, **Source Packages\JavaWeb DBJSPSQLPackage**, to open it and enter the codes shown in Fig. 9.108 into the bottom of this file. Let's have a closer look at this piece of codes to see how it works.

A. Two local variables, **insert** and **al**, are generated first. The former is a Boolean variable used to hold the running result of execution of our Web Service operation, **InsertCouse()**, and the latter is an instance of the ArrayList class, which is used to store seven pieces of information for a new inserted course record.
B. The ArrayList instance **al** is cleaned up by using the **clear()** method to make sure that the **al** is empty before it can be used to store any data.
C. A sequence of **add()** methods is used to add all seven pieces of new course information into the ArrayList instance **al**, which will be passed as an argument for our Web Service operation **InsertCourse()** later.

D. A **try-catch** block is used to call our Web operation **InsertCourse()** to insert a new course record into our sample database via our Web service. First a new Web service instance **service** is created based on our Web service class **WSCourse_Service**. Then the **getWSCoursePort()** method is executed to get the current port used by our Web service. This port is returned and assigned to a new Port instance **port**.
E. The Web Service operation **InsertCourse()** is executed with an argument **al** that contains seven pieces of new course information, and the running result is returned and assigned to the local Boolean variable **insert**.
F. If the returned Boolean value is **false**, which means that this data insertion action failed, a system method **println()** is used to indicate this situation. Otherwise this data insertion is successful.
G. The **catch** block is used to monitor and check any possible exception during this insertion process. A **false** is returned to the calling program if any error really occurred.
H. Otherwise a **true** is returned to indicate the success of this data insertion action.

Now we have finished all coding jobs for this new course insertion action. Let's build and run our client project to consume our Web Service to insert a new course record into the **Course** table in our sample database.

Prior to building and running our client project, make sure that our Web Service project **WebServiceCourse** has been built and deployed successfully.

Perform the following operations to build and run our client project **WebClientCourse**:

1) Click on the **Clean and Build Main Project** button to build our project, and exactly build our Java bean class file **CourseQuery.java**.
2) Right click on our client page **Course.jsp** from the **Projects** window, and select the **Compile File** item to compile this page.
3) Right click on our transaction page **CourseProcess.jsp** from the **Projects** window, and select the **Compile File** item to compile this page.
4) Right click on our client page **Course.jsp** from the **Projects** window, and select the **Run File** item to run our client project.

As the course page is opened, enter a valid faculty name, such as **Ying Bai**, into the Faculty Name box, and then click on the **Select** button to query all courses (**course_id**) taught by this faculty. All five courses (**course_id**) should have been retrieved from our database and displayed in the CourseList box.

Now let's test to insert a new course record into the **Course** table in our sample database. Keep the selected faculty member, **Ying Bai**, with no change, and enter the following six pieces of information as a new course record into the six related TextFields in this course page:

- Course ID: **CSE-565**
- Course Name: **Machine Learning**
- Schedule: **T-H: 9:30 – 10:45 AM**
- Classroom: **MTC-202**

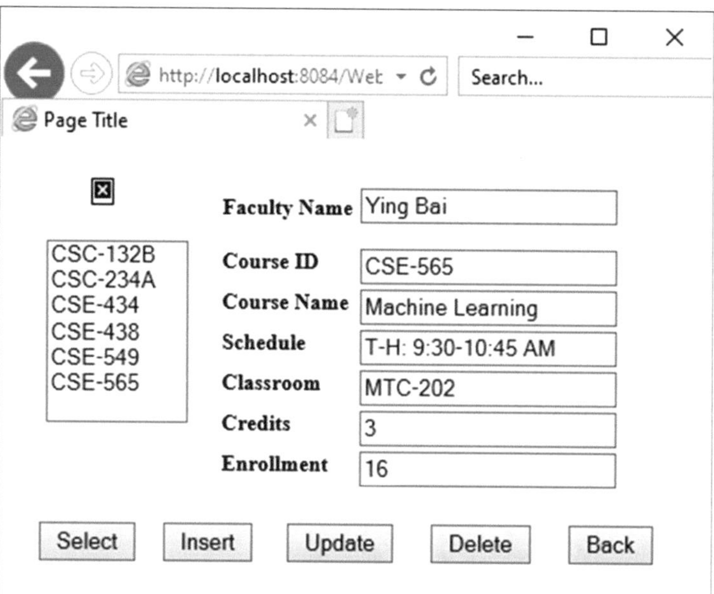

Fig. 9.109 The running status and result of inserting a new course record

- Credit: **3**
- Enrollment: **16**
- Faculty Name: **Ying Bai**

Now click on the **Insert** button to try to insert this new course record into the **Course** table in our sample database **CSE_DEPT**. If this insertion action is successful, the client page is refreshed to clean all contents on each TextField.

To check and confirm this data insertion, just click on the **Select** button to retrieve all courses (**course_id**) taught by the selected faculty member **Ying Bai**. One can find that the new inserted course, **CSE-565**, is retrieved and displayed in the CourseList box, as shown in Fig. 9.109.

Select this new inserted course from this CourseList box by clicking on it, and then click on the **Select** button by two times; the details about this new inserted course are displayed in six TextFields, as shown in Fig. 9.109. Click on the **Back** button to close our project.

Another way to confirm this data insertion is to open the **Course** table via the **Services** window in the NetBeans IDE. After opening the **Services** window, expand the **Databases** icon, and connect to our sample database by right clicking on our database URL. Select the **Connect** item, and enter the password, **Happy2020**, to connect to our sample database. After connection, expand the **URL\CSE_DEPT.dbo\Tables**. Right click on the **Course** table, and select the **View Data** item to open this table. One can find that the new course is really inserted into this **Course** table; exactly, it is located at the bottom line that has been highlighted, as shown in Fig. 9.110.

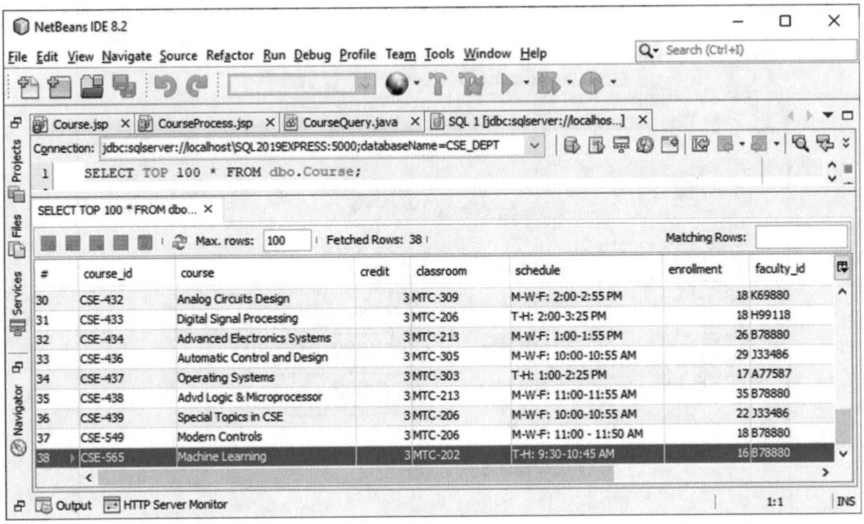

Fig. 9.110 The opened Course table in our sample database

Next let's build and develop the codes for our client project to access our Web Service to update a selected course in our **Course** table.

9.16.8 Build Our Client Project to Update Course Records via Our Web Service

Generally there is no need to update a **course_id** when updating a course record since a better way to do that is to insert a new course record and delete the old one. The main reason for this is that a very complicated cascaded updating process would be performed if a **course_id** was updated since it is a primary key in the **Course** table but a foreign key in the **StudentCourse** table. To update a primary key, one needs to update foreign keys first in the child tables and then update the primary key in the parent table. This will make our updating process very complicated and easy to be confused. In order to avoid this confusion, in this section, we will update a course record by changing any column except the **course_id**, and this is a popular way to update a table and widely implemented in most database applications.

Now let's develop the codes for the **Update** button in our client project, exactly in the client page **Course.jsp**, to update a course record via our Web Service. The main coding jobs are concentrated on two files, the transaction page **CourseProcess.jsp** and our Java bean class file **CourseQuery.java**. Let's first take care of the coding development for the transaction page **CourseProcess.jsp**.

```
  .........
  else if (request.getParameter("Update")!= null) {
    //process the course record updating
    %>
A   <jsp:useBean id="Update_Course" scope="session" class="JavaWebDBJSPSQLPackage.CourseQuery" />
    <jsp:setProperty name="Update_Course" property="*" />
    <%
B   boolean res = false;
C   String cid = request.getParameter("CourseIDField");
    String cname = request.getParameter("CourseNameField");
    String credit = request.getParameter("CreditField");
    String classroom = request.getParameter("ClassroomField");
    String schedule = request.getParameter("ScheduleField");
    String enroll = request.getParameter("EnrollmentField");
    String fname = request.getParameter("FacultyNameField");
D   String[] cupdate = {fname, cname, credit, classroom, schedule, enroll, cid};
E   res = cQuery.Update_Course(cupdate);
F   if (!res)
        response.sendRedirect("Course.jsp");
G   else {
        session.setAttribute("CourseIDField", null);
        request.setAttribute("CourseNameField", null);
        request.setAttribute("CreditField", null);
        request.setAttribute("ClassroomField", null);
        request.setAttribute("ScheduleField", null);
        request.setAttribute("EnrollmentField", null);
         }
    }
  else if (request.getParameter("Delete")!= null) {
     //process the course record deleting
    }
  .........
```

Fig. 9.111 The codes for the Update Course block in the CourseProcess.jsp page

The main function of this piece of codes is to coordinate the updating query and provide a valid interface between the client page and the Java bean to make that query smoother.

Double click on this page from the **Projects** window to open it, and enter the codes shown in Fig. 9.111 into this page, exactly into the **else if (request.getParameter("Update")!= null)** block.

Let's have a closer look at this piece of codes to see how it works.

A. Two JSP directives are declared first, and they are used to set up the Java bean, session, class, and property used on this JSP page. The **Update_Course()** method will be built in our Java bean class later, and the underscore between the **Update** and the **Course** is to distinguish this method with a similar operation, **UpdateCourse()**, in our Web Service. These two directives must not be enclosed by a pair of <%...%> symbols.
B. Starting from step **B**, the following codes will be Java codes to be embedded into this page; thus, an opening symbol **<%** is used to start this part. Since the Web operation **UpdateCourse()** in our Web Service returns a Boolean result, to hold it, a Boolean variable **res** is created and initialized first.
C. To set up an updated course record that contains six pieces of updated course information, seven system methods, **getParameter()**, are used to pick up each piece of updated course information (including **course_id**) from the related

```
   .........
   public boolean Update_Course(String[] upCourse){
A      boolean update = false;
       ArrayList al = new ArrayList();
B      al.clear();
C      al.add(0, upCourse[0]);        // faculty_name
       al.add(1, upCourse[1]);        // course_name
       al.add(2, upCourse[2]);        // credit
       al.add(3, upCourse[3]);        // classroom
       al.add(4, upCourse[4]);        // schedule
       al.add(5, upCourse[5]);        // enrollment
       al.add(6, upCourse[6]);        // course_id
D      try{
         org.ws.sql.WSCourse_Service service = new org.ws.sql.WSCourse_Service();
         org.ws.sql.WSCourse port = service.getWSCoursePort();
E        update = port.updateCourse(al);
F        if (!update)
           System.out.println("The data updating is failed!");
       }
G      catch (Exception e) {
         System.out.println("Error in Updating Statement! " + e.getMessage());
         return false;
       }
H      return update;
     }
```

Fig. 9.112 The added codes for the Update_Course() method in the Java bean

TextField in our client page, **Course.jsp**, and assign each of them to a local String variable.

D. Then a String[] array is created and initialized with those seven local variables (keep **course_id** with no change) to make an updated course record ready to be sent to the Java bean class in the next step.
E. The **Update_Course()** method that will be defined in our Java bean class is executed with the initialized String[] as the argument. The running result of this method is returned and assigned to our local Boolean variable **res**.
F. If a **false** is returned, which means that the execution of this method failed, then the client page, **Course.jsp**, is refreshed to make it ready for the next operation.
G. Otherwise the running of that method is successful, and the selected course record has been updated in the **Course** table in our sample database; thus, all TextFields in the client page will be reset to null to recover them to show the original record.

Next let's handle the coding process in our Java bean class file **CourseQuery.java**. Double click on this file from the **Projects** window, exactly under the folder, **Source Packages\JavaWeb DBJSPSQLPackage**, to open it and enter the codes shown in Fig. 9.112 into the bottom of this file. Let's have a closer look at this piece of codes to see how it works.

A. Two local variables, **update** and **al**, are generated first. The former is a Boolean variable used to hold the running result of execution of our Web Service operation, **UpdateCourse()**, and the latter is an instance of the ArrayList class, which is used to store seven pieces of information for an updated course record.
B. The ArrayList instance **al** is cleaned up by using the **clear()** method to make sure that the **al** is empty before it can be used to store any data.

C. A sequence of **add()** methods is used to add all six pieces of updated course information (including **course_id**) into the ArrayList instance **al**, which will be passed as an argument for our Web Service operation **UpdateCourse()** later.
D. A **try-catch** block is used to call our Web operation **UpdateCourse()** to update a selected course record in our sample database via our Web service. First a new Web service instance **service** is created based on our Web service class **WSCourse_Service**. Then the **getWSCoursePort()** method is executed to get the current port used by our Web service. This port is returned and assigned to a new Port instance **port**.
E. The Web Service operation **UpdateCourse()** is executed with an argument **al** that contains all pieces of updated course information, and the running result is returned and assigned to the local Boolean variable **update**.
F. If the returned Boolean value is **false**, which means that this data updating action failed, a system method **println()** is used to indicate this situation. Otherwise this data updating is successful.
G. The **catch** block is used to monitor and check any possible exception during this data updating process. A **false** is returned to the calling program if any error really occurred.
H. Otherwise a **true** is returned to indicate the success of this data updating action.

Now we have finished all coding jobs for this course updating action. Let's build and run our client project to consume our Web Service to update a selected course record in the **Course** table in our sample database.

Prior to building and running our client project, make sure that our Web Service project **WebServiceCourse** has been built and deployed successfully.

Perform the following operations to build and run our client project **WebClientCourse**:

1) Click on the **Clean and Build Main Project** button to build our project, and exactly build our Java bean class file **CourseQuery.java**.
2) Right click on our client page **Course.jsp** from the **Projects** window, and select the **Compile File** item to compile this page.
3) Right click on our transaction page **CourseProcess.jsp** from the **Projects** window, and select the **Compile File** item to compile this page.
4) Right click on our client page **Course.jsp** from the **Projects** window, and select the **Run File** item to run our client project.

As the course page is opened, enter a valid faculty name, such as **Ying Bai**, into the Faculty Name box, and then click on the **Select** button to query all courses (**course_id**) taught by this faculty. All five courses (**course_id**) should have been retrieved from our database and displayed in the CourseList box.

Now let's test to update an existing course record, **CSE-565**, from the **Course** table in our sample database. Keep the selected faculty member, **Ying Bai**, with no change, and click on the course **CSE-565** from the CourseList box to select it, and click on the **Select** button by two times to get details about this course. Then enter

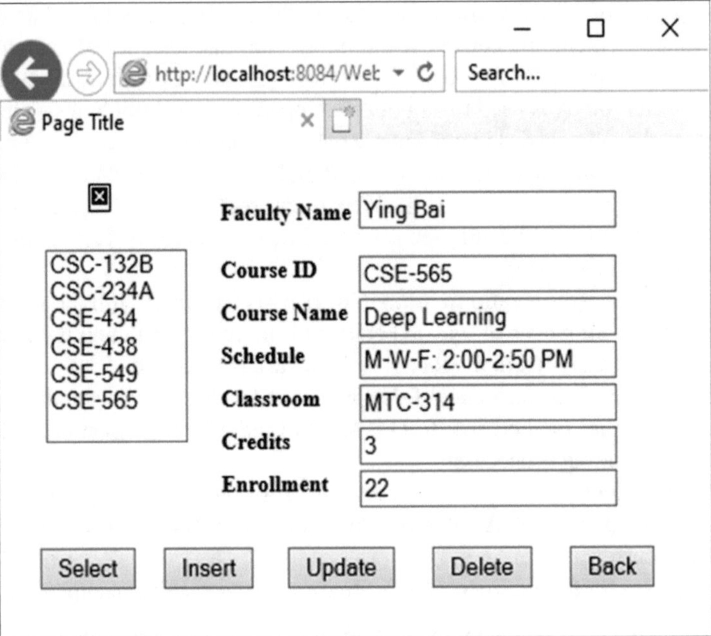

Fig. 9.113 The updated result for course CSE-565

the following five pieces of information as an updated course record into the six related TextFields in this course page:

- Course Name: **Deep Learning**
- Schedule: **M-W-F: 2:00 – 2:50 PM**
- Classroom: **MTC-314**
- Credit: **3**
- Enrollment: **22**
- Faculty Name: **Ying Bai**

Now click on the **Update** button to try to update this course record from the **Course** table in our sample database **CSE_DEPT**. If this updating action is successful, the client page is refreshed to clean up all contents on each TextField.

To check and confirm this data updating, just click on the **Select** button to retrieve all courses (**course_id**) taught by the selected faculty member **Ying Bai**. One can find that the course, **CSE-565**, has been updated and its result is displayed in the CourseList box, as shown in Fig. 9.113.

Select this updated course from this CourseList box by clicking on it, and then click on the **Select** button by two times; the details about this updated course are displayed in six TextFields, as shown in Fig. 9.113. Click on the **Back** button to close our project.

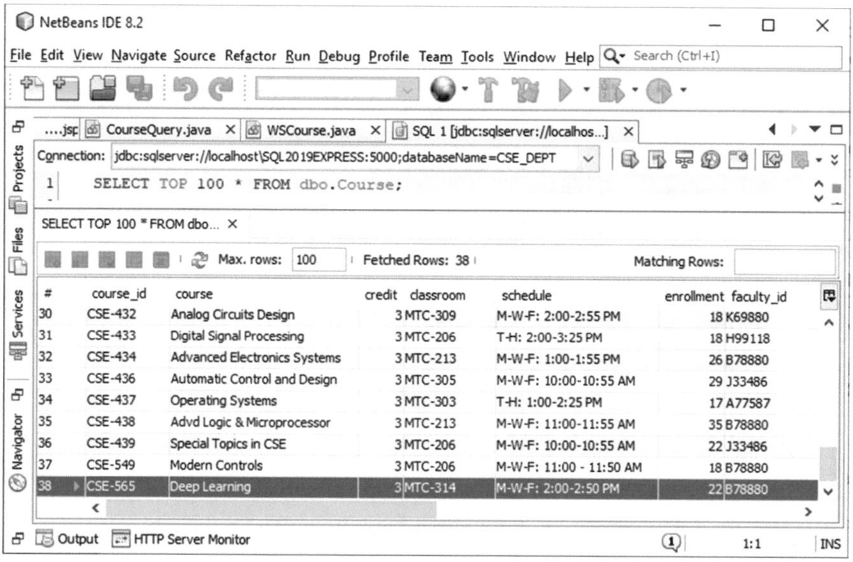

Fig. 9.114 The updated course CSE-565 in the Course table

Another way to confirm this data updating is to open the **Course** table via the **Services** window in the NetBeans IDE. After opening the **Services** window, expand the **Databases** icon, and connect to our sample database by right clicking on our database URL. Select the **Connect** item, and enter the password, **Happy2020**, to connect to our sample database. After connection, expand the **URL\CSE_DEPT.dbo\Tables**. Right click on the **Course** table, and select the **View Data** item to open this table. One can find that the course **CSE-565** is really updated in this **Course** table, and exactly it is located at the bottom line that has been highlighted, as shown in Fig. 9.114.

Next let's build and develop the codes for our client project to access our Web Service to delete a selected course in our **Course** table.

9.16.9 Build Our Client Project to Delete Course Records via Our Web Service

Now let's build the codes for the **Delete** button in our client project, exactly in the client page **Course.jsp**, to delete a course record via our Web Service. The main coding jobs are still concentrated on two files, the transaction page **CourseProcess.jsp** and our Java bean class file **CourseQuery.java**. Let's first take care of the coding development for the transaction page **CourseProcess.jsp**.

```
  .........
  else if (request.getParameter("Delete")!= null) {
    //process the course record deleting
    %>
A   <jsp:useBean id="Delete_Course" scope="session" class="JavaWebDBJSPSQLPackage.CourseQuery" />
    <jsp:setProperty name="Delete_Course" property="*" />
    <%
B   boolean res = false;
C   String cid = request.getParameter("CourseIDField");
D       res = cQuery.Delete_Course(cid);
E       if (!res)
          response.sendRedirect("Course.jsp");
F       else {
          session.setAttribute("CourseIDField", null);
          session.setAttribute("CourseNameField", null);
          session.setAttribute("CreditField", null);
          session.setAttribute("ClassroomField", null);
          session.setAttribute("ScheduleField", null);
          session.setAttribute("EnrollmentField", null);
          }
      }
  else if (request.getParameter("Back")!= null) {
      //process the course record deleting
   }
```

Fig. 9.115 The codes for the Delete Course block in the CourseProcess.jsp page

The main function of this piece of codes is to coordinate the deleting query and provide a valid interface between the client page and the Java bean to make that query smoother.

Double click on this page from the **Projects** window to open it, and enter the codes shown in Fig. 9.115 into this page, exactly into the **else if (request. getParameter("Delete")!= null)** block.

Let's have a closer look at this piece of codes to see how it works.

A. Two JSP directives are declared first, and they are used to set up the Java bean, session, class, and property used on this JSP page. The **Delete_Course()** method will be built in our Java bean class later, and the underscore between the **Delete** and the **Course** is to distinguish this method with a similar operation, **DeleteCourse()**, in our Web Service. These two directives must not be enclosed by a pair of <%...%> symbols.
B. Starting from step **B**, the following codes will be Java codes to be embedded into this page; thus, an opening symbol **<%** is used to start this part. Since our Web operation **DeleteCourse()** in our Web Service returns a Boolean result, to hold it, a Boolean variable **res** is created and initialized first.
C. To set up a course record that will be deleted from the **Course** table in our sample database, a system method, **getParameter()**, is used to pick up the selected **course_id** that is related to a course record to be deleted from the related TextField in our client page, **Course.jsp**, and assign it to a local String variable **cid**.
D. The **Delete_Course()** method that will be defined in our Java bean class is executed with the initialized **cid** as the argument. The running result of this method is returned and assigned to our local Boolean variable **res**.

```
   .........
   public boolean Delete_Course(String dCourse){
A      boolean delete = false;
B      try{
          org.ws.sql.WSCourse_Service service = new org.ws.sql.WSCourse_Service();
          org.ws.sql.WSCourse port = service.getWSCoursePort();
C         delete = port.deleteCourse(dCourse);
D         if (!delete)
            System.out.println("The data deleting is failed!");
       }
E      catch (Exception e) {
          System.out.println("Error in Deleting Statement! " + e.getMessage());
          return false;
       }
F      return delete;
   }
```

Fig. 9.116 The added codes for the Delete_Course() method in the Java bean

E. If a **false** is returned, which means that the execution of this method failed, then the client page, **Course.jsp**, is refreshed to make it ready for the next operation.
F. Otherwise the running of that method is successful, and the selected course record has been deleted from the **Course** table in our sample database; thus, all TextFields in the client page will be reset to null to recover them to show the original record.

Next let's handle the coding process for our Java bean class file **CourseQuery.java**. Double click on this file from the **Projects** window, exactly under the folder, **Source Packages\JavaWeb DBJSPSQLPackage**, to open it and enter the codes shown in Fig. 9.116 into the bottom of this file. Let's have a closer look at this piece of codes to see how it works.

A. A local Boolean variable, **delete**, is generated first and it is used to hold the running result of execution of our Web Service operation, **DeleteCourse()**, later.
B. A **try-catch** block is used to call our Web operation **DeleteCourse()** to delete a selected course record from our sample database via our Web service. First a new Web service instance **service** is created based on our Web service class **WSCourse_Service**. Then the **getWSCoursePort()** method is executed to get the current port used by our Web service. This port is returned and assigned to a new Port instance **port**.
C. The Web Service operation **DeleteCourse()** is executed with a String argument **dCourse** that is a valid **course_id**, which is related to a course record to be deleted from our database.
D. If the returned Boolean value is **false**, which means that this data deleting action failed, a system method **println()** is used to indicate this situation. Otherwise this data deleting is successful.
E. The **catch** block is used to monitor and check any possible exception during this data deleting process. A **false** is returned to the calling program if any error really occurred.
F. Otherwise a **true** is returned to indicate the success of this data deleting action.

Now we have finished all coding jobs for this course deleting action. Let's build and run our client project to consume our Web Service to delete a selected course record from the **Course** table in our sample database.

Prior to building and running our client project, make sure that our Web Service project **WebServiceCourse** has been built and deployed successfully.

Perform the following operations to build and run our client project **WebClientCourse**:

1) Click on the **Clean and Build Main Project** button to build our project, and exactly build our Java bean class file **CourseQuery.java**.
2) Right click on our client page **Course.jsp** from the **Projects** window, and select the **Compile File** item to compile this page.
3) Right click on our transaction page **CourseProcess.jsp** from the **Projects** window, and select the **Compile File** item to compile this page.
4) Right click on our client page **Course.jsp** from the **Projects** window, and select the **Run File** item to run our client project.

As the course page is opened, enter a valid faculty name, such as **Ying Bai**, into the Faculty Name box, and then click on the **Select** button to query all courses (**course_id**) taught by this faculty. All five courses (**course_id**) should have been retrieved from our database and displayed in the CourseList box.

Now let's test to delete an existing course record, **CSE-565**, from the **Course** table in our sample database. Keep the selected faculty member, **Ying Bai**, with no change, and click on the course **CSE-565** from the CourseList box to select it; click on the **Select** button by two times to get details about this course. Then click on the **Delete** button to try to remove this course record from the **Course** table in our sample database.

To confirm or test this data deleting action, keep the selected faculty member **Ying Bai** with no change, and click on the **Select** button again to try to retrieve back all courses (**course_id**) taught by this faculty. Immediately one can find that all five courses (**course_id**) are returned and displayed in the CourseList box without course **CSE-565**, as shown in Fig. 9.117. This is an evidence that our course **CSE-565** has been deleted successfully from the Course table in our sample database.

One can also open the **Course** table in our sample database **CSE_DEPT** by opening the **Services** window in the NetBeans IDE environment. The course **CSE-565** cannot be found from this table, which means that it has been deleted from this **Course** table.

It is highly recommended to recover any deleted record to keep our database clean and neat. An easy way to do this recovery job is to perform another inserting action via the **Insert** button on our client page to get this course record to be inserted into this **Course** table. Refer to course details displayed in six TextFields shown in Fig. 9.117 to do this recovery job.

Click on the **Back** button to exit our client project.

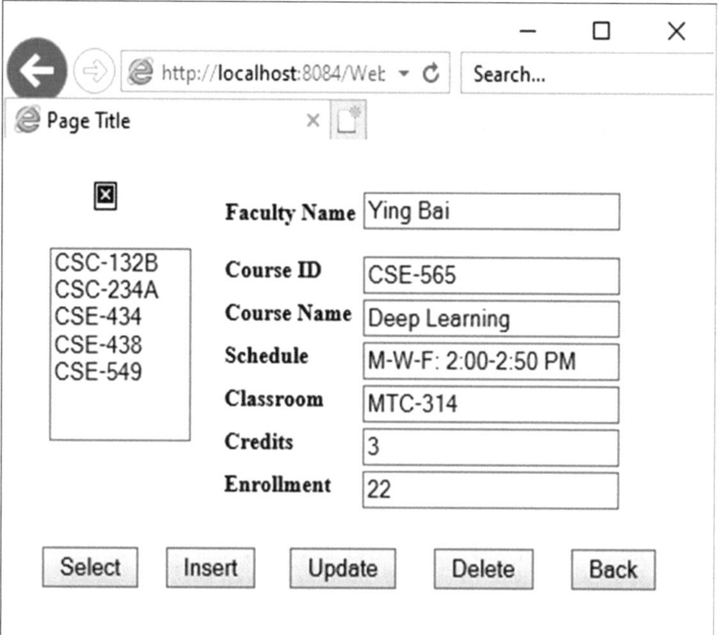

Fig. 9.117 The running and testing result of deleting a course record

9.17 Chapter Summary

A detailed discussion and analysis of the structure and components about Java Web services are provided in this chapter. Two popular Java Web services, REST-Based and SOAP-Based services, are discussed in detail with real projects. The procedure of building a typical SOAP-Based Web service project is introduced with a real project example.

At Sect. 9.3, an example testing SOAP-Based Web Service project, **WSTest**, is discussed and analyzed to provide users a completed picture with detailed procedure to illustrate how to build, deploy, and consume a Web Service project step by step.

Starting Sect. 9.5, some typical SOAP-Based Web service projects, such as **WebServiceSQLApp** and **WebServiceCourse** that are used to access and manipulate data against a SQL Server 2019 database, are discussed and analyzed in detail with some real project examples.

To consume these kinds of Web services, eight real client projects are developed and built with detailed coding processes and illustrations:

- **WinClientSelect**: a Window-Based Web client project to consume the Web service **WebServiceSQLApp** to perform data query to the **Faculty** table in our sample SQL Server 2019 Express database

- **WinClientInsert**: a Window-Based Web client project to consume the Web service **WebServiceSQLApp** to perform data insertion actions to the **Faculty** table in our SQL Server 2019 Express sample database
- **WinClientUpdtDelt**: a Window-Based Web client project to consume the Web service **WebServiceSQLApp** to perform data updating and deleting actions to the Faculty table in our sample SQL Server 2019 Express database
- **WebClientSelect**: a Web-Based Web client project to consume the Web service **WebServiceSQLApp** to perform data query to the **Faculty** table in our sample SQL Server 2019 Express database
- **WebClientInsert**: a Web-Based Web client project to consume the Web service **WebServiceSQLApp** to perform data insertion actions to the **Faculty** table in our sample SQL Server 2019 Express database
- **WebClientUpdtDelt**: a Web-Based Web client project to consume the Web service **WebServiceSQLApp** to perform data updating and deleting actions to the **Faculty** table in our sample SQL Server 2019 Express database
- **WinClientCourse**: a Window-Based Web client project to consume the Web service **WebServiceCourse** to perform data query and manipulations to the **Course** table in our sample SQL Server 2019 Express database
- **WebClientCourse**: a Web-Based Web client project to consume the Web service **WebServiceCourse** to perform data query and manipulations to the **Course** table in our sample SQL Server 2019 Express database

All of these real projects have been tested and debugged and can be used without modifications. To use these project examples, one needs to install

- Glassfish v4.1.1 Web application server
- Microsoft SQL Server 2019 Express database
- Microsoft SQL Server Management Studio 18
- Microsoft SQL Server JDBC Driver

All of these software tools and drivers can be downloaded and installed on the users' computer with free of charge. Refer to Appendices to finish these downloading and installation processes.

Homework

I. <u>True/False Selections</u>

____1. Unlike Java Web applications, the Java Web Services provide an automatic way to search, identify, and return the desired information required by the user through a set of methods installed in the Web server.

____2. Java Web services provide graphic user interfaces (GUIs) to enable users to access the Web services via the Internet.

____3. Web Services can be considered as a set of methods installed in a Web server and can be called by computer programs installed on the clients through the Internet.

____4. Two popular Java Web services are REST-Based and SOAP-Based services, and both are supported by NetBeans IDE.

____5. Both Web service models, JAX-WS and JAX-RPC, are popular and updated models used in Web service developments.

____6. Compared with REST-Based service, SOAP-based Web services are more suitable for heavyweight applications using complicated operations and for applications requiring sophisticated security and reliability.

____7. Unlike ASP.NET Web services, a Java SOAP-based Web service project is involved in a Java Web application project in which the Web service can be deployed based on an appropriate container.

____8. To access a Web service, one does not have to call any operation defined in the Web service.

____9. Before one can call a Web service operation, a Web service reference must have been established for the client project.

___10. It is unnecessary to update a Web service each time when consuming it in a client project; however, one must deploy that Web service each time when starting it from NetBeans IDE.

II. Multiple Choices

1. In a SOAP-Based Java Web Service, the SOAP means ________________.

   (a) Statement Object Access Protocol
   (b) Simplified Object Access Protocol
   (c) Simple Object Access Protocol
   (d) Structure Object Access Protocol

2. In a REST-Based Java Web Service, the REST means ________________.

   (a) REpresentational State Transfer
   (b) REpresentational State Transmitter
   (c) REpresentational Status Transfer
   (d) Rapid Essential State Transfer

3. When using a REST-Based Web service, only four methods are available: __________.

   (a) INPUT, OUTPUT, POST, and DELETE
   (b) SAVE, PUT, POST, and DELETE
   (c) GET, EXECUTE, POST, and DELETE
   (d) GET, PUT, POST, and DELETE

4. The protocol used in the REST-Based Web services is __________.

   (a) FTP
   (b) XML
   (c) HTTP
   (d) TCP/IP

5. To effectively find, identify, and return the target information required by computer programs, a SOAP-based Web Service needs the following components, ___________.

   (a) XML and WSDL
   (b) SOAP, UDDI and WSDL
   (c) UDDI, XML and SOAP
   (d) WSDL, XML, UDDI and SOAP

6. SOAP is a simple ________-based protocol to help applications developed in different platforms and languages to exchange information over ___________.

   (a) HTML, HTTP
   (b) XML, HTTP
   (c) FTP, TCP/IP
   (d) XML, Internet

7. In WSDL terminology, each Web Service is defined as a ________ and each Web method is defined as an abstract ____________.

   (a) Method, function
   (b) Service, operation
   (c) Endpoint, function
   (d) Port, operation

8. SOAP is used to wrap and pack the data tagged in the ________ format into the messages represented in the ________ protocol.

   (a) XML, SOAP
   (b) HTML, HTTP
   (c) FTP, TCP/IP
   (d) SOAP, XML

9. When building a Java Web service, a ______________ that contains Web container for the ______________ must be built first.

   (a) Web service, Web application
   (b) Web client, Web consuming project
   (c) Web service, Web client project
   (d) Web application, Web service

10. To consume a Web service, a _____________ must be established in the client project.

    (a) Web service reference
    (b) Web service operation
    (c) Web service directory
    (d) All of them

III. Exercises

1. Provide a brief description about the advantages of using a SOAP-Based Web service.
2. Illustrate the structure and components of SOAP-Based Web services.
3. Provide a brief description about procedures of building a typical SOAP-Based Web service project.
4. Provides a brief description about how to establish a Web service reference for a given client project to enable the latter to consume that Web service.
5. Explain the operational sequence of adding a Web service operation into a method in a client project to enable the latter to call that operation.
6. Use the structure shown in Fig. 9.118 to build a Web Service project **WebServiceStudent**, and use the Web Service with Java runtime objects to perform data actions against the **Student** table in our SQL Server 2019 Express database.

   Hint1: Create a new Web Application project **WebServiceStudentApp** first, and then add a Web Service project **WebServiceStudent** into that Web Application project.
   Hint2: Refer to project **WebServiceSQLApp** to complete this project.

7. Develop a Window-based consuming project **WinClientStudentSelect** to consume the Web Service project built in above exercise to access and query data against the **Student** table in our sample SQL Server 2019 Express database.
8. Develop a Window-based consuming project **WinClientStudentInsert** to consume the Web Service project built in above exercise to insert new student records against the **Student** table in our sample SQL Server 2019 Express database.
9. Develop a Web-based consuming project **WebClientStudentSelect** to consume the Web Service project built above to query data from the **Student** table in our sample SQL Server 2019 Express database.

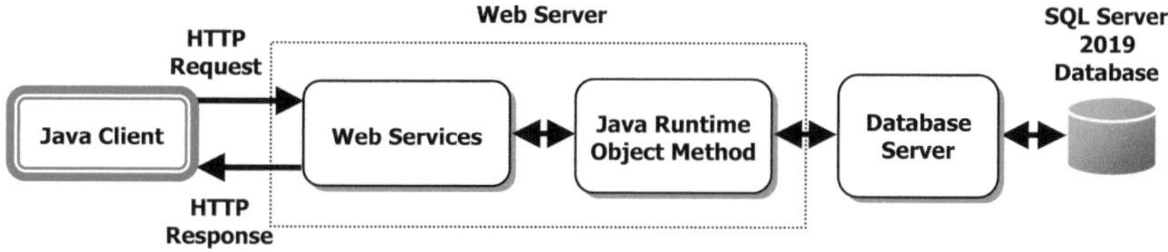

Fig. 9.118 The structure of building a new Web service project

Appendices

Appendix A: Install and Configure SQL Server 2019 Express Database and SQL Server Management Studio

This installation and configuration process is divided into three parts:

- Install SQL Server 2019 Express Database.
- Install SQL Server 2018 Management Studio.
- Configure and Setup SQL Server 2019 Express Connection Parameters.

Install SQL Server 2019 Express Database

1. Go to https://www.microsoft.com/en-us/sql-server/sql-server-downloads to open the Microsoft SQL Server 2019 downloading site, which is shown in Fig. A.1.

Y. Bai, *SQL Server Database Programming with Java*,
https://doi.org/10.1007/978-3-031-06553-8

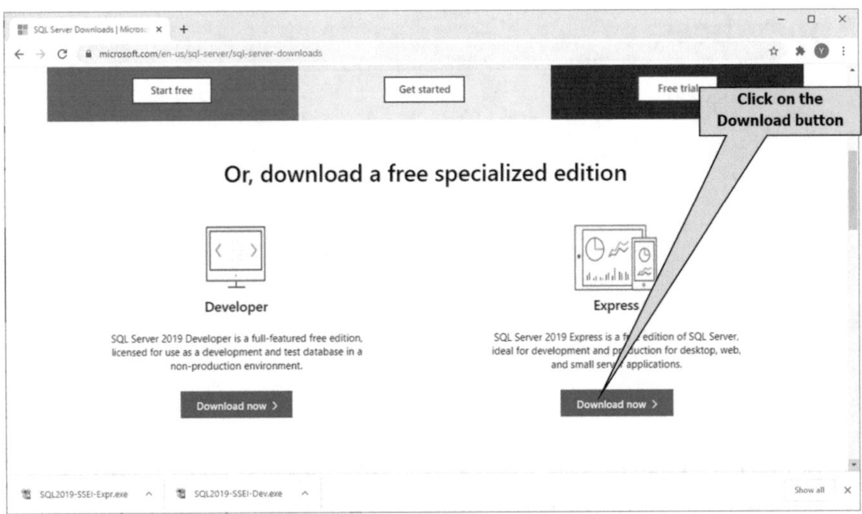

Fig. A.1 The opened downloading page

2. Click the **Download now** button under the **Express** icon to download an .exe file **SQL2019-SSEI-Expr.exe** into your computer or to the **Download** folder. Then double click it to open the Installation wizard (Fig. A.2).

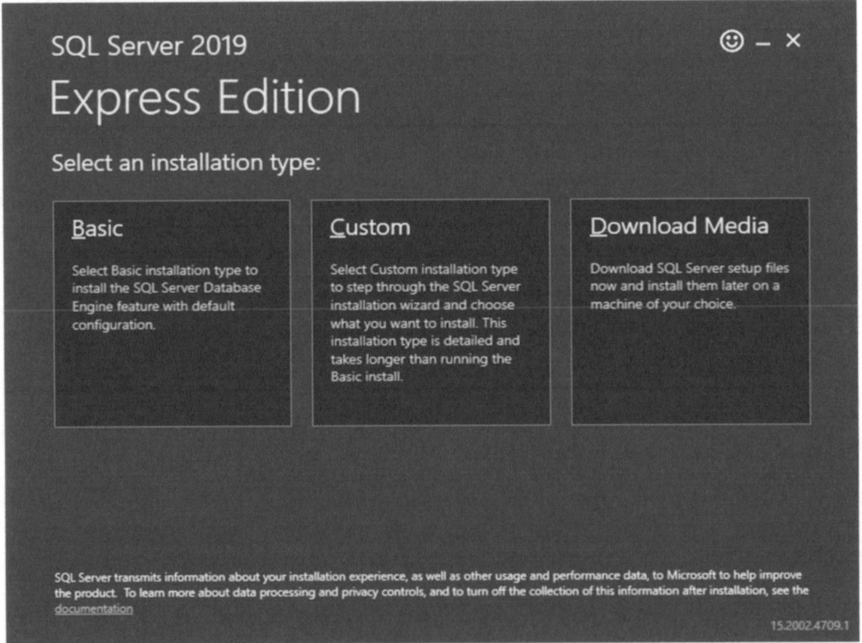

Fig. A.2 The installation option wizard

3. Select the **Custom** box by clicking on it to open the **SQL Server media download target location** page, as shown in Fig. A.3. Click on **Installation** button to begin the installation process.

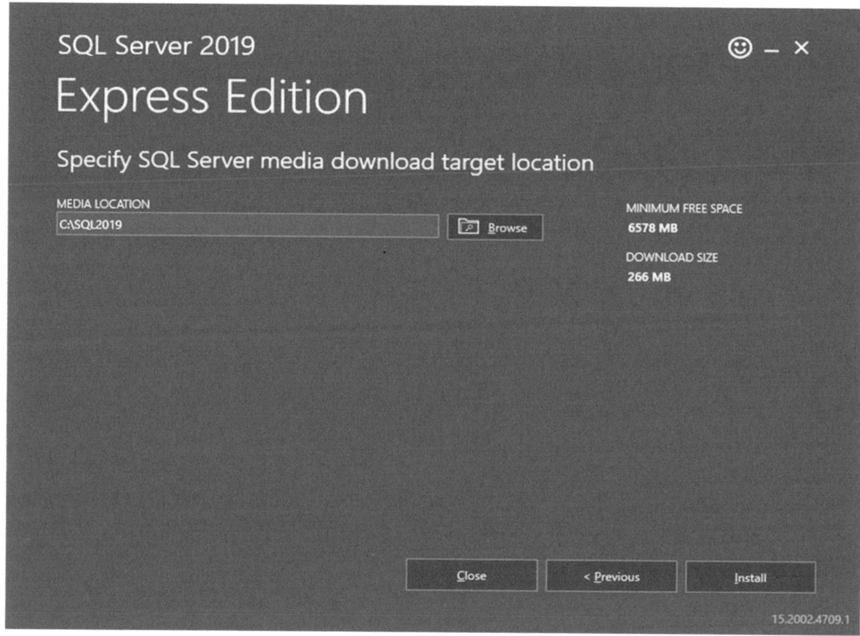

Fig. A.3 The SQL server media download target location page

4. The installation process beings with the file extraction process. An option wizard or the **SQL Server Installation Center** wizard is displayed when the extraction process is done to allow users to select different installations, as shown in Fig. A.4.

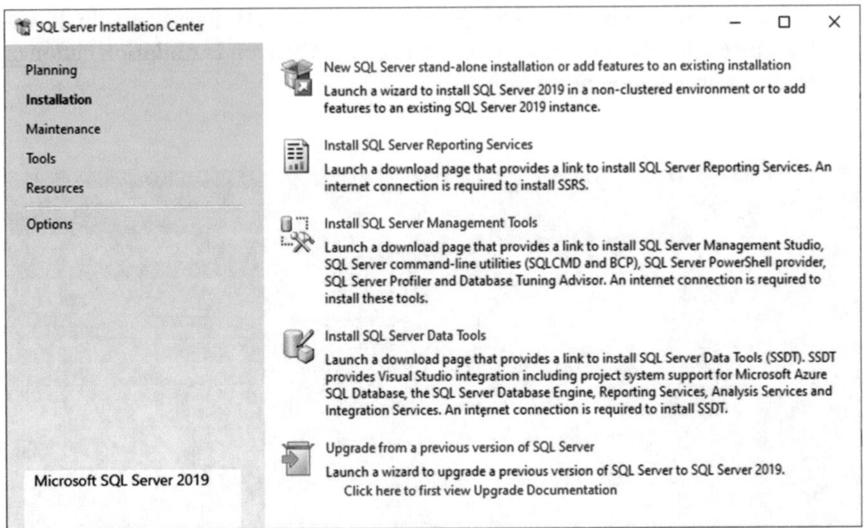

Fig. A.4 The SQL server installation center wizard

5. Click the first item, **New SQL Server standard alone installation**, to install SQL Server 2019 Express database. The **Setup** wizard is displayed, as shown in Fig. A.5.

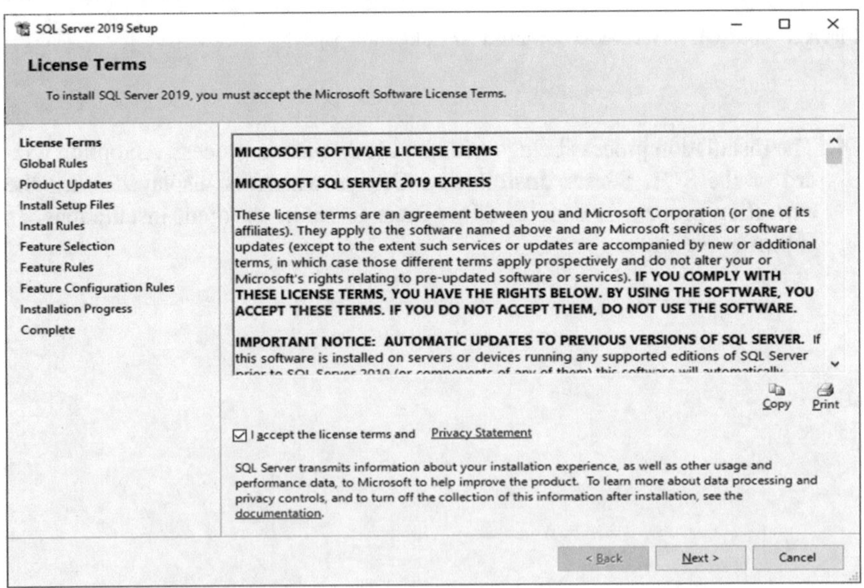

Fig. A.5 The setup wizard

6. Check *I accept the license terms* checkbox and the **Next** button to start this installation.
7. An intermediate system checking results are shown on next page, as shown in Fig. A.6. Click on the **Next** button to continue.

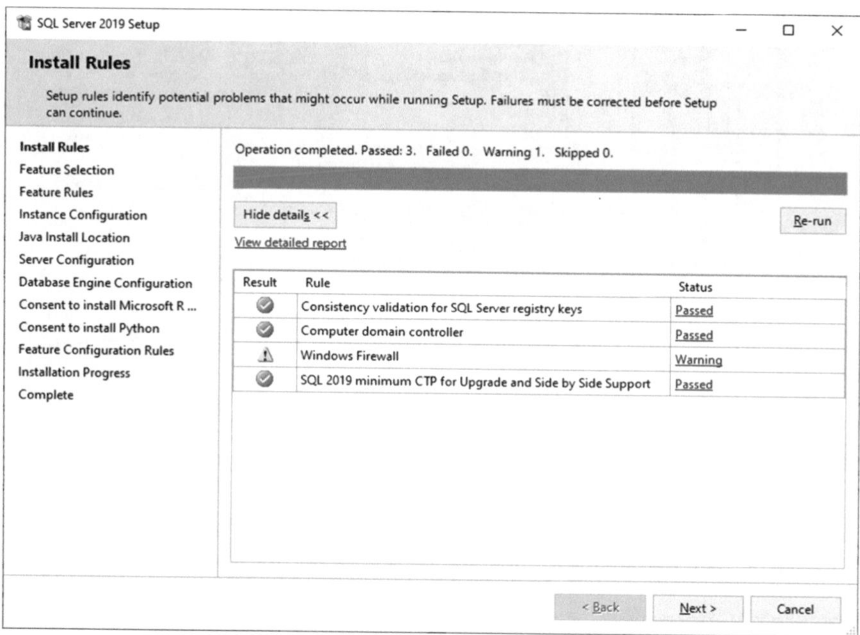

Fig. A.6 The intermediate checking results page

8. On the **Feature Selection** page (Fig. A.7), keep all default items and click the **Next** button.

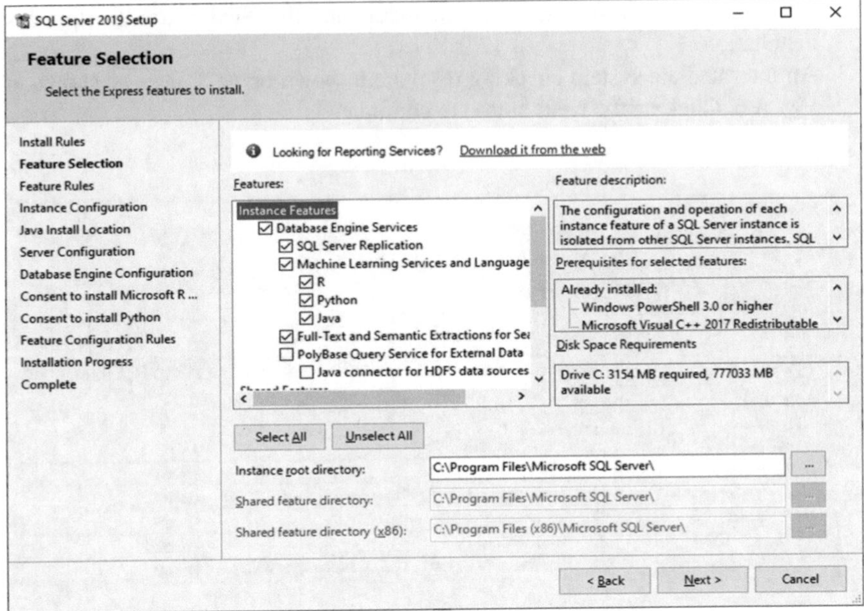

Fig. A.7 The database instance feature selection page

9. In the **Instance Configuration** page (Fig. A.8), enter **SQL2019EXPRESS** into both **Named instance** and **Instance ID** boxes, and click on the **Next** button.

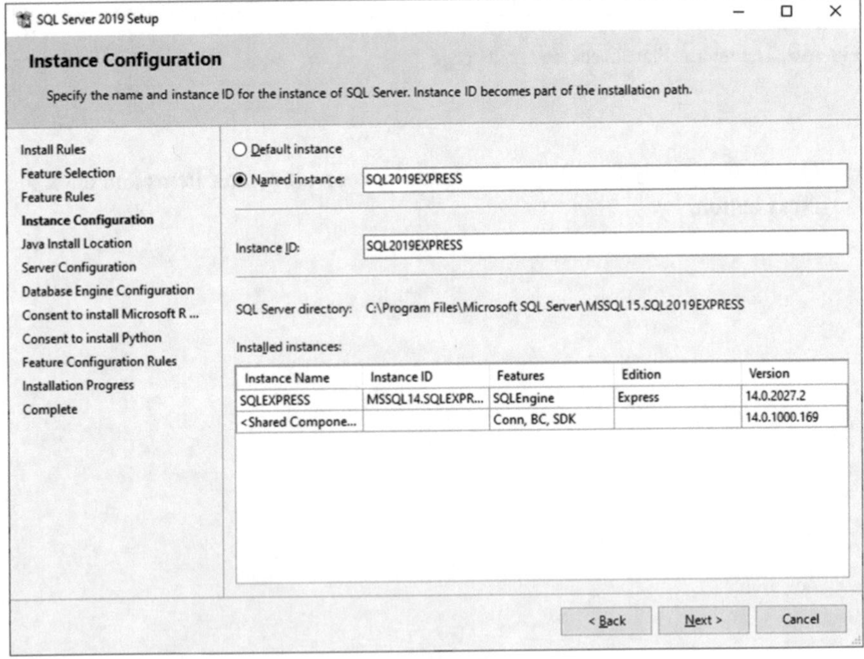

Fig. A.8 The database engine configuration page

10. On the **Java Install Location** page (Fig. A.9), keep default settings and click the **Next** button.

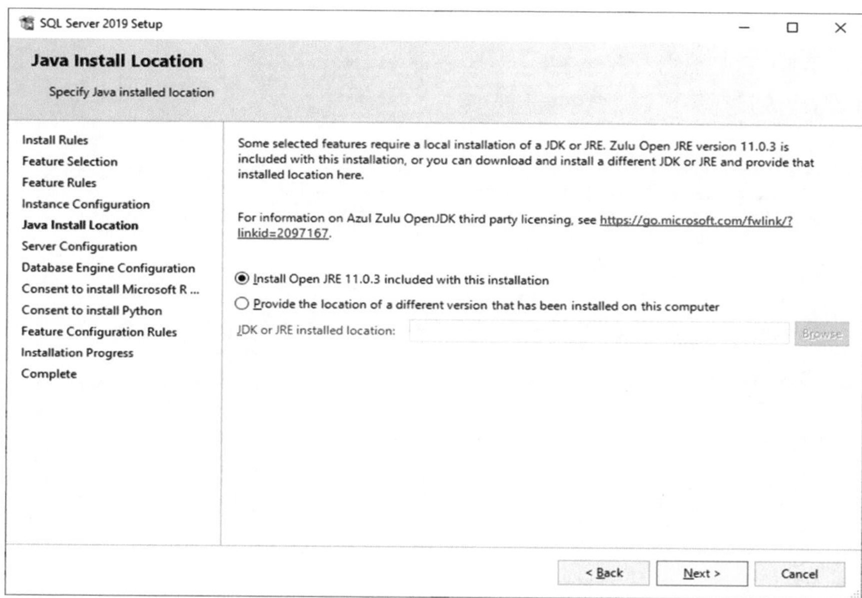

Fig. A.9 The Java install location page

11. On the next page, **Server Configuration** page, click the **Next** button to keep default settings.
12. On the next page, **Database Engine Configuration** page (Fig. A.10), keep default settings and click on the **Next** button to continue.

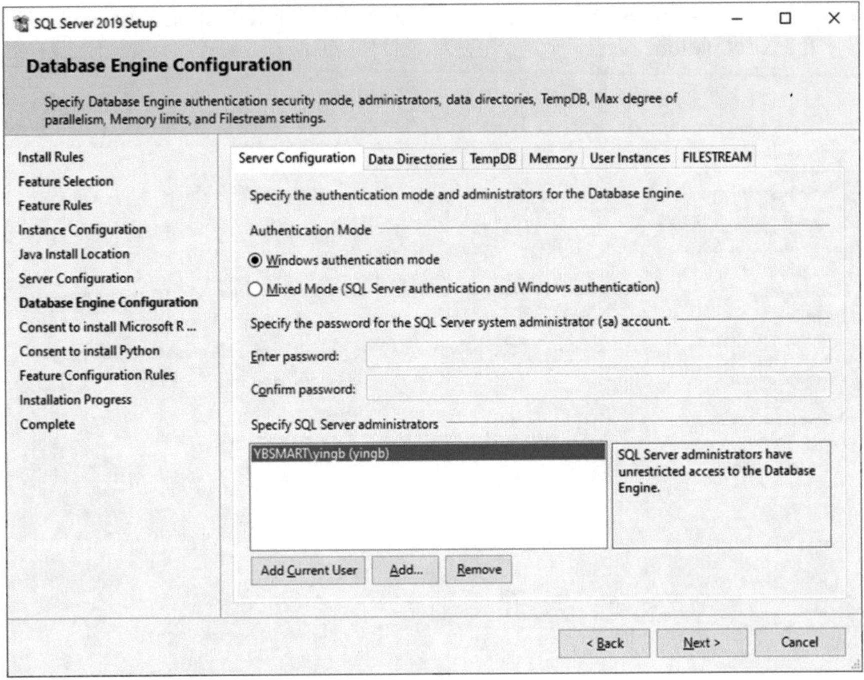

Fig. A.10 Database engine configuration page

13. On the next page, **Content to install Microsoft R Open** page, click on the **Accept** button and the **Next** button to continue.
14. On the next page, **Content to install Python**, just click on the **Accept** and the **Next** button to continue.
15. The Installation process starts, as shown in Fig. A.11.

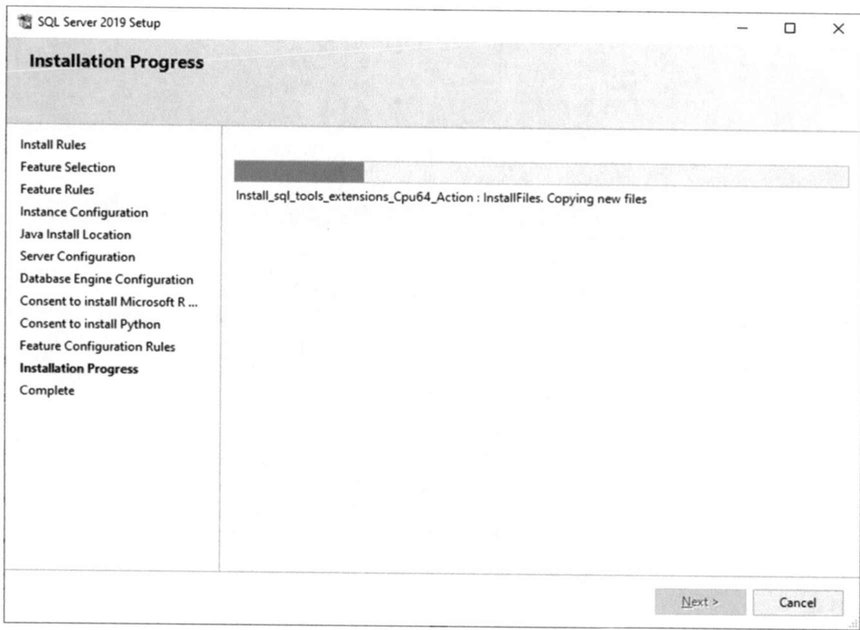

Fig. A.11 The installation process

16. During the installation process, the **Next** button is disabled. This button will be reactivated after the installation is completed.
17. As the installation process is completed, the **Complete** wizard is displayed, as shown in Fig. A.12. Click on the **Close** button to complete this installation process.

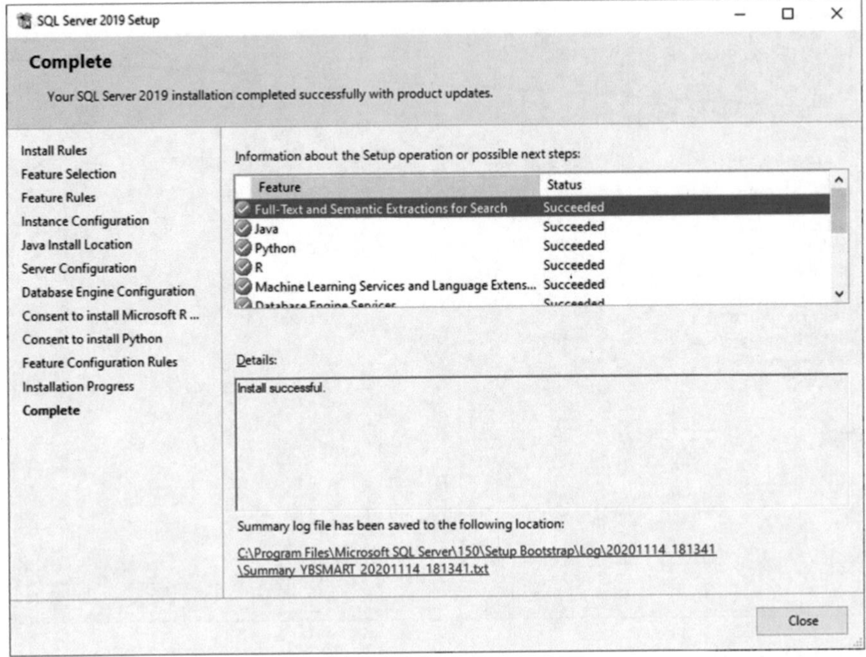

Fig. A.12 The installation is completed

Next, we need to install SQL Server 2018 Management Studio since we need it to access installed SQL Server Express to create, edit, and build our sample database used for this book.

Install SQL Server Management Studio

1. Return to **SQL Server Installation Center** wizard (Fig. A.4), or go to **Start|SQL Server 2019 Installation Center** to open it, select the **Installation** item from the left pane and select the item **Install SQL Server Management Tools** to begin this installation process. A new Web page, which is shown in Fig. A.13, is opened to install SQL Server Management Studio (SSMS).

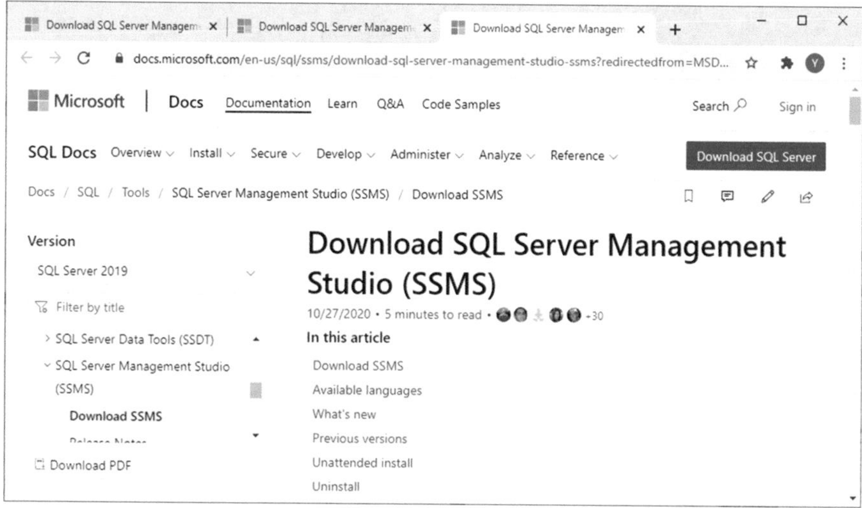

Fig. A.13 Opened Web page to install SSMS 18.7.1

2. Depends on the current version (for our case, the most updated version is SSMS 18.7.1), thus scroll down that page to find a link: **Download SQL Server Management Studio**. Then click that link to download an .exe file, **SSMS-Setup-ENU.exe**. Double click on this executable file to begin to install this SSMS when the downloading process is done.
3. On the opened Installation wizard, click on the **Install** button to start this process, as shown in Fig. A.14. Click the **Close** button when the installation process is done.

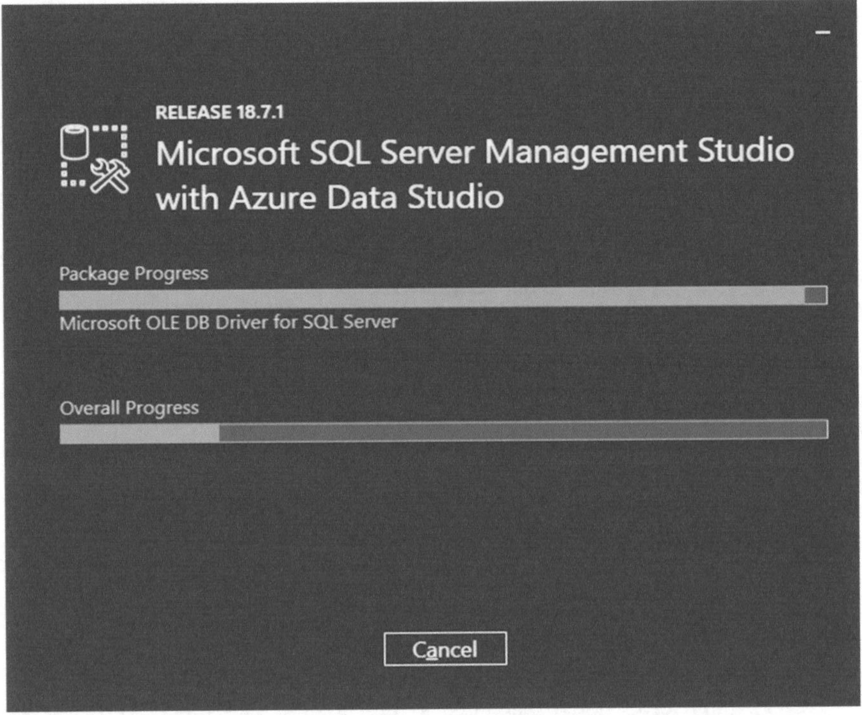

Fig. A.14 The installation processing page

Before we can connect to our installed SQL Server 2019 Express database via SSMS, we need to configure and setup some important parameters.

Configure and Setup SQL Server 2019 Express Connection Parameters

1. Open the **SQL Server 2019 Configuration Manager** by going to item **Start|SQL Server 2019 Configuration Manager** in your computer, as shown in Fig. A.15.

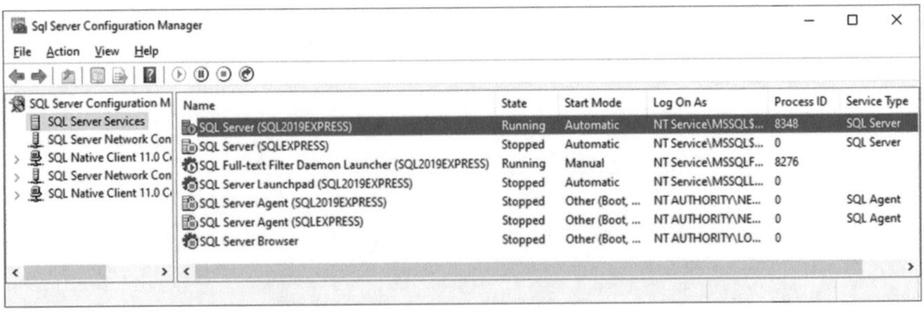

Fig. A.15 Check the port number used by the SQL server

2. Now we need to check the port number used by the SQL Server. In the left pane, select **SQL Server Services** icon, and then select the **SQL Server (SQL2019EXPRESS)** item on the right pane as shown in Fig. A.15. The port number of this SQL Server used is indicated as **Process ID** column. In our case, it is **8348**. Write this number and we will use it later to assign this port to the TCP/IP and Firewall to allow firewall to pass this port.
3. Expand the **SQL Server Network Configuration** icon on the left pane, and click on the **Protocols for SQL2019EXPRESS** item, as shown in Fig. A.16.

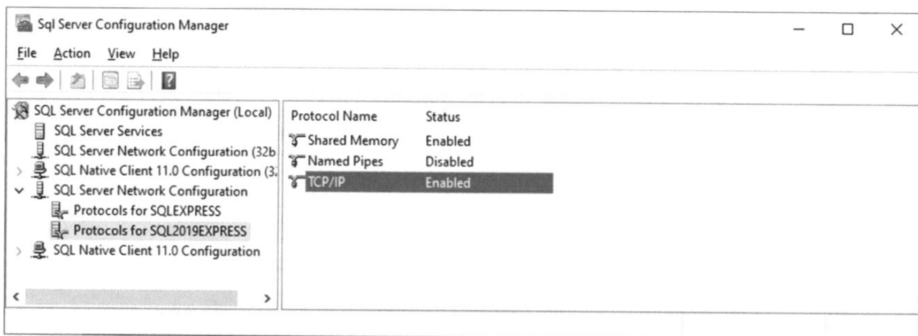

Fig. A.16 The opened SQL server configuration manager wizard

4. On the right pane, right-click on the **TCP/IP** item and select **Enable** to enable the TCP/IP communication protocol for this SQL Server port.
5. Now we need to configure the Firewall installed in your computer to enable it to know this SQL Server and its port. On the **Start** menu, type **WF.msc**, and then press the **Enter** key.
6. In the opened **Windows Defender Firewall with Advanced Security** wizard, from the left pane first click on the **Inbound Rules** icon, and then right-click on this **Inbound Rules** icon again, and then click **New Rule** in the action pane to open the **New Inbound Rule** wizard, as shown in Fig. A.17. Check the **Port** radio button and click on the **Next** button.

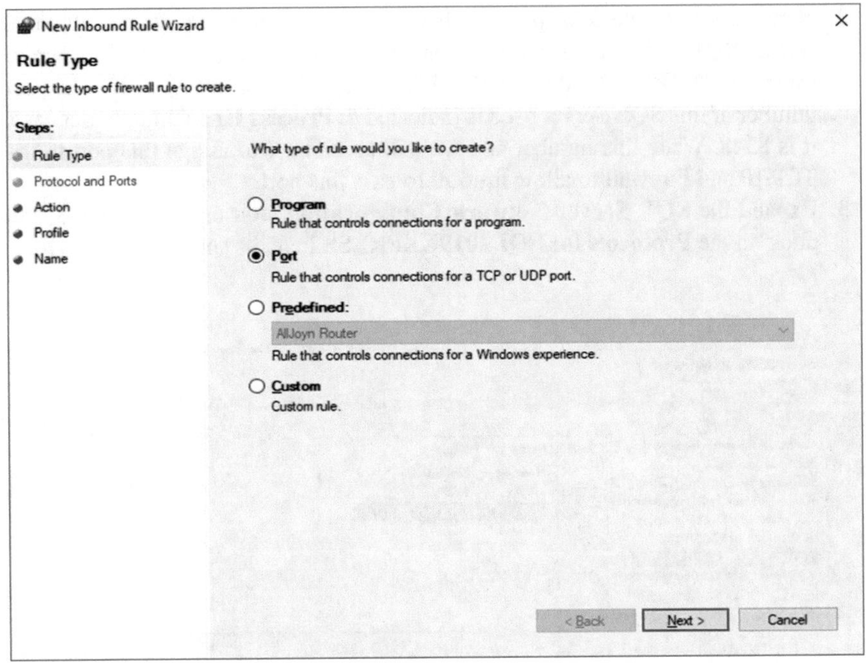

Fig. A.17 The opened new inbound rule wizard

7. On the opened **Protocol and Ports** wizard shown in Fig. A.18, enter **8348** into the **Specific local ports** textbox and click on the **Next** button to go to the next page, **Action** page.

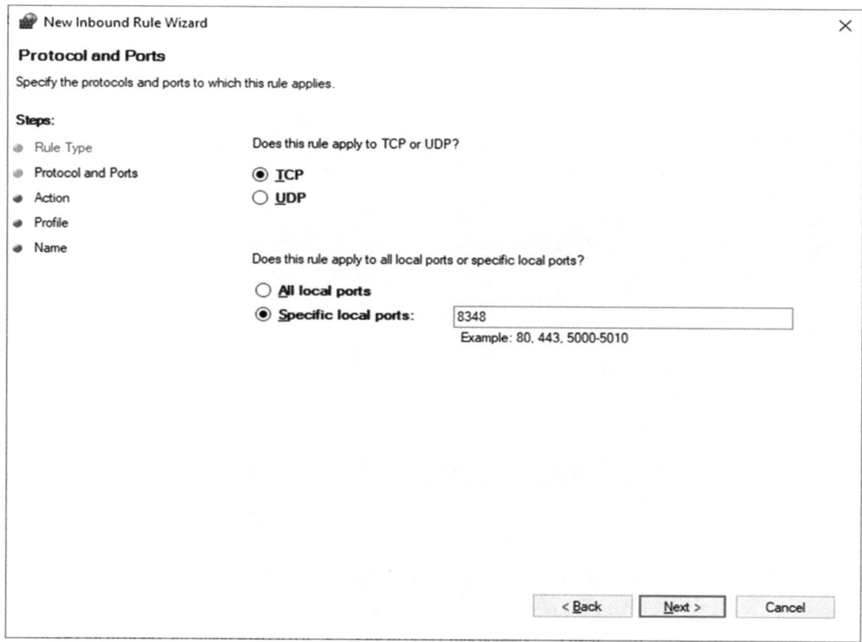

Fig. A.18 The opened protocol and ports wizard

8. In the opened **Action** page, keep the default selection for the radio button, **Allow the connection**, and click on the **Next** button to go the **Profile** page.
9. In the **Profile** page, keep all default settings and click on the **Next** button.
10. In the opened **Name** page (Fig. A.19), enter **SQL Server 2019 Connection** into the **Name** box and click on the **Finish** button to complete this setup.

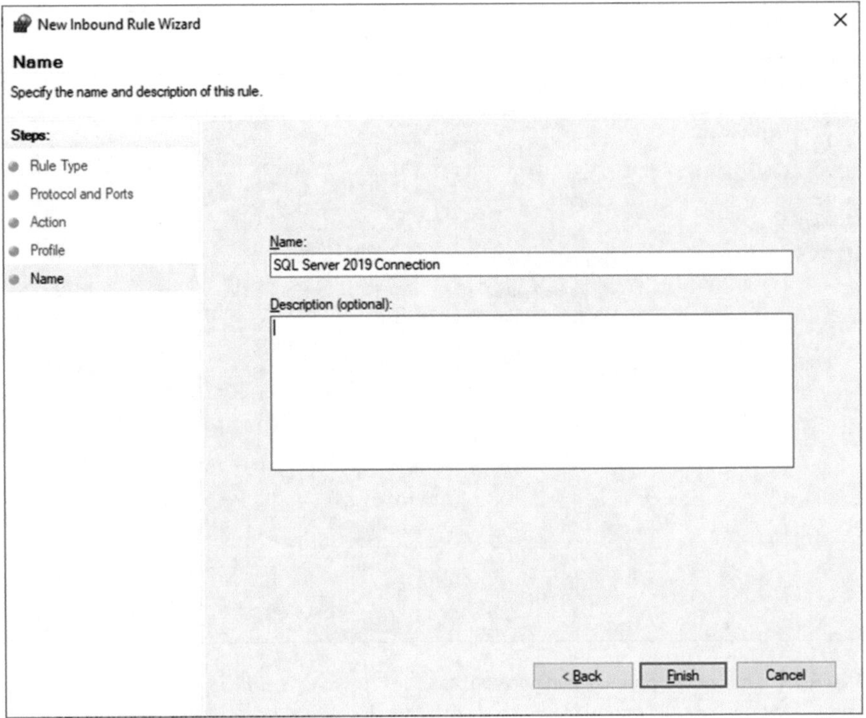

Fig. A.19 The opened name wizard

11. Now you can find that this new rule with the name: **SQL Server 2019 Connection** has been added into this **Inbound Rules** box on the top of that wizard, as shown in Fig. A.20. Now you can close the **Windows Defender Firewall with Advanced Security** wizard and **SQL Server 2019 Configuration Manager** wizard.

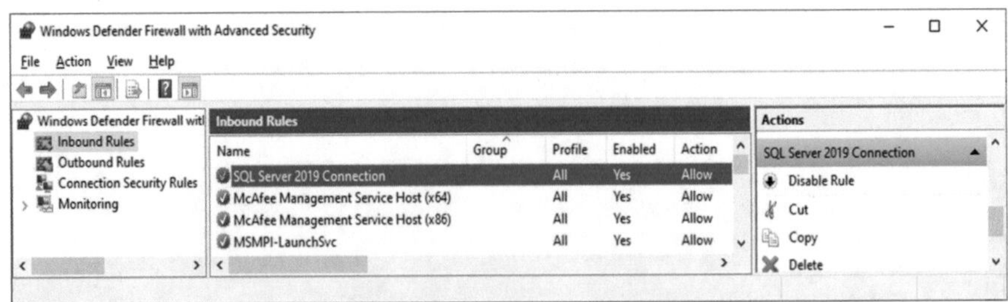

Fig. A.20 The completed inbound rules addition

Before we can test this connection, we need to know the name of your computer in which the SQL Server is installed. The actual situation is: a SQL Server is installed in your computer, but your computer also works as a client to communicate to that SQL Server. Thus both a SQL Server and a client are installed in your single computer; however, we still need the name of your computer to access the Server. In other words, any times when one needs to access a Server installed on a computer, a full name of the Server, which includes both the name of computer and the name of the Server, is needed.

1. Open the Control Panel and go to **System** page to open the **System** wizard, as shown in Fig. A.21.

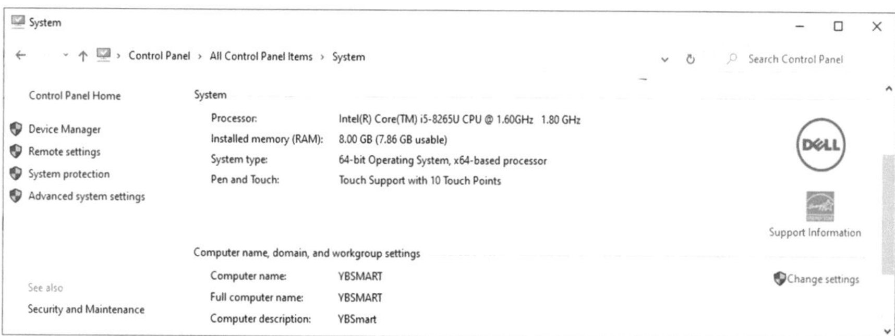

Fig. A.21 The opened system wizard on the control panel

2. You can find the name of your computer in the Computer name group line (Fig. A.21). In our case, it is **YBSmart**.

Now let's test our SQL Server 2019 Express database connection.

Open the Microsoft SQL Server Management Studio from your computer by going to **Start|Microsoft SQL Server Tools 18|Microsoft SQL Server Management Studio 18** menu item. The **Connect to Server** wizard is displayed as shown in Fig. A.22.

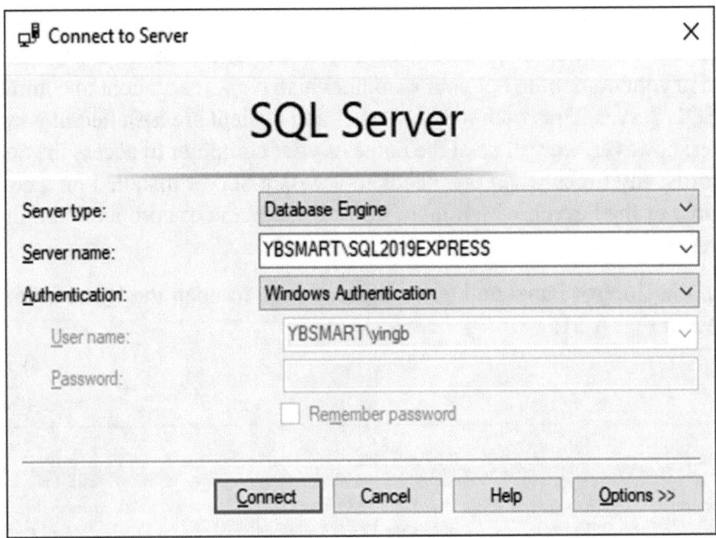

Fig. A.22 The started SQL server 2019 express

Enter the database FULL name **YBSmart\SQL2019Express** into the **Server name** box, and keep the default Windows Authentication and username with no change, as shown in Fig. A.22, and click on the **Connect** button to connect to the database. After the SQL Server is found and connected, all folders related to SQL Server 2019 Express database are displayed, as shown in Fig. A.23.

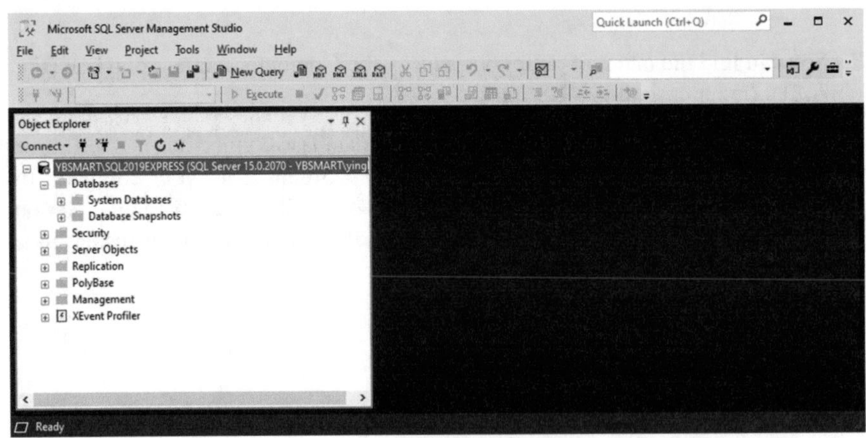

Fig. A.23 The connected SQL server 2019 express database

Our download and install Microsoft SQL Server 2019 Express, and install and configure Microsoft SQL Server Management Studio, is complete. Now you may also close the **SQL Server Installation Center** wizard if you have not done so.

Appendix B: Download and Install JDK 14 and Apache NetBeans 12

Prior to installing Apache NetBeans 12, a Java Development Kits (JDK) must be installed. Go to the link: https://www.oracle.com/java/technologies/javase/jdk14-archive-downloads.html

to install JDK 14.0.1 since this is the most updated version of JDK.

1. On the opened wizard, scroll down to find **Java SE Development Kit 14.0.1**. For most updated cases and applications, one can select to install either JDK 14.0.2 or JDK 14.0.1. Here we are using JDK 14.0.1 as an example to illustrate the installation process.
2. Browse to **Windows x64 Installer** under **Java SE Development Kit 14.0.1** tag, as shown in Fig. B.1, click on that link to begin the downloading process.

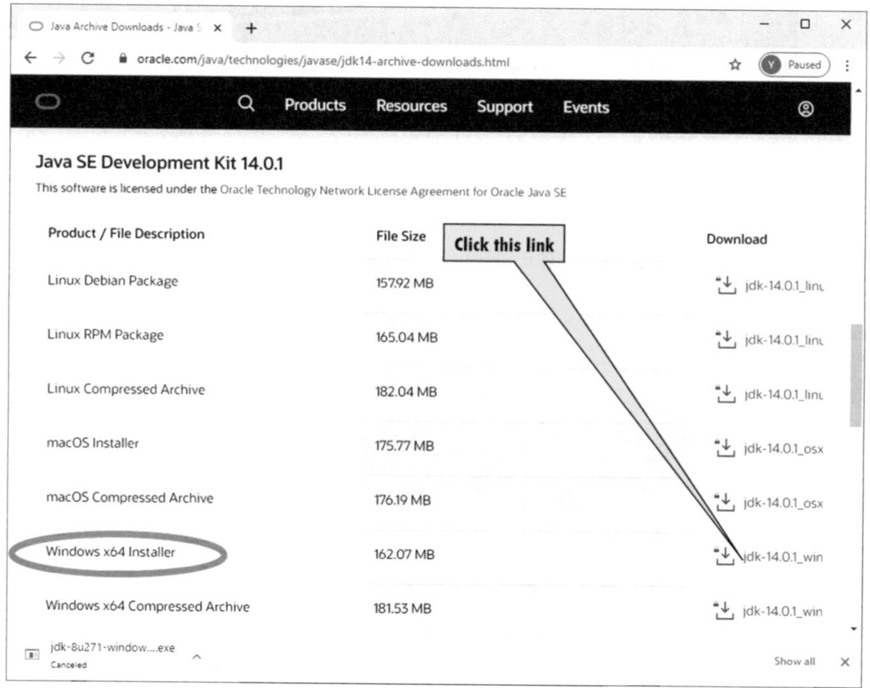

Fig. B.1 The opened Java SE JDK downloading wizard

3. On the next wizard, check the **License Agreement** checkbox and click on the **Download jdk-14.0.1_windows-x64_bin.exe** button to continue.
4. Complete the **LogIn** process on the next wizard. You may need to create a new Oracle account to complete this step. Then the downloading process starts.
5. Double click on the downloaded file when this process is completed to start the JDK 14.0.1 installation process.

6. On the next wizard, click on the **Next** button on the Installation wizard to continue, as shown in Fig. B.2.

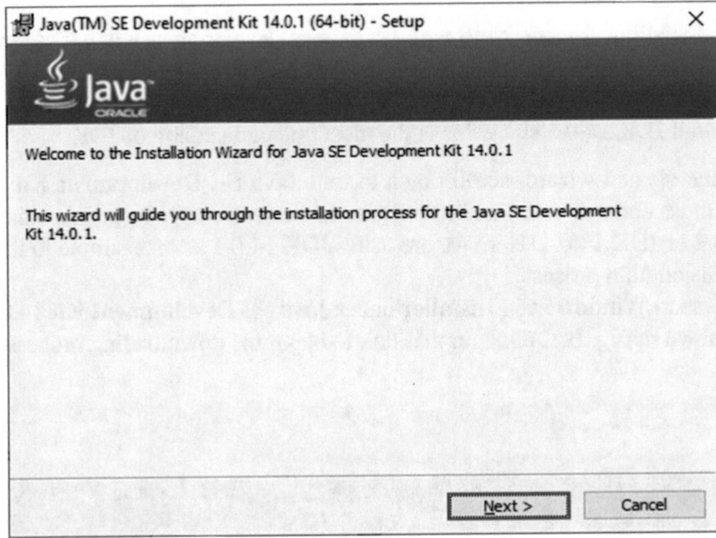

Fig. B.2 The opened Java SE JDK 14.0.1 installation wizard

7. On the next wizard, keep all the default items and default location, and click on the **Next** button again.
8. The installation process starts, as shown in Fig. B.3.

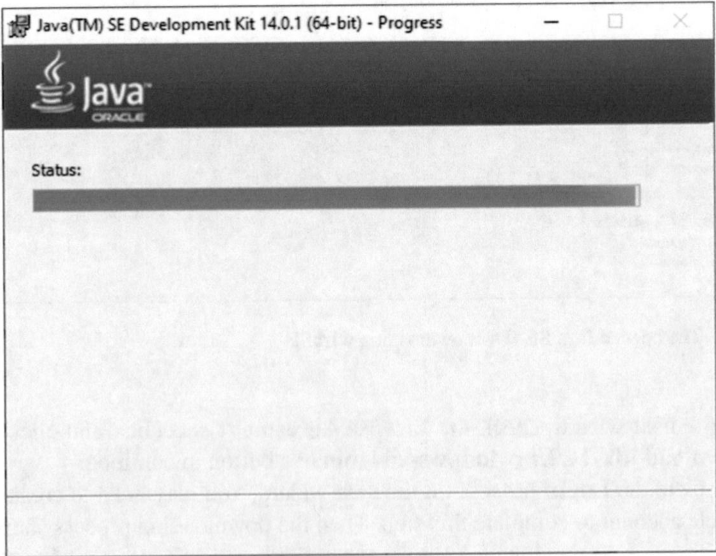

Fig. B.3 The pre-installation process starts

9. When this process is done, click on the **Close** button to complete this installation process.

Now let's start the downloading and installation process for Apache NetBeans 12.

1. Go to link: https://netbeans.apache.org/download/nb120/nb120.html to open the downloading and installing page.
2. Click on the link: Apache-NetBeans-12.0-bin-windows-x64.exe (SHA-512, PGP ASC) to begin this downloading process.
3. Click on the top link, **https://apache.claz.org/netbeans/netbeans/12.0/Apache-NetBeans-12.0-bin-windows-x64.exe**, which is under the **HTTP** tag to start this downloading and installing process (Fig. B.4). It may take a while to complete this downloading due to the large size of the file (358 MB).

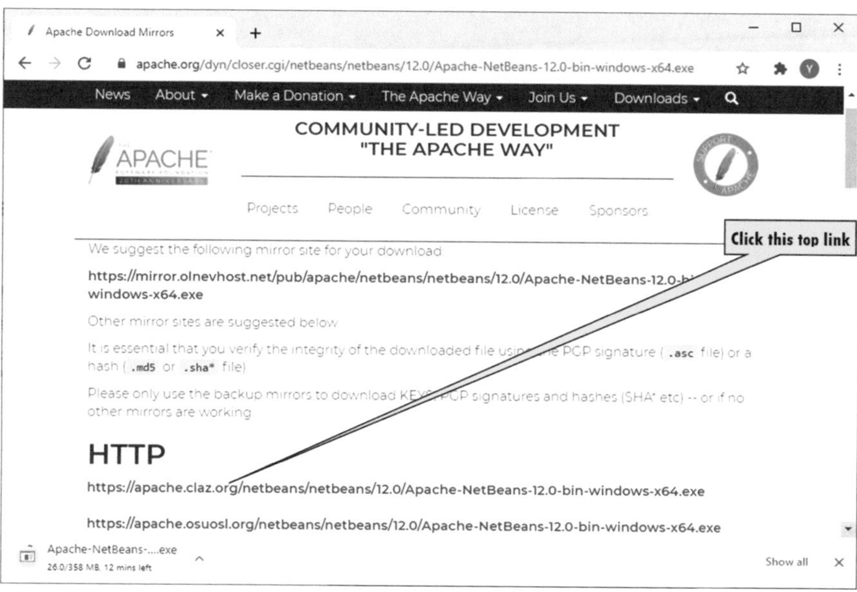

Fig. B.4 The opened wizard for downloading the Apache NetBeans 12

4. When the downloading process is done, double click on it to open the installing wizard. Then click on the **Next** button to keep all default settings with no change and continue this process.
5. Check the License Agreement checkbox and **Next** button to continue.
6. Click on the **Next** button on the next wizard to keep the default location and continue this installation process.
7. Click on the **Install** button on the next wizard to start this installation process, as shown in Fig. B.5.

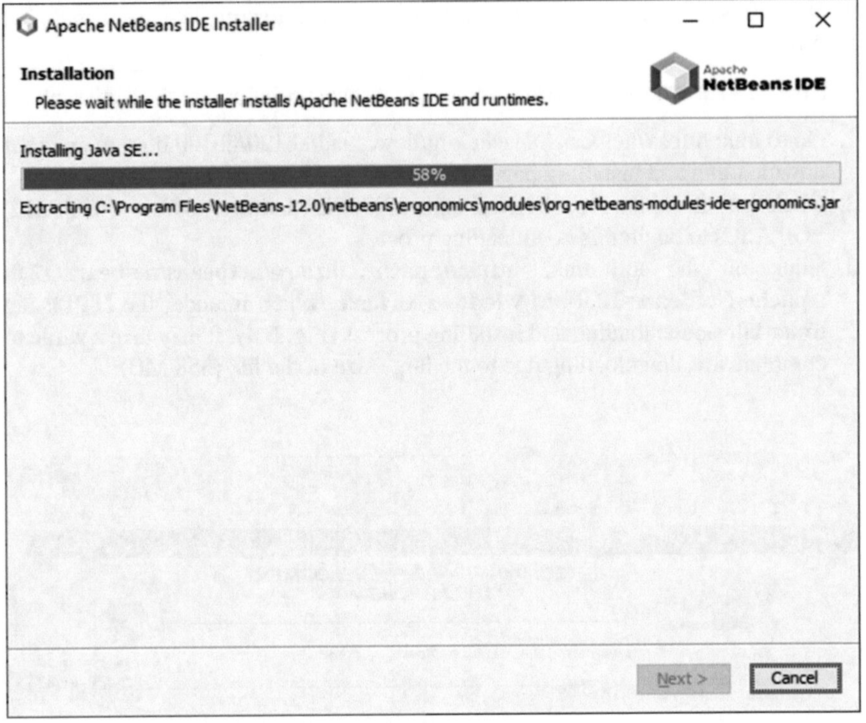

Fig. B.5 The installation process starts

8. When the installation process is done, as shown in Fig. B.6, click on the **Finish** button to complete this process.

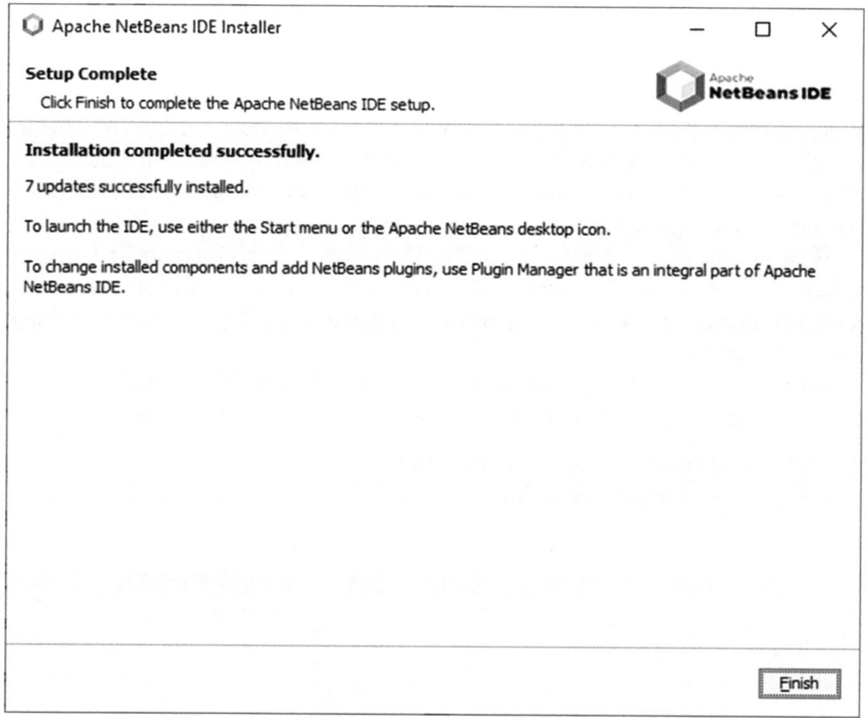

Fig. B.6 The installation process finished

Appendix C: Download and Install DevExpress .NET UI Controls

When building Faculty and Student tables, we need to store faculty and student images into the SQL Server 2019 Express database directly. Due to the new property of SQL Server 2019 database, an image can be directly stored into the database column as an image object (in fact, it is a binary data type).

With the help of a product developed by Developer Express Incorporated, exactly a user interface component, WindowsUI, we can directly insert an image into a SQL Server database's column via Microsoft Visual Studio.NET platform without any coding process.

In order to use this component, one needs to download this WindowsUI. Perform the following operations to complete this download and installation process.

1. Go to https://www.devexpress.com/#ui site.
2. Click on **WinForms Suites** link (Fig. C.1) to open the 30-day free trial dialog.

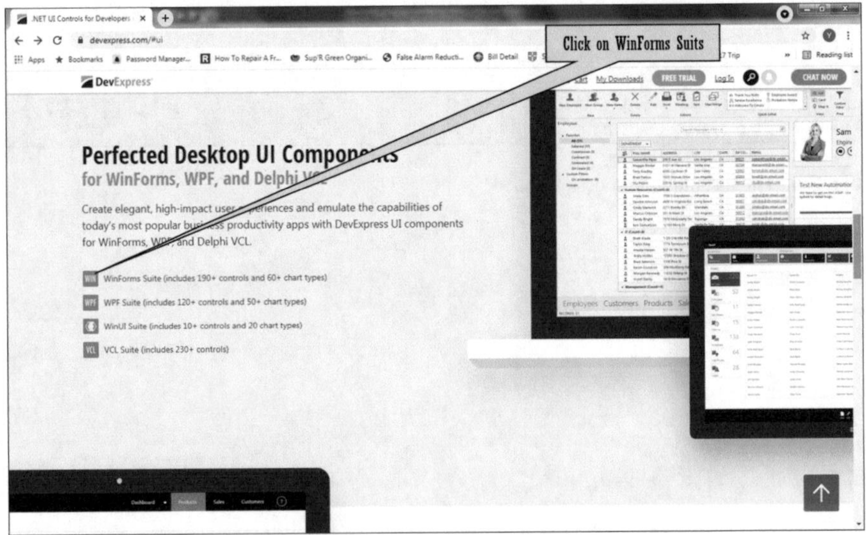

Fig. C.1 The opened site for WindowsUI component

3. Click on **FREE 30-DAY TRIAL** button to begin this downloading process. An executable file: **DevExpressUniversalTrialSetup-20,210,401.exe** is downloaded to your computer under the **Downloads** folder. Double click on that file to run it.
4. Click on the **Trial Installation** button to start the installation process.
5. Click on all icons, except the **WinForms Controls** and **CodeRush** icons (Fig. C.2), and the **Next** button to install this component.

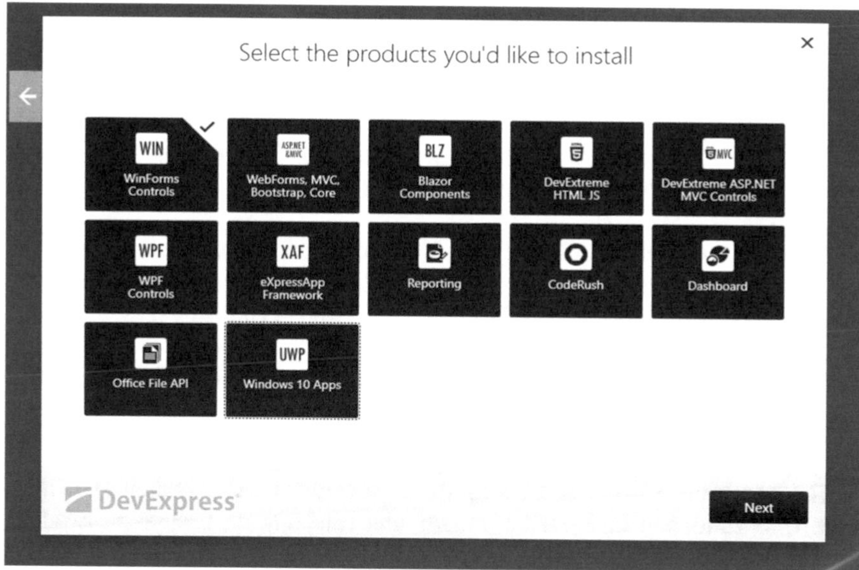

Fig. C.2 Select WinForms controls to install the WindowsUI component

6. Click on the **Accept & Continue** button for the next page to continue.
7. On next page, select either **Yes** or **No**, to participate in a customer experience program, and click the **Install** button to start this process.
8. The downloading and installation process starts, as shown in Fig. C.3.

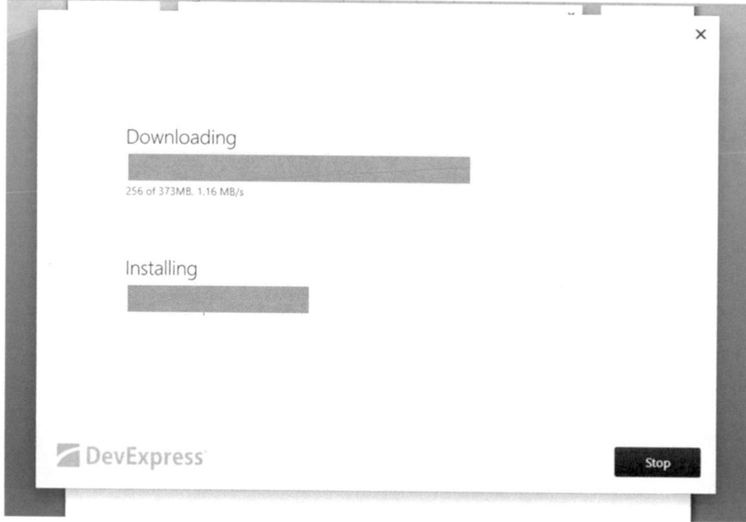

Fig. C.3 The downloading and installation process starts

9. When the installation is completed, click on the **Finish** button.

Appendix D: How to Use Sample Database

This sample database **CSE_DEPT** that is related to Microsoft SQL Server 2019 Express is provided for this book and it can be used by all projects developed in this book.

The sample database file is located under the folder **Sample Database** that is located at both the **Faculty** and **Students** folder in the Wiley ftp site (refer to Fig. 1.2 in Chap. 1).

To use this sample database file, one needs to follow the instructions discussed below. The prerequisite to use this sample database is that a Database Management Studio (DBMS) and Microsoft SQL Server 2019 Express Database must have been installed in your machine.

Refer to Appendix A to install Microsoft SQL Server Management Studio and Microsoft SQL Server 2019 Express Database if you have not installed.

D.1 Configure Advanced Security Settings to Access the DATA Folder.

The sample database **CSE_DEPT.mdf** we created in Chap. 2 contains two files, **CSE_DEPT.mdf** and **CSE_DEPT_log.ldf**. One can copy and paste these two files into the user's default SQL Server Database folder in the user's machine to use this sample database. However, the default SQL Server Database folder, **C:\Programm Files\Microsoft SQL Server \MSSQL15.SQL2019EXPRESS\MSSQL\DATA**, is not allowed to be accessed by users generally. To perform the copy and paste function to that folder, one needs to configure the Advanced Security Settings of that **DATA** folder to enable users to access the folder to perform those functions.

To configure this Advanced Security Settings, perform the following operations:

1. Go to the default SQL Server Database folder in the user's machine, **C:\ Programm Files\Microsoft SQL Server \MSSQL15.SQL2019EXPRESS\ MSSQL\DATA**.
2. Right click on the **DATA** folder and select the Properties item to open the **DATA** Properties wizard.
3. Click on the **Security** tab and **Advanced** button to open the Advanced Security Settings for DATA wizard, which is shown in Fig. D.1.

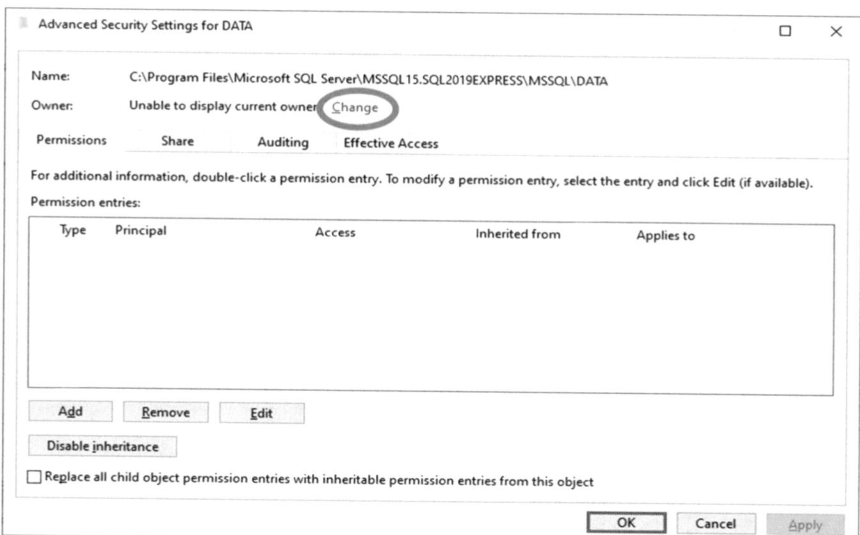

Fig. D.1 The opened advanced security settings for DATA wizard

4. Click on the **Change** item after the current owner, **Administrator (YBSMART\Administrator)** to open the Select User or Group wizard.
5. Then click on the **Advanced** button and the **Find Now** button, as shown in Fig. D.2.

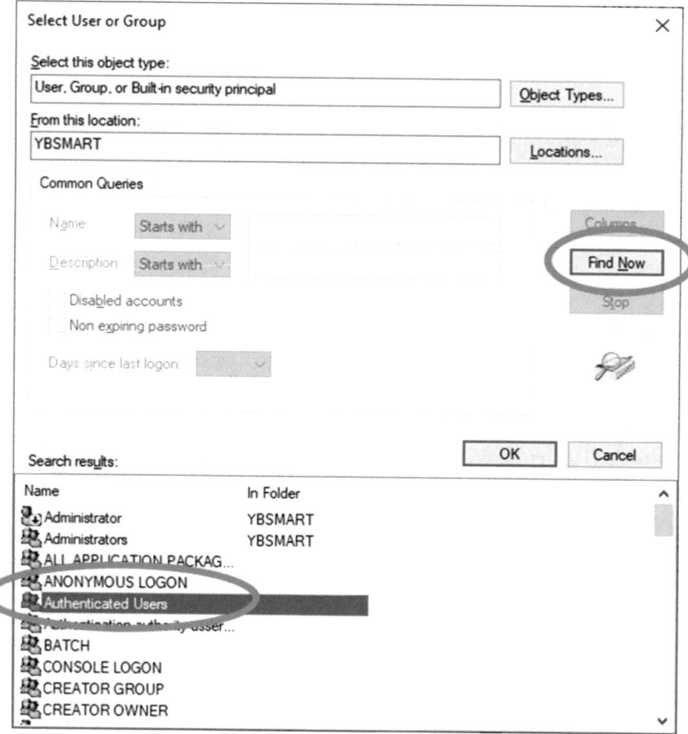

Fig. D.2 The opened Select User or Group wizard

6. Select the **Authenticated Users** from the bottom list, as shown in Fig. D.2, and click on the **OK** button to add this user as a new owner.
7. Click on the **OK** button again on return to the Advanced Security Settings wizard. Then click on the **Add** button to add this new owner into the **Permission entries** list on the bottom.
8. On the next wizard, the **Permission Entry for DATA** wizard, which is shown in Fig. D.3, click on the **Select a principal** item on the top. Then click on the **Advanced** button on the opened Select User or Group wizard, click on the **Find Now** button again and select the **Authenticated Users** item from the bottom list.

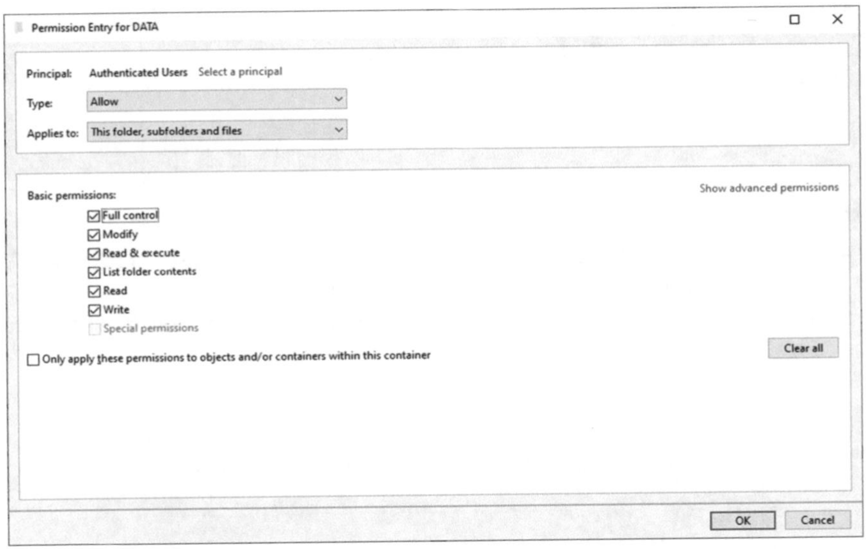

Fig. D.3 The opened and finished Permission Entry for DATA wizard

9. Click on the **OK** button for next two wizards to return to the **Permission Entry for DATA** wizard. Then check the top two checkboxes, Full Control and Modify, to enable the selected new user, **Authenticated Users**, to have full control ability to this DATA folder.
10. Your finished **Permission Entry for DATA** wizard should match one that is shown in Fig. D.3. Click on the **OK** button to complete this configuration process.
11. Now you can find that this new owner has been added into the Permission entries list, as shown in Fig. D.4. Click on the **Apply** button to make this configuration take effect. Click on the **Yes** button for the popup Messagebox.

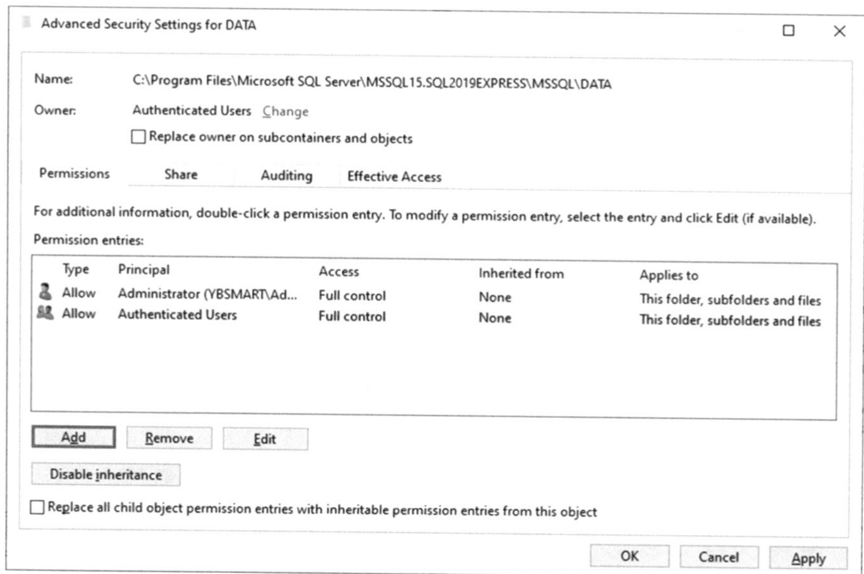

Fig. D.4 The finished Advanced Security Settings for DATA wizard

12. Click on the **OK** button to close the **DATA** Properties wizard.

Now you can access the SQL Server 2019 Database default **DATA** folder, **C:\Programm Files\Microsoft SQL Server\MSSQL15.SQL2019EXPRESS\MSSQL\DATA** on your machine to perform copy and paste sample database function.

The reason we add this **Authenticated Users** as a permissive user to access the SQL Server 2019 Express Database is that this user was selected as a login user (**Windows Authentication**) when we connected to that database and created our sample database **CSE_DEPT** at Chap. 2. You may need to select your desired user if you use different user to connect to SQL Server 2019 Express Database server and create your database.

D.2 Use Microsoft SQL Server 2019 Express Sample Database File.

The sample Microsoft SQL Server 2019 database file **CSE_DEPT.mdf** can be found from the folder **Sample Database** located at the Wiley ftp site (refer to Fig. 1.2 in Chap. 1) under the **Students** folder. To use this database file in any sample database programming project that used a SQL Server Data Provider in this book, you need to perform the following operations (suppose the Microsoft SQL Server Management Studio has been installed in your machine):

1. Copy the sample database files **CSE_DEPT.mdf** and **CSE_DEPT_log.ldf** from the folder **Sample Database** located at the Wiley ftp site (refer to Fig. 1.2 in Chap. 1) and paste it to the Microsoft SQL Server default database file folder, **C:\Programm Files\Microsoft SQL Server\MSSQL15.SQL2019EXPRESS\MSSQL\DATA** in your machine.

2. Open the Microsoft SQL Server Management Studio and connect to our SQL 2019 Express database server.
3. Right click on the **Databases** folder, and select **Attach** folder to open the Attach Database wizard, as shown in Fig. D.5.

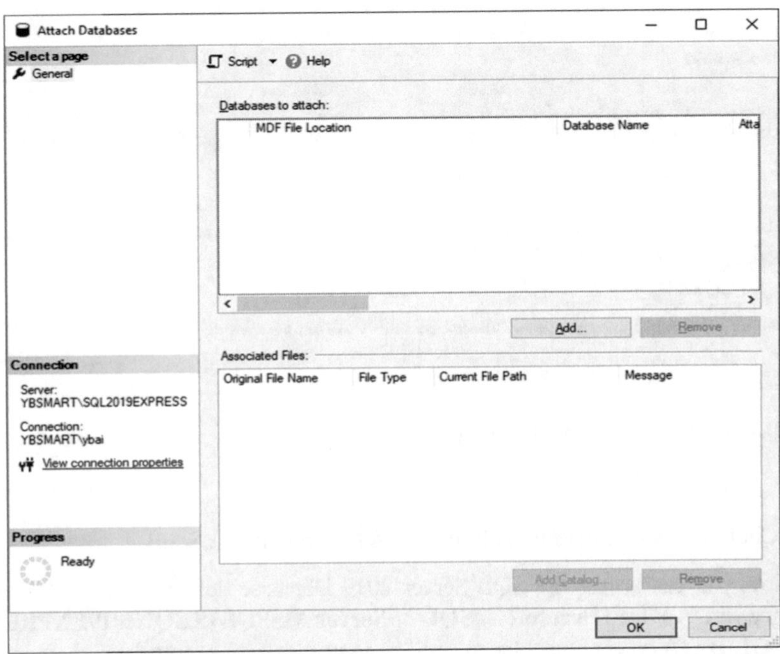

Fig. D.5 The opened attach databases wizard

4. Click on the **Add** button that is under the **Databases to attach** Textbox, and browse to our pasted sample database file **CSE_DEPT.mdf** that is located at the default folder shown in step 1, as shown in Fig. D.6. Click on that file to select it. Then click on the **OK** button to add it into our database.

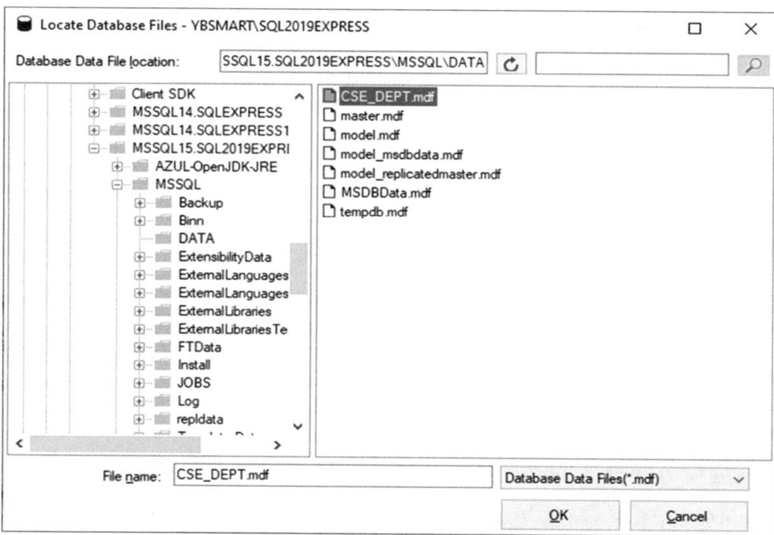

Fig. D.6 The opened database file selection wizard

5. The resulted wizard is shown in Fig. D.7. Click on the **OK** button to attach this database file into our database.

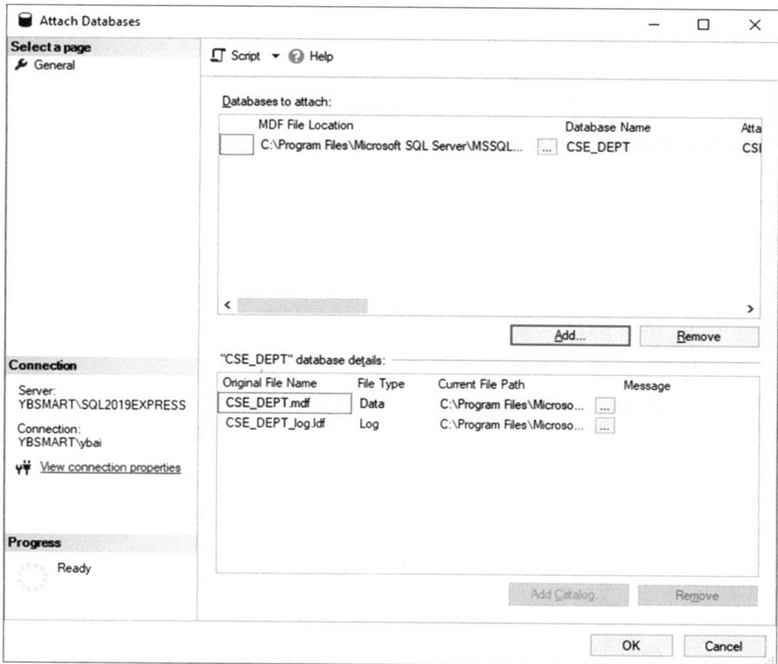

Fig. D.7 The finished attach databases wizard

6. Now if you expand the **Databases** folder from the Microsoft SQL Server Management Studio, you can find that our sample database **CSE_DEPT** has been added into our database server, as shown in Fig. D.8.

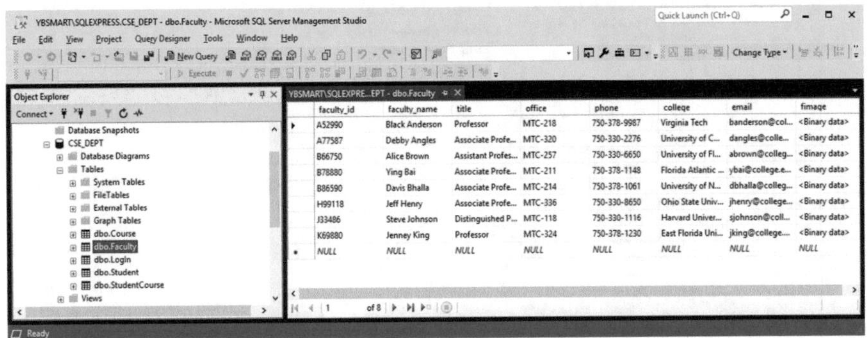

Fig. D.8 The attached database CSE_DEPT and tables

7. Now expand this attached database **CSE_DEPT**, you can find all five tables, **dbo.LogIn, dbo.Faculty, dbo.Course, dbo.Student**, and **dbo.StudentCourse**, under this database.

You can check some tables to confirm this attach action. For example, to check the **Faculty** table, just right click on the **dbo.Faculty** table and select **Edit Top 200 Rows** item. All faculty members in this table are shown up, as shown in Fig. D.8.

Refer to Sect. 6.1.4 in Chap. 6 to add this database file as a new Data Source into your sample project if you want to develop a data-driven application using Visual Studio.NET Design Tools and Wizards method.

Refer to Sect. 6.3.3.3 in Chap. 6 to add this database file as a new Data Source into your sample project if you want to develop a data-driven application using Run-Time object method.

Appendix E: Data Type Mappings Between SQL Statements and Java Applications

E1: Java Primitive Data Types Mapped to SQL Data Types (Table E.1).

E2: SQL Data Types Mapped to Java Types.

Data types mapping between the SQL data types and Java types are shown in Table E.2.

E3: Java Object Types Mapped to SQL Data Types.

Table E.1 Java primitive data types mapped to SQL data types

Java Type	SQL Data Type
boolean	BIT
Byte[]	VARBINARY or LONGVARBINARY
Double	DOUBLE
float	REAL
int	INTEGER
java.lang.Bignum	NUMERIC
java.sql.Date	DATE
java.sql.Time	TIME
java.sql.Timestamp	TIMESTAMP
Long	BIGINT
String	VARCHAR or LONGVARCHAR

Table E.2 Methods defined in the DriverManager class

SQL Data Type	Java Type
CHAR	String
VARCHAR	String
LONGVARCHAR	String
NUMERIC	java.lang.Bignum
DECIMAL	java.lang.Bignum
BIT	boolean
TINYINT	Integer
SMALLINT	Integer
INTEGER	Integer
BIGINT	Long
REAL	Float
FLOAT	Double
DOUBLE	Double
BINARY	Byte[]
VARBINARY	Byte[]
LONGVARBINARY	Byte[]
DATE	java.sql.Date
TIME	java.sql.Time
TIMESTAMP	java.sql.Timestamp

Data types mapping between the Java object types and SQL data types are shown in Table E.3.

Table E.3 Java object types mapped to SQL data types

Java Type	SQL Data Type
Boolean	BIT
byte[]	VARBINARY or LONGVARBINARY
Double	DOUBLE
Float	REAL
Integer	INTEGER
java.lang.Bignum	NUMERIC
java.sql.Date	DATE
java.sql.Time	TIME
java.sql.Timestamp	TIMESTAMP
Long	BIGINT
String	VARCHAR or LONGVARCHAR

E4: SQL Data Types Mapped to Java object Types.

Data types mapping between the SQL data types and Java object types are shown in Table E.4.

Table E.4 Methods defined in the DriverManager class

SQL Data Type	Java Type
CHAR	String
VARCHAR	String
LONGVARCHAR	String
NUMERIC	java.lang.Bignum
DECIMAL	java.lang.Bignum
BIT	Boolean
TINYINT	Integer
SMALLINT	Integer
INTEGER	Integer
BIGINT	Long
REAL	Float
FLOAT	Double
DOUBLE	Double
BINARY	byte[]
VARBINARY	byte[]
LONGVARBINARY	byte[]
DATE	java.sql.Date
TIME	java.sql.Time
TIMESTAMP	java.sql.Timestamp

E5: Data Mapping for ResultSet get() Method.

Data mappings for ResultSet **get**() method are shown in Table E.5.

Table E.5 Data mappings for ResultSet get() method

	Numeric	Decimal	Tinyint	Binary	Varbinary	Bit	Date	Double	Float	Real	Integer	Bigint	Smallint	Char	Varchar	Time	Timestamp	Longvarchar	Longvarbinary
getBigDecimal()	■	■	▲			▲		▲	▲	▲	▲	▲	▲	▲	▲			▲	
getByte()	▲	▲	■			▲		▲	▲	▲	▲	▲	▲	▲	▲			▲	
getBytes()				■	■														▲
getBoolean()	▲	▲	▲	▲	▲	■		▲	▲	▲	▲	▲	▲	▲	▲			▲	
getDate()							■							▲	▲		▲	▲	
getDouble()	▲	▲	▲	▲	▲	▲		■	■	▲	▲	▲	▲	▲	▲			▲	
getFloat()	▲	▲	▲	▲	▲	▲		▲	▲	■	▲	▲	▲	▲	▲			▲	
getInt()	▲	▲	▲	▲	▲	▲		▲	▲	▲	■	▲	▲	▲	▲			▲	
getLong()	▲	▲	▲	▲	▲	▲		▲	▲	▲	▲	■	▲	▲	▲			▲	
getObject()	▲	▲	▲	▲	▲	▲	▲	▲	▲	▲	▲	▲	▲	▲	▲	▲	▲	▲	▲
getShort()	▲	▲	▲	▲	▲	▲		▲	▲	▲	▲	▲	■	▲	▲			▲	
getString()	▲	▲	▲	▲	▲	▲		▲	▲	▲	▲	▲	▲	■	■	▲		▲	
getTime()														▲	▲	■	▲	▲	
getTimeStamp()							▲							▲	▲		■	▲	
getAsciiStream()				▲	▲									▲	▲			■	▲
getBinaryStream()				▲	▲									▲	▲			■	▲
getUnicodeStream()				▲	▲									■					■

■ = Preferred get() method for this SQL data type
▲ = Acceptable data type for this get() method

Appendix F: Download and Install Java JDK 8

1. Go to https://www.oracle.com/java/technologies/javase/javase-jdk8-downloads.html to open the downloading page for JDK 8, as shown in Fig. F.1.

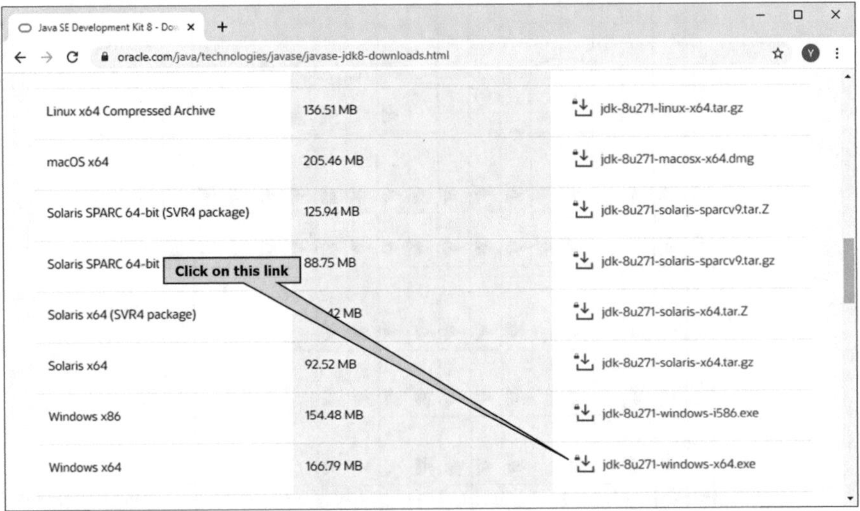

Fig. F.1 The opened downloading page for JDK 8 (Copyrighted by Oracle and used with permission)

2. Click on the **Accept License** checkbox and the **Download jdk-8u271-windows-x64.exe** button to begin this downloading process. You may need a login process to start this process.
3. When the downloading process is done, click on that downloaded file to run this installation. On the next wizard, as shown in Fig. F.2, click on the **Next** button to start.

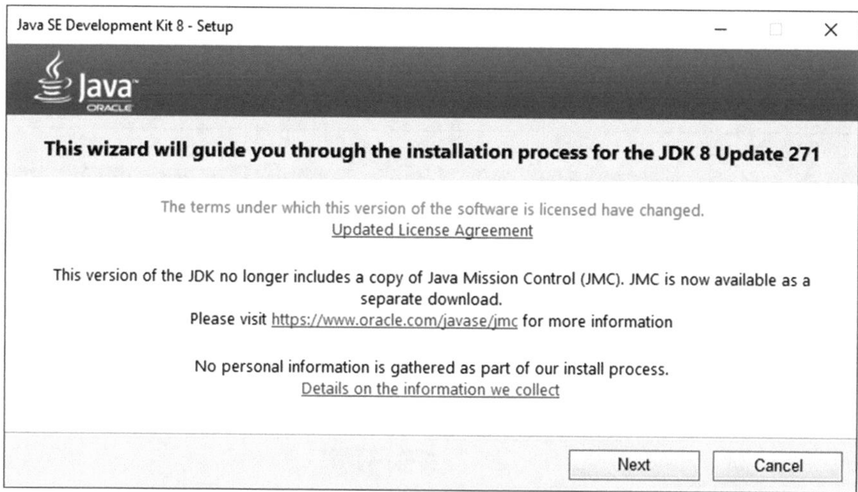

Fig. F.2 The pre-installation process starts (Copyrighted by Oracle and used with permission)

4. Click on the **Next** button on the next wizard to select the default location, **C:\Program Files\Java/jdk1.8.0_271**, to begin this pre-installation process, as shown in Fig. F.3.

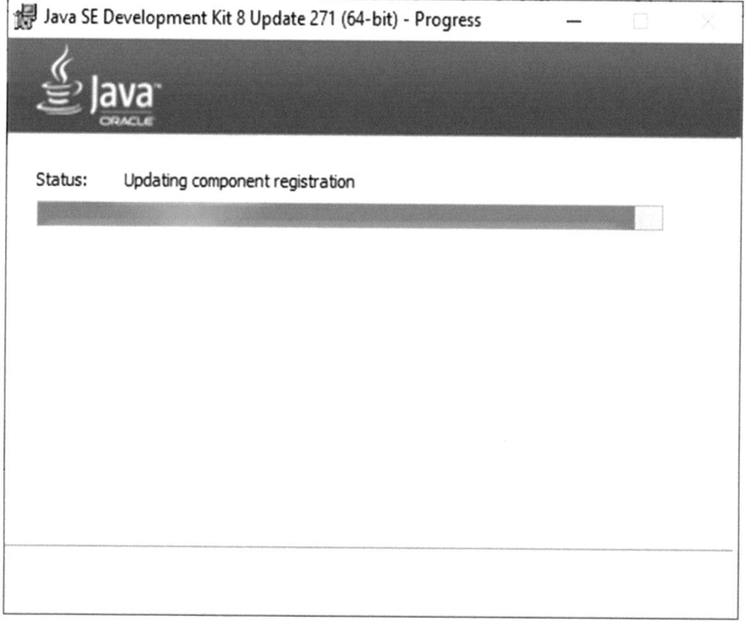

Fig. F.3 The pre-installation process starts (Copyrighted by Oracle and used with permission)

5. The pre-installation process starts, as shown.
6. Click on the **Next** button on the next wizard to confirm the installation target location. The installation process starts, as shown in Fig. F.4.

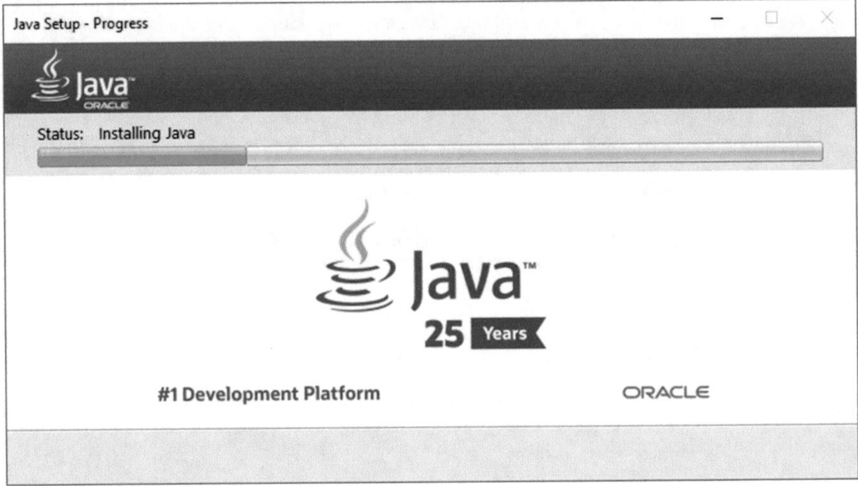

Fig. F.4 The installation process starts (Copyrighted by Oracle and used with permission)

When the installation process is completed, as shown in Fig. F.5, click on the **Close** button.

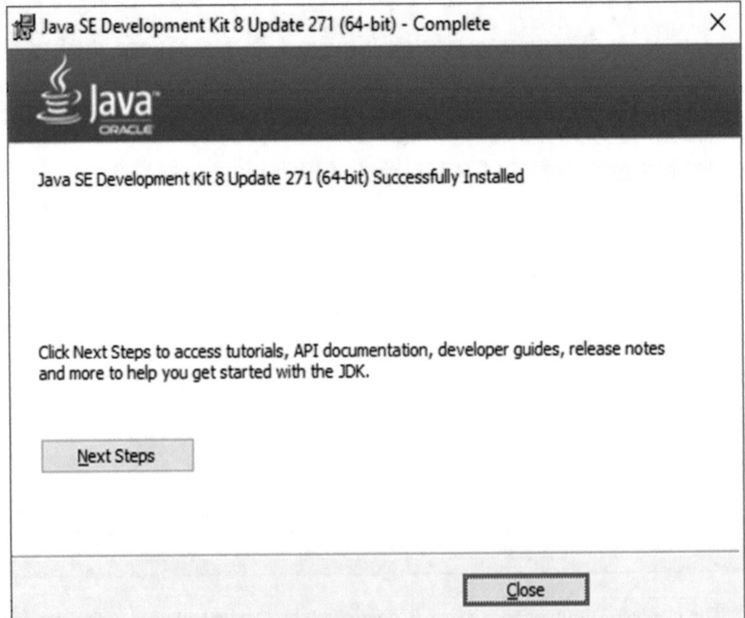

Fig. F.5 The installation process is completed (Copyrighted by Oracle and used with permission)

Appendix G: Download and Install JDBC 4.2

1. Go to https://www.microsoft.com/en-us/download/details.aspx?id=54671 to open this downloading page, as shown in Fig. G.1.

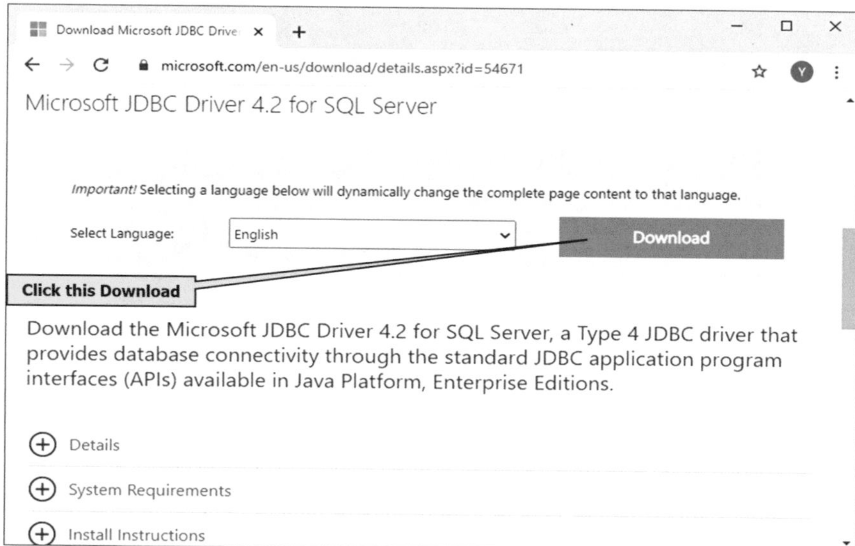

Fig. G.1 The opened downloading page (Copyrighted by Oracle and used with permission)

2. Click on the **Download** button to begin this downloading process.
3. Check on the **sqljdbc_4.2.8112.200_enu.exe** checkbox, as shown in Fig. G.2, and click on the **Next** button.

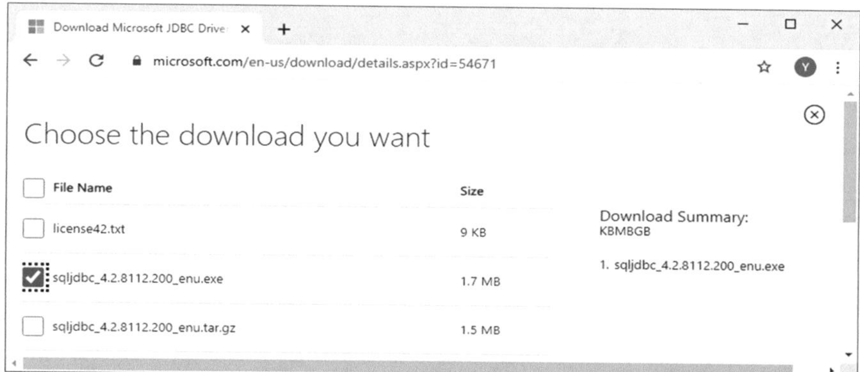

Fig. G.2 The opened downloading component selection page (Copyrighted by Oracle and used with permission)

4. The downloading process starts. Click on the downloaded file to run it as this process is done.
5. Click on the Browse button to select a desired location to unzip this file. In our case, we selected **C:\Temp** folder to store this unzipped file, which is shown in Fig. G.3. Then click on the **Unzip** button to unzip this file.

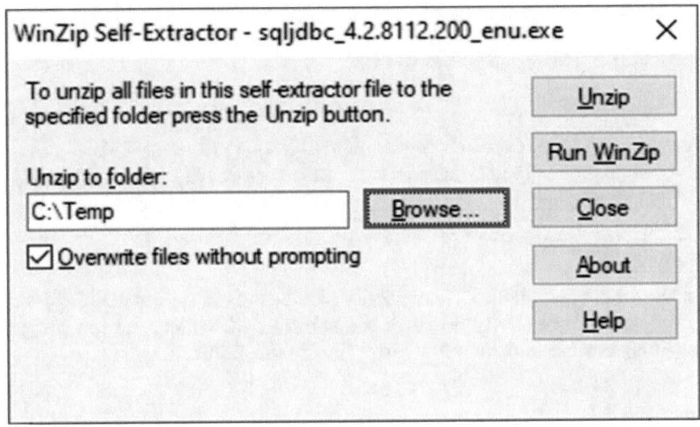

Fig. G.3 The opened unzip wizard

6. Click on the **Close** button to close this unzip process as it is done.
7. Then go to the **C:\Temp** folder and the unzipped folder **sqljdbc_4.2** is in there. Copy that entire folder to the **C:\Program Files** folder in your computer.
8. Now open the Windows Explorer and browse to the folder, **C:\Program Files\sqljdbc_4.2**, you can find that two JDBC driver files, **sqljdbc41.jar** and **sqljdbc42.jar**, are located at two folders, **jre7** and **jre8**, as shown in Fig. G.4. In our applications, we prefer to use the **sqljdbc41.jar**.

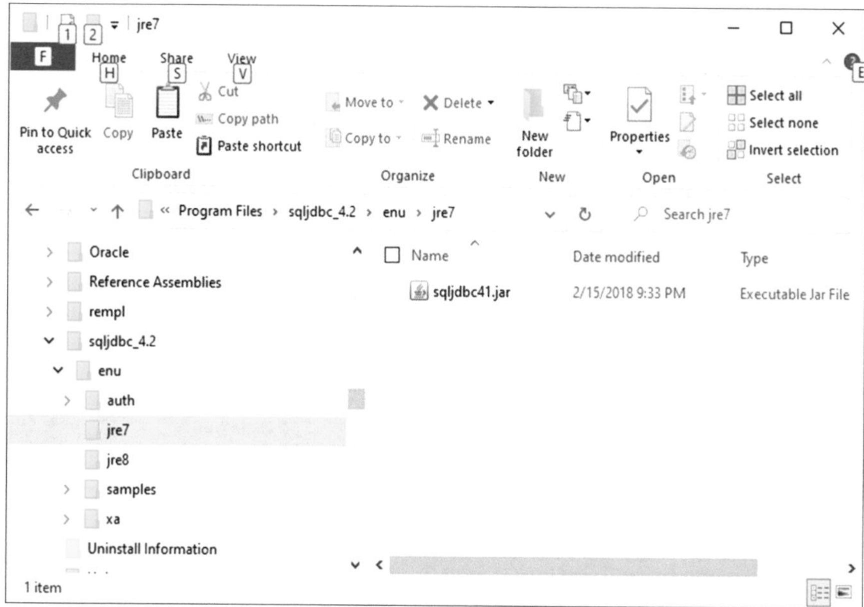

Fig. G.4 The location of installed JDBC driver

Appendix H: Download and Install NetBeans IDE 8.2 and Glassfish Server

1. Go to https://netbeans.org/downloads/old/8.2/ to open the download page, as shown in Fig. H.1.

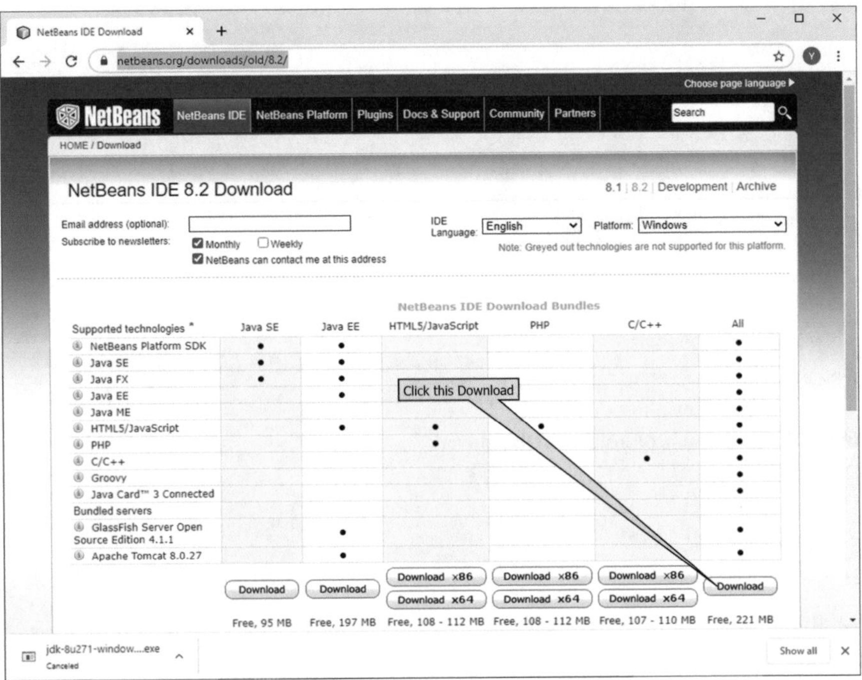

Fig. H.1 The opened download page for NetBeans IDE 8.2

2. Click on the **Download** button under the **All** column to download all popular components on this NetBeans 8.2 IDE.
3. When the downloading process is done, click it to run this file. The pre-installation process starts, as shown in Fig. H.2.

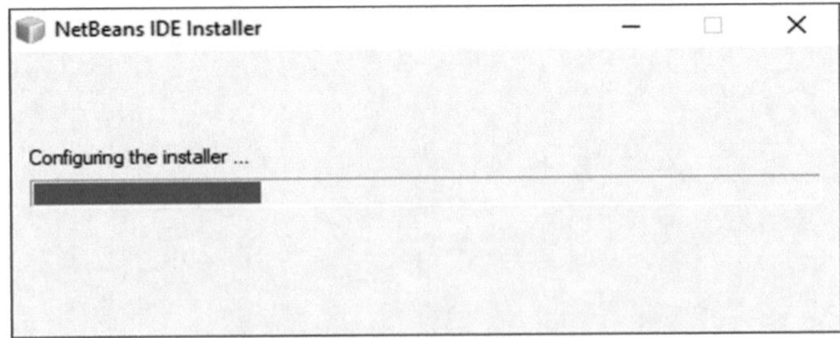

Fig. H.2 The pre-installation starts

4. The configuration of the installer process also starts, as shown in Fig. H.3.

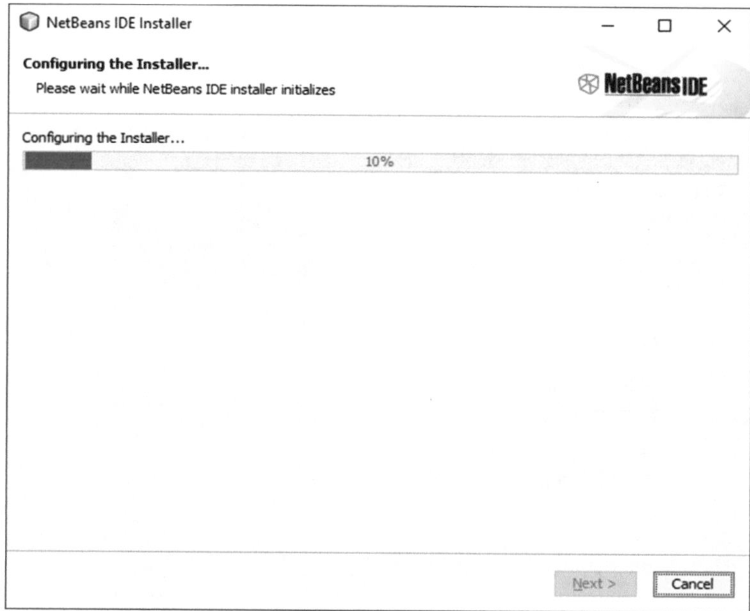

Fig. H.3 The configuration of the installation wizard

5. Then the installation panel appears, as shown in Fig. H.4. Click on the **Customize** button to involve the Tomcat server into this installation process.

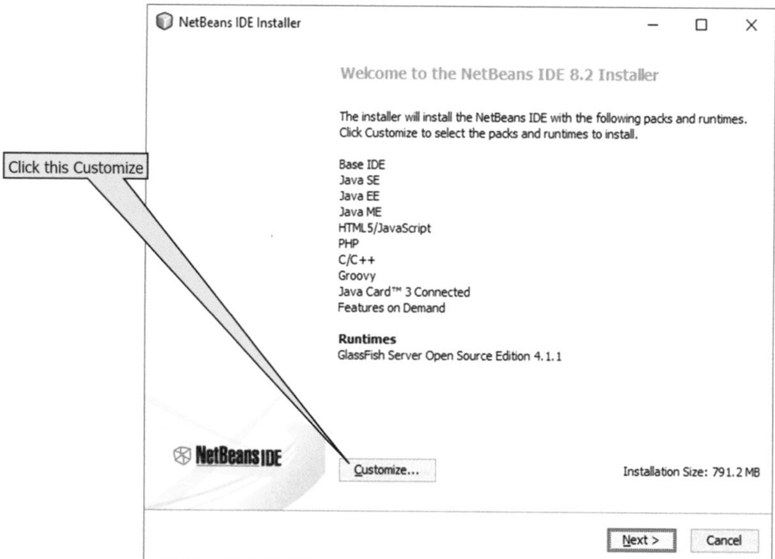

Fig. H.4 The opened installation panel

6. On the opened Customize Installation wizard, as shown in Fig. H.5, check the checkbox, **Apache Tomcat 8.0.27**, located at the bottom to bundle this Web server into this installation. Click on the **OK** button to continue.

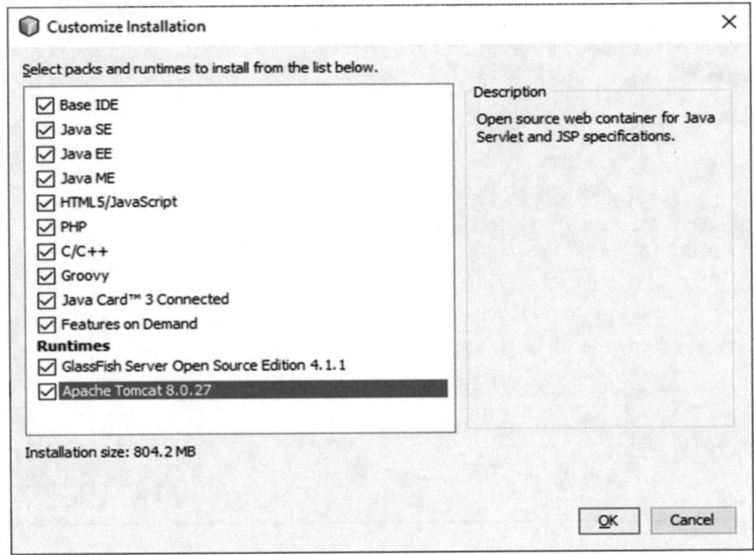

Fig. H.5 The opened cstomize installation wizard

7. Then click on the **Next** button to start this installation.
8. Click on the **Accept License** checkbox and click on the **Next** button to continue.
9. Confirm the installation locations for this IDE and related JDK, as shown in Fig. H.6, and click on the **Next** button.

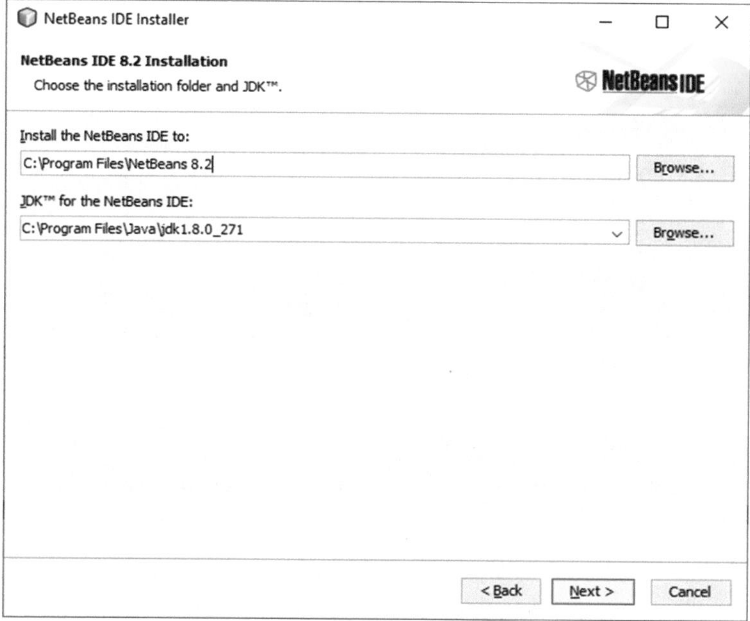

Fig. H.6 The opened installation of NetBeans and JDK locations wizard

10. Confirm the locations to install the GlassFish server and related JDK, as shown in Fig. H.7, and click on the **Next** button.

Fig. H.7 The opened installation of GlassFish and JDK locations wizard

11. On the next wizard, as shown in Fig. H.8, confirm the location of installing the Tomcat server, and click on the **Next** button.

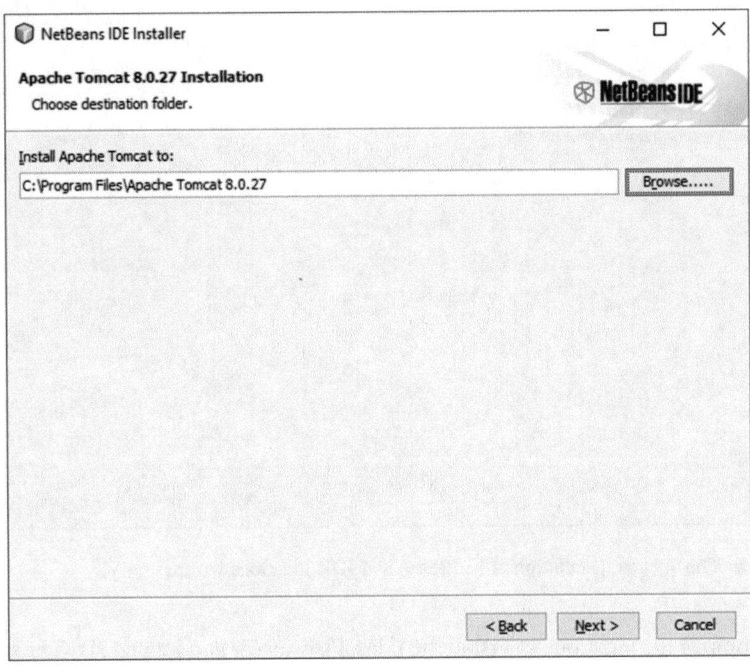

Fig. H.8 The default installation location for Tomcat server

12. Then click on the **Install** button on the next wizard to start this installation process. The installation process is started, as shown in Fig. H.9.

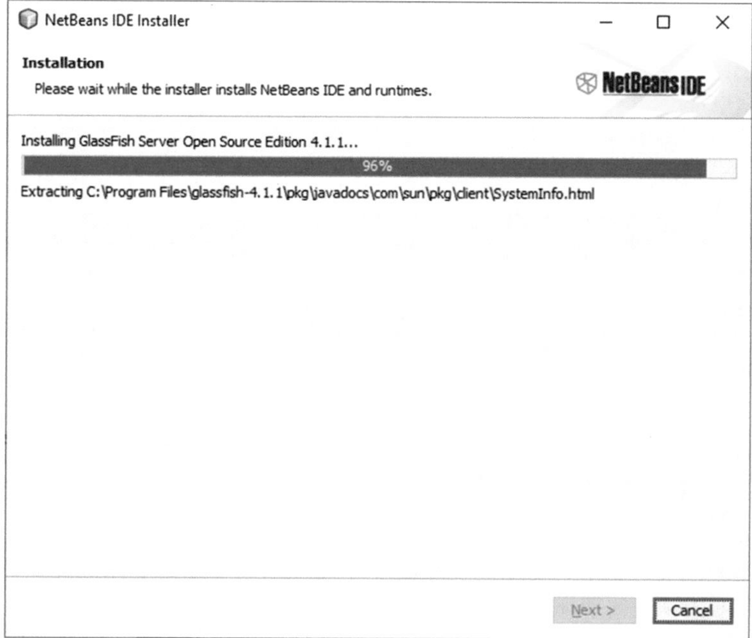

Fig. H.9 The installation process starts

13. When the installation process is completed, as shown in Fig. H.10, click on the **Finish** button to complete this installation process.

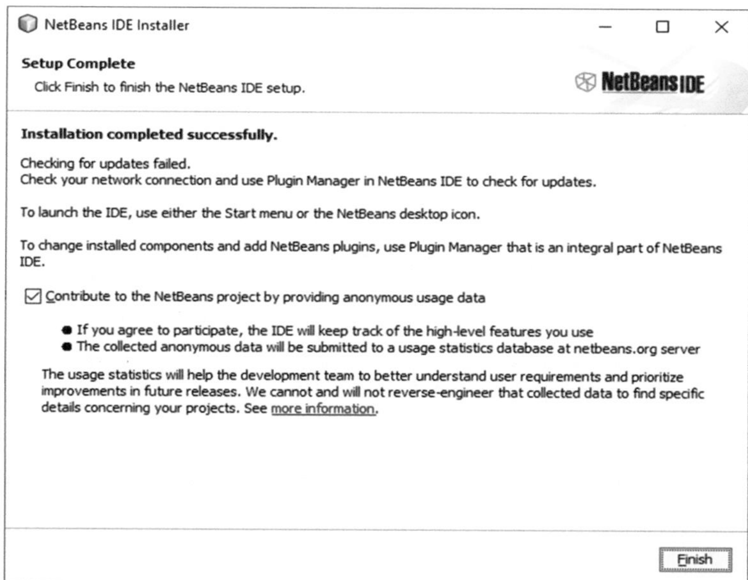

Fig. H.10 The installation completing wizard

Now open the Windows Explorer, you can find that a folder, **Apache Tomcat 8.0.27**, has been added under the Program Files folder, as shown in Fig. H.11, in which the Tomcat server is installed.

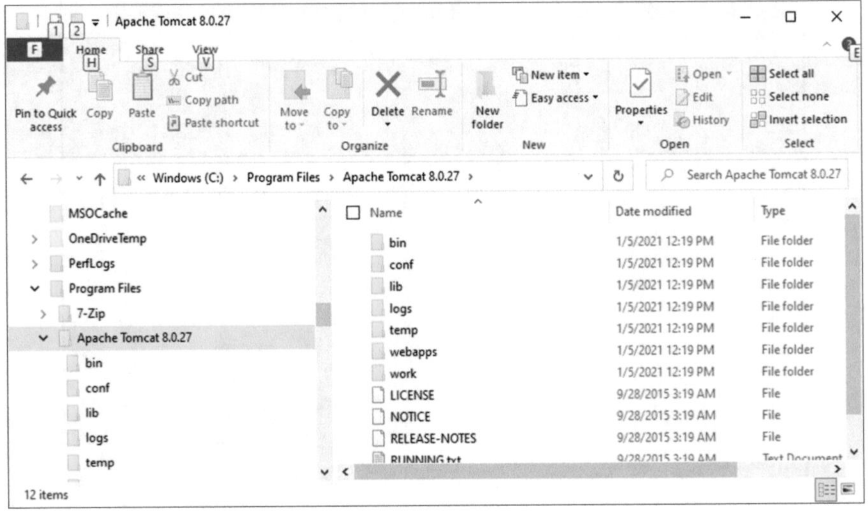

Fig. H.11 The installed folder for Apache Tomcat

Remember this folder and we may need to use this location to add the Tomcat server into our projects later when we configure the NetBeans IDE to build our Web applications.

Appendix I: Modify the HTTP Port Number for Tomcat Server

In most cases, the default HTTP Port used by the Tomcat server is **8080**, and it works for most applications. However, this port may be occupied by the other devices in some computers. In that case, in order to enable the Tomcat server to work properly in your machine, we need to modify this HTTP Port number manually.

First you need to check and confirm the HTTP Port number that is being used by your Tomcat server. Perform the following operational steps to do this checking:

1. Open the NetBeans 8.2 IDE if it has not been opened and your Web application project.
2. Click on the **Services** tab to open the **Services** window on the left.
3. Then expand the **Servers** node and right click on the used Tomcat server, in our case, it is **Apache Tomcat or TomEE**, and click on the **Properties** item on the bottom from the popup menu to open the Properties wizard, as shown in Fig. I.1.

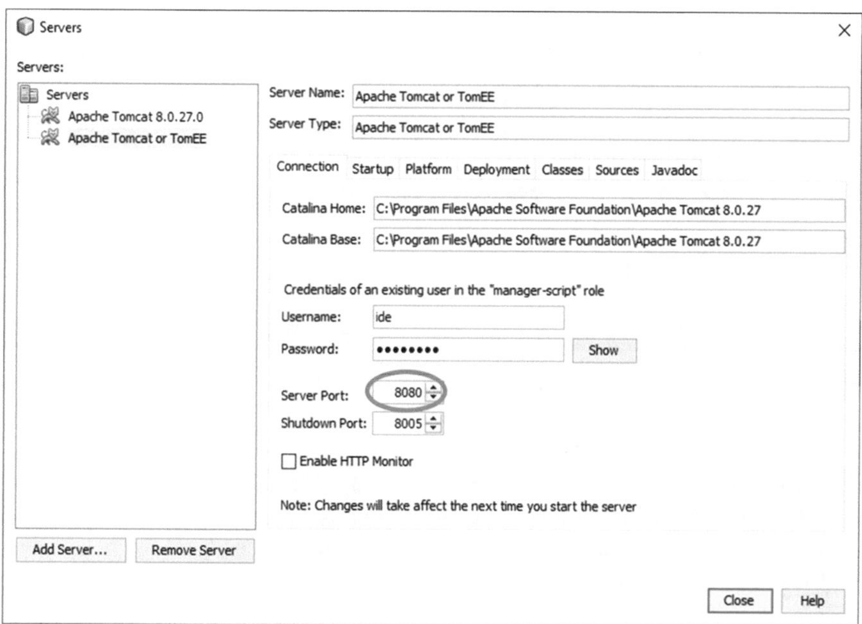

Fig. I.1 The opened Tomcat server Properties wizard

4. You can see the current HTTP Port number in the **Server Port** box, which in our case it is **8080** (do not worry about the Shutdown Port).
5. Click on the **Close** button to close this wizard.

Keep this HTTP Port number in mind, and you can modify it if you encountered some port number conflicting error as you run your Web application projects.

Perform the following operations to do this modification:

1. Go to the location where the configuration file of the Tomcat server is installed on your machine, in our case, it is **C:\Program Files\Apache Software Foundation\Apache Tomcat 8.0.27\conf**.
2. Then open the Tomcat server configuration file **server.xml** in the Notepad format by right clicking on that configuration file and selecting the **Open With** to use the Notepad app to open it.
3. Scroll down along this file to lines 69 and 75, or until you find the port definition part, which is shown in Fig. I.2.

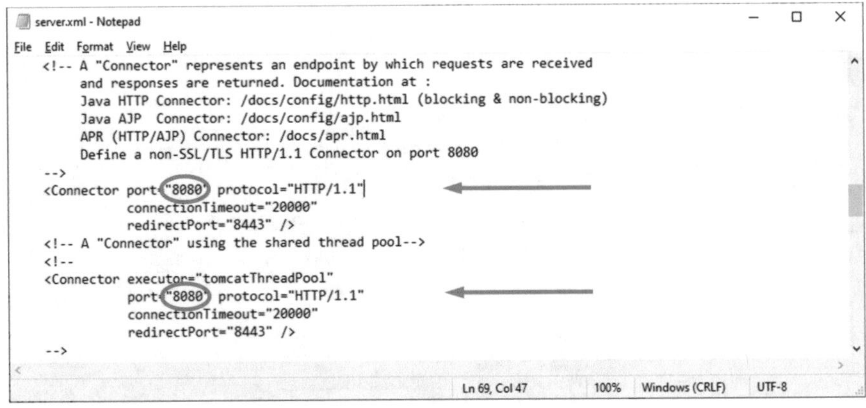

Fig. I.2 The opened Tomcat server configuration file

4. Change the port number from "**8080**" to any other desired number, such as "**8084**" or "**8086**" for both lines, as shown in Fig. I.2.
5. Click on the **File > Save** item to save this modification.
6. Close this editable version of this file.

If you experienced some authority or permission issue and cannot open this configuration file, refer to Appendix D to solve this issue.

Index

Y. Bai, *SQL Server Database Programming with Java*,
https://doi.org/10.1007/978-3-031-06553-8

D

G

H

I

L

M

T

Printed in the United States
by Baker & Taylor Publisher Services